Fodor's

ESSENTIAL PORTUGAL

Contents

MAPS

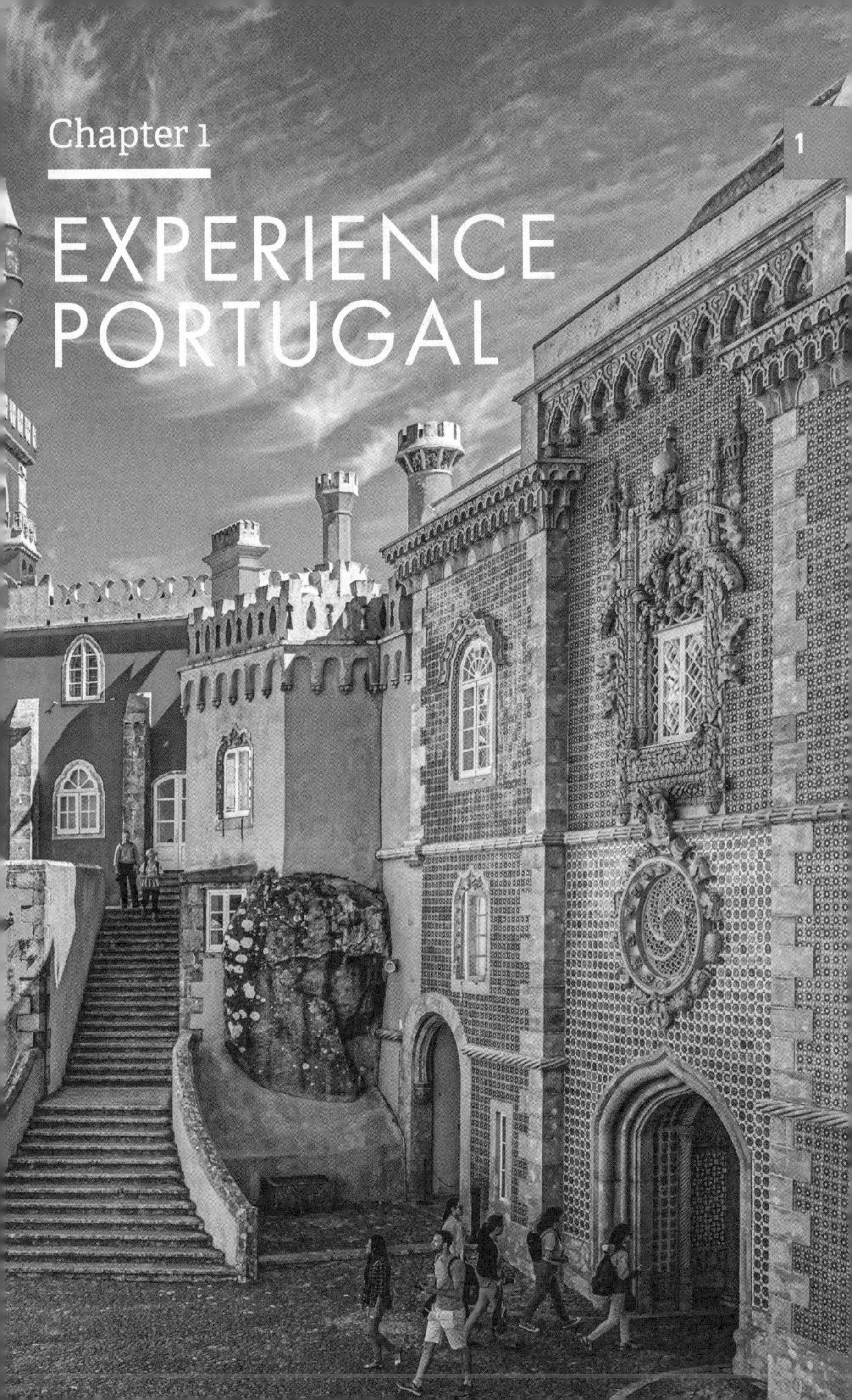

Chapter 1

EXPERIENCE PORTUGAL

20 ULTIMATE EXPERIENCES

Portugal offers terrific experiences that should be on every traveler's list. Here are Fodor's top picks for a memorable trip.

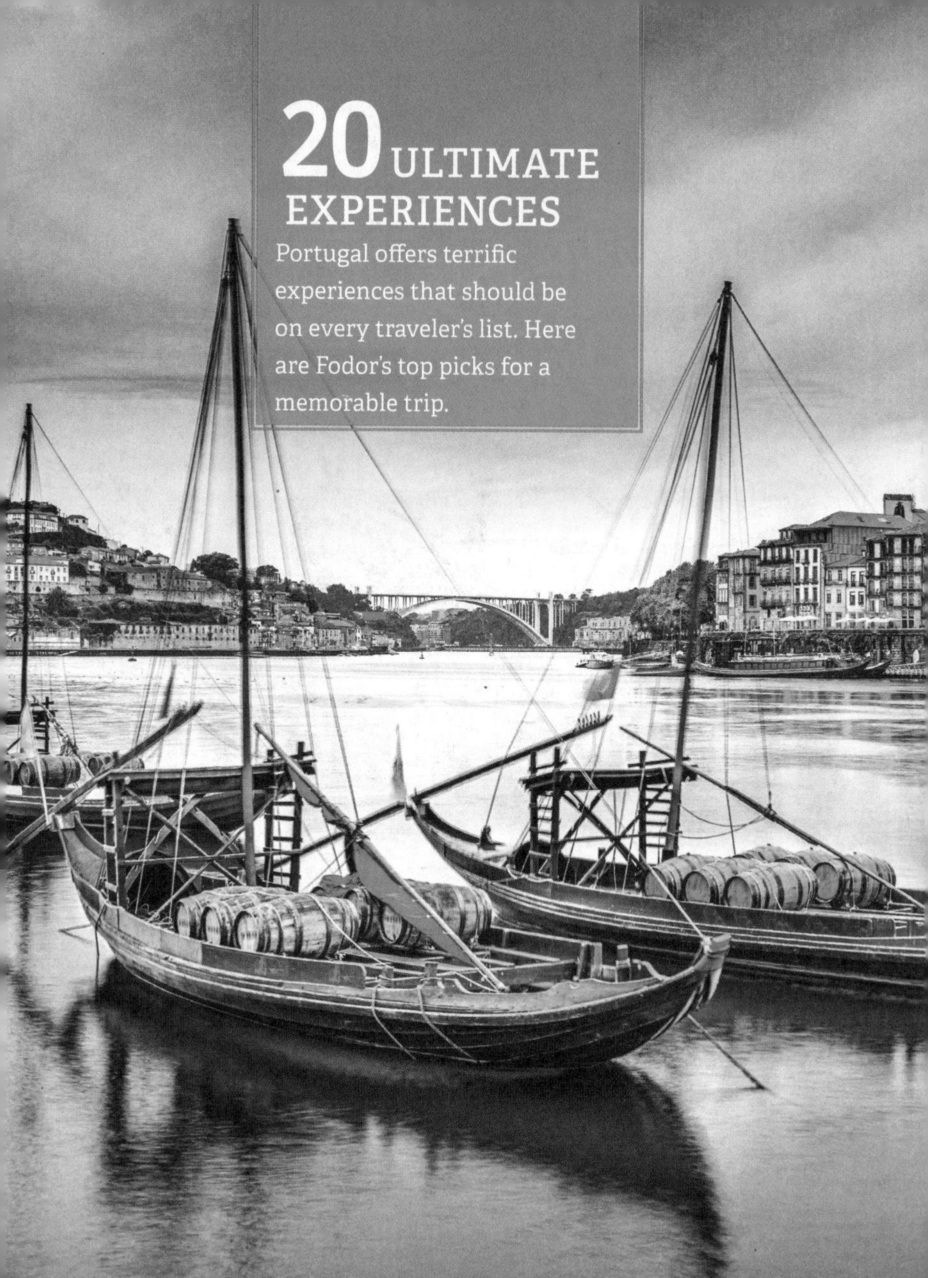

1 Porto

Porto is a travel destination in its own right, with internationally known restaurants, restored historic sites, and breathtaking beaches. *(Ch. 9)*

2 Listening to Fado

Don't miss a performance of this unique musical style at a fado house. Singers croon plaintive tunes to soulful Portuguese guitar accompaniment. *(Chs. 3, 9)*

3 Sampling Seafood

Portugal is known for its fabulous seafood. From the ubiquitous codfish to octopus and limpets, there are plenty of delicacies from the ocean to try. *(Chs. 3, 4. 7, 11)*

4 Touring Hilltop Villages

Fortified medieval walls, narrow streets, dramatic castles, and spectacular views of the countryside make these stunning settlements irresistible. *(Chs. 6, 8, 10)*

5 Santos Populares

From big cities like Lisbon and Porto to the small towns, every summer locals gather to celebrate their patron saints with alfresco dining and live music. *(Chs. 3, 9)*

6 Paiva Walkways

This zigzag wooden walkway, located near Aveiro, offers scenic views of the Paiva River and the Arouca Geopark. *(Ch. 8)*

7 Port Wine Tasting

Near Porto, you can tour the caves that store Portugal's most famous drink. Top off the experience with generous tasting sessions. *(Ch. 9)*

8 The Azores

Beyond the mainland, Portugal's islands are worth discovering. Don't miss the Azores, where old volcano craters form lakes and steaming thermal baths. *(Ch. 11)*

9 Lisbon

The vibrant capital encompasses cobblestoned streets, funicular railways, world-class museums, and top-notch dining, shopping, and nightlife. *(Ch. 3)*

10 Hiking the Rota Vicentina

Stretching from Alentejo to the Algarve, the 250-mile Rota Vicentina is one of the most beautiful coastal trails in Europe. For a shorter and less demanding walk, take one of the circular routes. *(Ch. 7)*

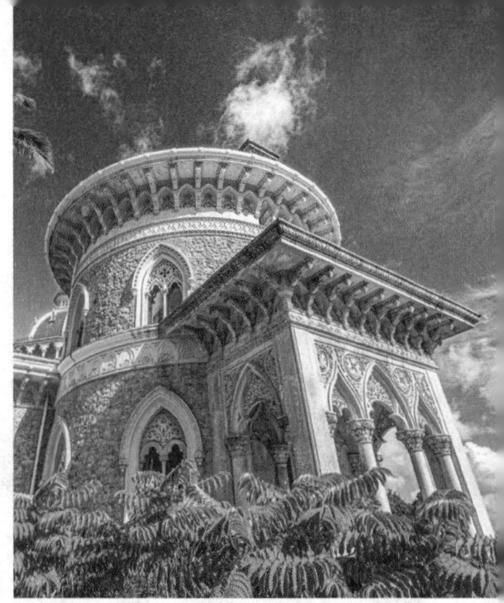

11 Sintra

A UNESCO World Heritage Site, the town of Sintra is resplendent with gorgeous palaces and gardens. The surrounding hills form a romantic backdrop for its historic charms. *(Ch. 4)*

12 Cafés and Pastelarias

You're never far from a café or pastry shop in Portugal. Be sure to take frequent breaks to savor coffee and delicious pastries like the *pastel de nata*, an egg-custard tart. *(Ch. 3)*

13 Peneda-Gerês National Park

Gentle grass mountains, medieval villages, and thermal baths make up the scenery of this natural park. Come for a swim or take a hike along the hills where wildlife abounds. *(Ch. 10)*

14 Admiring the Azulejos

Brightly colored ceramic tiles adorn numerous fountains, churches, and palaces, including the Queluz National Palace, throughout the country. *(Ch. 4)*

15 Surfing

With waves hitting 100 feet, Portugal is a surfers' paradise. The main surf towns are Sagres, Ericeira, and Nazaré, where Garrett McNamara surfed the largest wave on record. *(Chs. 5, 7, 9)*

16 Cruising the Douro River

A cruise is a relaxing way to explore the eye-opening landscapes of the Douro River Valley, with its steeply terraced vineyards. *(Ch. 10)*

17 Évora

One of Portugal's best-preserved medieval towns, Évora has fortified walls and winding cobblestone lanes lined with Roman and Gothic architecture. *(Ch. 6)*

18 Celebrate Carnival

Hand-carved wooden masks are worn during this festival in the village of Lazarim. Visit on Shrove Tuesday to experience one of Portugal's most authentic carnival parades.

19 Beaches

Take your pick of beautiful beaches—from windswept surfing hubs to unspoiled, sheltered coves—on the long Atlantic coastline. *(Chs. 4, 7, 10)*

20 Stay in a Pousada

Spice up your trip with a stay in a pousada. These lodgings in restored castles, monasteries, and historic buildings meld luxury with regional charm.

WHAT'S WHERE

1 **Lisbon.** One of Europe's smallest and sunniest capitals, Lisbon juxtaposes the old with the new and hip, all with increasing crowds of tourists.

2 **Sintra, the Estoril Coast, and the Setúbal Peninsula.** The fairy-tale castles of Sintra are just a short train ride from Lisbon; windswept surf beaches lie nearby in Cascais and Estoril. South of the River Tagus lie the dramatic mountains and pine forests of Serra da Arrábida, fresh seafood in Sesimbra, and endless white-sand beaches on the Setúbal Peninsula.

3 **Estremadura and the Ribatejo.** North and east of Lisbon are several UNESCO World Heritage Sites, including the headquarters of the Knights Templar, the Convento de Cristo, not to mention the coast's monster waves.

4 **Évora and the Alentejo.** In Évora, medieval walls encircle palatial buildings and a Roman temple. The Alentejo is bracketed by spectacular but windy Atlantic beaches and the striking Guadiana Valley, where nearly half the *vinho* in the country is produced.

5 **The Algarve.** Sheltered by the Serra de Monchique and Serra do Caldeirão ranges to the north and lapped by the Atlantic to the south, the Algarve is Portugal's main beach destination.

6 **Coimbra and the Beiras.** The central Beiras region contains Portugal's most spectacular mountain range, the Serra da Estrela, ringed by towns that are home to superb Renaissance art. Inland is the university city of Coimbra.

7 **Porto.** Porto is a mix of medieval and modern. There's also a lively fashion scene, excellent gastronomy, and Portugal's finest producers of port wine.

8 **Northern Portugal.** The green Minho region is home to *vinho verde.* The Douro Valley—with its steep terraced slopes and sparkling river—produces some of Portugal's best wine, as well as the port for which it is famous.

9 **The Azores.** Nature lovers come to these remote islands to witness their stunning beauty, impressive volcanoes, natural swimming holes, and—in spring—hydrangeas exploding into bloom.

ATLANTIC OCEAN
SPAIN
Valença
Viana do Castelo
Barcelos
Braga
Póvoa de Varzim
Guimarães
Vila do Conde
Amarante
Porto
Penafiel
Espinho
Chaves
Bragança
Mirandela
Mogadouro
DOURO VALLEY
Vila Real
Lamego
Moimenta da Beira
Oliveira dos Azeméis
S. Pedro do Sul
Albergaria-a-Velha
Aveiro
Viseu
Pinhel
Sta. Comba Dão
Mealhada
Mira
Cantanhede
Guarda
Coimbra
Covilhã
Arganil
Figueira da Foz
Fundão
Penamacor
Serra da Gardunha
Pombal
Leiria
Ourém
Proença-a-Nova
Castelo Branco
Batalha
Nazaré
Tomar
Alcobaça
Fátima
Convento do Cristo
Abrantes
Caldas da Rainha
Torres Novas
Nisa
Óbidos
Marvão
Aveiras de Cima
Santarém
Ponte de Sor
Portalegre
Torres Vedras
Mafra
Vila Franca de Xira
Sintra
Avis
Lisbon
Estremoz
Badajoz
Cascais
Estoril
Seixal
Arraiolos
Elvas
Montemor-o-Novo
Vila Viçosa
Setúbal
SETUBAL PENINSULA
Cabo Espichel
Sesimbra
Serra da Arribida
Évora
Reguengos
Alcácer do Sal
TO THE AZORES
Ferreira do Alentejo
Moura
Vilaverde de Ficalho
Sines
Cabo de Sines
Santiago do Cacem
Beja
GUADIANA VALLEY
Serpa
Castro Verde
Odemira
Ourique
Mértola
TO MADEIRA ISLAND
SERRA DE MONCHIQUE
Almodovar
Monchique
SERRA DO CALDEIRÃO
ALGARVE
S. Brás de Alportel
Vila do Bispo
Portimão
Lagos
Albufeira
Tavira
Vila Real de S. António
Cabo de S. Vicente
Sagres
Faro
Olhão
Minho
Lima
Serra do Gerês
Tâmega
Douro
Sabor
Vouga
Mondego
Serra da Estrêla
Zêzere
Tagus
Sra. do Aire
Sorraia
Sra. de Ossa
Guadiana
Sado
Mira
Chança
N101
N103
A3/IP1
A4/IP4
N102/IP2
IP5
A1/IP1/E1
N109
N110
N233
IP2
IP6
N118
N8
N10
A2/IP1
A6/IP1
A6
A2
IP1/E1
N2
N122
N120
E1/IP1
EN125
A22
IP1
1
2
3
4
5
6
7
8
9
0
50 miles
0
50 km

What to Eat and Drink in Portugal

CATAPLANA DE MARISCO
This traditional Portuguese stew made from fresh fish, shrimp, mussels, herbs, and vegetables, hails from the Algarve region. The copper pan it's cooked in is called *cataplana*, and its clamlike shape helps contain the heat and keeps all the flavors simmering together.

BACALHAU À BRÁS
Portugal's national dish is codfish, better known as *bacalhau*, and one of the many creative cod-based recipes to try is *bacalhau à brás*, scrambled eggs with shredded cod, onion, and thin potato sticks topped with black olives.

AMÊIJOAS À BULHÃO PATO
Amêijoas à Bulhão Pato is a delicious clam dish named after the Portuguese writer António de Bulhão Pato. It's the mix of garlic, olive oil, white wine, and coriander drizzled over the clams that makes this dish a must-try.

POLVO À LAGAREIRO
Like its neighboring countries, olive oil is an essential part of the Portuguese diet. *Polvo à Lagareiro* is the epitome of that, a typical octopus meal served with baked potatoes and doused with nothing but olive oil and garlic.

GRILLED SARDINES
You know summer's arrived in Portugal when the streets (and all your clothes) smell of sardines. Tossed on a grill and sprinkled with a bit of salt, sardines are one of the most traditional Portuguese meals, especially around Lisbon. You can eat them with potatoes, a bell pepper salad, or on a slice of bread, head and all.

PREGO
Ask for a *prego* in Portugal and you'll either get a nail or a sandwich. Of course, if you're at a restaurant, odds are you'll get the latter, a beef sandwich, with a slice of meat that is often bigger than the bread itself.

FRANCESINHA
A *francesinha* is more than a ham and cheese sandwich—it's a full-on meal. Served between toasted bread slices, it has ham, roast beef, and a sausage called *linguiça*, followed by cheese and a spicy beer-and-tomato sauce.

PICA-PAU
A toothpick and a bit of bread are all you need to eat *pica-pau*. The concept of the dish is simple—little chunks of meat marinated with garlic and served in a small bowl to share. Usually it comes with pork, but you can also find it with beef. Every restaurant has its own special recipe.

LEITÃO À BAIRRADA
In a nutshell, *leitão* means suckling pig, most often a Bísaro pig less than a month old. The leitão is slowly roasted on a spit in a wooden oven for nearly two hours. Meanwhile, it's sprayed with white wine and brushed with a spice mix that includes salt, pepper, garlic, lard, and bay leaf.

Polvo à Lagareiro

PASTÉIS DE NATA
Portugal has plenty of tasty pastries, but if you can only pick one, make it the *pastel de nata*—Portugal's custard tart, best purchased in a specialized store. Egg yolk, milk, and sugar are the main ingredients used in the creamy filling, which is held together by a flaky pastry cup.

AZORES TEA
Introduced by the Chinese, tea has been growing in the Azores since the 19th century. The region's subtropical climate and the volcanic soils provide the perfect conditions for tea production, including green and black varieties.

GINJINHA
From early in the morning to late at night, you can drink *ginjinha* without anyone raising an eyebrow. This sweet liqueur with red velvet color is famous all over Portugal, but it's in Lisbon that you'll find bars solely dedicated to this brandylike drink.

VINHO DO PORTO
Port wine comes from the Douro Valley, located near the city of Porto, which is how it got its name. Often served with dessert, there are several varieties of port, ranging from the citrusy white to more caramel and nutty aromas like the tawny and ruby.

MOSCATEL
This fortified wine, with a sweet fruity flavor, has two types, both drunk either as an aperitif or a dessert wine. There's Moscatel de Favaios, made in the Douro Valley, and there's Moscatel de Setúbal, which comes from a fishing town a few miles away from Lisbon.

VINHO VERDE
There's nothing like a chilled glass of wine in the summer—and for Portuguese people, that means *vinho verde*. Though produced exclusively in the region between Minho and Douro, this popular wine (sometimes slightly effervescent) is available all over the country.

Cool Castles and Fortified Cities in Portugal

CASTELO DE GUIMARÃES

Guimarães, not Lisbon, was Portgual's first capital. It was here, circa 1109, that the nation's first king, Dom Afonso Henriques, was born. At the time, the whole city was protected by walls, but today you can only see fragments. The Castelo de Guimarães, however, is still standing strong.

CASTELO DOS MOUROS

Long before Sintra had its cluster of fairy-tale palaces, the 9th-century Castelo dos Mouros was already standing tall. In the hands of the Moors until it was taken over during the Christian conquest of Portugal, its fortified stone walls offer beautiful panoramic views.

FORTE DE SANTA LUZIA

The unassuming town of Elvas is where you'll find one of the best examples of bulwarked, star-shaped fortifications in Portugal. Beyond its numerous forts, Elvas is also home to a 13th-century castle, which offers spectacular views over the old town and far into the Spanish frontier.

CASTELO DE ÓBIDOS

The town of Óbidos is home to one of the best-preserved castles in Portugal. Its walls surround a maze of cobblestone lanes lined with picturesque houses and churches. The Moors might have laid the first foundations, but the castle you see today dates back to the 12th century. In July, the town is transformed into a medieval village with jousting knights and fire jugglers taking over the streets, and when Christmas arrives, the walls are lit up at night.

CASTELO DE PENEDONO

Not far from the Douro Valley, and with a little less than 3,000 residents, is the town of Penedono. There's not much here, other than the castle, but it's one you shouldn't miss. Dating back to the 14th century, it has a distinctive hexagonal shape and five towers with pointy tops. A cobblestone stairway leads the way to the entrance, and from there you can climb up to enjoy the views over the rolling hills.

CASTELO DE MARVÃO

In the northern reaches of Alentejo, clinging to a rocky crag, you'll find the fortified town of Marvão. As you enter the gates, follow the battlements and before long the Castelo de Marvão will appear. Built by King Dinis in the 13th century, the castle provides astonishing views past the São Mamede Natural Park and all the way to the Spanish border. Shout out inside the cistern by the entrance and listen to your voice echo through the historic walls.

Castelo de Marvão

CIDADELA

Standing at the foot of the Montesinho Natural Park, the town of Bragança is in the remote region of Trás-os-Montes. The medieval Cidadela divides the city into two sections: the new town, outside the fortified walls, and the old town, with its whitewashed houses clustered around the castle. Dating back to the 12th century, the castle is visible from afar thanks to its prominent keep. There are several attractions inside the walls, including a church, the city hall, and a military museum.

FORTALEZA DE VALENÇA DO MINHO

The fortified city of Valença do Minho stands shoulder to shoulder with Spain, with only the Minho River separating the two countries. Its location along the border made it one of the most important defensive points during the wars between Portugal and Spain. The fortress emerged in the 13th century, but it was only in the 18th century that it gained its emblematic bulwarked structure. Stretching for 5 km, it surrounds the city's historic center and offers incredible views of the river and the neighboring town of Tui. Inside the fortress, you'll come across old cannons, several churches, and a Roman milestone.

CASTELO DE ALMOUROL

You'll need a boat to reach this castle in the middle of the Tagus River. Belonging to the Order of the Knights Templar, the Castle of Almourol was built in the 12th century where a Roman fort once stood. To get to the islet, you can board a boat near the train station of nearby Almourol.

TEMPLO ROMANO

History buffs will love a visit to Évora. Built between the 14th and the 15th century, the Cerca Medieval (also known as the Cerca Nova) is the ancient city wall that encloses this UNESCO World Heritage Site.

Spectacular Gothic Churches in Portugal

MOSTEIRO DA BATALHA
Built to commemorate a decisive Portuguese victory over the Spanish during the Battle of Aljubarrota in 1385, the Mosteiro da Batalha, a UNESCO World Heritage Site, is a masterly combination of Gothic and Manueline styles with magnificent chapels, cloisters, and stained-glass windows.

CONVENTO DO CARMO
The Carmelite Convent—once Lisbon's largest—was almost completely destroyed during the 1755 earthquake. The ruins of the Gothic Church of Our Lady of Mount Carmel on the southern facade of the convent is now one of the city's main reminders of the power of nature.

SÉ DA GUARDA
Construction on the fortresslike Sé da Guarda started in 1390 but wasn't completed until 1540. As a consequence, the imposing Gothic building also shows Renaissance and Manueline influences. Inside, a magnificent four-tier relief contains more than 100 carved figures.

CONVENTO DE SÃO FRANCISCO
The construction of this convent in Santarém goes back to 1242, when King Sancho II ordered its construction along with the sister convent of Santa Clara. King Fernando added his own flourishes in the 14th century, so styles from Gothic to baroque are clearly evident in the facade.

IGREJA DE SÃO DOMINGOS
The origins of this church go back to the construction of the first Dominican monastery in the city of Guimarães, built during 1271 and 1278. During the 18th and 19th centuries the original structure was embellished with elements.

SÉ CATEDRAL DE ÉVORA
Soon after being reconquered from the Moors in 1166, Évora began construction of this spectacular cathedral. The structure received several additions through time, such as the Gothic cloisters and the Manueline chapel. It is the largest of the medieval cathedrals in Portugal.

MOSTEIRO DOS JERÔNIMOS
This 16th-century monastery is the resting place of such luminaries as explorer Vasco da Gama and poet Luís de Camões. A UNESCO World Heritage Site, the Mosteiro dos Jerônimos is a prominent example of the late-Gothic Manueline style of architecture in Lisbon.

IGREJA DE SÃO FRANCISCO
The Church of St. Francis is the most prominent Gothic monument in the port city of Porto. While the exterior is rather undistinguished, the late-14th-century building's interiors have astounding baroque ornamentations, with gilded carvings filling it floor to ceiling.

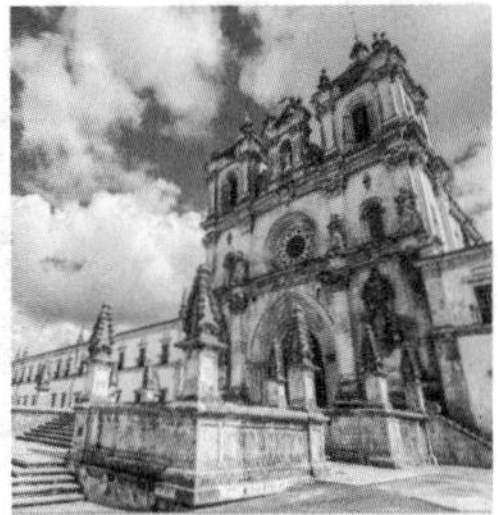

MOSTEIRO DE ALCOBAÇA
With construction starting in 1153 under the orders of the first Portuguese king, Afonso Henriques, the awe-inspiring Mosteiro de Alcobaça is considered the country's first example of Gothic architecture. It was dedicated to St. Bernard and the Cistercian Order following the Portuguese's conquest of the city of Santarém.

CONVENTO DE SANTA CLARA-A-VELHA
Built in the 14th century, restorers have long been excavating the interior of the ruined Convento de Santa Clara-a-Velha in Coimbra. The Gothic building was abandoned by its resident nuns 1677. Today, one can visit the restored main building as well as the adjacent open-air ruins and a nearby museum about the site's history.

Best Vineyards in Portugal

QUINTA DA BACALHÔA
Only a 40-minute drive from Lisbon, the beautifully restored vineyard, with a gorgeous hedged garden, was once the property of the Portuguese royal family before being transformed into a museum and famed winery in the 1970s.

QUINTA DO PANASCAL
Quinta do Panascal was one of the first estates in the Douro Valley to open its doors to visitors back in 1992. The estate, overlooking the Távora River, makes the respectable Fonseca Vintage port. Guests can take an audio-guide tour and sample three ports.

QUINTA DO CARMO
Producing wines of the Bacalhôa label in Alentejo, Quinta do Carmo's history goes back to the 17th century. The beautiful estate is in typical Alentejo style, and you enter the grounds through an ornate gate. Visits include vineyard and cellar tours as well as wine tastings.

QUINTA DOS MURÇAS
If you want to experience what life is like on a vineyard, head to Quinta dos Murças. The estate's eight terroirs produce a wide variety of reds, whites, and rosés. There are a number of 30- and 60-minute tasting tours on offer, but an even better way to participate in the estate's daily activities is by staying at the beautiful five-bedroom house with a terrace overlooking the Douro River.

QUINTA DO VALLADO
Established in 1716, Quinta do Vallado is one of the oldest quintas in the Douro Valley. Back in the day, it belonged to Antónia Adelaide Ferreira, a businesswoman known for her leadership in the cultivation of port wine. The estate is still owned by the Ferreira family, but today its portfolio has expanded well beyond port. There are tours and tastings year-round, as well as a number of other offerings such as private tours and wine workshops. Like many other quintas throughout the region, it also has rooms for guests.

QUINTA DE LA ROSA
This family-owned estate is one of the pioneers of red wine in the region. Production started in the 1990s, when most estates in the Douro Valley were focused solely on port. At Quinta de la Rosa you can learn everything about wine making, from harvest to bottling. It's also possible to stay at the quinta, and all 23 rooms (as well as the swimming pool) overlook the valley.

Quinta do Vallado

QUINTA DO CRASTO

Dating back to 1616, this large wine estate on the north bank of Rio Douro was marked on the first Douro Demarcated Region Map in 1843. It is managed by the fourth generation of the Roquette family, who have expanded the vineyards and wine tourism activities to include not only the standard visit of the estate but also lunches, dinners, and boat trips on the river. Quinta do Crasto regularly crops up in listings of top wine estates in the world, and has hosted the likes of Harrison Ford and Ronnie Wood over the years.

HERDADE DO ESPORÃO

This famed 1,700-acre wine estate in Évora produces Esporão, one of Portugal's top labels and also fine olive oil. The estate's restaurant serves locally sourced dishes and the cellar has an impressive collection of bottles.

QUINTA DO BOMFIM

The lovely Quinta do Bomfim has been run by a British-Portuguese family for five generations. The estate produces renowned Porto wines as well as other varieties. Among the estate's offerings are walking tours of varying distances and difficulties, and picnics on the terrace overlooking the river.

QUINTA DAS CARVALHAS

The Quinta das Carvalhas is one of the largest wineries in the Douro. Sitting atop a hill, it has privileged views over the valley. The property is about 1,500 acres and encompasses forests, olive groves, and fields, which visitors can tour accompanied by an expert grape cultivator.

Best Beaches in Portugal

NAZARÉ

Famed for its monster winter waves, the sands of Nazaré have plenty of appeal even to less adventurous visitors. The long, wide, half-moon of sand is dotted with colorful beach tents during the summer, when you can swim at the region's beaches.

PENICHE

Drive just 40 minutes north of Lisbon and you'll start to see the famous surf beaches of Peniche, an otherwise unassuming seaside town surrounded by soft sandy strands with breaks that attract serious surfers from across the world. You don't need to be a water sports enthusiast to enjoy the natural beauty of these beaches; while there's no scope for swimming at the long, windswept strand of golden sands at Praia Azul, the gorgeous beach at Foz do Arelho has everyone covered. On one side are crashing Atlantic waves, on the other side, the calm waters of a saltwater lagoon. Kids can splash around here to their hearts' content, adults can enjoy a leisurely swim, and the water is reputed to have healing properties.

PRAIA DA MARINHA

The quintessential Portuguese paradise beach, this pocket-sized Algarve beach boasts clear waters that lap against curious rock formations that have formed coves and caves from orange limestone. The same brightly hued rock makes a dramatic backdrop to snorkeling and sunbathing in this idyllic spot and, although it's located in prime tourist territory in the middle of the Algarve coast, the relatively challenging descent means it's less visited than other beaches in the region and maintains a hidden treasure appeal.

TROIA PENINSULA

If the packed beaches of Cascais and Estoril don't appeal as a day trip from Lisbon, head south of the city to the colorful small city of Setúbal. Although less polished than its beautiful sister city, Setúbal is rich in handsome historic buildings and manicured gardens, and its bay is officially ranked among the most beautiful in the world. The real treasures for beachgoers lie across the dolphin-filled waters, though, at the Troia Peninsula, where almost 11 miles of sandy beaches offer plenty of space and crowds are conspicuous by their absence. From here, visitors can head back to Lisbon or embark on a beach-hopping road trip along the Alentejo coast and down to the Algarve.

PORTINHA DA ARRABIDA

Located in the middle of the beautiful Arrabida National Park, where pine-covered mountains and rocky cliffs give way to pristine hidden beaches, Portinho da Arrabida is frequently cited among the most beautiful beaches in Portugal thanks to its clear, multihued waters and gorgeous setting. It's a relatively short drive from either Lisbon or the colorful port town of Setubal, and there are a handful of simple restaurants serving superfresh seafood to hungry beachgoers.

Praia da Rocha

PRAIA DE MIRAMAR

It may lack Lisbon's sunshine, but the Porto coast still has picture-perfect beaches. Just 6 miles south of the city is the pretty seaside town of Miramar, where 17th-century chapel Capela do Senhora Pedra sits proudly amid the waves on a rocky headland that juts out from the sandy beach. Still pleasantly uncrowded, Praia de Miramar is good for swimming in the summer.

PRAIA DA ROCHA

Many Portuguese beaches are notable for the curious rock formations that form nooks and crannies among the sands, and the popular Praia da Rocha is a prime example. The name literally means "Beach of the Rocks," and visitors can explore caves and caverns and swim through natural arches carved from the craggy yellow stone. And with many hidden spots among the rocks, it's easy to escape the crowds.

PRAIA DO GUINCHO

Flanked by rocky cliffs and dotted with sand dunes, this gorgeous beach on the western side of Lisbon's coast draws serious surfistas from Lisbon and abroad thanks to the near-constant winds that whip the water into giant waves. Although it's just a short hop from Lisbon, it feels like a real escape. If it looks oddly familiar, that may be because the beach appeared in the pre-titles sequence of the 1969 James Bond film *On Her Majesty's Secret Service*, and the area's protected status means little has changed since the scenes were recorded.

PRAIA DA COMPORTA

Portugal's Alentejo coast is often overlooked by beachgoers in favor of the Algarve or the Lisbon coast, but this scenic region is home to some of the finest beaches in Europe. While some are difficult to access, others, such as the beautiful Praia da Comporta, are well equipped to cater for visitors. Here, snow-white sands are dotted with sun loungers and straw-roofed beach huts selling cocktails as well as fresh seafood.

PRAIA DO RIBEIRA DO CAVALO

This picture-perfect beach is renowned as one of the most beautiful in Portugal, but the steep cliff-side scramble to reach it has defeated many a would-be beachgoer. From Sesimbra, 40 minutes from Lisbon, visitors need to abandon their cars midway up a steep road, and follow a less-than-obvious trail through gorse bushes before being rewarded with a view to die for. It may be easier to kayak from Sesimbra or jump aboard a fishing boat for a less strenuous journey.

What's New in Portugal

It's something of a mistake to say that Portugal's golden age was 500 years ago, when it was the richest country in the world. Sure, this was when Vasco da Gama and other explorers were heading out on the high seas in search of wealth, and when the most beautiful churches, convents, and national monuments were being built. In the 21st century, Portugal is going through a second golden age; the country is seeing growth like it hasn't encountered in decades, foreign investment is pouring in, and local economies are on the upswing. Construction is booming, with cranes dotting the skylines in the major cities, once-neglected older buildings being restored, and near-abandoned neighborhoods suddenly becoming trendy.

AN EXPANDING ECONOMY

The economic crisis that began more than a decade ago is largely a thing of the past. The austerity measures that were instituted have mostly been lifted. Portugal is not without some formidable challenges, but there is a sense of optimism. Some of the country's young people who went abroad to find jobs are returning because the country provides them with a good quality of life, a buzzing creative scene, and opportunities in burgeoning fields like technology. Immigrants of all stripes are joining them, giving the cities an increasingly international vibe.

Portuguese ingenuity and creativity are undiminished. In industries like textiles that were hard hit by globalization, companies fought back by producing better and better products. Portuguese winemakers raised their international profile, applying new methods to a unique roster of native grape varieties. Portuguese chefs finally caught up with their Spanish peers in applying new techniques to traditional dishes. And an industry of renewable energy—produced by wind, sun, and even tides—is branding Portugal the new "West Coast of Europe."

TOURISM IS BOOMING

The sluggish growth in tourism that has affected many other countries has left Portugal unscathed. That's thanks in part to its presence on seemingly every "hot new destinations" list in recent years. A steady stream of restaurants has opened in the major cities, and hotel occupancy has been rising steadily. By 2018, the number of travelers exploring the country was close to 13 million. The Lisbon area is now a leading destination for corporate conferences, thanks to year-round mild weather, relatively affordable facilities, and friendly locals. And with an increase in flights from North America and Europe, Porto is also emerging as one of Europe's top destinations.

Until recently, Portugal was hands down the best-value destination in Western Europe. That has started to change as popular spots like Lisbon and Porto have gotten more expensive, but everything from dinner in a nice restaurant to a stay at an upscale resort hotel has remained relatively affordable. You can eat delicious traditional food for as little as €8 for a main dish—a fraction of what you'd pay in a North American city—and it will be complemented by a flavorful local wine that's often cheaper than bottled water. Portugal is dotted with comfortable bed-and-breakfast accommodations at affordable prices. And all forms of transportation, even in the cities, remain affordable, with a one-way ride anywhere in the Lisbon subway system costing just €1.50.

WINES ATTRACT LOTS OF ATTENTION

It wasn't long ago that foreign wine drinkers knew just a couple of varieties from Portugal, especially the old standards of port and Madeira. But in the past several years, exports of dozens of different wines have skyrocketed. In the United States alone, imports of Portuguese wines more than tripled between 2000 and 2017. Regions that foreign drinkers had scarcely heard of, such as northern Portugal's Douro Valley, have become favorites on the international market.

Portugal produces many excellent dry wines, both high-end and ageworthy, as well as honest and straightforward youthful ones that you can buy inexpensively. If you're looking to try something different, Portugal has more than 300 native grape varieties in use, which makes for an endless procession of delicious experiments. Portuguese wines also come in a wide variety of wine styles, including sparkling, still, rosé, dessert, and fortified wines. At mealtimes in restaurants it is common for house wine to be brought out in jugs. The white is often served *à pressão*—from a pressurized tap—and is lightly sparkling. Don't be afraid to try it—these table wines are usually astonishingly cheap and surprisingly pleasant.

RENEWED PRIDE IN ITS TRADITIONS

Throughout the year, traditional *festas* are held up and down the country on local saints' days or in line with ancient pagan traditions. These often involve processions in traditional dress, neighborhood dance competitions, and rustic, traditional food tied to certain celebrations and regions. Far from being staged for tourists' benefit, festivals are a central part of Portuguese life, and emigrants generally try to ensure that trips home coincide with the local festa, particularly the ones that take place across the country during the month of June. Youngsters these days have a renewed interest in their heritage, and are taking an active part in keeping festival traditions alive—although they also flock to a world-class roster of vibrant rock festivals.

COMMITMENT TO RENEWABLE ENERGY

Portugal garnered global attention with its massive investment in renewable energy; according to the most recent figures available, it is now one of the top countries in the European Union in terms of capacity relative to population, with a ratio that is well above the continent's average. The EU has committed to getting 20% of energy from renewable sources, but Portugal set more ambitious goals of 31%. More than half its electricity already comes from wind, solar, or hydroelectric power—saving $1.1 billion a year in oil imports. The country's hydroelectic production has in some years been affected by droughts, but scientists are pursuing other solutions. The country has been promoting wave-power projects, and has rolled out a nationwide network of charging points for electric cars, as well as urban networks of shared electric bicycles and scooters.

Art, Architecture, and Azulejos

Portuguese artistic styles were inspired first by the excitement of the newly emerging nation and then by the baroque experimentation that wealth from the colonies made possible.

Painting came into its own in the 15th century with the completion of Nuno Gonçalves's Flemish-inspired polyptych of São Vicente (St. Vincent), which portrayed the princes and knights, monks and fishermen, court figures and ordinary people of imperial Portugal. It's on display in Lisbon's Museu Nacional de Arte Antiga. The work of the next great Portuguese painter, the 16th-century Vasco Fernandes (known as Grão Vasco, or the Great Vasco), has an expressive, realistic vigor. His masterpieces are on display in Viseu.

The elaborate decoration that is the hallmark of Manueline architecture is inspiring in its sheer novelty. Structures are supported by twisted stone columns and studded with emblems of seaborne exploration and conquest—particularly under Dom Manuel I (1495–1521)—with representations of anchors, seaweed, and rigging mingling with exotic animals.

Following the discovery of gold in Brazil at the end of the 17th century, churches in particular began to be embellished in a rococo style that employed *talha dourada* (polychrome and gilded carved wood) to stupendous effect. There are superb examples at the churches of São Francisco in Porto and Santo António in Lagos, and at the Convento de Jesus at Aveiro. For rococo at its most restrained, visit the royal palace at Queluz, near Lisbon.

In the 18th century, the sculptor Machado de Castro produced perhaps the greatest equestrian statue of his time, that of Dom José I in Lisbon's Praça do Comércio. Domingos António Sequeira (1768–1837) painted prominent historic and religious subjects. Portrait and landscape painting became popular in the 19th century; works by José Malhoa and Miguel Ângelo Lupi can be seen in the Museu de José Malhoa in Caldas da Rainha. The Museu Soares dos Reis in Porto—named after the 19th-century sculptor of that name (1847–89)—was the country's first national museum. His pupil António Teixeira Lopes (1866–1942) achieved popular success and has a museum named after him in Vila Nova de Gaia, near Porto.

Of all Portugal's artistic images, its *azulejos* (painted ceramic tiles) are perhaps the best known. It is thought the Moors introduced these tiles to Iberia, and although many are blue, the term "azulejo" may not come from *azul,* the Portuguese word for that color, but rather from the Arabic *az-zulayj* (little stones). By the 17th century whole panels depicting religious or secular motifs were common, for example at the Fronteira palace on the outskirts of Lisbon.

Tiles in a wide variety of colors adorn many fountains, churches, and palaces. The Paço Real (Royal Palace) in Sintra is one remarkable example of their decorative effect, but there are delightful combinations on the nation's *quintas* or *solares* (country residences) with interesting examples in the Minho region in the north. There are also well-preserved works on display in several museums, including Lisbon's Museu Nacional do Azulejo and Museu Nacional de Arte Antiga and Coimbra's Museu Machado de Castro.

Chapter 2

TRAVEL SMART

Updated by
Alison Roberts

★ **CAPITAL:**
Lisbon

POPULATION:
10 million

LANGUAGE:
Portuguese

$ CURRENCY:
Euro

AREA CODE:
351

EMERGENCIES:
112

DRIVING:
On the right

ELECTRICITY:
220-240V; electrical plugs have two round prongs

TIME:
Five hours ahead of New York

WEB RESOURCES:
www.visitportugal.com

AIRPORTS:
LIS, OPO, FAO

North Atlantic Ocean

PORTUGAL

Lisbon

What to Know Before You Go

When should you go? What should you pack (i.e. bathing suit or coat)? Should you tip? What time do you eat dinner? Should you try green wine? When should you drink coffee? Is Spanish the same as Portuguese? We've got answers and a few tips to help you make the most of your visit.

TIPS FOR TRIPS

Taxis are still found everywhere in Portugal, but Uber has muscled into Lisbon, Porto, Coimbra, and the Algarve, as has a budget-minded competitor called Bolt. In Lisbon and Porto there's also Kapten and Cabify (the latter has also made inroads in the Algarve). There's even an app for those old-style taxis, dubbed Free Now.

SLOW FOOD

Some visitors to Portugal complain about slow or inefficient service, and it's true that most locals value genuine human interaction over brisk efficiency. In restaurants, it may be worth adjusting your expectations and making a point of exchanging pleasantries with staff, who often respond with real warmth. If you are in a rush to eat, decent fare can be had at the counter of most *pastelerias* (pastry shops).

THERE'S A COOL WIND BLOWING

Portugal is not, strictly speaking, a Mediterranean country, but an Atlantic one. The ocean has a strong influence on the climate, particularly along the coastal strip where 85% of the population lives. Temperatures often plummet and the wind picks up even on summer nights, so pack a jacket or shawl in July or August.

GET CARDED

Portugal is a reasonably priced destination, but things like transportation in and around the major cities can add a lot to your bottom line. There's usually a discount card available that will make things a lot cheaper. In Lisbon it's the Lisboa Card, which gets you free transportation on subways, buses, trams, and other forms of transportation, but also provides free access to three dozen museums and galleries. Pick one up at any local tourist office.

MAKE SURE TO TASTE GREEN WINE

Northern Portugal has the country's largest demarcated region. Here they grow *vinho verde*, which translates to "green wine," referring not to the wine's color but to its youthful freshness from its particular production methods. Made from a mix of native white grapes, it can be naturally gently sparkling due to its high acidity, with a delicate, fruity flavor, although some producers of cheaper wines cheat with artificial carbonation. Vinho verde goes well with any kind of seafood and can even age well while still maintaining its sprightliness.

INDULGE YOUR SWEET TOOTH

Pastry making started off in convents, where egg whites were used for pressing and starching nuns' habits. The sisters used those leftover egg yolks along with sugar and cinnamon to make little egg sweets. Nowadays, pastries are so popular you cannot walk down a street in Portugal without encountering at least a couple of cafés or pastelerias. With all these sweets, it's no surprise then that the Portuguese also have some excellent espresso to enjoy with them; two of the favorite national brands are Delta and Nicola.

SAMPLE TRADITIONAL DISHES

The heart of traditional Portuguese cuisine is all about simple yet flavorful home-style comfort food to be enjoyed leisurely with family and friends. Historically, the majority of the Portuguese population were poor farmers, and families depended on what they could grow, raise, fish, or hunt. From these ingredients, families cooked up whatever could be used, with nothing going to waste. Today, much of this family-style cooking and serving remains ingrained in the cuisine, with an emphasis on simple local produce, grains, meats, and fish.

NIBBLE LOCAL SNACKS AT THE BAR

A common nibble in drinking dens is a plate of *tremoços* (soaked yellow lupin seeds), which bar staff occasionally hand you for free. Break the skin with your teeth and suck out the flesh (or eat them skin at all); they're salty but strangely addictive. In Lisbon and the south of Portugal, locals might order a plateful of *caracóis*—snails cooked in an herb broth—to accompany their afternoon beer. They're smaller (and cheaper) than the ones you might have sampled in France, and skewering them with a wooden toothpick can be quite a challenge. A chewier snack is *orelha* (pig's ear), usually flavored with cilantro.

ADJUST YOUR SCHEDULE

Restaurants in the the more touristy parts of town might start serving dinner at 7, but most Portuguese people wouldn't dream of dining at that hour. During the week, 8:30 or 9 would be a more normal time for locals to gather, and on Friday or Saturday it would probably be later still. As for going out on the town, don't even bother turning up at a nightclub before 2 am unless you're happy to be the only person on the dance floor.

SPANISH ISN'T THE SAME AS PORTUGUESE

In large cities and major resorts towns many people speak English and will immediately switch languages if you seem to be struggling. But off the beaten path they might not speak any English. Any attempt you make to speak Portuguese will be well received; a smattering of Spanish less so. You need not strive for fluency, as Portuguese can be difficult for newcomers to pronounce and understand; even just mastering a few basic words and terms is bound to make chatting with the locals more rewarding.

THE CORRECT WAY TO DRINK YOUR COFFEE

Milky coffee is all very well in the morning, but ordering it after a meal definitely marks you as a tourist. The standard local style is a strong espresso served neat, or at most with a drop of milk (as a *pingado*), and perhaps with a packet of sugar stirred in. Decaf (*descafeinado*) is now widely available in cafés and restaurants.

ROOT FOR THE HOME TEAM

Watch the big weekend soccer match, but not necessarily at the massive Estádio Sport Lisboa. The best place is the bar or café nearest your hotel. At any time during the week, one surefire way to get a conversation going is to ask about how Benfica—the professional football club based in Lisbon—is doing these days. At least a third of the country's population is said to support the club. To really get in tune with the locals, order an *imperial* (small draft beer).

GET YOUR TIMING RIGHT

With so many foreign tourists visiting Portugal throughout the year, few businesses continue the old tradition of closing up shop for the whole of August. Still, high summer is not the best time to enjoy this country, particularly the baking hot interior. If you want good weather but smaller crowds, time your visit for the shoulder seasons of June or September, when prices are well below the summer peak.

Getting Here

Air

The major gateway to Portugal is Lisbon's Aeroporto Humberto Delgado (LIS), located about 8 km (5 miles) northeast of the city center. The quickest way to get downtown is the Lisbon Metro, which departs every few minutes from Terminal 1. The 16-minute ride costs €1.50. Two different AeroBus routes depart every 20 minutes from outside the Arrivals Terminal and arrive downtown in about 45 minutes. The fare is €4. A third route runs on weekends and takes about 25 minutes to reach Sete Rios bus station.

Porto's Aeroporto Francisco Sá Carneiro (OPO) is handling more and more international flights. Like Lisbon, Porto has an efficient Metro running to the city center. The trip takes 30 minutes and costs €2. Local bus companies shuttle passengers between the airport and downtown for about €2.80. The Aeroporto de Faro (FAO) handles the largest number of charter flights because of its location in the popular tourist destination of the Algarve. Several buses make the 20-minute trip to downtown Faro and charge about €2.25.

The flying time to Lisbon is 6½ hours from New York on a direct flight; it's 10 hours from Chicago and 15 hours from Los Angeles on indirect flights. The flight from London to Lisbon is just under 3 hours.

The organization that oversees Portugal's airports, Aeroportos de Portugal (ANA), has a handy website with information in English.

FLIGHTS

TAP Air Portugal, the country's national airline, has daily nonstop flights to Lisbon from New York's John F. Kennedy International Airport and several nonstop flights during the week from New Jersey's Newark Liberty International Airport to Lisbon and Porto. United's daily nonstop flights between Newark and Lisbon are scheduled to provide convenient connections from destinations elsewhere in the eastern and southern United States.

British Airways, TAP, Ryanair, and easyJet have regular nonstop flights from the United Kingdom to several destinations in Portugal. From Spain, TAP, Iberia, Vueling, and easyJet have daily Madrid–Lisbon flights and Ryanir has flights twice weekly; TAP, Vueling, and Iberia fly daily nonstop from Barcelona to Lisbon. From the Netherlands, KLM, TAP, easyJet, and Transavia have frequent nonstop flights from Amsterdam to several Portuguese cities.

Domestic air travel can be a good value between major cities, such as Lisbon and Porto or Lisbon and Faro, though prices tend to increase during the busy summer months.

Bus

Portugal's network of regional bus service is comprehensive, punctual, and comfortable. It's a relatively inexpensive way to get around the country, and the views from your window are often spectacular. The only downside is that the great distances between the country's northern and southern reaches mean that if you want to see several different regions you'll spend a lot of time sitting.

Three of the largest bus companies are Rede Expressos, which serves much of the country; Rodo Norte, which serves the north; and Eva Transportes, which covers the Algarve the Alentejo. For major bus lines, you can buy a ticket online before you depart. For smaller rural lines, look for the schedules posted in the local bus station or at the local tourist offices. It's always wise to reserve a ticket at least a day ahead, particularly in summer when a lot of people are traveling.

There are three classes of bus service: *expressos* are comfortable, fast, direct buses between major cities; *rápidas* are fast regional buses; and *carreiras* stop at every crossroad. Expressos are generally the best cheap way to get around (particularly for long trips, where per-kilometer costs are lowest).

 Car

Many main national highways (labeled "N" with a number) have been upgraded to toll-free, two-lane roads, identified with "IP" (Itinerario Principal) and a number; highways of mainly regional importance have been upgraded to IC (Itinerario Complementar). Roads labeled with "E" and a number are routes that connect with the Spanish network.

Commercially operated *autoestradas* (toll roads with two or more lanes in either direction identified with an "A" and a number) link larger cities with Lisbon, circumventing congested urban centers. The A6 via Évora links Lisbon with Portugal's eastern border with Spain at Badajoz (from which the highway leads to Madrid).

Autoestrada tolls are steep, costing, for example, €22.55 between Lisbon and Porto, but time saved by traveling these roads usually makes them worthwhile. Minor roads are often poor and winding, with unpredictable surfaces.

Heading out of Lisbon, there's good, fast access to Setúbal and to Évora and other Alentejo towns, although rush-hour traffic on the Ponte 25 de Abril across the Tagus River can be frustrating. An alternative is taking the 17-km-long (11-mile-long) Ponte Vasco da Gama (Europe's longest bridge) across the Tejo estuary to Montijo; you can then link up with southbound and eastbound roads.

Some highways in Portugal—including the east-west A22 in the Algarve—now use electronic tolls only, with no method of payment accepted on the roads themselves. To avoid getting fined for not paying the tolls, if you rent a car in Portugal, make sure the rental car company installs an electronic device that adds the costs of the tolls to your final bill.

CAR RENTALS

To rent a car in Portugal you must be a minimum of 21 years old (with at least one year's driving experience) and a maximum of 75 years old and have held your driving license for over a year. Some car-rental companies may require you to have an International Driving Permit (IDP), which can be used only in conjunction with a valid driver's license and which translates your license into 10 languages.

Red tape–wise, your driver's license from home is recognized in Portugal. However, you should learn the international road-sign system (charts are available to members of most automobile associations).

RULES OF THE ROAD

Driving is on the right. The speed limit on the autoestrada is 120 kph (74 mph); on other roads, it's 90 kph (56 mph), and in built-up areas, 50 kph (30 mph).

At the junction of two roads of equal size, traffic coming from the right has priority. Vehicles already in a traffic circle have priority over those entering it from any point. The use of seat belts is obligatory. Horns shouldn't be used in built-up areas, and you should always carry your

Getting Here

driver's license, proof of car insurance, a reflective red warning triangle, and EU-approved reflective jacket for use in a breakdown.

Children under 12 years old *must* ride in the back seat in age-appropriate restraining devices (facing backwards for children under 18 months). Motorcyclists and their passengers must wear helmets, and motorcycles must have their headlights on day and night.

 Cruise

Portugal is a popular port of call for many cruise liners. Most stop at Lisbon, while a few include Madeira in their itinerary. There are also companies that offer more localized cruising opportunities, including River Cruise Tours, which offers luxury boat trips along the Douro River from Porto to the Spanish border.

 Train

Portugal's train network, Comboios de Portugal, covers most of the country, though it's thin in the Alentejo region. The cities of Lisbon, Coimbra, Aveiro, Porto, Braga, and Faro are linked by the fast, extremely comfortable Alfa Pendular services.

Most other major towns and cities are connected by Intercidade trains, which are reliable, although a bit slower and less luxurious than the Alfa trains. The regional services that connect smaller towns and villages tend to be infrequent and slow, with stops at every station along the line.

Advance booking is recommended along the main train lines. Reservations are also advisable for other trains if you want to avoid long lines in front of the ticket window on the day the train leaves. You can avoid a trip to the station to make the reservation by booking it online.

Travelers under 25 benefit from a 25% reduction in the price of all train tickets. Those over 65 get 50% off. In both cases, just show official ID with proof of your age, such as a driving license or passport.

Essentials

Dining

The dining scene in Portugal has changed dramatically over the past few years, with the country's best chefs taking a cue from their counterparts in Spain and around Europe. In cities like Lisbon and Porto, it's not hard to find upscale places that have won international awards for their inventive takes on Portuguese fare. But locals will tell you that the best food by far tends be found in the moderately priced and less-expensive spots. Don't expect much in the way of decor, and if you have trouble squeezing in, remember the rule of thumb: if it's packed, it's probably good.

Restaurants featuring charcoal-grilled meats and fish, called *churrasqueiras,* are also popular (and often economical) options, and the Brazilian *rodízio*-type restaurant, where you are regaled with an endless offering of spit-roasted meats, is entrenched in Lisbon, Porto, and the Algarve.

Shellfish restaurants, called *marisqueiras,* are numerous along the coast; note that lobsters, mollusks, and the like are fresh and good but pricey. Restaurant prices fall appreciably when you leave the Lisbon, Porto, and Algarve areas, and portion sizes increase the farther north you go.

Portuguese restaurants serve a *menu do dia,* or set menu of two or three courses, usually including a drink and coffee. This can be a real bargain—usually at least 20% less than the courses ordered separately.

Vegetarians can have a tough time in Portugal, although *sopa de legumes* (vegetable soup) is often included as a starter, together with the inevitable *salada* (salad). In general, in traditional restaurants the only other option (for vegetarians) are omelets, although more modern places nowadays tend to have at least one decent alternative. The larger cities have a few vegetarian restaurants, and Chinese, Italian, and Indian restaurants are increasingly common and always have plenty of vegetarian and vegan options.

MEALS AND MEALTIMES

Breakfast (*pequeno almoço*) is the lightest meal, usually consisting of nothing more than a croissant or pastry washed down with coffee; lunch (*almoço*), the main meal of the day, is served between noon and 3 pm, although nowadays, office workers in cities often grab a quick sandwich in a bar instead of stopping for a big meal. Some cafés and snack bars serve light meals throughout the afternoon.

Around 5 pm, there's a *lanche* break for coffee or tea and a pastry; dinner (*jantar*) is eaten around 8 pm, and restaurants generally serve until about 10 pm. Monday is a common day for restaurants to close, so check ahead.

Unless otherwise noted, the restaurants listed in this guide are open daily for lunch and dinner.

WHAT IT COSTS In Euros

$	$$	$$$	$$$$
AT DINNER			
Under €16	€16–€20	€21–€25	over €25

Essentials

Lodging

There are many different types of lodging options in Portugal, ranging from *residências* and *pensões* (simple accommodations which serve breakfast) to international chain hotels with every amenity you can name. Many who travel to the beachfront communities in the Algarve or along the Estoril Coast check themselves into luxurious resorts and never step outside them, thanks to amenities such as swimming pools, tennis courts, and a golf course.

The most unique type of lodging in Portugal is the *pousada.* The term is derived from the Portuguese verb *pousar* (to rest). Portugal has several dozen of these in restored castles, palaces, monasteries, convents, and other charming buildings. Each pousada is in a particularly scenic and tranquil part of the country and is tastefully furnished with regional crafts, antiques, and artwork. All have restaurants that serve local specialties; you can stop for a meal or a drink without spending the night. Rates are reasonable, considering that most pousadas are four- or five-star hotels. Some have 10 or fewer rooms, so make reservations well in advance, especially for stays in summer.

Throughout the country, though particularly in the north, many *solares* (manors) and *casas no campo* (farmhouses) have been remodeled to receive guests. These guesthouses are in bucolic settings, near parks or monuments or in charming villages. Some even let you help out with the work on the farm or in the vineyards.

Concentrated mostly in the northern half of the country is a profusion of *termas* (thermal springs), whose waters reputedly can cure whatever ails you. In the smaller spas, hotels are rather simple; in the more famous ones, they're first-class and are likely to have multiples pools, saunas, hot tubs, and treatment rooms.

WHAT IT COSTS In Euros

$	$$	$$$	$$$$
FOR TWO PEOPLE			
Under €140	€140–€200	€201–€260	over €260

Tipping

Service is not always included in café, restaurant, and hotel bills. Waiters and other service people are sometimes poorly paid, and leaving a tip of around 5%–10% will be appreciated (though locals often don't tip at all). If, however, you received bad service, never feel obligated (or intimidated) to leave a tip. Also, if you have something small, such as a sandwich or *petiscos* (appetizers) at a bar, you can leave just enough to round out the bill to the nearest €1.

When to Go

High Season: June through September is the busiest, hottest, and most expensive time to visit Portugal. While the north of the country remains cooler and quieter (except for a few days in August when Portuguese emigrants flood back to their town or village for its annual festival), Lisbon and the Algarve can be sweltering. Most Lisbon locals head south for the summer holidays.

Low Season: Winter in Portugal is growing in popularity due to the agreeable temperatures year-round and lower hotel

Tipping Guidelines for Portugal

Bartender	€1 per drink
Bellhop	€1 per bag
Hotel Concierge	€5 or more, if he or she performs a service for you
Hotel Doorman	€1–€2 if he helps you get a cab
Hotel Maid	€1–€3 per day (either daily or at the end of your stay, in cash)
Hotel Room-Service Waiter	€1–€2 per delivery, even if a service charge has been added
Skycap at Airport	€1–€3 per bag checked
Taxi Driver	Round up the fare to the next euro
Tour Guide	€5
Valet Parking Attendant	€1–€2, but only when you get your car
Waiter	5%–10%, nothing additional if a service charge is added to the bill

prices. Off-season activities are still varied and plentiful, and while the beach may be off the menu, pleasant strolls and cozy evenings are definitely on it.

Shoulder Season: Spring and autumn are both stunning seasons in which to visit Portugal. In April and October you may be lucky enough to enjoy a bracing dip in the pool or sea. Almond and orange blossoms perfume the air, key regions are quieter, and room prices have not yet peaked.

Great Itineraries

Lisbon to Porto

If this is your first trip to Portugal, this classic itinerary gives you a taste of the major cities of Lisbon and Porto, as well as the most fascinating stopovers along the way. As you drive north you'll see picturesque coastline, dramatic river valleys, and tree-covered mountains.

Fly in: Lisbon Airport, 7 km (4½ miles) north of the city center (LIS).

Fly out: Porto Airport, 11 km northwest of the city center (OPO).

DAYS 1–2: LISBON

Put on your walking shoes and range across the seven hills of the Portuguese capital city. If your knees can't cope, hop on one of the vintage street trams that traverse the city or one of the funiculars that carry you up to more lofty neighborhoods. Mosteiro dos Jerónimos and Torre de Belém—both UNESCO World Heritage Sites—should be on your itinerary, as should museums like Museu Colecção Berardo and Museu Gulbenkian. *Chapter 3*

DAY 3: SINTRA

On your way north from Lisbon, stop for a day to see Sintra's roster of fairy-tale palaces, castles, and romantic gardens, which together make it another UNESCO World Heritage Site. The leafy Serra de Sintra range is a lovely place for walks, and you could easily spend an extra day or more here. *Chapter 4*

DAY 4: MAFRA AND ÓBIDOS

After all that trudging, take it easy with a meandering drive through the fertile Estremadura region. On your way to the enchanting walled village of Óbidos, you'll pass Mafra, an otherwise unassuming town that is home to an ostentatious 18th-century palace, whose construction was financed by gold from Brazil. Famous for its cherry liquor and chocolate, Óbidos is a wonderful place to rest for a night after the hectic pace of touring Lisbon and its environs. You can even sleep in a castle-turned-pousada. *Chapter 5*

Tips

- Sintra is best avoided on summer weekends, when it gets very crowded. Consider an overnight stay so you can see the sights in the morning before the day-trippers arrive or in the late afternoon after their tour buses have departed. You'll also be able to enjoy a more leisurely meal at one of the city's highly regarded eateries.

- Drop into any of the tourist information offices in Lisbon and buy a one-, two-, or three-day Lisboa Card, which will save you significant time and euros on public transportation and admission to museums and monuments. The rechargable Viva Viagem card is another good option, but it covers only transportation.

- Plan your time carefully, as many major monuments and museums are closed on Monday, but others are closed Tuesday or Wednesday. If you're looking to save money, admission to some museums and monuments is free the first Sunday of every month, while others offer free entrance until 2 pm every Sunday.

DAY 5: COIMBRA

Coimbra boasts heady architecture, a sophisticated shopping scene, and romantic squares and gardens. The place oozes history: Portugal's first king was born and buried here. It's a hilly city, so be prepared, but the center is reasonably compact and you should be able to cover all the main sights easily in a day. Kids will love the mini-monuments at Portugal dos Pequenitos, where the entire country has been shrunk to child-size proportions. Don't miss the quirky *elevador*—a combination of funicular, elevator, and walkway—or fado, the most characteristic of Portugal's folk music. *Chapter 8*

DAY 6: BRAGA

The country's religious nerve center, Braga is an ecclesiastical heavyweight with a massive archbishop's palace at the center. A tiara of impressive religious buildings and sanctuaries encircles the town, including the extravagant Bom Jesus baroque pilgrim church, located 5 km (3 miles) to the east. Braga is a city for strolling. If you have the time, it's an easy day trip from Braga to medieval Guimarães with its lovely town center and magnificent palace of the dukes of Bragança. *Chapter 10*

DAY 7: VIANA DO CASTELO

A low-key Portuguese resort and the country's folkloric capital, this elegant seaside town has grandiose 16th-century buildings, superb restaurants, and sweeping beaches. Chug across the Rio Lima by ferry to the local strip of sand, stroll around the picturesque town center, and, if your timing permits, visit the bustling Friday market to pick up a few hand-embroidered linens as gifts for the folks back home. *Chapter 10*

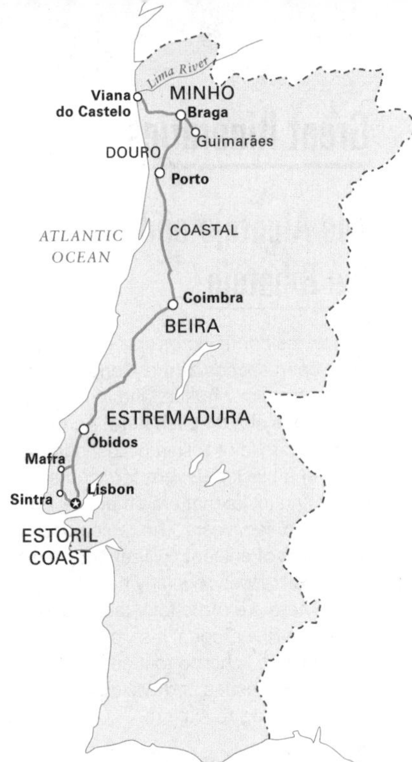

DAYS 8–9: PORTO

Portugal's second city and gateway to the north, Porto has a beguiling air of faded grandeur, with its peeling buildings and medieval tangle of riverfront streets. It's gaining in popularity as a city break destination, and has a lively nightlife scene as well as ample opportunities to sample port wine. Start by picking up a map at the tourist office and heading for the atmospheric Ribeira embankment, with its buildings strung with laundry and superb *tascas*, where you can tuck into fresh fish and admire the colorful lights of the impressive port lodges across the water. Some visitors might want to take a half-day boat trip up the Douro River, whose amazing terraced vineyards form another World Heritage Site. *Chapter 9*

Great Itineraries

The Alentejo and the Ribatejo

Lisbon residents increasingly see the wide-open spaces of the Alentejo as a refuge from city hustle, and life definitely moves at a slower pace here. Across mile after mile of rolling plains, sheep graze and black pigs root for acorns under cork oaks that are stripped of their bark every few years. The region bears the marks of ancient civilizations, and hilltop fortresses regularly heave into view. There are more fairy-tale castles along the River Tagus, just to the west. The Ribatejo is home to a number of impressive castles and walled cities that are fascinating to explore.

Fly in: Lisbon Airport, 7 km (4½ miles) north of the city center (LIS).

Fly out: Lisbon Airport, 7 km (4½ miles) north of the city center (LIS).

DAY 1–2: LISBON

If you've already seen Lisbon, you'll probably bypass the most touristy areas of Baixa and Belém in favor of more far-flung neighborhoods where you'll see more locals. You should plan on enjoying at least one meal by the river on a terrace and drinks at one of the many hilltop *quiosques* (refreshment stands) which have magnificent views. Take in a fado show as well, and stay up late for the unmatched nightlife. *Chapter 3*

DAY 3: ARRAIOLOS AND ÉVORA

On your third day, drive due east toward Évora, one of Portugal's most beautiful cities. Just before you get there, stop for lunch in the beautiful village of Arraiolos, famed for its handmade tapestries. The capital of the Upper Alentejo, Évora is a walled town known around the globe for its status as a UNESCO World Heritage Site. Lose yourself in the Cidade Velha, but be sure to see the main square, the Praça do Giraldo, the impressive Roman temple to Diana, and the haunting chapel of bones. Évora has some of the region's best restaurants and lodgings. *Chapter 6*

DAY 4: VILA VIÇOSA AND ESTREMOZ

Before leaving the Évora area, consider stopping off at a local cromlech or dolmen—prehistoric stone monuments—that sprout up in open fields and other unexpected locations. Then head east to Vila Viçosa and Estremoz, two of region's most important "marble towns" (Portugal is Europe's second-biggest

Tips

- Avoid heading inland to the Alentejo in August, when temperatures can be scorching (quite literally, as wildfires are often a threat in the hottest months of summer). Spring, on the other hand, is delightful, with wildflowers galore. Fall sees many food-related festivals taking place in the region.
- The driving conditions are relatively relaxing and easy in this region, with long-distance roads that are fairly flat and gently curving. The Alentejo is not well served by trains but express and local bus service is speedy and reliable.
- The Alentejo is a noted wine-producing region (not many people know this, but half of all Portuguese wine is produced in the Alentejo). Many vineyards are pleased to welcome visitors, but make sure to reserve ahead.

producer, after Italy). Vila Viçosa's huge Praça da Republica, lined with orange trees and anchored by a castle on one end and a 17th-century church on the other, is one of the finest squares in all of the Alentejo. These towns have lovely pousadas where you can spend the night in style. *Chapter 6*

DAYS 5–6: PORTALEGRE

Base yourself in the Portalegre area for a couple of days. Though the charms of the town itself are fairly soon exhausted, many stimulating trips out are possible: to the stunning hilltop villages of Castelo de Vide and Marvão, with its ancient battlements; to the Parque Natural da Serra de São Mamede—a lovely area for walking; or to the former royal stud farm at Alter do Chão. *Chapter 5*

DAY 7: ABRANTES

Head northwest toward the Tagus River, sighting the spectacular castle at Belver on your way. The flower-bedecked village of Sardoal makes for an enjoyable stop on the way to Abrantes—and yet another hilltop castle. *Chapter 4*

DAY 8: TOMAR AND FÁTIMA

Head to the pretty little town of Tomar, dominated by the hilltop Convento de Cristo (Convent of Christ) that was built in the 12th century by the Knights Templar. Nearby is the pilgrimage site of Fátima, which has one of the largest Catholic churches in the world. *Chapter 5*

DAY 9: SANTARÉM AND LISBON

If you don't need to head straight back to Lisbon to catch a flight, spend at least half a day in the regional capital of Santarém, with its impressive Gothic church and fine views over the plains that you have just traversed. *Chapter 4*

On the Calendar

January

Cantar as Janeiras. In many parts of Portugal it is still common to *Cantar as Janeiras*—sing January in. From January 1 to 6 groups of friends go door to door, proclaiming Jesus's birth and wishing their listeners a happy new year. This is often accompanied by traditional instruments. (Originally it was done in the hope householders might hand out Christmas leftovers.)

Feira do Fumeiro. The Feira do Fumeiro, a celebration of smoked and cured sausages and hams in the village of Montalegre in Trás-os-Montes, is a major gastronomic event in northern Portugal and draws thousands of visitors in January every year. A similar event in the same region takes place in February in Vinhais, the self-proclaimed *capital do fumeiro*.

February–March

Carnaval (*Carnival*). The final festival before Lent, Carnaval is held throughout the country, with processions of masked participants, parades of decorated vehicles, and displays of flowers. Nowadays it is influenced by the wilder Brazilian celebrations; the most genuinely Portuguese events are held in Ovar, Nazaré, Loulé, and Portimão, though there's a big one near Lisbon at Torres Vedras.

Feira do Queijo do Alentejo. One of Portugal's most prized cheeses comes from Serpa, a charming walled city in Baixo Alentejo, which hosts the country's biggest cheese festival each February. There are cheese-making demonstrations, sheep shearing and milking, and street dances with choral performances.

March

Essência do Vinho. Portugal's biggest wine showcase is Essência do Vinho, with thousands flocking to the Palácio da Bolsa in Porto, the city's old stock exchange, to sample the products of vineyards around the country. Check the website for wine events throughout the country all year. 🌐 *www.essenciadovinho.com.*

March–April

Semana Santa (*Holy Week*). Festivities for Semana Santa are held in Braga, Ovar, Póvoa de Varzim, and other cities and major towns, with the most important events taking place on Monday, Thursday, and Good Friday. Easter also marks the start of the bullfighting season and—outside Lisbon's Campo Pequeno arena at any rate—protests by animal rights groups.

April

Peixe em Lisboa. Lisbon's biggest gastronomic event, Peixe em Lisboa, or Lisbon Fish and Flavors as it's called in English, features top Portuguese and foreign chefs, who set up food stalls and do cooking demonstrations and talks. It's usually held in the second week of April; check the website for specific dates and venues. 🌐 *www.peixemlisboa.com.*

25 de Abril. The anniversary of the 1974 Carnation Revolution (actually an almost-bloodless coup) that brought down a dictatorship of four decades in Portugal is known simply as 25 de Abril.

May

Festas das Cruzes (*Festival of the Crosses*). Legend has it that, in the early 16th century, a peasant who insisted on working on the Day of the Holy Cross saw a perfumed, luminous cross appear on the ground where he was digging. Ever since, in late April or early May, Barcelos has held the colorful Festas das Cruzes, with a large fair, concerts, an affecting procession, and a fireworks display on the Rio Cávado.

Peregrinação de Fátima. Every May, thousands make the pilgrimage to the town of Fátima from all over the world to commemorate the first apparition of the Virgin to the shepherd children on May 13, 1917. These are repeated monthly through October 13, the anniversary of the last vision. 🌐 *www.fatima.pt.*

Estoril Open. Portugal's biggest and most famous tennis tournament, the Estoril Open—currently sponsored by the Millennium BCP bank— takes place on the clay court at the Clube de Ténis do Estoril. The tournament usually draws one or two top international players, and some up-and-coming Iberian stars. It usually falls in the last week of April, or first week in May. 🌐 *www.millenniumestorilopen.com.*

Rock in Rio Lisboa. Late May sees the start of the music festival season: in even years Rock in Rio Lisboa (the events were initially held in Rio de Janeiro before crossing the Atlantic) is first off the blocks with its family-friendly layout and predominately mainstream fare. Portugal's growing number of rock fests are a great place to see your favorite bands—tickets are cheaper than for events in most of Europe and generally mud-free. 🌐 *rockinriolisboa.sapo.pt.*

June

Festa de São Gonçalo. Amarante hosts the fertility-focused Festa de São Gonçalo, when St. Gonçalo (a locally born priest) is commemorated by the baking of phallus-shape cakes, which are then exchanged between unmarried men and women. Events also include a fair, folk dancing, and traditional singing.

Festa de Santo António. This festival is the first of June's Festas Populares, and the biggest party of the year in Lisbon (and a number of other towns around the country). On June 12, trestle tables are set up in the city's traditional neighborhoods (and some modern ones); colorful flags are strewn overhead, and grilled sardines and sangria are served. Throughout the month, there are free concerts and other events around town, and the streets of the Bairro Alto throng with revelers dancing to *pimba* (Portuguese pop music) through the night. 🌐 *www.festasdelisboa.com.*

Festa de São João. This festival is especially colorful in Porto, where the whole city erupts with bonfires and barbecues and every neighborhood has its own *baile* (open-air dancing). Locals roam the streets, hitting passersby on the head with, among other things, plastic hammers.

Festival de Sintra. One of Portugal's longest-running annual cultural events, the Festival de Sintra includes classical music and ballet performances by international and Portuguese groups. 🌐 *festivaldesintra.pt.*

On the Calendar

July

Festival Estoril Lisboa. This music festival in June or July includes concerts by leading Portuguese and foreign artists in several towns along the Estoril Coast, with an emphasis on performers from Mediterranean countries. 🌐 *www.festori-lisbon.com.*

Festa dos Tabuleiros. Every four years, Tomar hosts the spectacular Festa dos Tabuleiros in which young women march through town with trays on their heads piled absurdly high with bread and flowers. That main parade is on the second Sunday of the month; there are plenty of lesser but still spectacular events in the week preceding it. 🌐 *www.tabuleiros.org.*

NOS Alive. The biggest of Portugal's outdoor summer rock festivals, NOS Alive is held in Lisbon's riverside Algés district with a lineup that spans the musical spectrum, from indie rock to electronica. It's held over three days, and revelers can enjoy mud-free camping or buy day tickets and retreat to the comfort of a hotel bed at night. With impressive lineups each year, NOS Alive is often cited as one of Europe's best (and sunniest) music fests. 🌐 *nosalive.com.*

August

Festas da Nossa Senhora da Agonia. In mid-August every year, the Festas da Nossa Senhora da Agonia, at Viana do Castelo, is just one of myriad summer events in the Minho Province that features processions, folk music and dancing, greasy pastries, and fireworks. Usually held a week later, the Festa da Nossa Senhora dos Remédios in Lamego is a similar party. 🌐 *www.vianafestas.com.*

Festas da Nossa Senhora da Boa Viagem. In the Festas da Nossa Senhora da Boa Viagem, at Peniche, locals organize processions on land and sea in honor of the patron saints they hope will keep fishermen safe. It's celebrated on the first Sunday of August.

Festival Sudoeste. Another of Portugal's major outdoor music events, Festival Sudoeste is held near the otherwise-sleepy town of Zambujeiro on the Alentejo coast in the first full week of August. Expect up to five days of rock concerts and dance music, with top national and international names. 🌐 *www.sudoeste.meo.pt.*

September

Festa das Vindimas de Palmela (*Grape Harvest*). This festival in the historic town of Palmela, near Lisbon, has a symbolic treading of the grapes and a blessing of the harvest, accompanied by a parade of harvesters, wine tastings, the election of the Queen of the Wine, and fireworks. 🌐 *www.festadasvindimas.org.*

Queer Lisboa. In Lisbon, an active film festival season kicks off after the summer holidays with Queer Lisboa, one of the leading gay and lesbian events of its kind in Europe, in late September. The months that follow see showcases and competitive events focusing on genres from documentaries to horror movies. 🌐 *queerlisboa.pt/en.*

October

Festival Nacional de Gastronomia (*National Gastronomy Festival*). This festival in Santarém—the largest of its kind in Portugal—consists of cooking contests, lectures, and the preparation (and consumption) of traditional regional dishes. It takes place from late October to early November. 🌐 *www.festivalnacionaldegastronomia.pt.*

November

Festa de São Martinho. On November 11, the Festa de São Martinho is celebrated above all by *magustos*—tastings of the first barrels of the year's new wine, accompanied by roasted chestnuts. Celebrations, sometimes called the Festa da Castanha or Festa do Castanheiro (chestnut festival), are held in villages across the country. One of the most famous ones is in Marvão, in Alto Alentejo.

Feira Nacional do Cavalo (*National Horse Fair*). This festival in Golegã, in the Ribatejo region, combines parades of saddle and bullfighting horses with riding competitions, handicrafts exhibitions, and wine tastings in the first week and a half of November. 🌐 *fnc.cm-golega.pt*

December

Festa dos Rapazes. The remote Trás-os-Montes region unsurprisingly retains some of Portugal's most ancient pagan traditions. The Festa dos Rapazes in the villages around Bragança is one example; in the period between Christmas and the Noite dos Reis (the night of January 5) young people dress up in straw costumes to scare each other.

Contacts

Air

AIRLINES Azores Airlines. *296 209 720* *www.azoresairlines.pt.* **Sevenair.** *214 444 545* *www.sevenair.com.* **TAP Portugal.** *707 205 700* *www.flytap.com.*

AIRPORT INFORMATION Aeroporto de Faro. *289 800 800.* **Aeroporto Francisco Sá Carneiro.** *229 432 400.* **Aeroporto Humberto Delgado.** (*Portela*). *www.aeroportolisboa.pt.*

AIR TRAVEL RESOURCES ANA. *www.ana.pt.*

Bus

BUS CONTACTS Eva Transportes. *707 223 344* *www.eva-bus.com.* **Rede Expressos.** *707 223 344, 217 524 524* *www.rede-expressos.pt.* **Rodo Norte.** *259 340 710* *www.rodonorte.pt.*

Car

EMERGENCY SERVICES Automóvel Clube de Portugal. *808 222 222 for 24-hour emergency help* *www.acp.pt.*

TOLL INFORMATION Portugal Tolls. *707 500 501* *www.portugaltolls.com.*

Train

TRAIN INFORMATION CP. *www.cp.pt.*

Lodging

CONTACTS Associação das Termas de Portugal. *217 971 338* *termasdeportugal.pt.* **Central Nacional do Turismo no Espaço Rural.** *258 931 750* *www.center.pt.* **Pousadas de Portugal.** *218 442 001 reservations, 833 341 2401 toll-free from U.S.* *www.pousadas.pt/en.*

Visitor Information

Visit Lisbon
210 312 700 *www.visitlisboa.com/en.*

Visit Porto
300 501 920 *visitporto.travel.*

Visit Portugal
211 140 200 *www.visitportugal.com.*

Wines of Portugal
213 569 890 *www.winesofportugal.info.*

Chapter 3

LISBON

3

Updated by
Lucy Bryson

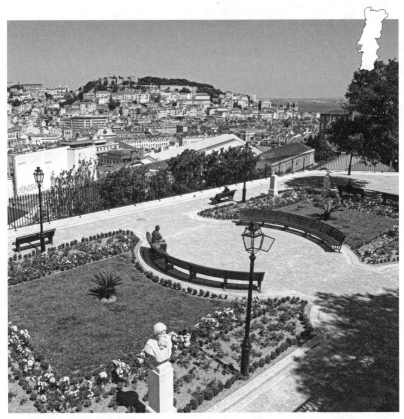

Sights	Restaurants	 Hotels	 Shopping	 Nightlife
★★★★★	★★★★★	★★★★★	★★★★☆	★★★★★

WELCOME TO LISBON

TOP REASONS TO GO

★ **National Treasures:** Mosteiro dos Jerónimos and Torre de Belém—both UNESCO World Heritage Sites—are grand monuments reflecting Portugal's proud seafaring past.

★ **World-Class Museums:** The Museu Colecção Berardo and Museu Gulbenkian are just two of the dozens of museums that make the city the region's cultural capital.

★ **A Step Back in Time:** Explore Lisbon on historic trams that wind through narrow cobbled streets where washing flaps from the windows of pastel-color houses and sardines sizzle on the grill.

★ **Buzzing Nightlife:** Lisbon has a reputation across Europe as a great place to hit the town, with venues ranging from laid-back bars to energetic nightclubs where people dance until dawn.

★ **Taking in the Views:** This is a city built on seven hills, so no matter where you are eating or drinking, you're likely to have eye-popping vistas.

1 **Baixa.** The center of Lisbon was built after the 1755 earthquake and tidal wave.

2 **Chiado and Bairro Alto.** The city's classy shopping and dining districts.

3 **Avenida da Liberdade, Príncipe Real, and Restauradores.** Notable for its parks and upmarket shopping and dining scene.

4 **Alfama.** The old Moorish quarter, which survived the 1755 earthquake.

5 **Alcântara, Cais do Sodré, and Santos.** Formerly run-down areas that are now hip nightlife centers.

6 **Estrela, Campo de Ourique, Lapa.** Relaxed and less touristy areas that are still within the city center.

7 **Intendente, Maritim Moniz, and Mouaria.** Vibrant, multicultural neighborhoods.

8 **Belém.** Beautiful area with several of the city's best cultural centers.

9 **Avenida Novas.** Modern Lisbon, popular with business travelers.

10 **South of the River.** Bars and restaurants a quick ferry ride from downtown.

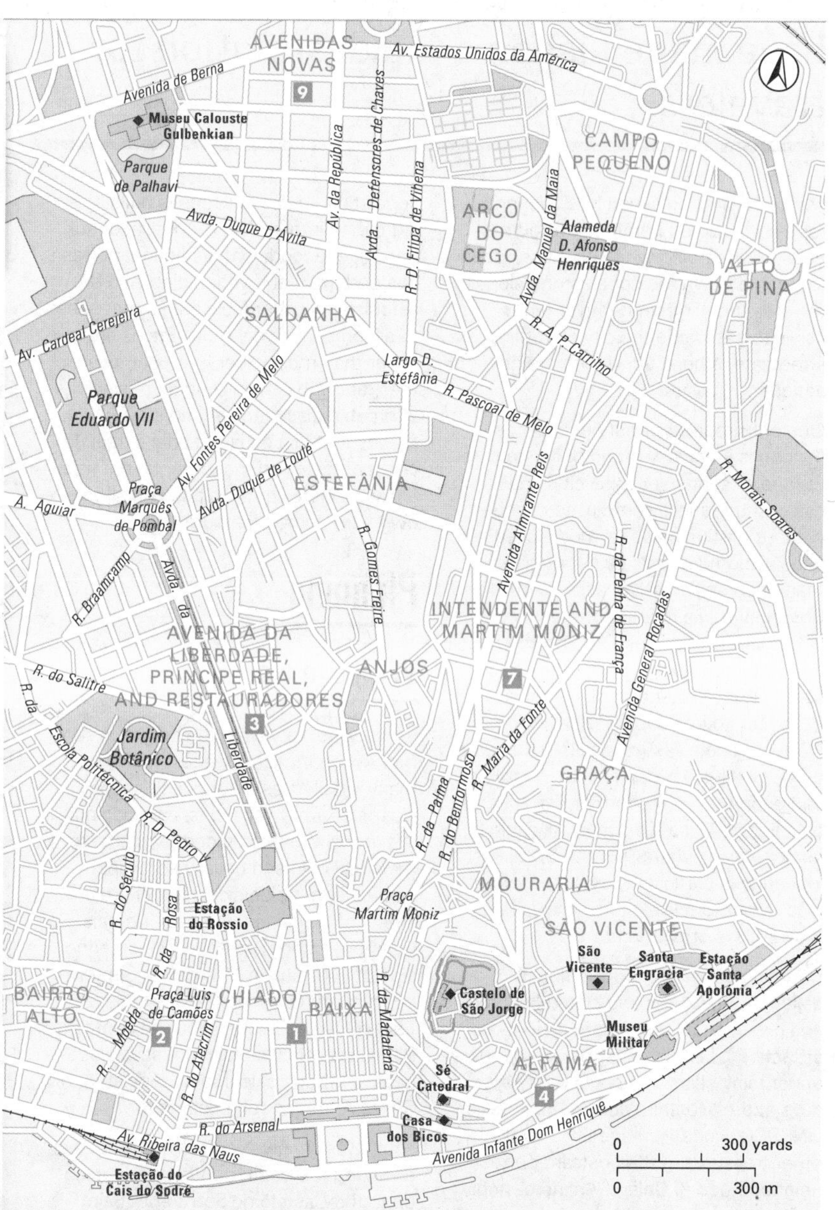
AVENIDAS NOVAS
Av. Estados Unidos da América
Avenida de Berna
Museu Calouste Gulbenkian
Parque de Palhavi
CAMPO PEQUENO
ARCO DO CEGO
Alameda D. Afonso Henriques
ALTO DE PINA
Avda. Duque D'Ávila
Av. da República
Avda. Defensores de Chaves
R. D. Filipa de Vilhena
Avda. Manuel da Maia
SALDANHA
Av. Cardeal Cerejeira
R. A. P. Carrilho
Largo D. Estéfânia
R. Pascoal de Melo
Parque Eduardo VII
Av. Fontes Pereira de Melo
Avda. Duque de Loulé
ESTEFÂNIA
R. Morais Soares
Praça Marquês de Pombal
A. Aguiar
R. Gomes Freire
Avenida Almirante Reis
R. da Penha de França
R. Braamcamp
Avda. da Liberdade
INTENDENTE AND MARTIM MONIZ
Avenida General Roçadas
AVENIDA DA LIBERDADE, PRINCIPE REAL, AND RESTAURADORES
ANJOS
R. do Salitre
R. da Escola Politécnica
Jardim Botânico
R. Maria da Fonte
R. do Benformoso
R. da Palma
GRAÇA
R. D. Pedro V
MOURARIA
R. do Século
R. da Rosa
Estação do Rossio
Praça Martim Moniz
SÃO VICENTE
São Vicente
Santa Engracia
Estação Santa Apolónia
BAIRRO ALTO
Praça Luis de Camões
CHIADO
BAIXA
R. da Madalena
Castelo de São Jorge
R. Moeda
R. do Alecrim
Museu Militar
ALFAMA
Sé Catedral
R. do Arsenal
Casa dos Bicos
Av. Ribeira das Naus
Avenida Infante Dom Henrique
Estação do Cais do Sodré
0 300 yards
0 300 m

An alluring combination of glorious architecture, deep-rooted musical traditions, and thoroughly modern flair have made Lisbon a top destination for travelers.

Famously built on seven hills, Lisbon's terra-cotta-roofed homes, turreted castles, and gleaming white basilicas appear to tumble down the cobblestone slopes towards the glimmering River Tagus as visitors traverse the city on rattling streetcars or head uphill with the help of antique funiculars.

One of Europe's hottest destinations (Lisbon is justifiably proud of its status as Europe's "sunniest capital city"), Lisbon has enthusiastically embraced change without casting aside its much-loved heritage. Colorful murals by internationally renowned street artists such as Vhils and Bordalo II make it one of the best cities in Europe to see street art. The city has gained a reputation as one of the best spots on the continent for live music—from rock to jazz and classical—with many outdooor festivals held in the city's numerous leafy green spaces. Brazilians and people from the former Portuguese colonies in Africa are continually enriching the city's cultural life. The Brazilian influence is particularly evident—young locals are more likely to sip a caipirinha than a glass of port wine.

Counting some of Europe's finest galleries, museums and cultural centers, and a vast aquarium among its indoor attractions, Lisbon's charms do not abate under rainy skies. You could easily spend days at the Mosteiro dos Jerónimos—a UNESCO World Heritage Site—and other treasures in the postcard-perfect neighborhood of Belém. An increasingly sophisticated dining scene is building on a growing international appreciation for Portuguese food, with its abundant fresh seafood, fruit, and vegetables, and the astonishingly affordable wines that seem to accompany every meal. Prices are still lower than most other European countries, and you can still find surprisingly affordable places to eat and stay. All this means that Lisbon is not only a treasure chest of historical monuments, but also a place where you won't use up all your own hard-earned treasure.

Planning

When to Go

It's best not to visit at the height of summer, when the city swelters in the heat, many smaller restaurants and shops close for family vacations, and lodging is expensive and crowded. Winters are generally mild and usually accompanied by bright blue skies, and there are plenty of bargains to be had at hotels. For optimum Lisbon weather, visit on either side of summer, in May or late September through October. The city's major festivals are in June, when the Santos Populares (popular saints) festivals see days of riotous celebration dedicated to Saints Anthony, John, and Peter.

You'll want to give yourself a day at least exploring the *bairro* of Alfama, climbing up to the Castelo de São Jorge (Saint

George's castle) for an overview of the city; another in the monumental downtown area, Baixa, and in the neighboring fancy shopping district of Chiado, and perhaps also in the funkier shops of Bairro Alto. Another again could be spent in historic Belém, with its many museums and monuments. Note that many are closed Monday, and churches often close for a couple of hours at lunchtime. Leave time in your schedule to take the ferry across the river to Cacilhas, for excellent fish restaurants and a handful of hidden waterfront bars that offer superb views of Lisbon.

Getting Here and Around

AIR

Lisbon's small, modern airport, sometimes known as Aeroporto de Portela, is 7 km (4½ miles) north of the center. Getting downtown is simple and inexpensive thanks to a metro extension that goes via the Gare do Oriente rail station, and to the special Aerobus shuttles. Line 1, which departs every 20 minutes between 7 am and 11:20 pm, drops passengers off near major downtown hotels at the Marquês de Pombal, Avenida da Liberdade, and Rossio stops. Line 2 departs every 20 minutes from 8:10 am to 9:10 pm, passing near tourists areas at the Martim Moniz and Rossio stops. A third line serves a direct route to Sete Rios train station, departing every hour on the hour between 9 am and 5 pm.

Tickets from the driver cost €4, or you can buy them online for €3.60; these are valid for all local buses for the next 24 hours. Two 24-hour Aerobus tickets cost €6 (or €5.40 online). The cheaper (€1.80) city Bus 744 departs every 15–30 minutes between 5 am and 1:40 am from the main road in front of airport arrivals. At night, Bus 208 plies a route between Oriente station and Cais do Sodré that takes in the airport.

For a taxi, expect to pay €20 to €30 to get downtown, plus a €1.60 surcharge for each item of luggage in the trunk. To avoid hassle, a prepaid taxi voucher (from €16 for downtown in daytime) may be bought at the tourist desk in the airport: you'll pay a little more but won't be taken for an extra-long ride. Uber users will find it quick and easy to order a ride from the airport, and most drivers speak English. Uber is often a cheaper alternative for getting around downtown, and many Lisboetas use this and similar apps in place of regular cabs.

BUS

Lisbon's main bus terminal is the Gare do Oriente, adjacent to Parque das Nações. Most international and national express buses operate from the Sete Rios terminal. TST buses bound for destinations south of the River Tagus depart from a terminal at Praça de Espanha. All of these stations are easily accessible by subway.

Few tourists take buses for travel within the city, as subway and tram service is fast and convenient.

FERRY

There are bridges across the Rio Tejo, but ferries are a quicker and much nicer option when you're headed to neighborhoods south of the city. Besides avoiding the traffic, you get amazing views of the Lisbon skyline. Ferries to nearby communities of Almada and Cacilhas are run by Transtejo Soflusa from terminals at Belém, Cais do Sodré, and Terreiro do Paço.

CONTACTS Transtejo Soflusa. ☎ *210 422 400* 🌐 *www.transtejo.pt.*

PUBLIC TRANSPORT

Lisbon's transit system includes trams, buses, ferries, and funiculars, and elevators linking high and low parts of the city. For all these forms of transport, paying as you board means paying much more—€2 a ride for each trip on a bus, €3 a tram, €3.80 for a funicular, and €5.30 for

These charming yellow trams are a fun way to explore Lisbon.

the Santa Justa Elevator. It's better to purchase a 7 Colinas or Viva Viagem travel card, rechargable cards that can be used on all forms of public transportation. A one-day card costs €6.40 and is valid on all of Lisbon's buses, trams, and subways. Buy them at transportation terminals and at the foot of the Elevador de Santa Justa. Public transportation in the city is operated by Carris.

Run by the Metropolitana de Lisboa, Lisbon's modern metro system (station entrances are marked with a red "M") is cheap and speedy, though it misses many sights and gets crowded during rush hour and for big soccer matches. For €1.40, you get one hour's access to buses, trams, and the metro: choose the "Zapping" option to load larger amounts onto your card if you intend to make multiple journeys.

Yellow Bus, now operated by Carristur, operates a special Hills Tramcar Tour that rattles through the most scenic parts of old Lisbon. The fare is €18 per person. It also offers an all-in-one ticket giving you hop-on, hop-off access to all its bus, boat, and tram tours for 72 hours. The fare is €40. **■ TIP→ Keep a close eye on your belongings when using public transportation, especially Tram 28, during busy times. Pickpockets ply their trade on crowded trains, buses, and trams.**

CONTACTS Carris. ☎ *218 503 225* 🌐 *www.carris.pt.* **Metropolitano de Lisboa.** ☎ *213 500 115* 🌐 *www.metrolisboa.pt.*

TAXI

Taxis in Lisbon are relatively cheap, and the airport is so close to the city center that many visitors make a beeline for a cab queue outside the terminal. To avoid any hassle over fares you can buy a prepaid voucher (which includes gratuity and luggage charges) from the tourist office booth in the arrivals hall. Expect to pay €15 to €25 to the city center and €45 to €50 if you're headed for Estoril or Sintra. Uber is also very popular in Lisbon, and it's worth downloading the app even if you're not a regular user.

Drivers use meters but can take out-of-towners for a ride, literally, by not taking the most direct route. If you book a cab from a hotel or restaurant, have someone speak to the driver so there are no "misunderstandings" about your destination. The meter starts at €3.25 during the day and €3.90 at night and on weekends. You pay what is on the meter. Supplementary charges are added for luggage (€1.60) and if you phone for a cab (€0.80). The meter isn't always used for long-distance journeys outside Lisbon.

You may hail cruising vehicles, but it's sometimes difficult to get drivers' attention; there are taxi stands at most main squares. Contrary to the norm in many countries, when the green light is on it means the cab is already occupied. Tips of up to 10% are appreciated, but not obligatory.

CONTACTS Autocoope. ☎ *217 932 756* 🌐 *autocoope.pai.pt.* **Retális.** ☎ *218 119 000* 🌐 *www.retalis.pt.* **Teletáxis.** ☎ *218 111 100* 🌐 *www.teletaxis.pt.*

TRAIN

International and long-distance trains arrive at Santa Apolónia station, to the east of Lisbon's center, after passing through Gare do Oriente, where commuter trains from south of the river, and fast trains from the Algarve also stop. Services to Sintra use Rossio station, a neo-Manueline building just off Rossio square itself. Trains along the Estoril Coast terminate at the waterfront Cais do Sodré station.

Travel within in the city is more convenient by subway or tram, but the Cascais train line departing from Cais do Sodré is handy for some destinations in neighborhoods like Santos, Alcântara, and Belém.

Hotels

Lisbon's lodgings have evolved dramatically in recent years, as the city's tourism boom has brought with it an unprecedented demand for accommodation in every budget range. Many of the city's grand town houses have been transformed into chic boutique hotels. Visitors are certainly not short of options for hotel stays: from luxury riverfront properties with award-winning restaurants and rooms in historic palaces to tiny B&Bs. Street noise can be a problem, especially in busy nightlife areas like Bairro Alto and Cais do Sodré. Some hotels charge the same rate for each of their rooms, so by checking out a couple you might be able to get a better room for the same price. This is especially true of the older hotels and inns, where no two rooms are exactly alike.

Lisbon is busy year-round, so it's best to secure a room well in advance of your trip. Prices have surged in line with the increased demand, but there are some good bargains to be had outside peak tourist season from June through September. Despite the high year-round occupancy, substantial discounts—sometimes 30%–40%—abound from November through February.

The Lisboa Card

The Lisboa Card (🌐 *www.visitlisboa.com/en/shop/lisbon-card*) is a special rechargable card that allows free travel on all public transportation (including trains to Sintra, Estoril, and Cascais) as well as free entry to more than two dozen museums, monuments, and galleries. The card is valid for 24, 48 hours, or 72 hours, and is activated the first time you use it. It's sold at airport kiosks, at Ask Me Lisboa tourist information offices, and at many other places around the city.

Restaurant prices are per person for a main course at dinner, including value-added sales tax. Prices in the reviews are the lowest cost of a standard double room in high season (off-season rates may be lower). For expanded hotel and restaurant reviews, visit Fodors.com.

WHAT IT COSTS In Euros			
$	$$	$$$	$$$$
RESTAURANTS			
€16 or under	€17–€22	€23–€30	over €30
HOTELS			
€140 or under	€141–€200	€201–€260	over €260

Nightlife

Newcomers to Lisbon often hit the bars around 9 pm and head home at midnight thinking that the bar scene is rather quiet. In fact, Lisbon bars don't get going until after midnight, clubs even later. On weekends, lively groups spill out of bars and stand shoulder to shoulder in the streets, especially in the lively Bairro Alto and the revitalized Cais do Sodré. Many places are rather quiet from Sunday through Wednesday although, in the summer high season, bars fill every night of the week with partiers who don't need to rise early the next day.

Some dance clubs charge a cover of €15 to €20 (more on weekends), which usually includes one or two drinks. Early birds sometimes get in free. Clubs are open from about 10 or 11 pm (but only start filling up well after midnight) until 4 or 5 am; a few stay open until 8 am. Be aware that some unscrupulous door staff will try to overcharge out-of-towners; if the price seems too inflated, walk away.

For a less boisterous evening out, visit a café-bar or a *casa de fado,* where performers sing the city's world-renowned, beautifully mournful style of music.

Lisbon has a well-established gay and lesbian scene, concentrated primarily in and around the Bairro Alto and the neighboring Príncipe Real area.

Performing Arts

Lisbon has a thriving arts scene, and there are listings of concerts, plays, and films in the monthly *Agenda Cultural,* available from the tourist office and in many museums and theaters. Also, the Friday editions of both the *Diário de Notícias* and *O Independente* newspapers have separate magazines with entertainment listings. The weekly Portuguese-language magazine *Time Out Lisboa* is even more comprehensive. An English version (*Time Out Lisboa: Lisbon for Visitors*) is published each spring and autumn, and available at newsstands all year.

Restaurants

Lisbon's dining scene has evolved dramatically in recent years to include any number of eateries with celebrity chefs, international reputations, and a menu of elaborate examples of New Nordic cuisine. But don't be fooled into thinking that all that locals eat is gourmet fare. The city's simplest and most traditional *tascas*—the family-run eateries serving traditional dishes—still do a roaring trade. Vegetarians and vegans, who until recently would have had a tough time in Lisbon, are now relatively well catered for thanks to an increased demand.

The city's colonial legacy is increasingly evident in its food scene, too: you can sample the flavors of Goa, Macau, and Mozambique, while the city's rapidly-swelling Brazilian population has contributed any number of places to enjoy a mighty meat barbecue or street food such as *coxinha de frango* (breaded chicken croquettes).

It's not hard to eat on a budget in Lisbon. Many restaurants have an *ementa turistica* (tourist menu), a set-price meal, most often served at lunchtime. Note that you'll be charged a few euros if you eat any of the *couvert* items—typically appetizers such as bread and butter, olives, and the like—that are brought to your table without being ordered.

Lisbon's restaurants usually serve lunch from noon or 12:30 until 3 and dinner from 7:30 until 11; many establishments are closed Sunday or Monday. Inexpensive restaurants typically don't accept reservations. Throughout Lisbon, dress for meals is usually casual.

Shopping

Shopping in Lisbon is less about international chains and more about locally owned shops. Here you'll find ceramics and lace made by local craftspeople, food and wine that impart the nation's flavor, and clothes by new and established designers. Shopping at the city's markets is fun and can yield bargains: two good places to start are the morning produce market that still occupies one half of the Mercado da Ribeira in Cais do Sodré (the other half is now a hugely popular food hall); and at the huge Feira da Ladra flea market, held each Tuesday and Saturday in Alfama.

Bairro Alto is one of the shopping hubs of Lisbon's flourishing fashion scene. The brightly lighted modern shops of local designers stand in stark contrast to the area's 16th-century layout and dark, narrow streets. The Príncipe Real area is home to one of the best spots in the city for boutique browsing at the grand Embaixada gallery. Many antiques stores can be found on a single long street that changes its name four times as it runs southward from Largo do Rato: Rua Escola Politécnica, Rua Dom Pedro V, Rua da Misericórdia, and Rua do Alecrim. There's also a cluster of antiques shops on Rua Augusto Rosa, between the Baixa and Alfama districts.

Several excellent shops in Baixa sell chocolates, marzipan, dried and crystallized fruits, pastries, and regional cheeses and wines—especially varieties of port, one of Portugal's major exports. Baixa is also a good place to look for jewelry. What is now called Rua Áurea was once Rua do Ouro (Gold Street), named for the goldsmiths' shops installed on it under Pombal's 18th-century city plan. The trade has flourished here ever since.

Tours

BUS TOURS

Many companies organize half-day group tours of Lisbon starting at about €35. Reservations can be made online, through your hotel, or at Ask Me Lisboa kiosks. Carris has hop-on, hop-off tram and bus tours of the city, as do several other companies like Cityrama Gray Line. HIPPOtrip uses amphibious vehicles that plunge into the Tagus River.

Cityrama Gray Line Portugal

BUS TOURS | **FAMILY** | This well-established tour company operates hop-on, hop-off sightseeing tours of Lisbon by bus and boat, as well as group tours out to tourist hot spots such as Sintra and the beaches of the Estoril Coast. ✉ *Areeiro* ☎ 🌐 *www.cityrama.pt* 🎫 *€35.*

★ **HIPPOtrip**

BUS TOURS | **FAMILY** | These lively, family-friendly trips aboard amphibious vehicles take a road tour of the city's major sites before plunging into water for a float on the River Tagus. Trips depart from Alcântara and last 90 minutes. ✉ *Doca do Santo Amaro, Alcântara* ☎ *211 922 030* 🌐 *www.hippotrip.com* 🎫 *€28.*

PRIVATE TOURS

To arrange private tour guides, contact AGIC or Lisbon Tour Guides. An English-speaking guide for a half day starts at €70, while a full day is €100. The well-regarded Rota Monumental offers private tours of the city in comfortable vans. For fun tours by jeep, motorbike, or side car, contact Bike My Side.

AGIC

GUIDED TOURS | The Associação Portuguesa dos Guias-Intérpretes e Correios de Turismo (Portuguese Association of Tourist Guides and Tour Managers) provides knowledgeable guides for individual and group tours of the city and further afield. Contact booking@agicportugal for booking and pricing information. ☎ *931 108 540* 🌐 *www.agicportugal.com/en.*

★ Bike My Side

DRIVING TOURS | For a unique experience, try taking a motorcycle sidecar ride around the steep streets of Lisbon with Bike My Side. Guide Daniel Coelho is a wealth of information about the city and its history and can advise you on the hottest new hangouts. Bike My Side also runs motorbike tours of the most interesting neighborhoods and jeep tours out to the surrounding hills. ✉ *Lisbon* ☎ *962 554 610* 🌐 *www.bikemyside.com* 🎫 *From €160.*

Lisbon Tour Guides

GUIDED TOURS | Friendly, experienced tour guides lead visitors on full- and half-day walking tours of Lisbon and daylong excursions to nearby Sintra and Óbidos. 🌐 *lisbontourguides.pt* 🎫 *From €50.*

Rota Monumental

DRIVING TOURS | **FAMILY** | The knowledgeable and enthusiastic English-speaking guides at Rota Monumental take visitors on individual and group driving tours of Lisbon and the surrounding area. ☎ *916 306 682* 🌐 *www.rotamonumental.com* 🎫 *From €49.*

★ We Hate Tourism Tours

GUIDED TOURS | This quirky company prides itself on knowing the ins and outs of Lisbon, offering expert guides who are happy to share their favorite bars, restaurants, and attractions. Its wide range of tours includes dinner at tucked-away eateries only locals know about and walks through "the real Lisbon." The offbeat headquarters is worth a visit for the T-shirts. ✉ *LX Factory, Rua Rodrigues de Faria 103, Alcântara* ☎ *913 776 598* 🌐 *www.wehatetourismtours.com* 🎫 *From €47.*

SPECIALTY TOURS

For foodie insights into Lisbon and its many cultural flavors, Eating Europe's Undiscovered Lisbon Tours run daily, and take in spots you'd be unlikely to find without a guide. For private wine-themed tours to Lisbon's hinterland, contact Have a Wine Day. Like to surf? You can find the best breaks with Surf Bus.

Have a Wine Day

SPECIAL-INTEREST | The scenic hills and valleys surrounding Lisbon are liberally sprinkled with vineyards, and Have a Wine Day offers flexible individual and group tours to the best wine-producing regions. Trips include visits to historic towns such as Sintra and Palmela. ☎ *916 470 995* 🌐 *www.haveawineday.com* 🎫 *From €55.*

★ Lisbon Food Tours by Eating Europe

WALKING TOURS | This company has won rave reviews for its insightful foodie walking tours in cities such as Paris, Rome, and London, and the plaudits are already pouring in for these four-hour food-focused tours of Lisbon. Beginning in the Baixa, tours led by knowledgable locals wind through Mouraria and Alfama, stopping to enjoy street-food treats and sit-down meals and along the way. Walkers also sample wonderful wines from different regions of Portugal. ☎ *308 810 685* 🌐 *www.eatingeurope.com/lisbon* 🎫 *From €69.*

Surf Bus

BUS TOURS | This well-established outfit offers trips to the best surf beaches surrounding Lisbon, including Guincho, Costa da Caparica, and Praia Grande. Full-day tours can take in farther-flung spots such as Ericeira or Peniche. Hotel pickup, lessons, and equipment are available. ☎ *913 587 655* 🌐 *www.surfbus.pt* 🎫 *From €15.*

WALKING TOURS

These tours of Lisbon require strong legs and sturdy shoes, but walkers are well rewarded with incredible views and unique insights into the city and its history. You can take free tours of Lisbon with Lisbon Chill-Out Free Tour, or pay around €20 for more personalized trips with outfits such as Inside Lisbon. Lisbon Walker does tailor-made walks with themes like Jewish Lisbon, African Lisbon, and even Lisbon: City of Spies.

★ Inside Lisbon

GUIDED TOURS | Inside Lisbon offers insightful and energetic walking tours that take in the highlights of the city, as well as less strenuous excursions to nearby spots like the castles of Sintra and the wine-tasting region in the hills of Arrábida. ☎ *211 914 545* 🌐 *www.insidelisbon.com* 🎫 *From €38.*

Lisbon Chill-Out

WALKING TOURS | Multilingual guides give the inside scoop on their favorite hangouts as well as insights into the history of the city. The free tours—you tip the guide whatever you think is appropriate—are three hours long and take in lots of hills, so bring water and wear comfortable shoes. The company also runs literature-themed tours and pub crawls. ✉ *Praça Luís de Camões, Baixa* ☎ *916 060 768* 🌐 *www.lisbon-chillout-freetour.com* Ⓜ *Baixa-Chiado.*

Lisbon Explorer

WALKING TOURS | This company takes pride in offering "tours for the culturally curious," with themes ranging from the city's Jewish history to a secret world of spies and subterfuge. Priced by tour, not by person, this is a good value for groups. ✉ *Praça Dom Pedro IV, Rossío* ☎ *966 042 993* 🌐 *www.lisbonexplorer.com* 🎫 *From €160 per tour* Ⓜ *Rossio.*

Lisbon Walker

GUIDED TOURS | Culturally curious visitors to Lisbon can discover the city's secrets, from hidden foodie haunts to the best shops only locals know about. Meet at the northwest corner of Praça do Comércio. ✉ *Lisbon* ☎ *218 861 840* 🌐 *www.lisbonwalker.com* 🎫 *From €20.*

Visitor Information

Your first stop in Lisbon should be the Ask Me Lisboa welcome center at the Praça do Comércio. English-speakers offer advice on everything from navigating public transportation to booking tours. There are pamphlets offering all manner of officially approved tours. You can also pick up a Lisboa Card, which offers unlimited travel on public transportation and discounted or free access to many major tourist attractions. There are also branches at the airport and at sights like Palacio Foz, Cais do Sodré, and the Lisboa Story Centre.

CONTACTS Ask Me Lisboa. ✉ *Rua do Arsenal 15, Baixa* ☎ *210 312 810* 🌐 *www.askmelisboa.com* Ⓜ *Terreiro do Paço.*

Baixa

The earthquake of 1755, and the ensuing massive tidal wave and fires, killed thousands of people and reduced 18th-century Lisbon to rubble. But within a decade, frantic rebuilding under the direction of the king's minister, the Marquês de Pombal, had given the Baixa, or downtown, a neoclassical look. Full of restaurants and shops, it stretches from the riverfront Praça do Comércio northward to the square known as the Rossio. Pombal intended the various streets to house workshops for various trades, something that's still reflected in street names such as Rua dos Sapateiros (Cobblers' Street) and Rua da Prata (Silversmiths' Street).

Near the neoclassical arch at the bottom of Rua Augusta you'll find street vendors selling jewelry. Northeast of Rossio, the Rua das Portas de Santo Antão has seafood restaurants, while the area also has three surviving *ginjinha* bars—cubbyholes where local characters throw down shots of the wild-cherry liqueur. One is in Largo de São Domingos itself, another a few doors up Rua das Portas de Santo Antão, and the third 66 feet east along Rua Barros Queiroz.

GETTING HERE AND AROUND

Baixa is Lisbon's downtown, so the area is well served by public transport. Local metro stations include Terreiro do Paço, Baixa-Chiado, and Rossio; large numbers of buses also ply the north–south streets of its regular grid, though their stops are all at its northern and southern ends, on Rossio and on or near Praça do Comércio.

Sights

Arco da Rua Augusta
BUILDING | **FAMILY** | Capping the postearthquake restoration of Lisbon's downtown, Lisbon's answer to the Parisian Arc de Triomphe offers a splendid viewpoint from which to admire the handsome buildings around the Praça do Comércio. Access to the arch is via an elevator and then up two narrow, winding flights of stairs. Once at the top, young visitors delight in ringing a giant bell, while the grown-ups can admire views of the Tagus River in one direction and the shopping strip of Rua Augusta in the other. The red-roofed houses and grand religious buildings that climb up the surrounding hillsides complete the scene. ✉ *Rua Augusta 2, Baixa* 🎫 *€3.25* Ⓜ *Blue Line to Terreiro do Paço.*

Elevador de Santa Justa (*Santa Justa Elevator*)
VIEWPOINT | The Santa Justa Elevator is one of Lisbon's more extraordinary structures. Designed by Raul Mésnier, who studied under French engineer Gustave Eiffel, the Gothic-style tower was built in 1902. Queues are often frustratingly long in high season, but once you're to the front of the line it's an enjoyable ride up to the top. On the upper level you can either take the walkway leading to the historic square of Largo do Carmo or climb the staircase to the *miradouro* (viewpoint) one level up for views of the entire neighborhood. The return ticket sold on board includes access to the miradouro, but at €5.30 it's a poor value—a 24-hour 7 Colinas or Viva Viagem public transportation card costs €6.40 and is valid on the elevator as well as all of the city's buses, trams, and subways. A Lisboa Card also includes admission to the elevator. ✉ *Rua do Ouro, Baixa* 🎫 *€5.30* Ⓜ *Blue or Green Line to Baixa-Chiado.*

★ **Fundação Millennium BCP Núcleo Arqueológico** (*Millennium BCP Foundation Archaeological Site*)
MUSEUM | More than 2,500 years of history is on display at this archaeological treasure trove hidden beneath a bank on one of Lisbon's busiest shopping streets. The buried network of tunnels occupies almost a whole block in Lisbon's historic center and was unearthed in the 1990s during excavation works carried out by the bank Millennium BCP. The digs revealed homes and artifacts from the Roman, Visigoth, Islamic, medieval, and Pombaline periods, and much of the space was used as a major-scale Roman fish-salting factory. It was later used as a Christian burial ground, and there's even a well-preserved skeleton to be seen. Free guided tours in English or Portuguese lead through underground walkways and around the foundations of ancient buildings. ✉ *Rua dos Correeiros 21, entrance on Rua Augusta, Baixa* ☎ *211 113 1004* 🌐 *www.fundacaomillenniumbcp.pt/en/nucleo-arqueologico* 🕒 *Closed Sun.* Ⓜ *Blue or Green Line to Baixa-Chiado, Blue Line to Terreiro do Paço.*

A Short History of Lisbon

Lisbon's geographical location, sitting alongside the wide and natural harbor of the Tagus River (Rio Tejo), has made it strategically important as a trading seaport throughout the ages. The city was probably founded around 1200 BC by the Phoenicians, who traded from its port and called it Alis-Ubbo. The Greeks came next, naming it Olisipo. But it wasn't until 205 BC that Lisbon prospered, when the Romans, calling it in their turn Felicitas Julia, linked it by road to the great Spanish cities of the Iberian Peninsula. The Visigoths followed in the 5th century and built the earliest fortifications on the site of the Castelo de São Jorge, but it was with the arrival of the Moors in AD 714 that Lisbon, then renamed Al-Ushbuna, came into its own.

The city flourished as a trading center during the four centuries of Moorish rule, and the Alfama—Lisbon's oldest district—retains its intricate Arab-influenced layout. In 1147 the Christian army, led by Dom Afonso Henriques and with the assistance of northern Crusaders, took the city after a ruthless siege. To give thanks for the end of Moorish rule, Dom Afonso planned a cathedral on the site of a mosque, and the building was dedicated three years later. A little more than a century after that, in 1255, the rise of Lisbon was complete when the royal seat of power was transferred here from Coimbra by Afonso III, and Lisbon was declared capital of Portugal.

The next great period—that of *os descobrimentos* (the discoveries)—began with the 15th-century voyages led by the great Portuguese navigators to India, Africa, and Brazil. During this era, Vasco da Gama set sail for the Indies in 1497–99 and Brazil was discovered in 1500. The wealth realized by these expeditions was phenomenal: gold, jewels, ivory, porcelain, and spices helped finance grand buildings and impressive commercial activity. Late-Portuguese Gothic architecture—called Manueline (after Dom Manuel I)—assumed a rich, individualistic style, characterized by elaborate sculptural details, often with a maritime motif. The Torre de Belém and the Mosteiro dos Jerónimos (Belém's tower and monastery) are supreme examples of this period.

A dynastic coup led to a few decades of rule from Madrid, which ended in 1640. With the assumption of the throne by successive dukes of the house of Bragança, Lisbon became ever more prosperous, only to suffer calamity on November 1, 1755, when it was hit by the last of a series of earthquakes. Two-thirds of Lisbon was destroyed, and tremors were felt as far north as Scotland; 40,000 people in Lisbon died, and entire sections of the city were swept away by a tidal wave.

Under the direction of the prime minister, Sebastião José de Carvalho e Melo, later to be named Marquês de Pombal in reward for his efforts, Lisbon was rebuilt quickly and ruthlessly. The medieval quarters were leveled and replaced with broad boulevards; the commercial center, the Baixa, was laid out in a grid; and the great Praça do Comércio, the riverfront square, was planned. Essentially, downtown Lisbon has an elegant 18th-century layout that remains as pleasing today as it was intended to be 250 years ago.

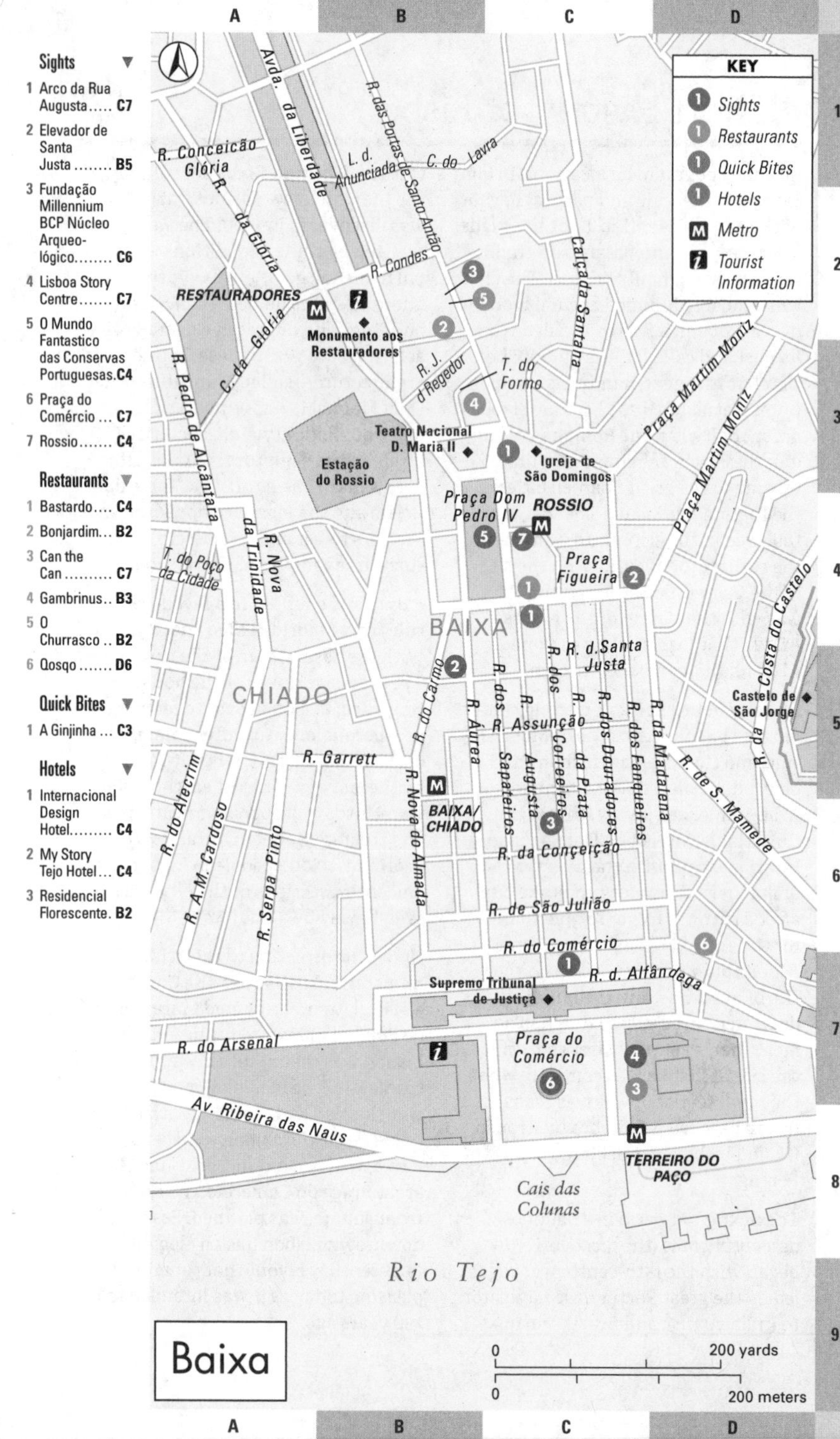
A
B
C
D
Sights
1 Arco da Rua Augusta C7
2 Elevador de Santa Justa B5
3 Fundação Millennium BCP Núcleo Arqueológico C6
4 Lisboa Story Centre C7
5 O Mundo Fantastico das Conservas Portuguesas. C4
6 Praça do Comércio ... C7
7 Rossio C4
Restaurants
1 Bastardo C4
2 Bonjardim ... B2
3 Can the Can C7
4 Gambrinus .. B3
5 O Churrasco .. B2
6 Qosqo D6
Quick Bites
1 A Ginjinha ... C3
Hotels
1 Internacional Design Hotel C4
2 My Story Tejo Hotel ... C4
3 Residencial Florescente. B2
KEY
Sights
Restaurants
Quick Bites
Hotels
Metro
Tourist Information
1
2
3
4
5
6
7
8
9
Avda. da Liberdade
R. das Portas de Santo Antão
L. d. Anunciada
C. do Lavra
R. Conceicão Glória
R. da Glória
R. Condes
Calçada Santana
RESTAURADORES
Monumento aos Restauradores
C. da Glória
R. J. d Regedor
T. do Formo
Praça Martim Moniz
Praça Martim Moniz
R. Pedro de Alcântara
Teatro Nacional D. Maria II
Estação do Rossio
Igreja de São Domingos
Praça Dom Pedro IV
ROSSIO
Praça Figueira
T. do Poço da Cidade
da Trinidade
R. Nova
BAIXA
Costa do Castelo
R. d. Santa Justa
CHIADO
R. do Carmo
R. Áurea
R. dos Sapateiros
R. Augusta
R. dos Correeiros
R. da Prata
R. dos Douradores
R. dos Fanqueiros
R. da Madalena
R. Assunção
Castelo de São Jorge
R. da
R. de S. Mamede
R. Garrett
R. do Alecrim
R. A.M. Cardoso
R. Serpa Pinto
R. Nova do Almada
BAIXA/ CHIADO
R. da Conceição
R. de São Julião
R. do Comércio
R. d. Alfândega
Supremo Tribunal de Justiça
R. do Arsenal
Praça do Comércio
Av. Ribeira das Naus
TERREIRO DO PAÇO
Cais das Colunas
Rio Tejo
Baixa
0
200 yards
0
200 meters

★ **Lisboa Story Centre**

INFO CENTER | FAMILY | This family-friendly museum uses multimedia exhibits to bring Lisbon's history to life. Over the course of an hour, the story is broken down into chapters, with a focus on the country's golden age of maritime adventures. A multilingual audio guide takes visitors through a series of exhibits. Midway through, a small cinema shows a short but dramatic reenactment of the 1755 earthquake and the fiery aftermath. ✉ *Praço do Comércio 78–81, Baixa* ☎ *211 941 099* 🌐 *lisboastorycentre.pt/en* 🎫 *€7, €8 includes Rua Augusta Arch* Ⓜ *Blue Line to Terreiro do Paço.*

O Mundo Fantastico das Conservas Portuguesas (*The Fantastic World of Portuguese Sardines*)

LOCAL INTEREST | FAMILY | If Willy Wonka turned his attention to canned fish, it would probably look something like this flamboyant shop on Rossio Square. A riot of color, complete with a miniature sardine-themed Ferris wheel, the Fantastic World of Portuguese Sardines is a gift shop and sightseeing experience all in one. ✉ *Rua Dom Pedro IV 39, Rossío* ☎ *211 349 044* 🌐 *www.mundofantasticodasardinha.pt* Ⓜ *Green Line to Rossio.*

★ **Praça do Comércio**

PLAZA | FAMILY | Known to locals as the Terreiro do Paço after the royal palace that once stood on this spot, the Praça do Comércio is lined with 18th-century buildings fronted by expansive esplanades. Down by the river, steps and slopes—once used by occupants of the royal barges that docked here—lead up from the water, and sunbathers strip down to catch rays during the summer. The equestrian statue in the center is of Dom José I, king at the time of the earthquake and subsequent rebuilding. In 1908, amid unrest that led to the declaration of a republic, King Carlos and his eldest son, Luís Filipe, were assassinated as they rode through the square in a carriage. In the summer, live samba bands play at sunset while vans sell potent cocktails. ✉ *Praça do Comércio, Baixa* Ⓜ *Blue Line to Terreiro do Paço.*

★ **Rossio**

PLAZA | FAMILY | The formal name for this grand public square is Praça Dom Pedro IV, but locals stick to the previous name, Rossio. Built in the 13th century as Lisbon's main public space, it remains a bustling social hub and—traffic noise aside—it's still impressive, and crowds socialize among baroque fountains beneath a statue of Dom Pedro atop a towering column. Visitors can admire the dramatic wave-pattern cobblestones, famously reconstructed on the beach promenades of Rio de Janeiro. The square was founded as the largest public space in the city and has seen everything from bullfights to public executions. On nearby Largo de São Domingos, where thousands were burned, there's a memorial to Jewish victims of the Portuguese Inquisition. Today, locals come here to relax with a newspaper, have their boots polished by the shoe shiners, or sip a ginjinha (traditional sour-cherry liqueur) at one of the bars. ✉ *Praça Dom Pedro IV, Rossío* Ⓜ *Green Line to Rossio.*

Coffee and Quick Bites

A Ginjinha

$ | PORTUGUESE | A tourist attraction in its own right, this tiny bar facing a beautiful square is the best place in the Baixa to sample Lisbon's famous *ginja (* cherry liqueur). Open since 1840, when the Galician Francisco Espinheira became the first purveyor of the spirit in Lisbon, the bar serves the sweet drink with or without cherries (opt for the version with fruit it you want to convince yourself you're getting some vitamins). **Known for:** whenever you come it's a standing-room-only crowd; bottles of the liqueur stacked up to the ceiling; tasty espresso coffees. $ *Average main: €2* ✉ *Largo de São Domingos 8, Baixa* ☎ *218 145 374* 💳 *No credit cards* Ⓜ *Green Line to Rossio.*

The historic Gothic-style Santa Justa Elevator is a popular stop on Lisbon's tourist trail.

Restaurants

★ Bastardo

$$ | **CONTEMPORARY** | The cool, colorful restaurant at the Internacional Design Hotel is as cheeky and irreverent as its name suggests. Expect the unexpected on the menu, which takes the country's culinary traditions on fantastic flights of fancy in dishes like shrimp with asparagus, foie gras, and roasted padrón peppers. **Known for:** innovative and eclectic dinner menu; playful interior design; bar serves potent cocktails. *Average main: €17 ✉ Internacional Design Hotel, Rua Betesga 3, Rossío ☎ 213 240 993 🌐 restaurantebastardo.com Ⓜ Green Line to Rossio.*

Bonjardim

$ | **PORTUGUESE** | In an alley between Praça dos Restauradores and Rua das Portas de Santo Antão, this eatery known locally as Rei dos Frangos (King of Chickens) specializes in spicy, spit-roasted *peri peri* chicken. The restaurant and adjacent esplanade are crowded at dinner, but watching the frenzied waiters is a lesson in the service industry. **Known for:** if you can't wait, there's always take-out; extremely popular with locals; handsome dining room. *Average main: €12 ✉ Travessa de Santo Antão 11–12, Baixa ☎ 213 427 424 Ⓜ Green Line to Rossio.*

Can the Can

$$ | **PORTUGUESE** | **FAMILY** | The Portuguese take their canned fish seriously. Find out what all the fuss is about at this funky restaurant where the chefs incorporate canned goods into all manner of dishes—it sounds gimmicky, but the results are delicious. **Known for:** delicious dishes you can't imagine come from a can; prime location facing Terreiro do Paço; terrace seating. *Average main: €19 ✉ Praça do Comércio 82–83, Baixa ☎ 218 851 392 🌐 canthecan.net Ⓜ Blue Line to Terreiro do Paço.*

Gambrinus

$$$$ | **SEAFOOD** | In business for more than seven decades, Gambrinus has plenty of historical drama in its decor, including arched wooden ceilings and stained-glass depictions of beer-swilling royals.

Prawns, lobster, and crab are always available, and seasonal choices like sea bream, sea bass, sole are offered grilled or garnished with clam sauce. **Known for:** eye-catching mural across an entire wall; seafood doesn't get any fresher; attentive service. *Average main: €34 Rua das Portas de Santo Antão 23–25, Restauradores 213 421 466 www.gambrinuslisboa.com Blue Line to Restauradores, Blue or Green Line to Rossio.*

O Churrasco

$$ | **PORTUGUESE** | **FAMILY** | On a street lined with tourist traps, O Churrasco is the local favorite and deservedly so. The paneled dining room serves top-notch peri peri chicken, sizzling steaks, and perfectly grilled fish. **Known for:** ideal location near all of the major sights; scattering of tables on the street; old-fashioned service. *Average main: €17 Rua das Portas de Santo Antão 83–85, Restauradores 213 423 059 restauranteo-churrasco.business.site Blue Line to Restauradores, Green Line to Rossio.*

★ **Qosqo**

$$ | **PERUVIAN** | Fans are adamant that this longtime favorite serves the best ceviche outside Peru, and it's hard to argue with that. The bartender mixes up excellent pisco sours, too. **Known for:** excellent takes on South American cuisine; gets all the little details right; relaxed dining room. *Average main: €17 Rua dos Bacalhoeiros 26A, Baixa 916 046 197 Closed Mon. No dinner Sun. Blue Line to Terreiro do Paço.*

Hotels

Internacional Design Hotel

$$ | **HOTEL** | Rooms at this fun and funky design hotel overlooking the Rossio are themed by design as well as by scent—take your pick from Urban, Tribal, Zen, and Pop. All of the rooms have unique designs with strikingly modern artworks, and some have private terraces with views of the bustling square and the shopping street of Rua Augusta. **Pros:** double-glazed windows to keep out the noise; stylishly decorated common areas; perfect location. **Cons:** some rooms don't have those great views; street-facing rooms still get some noise; no exercise facilities. *Rooms from: €160 Rua da Betesga 13, Baixa 213 240 990 www.idesignhotel.com 55 rooms Free Breakfast Green Line to Rossio.*

My Story Tejo Hotel

$$ | **HOTEL** | Just a few steps away from the busy Praça da Figueira, this hotel offers smart, modern rooms in a nicely restored 19th-century building. **Pros:** central location not far from the Rossio; renovations have preserved period details; restaurant serves Portuguese dishes. **Cons:** tends to get very busy in high season; some rooms tucked into odd spaces; not all rooms have views. *Rooms from: €170 Rua Condes de Monsanto 2, Baixa 218 866 182 www.mystoryhotels.com/mystorytejo 58 rooms Free Breakfast Green Line to Rossio.*

Residencial Florescente

$ | **B&B/INN** | If you're looking for a great location for sightseeing, check into one of the bright and cheerful rooms on the five azulejo-tile-lined floors of the Residencial Florescente. **Pros:** Rossio and Restauradores are steps away; gleaming white-marble bathrooms; family-friendly atmosphere. **Cons:** the smallest rooms are very small; front rooms are a little dark; some street noise at night. *Rooms from: €95 Rua Portas de Santo Antão 99, Baixa 218 842 000 www.residencialflorescente.com 68 rooms Free Breakfast Blue Line to Restauradores.*

Nightlife

BARS

★ Trobadores Taberna Medieval

BARS/PUBS | Drink mead from a ceramic mug and pretend you're back in medieval times at this offbeat and off-the-tourist-trail tavern. Exposed rafters, flickering candles, and live folk performances add to the old-world ambience. ✉ *Rua de São Julião 27, Baixa* ☎ *218 850 329* Ⓜ *Blue or Green Line to Baixa-Chiado.*

Performing Arts

THEATERS

★ Teatro Nacional de São Carlos

THEATER | Inaugurated in 1793, this grand neoclassical theater was inspired by classics from Naples and Milan. You have to see the main hall to appreciate the building's splendor. The stage itself is rather plain, but the five tiers of private boxes on either side draw the eye to the domed royal box, awash with gold leaf and held aloft by soaring columns. Two cherubs hold aloft the royal coat of arms. Originally an opera house, the space is now home to the Portuguese Symphonic Orchestra and hosts music and dance performances. Book guided tours in advance. ✉ *Rua Serpa Pinto 9, Baixa* ☎ *213 253 045* 🌐 *www.tnsc.pt* Ⓜ *Blue or Green Line to Baixa-Chiado.*

Teatro Nacional Dona Maria II

THEATER | Dominating the northern side of the Rossio, this Palladian-style building finished in 1846 is one of the city's crowning glories. The six ionic columns draw your eye upward to a carving of Apollo singing to the Muses. In addition to theatrical performances, there are regular art exhibits that are usually well worth a look. English-language guided tours are held every Monday (advance booking is required). ✉ *Praça Dom Pedro IV, Rossío* ☎ *800 213 250* 🌐 *www.tndm.pt/pt* Ⓜ *Green Line to Rossio.*

Shopping

CLOTHING

A Outra Face da Lua

CLOTHING | This surprisingly spacious shop is about as unconventional as it gets in Lisbon. Prepare to be completely engaged by the eclectic mix of vintage clothes, needlepoint purses, and boxes of costume jewelry—you name it, really. Plus there's a café in the middle. ✉ *Rua da Assunção 22, Baixa* ☎ *218 863 430* 🌐 *www.aoutrafacedalua.com* Ⓜ *Blue or Green Line to Baixa-Chiado.*

FOOD AND WINE

★ Conserveira de Lisboa

FOOD/CANDY | There's a feast for the eyes at this shop, whose walls are lined with colorful tins of sardines and other seafood, as well as fruit preserves and other delicacies. The staff serves you from behind an antique wooden counter. ✉ *Rua dos Bacalhoeiros 34, Baixa* ☎ *218 864 009* 🌐 *www.conserveiradelisboa.pt* Ⓜ *Blue Line to Terreiro do Paço.*

★ Garrafeira Nacional

WINE/SPIRITS | In business for almost a century, this low-pressure wine merchant has a knowledgeable English-speaking staff that will let you know everything about the vintage you've selected. Bottles are stacked from floor to ceiling and packed in glass vitrines like museum displays. Garrafeira Nacional is also known for its selection of Portuguese spirits. ✉ *Rua Santa Justa 18, Baixa* ☎ *218 879 080* 🌐 *www.garrafeiranacional.com/en/lojas* Ⓜ *Blue or Green Line to Baixa-Chiado.*

Garrafeira Napoleão

WINE/SPIRITS | It doesn't look like they could fit one more bottle on the shelves at Garrafeira Napoleão, sister shop to Garrafeira Nacioinal. The English-speaking staff at this wine store can recommend vintages. Everything is clearly marked with colorful labels. ✉ *Rua da Conceição 20/26, Baixa* ☎ *218 861 108* 🌐 *www.napoleao.eu/* Ⓜ *Green Line to Rossio.*

The waterfront Praça do Comércio is one of Lisbon's most spectacular squares.

Manuel Tavares

FOOD/CANDY | Just off the Rossio, this enticing shop dating back to 1860 stocks cheeses, preserves, vintage port, and other fine Portuguese products. ⊠ *Rua da Betesga 1AB, Baixa* ☎ *213 424 209* 🌐 *www.manueltavares.com* Ⓜ *Green Line to Rossio.*

Queijaria Nacional

FOOD/CANDY | A long glass display counter showcases the country's wealth of cheeses and meats. If a nibble isn't enough, order a platter and take a seat in the dining room in the rear. ⊠ *Rua da Conceição 8, Baixa* ☎ *912 082 450* Ⓜ *Blue or Green Line to Baixa-Chiado.*

JEWELRY

★ Margarida Pimentel

JEWELRY/ACCESSORIES | This Portuguese designer crafts gold and silver into incredible shapes for showstopping rings, bracelets, and necklaces. ⊠ *Rua Augusta 55, Belém* ☎ *219 992 479* Ⓜ *Blue or Green Line to Baixa-Chiado.*

★ W. A. Sarmento

JEWELRY/ACCESSORIES | One of the city's oldest goldsmiths, this shop that first opened its doors in 1870 produces characteristic Portuguese gold and silver filigree work. ⊠ *Rua Áurea 251, Baixa* ☎ *213 426 774* 🌐 *ourivesariasarmento.pt* Ⓜ *Blue or Green Line to Baixa-Chiado.*

MUSIC

★ Discoteca Amália

MUSIC STORES | You'll know you're close to this legendary record store when you hear tear-inducing fado tunes blasting out into the street. Come for soulful music by Amália Rodrigues and other leading *fadistas.* ⊠ *Rua Áurea 272, Baixa* ☎ *213 420 939* Ⓜ *Green Line to Rossio.*

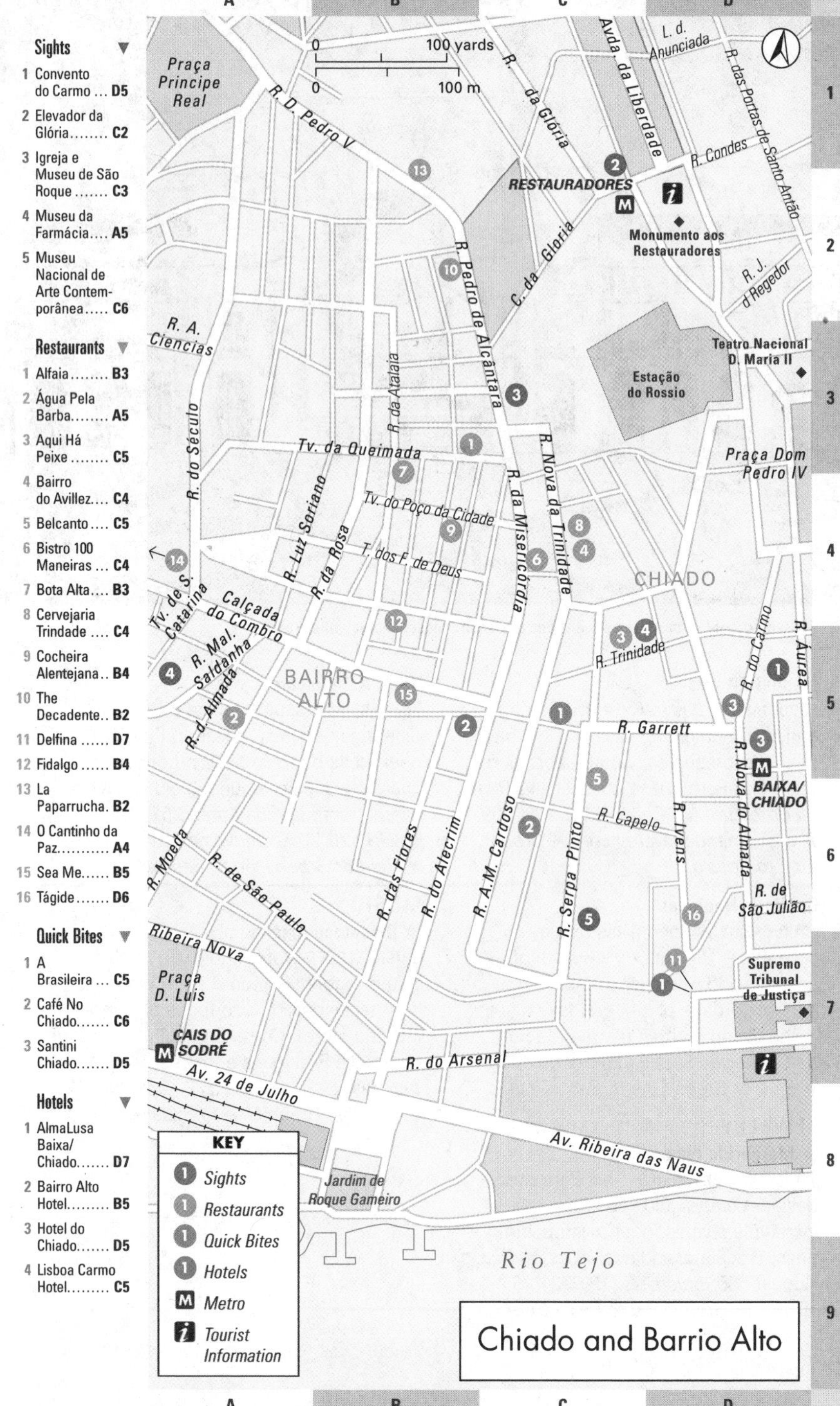
A
B
C
D
1
2
3
4
5
6
7
8
9
Sights
1 Convento do Carmo ... D5
2 Elevador da Glória........ C2
3 Igreja e Museu de São Roque C3
4 Museu da Farmácia.... A5
5 Museu Nacional de Arte Contemporânea..... C6
Restaurants
1 Alfaia........ B3
2 Água Pela Barba........ A5
3 Aqui Há Peixe C5
4 Bairro do Avillez.... C4
5 Belcanto C5
6 Bistro 100 Maneiras ... C4
7 Bota Alta.... B3
8 Cervejaria Trindade C4
9 Cocheira Alentejana.. B4
10 The Decadente.. B2
11 Delfina D7
12 Fidalgo B4
13 La Paparrucha. B2
14 O Cantinho da Paz........... A4
15 Sea Me...... B5
16 Tágide....... D6
Quick Bites
1 A Brasileira ... C5
2 Café No Chiado....... C6
3 Santini Chiado....... D5
Hotels
1 AlmaLusa Baixa/ Chiado....... D7
2 Bairro Alto Hotel......... B5
3 Hotel do Chiado....... D5
4 Lisboa Carmo Hotel......... C5
0
100 yards
0
100 m
Praça Principe Real
R. D. Pedro V
R. da Glória
Avda. da Liberdade
L. d. Anunciada
R. das Portas de Santo Antão
R. Condes
RESTAURADORES
Monumento aos Restauradores
C. da Gloria
R. Pedro de Alcântara
R. J. d Regedor
R. A. Ciencias
Estação do Rossio
Teatro Nacional D. Maria II
R. da Atalaia
R. do Século
Tv. da Queimada
R. Nova da Trinidade
Praça Dom Pedro IV
Tv. do Poço da Cidade
R. da Misericórdia
R. Luz Soriano
R. da Rosa
T. dos F. de Deus
CHIADO
Tv. de S. Catarina
Calçada do Combro
R. Mal. Saldanha
R. Trinidade
R. do Carmo
R. Áurea
BAIRRO ALTO
R. d. Almada
R. Garrett
BAIXA/ CHIADO
R. Nova do Almada
R. Capelo
R. Ivens
R. Moeda
R. de São Paulo
R. das Flores
R. do Alecrim
R. A.M. Cardoso
R. Serpa Pinto
R. de São Julião
Ribeira Nova
Praça D. Luis
Supremo Tribunal de Justiça
CAIS DO SODRÉ
R. do Arsenal
Av. 24 de Julho
Av. Ribeira das Naus
KEY
Sights
Restaurants
Quick Bites
Hotels
Metro
Tourist Information
Jardim de Roque Gameiro
Rio Tejo
Chiado and Barrio Alto

Chiado and Bairro Alto

West of Baixa is the fashionable shopping district of Chiado. Although a calamitous 1988 fire destroyed much of the area, an ambitious rebuilding program restored some of the fin de siècle facades. A chic retail complex and hotel on the site of the old Armazéns do Chiado—once Lisbon's most celebrated department store—has given the district a modern focus. Along Rua Garrett and Rua do Carmo are some of Europe's best shoe stores, as well as glittering jewelry shops, hip boutiques, and a host of delis and cafés.

Chiado's narrow, often cobbled streets lead to the Bairro Alto and often follow contours of the hills, which can make getting around confusing. Although the settlement of Bairro Alto dates to the 17th century, most of the buildings are from the 18th and 19th centuries and are an appealing mixture of small churches, warehouses, antiques and art galleries, artisans' shops, and town houses with wrought-iron balconies. It's most famous as a nightlife district, and the narrow alleyways and wide stairwells throng with partiers after dark.

GETTING HERE AND AROUND

Chiado is served by the Baixa-Chiado metro station, with a series of escalators inside the station bearing passengers up from the Baixa entrance under Rua Garrett to Largo do Chiado. Tram 28 rumbles through on its way between the Baixa and Estrela, passing through Chiado and Bairro Alto. Farther uphill, Bairro Alto can be reached by the Santa Justa elevator or the Elevador da Glória funicular, which steams up from a standing start on Praça dos Restauradores. Another approach to Bairro Alto is from Rato metro station, passing the Jardim Botânico and the Jardim do Príncipe Real on the way. Head this way for superchic shopping at the grand Embaixada gallery of upscale boutiques.

TIMING

Both Chiado and Bairro Alto are remarkably compact, and it takes little time to walk from one end to the other; an hour would cover it. But once you start diving off into the side streets and lingering in the shops, galleries, and bars, you'll find you can happily spend a morning or afternoon here (or a night in the case of the late-opening Bairro Alto). After midnight the streets get very busy, especially on weekends, when seemingly half of Lisbon comes here to eat, drink, and party.

SAFETY AND PRECAUTIONS

Bairro Alto has always had a reputation as being rather rough-and-ready, and there are still back alleys, particularly in its northern reaches, where it would be unwise to venture after dark. But if you avoid the more deserted streets, it's safe to walk around.

Sights

Convento do Carmo (*Carmelite Convent*)
MUSEUM | The Carmelite Convent—once Lisbon's largest—was built in 1389 and all but ruined by the 1755 earthquake. Its sacristy houses the **Museu Arqueológico do Carmo** (Carmelite Archaeological Museum), a small collection of ceramic tiles, ancient coins, and other city finds. The tree-shaded square outside—accessible via a walkway from the top of the Elevador de Santa Justa—is a great place to dawdle over a coffee. ✉ *Largo do Carmo, Chiado* ☎ *21 460 473* 🌐 *www.museuarqueologicodocarmo.pt* 🎫 *€5, guided tour €5.50* 🕓 *Closed Sun.* Ⓜ *Blue or Green Line to Baixa-Chiado or Green Line Rossio.*

Elevador da Glória
TRANSPORTATION SITE (AIRPORT/BUS/FERRY/TRAIN) | **FAMILY** | One of the finest approaches to the Bairro Alto is via this funicular railway, also known as Ascensor da Glória. Inaugurated in 1888 on the western side of Avenida da Liberdade, it's located near Praça dos Restauradores.

It runs up the steep hill and takes only about a minute to reach the São Pedro de Alcântara Miradouro, a viewpoint that looks out over the castle and the Alfama. ✉ *Calçada da Glória 6, Bairro Alto* 🎫 *€3.80 round-trip* Ⓜ *Blue Line to Restauradores.*

Igreja e Museu de São Roque (*Sao Roque Church and Museum*)
RELIGIOUS SITE | Completed in 1574, this church was one of the earliest Jesuit buildings in the world. While the exterior is somewhat plain and austere, the inside is dazzling, with abundant use of gold and marble. Eight side chapels have statuary and art dating to the early 17th century. The last chapel on the left before the altar is the extraordinary 18th-century **Capela de São João Baptista** (Chapel of St. John the Baptist), designed and built in Rome. The chapel was taken apart, shipped to Lisbon, and reassembled here in 1747. The museum adjoining the church displays a surprisingly engaging collection of clerical vestments and liturgical objects. There is also a stylish café with patio. ✉ *Largo Trindade Coelho, Bairro Alto* ☎ *213 235 065* 🌐 *www.museudesaoroque.com* 🎫 *Church free, museum €2.50* ⏱ *Closed Mon. until 2 pm* Ⓜ *Blue Line to Restauradores, then Elevador da Glória.*

Museu da Farmácia (*Pharmacy Museum*)
MUSEUM | Within an old palace, the Museum of Pharmacy covers more than 5,000 years of pharmaceutical history, from prehistoric cures to the fantastic world of fictive potions à la Harry Potter. Ancient objects related to pharmaceutical science and art—from Mesopotamian, Egyptian, Roman, and Incan civilizations—are on display in well-lighted showcases, as are those from Europe. Whole pharmacies have been transported here intact from other parts of Portugal, even a traditional 19th-century Chinese drugstore from Portugal's former territory of Macau. There's also a smart bar and restaurant called Pharmacia that serves lunch and dinner as well as afternoon *petiscos* (tasty snacks). ✉ *Rua Marechal Saldanha 1, Bairro Alto* ☎ *213 400 680* 🌐 *www.museudafarmacia.pt* 🎫 *€6.50* ⏱ *Closed Sun.* Ⓜ *Blue or Green Line Baixa-Chiado.*

Museu Nacional de Arte Contemporânea
MUSEUM | Also known as the Museu do Chiado, this museum housed in a former convent specializes in Portuguese art from 1850 to the present day, covering various movements like naturalism, surrealism, and modernism. The museum also hosts temporary exhibitions of paintings, sculpture, and multimedia installations, as well as summer jazz concerts in its small walled garden. ✉ *Rua Serpa Pinto 4, Chiado* ☎ *213 432 148* 🌐 *www.museuartecontemporanea.gov.pt* 🎫 *€4.50* ⏱ *Closed Mon.* Ⓜ *Blue or Green Line to Baixa-Chiado.*

Coffee and Quick Bites

A Brasileira
$ | **PORTUGUESE** | Dating from 1905, Lisbon's most famous café maintains its dazzling art deco interior, though you'll probably prefer to take a quick peek and then settle in at one of the handful of tables outside. The coffee no longer comes exclusively from the former colony that gave the place its name, but it still serves some of the best in town, alongside some tasty cakes and pastries. **Known for:** statue of poet Fernando Pessoa sitting at a table outside; paintings by major artists like Almada Negreiros; well-priced set meals at lunch and dinner. $ *Average main: €9* ✉ *Rua Garrett 120–122, Chiado* ☎ *213 520 335* 🌐 *abrasileira.pt/site* Ⓜ *Blue or Green Line to Baixa-Chiado.*

Café no Chiado
$$ | **CAFÉ** | The tables outside this reliable café are the perfect place to watch the old trams go by. Less touristy than some of the others nearby, it attracts artists

The Church of São Roque is known for its ornate interior and numerous side chapels.

from the neighboring theaters who still stop for a drink as they read international newspapers. **Known for:** grab one of the coveted seats on the shaded terrace; Iberian-style tapas perfect for sharing; perfect for an afternoon glass of wine. *Average main: €17 Largo do Picadeiro 10–12, Chiado 213 460 501 www.cafenochiado.com Blue or Green Line to Baixa-Chiado.*

Santini Chiado

$ | **ITALIAN** | **FAMILY** | For some of the best ice cream in town, drop into this branch of a family-run shop founded in 1949. Different flavors are introduced regularly, and may include Azorean pineapple, Brazilian açai, or even more exotic options. **Known for:** genuine Italian-style gelato; delicious milk shakes; perfect pastries. *Average main: €6 Rua do Carmo 9, Chiado 213 468 431 www.santini.pt Blue or Green Line to Baixa-Chiado.*

Restaurants

Água Pela Barba

$ | **SEAFOOD** | Famously the kind of eatery that locals love for being "bom e barato" (good and inexpensive), this seafood-focused spot features a menu with just half-a-dozen regular entrées but there are many more small plates. The fried fish tacos are always a crowd-pleaser. **Known for:** Portuguese wines from all over the region; compact dining room is usually packed; vegetarians have some imaginative options. *Average main: €15 Rua do Almada 29–31, Bairro Alto 213 461 376 No lunch Mon. Tram 28 to Calhariz-Bica stop.*

Alfaia

$$ | **PORTUGUESE** | In this traditional restaurant, one of the oldest in Lisbon, the courteous staff serve up Portuguese classics and pair them with one of the 600 choices on the wine list. In the charmingly old-fashioned dining room, bottles are on display llike works of art. **Known for:**

also runs a wine-and-tapas bar across the street; handful of tables ouside for alfresco dining; grilled sardines and other local favorites. *Average main: €17 Travessa da Queimada 22, Bairro Alto 213 461 232 www.restaurantealfaia.com Blue or Green Line to Baixa-Chiado.*

★ Aqui Há Peixe

$$$ | **SEAFOOD** | This restaurant's name translates to "There's Fish Here," and make no mistake: it's one of the top places in town to savor the catch of the day served fried, grilled, or roasted. Dinner attracts a youngish crowd who enjoy solid options like cuttlefish with black rice and saffron mayonnaise. **Known for:** fresh fish from the coast near Lisbon; affordable lunch specials; boozy dessert options. *Average main: €23 Rua da Trindade 18A, Chiado 213 432 154 www.aquihapeixe.pt Closed Mon. No lunch weekends Blue or Green Line to Baixa-Chiado.*

★ Bairro do Avillez

$$$$ | **PORTUGUESE** | José Avillez, one of the city's most distinguished chefs, has created his own dining destination incorporating a spectacular two-story dining room called Páteo (a wrought-iron balcony encircles the room, which is illuminated by a soaring skylight) and a more casual tavern called Taberna (the kind of place where haunches of ham hang over the bar). Then there's Beco, a cabaret space behind a hidden passageway where you can enjoy dinner and a show. **Known for:** Lisbon's most renowned chef shows off his skills; cabaret space is like stepping into the 1920s; restaurant features 12-course tasting menu. *Average main: €30 Rua Nova da Trindade 18, Chiado 215 830 290 www.bairrodoavillez.pt Blue or Green Line to Baixa-Chiado.*

★ Belcanto

$$$$ | **ECLECTIC** | Another jewel in the crown of celebrity chef José Avillez, Belcanto has garnered international acclaim for its inventive cuisine that uses the latest gastronomic techniques to update traditional dishes (which is why dishes on the tasting menu have names like *leitão revisitado*, meaning "suckling pig revisited). The dining room is just as refined, with every course placed before you with a flourish by an expert staff. **Known for:** reservations weeks or months ahead are essential; huge list of the finest regional wines; witty presentations. *Average main: €50 Largo de São Carlos 10, Chiado 213 420 607 belcanto.pt Closed Sun. and Mon. Blue or Green Line to Baixa-Chiado.*

★ Bistro 100 Maneiras

$$$$ | **ECLECTIC** | Sarajevo-born chef Ljubomir Stanisic won rave reviews for his flagship restaurant's innovative menu, so locals were nervous when he opened this bistro in a stunning art deco town house. Anyone who thought lightning couldn't strike twice was relieved that the sophisticated dining room wins awards, but so does the food, which draws on interesting dishes from across Europe. **Known for:** intimate bar serves gin-infused creations; bold dishes like octopus in spiced honey; stays busy until late at night. *Average main: Largo da Trindade 9, Bairro Alto 910 307 575 100maneiras.com Blue or Green Line to Baixa-Chiado.*

Bota Alta

$ | **PORTUGUESE** | This brilliant blue taverna is one of the Bairro Alto's oldest and most popular—lines form outside early in the evening and diners are packed in like sardines until late at night. The busy atmosphere is part of the charm, and the menu is strong on traditional Portuguese dishes like grilled salmon that are best washed down with a carafe of house wine. **Known for:** bacalhau real is one of several sensational cod dishes; all the dishes are from traditional recipes; generous portions and fair prices. *Average main: €14 Travessa da Queimada 37, Bairro Alto 213 427 959 Closed Sun. No lunch Sat. or Mon. Tram 24E to Largo Trindade Coelho.*

Cervejaria Trindade

$$$ | **PORTUGUESE** | For many of those in the know, a visit to this eatery—once the refectory of a 13th-century monastery—is a quintessential Lisbon experience. Transformed into a beer hall in 1836, it's now one of the city's most popular seafood restaurants, packing a lot of locals and tourists into the space under the vaulted ceiling lined with colorful azulejo tiles. **Known for:** huge variety of shellfish, priced by weight; feels like traveling back into time; can get noisy and crowded. *Average main: €24 Rua Nova da Trindade 20, Chiado 213 423 506 www.cervejariatrindade.pt Blue or Green Line to Baixa-Chiado.*

Cocheira Alentejana

$ | **PORTUGUESE** | This place hasn't changed a bit over the years, from the beams across the ceiling to the harnesses and wagon wheels that serve as decor. It's a favorite among locals, who prefer the old-fashioned dishes and respectful service, along with tourists looking for an authentic experience. **Known for:** black pork and other specialties from the Alentejo region; açorda de gambas (prawn and bread stew); traditional decor. *Average main: €14 Travessa do Poço da Cidade 19, Bairro Alto 213 464 868 cocheiraalentejana.pt Closed Sun. No lunch Sat. Tram 24E to Largo Trindade Coelho.*

The Decadente

$ | **PORTUGUESE** | A lively crowd gathers in this eatery's chic dining room (this was once the Swiss ambassador's residence), packs into the backyard terrace, and jostles for a spot at the cocktail bar. The menu, which changes regularly, focuses on fresh seasonal ingredients and creative versions of traditional dishes like *plumas de porco preto* (pork cutlets). **Known for:** young crowd from the attached hostel; trendy bar with excellent cocktails; imaginative set meals at lunch. *Average main: €14 Independente Hostel, Rua São Pedro de Alcântara 81, Bairro Alto 213 461 381 www.thedecadente.pt Tram 24 to S. Pedro Alcântara.*

★ **Delfina**

$$ | **PORTUGUESE** | Occupying a corner of one of downtown's grandest squares, Delfina Cantina Portuguesa bills itself as an upscale Portuguese deli. It's the house restaurant at the chic AlmaLusa boutique hotel, but all are welcome to enjoy the tapas-style small plates throughout the day and night, as well as more substantial meals like *bacalhau à brás* (shredded cod). **Known for:** great location overlooking a monumental square; delicious flour-free chocolate cake; cozy vintage-chic interior. *Average main: €19 AlmaLusa, Praça do Município 21, Baixa 212 697 445 www.almalusahotels.com/delfina/m/en Blue or Green Line to Baixa-Chiado, Green Line to Cais do Sodré.*

Fidalgo

$ | **PORTUGUESE** | Don't let the strikingly contemporary decor fool you—this is one of Bairro Alto's oldest restaurants, and still wins awards for its traditional cuisine. Longtime fans come for the grilled fish and seafood, priced by weight. **Known for:** friendly waitstaff; ample wine list with many regional choices; profiteroles with hot chocolate for dessert. *Average main: €14 Rua da Barroca 27, Bairro Alto 213 422 900 www.restaurantefidalgo.com Closed Sun. Blue or Green Line to Baixa-Chiado.*

La Paparrucha

$$$ | **ARGENTINE** | **FAMILY** | The inspiration for this restaurant's menu comes from Argentina, so expect a meat-heavy menu that has long made it a favorite among Lisbon's carnivores. You'll also find fish dishes borrowed from traditional Portuguese cuisine, and a couple of vegetarian options on the menu, too. **Known for:** panoramic views and some tables on the terrace; set menus make this a more affordable choice; family-friendly vibe and children's menu. *Average main: €24*

✉ *Rua D. Pedro V 18–20, Príncipe Real* ☎ *213 425 333* 🌐 *www.lapaparrucha.com* Ⓜ *Tram 24E to São Pedro de Alcântara.*

O Cantinho da Paz

$ | **INDIAN** | This wood-paneled restaurant specializes in foods from the former Portuguese colony of Goa—otherwise surprisingly hard to find in Lisbon. The dishes reveal Goa's unique mix of Portuguese and Indian influences, and the English-speaking staff can guide you through the menu. **Known for:** crab curry and other special dishes just on weekends; lobster curry for two is great for romantic meals; relaxed dining room. Ⓢ *Average main: €14* ✉ *Rua da Paz 4, off Rua dos Poiais de São Bento, Bairro Alto* ☎ *213 901 963* ⏲ *Closed Sun.* Ⓜ *Tram 28E to R. Poiais S. Bento.*

★ **Sea Me**

$$$ | **JAPANESE FUSION** | At this modern fish market, you buy fresh fish to prepare at home (which is what the locals do), or you can have it prepared on the spot in a variety of ways, whether it's dunked whole into the cooking pot or fileted and tossed onto the grill. The cooking has a strong Japanese influence, and a large portion of the menu is devoted to sushi and sashimi. **Known for:** seafood platters that are big enough to share; huge list of mostly Portuguese wines; catch of the day displayed on ice. Ⓢ *Average main: €25* ✉ *Rua do Loreto 21, Chiado* ☎ *213 461 564* 🌐 *peixariamoderna.com* Ⓜ *Blue or Green Line to Baixa-Chiado.*

Tágide

$$$$ | **PORTUGUESE** | Named after the mythical nymphs that live in the Tagus River, this place is divided into two parts: a sleek, modern dining room serving refined versions of Portuguese dishes upstairs and a more relaxed wine-and-tapas bar downstairs. Both spaces face the river, so the tables by the windows are some of the most coveted in town. **Known for:** perfect for romantic dinner for two or a big meal with friends; classical decor highlighted with 18th-century tiles; choose between a tasting menu and à la carte options. Ⓢ *Average main: €28* ✉ *Largo Academia Nacional de Belas Artes 18–20, Chiado* ☎ *213 404 010* 🌐 *www.restaurantetagide.com* ⏲ *Closed Sun.* Ⓜ *Blue or Green Line to Baixa-Chiado.*

Hotels

★ **AlmaLusa Baixa/Chiado**

$$ | **HOTEL** | In an artfully restored 18th-century showplace, this chic boutique hotel retains many of its original features, including rough-hewn wooden beams, graceful arches, and a serving hatch from a store that once stood on the site. **Pros:** faces the historic Praça do Município; highly knowledgeable concierge; outdoor terrace dining. **Cons:** no swimming pool or fitness area; not all views are created equal; rooms on the small side. Ⓢ *Rooms from: €200* ✉ *Praça do Munícipio 21, Baixa* ☎ *212 697 440* 🌐 *www.almalusahotels.com* 🛏 *28 rooms* 🍽 *Free Breakfast* Ⓜ *Blue or Green Line to Baixa-Chiado.*

★ **Bairro Alto Hotel**

$$$$ | **HOTEL** | Lisbon's first boutique hotel was treated to a top-to-toe redesign courtesy of Pritzker Prize–winning Portuguese architect Eduardo Souto de Moura, and it's now one of the finest places to stay in the heart of the city. **Pros:** rooftop terrace is a photographer's dream; close to the city's best nightlife; thoughtful design. **Cons:** some rooms are small; often packed with nonguests; books up fast in high season. Ⓢ *Rooms from: €290* ✉ *Praça Luís de Camões 2, Bairro Alto* ☎ *213 408 288* 🌐 *www.bairroaltohotel.com* 🛏 *87 rooms* 🍽 *Free Breakfast* Ⓜ *Blue or Green Line to Baixa-Chiado.*

Hotel do Chiado

$$$$ | **HOTEL** | Occupying the sixth to eighth floors of the Grandes Armazéns do Chiado shopping complex, this boutique hotel blends elements of 16th-century Portugal with 21st-century

amenities. **Pros:** afternoon tea has become something of an institution; location is perfect for shopping and sightseeing; beautifully restored building. **Cons:** terrace bar is often crowded with nonguests; design can feel a little staid; breakfast not included. *Rooms from: €270 Rua Nova de Almada 114, Chiado 213 256 100 www.hoteldochiado.pt 40 rooms No meals Blue or Green Line to Baixa-Chiado.*

★ Lisboa Carmo Hotel

$$$$ | **HOTEL** | This boutique charmer, located on beautiful Largo do Carmo in the hilly Chiado neighborhood, has amazing views of the historic square, the red rooftops of the city, and the Tagus River. **Pros:** prime location for sightseeing and barhopping; facing one of the city's most charming squares; extremely comfortable room furnishings. **Cons:** some rooms are on the small side; not all views are created equal; breakfast not included in rates. *Rooms from: €280 Rua da Oliveira ao Carmo, 1, 2, 3, Largo do Carmo, Chiado 213 264 710 carmo.luxhotels.pt/ 45 rooms No meals Baixa-Chiado.*

Nightlife

Bairro Alto, long the center of Lisbon's nightlife, is still one of the best places in the city for barhopping. There's a street-party vibe on weekends, when revelers take their drinks outdoors. A number of bars here have a predominately gay clientele, but invariably welcome all.

BARS

Artis

BARS/PUBS | Although it has changed over the years, this cozy wine bar has consistently been one of Bairro Alto's most popular drinking establishments since the 1980s. To accompany the wines there's a surprisingly long list of Portuguese petiscos, so it's also possible to have practically a full meal here. *Rua do Diário de Notícias 95, Bairro Alto 918 176 736 Blue or Green Line to Baixa-Chiado.*

Bairru's Bodega

BARS/PUBS | At this welcoming bar, Portugal's finest wines can be sampled by the glass or bottle. Along with regional cheeses, hams, and sausages, you can sample homemade ginjinha (sour-cherry liqueur) or enjoy a classic gin and tonic. *Rua da Barroca 3, Bairro Alto 213 469 060 Baixa-Chiado.*

★ Garrafeira Alfaia

BARS/PUBS | Barrels are used as tables at this at this tiny wine bar, where the various vintages are accompanied by platters of local cheeses and sausages. The knowledgeable staff will help you discover the different varieties of port and other Portuguese wines. If you like what you taste, buy a bottle to take with you. *Rua do Diário de Notícias 125, Bairro Alto 213 433 079 www.garrafeiraalfaia.com Blue or Green Line to Baixa-Chiado.*

Maria Caxuxa

BARS/PUBS | This former bakery (complete with giant kneading machine) is often packed with young people who've turned out to hear the hottest local DJs. While this bar is more spacious than others in the neighborhood, almost everyone prefers to grab a drink and head outside. The toasted sandwiches are perfect for late-night munchies, while the famous shots of strong spirits can ramp up a night on the town. Closed Sunday and Monday. *Rua da Barroca 6–12, Bairro Alto 213 461 311 Blue or Green Line to Baixa-Chiado.*

O Purista

BARS/PUBS | A bar that doubles as a barbershop, or vice versa, this is where Lisbon's coolest guys get ready for a night on the town. The interior is decorated like a classic barbershop and is meant to be a comfortable space for men (and women) to relax at any time of the day or night. ✉ *Rua Nova da Trindade 16C, Chiado* ☎ *916 442 744* Ⓜ *Blue or Green Line to Baixa-Chiado.*

Park

BARS/PUBS | On warm evenings (and quite a few cooler ones) this terrace on the roof of a multilevel parking garage heaves with young people drinking in the stunning sunset views and well-mixed cocktails. Live music and excellent local DJs provide the soundtrack (the place even has its own spin-off record label and radio station). ✉ *Calçada do Combro 58, Bairro Alto* ☎ *215 914 011* Ⓜ *Tram 28E to Calhariz (Bica).*

Portas Largas

BARS/PUBS | Partiers spills out into the street from the massive front doors of this mixed club, which often offers live Brazilian music. Sangria and caipirinha are the house drinks. Things get crowded after midnight. ✉ *Rua da Atalaia 105, Bairro Alto* ☎ *213 346 6379* Ⓜ *Tram 28E to Calhariz (Bica).*

DANCE CLUBS

Silk

BARS/PUBS | Once reserved for members, this fancy rooftop bar is now open to everyone (but be sure that you dress to impress). It's at the top of a small shopping gallery, offering stunning panoramic views from the terrace and through the glass walls. Cocktails and bottles of wine are served at your table on Friday and Saturday night. ✉ *Rua da Misericórdia 14, 6th fl., Chiado* ☎ *913 009 193* 🌐 *silk-club.com* Ⓜ *Blue or Green Line to Baixa-Chiado.*

GAY AND LESBIAN CLUBS

As Primas

BARS/PUBS | This laid-back bar is a popular lesbian hangout, although everyone drops by for the cheap drinks and to hear the 1980s music on the jukebox. ✉ *Rua da Atalaia 154–156, Bairro Alto* ☎ *213 425 925* Ⓜ *Tram 24E at Largo Trindade Coelho.*

Purex Clube

BARS/PUBS | On weekends, DJs pack the dance floor at this local favorite, a tiny space that's nevertheless more of a club than a bar. It's usually quite crowded, although many patrons grab a drink and enjoy it on the street. ✉ *Rua das Salgadeiras 28, Bairro Alto* ☎ *933 948 764* Ⓜ *Baixa-Chiado; Tram 28.*

★ Trumps

DANCE CLUBS | One of Lisbon's most iconic gay clubs, Trumps has attracted the city's trendiest crowds since it opened in the 1980s. There are two separate dance floors (one playing pop hits, another house music) with dazzling light displays that are packed with the mostly male clientele. ✉ *Rua da Imprensa Nacional 104B, Príncipe Real* ☎ *915 938 266* 🌐 *www.trumps.pt* Ⓜ *Yellow line to Rato.*

Shopping

ART GALLERIES

Galeria Graça Brandão

ART GALLERIES—ARTS | Founded in Porto, this gallery moved to Lisbon and took over an old printing house. It presents works by Portuguese and Brazilian artists. ✉ *Rua dos Caetanos 26, Bairro Alto* ☎ *213 469 183* 🌐 *www.galeriagracabrandao.com* Ⓜ *Tram 24E to Praça Luís de Camões.*

CERAMICS

★ Fábrica Sant'Anna

CERAMICS/GLASSWARE | Established in 1741, this factory uses century-old techniques, including painting and glazing entirely by hand, to create contemporary designs and reproductions of antique tiles. ✉ *Rua do Alecrim 95, Chiado* ☎ *213 638 292* 🌐 *www.fabrica-santanna.com* Ⓜ *Blue or Green Line to Baixa-Chiado.*

Vista Alegre

CERAMICS/GLASSWARE | Originally a royal factory founded in 1817, this is now one of Europe's most prestigious porcelain manufacturers. The flagship store in Chiado presents its ever-changing collections, which are often signed by national and international artists. ✉ *Largo do Chiado 20–23, Chiado* ☎ *213 461 401* 🌐 *vistaalegre.com* Ⓜ *Blue or Green Line to Baixa-Chiado.*

CLOTHING

A Fábrica dos Chapéus

CLOTHING | The young proprietor of this funky store stocks a huge range of hats—more than 3,000—and also makes exclusive designs to order. ✉ *Rua da Rosa 118, Bairro Alto* ☎ *219 914 579.* 🌐 *www.afabricadoschapeus.com* Ⓜ *Tram 24E to Largo Trindade Coelho.*

Cantê

CLOTHING | Exclusivity is guaranteed at this beachware store: it sells only its own inventive designs and stocks no more than eight of each model. Everything here is made in Portugal. ✉ *Calçada Nova de São Francisco 10, Chiado* ☎ *210 142 912* 🌐 *www.cantelisboa.com* Ⓜ *Blue or Green Line to Baixa-Chiado.*

Soul Mood

CLOTHING | This small, minimalist concept store offers the avant-garde fashions of lesser-known European designers. It's laid out almost like a gallery, with the curated collections on color-coordinated display. In addition to fashion and accessories, you may find jewelry by local designers like Valentim Quaresma, whose pieces have been featured in Lady Gaga videos. ✉ *Travessa do Carmo 1, Chiado* ☎ *213 463 179* Ⓜ *Blue or Green Line to Baixa-Chiado.*

★ Storytailors

CLOTHING | For some fairy-tale shopping, browse the racks here filled with fantastical frocks, capes, and more. Madonna is whispered to be among the celeb customers to have done so. ✉ *Calçada do Ferragial 8, Chiado* ☎ *213 432 306* 🌐 *www.storytailors.pt* Ⓜ *Blue or Green Line to Baixa-Chiado.*

CRAFTS AND SOUVENIRS

★ A Vida Portuguesa

CRAFTS | The former storeroom of an old perfumery has become one of Lisbon's most beloved stores. This is the flagship store of a brand that sells traditional Portuguese products that have been passed on from generation to generation and that have now become must-haves. Those include luxurious soaps of the Ach. Brito and Claus Porto brands and colorful Bordallo Pinheiro pottery—all displayed in beautifully restored antique glass cases. ✉ *Rua Anchieta 11, Chiado* ☎ *213 465 073* 🌐 *www.avidaportuguesa.com* Ⓜ *Blue or Green Line to Baixa-Chiado.*

Cork & Co

CRAFTS | Portugal's abundant cork forests are the basis for all the products showcased here (as well as worldwide at such design-forward stores as Milan Triennale and the MoMA Design Store in New York). Look for eye-catching designs for handbags, jewelry, and accessories. ✉ *Rua das Salgadeiras 10, Bairro Alto* ☎ *216 090 231* 🌐 *www.corkandcompany.pt* Ⓜ *Baixa-Chiado.*

★ Fabrica Features

CRAFTS | Overlooking the the busiest part of Chiado, this shop has a particularly Instagram-worthy view of the cobblestone pavement from above. When you arrive, you may also be tempted to photograph one of Europe's oldest (and most beautiful) elevators, with its well-preserved art-nouveau features from more than a century ago. The collection of bags, stationery, ceramics, and other products designed in Portugal and abroad are worth considering for more than just a photograph. ✉ *Rua Garrett 83, 4th fl., Chiado* ☎ *213 420 596* 🌐 *www.fabrica-features.com* Ⓜ *Blue or Green Line to Baixa-Chiado.*

FOOD AND WINE

Baco Alto

FOOD/CANDY | At this Bairro Alto favorite, you can sample wines and fine foods from around Portugal before buying.

The knowledgeable staff will recommend the right wine for you. ✉ *Rua do Norte 33, Bairro Alto* ☎ *912 456 066* Ⓜ *Baixa-Chiado.*

Casa Pereira

FOOD/CANDY | Step into this charming old store with its original 1930s decor to buy exotic coffees, teas, and chocolates, mainly from former Portuguese colonies (Brazil, Cape Verde, and São Tomé in particular). It's also a good place to grab a bottle of port wine. ✉ *Rua Garrett 38, Chiado* ☎ *213 426 694* Ⓜ *Blue or Green Line to Baixa-Chiado.*

LEATHER GOODS

★ Luvaria Ulisses

SHOES/LUGGAGE/LEATHER GOODS | Lisbon's smallest shop is one of its most charming, selling nothing but custom-made, finely crafted gloves since 1925. It's the last place in Portugal where you can get these exclusive gloves, and it's recognized as one of the best stores of its kind in Europe. The well-preserved interior fits two customers at a time, who go through the process of trying on the different sizes and colors by placing their elbows on a small cushion and letting the fitter make the perfect adjustments. ✉ *Rua do Carmo 87, Chiado* ☎ *213 420 295* Ⓜ *Green Line to Rossio.*

MALLS

Armazéns do Chiado

SHOPPING CENTERS/MALLS | It calls itself "Lisbon's meeting point" for a reason. This former department store is where people of all ages meet before a night out on the town. Inside are national and international chain stores, but the main attraction is the food court on the top floor, which offers views of Chiado. ✉ *Rua do Carmo 2, Chiado* ☎ *213 210 600* 🌐 *www.armazensdochiado.com* Ⓜ *Blue or Green Line to Baixa-Chiado.*

Avenida da Liberdade, Príncipe Real, and Restauradores

Tree-lined Avenida da Liberdade was modeled after Paris's Champs-Élysées and is covered with some of Lisbon's most beautifully designed cobblestone pavements. It's home to most of the city's luxury stores, and down its central lanes are several food kiosks open throughout the day, each with its own specialty (from smoothies to seafood). Like the Parisian boulevard, it ends at a square with a traffic circle, Praça Marquês de Pombal, named after the man who oversaw downtown Lisbon's reconstruction following the Great Earthquake of 1755 and whose statue stands at the center, overlooking the city. Behind him is Lisbon's Central Park (Parque Eduardo VII), laid out in the 19th century and home to a beautiful greenhouse garden.

At the other end of the avenue is Praça Dos Restauradores, a square with an obelisk commemorating the restoration of the Portuguese crown in 1640, ending 60 years of the Iberian Union, when Portugal and Spain shared the same king. Surrounding it are a number of attractive buildings, most notably Foz Palace, built in 1777 with an interior inspired by the Palace of Versailles and home to a tourist office.

Rising up the hill to the west of the Avenida is romantic Príncipe Real, a neighborhood of stately mansions, trendy restaurants, concept stores, antiques traders, and green spaces, for a break. It's also known as Lisbon's "gayborhood," with discreet LGBT bars and clubs on quiet residential streets.

GETTING HERE AND AROUND

Avenida da Liberdade is best reached by metro and is accessible from three stations on the Blue Line: Marquês de

Pombal, Avenida, and Restauradores. Príncipe Real can be reached by walking up the hill from Avenida da Liberdade or by taking the metro (Rato station on the Yellow Line) or Tram 24 that departs from Praça Luís de Camões in Chiado. Alternatively, take the Glória funicular by Praça Dos Restauradores that ends up in Bairro Alto and is just a few feet from Príncipe Real's main street (Rua Dom Pedro V).

Sights

Avenida da Liberdade (*Liberty Avenue*)
NEIGHBORHOOD | Liberty Avenue was laid out in 1879 as an elegant Parisian-style boulevard modeled on the Champs-Élysees. It has since lost some of its allure: many of the late-19th-century mansions and art deco buildings that once graced it have been demolished; others have been turned into soulless office blocks. There are, however, still some notable survivors of the original boulevard, now turned into luxury hotels and international fashion outlets. It's worth a leisurely stroll up the 1½-km (1-mile) length of the avenue, past ponds, fountains, and statues, from Praça dos Restauradores to Parque Eduardo VII, at least once, if only to cool off with a drink in one of the *quiosques* (refreshment kiosks) beneath the trees and to admire the iconic designs of the cobblestone pavements. ✉ *Av. da Liberdade, Avenida da Liberdade* Ⓜ *Blue Line to Avenida.*

Casa-Museu Medeiros e Almeida (*Medeiros e Almeida House and Museum*)
MUSEUM | One of Lisbon's lesser-known but most extraordinary museums, this is the former residence of collector António de Medeiros e Almeida. Every room of his late-19th-century mansion is filled with works of art ranging from paintings to ceramics, sculptures to furnishings. Highlights include paintings by Rubens and Tiepolo, a Rembrandt portrait, a silver tea set used by Napoléon, fountains originally from the Palace of Versailles, and what's said to be the world's most notable private collection of clocks. ✉ *Rua Rosa Araújo 41, Avenida da Liberdade* ☎ *213 547 892* 🌐 *www.casa-museumedeirosealmeida.pt* 🎫 *€5* ⏲ *Closed Sun.* Ⓜ *Blue or Yellow Line to Marquês de Pombal.*

Cinemateca Portuguesa (*Portuguese Cinema Museum*)
FILM | With a beautiful Moorish-style atrium, the city's movie museum hosts exhibitions on film history and screens classics from all over the world, usually in the original language and with Portuguese or English subtitles. Arrive early to check out the treasures displayed around the building, like the first Lumiére projector used in the country. There's a café with a pleasant terrace. ✉ *Rua Barata Salgueiro 39, Avenida da Liberdade* ☎ *213 140 429* 🌐 *www.cinemateca.pt* ☞ *Closed Sun.* Ⓜ *Blue Line to Avenida.*

Jardim Botânico de Lisboa (*Lisbon Botanical Garden*)
GARDEN | **FAMILY** | Lisbon's main botanical garden was first laid out in 1874 to teach students about botany. Hidden behind the small **Museu de História Natural** about 2 km (1 mile) north of the Bairro Alto, the garden has 10 acres of paths through nearly 15,000 species of subtropical plants. ✉ *Rua da Escola Politécnica 58, Príncipe Real* ☎ *213 921 800 Natural History Museum* 🌐 *museus.ulisboa.pt/pt-pt/jardim-botanico-lisboa* 🎫 *€3* Ⓜ *Yellow Line to Rato.*

★ **Parque Eduardo VII** (*Eduardo VII Park*)
NATIONAL/STATE PARK | **FAMILY** | Formerly Parque da Liberdade, this park was renamed in 1903 when England's Edward VII visited Portugal. Its large central promenade has manicured lawns featuring traditional Portuguese cobblestone pavement with geometric designs and views of the city center. The beautifully kept **Estufa Fria** is a sprawling 1930s greenhouse garden whose various habitats are arranged around a pretty pool. It's a romantic oasis in the middle of the city. ✉ *Praça Marquês de Pombal,*

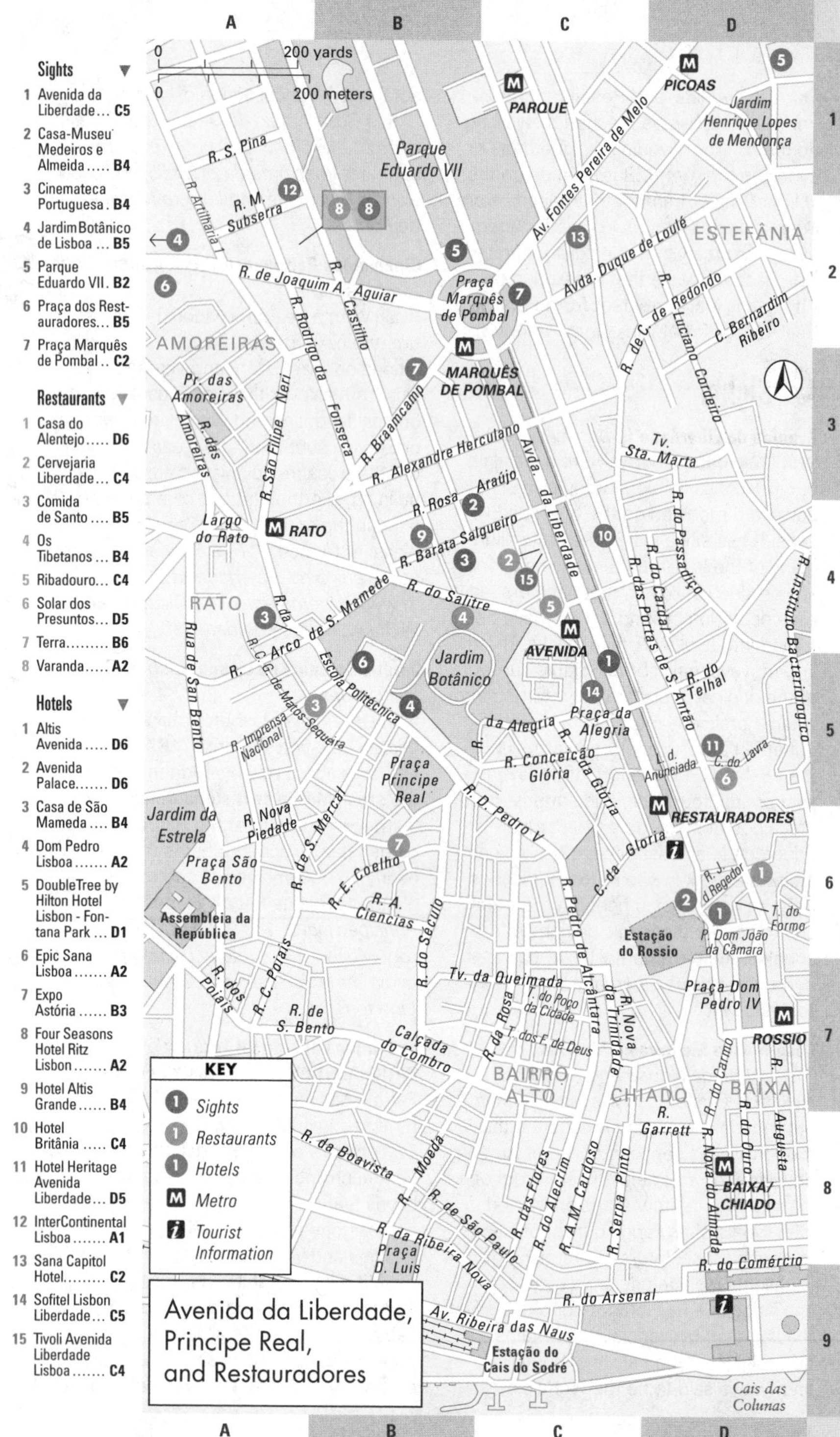

Sights
1 Avenida da Liberdade... C5
2 Casa-Museu Medeiros e Almeida..... B4
3 Cinemateca Portuguesa. B4
4 Jardim Botânico de Lisboa ... B5
5 Parque Eduardo VII. B2
6 Praça dos Restauradores... B5
7 Praça Marquês de Pombal.. C2
Restaurants
1 Casa do Alentejo..... D6
2 Cervejaria Liberdade... C4
3 Comida de Santo.... B5
4 Os Tibetanos... B4
5 Ribadouro... C4
6 Solar dos Presuntos... D5
7 Terra......... B6
8 Varanda..... A2
Hotels
1 Altis Avenida..... D6
2 Avenida Palace....... D6
3 Casa de São Mameda.... B4
4 Dom Pedro Lisboa....... A2
5 DoubleTree by Hilton Hotel Lisbon - Fontana Park... D1
6 Epic Sana Lisboa....... A2
7 Expo Astória...... B3
8 Four Seasons Hotel Ritz Lisbon....... A2
9 Hotel Altis Grande...... B4
10 Hotel Britânia..... C4
11 Hotel Heritage Avenida Liberdade... D5
12 InterContinental Lisboa....... A1
13 Sana Capitol Hotel......... C2
14 Sofitel Lisbon Liberdade... C5
15 Tivoli Avenida Liberdade Lisboa....... C4
A
B
C
D
1
2
3
4
5
6
7
8
9
0
200 yards
200 meters
PARQUE
PICOAS
Jardim Henrique Lopes de Mendonça
Parque Eduardo VII
R. S. Pina
R. Artilharia 1
R. M. Subserra
Av. Fontes Pereira de Melo
ESTEFÂNIA
Avda. Duque de Loulé
R. de Joaquim A. Aguiar
Praça Marquês de Pombal
R. Castilho
R. Rodrigo da Fonseca
R. de C. de Redondo
R. Luciano Cordeiro
C. Bernardim Ribeiro
AMOREIRAS
MARQUÊS DE POMBAL
Pr. das Amoreiras
R. das Amoreiras
R. São Filipe Neri
R. Braamcamp
R. Alexandre Herculano
Avda. da Liberdade
Tv. Sta. Marta
R. Rosa Araújo
R. do Passadiço
Largo do Rato
RATO
R. Barata Salgueiro
R. do Cardal
R. das Portas de S. Antão
R. Instituto Bacteriologico
R. do Salitre
RATO
R. de S. Mamede
R. da Arco
R. C. G. de Matos Sequeira
Rua de San Bento
Escola Politécnica
Jardim Botânico
AVENIDA
R. do Telhal
R. Imprensa Nacional
R. da Alegria
Praça da Alegria
R. Conceição Glória
R. da Glória
L. d. Anunciada
C. do Lavra
Praça Principe Real
R. D. Pedro V
RESTAURADORES
Jardim da Estrela
R. Nova Piedade
R. de S. Mercal
C. da Glória
Praça São Bento
R. E. Coelho
R. J. d Regedor
T. do Formo
Assembleia da República
R. A. Ciencias
R. do Século
R. Pedro de Alcântara
Estação do Rossio
P. Dom João da Câmara
R. dos Poiais
R. C. Poiais
Tv. da Queimada
T. do Poço da Cidade
Praça Dom Pedro IV
R. de S. Bento
R. da Rosa
T. dos F. de Deus
R. Nova da Trinidade
ROSSIO
Calçada do Combro
BAIRRO ALTO
CHIADO
R. do Carmo
BAIXA
R. Garrett
R. do Ouro
R. Augusta
R. da Boavista
R. Moeda
R. das Flores
R. do Alecrim
R. A. M. Cardoso
R. Serpa Pinto
R. Nova do Almada
BAIXA/ CHIADO
R. de São Paulo
R. da Ribeira Nova
Praça D. Luis
R. do Comércio
R. do Arsenal
Av. Ribeira das Naus
Estação do Cais do Sodré
Cais das Colunas
KEY
Sights
Restaurants
Hotels
Metro
Tourist Information
Avenida da Liberdade, Principe Real, and Restauradores

Avenida da Liberdade 🅿 *Park free, Estufa Fria €4* Ⓜ *Blue Line to Parque or Marquês de Pombal.*

Praça dos Restauradores (*Restauradores Square*)

PLAZA | Adjacent to Rossio Train Station, this square marks the beginning of modern Lisbon. Here the broad, tree-lined Avenida da Liberdade starts its northwesterly ascent. *Restauradores* means "restorers," and the square commemorates the 1640 uprising against Spanish rule that restored Portuguese independence. An 1886 obelisk commemorates the event. Note the elegant 18th-century Foz Palace on the square's west side. Before World War I, it was a casino; today it houses a tourist office, a sports museum, and a shop selling reproductions from the country's state museums. The only building to rival the palace is the restored Éden building, just to the south. This art deco masterpiece of Portuguese architect Cassiano Branco now contains a hotel. You'll also see the Elevador da Glória, the funicular that traveles up to Bairro Alto and its famous viewpoint. ✉ *Avenida da Liberdade* Ⓜ *Blue Line to Restauradores.*

Praça Marquês de Pombal (*Marquês de Pombal Square*)

PLAZA | Dominating the center of Marquês de Pombal Square is a statue of the marquis himself, the man responsible for the design of the "new" Lisbon that emerged from the ruins of the 1755 earthquake. On the statue's base are representations of both the earthquake and the tidal wave that engulfed the city; a female figure with outstretched arms signifies the joy at the emergence of the refashioned city. The square is effectively a large roundabout and a useful orientation point, since it stands at the northern end of Avenida da Liberdade. ✉ *Praça Marquês de Pomba, Avenida da Liberdade* Ⓜ *Blue or Yellow Line to Marquês de Pombal.*

Restaurants

★ Casa do Alentejo

$ | **PORTUGUESE** | Originally a social club for the people hailing from the region of Alentejo, this hidden restaurant is found on the upper floor of a Moorish-style building from the 1800s. With a pair of dining rooms lined with blue-and-white tiles, the place is known for classic northern Portuguese dishes like *carne de porco à alentejana* (pork with clams). **Known for:** one of the city's most stunning eateries; beautiful Louis XVI–style ballroom; guided tours with tastings. 💲 *Average main: €15* ✉ *Rua Portas de Santo Antão 58, Avenida da Liberdade* ☎ *213 405 140* 🌐 *www.casadoalentejo.com.pt* Ⓜ *Blue Line to Avenida.*

★ Cervejaria Liberdade

$$$$ | **SEAFOOD** | Lisbon's beer halls tend to be noisy, crowded places, but those looking for more sophisticated atmosphere should head to this upmarket eatery with towering murals and handsome wood paneling tucked inside the Tivoli Avenida Liberdade. You'll find the traditional fish dishes listed on the menu, but they're served with flair by an attentive staff. **Known for:** fresh oysters and prawns from the Algarve; impressive lists of wines and local beers; cocoa mousse for dessert. 💲 *Average main: €29* ✉ *Tivoli Avenida Liberdade, Av. da Liberdade 185, Avenida da Liberdade* ☎ *213 198 620* 🌐 *www.tivolihotels.com/en/tivoli-avenida-liberdade-lisboa/restaurants/cervejaria-liberdade* Ⓜ *Blue Line to Avenida.*

★ Comida de Santo

$ | **BRAZILIAN** | Tropical blues, greens, and yellows make this dining room a standout, as does the lively soundtrack coming from the speakers and the excellent dishes from northeast Brazil. Enjoy classic Bahian dishes, sip a potent caipirinha, and finish your meal with a traditional dessert made with tropical fruit. **Known for:** South American favorites like feijoada à brasileira (black bean stew); specialties like moqueca de peixe (fish stew with coconut milk); dining room is packed until late at night. *Average main: €14 Calçada Engenheiro Miguel Pais 39, Príncipe Real 213 963 339 www.comidadesanto.pt Closed Tues. No lunch in Aug. Yellow Line to Rato.*

Os Tibetanos

$ | **VEGETARIAN** | Delicious meat-free dishes (think mango-and-tofu curry, seitan steak, and spinach-filled Tibetan *momo* dumplings) ensure that there's always a line for a table in this restaurant's extremely colorful dining room or on the pleasant patio. It's part of a Buddhist center where a small shop stocks books, incense, homeopathic medicines, and other products, and yoga and meditation classes take place upstairs. **Known for:** foods inspired by world cuisines; good-value lunch menu; casual atmosphere. *Average main: €13 Rua do Salitre 117, Avenida da Liberdade 213 142 038 tibetanos.com No credit cards Closed Sun. Blue Line to Avenida.*

Ribadouro

$$ | **SEAFOOD** | What you see is what you get at Ribadouro, one of Lisbon's best-known seafood spots: take your pick of the lobster, mantis shrimp, tiger shrimp, whelks, oysters, and clams on display and the staff will create a seafood platter to your specifications. The presentations are simple and elegant, with all the flavor and none of the fuss of fancier places. **Known for:** evenings and weekends can be very busy; grilled steaks are also tasty; good for late-night dinners. *Average main: €20 Av. da Liberdade 155, Avenida da Liberdade 213 549 411 www.cervejariaribadouro.pt Blue Line to Avenida.*

★ Solar dos Presuntos

$$$$ | **PORTUGUESE** | Framed photographs of celebrities who've visited (from singer Adele to soccer star Cristiano Ronaldo) cover every inch of the walls of this bustling eatery. In business since 1947, it's known for the dry-cured ham that gave the place its name, but there are also many meat and seafood dishes on the menu. **Known for:** authentic dishes from northern Portugal; lobster rice and other seafood standouts; reservations are essential. *Average main: €26 Rua das Portas de Santo Antão 150, Avenida da Liberdade 213 424 253 www.solardospresuntos.com Closed Sun. Blue Line to Avenida.*

Terra

$$ | **VEGETARIAN** | **FAMILY** | One of the best-regarded vegetarian restaurants in town, Terra offers colorful, flavorful dishes that have been known to convert staunch carnivores to the meat-free cause. From the enormous array of dishes at the lunch buffet to mouthwatering vegan desserts, everything here is a delight for the senses. **Known for:** Mediterranean-inspired dishes; alfresco dining in the garden; organic and kosher wines. *Average main: €16 Rua da Palmeira 15, Príncipe Real 213 421 407 www.restauranteterra.pt Closed Mon. Yellow line to Rato.*

Varanda

$$$$ | **PORTUGUESE** | The most popular restaurant at the Four Seasons Hotel Ritz, Varanda is consistently at the top of its game thanks to the keen eye of French-Canadian executive chef Pascal Meynard. He oversees a seasonally changing tasting menu at dinner (the octopus confit is a feast for the eyes as well as the stomach) and a wide range of à la carte dishes throughout the day. **Known for:** Lisbon's best weekend brunch buffet; stellar views of Parque Eduardo VII; desserts from in-house pastry chef. *Average main: €45 Four Seasons Hotel Ritz, Rua Rodrigo de Fonseca 88, Avenida da Liberdade 213 811 400 Blue or Yellow Line to Marquês de Pombal.*

Hotels

★ Altis Avenida

$$$$ | **HOTEL** | Occupying an elegant art decó building that has been classified as a historic landmark, the monumental Altis Avenida offers glamour and luxury in a central location that makes it ideal for sightseeing. **Pros:** upstairs eatery serves delicious small plates perfect for sharing; sunny rooftop terrace lets you catch a few rays; pleasant staff and excellent service. **Cons:** some rooms are rather small; no on-site swimming pool; can be pricey. *Rooms from: €280 Rua 1° de Dezembro 120, Restauradores 210 440 000 www.altisavenidahotel.com 118 rooms Free Breakfast Restauradores.*

Avenida Palace

$$$$ | **HOTEL** | Built in 1892, the city's first luxury hotel combines regal elegance, modern comforts, and a romantic Belle Époque style. **Pros:** British-inspired bar serves delicious cocktails; suites are decorated to reflect historic period; regal lobby with soaring columns. **Cons:** some may find the atmosphere overly formal; no restaurant on the premises; no swimming pool. *Rooms from: €280 Rua 1° de Dezembro 123, Restauradores 213 218 100 www.hotel-avenida-palace.pt 82 rooms Free Breakfast Restauradores.*

Casa de São Mamede

$ | **B&B/INN** | **FAMILY** | One of the first private houses to be built in Lisbon after the 18th-century earthquake, Casa de São Mamede has been transformed into a relaxed boutique guesthouse endowed with a tiled dining room, a grand staircase, and stained-glass windows. **Pros:** 10-minute walk from the Bairro Alto; generous breakfast included in the rates; family-friendly vibe. **Cons:** a little staid for some travelers; no pool or fitness facilities; no parking available. *Rooms from: €120 Rua da Escola Politécnica 159, Rato 213 963 166 www.casadesaomamede.pt 26 rooms Free Breakfast Yellow Line to Rato.*

Dom Pedro Lisboa

$$ | **HOTEL** | This gleaming high-rise has guest rooms with the rich fabrics and polished-wood furnishings that appeal to the prosperous business executives who make up a big part of the clientele. **Pros:** upper floors have expansive views all the way to the river; spa has indoor pool, sauna, hot tub, and treatment rooms; shopping opportunities abound. **Cons:** 10-minute walk to nearest subway station; decor can feel a little dated; breakfast not included. *Rooms from: €160 Av. Engenheiro Duarte Pacheco 24, Amoreiras 213 896 600 www.dompedro.com 262 rooms No meals.*

DoubleTree by Hilton Hotel Lisbon–Fontana Park

$$ | **HOTEL** | It's worth considering the superior rooms at this contemporary hotel, especially those that have private balconies and floor-to-ceiling windows letting in lots of sunlight. **Pros:** short stroll to the Saldanha subway station; small garden with a gushing fountain; 24-hour fitness center. **Cons:** not close to the city's main sights; surrounding area still up and coming; rooms in older wing are a little dark. *Rooms from: €170 Rua Engenheiro Vieira da Silva, Saldanha 210 410 600 doubltree3.hilton.com 139 rooms No meals Saldanha.*

Epic Sana Lisboa

$$$ | **HOTEL** | **FAMILY** | With a heated infinity pool on the rooftop, an indoor pool in the enormous spa, and a well-equipped fitness center that looks out onto a beautiful botanical garden, this well-located hotel draws an active crowd. **Pros:** great amenities for families; good location for shopping; some great views. **Cons:** far from most of the city's sights; some rooms a little cramped; lacks any local flavor. *Rooms from: €230 Av. Engenheiro Duarte Pacheco 15, Marquês*

de Pombal ☏ 211 597 300 ⊕ www.lisboa.epic.sanahotels.com ⇨ 311 rooms ¶ No meals.

Expo Astória

$ | **HOTEL** | Housed in a fabulous art deco building, the fun and funky Expo Astória should appeal to those who find high-rise hotels a little lacking in soul. **Pros:** beautiful exterior with art deco flourishes; excellent service; lots of character. **Cons:** rooms are not very well soundproofed; spotty Wi-Fi access; bland decor. [$] *Rooms from: €130 ✉ Rua Braamcamp 10, Marquês de Pombal ☏ 213 861 317 ⊕ hotel-expo-astoria.lisbon-hotel.org ⇨ 113 rooms ¶ No meals [M] Marquês de Pombal.*

★ **Four Seasons Hotel Ritz Lisbon**

$$$$ | **HOTEL** | **FAMILY** | The feeling of luxury starts the minute you step into the Four Seasons Hotel Ritz Lisbon's marbled reception area and continues through to the lounge, whose terrace overlooks one of the city's prettiest parks. **Pros:** rooftop gym and full-size running track; stunning spa with all types of pampering; outstanding restaurant. **Cons:** some of the most expensive rooms in Lisbon; extra charge for parking and other amenities; decor may feel stuffy to some guests. [$] *Rooms from: €580 ✉ Rua Rodrigo da Fonseca 88, Marquês de Pombal ☏ 213 811 471 ⊕ www.fourseasons.com/lisbon ⇨ 282 rooms ¶ No meals [M] Blue or Yellow Line to Marquês de Pombal.*

★ **Hotel Altis Grand**

$$$ | **HOTEL** | This upscale lodging is every bit as refined and stately as you'd expect, from the welcoming lounge in the lobby area to the lively rooftop terrace bar where you can gaze out over the city. **Pros:** impeccable service from the moment you walk in the door; excellent fitness area with modern equipment; breakfast is a lavish buffet. **Cons:** swimming pool area can get very hot; some lower-floor rooms lack views; location is not particularly scenic. [$] *Rooms from: €240 ✉ Rua Castilho 11, Marquês de Pombal ☏ 213 106 000 ⊕ www.altishotels.com ⇨ 300 rooms ¶ Free Breakfast [M] Blue or Yellow Line to Marquês de Pombal.*

★ **Hotel Britânia**

$$$ | **HOTEL** | The art deco touches throughout Hotel Britânia are the key selling point—from the porthole windows flanking the arched doorway to the marble columns in the lobby to the historic murals in the bar. **Pros:** complimentary afternoon tea is a real treat; staff members are welcoming and friendly; lots of architectural flourishes. **Cons:** room decor is a little dated; missing amenities like a gym; no on-site restaurant. [$] *Rooms from: €220 ✉ Rua Rodrigues Sampaio 17, Avenida da Liberdade ☏ 213 155 016 ⊕ www.hotel-britania.com ⇨ 33 rooms ¶ No meals [M] Blue Line to Avenida.*

Hotel Heritage Avenida Liberdade

$$$$ | **HOTEL** | With an excellent location next to the Praça dos Restauradores, this style-conscious boutique hotel is located in an 18th-century town house styled by the Portuguese architect Miguel Cancio Martins. **Pros:** inviting common areas where guests can socialize; excellent location for sightseeing; bright and sunny rooms. **Cons:** more expensive than most of the city's top hotels; rather small indoor swimming pool; no on-site parking. [$] *Rooms from: €370 ✉ Av. da Liberdade 28, Avenida da Liberdade ☏ 213 404 040 ⊕ www.heritage.pt/en/heritage-avenida-liberdade/hotel ⇨ 42 rooms ¶ No meals [M] Blue Line to Restauradores.*

InterContinental Lisboa

$$$$ | **HOTEL** | Business travelers like this upscale hotel's location near Parque Eduardo VII, which makes it a hit with vacationers as well. **Pros:** 24-hour business center and other business facilities; plenty of on-site dining options; excellent service. **Cons:** not the best location for most of the city's sights; definitely focuses on business executives; some areas feel like a chain hotel. [$] *Rooms*

from: €290 ✉ Rua Castilho 149, Marquês de Pombal ☎ 213 818 700 🌐 www.ihg.com/intercontinental/hotels/gb/en/lisbon/lisha/hoteldetail 🛏 331 rooms 🍽 No meals Ⓜ Blue or Yellow Line to Marquês de Pombal.

Sana Capitol Hotel

$$ | **HOTEL** | **FAMILY** | Facing a quiet backstreet near Praça Marquês de Pombal, this hotel offers an exceptional location, lots of creature comforts, and high-tech touches. **Pros:** free parking and other thoughtful touches; modern, attractive decor; good breakfast. **Cons:** lacks a gym and other usual amenities; some taxi drivers have trouble finding it; restaurant only serves breakfast. $ *Rooms from: €140 ✉ Rua Eça de Queiroz 24, Marquês de Pombal ☎ 213 536 811 🌐 capitol.sanahotels.com/en 🛏 58 rooms, 1 suite 🍽 Free Breakfast Ⓜ Blue or Yellow Line to Marquês de Pombal.*

Sofitel Lisbon Liberdade

$$$ | **HOTEL** | Facing bustling Avenida da Liberdade, the opulent Sofitel has comfortably appointed rooms decorated in sophisticated variations of black, white, and gold and outfitted with high-tech touches. **Pros:** spacious rooms have a plush feel; free Wi-Fi and other amenities; lots of extras for families. **Cons:** often packed with conference participants; gym is on the small side; a little impersonal. $ *Rooms from: €240 ✉ Av. da Liberdade 127, Liberdade ☎ 213 228 300 🌐 www.sofitel-lisboa.com 🛏 163 rooms 🍽 No meals Ⓜ Blue Line to Avenida.*

Tivoli Avenida Liberdade Lisboa

$$$ | **HOTEL** | There's enough marble in the public areas of this grande dame to make you fear for the future supply of the stone, but the grandness gives way to comfort in the rooms, which are characterized by stylish dark wood and plush furnishings. **Pros:** leafy garden offers offers a respite from the hustle and bustle; top-notch spa and outdoor swimming pool; outstanding rooftop views. **Cons:** rooftop bar and restaurant often packed; some decor is a bit basic; can feel impersonal. $ *Rooms from: €240 ✉ Av. da Liberdade 185, Liberdade ☎ 🌐 www.tivolihotels.com/en/tivoli-avenida-liberdade-lisboa 🛏 285 rooms 🍽 Free Breakfast Ⓜ Blue Line to Avenida.*

Nightlife

BARS

★ Cinco Lounge

BARS/PUBS | With moody lighting, rococo furnishings, and potent cocktails, this spot is frequently cited as Lisbon's best cocktail bar. The creativity and innovation comes from the British owner, who mixed cocktails in his homeland (as well as Australia and the United States) before deciding to open his own place in Lisbon. *✉ Rua Ruben Leitão 17A, Príncipe Real ☎ 🌐 www.cincolounge.com Ⓜ Yellow Line to Rato.*

★ Pavilhão Chinês

BARS/PUBS | For a quiet drink in an intriguing setting, you can't beat this speakeasy. It's filled to the brim with fascinating junk collected over the years—from old toys to miniature statues—and it has two snooker tables where locals just might challenge you to a game. Cocktails and service are spot-on, and you may be reluctant to leave once you've settled into one of the comfy chairs. *✉ Rua Dom Pedro V 89, Príncipe Real ☎ 213 424 729 Ⓜ Yellow Line to Rato.*

★ Red Frog

BARS/PUBS | Inspired by clubs from the 1920s, this tucked-away cocktail bar is named for the huge amphibian you'll spot over the otherwise unmarked door (in true speakeasy fashion, ring the nearby bell to enter). A soft soundtrack of jazz, soul, and swing plays in the wood-paneled interior. The signature drink is the Spiced Rusty Cherry, ranked among the best cocktails in the world. *✉ Rua do Salitre 5A, Avenida da Liberdade ☎ 215 831 120 🌐 www.redfrog.pt Ⓜ Blue Line to Avenida.*

GAY AND LESBIAN CLUBS

★ Finalmente

DANCE CLUBS | Open for more than 40 years, the city's oldest gay club remains a hugely popular hangout, thanks in no small part to the wonderfully flamboyant drag shows. The biggest star is Deborah Kristall, who regularly calls on audience members to join in the onstage singing and dancing. On weekends DJs spin electronic music and the dance floor is absolutely packed by the time the drag show starts at 3 am. ✉ *Rua da Palmeira 38, Príncipe Real* ☎ *213 479 923* 🌐 *www.finalmenteclub.com* Ⓜ *Yellow Line to Rato.*

MUSIC CLUBS

★ Hot Clube de Portugal

MUSIC CLUBS | Europe's oldest jazz club started in a tiny basement in 1948, and all these decades later Hot Clube de Portugal remains the place for live jazz performances. It features local and international acts and has almost daily performances. ✉ *Praça da Alegria 47–49, Avenida da Liberdade* ☎ *212 460 305* 🌐 *www.hcp.pt* ⏲ *Closed Sun. and Mon.* Ⓜ *Blue Line to Avenida.*

Performing Arts

Coliseu dos Recreios

ARTS CENTERS | Constructed in 1890, this circular concert hall is a Lisbon cultural landmark. The great acoustics have made it one of the city's most important venues for performances ranging from classical music to rock. The smaller Sala hosts more intimate events like stand-up comedy. ✉ *Rua das Portas de Santo Antão 96, Restauradores* ☎ *213 240 585* 🌐 *www.coliseulisboa.com* Ⓜ *Green Line to Rossio.*

Shopping

ANTIQUES

J. Andrade Antiguidades

ANTIQUES/COLLECTIBLES | Museum curators are among the regulars poring over the unusual objects, paintings, sculptures, and furniture to be found in this store, run by two brothers since 1985. ✉ *Rua da Escola Politécnica 39, Príncipe Real* ☎ *213 424 964* 🌐 *www.jandrade-antiguidades.com* Ⓜ *Yellow Line to Rato.*

Solar Antiques

ANTIQUES/COLLECTIBLES | One of Lisbon's best-known antiques shops, Solar specializes in azulejo panels and also stocks 16th- to 18th-century Portuguese furnishings and paintings, most of them salvaged from old mansions, churches, and palaces. ✉ *Rua Dom Pedro V 68–70, Príncipe Real* ☎ *213 465 522* 🌐 *solar.com.pt* Ⓜ *Yellow Line to Rato.*

CLOTHING

Fashion Clinic

CLOTHING | Dozens of luxury labels (from Christian Louboutin to Stella McCartney to YSL) are represented at this store, which is a favorite of Lisbon's fashionistas. In addition to finding the perfect outfit for their most glamorous nights out, they can choose from a large selection of handbags and shoes, elegantly displayed in the well-designed space. ✉ *Tivoli Forum, Av. da Liberdade 180, Avenida da Liberdade* ☎ 🌐 *www.fashionclinic.com* Ⓜ *Blue Line to Avenida.*

Fly London

CLOTHING | Despite the name, this is the flagship store of one of Portugal's most successful footwear brands. It's known for its funky yet comfortable styles, and has more recently branched into clothing and accessories. ✉ *Av. da Liberdade 230, Avenida da Liberdade* ☎ *910 594 564* 🌐 *www.flylondon.com* Ⓜ *Blue Line to Avenida.*

GIFTS AND SOUVENIRS

Movimento Arte Contemporânea

ART GALLERIES—ARTS | Founded in 1993 with the aim of fostering cultural exchange between artists in Portugal and Portuguese-speaking countries such as Brazil, Angola, and Mozambique, this gallery displays contemporary paintings, sculptures, ceramics, and jewelry. ✉ *Rua do Sol ao Rato 9, Príncipe Real* ☎ *213 850 789* 🌐 *www.movimentoartecontemporanea.com* Ⓜ *Yellow Line to Rato.*

MALLS

★ **Embaixada**

SHOPPING CENTERS/MALLS | Shopping doesn't get any more stylish than at this grand 18th-century mansion, which has been transformed into a gallery showcasing some of the best of Portuguese design and even a few international brands. The bar and restaurant in the inner Moorish-style courtyard is an attractive place for a meal or drink. ✉ *Praça do Príncipe Real 26, Príncipe Real* ☎ *965 309 154* 🌐 *www.embaixadalx.pt* Ⓜ *Yellow Line to Rato.*

Alfama

Before there was Lisbon, there was Alfama. It's the oldest part of the city, and it remains a charming warren of narrow streets and alleyways. The neighborhood miraculously survived the devastating earthquake of 1755 that destroyed much of Lisbon, so its historic architecture is largely intact (or decaying in a glorious way). Now it's a must-stop on every visitor's itinerary, and one of the best places to buy traditional crafts, listen to traditional fado music, savor the stunning views, or simply allow yourself to get lost. It's also home to major landmarks including Castelo São Jorge and the 12th-century Sé Cathedral, the oldest in the city. Although the streets can be quite hilly, Alfama is best seen by foot, slowly, so as to allow its charms to unfold.

GETTING HERE AND AROUND

Alfama is the tourist heart of Lisbon, an uphill walk from Praça do Comércio and other major sites. The famous 28 tram runs right through the heart of it, but the area can also be accessed by taking the metro to Terreiro do Paço or Santa Apolónia or by taking the 759 bus. Part of joy of Alfama lies in getting lost among the maze of narrow alleyways. If you really lose your bearings, head downhill because eventually all roads lead to the riverfront.

Casa dos Bicos (*House of Spikes*)

HOUSE | This Italianate dwelling is one of Alfama's most distinctive buildings. It was built in 1523 for Bras de Albuquerque, the son of Afonso, who became the viceroy of India and conquered Goa and Malacca. The name translates as House of Spikes, and it's not hard to see why—it has a striking facade studded with pointed white stones in diamond shapes. The top two floors were destroyed in the 1755 earthquake, and restoration did not begin until the early 1980s. Since 2012 the building has housed the José Saramago Foundation, a cultural institute set up in memory of the only Portuguese-language winner of the Nobel Prize in Literature, with two floors dedicated to his life and works. ✉ *Rua dos Bacalhoeiros, Alfama* ☎ *218 802 040* 🌐 *www.josesaramago.org/onde-estamos* 🎫 **€3** 🕒 *Closed Sun.* Ⓜ *Blue Line to Terreiro do Paço.*

★ **Castelo de São Jorge** (*St. George's Castle*)

ARCHAEOLOGICAL SITE | **FAMILY** | Although St. George's Castle was constructed by the Moors, the site had previously been fortified by Romans and Visigoths. To your left as you pass through the main entrance is a statue of Dom Afonso Henriques, whose forces in 1147 besieged the castle and drove the Moors from Lisbon. The ramparts offer panoramic

A stunning sunset view of Castelo de São Jorge, which dominates the historic Alfama neighborhood.

views of the city's layout as far as the towering 25 de Abril suspension bridge. A residence of the kings of Portugal until the 16th century, the palace remnants now house a small museum showcasing archaeological finds, a snack bar, and a stately restaurant, Casa do Leão, offering dining with spectacular sunset views. From the *periscópio* (periscope) in the Torre de Ulísses, in the castle's keep, you can spy on visitors going about their business below. Beyond the keep, traces of pre-Roman and Moorish houses are visible thanks to recent archaeological digs, as well as the remains of a palace founded in the 15th century. The castle's outer walls encompass a small neighborhood, Castelo, the medieval church of Santa Cruz, restaurants, and shops. To get here, take Tram 28 (followed by an uphill walk) or Bus 737. ✉ *Rua de Santa Cruz do Castelo, Alfama* ☎ 🌐 *www.castelodesaojorge.pt* 🎫 *€10* Ⓜ *Tram 28E to São Tomé.*

Galeria Filomena Soares

ART GALLERIES—ARTS | Housed in a former warehouse not far from the Museu Nacional do Azulejo, this gallery is owned by, and bears the name of, one of Europe's leading female art dealers. Her roster includes leading local and international artists like Ângela Ferreira and Shirin Neshat. ✉ *Rua da Manutenção 80, Alfama* ☎ *218 624 122* 🌐 *gfilomenasoares.com/en* ☞ *Closed Sun., Mon., and Aug.* Ⓜ *Blue Line to Santa Apolónia.*

Miradouro de Santa Luzia (*St. Lucy's Overlook*)

$ | **VIEWPOINT** | | **FAMILY** |**VIEWPOINT** | **FAMILY** | Notable for its pretty terrace with blue-and-yellow azulejo tiles, the Miradouro de Santa Luzia has great views of the rooftops of Alfama and the boats along the Tagus River. Artists sell reasonably priced etchings of the scene. There's a pleasant kiosk serving coffee, cocktails, and snacks that you can enjoy at the nearby tables. ✉ *Largo de Santa Luzia, Alfama* ☎ *915 225 592* Ⓜ *Blue Line to Terreiro do Paço.*

Mosteiro de São Vicente de Fora

RELIGIOUS SITE | The Italianate facade of the twin-towered St. Vincent's Monastery heralds an airy church with a barrel-vault ceiling, the work of accomplished Italian architect Filippo Terzi (1520–97), finally completed in 1704. Its superbly tiled cloister depicts the fall of Lisbon to the Moors. The monastery also serves as the pantheon of the Bragança dynasty, which ruled Portugal from the restoration of independence from Spain in 1640 to the declaration of the republic in 1910. It's worth the admission fee to climb up to the rooftop terrace for a look over Alfama, the dome of the nearby Santa Engrácia, and the river. Guided tours of around 90 minutes run Tuesday to Saturday. ✉ *Largo de São Vicente, São Vicente* ☎ 🌐 *www.patriarcado-lisboa.pt/site/index.php?cont_=47&tem=356* 🎟 *€5* 🕒 *Closed Mon.* Ⓜ *Blue Line to Santa Apolónia.*

Museu do Teatro Romano (*Roman Theater Museum*)

ARCHAEOLOGICAL SITE | **FAMILY** | This small museum close to the cathedral displays some of the few visible traces of Roman Lisbon. The space was once a Roman amphitheater with capacity for 5,000 spectators and was built by Emperor Augustus in the 1st century BC. It fell into disrepair during the Middle Ages and lay buried and forgotten until reconstruction of the area began in the 18th century. Columns and other interesting artifacts are on display here, and multilingual touch-screen kiosks explain everything. ✉ *Rua de São Mamede 3A, Alfama* ☎ *218 172 450* 🌐 *www.museudelisboa.pt/en/* 🎟 *€3* 🕒 *Closed Mon.* Ⓜ *Blue Line to Terreiro do Paço, Blue or Green Line to Baixa-Chiado.*

Museu Militar de Lisboa (*Lisbon Military Museum*)

MILITARY SITE | **FAMILY** | The spirit of heroism is palpable in the sprawling barracks and arsenal complex of the Lisbon Military Museum, which houses one of the largest artillery collections in the world. You can ogle a 20-ton bronze cannon and admire Vasco da Gama's sword in a room dedicated to the explorer and his voyages. As you clatter through endless, echoing rooms of weapons, uniforms, and armor, you may be lucky enough to be followed—at a respectful distance—by a guide who can convey exactly how that bayonet was jabbed or that gruesome flail swung. In this ornate building there is also a collection of 18th- to 20th-century art. The museum is on the eastern edge of Alfama, at the foot of the hill and opposite the Santa Apolónia station. ✉ *Largo do Museu da Artilharia, Alfama* ☎ *218 842 310* 🎟 *€3* 🕒 *Closed Mon.* Ⓜ *Blue Line to Santa Apolónia.*

★ **Museu Nacional do Azulejo** (*National Tile Museum*)

MUSEUM | A tile museum might not sound thrilling, but this magnificent space dedicated to the city's eye-catching azulejo tiles is one of the city's top tourist attractions—and with good reason. Housed in the 16th-century Madre de Deus convent and cloister, it displays a range of individual glazed tiles and elaborate pictorial panels. The 118-foot-long *Panorama of Lisbon* (1730) is a detailed study of the city and its waterfront and is reputedly the country's longest azulejo mosaic. The richly furnished convent church contains some sights of its own: of note are the gilt baroque decoration and lively azulejo works depicting the life of St. Anthony. There are also a little café and a gift shop that sells tiles. ✉ *Rua da Madre de Deus 4* ☎ *218 100 340* 🌐 *www.museudoazulejo.gov.pt* 🎟 *€5* 🕒 *Closed Mon.* Ⓜ *Blue Line to Santa Apolónia.*

★ **Panteao Nacional** (*National Pantheon*)

BUILDING | The large domed edifice is the former church of Santa Engrácia. It took 285 years to build, hence the Portuguese phrase "a job like Santa Engrácia." Today the building doubles as Portugal's National Pantheon, housing the tombs of the country's former presidents as well as cenotaphs dedicated to its most famous

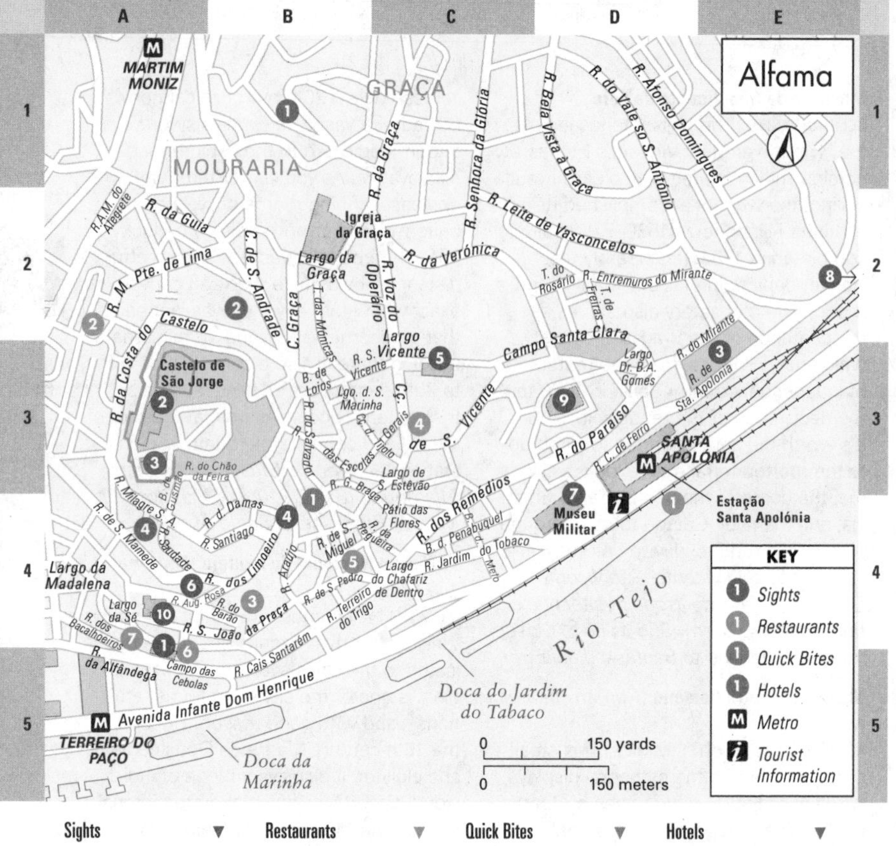

Sights

1 Casa dos Bicos **A4**
2 Castelo de São Jorge................ **A3**
3 Galeria Filomena Soares **E3**
4 Miradouro de Santa Luzia **B4**
5 Mosteiro de São Vicente de Fora..................... **C3**
6 Museu do Teatro Romano.......... **A4**
7 Museu Militar de Lisboa **D4**
8 Museu Nacional do Azulejo **E2**
9 Panteao Nacional **D3**
10 Sé de Lisboa............ **A4**

Restaurants

1 Bica do Sapato.......... **D4**
2 Cantinho do Aziz **A2**
3 Memmo Alfama Wine Bar & Terrace........... **B4**
4 Parreirinha de São Vicente........... **C3**
5 Santo António de Alfama................ **B4**
6 Solar dos Bicos **A5**
7 Taberna Moderna **A4**

Quick Bites

1 Portas do Sol........... **B4**

Hotels

1 Albergaria Senhora do Monte **B1**
2 Olissippo Castelo **B2**
3 Solar do Castelo **A3**
4 Solar dos Mouros....... **A4**

explorers and writers. A more recent arrival is fado diva Amália Rodrigues, whose tomb is invariably piled high with flowers from admirers. ✉ *Campo de Santa Clara* ☎ *218 854 820* 🌐 *www.patrimoniocultural.gov.pt/en/recursos/cedencia-e-aluguer-de-espacos/aluguer-de-espacos-panteao-nacional* 🎫 *€4* ⏲ *Closed Mon.* Ⓜ *Blue Line to Santa Apolónia.*

★ **Sé de Lisboa** (*Lisbon Cathedral*)
HISTORIC SITE | Lisbon's austere Romanesque cathedral was founded in 1150 to commemorate the defeat of the Moors three years earlier. To rub salt in the wound, the conquerors built the sanctuary on the spot where Moorish Lisbon's main mosque once stood. Note the fine rose window, and be sure to visit the 13th-century cloister and the treasure-filled sacristy, which contains the relics of the martyr St. Vincent, among other things. According to legend, the relics were carried from the Algarve to Lisbon in a ship piloted by ravens; the saint became Lisbon's official patron. The cathedral was originally built in the Romanesque style of the time but has undergone several rebuilds and refurbishments over the years, and today its rather eclectic architecture includes Gothic, baroque, and neoclassical adornments. **TIP→ Visitors are expected to dress respectfully.** ✉ *Largo da Sé, Alfama* ☎ *218 876 628* 🌐 *www.patriarcado-lisboa.pt/site* 🎫 *Cathedral free, cloisters €3* Ⓜ *Blue Line to Terreiro do Paço.*

Coffee and Quick Bites

Portas do Sol
$ | **INTERNATIONAL** | Unlike eateries at many of the city's scenic overlooks where the food definitely plays second fiddle to the views, Portas do Sol (meaning "doors to the sun") serves genuinely enticing cocktails and delightful dishes. Don't expect award-winning cuisine, but you could do far worse than a couscous or caprese salad washed down with a tangy caipirinha or freshly squeezed juice. **Known for:** appealing dining rooms for rainy days and chilly nights; excels with simple fare like salads and sandwiches; terrace with fantastic views to the river. Ⓢ *Average main: €9* ✉ *Largo das Portas do Sol, Beco de Santa Helena, Alfama* ☎ *218 851 299* 🌐 *portasdosol.pt* Ⓜ *Blue Line to Terreiro do Paço.*

Feira da Ladra Flea Market

If you're in Alfama on a Tuesday or Saturday, make sure to take in the Feira da Ladra flea market, which takes place on Campo de Santa Clara, from dawn to early afternoon (it runs a bit later on Saturday). The quality of the wares on offer varies tremendously, but it's a fun place for people-watching.

Restaurants

Bica do Sapato
$$$ | **ECLECTIC** | Partly owned by actor John Malkovich, this riverfront restaurant is known for its stylish interior with a minimalist look. The menu in the main dining room features modern takes on Portuguese fare, while the upstairs sushi bar offers a range of classic Japanese dishes. **Known for:** summertime tapas menu is a big hit; Sunday brunch from fall to spring; delicious dishes like swordfish steak. Ⓢ *Average main: €24* ✉ *Av. Infante Dom Henrique, Armazém B, Santa Apolónia* ☎ *218 810 320* 🌐 *www.bicadosapato.com* ⏲ *No dinner Sun. No lunch Mon.* Ⓜ *Blue Line to Santa Apolónia.*

Cantinho do Aziz
$ | **AFRICAN** | This Mozambican restaurant is a local institution and one of the best places in Lisbon to try African cuisine. The menu at the low-key, relaxed spot features fragrant and spicy meat dishes like *bakra* (spicy lamb ribs). **Known for:**

delicious dishes like nhama (beef with manioc, okra, and coconut); the spicy hot pepper sauce has many fans; lively outdoor terrace. $ *Average main: €12* ✉ *Rua de São Lourenço 5, Martin Moniz* ☎ *218 876 472* 🌐 *cantinhodoaziz.com* Ⓜ *Green Line to Martim Moniz.*

★ **Memmo Alfama Wine Bar & Terrace**

$$ | **PORTUGUESE** | The terrace at this popular eatery has some of the neighborhood's best views, with tables and chairs arranged around a small infinity pool. The menu centers around tapas-style small plates—the selection of Portuguese cheeses and meats, served with a basket of bread, is a good place to start. **Known for:** tasty dishes like peixinhos da horta (fried green beans); get here in late afternoon for sunset views; creative cocktails. $ *Average main: €18* ✉ *Memmo Alfama Hotel, Travessa das Merceeiras 27, Alfama* ☎ *210 495 660* 🌐 *www.memmo-hotels.com/alfama/wine-bar-amp-outdoor-pool.html* Ⓜ *Blue Line to Terreiro do Paço.*

Parreirinha de São Vicente

$ | **PORTUGUESE** | The food at this wood-paneled eatery around the corner from the Feira da Ladra flea market is expertly prepared and comes in portions big enough for two or three people to share. The brothers who run the place are from the northern Beiras region, and many of the dishes are meat-focused examples of its culinary traditions, but there are plenty of seafood options as well. **Known for:** handful of tables on the street; mostly patronized by locals; inexpensive lunch menu. $ *Average main: €12* ✉ *Calçada de São Vicente 54–58* ☎ *218 868 893* Ⓜ *Blue Line to Santa Apolónia.*

Santo António de Alfama

$$ | **PORTUGUESE** | This place is the opposite of a tourist trap—"We don't have sardines or fado," it proudly advertises—and the fact that it's still crowded is a testament to the great food and atmosphere. The simple but sophisticated dining room has lovely azulejo tiles and is hung with black-and-white photos of famous artists. **Known for:** pretty courtyard terrace shaded by trees; wide variety of seafood dishes; relaxed atmosphere. $ *Average main: €19* ✉ *Beco de São Miguel 7, Alfama* ☎ *218 881 328* 🌐 *www.siteantonio.com* Ⓜ *Blue Line to Terreiro do Paço.*

Solar dos Bicos

$ | **PORTUGUESE** | This charming restaurant with huge stone arches and a beautiful mural made of azulejo tiles offers typical regional cuisine at very reasonable prices. Grilled fish and seafood are the main attraction, but there are also plenty of no-nonsense meat dishes. **Known for:** good people-watching on the famous Casa dos Bicos; small pub next to the main restaurant; ample portions. $ *Average main: €15* ✉ *Rua dos Bacalhoeiros 8A, Alfama* ☎ *218 869 447* 🌐 *www.solardosbicos.pt* 🕓 *Closed for 2 wks in Dec.–Jan.* Ⓜ *Blue Line to Terreiro do Paço.*

Taberna Moderna

$$$ | **PORTUGUESE** | This updated version of the traditional Portuguese *tasca* (tavern) is an informal space where everyone seems to start off with a gin and tonic—there are 80 gins on the list, so there are plenty of variations. That said, food is hardly an afterthought as the kitchen turns out all sorts of delicious plates like black rice with cuttlefish or braised tuna that are the perfect size to share. **Known for:** one of the city's best places to go for a cocktail; lots of shareable dishes on the menu; umbrella-shaded tables on the street. $ *Average main: €21* ✉ *Rua dos Bacalhoeiros 18, Alfama* ☎ *218 865 039* 🌐 *tabernamoderna.com* 🕓 *Closed Sun. No lunch Mon.* Ⓜ *Blue Line to Terreiro do Paço.*

Hotels

Albergaria Senhora do Monte

$ | **HOTEL** | If you want expansive views of the castle and the entire neighborhood, book a room on one of the upper floors of this modern hotel perched atop the tallest of Lisbon's seven hills. **Pros:** amazing views from many rooms and common areas; in quiet residential neighborhood; friendly service. **Cons:** a long climb up a steep hill; not too many amenities; small breakfast selection. *Rooms from: €135 Calçada do Monte 39, Alfama 218 866 002 albergaria-senhora-do-monte.lisbon-hotel.org 28 rooms Free Breakfast.*

Olissippo Castelo

$$ | **HOTEL** | This small, elegant hotel near Castelo de São Jorge pampers guests with luxurious linens, elegant furnishings, and marble bathrooms. **Pros:** great views of the surrounding area; feels miles from the hustle and bustle; small bar serves light meals. **Cons:** you get here by climbing up a steep hill; very limited parking available; decor a bit basic. *Rooms from: €145 Rua Costa do Castelo 112–116, Alfama 218 820 190 www.olissippohotels.com/en/Hotels/Castelo/The-Hotel.aspx 24 rooms Free Breakfast.*

★ **Solar do Castelo**

$$$ | **B&B/INN** | Located in an 18th-century mansion within the walls of Castelo de São Jorge, this boutique hideaway has been lovingly restored. **Pros:** archaeological finds from the site are proudly put on display; beautiful breakfast area in the courtyard; pick-up from nearby bus stops. **Cons:** up a steep cobblestone road; some rooms don't have tubs; no restaurant. *Rooms from: €244 Rua das Cozinhas 2, Alfama 218 806 050 www.solardocastelo.com/en 20 rooms No meals.*

Solar dos Mouros

$ | **B&B/INN** | Done up in a pleasant shade of pink, this artistic town house has a great location near the Castelo de São Jorge. **Pros:** suites have their own spacious terraces; lovely views from just about everywhere; helpful staff. **Cons:** up a steep hill and stairs to climb; no parking is available; some bland decor. *Rooms from: €129 Rua do Milagre de Santo Antonio 6, Alfama 218 854 940 www.solardosmouros.com 13 rooms No meals.*

Nightlife

BARS

Caxin Bar

BARS/PUBS | Competition is fierce for a seat at this somewhat hidden lounge, but your patience will be rewarded with one of the friendliest drinking experiences in Alfama. It's officially a shisha lounge, but you don't need to be a hookah fan to appreciate the mysterious decor, tasty cocktails, and attentive service from the owner who brings snacks to your table for no extra charge. *Costa do Castelo 22, Alfama Blue or Green Line to Baixa-Chiado.*

★ **Damas**

MUSIC CLUBS | A former bakery, this cool restaurant, bar, and concert venue has maintained original interior features like the stainless steel work surfaces where bakers once rolled and kneaded the dough. Local and international bands and DJs take the stage around 11 on most nights. *Rua da Voz do Operário 60 964 964 416 Blue Line to Santa Apolónia.*

FADO CLUBS

★ **A Baiuca**

MUSIC CLUBS | The quality of both the food and the singing varies at this family-run establishment, but the setting—which calls to mind the dining room of a well-traveled older relative—is always welcoming. It's a fado *vadio* ("vagabond") spot, which means enthusiasm alone will get you onto the stage, and the night often ends with amateurs lined up outside, raring to perform. *Rua de São Miguel 20, Alfama 218 867 284 Blue Line to Terreiro do Paço.*

A Travessa do Fado

MUSIC CLUBS | Prominent fadistas, both traditional singers and next-generation artists who are expanding the boundaries

Fado

Fado is a haunting music that emerged in Lisbon from hotly disputed roots: African, Brazilian, and Moorish are among the contenders. A lone singer—male or female—is accompanied by a Spanish guitar and the 12-string Portuguese guitar, a closer relative of the lute. While Mouraria lays claim to be the birthplace of fado, today most *casas de fado* (fado houses) are in the Bairro Alto or Alfama.

They serve traditional Portuguese food (it's rarely anything special), and the singing starts at 9 or 10 and may continue until 2 am. Reservations for dinner are essential, but if you want to go along later just to listen, most establishments will let you do so if you buy drinks, usually around €10 minimum. Whenever you do arrive, fado etiquette is strict on one point: when the singing starts, all chatter must stop. *Silêncio, canta-se fado!*

of the form, perform most nights in this modern café attached to the city-run Fado Museum. Since this is a popular spot, reservations are essential in the evening. ✉ *Largo do Chafariz de Dentro 2, Alfama* ☎ *218 887 0144* 🌐 *www.museudofado.pt* Ⓜ *Blue Line to Terreiro do Paço.*

Clube de Fado
MUSIC CLUBS | An international crowd flocks to this spot to hear established performers—such as owner Mário Pacheco—and rising stars take turns at the microphone. Dinner is pricey at this two-story restaurant, but music fans arriving from around 10:30 pm can skip the food and concentrate on the music. ✉ *Rua S. João de Praça 86–94, Alfama* ☎ *218 852 704* 🌐 *www.clubedefado.pt/en* Ⓜ *Blue Line to Terreiro do Paço.*

★ **Mesa de Frades**
MUSIC CLUBS | All the rage among local fado lovers, this performance space is housed in a tiny, azulejo-lined former chapel. The quality of the food varies, but the music and atmosphere are always top rate. You can slip in at the end of the night, order a drink or two, and enjoy the show. ✉ *Rua dos Remédios 139A, Alfama* ☎ *917 029 436* Ⓜ *Blue Line to Santa Apolónia.*

★ **Parreirinha de Alfama**
MUSIC CLUBS | This little club has been owned by fado legend Argentina Santos since the 1960s, and although she no longer sings, she sits by the door most nights greeting newcomers and listening to other highly rated singers. Food plays second fiddle to the music, but you could do worse than grilled fish and a bottle of wine as the singers work their magic. ✉ *Beco do Espírito Santo 1, Alfama* ☎ *218 868 209* 🌐 *www.parreirinhadealfama.com* Ⓜ *Blue Line to Santa Apolónia.*

Performing Arts

★ **Chapitô**
CIRCUSES | A good way to break the language barrier is to see a show at this vibrant venue, where contemporary clowning, circus acts, and physical theater dominate. There's also the pleasant Chapitô à Mesa restaurant with fine views of the city and the bohemian Bartô bar with a mix of live music and DJs. ✉ *Costa do Castelo 1–7, Alfama* ☎ *218 855 550* 🌐 *chapito.org* Ⓜ *Blue Line to Terreiro do Paço.*

Shopping

ANTIQUES

M. Murteira Antiguidades

ANTIQUES/COLLECTIBLES | Several centuries are represented at this shop near the cathedral. It carries furniture, paintings, sculpture, and religious art from the 17th and 18th centuries as well as 20th-century artwork. ✉ *Rua Augusto Rosa 19–21, Alfama* ☎ *218 863 851* Ⓜ *Blue or Green Line to Baixa-Chiado.*

CERAMICS

Loja dos Descobrimentos

CERAMICS/GLASSWARE | You can often see artists at work in this shop specializing in hand-painted tiles. They ship worldwide, so there's no need to haul any breakables home in your bags. ✉ *Rua dos Bacalhoeiros 12A, Alfama* ☎ *218 865 563* 🌐 *www.loja-descobrimentos.com* Ⓜ *Blue Line to Terreiro do Paço.*

CRAFTS AND SOUVENIRS

★ **A Arte da Terra**

CRAFTS | In Lisbon Cathedral's former stables, A Arte da Terra uses the old stone mangers as display cases for traditional and modern crafts from around the country. As well as linen tablecloths, felt hats, and wool blankets, you can pick up fado and folk music and an amazing range of representations of Santo António, the city's favorite saint. ✉ *Rua Augusto Rosa 40, Alfama* ☎ *212 745 975* 🌐 *www.aartedaterra.pt* Ⓜ *Blue Line to Terreira do Paço.*

MARKETS

★ **Feira da Ladra**

OUTDOOR/FLEA/GREEN MARKETS | The so-called "thieves" market (it used to be said that stolen items invariably ended up here) is now the most famous flea market in Portugal. You'll need a few hours to browse all the stalls selling everything from vintage vinyl to antique furnishings. Running until about 2 pm on Tuesday and a little later into the afternoon on Saturday, it's a memorable shopping experience. ✉ *Campo de Santa Clara* Ⓜ *Blue Line to Santa Apolónia.*

Alcântara, Cais do Sodré, and Santos

Hipsters flock to this triangle of neighborhoods to hang out at the many independent bars, cafés, and boutique stores. Alcântara is synonymous with Lisbon's rebirth as Europe's Capital of Cool, thanks in large part to the funky revamped warehouses at LX Factory—now a miniature village packed with boho-chic bars, boutiques, and bookshops. Nearby Village Underground is a colorful collection of coworking spaces, art installations, and late-night party spots. A stroll along the banks of the Tagus takes visitors to Santos, where tapas restaurants, gin bars, and sushi joints sit side by side with family homes—residents grill sardines on the cobblestone streets and washing flaps from the windows. Nightlife steps it up a level in nearby Cais do Sodré, where partiers pack the famous Pink Street until dawn, and there's a chance to sample food from across Portugal at the Mercado da Ribeira, home of the hugely popular Time Out Market. A stroll along the riverfront takes you from one neighborhood to the next, or you can jump on a train to save time and energy; each of these hipster hot spots is on the railway line to Cascais.

GETTING HERE AND AROUND

Trains, metros, buses, and ferries arrive at and depart from Cais do Sodré, making it one of the best spots in the city for transportation. It's also flat, so walking is a breeze. Trains from Cais do Sodré stop at Alcântara and Santos on their way to Belém and the beaches of the Estoril coast. A second train station, Alcântara Terra, has connections to the Algarve, while a bus terminal nearby serves destinations south of the River Tagus. Santos has no metro stop, and parts of the neighborhood are hilly, with some narrow streets difficult to reach by

Alcântara, Cais do Sodre, and Santos

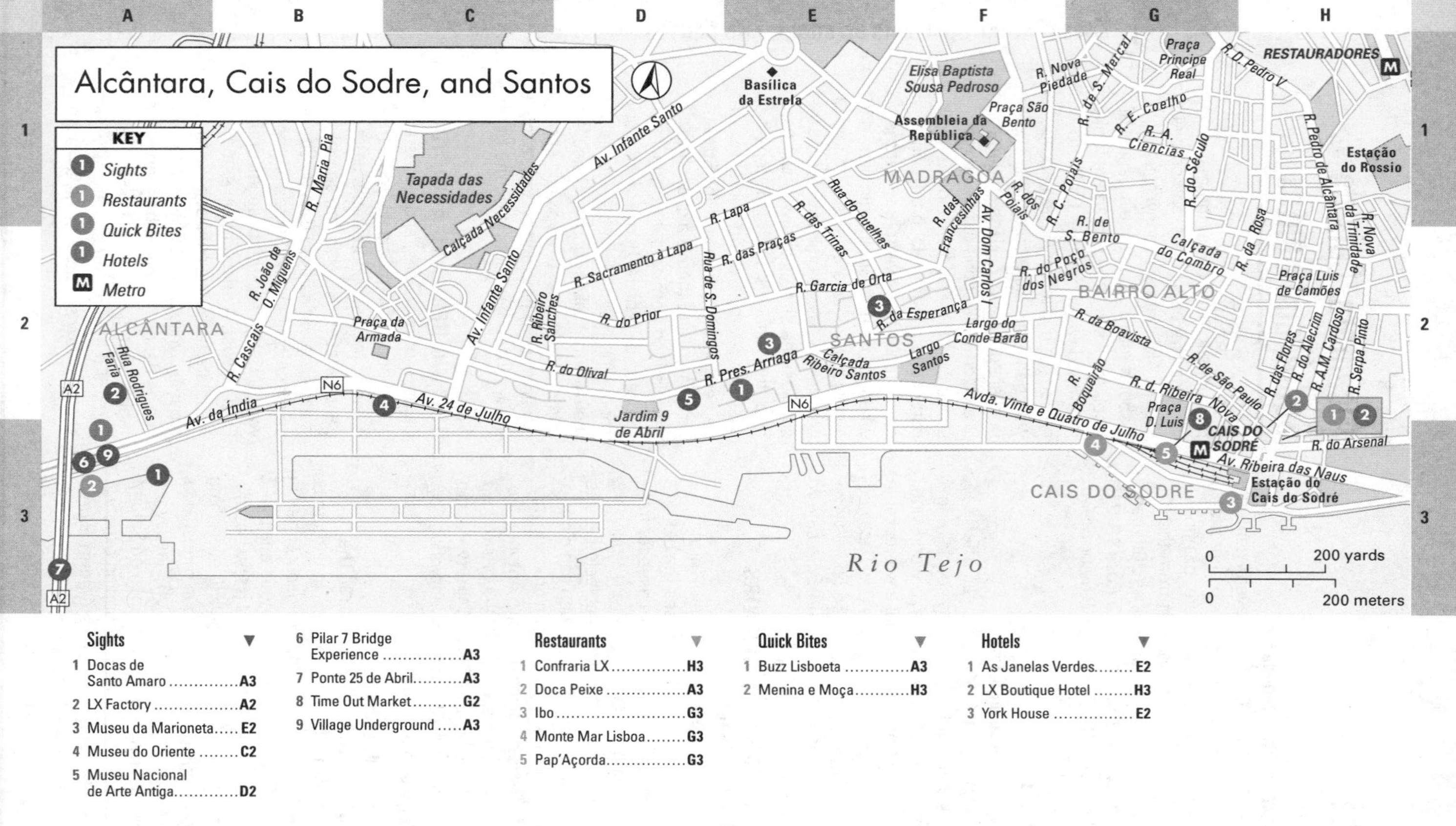

Sights

1 Docas de Santo Amaro A3
2 LX Factory A2
3 Museu da Marioneta..... E2
4 Museu do Oriente C2
5 Museu Nacional de Arte Antiga............ D2
6 Pilar 7 Bridge Experience A3
7 Ponte 25 de Abril.......... A3
8 Time Out Market.......... G2
9 Village Underground A3

Restaurants

1 Confraria LX.............. H3
2 Doca Peixe A3
3 Ibo G3
4 Monte Mar Lisboa........ G3
5 Pap'Açorda................ G3

Quick Bites

1 Buzz Lisboeta A3
2 Menina e Moça........... H3

Hotels

1 As Janelas Verdes........ E2
2 LX Boutique Hotel H3
3 York House E2

car—something to bear in mind in the heat of summer or if you're laden down with luggage.

Sights

Docas de Santo Amaro (*St. Amaro's Docks*)
PROMENADE | In the shadow of the huge Ponte 25 de Abril, the old wharves have been made over so that you can stroll along the riverfront all the way to Belém (taking about 30 minutes each way). At Docas de Santo Amaro, known to locals simply as Docas, a line of swanky restaurants and clubs now inhabit the shells of former warehouses. On the terrace in front of the marina, the party goes on until late into the night. ✉ *Av. Brasilia, Alcântara* Ⓜ *Tram 15E or 18E to Cais Rocha.*

★ **LX Factory**
ARTS VENUE | A former industrial area that's been transformed into a symbol of Lisbon's creative spirit, LX is a colorful collection of cafés, bars, and boutiques. A lively rooftop bar and restaurant—Rio Maravilha—offers drinking and dining with fabulous views across the river. Look out for the colorful female version of Almada's Cristo Rei (and Rio de Janeiro's Cristo Redentor) who stands on the rooftop with arms aloft, as though waiting to embrace her counterpart across the river. ✉ *Rua Rodrigues de Faria 103, Alcântara* ☎ *213 143 399* 🌐 *www.lxfactory.com* Ⓜ *Train (Cascais line) to Alcântara Mar.*

Museu da Marioneta
MUSEUM | **FAMILY** | Portugal has a rich history of using puppets—from cute to creepy—to tell stories, and this fascinating museum is an opportunity to see the marionettes and masks up close. The only one if its kind in Portugal, the Marionette Museum has expanded in recent years to include an impressive collection of African and Asian puppets alongside the Portuguese exhibits. The location, inside a former convent, adds an extra dash of drama to the proceedings, and there's a chance to get hands on with some of the puppets. ✉ *Convento das Bernardas, Rua da Esperança 146, Madragoa* ☎ *213 942 810* 🌐 *www.museudamarioneta.pt* 🎫 *€5* 🕒 *Closed Mon.* Ⓜ *Tram 25 to Santos-o-Velho.*

Museu do Oriente (*Museum of the Orient*)
MUSEUM | Housed in a former *bacalhau* (salt cod) warehouse with impressive bas-reliefs on its facade, the Museu do Oriente is one of Lisbon's most important cultural institutions. Funded by the Fundação Oriente (a legacy of colonial Macau and its gaming revenues), this dockside giant seeks to tell the story of the centuries-long Portuguese presence in Asia and to provide a showcase for Asian cultures. Highlights of the permanent collections include unique maps and charts from the golden age of Portuguese maritime exploration and stunning Chinese and Japanese painted screens. The museum hosts excellent, inexpensive concerts in its cozy auditorium. ✉ *Av. Brasília 352, Doca de Alcântara, Alcântara* ☎ *215 852 000* 🌐 *www.museudooriente.pt* 🎫 *€6, guided tours €7* 🕒 *Closed Mon.* Ⓜ *Tram 15E or 18E to Cais Rocha.*

★ **Museu Nacional de Arte Antiga** (*National Ancient Art Museum*)
MUSEUM | Portugal's National Ancient Art Museum is housed in an opulent 17th-century palace, built at the behest of the Count of Alvor and later occupied by the brother of the Marquis de Pombal. Try not to spend too much time gaping at the dramatic painted ceilings, stucco detailing, and baroque doorways or you'll miss the collection of more than 40,000 works, including the unsettling 1501 triptych *Temptation of Saint Anthony* by Hieronymus Bosch, one of the most important pieces in the country. A café set in lovely gardens is the perfect place for a bite. ✉ *Rua das Janelas Verdes, Santos* ☎ *213 192 800* 🌐 *www.museudearteantiga.pt* 🎫 *€6* 🕒 *Closed Mon.*

Tram 15 to Cais Rocha or Tram 25 to Santos-o-Velho.

Pilar 7 Bridge Experience

VIEWPOINT | FAMILY | At this innovative, interactive attraction you'll be whisked up to a glass-floored viewing platform high above the beautiful 25 de Abril suspension bridge. You'll learn how this engineering marvel was constructed, get a glimpse inside one of the massive pillars, and take a virtual reality tour of parts that nobody can otherwise reach. *Av. da Índia, Alcântara 211 117 880 www.visitlisboa.com/en/places/pilar-7-bridge-experience €6, €1.50 virtual reality experience Train to Alcântara Mar.*

Ponte 25 de Abril

BRIDGE/TUNNEL | Lisbon's first suspension bridge across the Tagus River, linking the Alcântara and Almada districts, is a double-decker that stands 230 feet above the water and stretches almost 2½ km (1½ miles). Reminiscent of San Francisco's Golden Gate Bridge, it's somewhat smaller, but still a spectacular sight from any direction. Overlooking the bridge from a hill on the south bank is the **Cristo Rei** (Christ the King) statue, which is smaller and stiffer than Rio de Janeiro's more famous Redeemer. *Ponte 25 de Abril, Alcântara Train (Cascais line) to Alcântara Mar.*

★ **Time Out Market** (*Ribeira Market*)

MARKET | A local landmark since 1892, the sprawling Mercado da Ribeira is worth a visit to see where locals go for stalls selling the city's freshest fruit, vegetables, fish, and seafood. A separate hall has been taken over by very popular and noisy food hall called the Time Out Market, where Lisbon's top chefs and restaurants present their best creations. The massive warehouse building is where tourists get an overview of local gastronomy and where locals find their favorite bites. *Av. 24 de Julho 49, Cais do Sodré www.timeoutmarket.com/lisboa/en Green Line to Cais do Sodré.*

Village Underground

NEIGHBORHOOD | Together with nearby LX Factory, Village Underground is a colorful symbol of Lisbon's rebirth as Europe's Capital of Cool. Beneath the river-spanning 25 de Abril Bridge, shipping containers and double-decker buses have been transformed into spaces for eating and drinking. DJ sets, vibrant murals, and that famous double-decker bus make it one of Lisbon's hottest hangouts for scenesters and the Instagram brigade. *Rua 1 de Maio 103, Alcântara 215 832 469 www.vu.lisboa.com Tram 15E or 18E to Alcântara–Av. 24 Julho.*

Coffee and Quick Bites

★ **Buzz Lisboeta**

$ | CAFÉ | Climb aboard this double-decker bus—and we do mean climb, as it's parked about 10 feet off the ground—for a range of sandwiches, salads, and strong coffee. The boozy brunches on the weekends are unforgettable. **Known for:** one of the city's liveliest eateries; attracts a trendy clientele; vegetarian and vegan fare. *Average main: €12 Village Underground, Rua 1 de Maio 103, Alcântara 911 115 533 Tram 15E or 18E to Calvário.*

Menina e Moça

$ | CAFÉ | This cute café-bar doubles as a bookstore, and it's not unusual to see local poets reading from their work. The bright primary colors and painted ceiling give it the look of a cozy kids' corner, but the coffees and mixed drinks are strictly for grown-ups. **Known for:** frequent live music performances; excellent brunch menu; literary clientele. *Average main: €12 Rua Nova do Carvalho 40–42, Cais do Sodré 218 272 331 Green Line to Cais do Sodré.*

Restaurants

Confraria LX

$$$ | **SUSHI** | Occupying a bright and breezy downstairs room at the LX Boutique Hotel, this eatery is widely regarded as one of the best places in town to eat sushi. There are vegan and vegetarian options alongside the usual tuna and salmon rolls. **Known for:** plenty of tapas that can be shared by everyone; impressive cocktail list; beautiful presentation. *Average main: €23 LX Boutique Hotel, Rua do Alecrim 12A, Cais do Sodré 213 426 292 www.lxboutiquehotel.com/restaurant Green Line to Cais do Sodré.*

Doca Peixe

$$$ | **SEAFOOD** | The display of the day's catch on ice at the entrance and the small aquarium clue you in to what's served at this well-regarded riverside spot. You might start with a tomato-and-mozzarella salad or prawns seared in cognac, then move on to sea bass with clams, or codfish baked in a cornbread crust served with turnip leaves. **Known for:** fresh-grilled fish is always the best choice; seafood stews using local ingredients; breezy terrace with river views. *Average main: €23 Doca de Santo Amaro, Armazém 14, Alcântara 213 973 565 www.docapeixe.com Tram 15E or 18E to Cais Rocha.*

Ibo

$$$ | **AFRICAN** | Spicy seafood curries from the fomer Portuguese colony of Mozambique blend beautifully with expertly prepared fish dishes at this formal dining room in a stylishly converted warehouse on the banks of the Tagus River. The terrace overlooking the waterfront promenade is perfect for dinner, especially around sunset. **Known for:** outdoor tables are hotly contested, so be sure to book ahead; sophisticated atmosphere; extensive wine list. *Average main: €22 Armazém A, Porta 2, Compartimento 2, Cais do Sodré 961 332 024 www.ibo-restaurante.pt Closed Mon. No dinner Sun. Green Line to Cais do Sodré.*

Monte Mar Lisboa

$$$ | **SEAFOOD** | A city-smart sister to the celebrated Monte Mar formal dining restaurant in Cascais, Monte Mar Lisboa offers the same superior seafood with a more relaxed riverfront ambience. Occupying one of the formerly disused warehouses along the revitalized docks, Monte Mar has a terrific view of the river, the 25 de Abril suspension bridge, and the Cristo Rei on the other side, while indoors it is all slick black and chrome. **Known for:** tasty spider crab, lobster, and other crustaceans; signature dish of hake fillet with cockle rice; lovely terrace with views over the river. *Average main: €25 Rua da Cintura do Porto de Lisboa Armazém 65, Cais do Sodré 213 220 160 www.mmlisboa.pt/en/restaurant-monte-mar-lisboa Closed Mon. Green Line to Cais do Sodré.*

★ **Pap'Açorda**

$$$ | **PORTUGUESE** | Bringing along the famously glitzy chandelier from its much-missed location in Bairro Alto, this cutting-edge restaurant is now located within the cool confines of the Time Out Market in Cais do Sodré. The menu still lists cutting-edge versions of Portuguese classics—tuna with allspice, and a famous *açorda*, that bread-based stew rich in seafood (the luxury version contains lobster) and flavored with garlic and cilantro. **Known for:** a good bet for late-night dining on weekends; legendary chocolate mousse for dessert; great wine and cocktail list. *Average main: €22 Time Out Market, Av. 24 de Julho 49, Cais do Sodré 211 200 479 papacorda.com Closed Mon. Green Line to Cais do Sodré.*

The Ponte 25 de Abril, a suspension bridge spanning the Tagus River, makes for a photo-worthy backdrop.

Hotels

★ As Janelas Verdes

$$$ | **B&B/INN** | This late-18th-century mansion maintains the proper period furnishings, paintings, and tilework in the common areas, and the guest rooms have been individually furnished with the same care and taste. **Pros:** guests get free admission to nearby Museu de Arte Antiga; some have access to the garden via an exterior staircase; location far away from the crowds of tourists. **Cons:** no subway station nearby; not many amenities; far from city center. *Rooms from: €240 Rua das Janelas Verdes 47, Lapa 213 968 143 www.asjanelasverdes.com 29 rooms Free Breakfast Green Line to Cais do Sodré.*

★ LX Boutique Hotel

$$$ | **HOTEL** | A hip location in one of Lisbon's hottest neighborhoods, the duck-egg-blue LX Boutique Hotel is perfect if you're looking forward to a night on the town, want to visit the historic sights at Belém, or spend some time on the beaches of the Estoril Coast. **Pros:** the suite has a retractable glass roof; restaurant serves excellent sushi; faces a beautiful square. **Cons:** rooms rather small; no exercise facilities; just four parking spots (fee). *Rooms from: €225 Rua do Alecrim 12, Cais do Sodré 213 474 394 www.lxboutiquehotel.com 61 rooms No meals Green Line to Cais do Sodré.*

York House

$$$ | **B&B/INN** | While each of the guest rooms at York House is unique, they share nice touches like four-poster beds, beautiful rugs, and period reproduction furnishings. **Pros:** authentic period charm everywhere you look; handy for the Museu de Arte Antiga; dine in the renowned A Confraria eatery. **Cons:** steep climb upstairs from the street; long distance from most attractions; extra charge for breakfast. *Rooms from: €210 Rua das Janelas Verdes 32, Cais do Sodré 213 962 435 www.yorkhouselisboa.com 32 rooms No meals Train to Santos.*

Nightlife

In Cais do Sodré, the famous Rua Cor da Rosa (which locals call Pink Street because of the rosy-colored pavement) rivals Bairro Alto for late-night partying. From this central locale, it's a couple of minutes on the train to the tapas bars and tascas of hilly Santos. One stop farther takes you to Alcântara, where hipsters flock to the collection of bars at LX Factory and well-heeled types hangout at smart nightspots on the waterfront.

BARS

★ Lounge

BARS/PUBS | This hip joint is where twenty- and thirtysomething vinyl lovers chat (or shout) to the pumping sound of dance music. There are regular live performances—think funky Brazilian or African sounds—that bring in the crowds on weekends. ✉ *Rua da Moeda 1, Cais do Sodré* ☎ *214 032 712* 🌐 *www.lounge-lisboa.com.pt* Ⓜ *Green Line to Cais do Sodré.*

★ Matiz Pombalina

BARS/PUBS | An upmarket cocktail bar whose decor is inspired by the Pombaline architecture of downtown Lisbon, Matiz Pombalina feels like the living room of an exceptionally stylish friend. The main focus is on gin but every cocktail on the extensive list can be customized to your tastes, and live jazz provides the perfect soundtrack to your sipping. The space is quite small, so it's worth reserving a table in advance. ✉ *Rua das Trinas 25, Santos* ☎ *214043 703* 🌐 *www.matiz-pombalina.pt/en* Ⓜ *Tram 15E or 18E to Santos.*

★ O Bom O Mau e O Vilão

BARS/PUBS | This film-themed bar (the name comes from the Portuguese title of *The Good, the Bad and the Ugly*) attracts an artsy young crowd thanks to its lengthy cocktail list and vintage-chic decor. DJs spin vinyl while patrons loaf in comfy armchairs or prop up the bar. ✉ *Rua Do Alecrim 21, Cais do Sodré* ☎ *963 982 094* 🌐 *thegoodthebadandtheuglybar.com* Ⓜ *Green Line to Cais do Sodré.*

★ Pensão Amor

BARS/PUBS | Housed in a former brothel, this offbeat hangout recalls its decadent past with velvet armchairs, tassled curtains, and a huge mural across the ceiling. Its warren of rooms houses an erotic bookshop, a bar, a café, and a dance floor. Burlesque shows add to the racy appeal, but it's more suggestive than sordid. ✉ *Rua do Alecrim 19, Cais do Sodré* ☎ *213 143 399* 🌐 *www.pensaoamor.pt* Ⓜ *Cais do Sodré.*

★ Rio Maravilha

BARS/PUBS | Occupying a former break room for factory workers, Rio Maravilha now offers Lisbon's creative types a chance to eat, drink, and be merry. The Brazil-themed decor is colorful, the ambience is relaxed, and the menu has plenty of creative small plates, but it's the views over 25 de Abril suspension bridge that steal the show. It's open until late on weekends, when DJs get the crowd going. ✉ *LX Factory, Rua Rodrigues de Faria 103, 4th fl., Alcântara* ☎ *966 028 229* 🌐 *www.riomaravilha.pt* Ⓜ *Tram 15E or 18E to Calvário.*

Sol e Pesca

BARS/PUBS | This former fishing-tackle shop kept much of the original decor—including fishing rods and life preservers—when it reopened as a trendy bar. It serves canned delicacies (mostly involving fish) and inexpensive draft beer. ✉ *Rua Nova do Carvalho 44, Cais do Sodré* ☎ *213 467 203* Ⓜ *Green Line to Cais do Sodré.*

LIVE MUSIC

Agua de Beber

MUSIC | This under-the-radar spot draws an extremely enthusiastic crowd for live Brazilian music. The excellent caipirinhas help get the party spirit flowing. ✉ *Travessa de São Paulo 8, Cais do Sodré* ☎ *214 039 956* Ⓜ *Green Line to Cais do Sodré.*

★ **B.Leza**

DANCE | Playing African beats for more than 20 years, B.Leza really packs them in at this riverfront warehouse. It has a strong Angolan influence, with *kizomba* dance workshops and regular live music and dance shows. ✉ *Cais da Ribeira Nova, Armazém B, Cais do Sodré* ☎ *210 106 837* Ⓜ *Green Line to Cais do Sodré.*

★ **MusicBox**

MUSIC CLUBS | Under the arches on the famous Pink Street—you can find it by the enormous mural overhead—MusicBox has well-known bands and popular DJs performing on the huge stage. Get here after midnight—the fun goes on until dawn. ✉ *Rua Nova do Carvalho 24, Cais do Sodré* ☎ *213 473 188* 🌐 *musicboxlisboa.com* Ⓜ *Green Line to Cais do Sodré.*

Estrela, Campo de Ourique, and Lapa

There are relatively few tourists in this part of town, but those who do step off the tram and choose to wander around the neighborhoods of Estrela, Campo de Ourique, and Lapa will discover a side of Lisbon often only experienced by locals. The affluent district of Lapa was laid out shortly after the Great Earthquake of 1755, on what were then considered the outskirts of the city. It was where the wealthier classes built their mansions, most of which have since been turned into embassies or hotels (the most notable examples are down Rua do Sacramento à Lapa). Other buildings follow a neoclassical style, with many featuring beautiful decorative tiles on their facades. In fact, this was where the Portuguese tradition of covering buildings with tiles was born. Today, Lapa remains a peaceful residential neighborhood that eventually leads to Estrela, where you'll find one of the prettiest parks in the city and a basilica whose large dome can be seen from almost anywhere in the city.

GETTING HERE AND AROUND

The famous Tram 28 rumbles up from downtown to Estrela, with a stop at the Basilica. Rato metro station is a 5- to 10-minute walk away—but with its narrow lanes, one-way streets, and steep stairs, much of Lapa needs to be explored on foot.

It's worth setting aside at least a day to explore these scenic parts of town; just be sure to wear comfortable shoes. The Basilica and nearby Jardim da Estrela merit an hour or so, and the café-bar, playground, and weekend craft markets at Jardim da Estrela may entice you to linger considerably longer. Leave 20 minutes or so for a downhill stroll past grand old buildings and narrow cobbled lanes to reach the Museu de Arte Antiga, which itself merits a couple of hours' contemplation, and allow another hour, plus around 15 minutes' walking time, if you plan to visit the Museu da Marioneta.

Sights

Aqueduto das Águas Livres (*Aqueduct of Free Waters*)

BUILDING | Stretching for more than 18 km (11 miles) from the water source on the outskirts of the city, the Aqueduct of Free Waters began providing Lisbon with clean drinking water in 1748. The most imposing section is the 35 arches—the largest of these is said to be the highest ogival (pointed) arch in the world—that stride across the Alcântara River Valley north of the Amoreiras Shopping Complex in the neighborhod of Campolide. Nearer the city center, another 14 arches run 200 feet along the Praça das Amoreiras, ending in the Mãe d'Agua, an internal reservoir capable of holding more than a million gallons of water. This extraordinary structure is open for visits, providing a chance to see the holding tank, lavish internal waterfall, and associated machinery. ✉ *Calçada da Quintinha 6, Campolide* ☎ *218 100 215* 🌐 *www.epal.pt/EPAL/en/menu/water-museum/* 🎫 *€3* ⏲ *Closed Mon.* Ⓜ *Tram 24 to Campolide.*

Basílica da Estrela (*Estrela Basilica*)
RELIGIOUS SITE | A standout on Lisbon's skyline, this gleaming white basilica was built in the baroque and neoclassical styles. Its location at the top of one of Lisbon's seven hills makes for dramatic views from its rococo *zimbório* (dome). It was built at the end of the 18th century under the command of Queen Maria I (whose tomb lies within the building) to fulfill a religious promise she made while praying for a male heir. The interior is striking, too, with black-and-pink marble walls and floors and a famously elaborate nativity scene displayed year-round. Estrela is a short walk west of Largo do Rato, where the metro's Yellow Line terminates. ✉ *Praça da Estrela, Lapa* 🎫 *Basilica free, dome €5* Ⓜ *Yellow Line to Rato, Tram 25 or 28 to Estrela.*

Fundação Arpad Szenes-Vieira da Silva (*Arpad Szenes-Vieira da Silva Foundation*)
MUSEUM | This small but beautiful museum in a former silk factory displays paintings, drawings, and prints by Maria Helena Vieira da Silva and her Hungarian husband, Árpád Szenes. The couple lived in Lisbon, Paris, and Rio de Janeiro and were influential artists after their participation in the 1937 World Exhibition in Paris. Most of Vieira da Silva's pieces are geometrical abstractions and can be seen over the two floors of the building that face the arches of the city's landmark aqueduct. Throughout the year the museum also hosts temporary exhibits of 20th-century and contemporary art. ✉ *Praça das Amoreiras 56, Amoreiras* ☎ *213 880 044* 🌐 *www.fasvs.pt* 🎫 *€5* ⏲ *Closed Mon.* Ⓜ *Yellow Line to Rato.*

Galeria Cristina Guerra
MUSEUM | This gallery regularly presents works by top Portuguese artists plus some big international names. Much of the artwork later appears in some of the world's leading art fairs. ✉ *Rua Santo António à Estrela 33, Estrela* ☎ *213 959 559* 🌐 *www.cristinaguerra.com* ☞ *Closed Sun. and Mon.* Ⓜ *Tram 25 or 28 to Rua Domingos Sequeira.*

★ **Mercado de Campo de Ourique** (*Campo de Ourique Market*)
MARKET | Started in 1934, this is one of Lisbon's oldest neighborhood markets and over the last few years has turned into one of the city's hottest food destinations. The stalls of fresh fruits and vegetables now surround tables where customers sit for meals prepared at the newer gourmet stalls. It's a lively place where you still find mostly locals, unlike at the bigger and more famous Time Out Market by the river. ✉ *Rua Coelho da Rocha, Campo de Ourique* ☎ *211 323 701* 🌐 *www.mercadodecampodeourique.pt* Ⓜ *Tram 25 or 28 to Igreja Sto. Condestável.*

Reservatório da Mãe d'Água das Amoreiras (*Mãe d'Agua Reservoir and Water Museum*)
HISTORIC SITE | The Mãe d'Agua—literally "Mother of the Water"—is a centuries-old reservoir that's an impressive feat of engineering from Hungarian architect Carlos Mardel, who designed the enormous Aguas Livres Aqueduct. A small museum here provides insights into the 1748 construction, and from here it's possible to walk along stretches of the aqueduct. A viewing platform offers terrific views over the city. ✉ *Praça das Amoreiras 8, Amoreiras* ☎ *218 100 215* 🌐 *www.epal.pt/EPAL/en/menu/water-museum/* 🎫 *€3* ⏲ *Closed Mon.* Ⓜ *Yellow Line to Rato.*

Restaurants

Casa dos Passarinhos
$ | **PORTUGUESE** | In business for nearly a century, this eatery is a lunchtime favorite for workers in the nearby office complex, and at night it draws mainly

Sights

1 Aqueduto das Águas Livres........ **B1**

2 Basílica da Estrela....... **B6**

3 Fundação Arpad Szenes-Vieira da Silva......... **D3**

4 Galeria Cristina Guerra....... **A6**

5 Mercado de Campo de Ourique..... **A4**

6 Reservatório da Mãe d'Água das Amoreiras .. **D4**

Restaurants

1 Casa dos Passarinhos **B4**

2 Clube de Jornalistas.. **B7**

3 Estórias na Casa da Comida...... **D3**

4 Loco......... **B6**

5 Tasca da Esquina..... **B5**

Hotels

1 Olissippo Lapa Palace...... **A7**

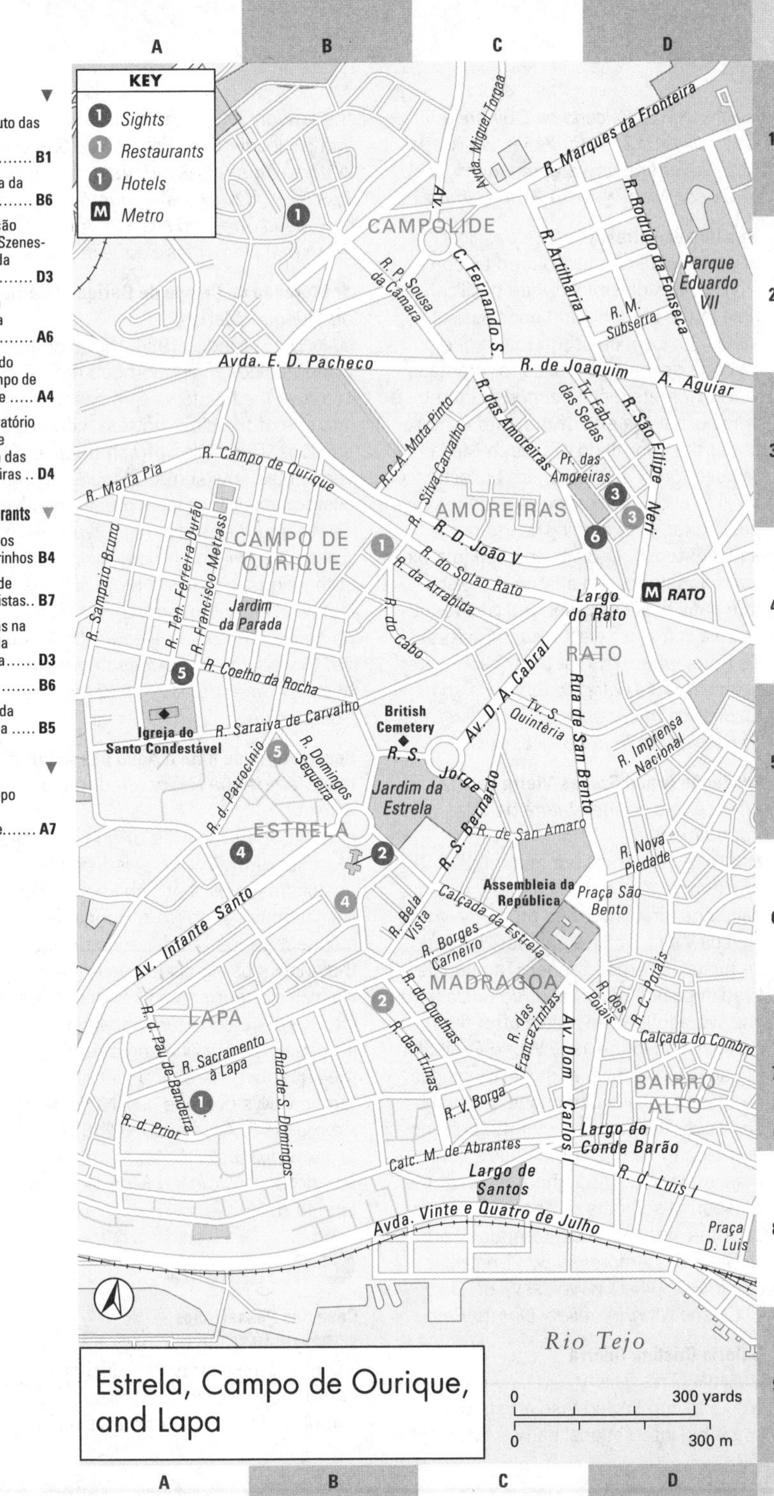

locals from the neighborhood in search of a home-cooked meal. Come for the house specialties, which include the famous *naco na pedra* (steak cooked on a hot stone), *vitela barrosã* (tender veal from the north), and *açorda de gambas* (shrimp and bread stew). **Known for:** a pair of charming dining rooms decorated in a rustic style; many dishes are served in the pots they were cooked in; affordable set lunches. *Average main: €12 Rua Silva Carvalho 195, Campo de Ourique 213 882 346 casadospassarinhos.com Closed Sun. and 2 wks in Aug. Yellow Line to Rato.*

★ Clube de Jornalistas

$$ | **INTERNATIONAL** | Although the name suggests it's only open to journalists, the Brazilian-owned Press Club is an excellent restaurant open to everyone. It has a cozy dining room lined with azulejo tiles, but everyone usually heads straight to the pleasant garden and plops down at one of the umbrella-shaded tables. **Known for:** classic 18th-century interior; creative international menu; delicious dessert sampler. *Average main: €19 Rua das Trinas 129, Lapa 213 977 138 www.restauranteclubedejornalistas.com Closed Sun. Tram 25 to Rua de São Domingos à Lapa.*

★ Estórias na Casa da Comida

$$$$ | **PORTUGUESE** | Design aficionados were wowed by this longtime favorite's sophisticated new interiors, and foodies applauded the innovations of chef Duarte Lourenço and sommelier Ricardo Morais. Snack on a superior line of *petiscos* (appetizers) in the cozy bar area, choose a few à la carte options in the handsome dining room, or opt for the eight-course "madness of the chef" tasting menu that features treats like juniper-smoked rabbit or fish cakes made from gooseneck barnacles and crab. **Known for:** a romantic terrace adds to the feel that this is someplace special; contemporary Portuguese cuisine with an international flavor; servers know the wine list inside and out. *Average main: €27 Travessa das Amoreiras 1, Amoreiras 213 860 889 www.casadacomida.pt/restaurante Closed Sun. No lunch Yellow Line to Rato.*

★ Loco

$$$$ | **PORTUGUESE** | In a dining room where the wide-plank floors and honey-colored wood tables provide the perfect backdrop, this award-winning restaurant offers tantalizing tasting menus by chef Alexandre Silva, who changes them every two weeks so he can take advantage of the freshest seasonal ingredients. Occasionally, he invites other top chefs from Lisbon and beyond to create special one-night-only menus in the dramatic open kitchen. **Known for:** each carefully presented dish resembles a work of art; high-quality yet little-known Portuguese wines; gorgeous interior design. *Average main: €80 Rua dos Navegantes 53B, Estrela 213 951 861 www.loco.pt Closed Sun. and Mon. No lunch Tram 25 or 28 to Estrela.*

Tasca da Esquina

$$ | **PORTUGUESE** | Vítor Sobral, one of the country's most famous chefs, has brought together the vibe of a traditional neighborhood eatery and sophisticated dishes that appeal to modern palates. The glass-walled space overlooking a cobblestone lane sits on a corner not far from the Basílica da Estrela. **Known for:** small plates that are perfect for sharing with the group; tasting menu with surprise dishes selected by chef; always packed, so be sure to book in advance. *Average main: €18 Rua Domingos Sequeira 41C, Campo de Ourique 219 837 255 www.tascadaesquina.com Tram 25 or 28 to Rua Saraiva Carvalho.*

Hotels

★ Olissippo Lapa Palace

$$$$ | **HOTEL** | Combining the elegance of a 19th-century manor house with the modern amenities of a luxury resort, the

Olissippo Lapa Palace is perched at the top of one of Lisbon's seven hills and has spectacular views. **Pros:** the higher your room, the better your views; indoor bar is a refined yet relaxed spot; live jazz bands many evenings. **Cons:** location isn't the best for sightseeing; rooms and restaurant are pricey; you have to take a taxi everywhere. *Rooms from: €370* *Rua Pau de Bandeira 4, Lapa* *213 949 494* *www.lapapalace.com* *109 rooms* *Free Breakfast.*

Nightlife

FADO CLUBS

★ Senhor Vinho

MUSIC CLUBS | This Lisbon institution attracts some of Portugal's most accomplished fado singers. It also serves better food than many *casas de fado* and is one of the few touristy spots that still attracts locals. The name literally means "Mister Wine," and as expected, there are some good bottles to choose from. *Rua do Meio à Lapa 18, Lapa* *213 972 681* *www.srvinho.com* *Tram 25 to Rua de São Domingos à Lapa.*

Shopping

FOOD AND WINE

★ Gleba

FOOD/CANDY | **FAMILY** | Sourdough loaves made by talented and passionate young baker Diogo Amorim attract carb-craving Lisboetas from across the city. Amorim learned his trade in the some of the world's top kitchens, and here he perfects the art, using flour prepared in an on-site stone mill. *Prior do Crato 16, Alcântara* *966 064 697 to order bread,* *www.gleba-nossa.pt* *Tram 15E or 18E to Alcântara–Av. 24 de Julho.*

Intendente, Martim Moniz, and Mouraria

Situated on the hillside below the São Jorge castle, these three neighborhoods are among the oldest in Lisbon, and a walk around their narrow hilly lanes can feel like a step back in time. And although there are no palaces and little cultural patrimony here, getting lost in the winding lanes, where the scent of grilled fish mingles with Asian spices and the sound of fado drifts from balconies overhead, is a true Lisbon experience.

These areas, along with neighboring Alfama, were among the only to survive the devastating earthquake of 1755, and the higgledy-piggledy streets, with laundry lines flapping between buildings, continue to evoke medieval Lisbon. In the past these areas were outside the city walls so traditionally only the poorest people lived here, but today, although rapidly gentrifying, they remain working-class neighborhoods. Many Asian and African immigrants live in the area as well, contributing to the lively, multicultural feel. You'll also find artists and other creatives living here, which also gives these neighborhoods a slightly alternative vibe—vintage stores, designer ateliers, and speakeasy-style bars rub shoulders with traditional restaurants, Chinese supermarkets, and sari shops. If you're looking to hear some fado, Portuguese folk music, Mouraria is its birthplace and remains one of the best places in the city to hear it sung.

GETTING HERE AND AROUND

Intendente and Martim Moniz have metro stops on the Green Line, but Mouraria is less well served by public transport. The 28 tram does run along the edge of Intendente and the 12 tram runs from Martim Moniz up Rua Cavaleiro, which saves you a few minutes' uphill walk into Mouraria, but its hilly location is unfortunately best reached on foot. From

Intendente, Martim Moniz, and Mouraria

Sights
1 Largo do Intendente .. C2
2 Praça Martim Moniz B3

Restaurants
1 Cantinho do Aziz C3
2 Infame C2
3 Prado C4

Quick Bites
1 Cafe O das Joanas C2

Hotels
1 Hotel Mundial B3

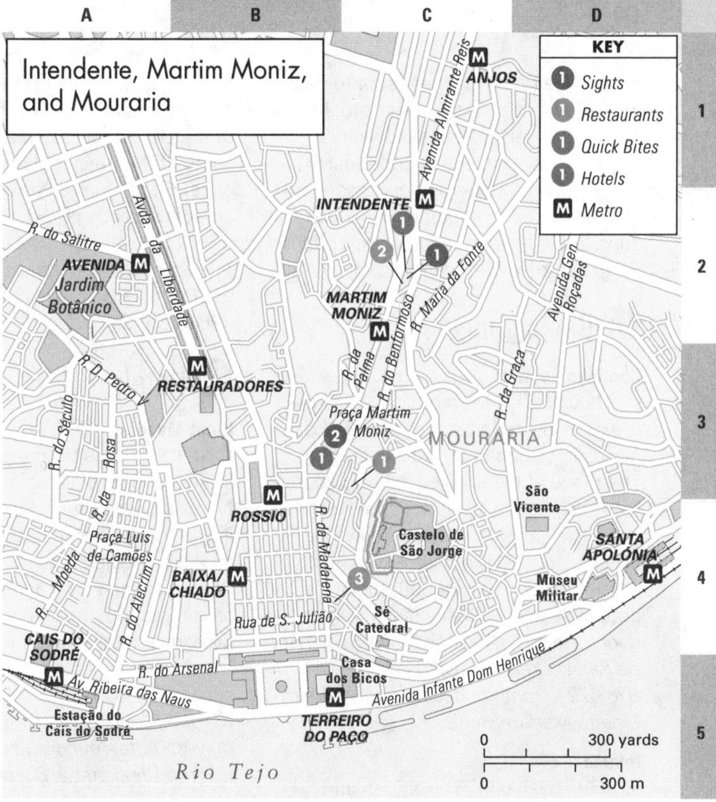

KEY
Sights
Restaurants
Quick Bites
Hotels
Metro

the Baixa you can also take the elevator (free) from Rua dos Fanqueiros to Rua da Madalena, at the base of Mouraria.

Sights

Largo do Intendente

PLAZA | This large square at the heart of Intendente is one of the most striking in the city. Neglected for many years, it's recently experienced a rebirth, and the buildings that surround it feature beautifully tiled facades and interesting architecture, including Lisbon's answer to New York's Flatiron Building, which is now a hotel at the top end of the square. Cafés with terraces offer plenty of opportunity for people-watching. ✉ *Largo do Intendente, Intendente* Ⓜ *Green Line to Intendente; Tram 28 to Largo do Intendente.*

Praça Martim Moniz

NEIGHBORHOOD | **FAMILY** | This large square at the heart of Lisbon's multicultural Martim Moniz neighborhood is the terminus of the 28 tram. There are fountains and shady benches perfect for relaxing and there's a small street food market with stalls serving Chinese, Indian, African, and Portuguese food and drinks. On weekends and special holidays, such as Chinese New Year, there are often dance and music performances and a craft market. ✉ *Praça Martim Moniz, Martin Moniz* Ⓜ *Green Line to Martim Moniz; Tram 28 or Tram 12 to Martim Moniz.*

Coffee and Quick Bites

Cafe O das Joanas

$ | **CAFÉ** | This local institution, popular with the artsy crowd, offers light breakfast and lunch options for reasonable prices. The terrace is great spot to relax and enjoy a beer or snack or both. **Known for:** snacks, salads, and sandwiches; alternative crowd; cheap draft beer. *Average main: €7 Largo do Intendente Pina Manique, Intendente Closed Tues. Green Line to Intendente; Tram 28 to Largo do Intendente.*

Restaurants

Cantinho do Aziz

$ | **AFRICAN** | This Mozambican restaurant is a local institution and one of the best places in Lisbon to try African cuisine. The menu at the low-key, relaxed spot features fragrant and spicy meat dishes like *bakra* (spicy lamb ribs). **Known for:** delicious dishes like nhama (beef with manioc, okra, and coconut); the spicy hot pepper sauce has many fans; lively outdoor terrace. *Average main: €12 Rua de São Lourenço 5, Martin Moniz 218 876 472 cantinhodoaziz.com Green Line to Martim Moniz.*

Infame

$$ | **CONTEMPORARY** | This stylish and welcoming restaurant has been tastefully designed to make the most of its historical building with a striking tiled floor, high ceilings, an exposed metal staircase, and windows on three sides. A pleasant place for brunch, lunch, or dinner, the eclectic menu features seafood, meat, and vegetarian options, many with Asian influences. **Known for:** modern, Asian-influenced menu; stylish and contemporary decor; weekend brunch that includes vegetarian options. *Average main: €19 Largo do Intendente Pina Manique 4, Intendente infame.pt Green Line to Intendente; Tram 28 to Largo do Intendente.*

★ Prado

$$$ | **CONTEMPORARY** | Seasonal ingredients are combined in unusual ways to create noteworthy dishes at this charming restaurant, where plants hang from the ceiling and contemporary furnishings keep things feeling serene. The presentation is on par with some of the city's best restaurants. **Known for:** some of the freshest farm-to-table produce; list of organic Portuguese wines; attracts a trendy crowd. *Average main: €25 Travessa das Pedras Negras 2, Intendente pradorestaurante.com Closed Mon. and Tues. Tram 28 or 12E to Sé (Cathedral).*

Hotels

Hotel Mundial

$$ | **HOTEL** | Steps from the Rossio and Restauradores squares, this large property looks uncompromisingly modern, but inside there's lots of good, old-fashioned charm combined with modern facilities. **Pros:** stunning views and great lounge bar on the rooftop; free Wi-Fi; friendly staff. **Cons:** unattractive exterior; no pool; Praça Martim Moniz is still an up-and-coming square. *Rooms from: €144 Praça Martim Moniz 2, Martin Moniz www.hotel-mundial.pt 349 rooms Free Breakfast Rossio.*

Nightlife

BARS

Bar Flamingo

BARS/PUBS | For a lively, late night with a local vibe, head to Bar Flamingo, an eclectic space that offers cocktails, music, dancing, and a party atmosphere. Totally unpretentious, the crowd is friendly and laid-back. *Largo do Terreirinho 16, Mouraria .*

★ Casa Independente

MUSIC CLUBS | This venue, styled as a series of rooms—a nod to its former life as an apartment building—attracts a young and stylish crowd for drinks, live music, and DJ sets. The upstairs rooms are more intimate, with a vintage-store aesthetic, and there's a roof terrace and downstairs bar and dance space. It's closed on Sunday and Monday. *Largo do Intendente Pina Manique 45,*

Intendente ☎ 🌐 *casaindependente.com* Ⓜ *Green Line to Intendente; Tram 28 to Largo do Intendente.*

FADO CLUBS

★ Maria da Mouraria

MUSIC | This small restaurant is one of the most authentic venues in Lisbon for listening to mournful and soulful fado music. On the site of the former house of famous fadista Maria Severa, the venue hosts regular concerts, sometimes luring big-name singers to perform. You can dine in the restaurant, which serves traditional Portuguese dishes, while you listen, or try your luck arriving just for the concert, but tables may be sold out. ✉ *Largo Severa 2B, Mouraria* ☎ 🌐 *mariadamouraria.pt.*

Shopping

★ A Vida Portuguesa

LOCAL SPECIALTIES | This large emporium stocks beautifully designed and finely packaged traditional Portuguese goods at every price point that range from soaps and shaving cream to glassware, ceramics, textiles, notebooks, food, and olive oils. Airy and spacious, this contemporary shop is a must-visit for gifts and mementos that truly reflect Portuguese life. ✉ *Largo do Intendente Pina Manique 23, Intendente* ☎ 🌐 *www.avidaportuguesa.com* Ⓜ *Green Line to Intendente; Tram 28 to Largo do Intendente.*

★ Cortiço & Netos

CERAMICS/GLASSWARE | The Portuguese love affair with tiles is evident on buildings across the country, but taking home a tile as a memento has implications, as many of those for sale have been stolen from historic buildings. For a more ethical option, Cortiço & Netos sells distinct and beautiful discontinued tiles from the 1950s onward. You can buy just one tile or by the square meter. ✉ *Calçada de Santo André 66, Intendente* ☎ 🌐 *www.corticoenetos.com* Ⓜ *Tram 12 to Calçada de Santo André.*

★ Prado Mercearia

FOOD/CANDY | With tiled floors and vintage fittings, this beautifully designed grocery store would fit right in in Brooklyn, as the shelves are stocked with seasonal, often organic, and all locally sourced products. Items include cheeses, tinned fish, bread, fruits and vegetables, and dry goods. There are also sandwiches, coffee, and homemade cake to take away or eat in. ✉ *Rua Pedras Negras 35, Intendente* ☎.

Belém

Some of Lisbon's grandest monuments and museums are in the district of Belém (the Portuguese word for Bethlehem). It was from here that the country's great explorers set out during the period of the discoveries. The wealth brought back from the New World helped pay for many of the neighborhood's structures, some of which are the best examples of the uniquely Portuguese late-Gothic architecture known as Manueline. The area's historical attractions are complemented by the modern and contemporary art and performances showcased in Lisbon's largest cultural center.

GETTING HERE AND AROUND

Belém is easily reached by train from Cais do Sodré station. Trains leave every few minutes, but make sure you catch a local train rather than an express. Alternatively, several buses will get you here from Lisbon's center, and the 30-minute ride on Tram 15 (plied by both antique and modern models) from the Baixa district's Praça do Comércio is very scenic. Tram 15 also passes close by or stops right at several of the important sights.

Sights

Fundação Champalimaud (*Fundação Champalimaud*)

BUILDING | In a prime riverside location, this giant medical research and clinical

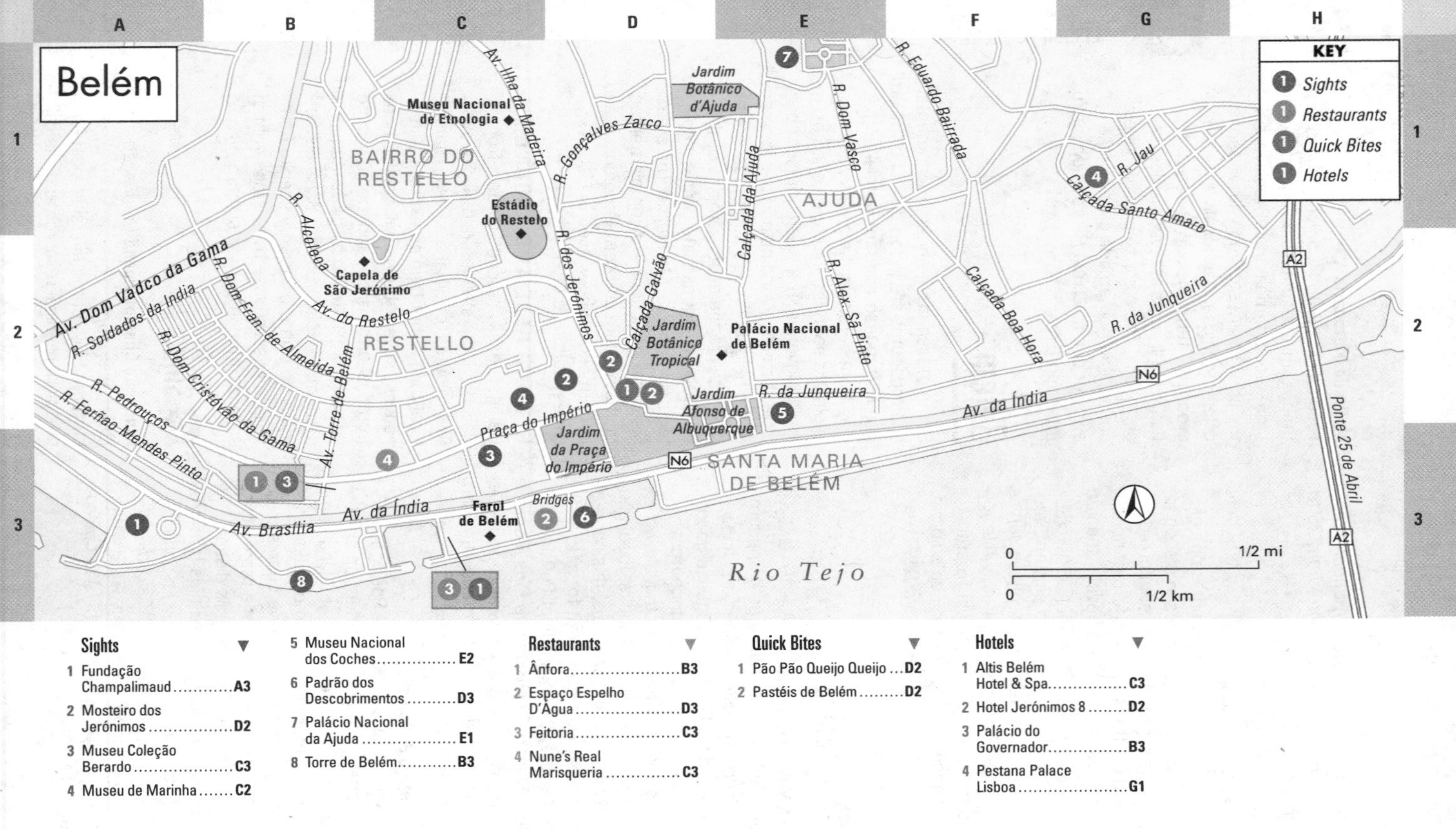

Sights

1 Fundação Champalimaud A3
2 Mosteiro dos Jerónimos D2
3 Museu Coleção Berardo C3
4 Museu de Marinha C2
5 Museu Nacional dos Coches E2
6 Padrão dos Descobrimentos D3
7 Palácio Nacional da Ajuda E1
8 Torre de Belém B3

Restaurants

1 Ânfora B3
2 Espaço Espelho D'Água D3
3 Feitoria C3
4 Nune's Real Marisqueria C3

Quick Bites

1 Pão Pão Queijo Queijo ... D2
2 Pastéis de Belém D2

Hotels

1 Altis Belém Hotel & Spa C3
2 Hotel Jerónimos 8 .... D2
3 Palácio do Governador B3
4 Pestana Palace Lisboa G1

facility designed by Pritzker Prize winner Charles Correa has become a pilgrimage site for architecture buffs. Darwin's Café restaurant is open to the public and has stunning river views, not least from its charming esplanade. ✉ *Av. Brasília, Belém* ☎ *210 480 200* 🌐 *fchampalimaud.org* Ⓜ *Tram 15E at Pedrouços.*

★ **Mosteiro dos Jerónimos** (*Jeronimos Monastery*)

ARCHAEOLOGICAL SITE | FAMILY | If you see only one historic landmark in Belém, make it this magnificent monastery. This UNESCO World Heritage Site is a supreme example of the Manueline style (named after King Dom Manuel I), which represented a marked departure from earlier Gothic architecture. Much of it is characterized by elaborate sculptural details, often with a maritime motif. João de Castilho was responsible for the southern portal, which forms the main entrance to the church: the figure on the central pillar is Henry the Navigator. Inside, the spacious interior contrasts with the riot of decoration on the six nave columns and complex latticework ceiling. This is the resting place of both explorer Vasco da Gama and national poet Luís de Camões. Don't miss the Gothic- and Renaissance-style double cloister, also designed to stunning effect by Castilho. ✉ *Praça do Império, Belém* ☎ *213 620 034* 🌐 *www.mosteirojeronimos.pt* 🎫 *€10* 🕓 *Closed Mon.* Ⓜ *Tram 15E to Mosteiro Jerónimos.*

★ **Museu Coleção Berardo** (*Berardo Collection Museum*)

MUSEUM | Housed in the minimalist Belém Cultural Center, the Berardo Collection Museum is a showcase for one of Europe's most important private collections of modern art. Works from this treasure trove—which range from Picasso and Warhol to Portugal's own Paula Rego—are regularly rotated through the galleries, and there are also excellent visiting exhibitions. There are several bookstores, cafés, and gift shops in the complex, including a terrace café on the upper floor with lovely views. ✉ *Praça do Império, Belém* ☎ *213 612 400* 🌐 *en.museuberardo.pt* 🎫 *€5* Ⓜ *Tram 15E to Centro Cultural Belém.*

Museu de Marinha (*Maritime Museum*)

MUSEUM | FAMILY | One of Lisbon's oldest museums (it was founded in 1853), the Maritime Museum showcases the importance of the seafaring tradition in Portugal. With its thousands of maps and maritime codes, navigational equipment, model ships, uniforms, and weapons, the museum appeals to visitors young and old. ✉ *Praça do Império, Belém* ☎ *210 977 388* 🌐 *ccm.marinha.pt/pt/museu* 🎫 *€6.50* Ⓜ *Tram 15E to Mosteiro Jerónimos.*

Museu Nacional dos Coches (*National Coach Museum*)

MUSEUM | FAMILY | Designed by Brazilian Pritzker Prize winner Paulo Mendes da Rocha, the National Coach Museum has a dazzling collection of gloriously gilded horse-drawn carriages. The oldest on display was made for Philip II of Spain in the late 1500s; the most stunning are three conveyances created in Rome for King John V in 1716. The museum, one of the country's most popular, is right next door to the official residence of the president of the republic, whose **Museu da Presidência** tells the story of the presidency, profiles the officeholders, and displays gifts they have received on state visits. ✉ *Av. da Índia 136, Belém* ☎ *210 732 319* 🌐 *www.museudoscoches.pt* 🎫 *€8* 🕓 *Closed Mon.* Ⓜ *Tram 15E to Altinho.*

★ **Padrão dos Descobrimentos** (*Monument of the Discoveries*)

MEMORIAL | FAMILY | The white, monolithic Monument of the Discoveries was erected in 1960 to commemorate the 500th anniversary of the death of Prince Henry the Navigator. It was built on what was the departure point for many voyages of discovery, including those of Vasco da Gama for India and—during Spain's occupation of Portugal—of the

Spanish Armada for England in 1588. Henry is at the prow of the monument, facing the water; lined up behind him are the Portuguese explorers of Brazil and Asia, as well as other national heroes. On the ground adjacent to the monument, an inlaid map shows the extent of the explorations undertaken by the 15th- and 16th-century Portuguese sailors. Walk inside and take the elevator to the top for river views. ✉ *Av. Brasília, Belém* ☎ *213 031 950* 🌐 *www.padraodosdescobrimentos.pt* 🎫 *€6* ⏲ *Closed Mon. Sept.–Mar.* Ⓜ *Tram 15E to Mosteiro dos Jerónimos.*

Palácio Nacional da Ajuda (*Ajuda National Palace*)
CASTLE/PALACE | Built in 1802 as a royal residence, the last regal occupant (Queen Maria) died here in 1911. Today, the ornate neoclassical building functions as a museum. Visitors can take a peek at how Portuguese monarchs lived, as well as admire 18th- and 19th-century paintings, furniture, and tapestries. It is also used for official ceremonies and functions by the Presidency of the Republic, and one wing houses the government's culture department. It's a 20-minute walk up Calçada da Ajuda from the Museu Nacional dos Coches. ✉ *Largo da Ajuda, Ajuda* ☎ *213 637 095* 🌐 *www.patrimoniocultural.gov.pt/pt/museus-e-monumentos/rede-portuguesa/m/palacio-nacional-da-ajuda/* 🎫 *€5* ⏲ *Closed Wed.* Ⓜ *Tram 18E to Cemitério Ajuda.*

★ **Torre de Belém** (*Belém Tower*)
BUILDING | **FAMILY** | A UNESCO World Heritage Site, the openwork balconies and domed turrets of the fanciful Belém Tower make it perhaps the country's purest Manueline structure. It was built between 1514 and 1520 on what was an island in the middle of the river Tagus, to defend the port entrance, and dedicated to St. Vincent, the patron saint of Lisbon. Today the chalk-white tower stands near the north bank—evidence of the river's changing course. Cross the wood gangway and walk inside to admire the cannons and descend to the former dungeons, before climbing the steep, narrow, winding staircase to the top of the tower for a bird's-eye view across the Tagus River. ✉ *Av. Brasília, Belém* ☎ *213 620 034* 🌐 *www.torrebelem.pt* 🎫 *€6* ⏲ *Closed Mon.* Ⓜ *Tram 15E to Largo da Princesa.*

Coffee and Quick Bites

Pão Pão Queijo Queijo
$ | **DELI** | **FAMILY** | This oddly named place—it translates as "Bread Bread Cheese Cheese"—serves much more than these two staples. Expect a huge variety of sandwiches, salads, and wraps, catering to everyone from staunch vegans to dedicated carnivores. **Known for:** Turkish-style meat kebabs; good array of salads; popular with locals. Ⓢ *Average main: €10* ✉ *Rua de Belém 126, Belém* ☎ *213 626 369* Ⓜ *Tram 15E to Mosteiro dos Jerónimos.*

★ **Pastéis de Belém**
$ | **CAFÉ** | **FAMILY** | This bakery specializes in *pastéis de nata*: delicious, warm custard pastries sprinkled with cinnamon and powdered sugar. Although these sweet treats are ubiquitous in Portugal, the version here is the most celebrated. **Known for:** the most famous custard tarts in Portugal; distinctive azulejo tile design; delicious espresso. Ⓢ *Average main: €8* ✉ *Rua de Belém 84–92, Belém* ☎ *213 637 423* 🌐 *pasteisdebelem.pt/en* Ⓜ *Tram 15E to Mosteiro Jerónimos.*

Restaurants

★ **Ânfora**
$$$ | **PORTUGUESE** | Named for the Roman amphorae uncovered beneath the site, the restaurant at the luxurious Palácio do Governador Hotel feels like dining in the vaulted halls of a castle. There's nothing old-fashioned about the food though: chef Vera Silva has created a spectacular menu of dishes that combine traditional

Climb the steps to the top of the 16th-century Belém Tower for beautiful Tagus River views.

ingredients with modern techniques. **Known for:** beautifully presented dishes; good advice on wine pairings; incredible desserts. *Average main: €22 Nau Palácio do Governador, R. Bartolomeu Dias 117, Belém 213 007 009 www.palaciogovernador.com/en/restaurant-and-bar.html Train (Cascais Line) to Belem.*

Espaço Espelho D'Água

$$ | **FUSION** | A favorite with the fashion press, this strikingly modern space on the banks of the river serves up small plates and more substantial dishes to a stylish clientele. There's a concert and exhibition space where you can catch live performances. **Known for:** gorgeous terrace with river views; live music and cultural events; elegantly presented plates. *Average main: €17 Edificio Espelho D'Agua, Av. Brasília, Belém Next to Padrao dos Descobrimentos 213 010 510 www.espacoespelhodagua.com Tram 15E to Centro Cultural Belém.*

★ **Feitoria**

$$$$ | **FUSION** | Expect culinary wizardry at this award-winning restaurant headed by one of Portugal's most acclaimed chefs, João Rodrigues. If your budget allows, the best way to sample his talents is to opt for one of the four or six-course set menus, one of which is entirely vegetarian. **Known for:** inventive set menus featuring treats such as caviar and truffles; dazzling dining room is a great backdrop for the food; vegetarian and vegan options. *Average main: €35 Hotel Altis Belém, Doca do Bom Successo, Belém 210 400 208 www.restaurantefeitoria.com Tram 15E to Centro Cultural Belém.*

Nune's Real Marisqueira

$$ | **SEAFOOD** | **FAMILY** | Crustaceans of every shape and size are the specialty at this well-regarded restaurant, but the fish dishes are also delicious. The atmosphere is relaxed, the chefs take their work seriously, and the restaurant attracts locals in droves. **Known for:** choose your dinner from the huge

tanks; dishes served in the frying pans; contemporary decor. *$ Average main: €20 ✉ Rua Bartolomeu Dias 112, Belém ☎ 213 019 899 🌐 www.nunesmarisqueira.pt ⏲ Closed Mon. Ⓜ Tram 15E to Largo da Princesa.*

Hotels

★ Altis Belém Hotel & Spa

$$$$ | **HOTEL** | The decor at this elegant riverside hotel harks back to Portugal's Age of Discovery, but that's not to say it's stuck in the past—the overall feel is light and modern and its relatively small size gives it an intimate feel. **Pros:** one of the chicest spots in town to meet for cocktails; convenient to Belém's many attractions; excellent spa area. **Cons:** not that convenient to public transport; restaurant and bar get packed; no local flair. *$ Rooms from: €280 ✉ Doca do Bom Sucesso, Belém ☎ 210 400 200 🌐 www.altishotels.com/EN/HotelAltisBelem ⇆ 49 rooms 🍽 Free Breakfast.*

Hotel Jerónimos 8

$$$ | **HOTEL** | Just around the corner from the monastery of the same name, Hotel Jerónimos 8 harmoniously blends past and present. **Pros:** breakfast pastries from the famous Pastéis de Belém; views of the nearby monastery; attracts a lively clientele. **Cons:** design may no longer be cutting edge; a long way from downtown sights; no pool or fitness area. *$ Rooms from: €210 ✉ Rua dos Jerónimos 8, Belém ☎ 213 600 900 🌐 www.almeida-hotels.pt/pt/hotel-lisboa-4-estrelas ⇆ 65 rooms 🍽 Free Breakfast.*

★ Palácio do Governador

$$$ | **HOTEL** | Layers of history are on display at this beautiful retreat that combines fascinating peeks into the past with the latest high-tech amenities. **Pros:** lovely outdoor pool, but vast indoor one steals the show; garden terrace is a lovely place to enjoy a drink; peaceful location away from the crowds. **Cons:** can be a little hard to find; neighborhood is not especially scenic; a bit far from the action. *$ Rooms from: €250 ✉ Rua Bartolomeu Dias 117, Belém ☎ 213 007 009 🌐 www.palaciogovernador.com/en ⇆ 60 rooms 🍽 Free Breakfast Ⓜ E15 Tram to Torre de Belem.*

★ Pestana Palace Lisboa

$$$$ | **HOTEL** | **FAMILY** | Madonna based herself here while house hunting in Lisbon, and it's not hard to see why the Queen of Pop fell in love with the place: the former home of the Marquis of Valle Flôr is a beloved local landmark that harbors a collection of fine 19th-century art. **Pros:** dine in the elegant Valle Flôr restaurant; beautiful outdoor and indoor swimming pools; spa offers an exclusive range of treatments. **Cons:** some distance from the major attractions; outdoor pool area busy in summer; all this luxury doesn't come cheap. *$ Rooms from: €295 ✉ Rua Jau 54, Ajuda ☎ 213 615 600 🌐 www.pestanacollection.com/en/hotel/pestana-palace ⇆ 193 rooms 🍽 Free Breakfast.*

Nightlife

BARS

Bar 38° 41'

BARS/PUBS | Perfectly made drinks and equally satisfying views over the river entice chic Lisboetas to the terrace bar at the luxurious Altis Belém Hotel and Spa. Get here well ahead of time if you want to snag a table at sunset. *✉ Altis Belém Hotel and Spa, Doca de Bom Successo, Belém ☎ 210 400 210 🌐 www.altishotels.com/PT/HotelAltisBelem/Bar3841 Ⓜ Tram 15E to Centro Cultural Belém.*

Topo Belém

BARS/PUBS | On the rooftop terrace of the Belém Cultural Center, this cool and contemporary space is all about the views. *✉ Centro Cultural de Belém, Praça do Império, Belém ☎ 213 010 524 Ⓜ Tram 15E to Centro Cultural Belém.*

★ Wine with a View
WINE BARS—NIGHTLIFE | There's literally nothing between you and the view—this smart vintage cart has a near-permanent pitch in the gardens of the Torre de Belém. It peddles Portuguese wines of every style and hue, which be sipped from disposable wine glasses while sightseeing. ✉ *Av. Brasília, Belém* ☎ *939 315 778* 🌐 *www.winewithaview.pt* Ⓜ *Tram 15E to Largo da Princesa.*

Performing Arts

Centro Cultural de Belém
ARTS CENTERS | This cultural center offers a huge range of reasonably priced events featuring national and international artists and musicians. ✉ *Praça do Império, Belém* ☎ *213 612 400* 🌐 *www.ccb.pt.*

Shopping

ART GALLERIES

Arte Periférica
ART GALLERIES—ARTS | This gallery and arts store at the Centro Cultural de Belém is a good source of contemporary art, particularly by emerging young talent. ✉ *Centro Cultural de Belém, Praça do Imperio, Loja 3, Belém* ☎ *213 617 100* 🌐 *www.arteperiferica.pt* Ⓜ *Tram 15E to Centro Cultural Belém.*

Avenidas Novas

Farmland with a few mansions scattered around became a sprawling modern residential and business district in the early 20th century. Long, broad avenues radiated from Marquês de Pombal Square, and spread to the northern and eastern parts of city, at first lined with elegant buildings, but later taken over by dull office and apartment blocks. People referred to them as the "avenidas novas" ("new avenues"), and that's what this district is officially called today. In the 1950s it was chosen as the site of the city's greatest museum (the Calouste Gulbenkian Museum), which is the main reason many tourists head to this part of town. While it may lack the soul of old Lisbon and doesn't have other major attractions besides the Gulbenkian, it's home to several large hotels, so it's also where many end up staying. Wider sidewalks and more pedestrian space have made the area much more inviting and led to the opening of new restaurants with outdoor seating and some kiosks serving light meals, like in the city's older neighborhoods.

GETTING HERE AND AROUND

The metro is the best way to reach Avenidas Novas. All four lines go through the district, but it's the Yellow Line that stops at the main avenues and squares. Unlike the other parts of the city, it does not have tram services, but Buses 736, 738, and 744 connect it to downtown and beyond.

Sights

Galeria 111
MUSEUM | This high-profile gallery is one of the few dating back to before the 1974 revolution, presenting some of the best contemporary Portuguese artists from the 20th and 21st centuries. You may find works by big names like Paula Rego and Vieira da Silva together with pieces by emerging artists. ✉ *Campo Grande 113* ☎ *217 977 418* 🌐 *www.111.pt* 🕒 *Closed Sun. and Mon.* Ⓜ *Green or Yellow Line to Campo Grande.*

Jardim Zoológico de Lisboa (*Lisbon Zoological Gardens*)
ZOO | **FAMILY** | Families should set aside a full day to explore this deservedly popular and immaculately maintained zoo, which is home to more than 3,000 animals from more than 330 species. The grounds are huge, but visitors can leap aboard a cable car to whiz from one attraction to another. Those who don't have a head for heights can board a miniature train (not

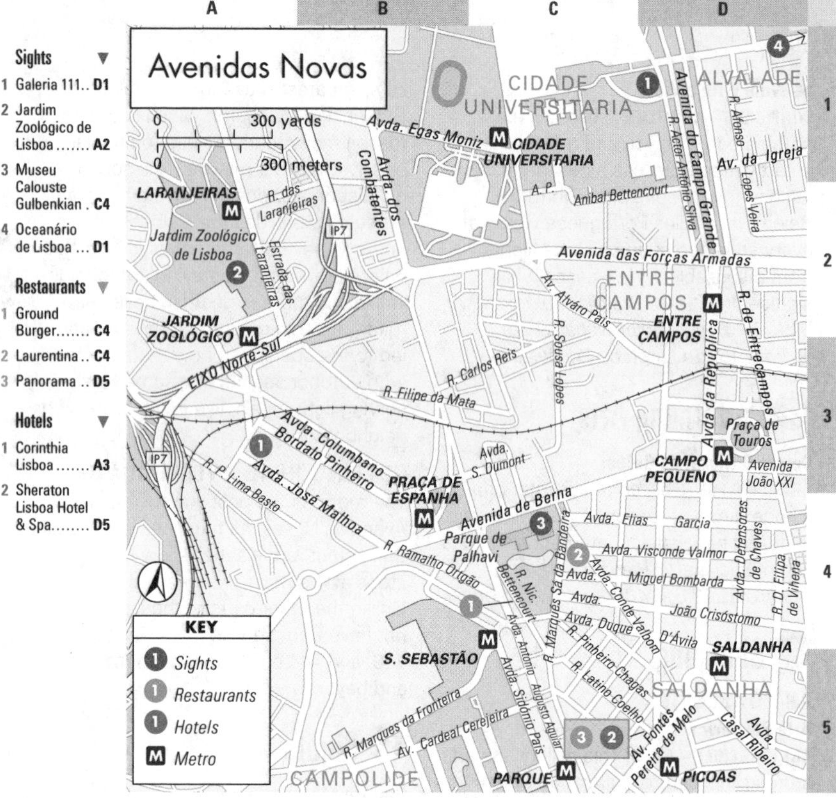

included in entrance price) that trundles around the gardens. There's a petting zoo and twice-daily animal shows (you have your pick of those featuring parrots, pelicans, dolphins, sea lions, reptiles, or lemurs). There are several cafés on the grounds, as well as picnic areas for those who prefer a packed lunch. ✉ *Praça Marechal Humberto Delgado, Sete Rios* ☎ *217 232 900* 🌐 *www.zoo.pt* 🎫 *€22* Ⓜ *Blue Line to Jardim Zoológico.*

★ **Museu Calouste Gulbenkian** (*Calouste Gulbenkian Museum*)

ARTS VENUE | Set in lovely gardens filled with leafy walkways, blooming flowers, and waddling ducks, the museum of the celebrated Calouste Gulbenkian Foundation houses treasures collected by Armenian oil magnate Calouste Gulbenkian. The collection is split in two: one part is devoted to Egyptian, Greek, Roman, Islamic, and Asian art, and the other to European acquisitions. The quality of the pieces is magnificent, and you should aim to spend at least two hours here. English-language notes are available throughout. A walk through the gardens leads to the foundation's Modern Collection: 9,000 pieces from the 20th and 21st centuries, including sculptures, paintings, and photography. There's a café with a pleasant terrace overlooking the gardens. ✉ *Av. de Berna 45* ☎ *217 823 000* 🌐 *gulbenkian.pt/museu/en* 🎫 *€10* 🕑 *Closed Tues.* Ⓜ *Blue Line to São Sebastião or Praça de Espanha.*

★ **Oceanário de Lisboa** (*Lisbon Oceanarium*)

ZOO | FAMILY | East of most of the city's sights in the sprawling Parque das Nações, Europe's largest indoor aquarium wows children and adults alike with a vast saltwater tank featuring a massive array of fish, including several types of shark. Along the way you pass through habitats representing the North Atlantic, Pacific, and Indian Oceans, where puffins and penguins dive into the water, sea otters roll and play, and tropical birds flit past you. You then descend to the bottom of the tank to watch rays float past gracefully and schools of silvery fish darting this way and that. To avoid the crowds, come during the week or early in the day. ✉ *Esplanada D. Carlos I, Parque das Nações* ☎ *218 917 000* 🌐 *www.oceanario.pt/en* 🎫 *€16* Ⓜ *Red Line to OrienteOriente.*

Restaurants

Ground Burger

$$ | **AMERICAN** | Located next to the Calouste Gulbenkian Museum, this is largely considered Lisbon's best burger joint. It serves American-style burgers, and there's a new one on the menu every month, plus a vegetarian option. **Known for:** 100% Black Angus burgers; American-style milk shakes; craft beers. $ *Average main: €16* ✉ *Av. António Augusto de Aguiar 148A* ☎ *21/371–7171* 🌐 *www.groundburger.com* Ⓜ *Blue or Red Line to São Sebastião.*

Laurentina

$$ | **PORTUGUESE** | In business since 1976, this is one of the top restaurants for traditional Portuguese food in the Avenidas Novas district. The plant-filled interior has been modernized, but the menu has been left largely untouched and includes a few Mozambican specialties (the restaurant's founder learned to cook in the former Portuguese colony). **Known for:** variety of cod dishes; good-value daily specials at lunchtime; long list of Portuguese wines. $ *Average main: €16* ✉ *Av. Conde Valbom 71A* ☎ *21/796–0260* 🌐 *www.restaurantelaurentina.com* Ⓜ *Blue or Red Line to São Sebastião.*

Panorama

$$$$ | **PORTUGUESE** | Located at the top of the Sheraton Lisboa Hotel, this restaurant offers bird's-eye views of Lisbon. A number of the city's top chefs had their start here before moving on to their own restaurants, and it has always been the place to try contemporary Portuguese cuisine that's mindful of the gastronomic traditions of Portugal's different regions. **Known for:** grilled fish and meat; good selection of international wines; cocktails. $ *Average main: €50* ✉ *Sheraton Lisboa Hotel, Rua Latino Coelho 1* ☎ *21/312–0000* 🌐 *www.panorama-restaurante.com* 🕒 *No lunch Mon.–Sat.* Ⓜ *Yellow Line to Picoas.*

Hotels

Corinthia Lisboa

$$$ | **HOTEL** | An excellent option for those looking to stay close to the airport, the luxe Corinthia Lisboa offers comfortable accommodations and impeccable service just a short hop from both the airport and the historic downtown. **Pros:** no less than three restaurants and two bars; walking distance to the Gulbenkian Museum; excellent swimming pool and spa area. **Cons:** long distance to downtown attractions; not Lisbon's most beautiful neighborhood; the building's exterior is uninspiring. $ *Rooms from: €210* ✉ *Corinthia Lisboa, Av. Columbano Bordalo Pinheiro 105, Saldanha* ☎ *217 236 300* 🌐 *www.corinthia.com/hotels/Lisbon* 🛏 *518 rooms* 🍽 *No meals.*

Sheraton Lisboa Hotel & Spa

$$$ | **HOTEL** | Traveling executives flock to this business hotel overlooking modern Lisbon for its many pluses: a huge reception area with a comfortable bar, a staff that goes above and beyond, and nicely appointed guest rooms. **Pros:** within walking distance of the historic downtown; convenient location in the business district; excellent fitness center. **Cons:** not the best location for sightseeing; building is not particularly attractive; lacks any

local flavor. $ *Rooms from: €245* *Rua Latino Coelho 1, Saldanha* *213 120 000* *www.marriott.com/hotels/travel/lissi-sheraton-lisboa-hotel-and-spa* *369 rooms* *No meals* *Yellow Line to Picoas.*

Performing Arts

Praça de Touros do Campo Pequeno (*Campo Pequeno Bullring*)
ARTS CENTERS | These days this monumental structure hosts more rock concerts than bullfights. Holding up to 9,000 people, the Moorish-style auditorium hosts big names like the Pixies or Vampire Weekend. *Av. da República, Campo Pequeno* *217 998 450* *www.campopequeno.com* *Yellow Line to Campo Pequeno.*

South of the River

Lisbon's secret is well and truly out, but it's still possible to dodge the crowds if you make the short hop across the river Tagus. A short ferry ride from downtown Lisbon, colorful Cacilhas is increasingly enticing Lisboeta night owls, while the views and handsome old buildings of Almada Velha offer a wealth of photo-snapping opportunities. Local foodies like to make the similarly short ferry hop from Belém to Trafaria, a fishing town known for its superior seafood. From here it's a short Uber ride to the fishing village of Cova do Vapor and surfer hangout Costa da Caparica.

GETTING HERE AND AROUND

Take the 10-minute passenger ferry from Cais do Sodré to Cacilhas (departures every 20 minutes), and Bus 203 from Cacilhas heads to Sesimbra and Caparica. Ferries between Belém and Trafaria are a little less regular and take around 20 minutes. Trains, buses, and cars cross the 25 de Abril suspension bridge or the sweeping Ponte Vasco da Gama. Drivers should expect to pay a couple of euros in tolls on either bridge. Regular buses leave from the Transportes Sul do Tejo (TST) terminal in Praça da Espanha for Sesimbra, calling at Alcântara Terra before crossing the river. There are also regular TST services between Alcântara Terra and Costa da Caparica.

Sights

★ **Elevador Panorâmico da Boca do Vento**
LOCAL INTEREST | Looking like an elevator they forgot to construct a building around, this lovely lift is a fun, free, and extremely photogenic way to travel between Almada's Old Town and the riverfront's pretty gardens and noteworthy restaurants. Enjoy the views from the glass-fronted cabin as you ascend or descend. It runs every day from 8 am to midnight. *Rua do Ginjal 72, Almada* *Free.*

★ **Santuario Nacional de Cristo Rei**
(*National Sanctuary of Christ the King*)
MEMORIAL | **FAMILY** | Lisbon's answer to Rio de Janeiro's Christ the Redeemer sits atop a giant concrete plinth high above the Tagus River. It was inaugurated in 1959 as a mark of thanks for Portugal's safety during the violence of World War II. Today, the Santuário Nacional do Cristo Rei is an important religious site, but most casual visitors come here primarily for the spectacular views from the 262-foot-high viewing platform, which is reached by elevator. Visiting the peaceful, scenic grounds is free. *Praceta do Cristo Rei 27A, Almada* *212 751 000* *€6.*

Coffee and Quick Bites

★ **Chá de Histórias**
$ | **CAFÉ** | This is a retro-chic spot for tea and cakes or cocktails and *petiscos* (small plates). The kitsch collectibles and bottle-filled cabinets make the space feel like being at someone's grandparents' house, and the board games and comic books add to the wholesome charm. **Known for:** toasted sandwiches with

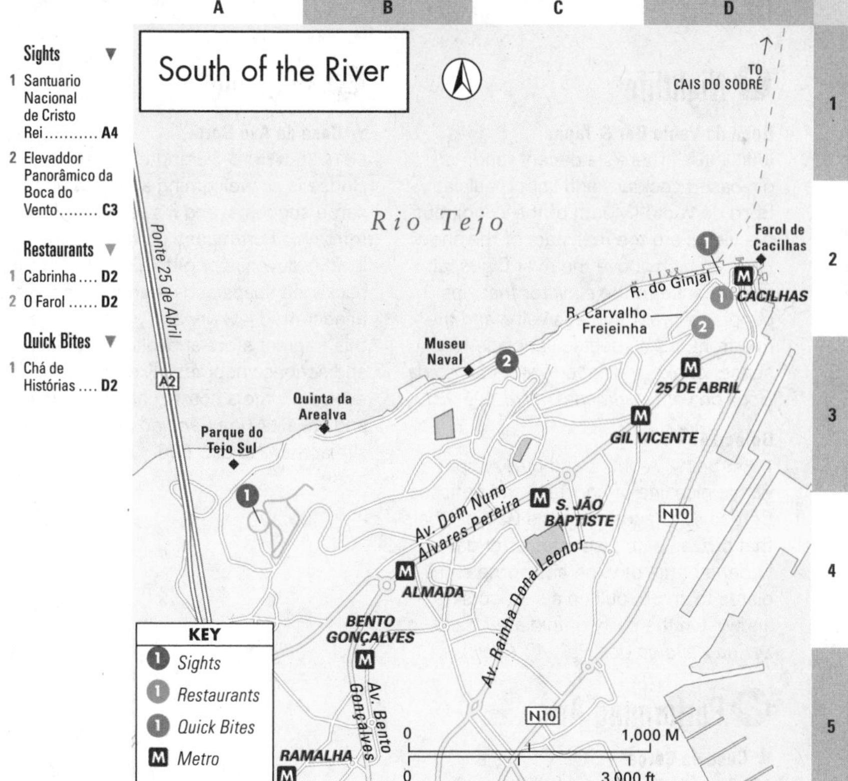

tasty fillings; delicious homemade cakes; weekend DJ sessions. *Average main: €8 Rua Cândido dos Reis 129, Cacilhas 272 744 084 No lunch. Closed Sun. and Mon.*

Restaurants

Cabrinha

$$ | PORTUGUESE | FAMILY | The largest of Cacilhas's many *marisqueiras* (traditional seafood restaurants), Cabrinha has been doing a roaring business among locals and out-of-towners for over 40 years. Crustaceans of all shapes and sizes are priced by weight, while steaks, grilled fish, and the famous seafood stew will satisfy a hearty appetite without blowing the budget. **Known for:** brisk, friendly service; lobster and giant prawns; tasty seafood rice. *Average main: €20 Beco Bom Sucesso 4, Cacilhas 212 764 732 www.cabrinha.com.pt Closed Mon.*

O Farol

$$ | PORTUGUESE | FAMILY | The oldest *cervejaria* (relaxed dining and drinking spot) in the region, O Farol has been serving cold beer, rich seafood stews, and delicious shellfish since 1890. The brightly lit space feels more functional than fashionable, but the crowds eating here are a testament to the outstanding seafood, and the sunset views over the river to Lisbon are magical. **Known for:** excellent location near the ferry terminal; efficient, friendly service; grilled fish and shrimp. *Average main: €20 Largo Alfredo Dinis 1, Cacilhas 212 765 248 restaurantefarol.com.*

Nightlife

Boca do Vento Bar & Tapas

BARS/PUBS | There's a decent range of gin-based cocktails and light meals at Boca do Vento (Mouth of the Wind), but the views are the real stars of the show. Perched high above the river Tagus, at the entrance to the elevator that zips people between Almada Velha and the riverfront, it's a spectacular place for sunset drinks on the terrace. ✉ *Largo da Boca do Vento, Almada* ☎ *914 406 981.*

Boteco 47

TAPAS BARS | A bright and breezy spot with a nice line of cocktails and petiscos, Boteco 47 is another of the Cacilhas bars that buzzes with Lisboetas after dark. Order a bottle of wine and some small plates to share, pull up a seat outside, and watch the party unfold after dark. ✉ *Rua Cândido dos Reis 47, Cacilhas.*

Performing Arts

★ **Casa da Cerca**

ART GALLERIES—ARTS | A contemporary art museum and live music venue set in a beautiful 18th-century building and surrounded by immaculately maintained grounds, Casa da Cerca more than merits the quick trip across the river. Permanent and visiting exhibitions and installations will appeal to art lovers, and a café-bar with incredible views across the Tagus and the 25 de Abril Bridge adds considerably to the appeal. From March to September, the Há Música na Casa da Cerca program hosts free concerts ranging from jazz and blues to fado. ✉ *Rua Cerca 2, Almada* ☎ *212 724 950* 🌐 *www.m-almada.pt.*

Shopping

★ **Casa da Avó Berta**

GIFTS/SOUVENIRS | Grandma Berta's House is as welcoming and cozy as the name suggests, and it's packed full of retro-chic Portuguese products that make lovely souvenirs or gifts. From beautifully packaged soaps and ceramic sardines to handcrafted jewelry and gourmet treats, this fragrant store appeals to browsers and serious shoppers alike. You can even sink into a comfy chair for coffee and cake. ✉ *Rua Cândido dos Reis 51A, Almada* ☎ *215 963 696.*

Chapter 4

SINTRA, THE ESTORIL COAST, AND THE SETÚBAL PENINSULA

Updated by
Lucy Bryson

Sights	Restaurants	Hotels	Shopping	Nightlife
★★★★★	★★★★★	★★★★☆	★★★☆☆	★★★☆☆

WELCOME TO SINTRA, THE ESTORIL COAST, AND THE SETÚBAL PENINSULA

TOP REASONS TO GO

★ **Fairy-tale getaway:** Sintra—a UNESCO World Heritage Site—has gorgeous palaces and gardens, and a landscape that inspires poetry. The combination makes it ripe for romantics.

★ **Endless beaches:** All along the Estoril Coast and from Costa da Caparica to Cabo Espichel and around Arrábida, beautiful beaches await. If lively ones are your style, head to Cascais and Caparica; tranquil alternatives are hidden among the cliffs around Guincho, Cabo da Roca, and Cabo Espichel.

★ **Divine wine:** The Setúbal Peninsula is home to Moscatel de Setúbal (a sweet fortified wine) and to several well-known wine producers, including JM Fonseca, Quinta da Bacalhoa, and João Pires (J.P. Vinhos). North of the Tagus are other historical wine regions, most notably Colares, near Sintra.

★ **Fabulous seafood:** *Marisqueiras* (seafood restaurants) are an essential component of Portuguese culture, and this region has some of the best in Portugal.

1 **Sintra.** The undeniable romance of Sintra makes it a UNESCO World Heritage Site. Here you'll find breathtaking castles and mist-shrouded palaces at every turn and the steep streets lined with cafés, restaurants, and wine-tasting rooms.

2 **Queluz.** A short journey by train from Lisbon or Sintra, the community of Queluz is best known for its magnificent 18th-century palace, which sits in equally splendid gardens.

3 **Estoril.** Famous for its swanky casino (said to have inspired James Bond creator Ian Fleming), Estoril has long attracted high-living types. But you don't need to be a millionaire to appreciate the string of family-friendly beaches.

4 **Cascais.** Like neighboring Estroril, the resort town of Cascais has a succession of beaches that appeal to everyone from parents looking for gentle waves to surfers in search of a challenge. It also has some notable museums and galleries.

5 **Guincho.** One of the most famous beaches in the area, Praia do Guincho is a wild, windswept stretch of sand that's hugely popular with surfers. Located within the Sintra-Cascais National Park, it has some excellent seafood restaurants.

6 **Azóia.** Europe's westernmost village, Azóia is a stone's throw from Cabo da Roca, famous for its atmospheric lighthouse and incredible ocean views.

7 **Costa da Caparica.** A short hop across the river from Lisbon, the Costa da Caparica attracts Lisbon's surfers and sunseekers with its seemingly endless string of beaches.

8 **Palmela.** Famous for its medieval castle, Palmela sits in the rolling hills surrounded by wineries and vineyards. The views from the hilltop castle stretch for miles.

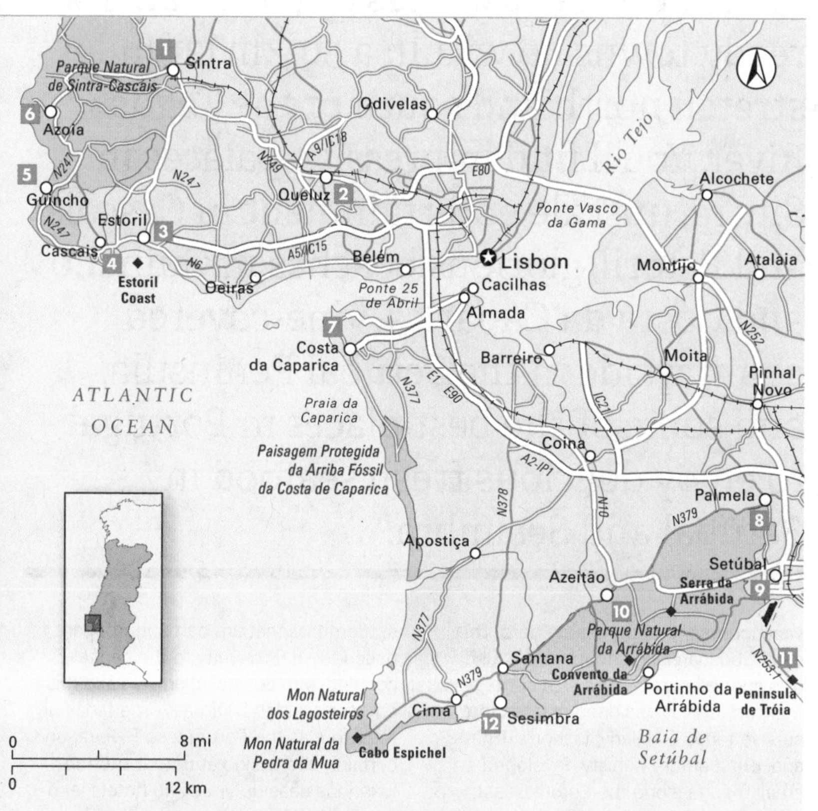

9 Setúbal. Not yet discovered by most travelers, Setúbal has sunny plazas, leafy parks, and a lively arts scene. You can take a dolphin-spotting boat trip from here, or just enjoy local specialties like *choco frito* (fried cuttlefish).

10 Azeitão. A top destination for wine buffs, Azeitão is home to some of the oldest cellars in Portugal. The pleasant historic center makes a good base for exploring the nearby vineyards. The local cheeses are noteworthy, too.

11 Peninsula de Tróia. This peninsula has some of the loveliest beaches in the region.

12 Sesimbra. The pretty beach town of Sesimbra has become a favorite destination for seafood lovers thanks to its centuries-old fishing traditions. Neighboring Arrábida National Park is home to some of the most beautiful (and secluded) beaches in Portugal.

The capital's backyard offers some seriously enticing side trips. A succession of attractive coastal resorts and camera-ready towns lie within a 50-km (31-mile) stretch north and south of the Tagus River. You'll find impressive palaces in Sintra, upscale entertainment in Cascais and Estoril, glorious beaches in Guincho and Costa da Caparica, vine-covered countryside in the Setúbal Peninsula, and some of the best places in Portugal to enjoy delicious fresh seafood in Setúbal and Sesimbra.

Vacationers are nothing new here. The early Christian kings adopted the lush hills and valleys of Sintra as a summer retreat and designed estates that survive today. Similarly, Lisbon's 18th- and 19th-century nobility developed small resorts along the Estoril Coast; the amenities and ocean views are still greatly sought after. For swimming, modern Lisboetas look a little farther afield—south across the Tagus River to the beaches and resorts of the Costa da Caparica and the southern Setúbal Peninsula. But whichever direction you travel and whatever your interests, you'll be delighted with all that's available within an hour of Lisbon.

MAJOR REGIONS

The Estoril Coast. The Estoril Coast extends for 32 km (20 miles) west of Lisbon, taking in the major towns of Estoril and Cascais as well as smaller settlements that are part suburb, part beach town. Proximity to the capital coupled with coastal charms make this a coveted residential area. Some fancifully refer to it as the Portuguese Riviera, and certainly the casino at Estoril and the luxurious seaside villas and hotels lend the area cachet.

Sintra and Queluz. The town of Sintra—a UNESCO World Heritage Site—is the jewel in this region's proverbial crown. Fortified by Moors, popularized by palace-building royals, and beloved by Romantic writers, its storied past manifests itself in stunning architecture. Moreover, it is blessed by natural beauty: the woods and valleys on the northern slopes of the Serra de Sintra are picturesque and provide the area with its own microclimate (it can be cool and misty in Sintra when Lisbon is sunny and warm). To the west, the Atlantic exerts its influence at windswept beaches and capes, including Cabo da Roca—the westernmost point in Europe. In the other direction, the town of Queluz, halfway between Lisbon and Sintra, is dominated by a magnificent baroque palace set in gardens dotted with statuary.

The Setúbal Peninsula. The Setúbal Peninsula, south of the Tagus River, is popular for its beaches in Costa da Caparica, Sesimbra, Arrábida, Tróia, and everywhere in between. These provide the cleanest ocean swimming closest to Lisbon. Other highlights include the delicious local seafood, pastries, and regional wines; the historic castles of Palmela and Sesimbra and the fort in Setúbal; plus the scenic mountain range—the Serra da Arrábida—that separates the port from the peninsula's southernmost beaches and fishing villages.

Planning

All the main towns and most of the sights are accessible by train or bus from Lisbon, so you can see the entire region on day trips from the capital. This is a particularly good way to explore the resorts on the Estoril Coast and the beaches of the Costa da Caparica, south across the Tagus River. The palace at Queluz also makes a good day trip; it is 20 minutes northwest of Lisbon by train. Using the capital as your base, a realistic time frame for visiting the major sights is four days: one each for the Estoril Coast, Queluz and Sintra, Caparica, and Setúbal.

When to Go

If you're planning to visit in summer, particularly July and August, you *must* reserve a hotel room in advance. If you can, travel to the coastal areas in spring or early fall: the crowds are much thinner, and it could be warm enough for a brisk swim in May and October.

Most of the region's festivals are held in summer. In São Pedro de Sintra, the Festa de São Pedro (St. Peter's Day) celebration is on June 29; there are summer music and arts festivals in Sintra, Cascais, and Queluz; September in Palmela sees the Festa das Vindimas (Grape Harvest Festival); the Feira de Santiago (St. James Fair) takes place in Setúbal at the end of July. Year-round markets include those in São Pedro de Sintra (second and fourth Sunday of every month) and Vila Nogueira de Azeitão (first Sunday of every month). Sesimbra holds a gigantic samba festival (the largest outside Brazil) each August, and its four-day Carnaval includes "Clowns Day," the largest gathering of clowns anywhere in the world.

Getting Here and Around

With a car you can cover most of the main sights north and south of the Tagus River in two days, although this gives you little time to linger. A week wouldn't be too long to spend, particularly if you plan to soak up the sun at a resort or take an in-depth look at Sintra, whose beautiful surroundings alone can fill two or three days.

BOAT AND FERRY

From the city of Setúbal, Atlantic Ferries provides 24-hour service for passengers and cars via ferry and catamaran from Setubal's bay across to the Tróia Peninsula where white sand beaches stretch all the way down to the Alentejo. The comfortable catamaran (€7.20 per person) takes 15 minutes, and the car ferry (€5.20 per person, €15.60 per car) takes 25 minutes. The return journey is free.

FERRY INFORMATION Atlantic Ferries. ☎ *265 235 101* 🌐 *www.atlanticferries.pt.*

BUS

Although the best way to travel from Lisbon to Sintra and most of the towns on the Estoril Coast is by train, there are some useful bus connections between these towns. From the bus terminal in Cascais, SCOTTurb buses travel to Guincho (15 minutes) and Sintra (30 minutes). Bus 417 is faster, but Bus 403 travels along a more scenic route.

Transportes Sul de Tejo (TST) buses run between Lisbon and destinations south of the Tagus, including Caparica, Sesimbra, and Setúbal. Service to beach destinations is more frequent in July and August than the rest of the year.

Tickets are cheap (less than €4 for most journeys), and departures are generally every hour (less frequently on weekends). Always arrive at least 15 minutes before your bus is scheduled to depart.

BUS CONTACTS SCOTTurb. ☎ *214 699 100* 🌐 *scotturb.com.* **Transportes Sul do Tejo.** (*TST*) ☎ *707 508 509* 🌐 *www.tsuldotejo.pt.*

CAR

Highways connect Lisbon with Sintra (A37), Estoril and Cascais (A5/IC15) and Setúbal (A2/IP1). Avoid departing from Lisbon at the start of a weekend or public holiday. The bridges crossing the Tagus—especially the Ponte 25 de Abril, but also the Ponte Vasco da Gama—can be very slow. Parking can be problematic too, particularly in summer along the Estoril Coast.

TAXI

Lisboetas use ride-hailing apps like Kapten (a local favorite) and Uber to visit the towns around Lisbon. If you take a traditional taxi, agree on a fixed price for the round-trip journey. Estoril should be about €40 each way, while Sintra should cost roughly €50 each way. Prices will be higher on weekends and public holidays.

TRAIN

Comboios de Portugal (CP) commuter trains travel the entire Estoril Coast, with departures every 15 to 30 minutes from the waterfront Cais do Sodré station in Lisbon, west of the Praça do Comércio. The scenic trip to Estoril takes about 30 minutes, and four more stops along the seashore to the end of the line at Cascais. A one-way ticket to either costs €2.25. Trains from Lisbon's beautiful Rossio station depart every 15 minutes to Queluz (20 minutes) and on to Sintra (40 minutes). One-way tickets cost €1.65 to Queluz and €2.25 to Sintra.

Fertagus trains from Lisbon's Roma–Areeiro, Entrecampos, Sete Rios, and Campolide stations head south via the Ponte 25 de Abril crossing the Tagus River. Passengers on the double-decker railcars benefit from pleasant views and soothing music on the way to Setúbal, a journey of around an hour. Tickets cost €4.55 one way.

From June to September, the Transpraia narrow-gauge railway runs for 8 km (5 miles) along the Costa da Caparica from the town of Caparica to Fonte da Telha, making 20 stops at beaches along the way. A one-way ticket to the end of the line costs €3. The "mini train" opens up stretches of coastline that are otherwise inaccessible without a car, and even makes a call at a nudist beach.

TRAIN CONTACTS Comboios de Portugal. (*CP*) ☎ *707 210 220* 🌐 *www.cp.pt/passageiros.* **Fertagus.** ☎ *211 066 363* 🌐 *www.fertagus.pt/.*

Restaurants

City dwellers make a point of heading to coastal communities south of the city for platefuls of *arroz de marisco* (rice with shellfish) or *linguado* (sole). One summertime delights is the smell of grilled sardines wafting from restaurants and beachside stalls. Seafood is the specialty along the Estoril Coast—even the inland villages here and on the Setúbal Peninsula are close enough to the sea to be assured a steady supply of fish, and the seaside fishing town of Sesimbra attracts seafood-loving foodies from across the country with its excellent seafront restaurants.

In Sintra, *queijadas* (sweet cheese tarts) are a specialty; in the Azeitão region of the Setúbal Peninsula locals swear by the *queijo fresco*, a delicious white cheese made either of goat's or sheep's milk. This region also produce good wines. From Colares comes a light, smooth red, a fine accompaniment to a hearty lunch; Palmela, a demarcated wine-growing district of Setúbal, produces distinctive amber-color wines of recognized quality; and a local specialty is a dessert wine called Moscatel de Setúbal.

Hotels

Accommodations are more limited once the bright lights of Lisbon have been left behind. But the options, both old and new, are truly diverse. Historic lodgings are understandably popular, and *pousadas*—inns, often in converted buildings, that generally have superior facilities—are the top pick for many travelers. The three in this region are at Queluz, Setúbal, and Palmela. Modern alternatives may not have the same cultural cred, but they compensate by having up-to-date amenities and, in some cases, an eco-friendly outlook. No matter what you choose, advance booking is essential in summer. Out of season, many places offer substantial discounts.

Restaurant and hotel reviews have been shortened. For expanded hotel reviews, visit Fodors.com. Restaurant prices are per person for a main course at dinner. Hotel prices are for a standard double room, including tax, in high season (off-season rates may be lower).

WHAT IT COSTS In Euros

	$	$$	$$$	$$$$
RESTAURANTS	under €16	€16–€20	€21–€25	over €25
HOTELS	under €140	€140–€200	€201–€260	over €260

Tours

Most travel agents and large hotels in Lisbon can reserve you a place on a guided tour. Sightseeing bus operators such as Cityrama Gray Line organize half- and full-day excursions to destinations like Sintra, Queluz, and Estoril. Tours typically cost €45 to €85, depending on the distance and duration. Half-day tours typically encompass visits to all the principal sights and some include wine tasting in Colares.

CONTACTS Cityrama Grayline. ✉ *Av. João XXI 78-E, Campo Pequeno* ☎ *213 191 090 Reservations* 🌐 *www.cityrama.pt.*

Visitor and Tour Information

Lisbon's tourist offices (AskMe Lisboa) can provide information on a vast range of trips and tours in Lisbon's outskirts, from surf trips to winery visits, as well as more standard sightseeing tours by bus. The main branch is located downtown at Terreiro do Paço (also known as Praça do Comercio). The staff here can sell you the Lisboa Card, valid for periods of 24, 48, or 72 hours (€20, €34, and €42); the card's benefits include free rail travel to Sintra and along the Estoril Coast and free or discounted access to many of the region's tourist attractions. Local tourist offices are usually open daily June to September. Their hours are greatly reduced after peak season, and most are closed Sunday.

Great Itineraries

If You Have 2 Days

Public transportation is preferable if you're just hitting the main sights, but hiring a car is a good way to get a little off the beaten track and pack a lot of experiences into a short time. Start in Lisbon and drive to **Estoril**, where you can soak up the atmosphere in the gardens and on the seafront promenade. From here, it's only a short distance to **Cascais**, the perfect place for an alfresco lunch. Afterward, explore the little cove beaches and the **Boca do Inferno.** The next day, it's less than an hour's ride north to **Sintra**, where before lunch you'll have time to see its palace and climb to the **Castelo dos Mouros.** After lunch, return to Lisbon, stopping in **Queluz** to see the Palácio Nacional. For dinner, you might cross the Rio Tejo from Lisbon to **Cacilhas** for seafood.

If You Have 4 Days

From Lisbon, head for **Queluz** and its Palácio Nacional. In the afternoon, make the short drive to **Sintra**, where you can spend the rest of the day seeing the sights in and around the town. Consider having dinner in the adjacent village of **São Pedro de Sintra.** Head out early the next day to the extraordinary **Palácio Nacional de Pena.** To contrast this haughty palace with a more humble sight, travel west to the **Convento dos Capuchos** before continuing to the headland of **Cabo da Roca.** Wind south to the wonderful beach at **Guincho** to catch the late-afternoon sun and have a bite to eat. Stick to the coastal road as it heads east toward **Cascais**, where you can spend the night.

On the third day, drive back into Lisbon through **Estoril.** Cross the Rio Tejo via the mighty Ponte 25 de Abril, and detour for lunch at either **Cacilhas** or **Costa da Caparica.** It's then only an hour's drive to the mighty hilltop castle at **Palmela**, from where it is possible to take in views over the entire region before driving (6 miles) down the road to soak up sunny plazas and colorful street art **Setúbal.** On the fourth morning drive through the **Serra da Arrábida**, taking in the jaw-dropping views and stopping for lunch at an esplanade restaurant in **Sesimbra.** From here, you can return to Lisbon in around 40 minutes.

CONTACTS AskMe Lisboa. ✉ *Terreiro do Paço, Baixa* ☎ *210 312 810* 🌐 *www.askmelisboa.com.*

Sintra

30 km (18 miles) northwest of Lisbon.

History buffs, architecture enthusiasts, literature lovers, and hopeless romantics all fall under Sintra's seductive spell. The lush northern slopes of the Serra de Sintra have been inhabited since prehistoric times, although the Moors were the first to build a castle on the peaks. Later Sintra became the summer residence of Portuguese kings and aristocrats, and its late-medieval palace is the greatest expression of royal wealth and power from the time. In the 18th and 19th centuries, English travelers, poets, and writers—including an enthusiastic Lord Byron—were drawn by the region's beauty. Poet Robert Southey described Sintra as "the most blessed spot on the whole inhabitable globe." Its historic importance has been recognized by UNESCO, which designated it a World Heritage Site in 1995.

GETTING HERE AND AROUND

By far the easiest way to get to Sintra is by train. Trains from Lisbon's Rossio Station run every 15 minutes to Sintra (40 minutes). One-way tickets cost €2.15. Sintra's small train station gets packed during the peak summer season (July–early September), and queues at the information desk are huge. Driving to Sintra takes around 30 minutes, but once you get there parking is a hassle.

Once you're in town, the nearest attractions are within walking distance. If you'd rather not tackle steep hills on foot, you can opt for a horse-drawn carriage ride, a guided tour (easily arranged through the tourist office), a hop-on, hop-off bus, or a tour by taxi. The most useful bus service for getting around Sintra is SCOTTurb Bus 434, which connects Sintra Station, the town center (there's a stop outside the tourist office), Castelo dos Mouros, and Pena Palace. The fare is €6.90, and is valid all day.

Tuk tuks are an increasingly popular way to make the ascent to castles and viewpoints, and several companies have started in the past several years. Drivers line up at the train station, in the historic center, and at key tourist hot spots. Expect to pay around €30 per hour for two passengers.

The Sintra Elétrico tram runs from the town center to the pleasant beach village of Praia das Maçãs, a scenic 45-minute ride costing €3 each way. The service is less frequent in winter.

TOURS

Eléctrico de Sintra

BUS TOURS | **FAMILY** | Antique red streetcars make the 45-minute scenic journey from the center of Sintra through the countryside and down the mountain to the ocean at Praia das Maçãs. Seafood restaurants line the beach at the last stop. During the summer season there are three trams a day in each direction. ✉ *Rua General Alves Roçadas* ☎ *219 236 114* 🌐 *www.aldeiadapraia.pt/tram-timetable-sintra-electrico* 🎫 *€3.*

Sintratur

CARRIAGE TOURS | Old-fashioned horse-and-carriage rides take you around the town. A short tour costs €30 for up to four people. ✉ *Av. Heliodoro Salgado 16* ☎ *925 585 384* 🌐 *www.sintratur.com.*

Turislua Turis Tuk

DRIVING TOURS | **FAMILY** | Following Lisbon's lead, the town has adopted tuk tuks for sightseeing. Turis Tuk's distinctive red tuk tuks zip around Sintra and beyond, saving tourists' legs as they visit the hilltop palaces, castles, and other key sights. Agree on a price before heading out. ✉ *2A Volta Duche* ☎ *219 243 881* 🎫 *€30.*

VISITOR INFORMATION

The main local tourist office, AskMe Sintra, has details on opening hours and prices, walking trails in the countryside, and the best local tour companies. There's also a branch in the train station.

CONTACTS AskMe Sintra. ✉ *Praça da República 23* ☎ *219 231 157* 🌐 *www.cm-sintra.pt.*

Sights

Castelo dos Mouros (*Moorish Castle*)

CASTLE/PALACE | **FAMILY** | The battlemented ruins of this 9th-century castle still give a fine impression of the fortress that finally fell to Christian forces led by Dom Afonso Henriques in 1147. Panoramic views from the serrated walls explain why the Moors chose the site. It's visible from various points in Sintra itself, but for a closer look follow the steps that lead up to the ruins from the back of the town center (40 minutes going up, about half that coming down). Alternatively, you can catch SCOTTurb Bus 434 or rent a tuk tuk in town. ✉ *Estrada da Pena* ☎ *219 237 300* 🌐 *www.parquesdesintra.pt* 🎫 *€8.*

Convento dos Capuchos (*Capuchin Convent*)

RELIGIOUS SITE | The entrance to this extraordinarily austere convent, 13 km (8 miles) southwest of Sintra, sets the tone for the severity of the ascetic living conditions within. From 1560 until 1834, when it was abandoned, seven monks—never any more, never any less—prayed in the tiny chapel hewn out of the rock and inhabited the bare cells, which were lined with cork in attempt to maintain a modicum of warmth. Impure thoughts meant a spell in the Penitents' Cell, an excruciatingly small space. ✉ *Convento dos Capuchos, Colares* ☎ *219/237 300* 🌐 *www.parquesdesintra.pt* 🎟 *€7.*

★ **NewsMuseum**

MUSEUM | Barack Obama and Queen Elizabeth II are among the famous faces peering from the windows of this modern museum dedicated to the workings of the mass media. Inside a handsome building with wrought-iron balconies, it combines interactive exhibits such as a giant touch-screen tablet highlighting world-changing events with thought-provoking examinations of how the media has covered various topics, including Portuguese soccer luminary Cristiano Ronaldo. The bright exhibits and interactive devices should keep younger visitors occupied for an hour or so. ✉ *Rua Visconde de Monserrate 26* ☎ *210 126 600* 🌐 *www.newsmuseum.pt/en* 🎟 *€8.*

★ **Palácio e Parque de Monserrate** (*Monserrate Park and Palace*)

HOUSE | **FAMILY** | This estate, 4 km (2½ miles) west of Sintra, was laid out by Scottish gardeners in the mid-19th century at the behest of a wealthy Englishman, Sir Francis Cook. The centerpiece is the Moorish-style, three-dome **Palácio de Monserrate.** The original palace was built by the Portuguese viceroy of India, and was later home to Gothic novelist William Beckford. The gardens, with their streams, waterfalls, and Etruscan tombs, are famed for an array of tree and plant species, though labels are lacking. ✉ *Estrada da Monserrate* ☎ *219 237 300* 🌐 *www.parquesdesintra.pt* 🎟 *€8.*

★ **Palácio Nacional de Sintra** (*Sintra Palace*)

CASTLE/PALACE | **FAMILY** | The enormous twin chimneys rising out of Sintra Palace are among the town's most iconic landmarks. There has probably been a palace here since Moorish times, although the current structure dates to the late 14th century. It is the only surviving royal palace in Portugal from the Middle Ages, and displays a combination of Moorish, Gothic, and Manueline architecture. The chapel has Mozarabic (Moorish-influenced) azulejos from the 15th and 16th centuries. The ceiling of the Sala das Armas is painted with the coats of arms of 72 noble families, and the grand Sala dos Cisnes has a remarkable ceiling of painted swans. The Sala das Pegas (magpies) figures in a well-known tale about Dom João I (1385–1433) and his dalliance with a lady-in-waiting. The king had the room painted with as many magpies as there were chattering court ladies, thus satirizing the gossips as loose-tongued birds. Bilingual descriptions in each room let you enjoy them at your own pace. ✉ *Largo Rainha D. Amélia* ☎ *219 237 300* 🌐 *www.parquesdesintra.pt* 🎟 *€10.*

★ **Parque e Palácio Nacional da Pena** (*Pena National Park and Palace*)

CASTLE/PALACE | **FAMILY** | The biggest draw in Sintra, this Disneylike castle is a glorious conglomeration of turrets and domes awash in pastels. In 1503 the Monastery of Nossa Senhora da Pena was constructed here, but it fell into ruins after religious orders were expelled from Portugal in 1832. Seven years later the ruins were purchased by Maria II's consort, Ferdinand of Saxe-Coburg. Inspired by the Bavarian castles of his homeland, Ferdinand commissioned a German architect, Baron Eschwege, to

Wear sturdy shoes when walking along the sometimes steep stone walls of Castelo dos Mouros, but the views are well worth it.

build the castle of his fantasies, in styles that range from Arabian to Victorian. Work was finished in 1885, by which time he was Fernando II. The surrounding park is filled with trees and flowers from every corner of the Portuguese empire, as well as hidden temples, grottoes, and Valley of the Lakes, where black swans sit regally. Portugal's last monarchs used the Pena Palace as a summer home, the last of whom—Queen Amália—went into exile in England after the Republic was proclaimed on October 5, 1910. Inside is an ostentatious and often bizarre collection of Victorian and Edwardian furniture, ornaments, and paintings. Placards explain each room. Visitors can walk along high castle walls, peek into turrets, and finally reward themselves with a drink and a snack at one of two on-site cafés. A path beyond an enormous statue (thought to be Baron Eschwege, cast as a medieval knight) on a nearby crag leads to the **Cruz Alta,** a 16th-century stone cross 1,782 feet above sea level, with stupendous views. ✉ *Estrada da Pena* ☎ *219 237 300* 🌐 *www.parquesdesintra.pt* 🎫 *€14 palace and park, €7.50 park only.*

★ Quinta da Regaleira

HOUSE | A five-minute walk along the main road past the tourist office takes you to one of Sintra's most intriguing privately owned mansions. Quinta da Regaleira was built in the early 20th century for a Brazilian mining magnate with a keen interest in Freemasonry and the Knights Templar (who made their 11th-century headquarters on this site). The estate includes gardens where almost everything—statues, water features, grottoes, lookout towers—is linked to one or the other of his pet subjects. Spookiest of all is the 100-foot-deep Poço do Iniciático (Initiation Well)—an inverted underground "tower." Audio guides in English are available at reception. ✉ *Rua Barbosa do Bocage 5* ☎ *219 106 650* 🌐 *www.regaleira.pt* 🎫 *€8.*

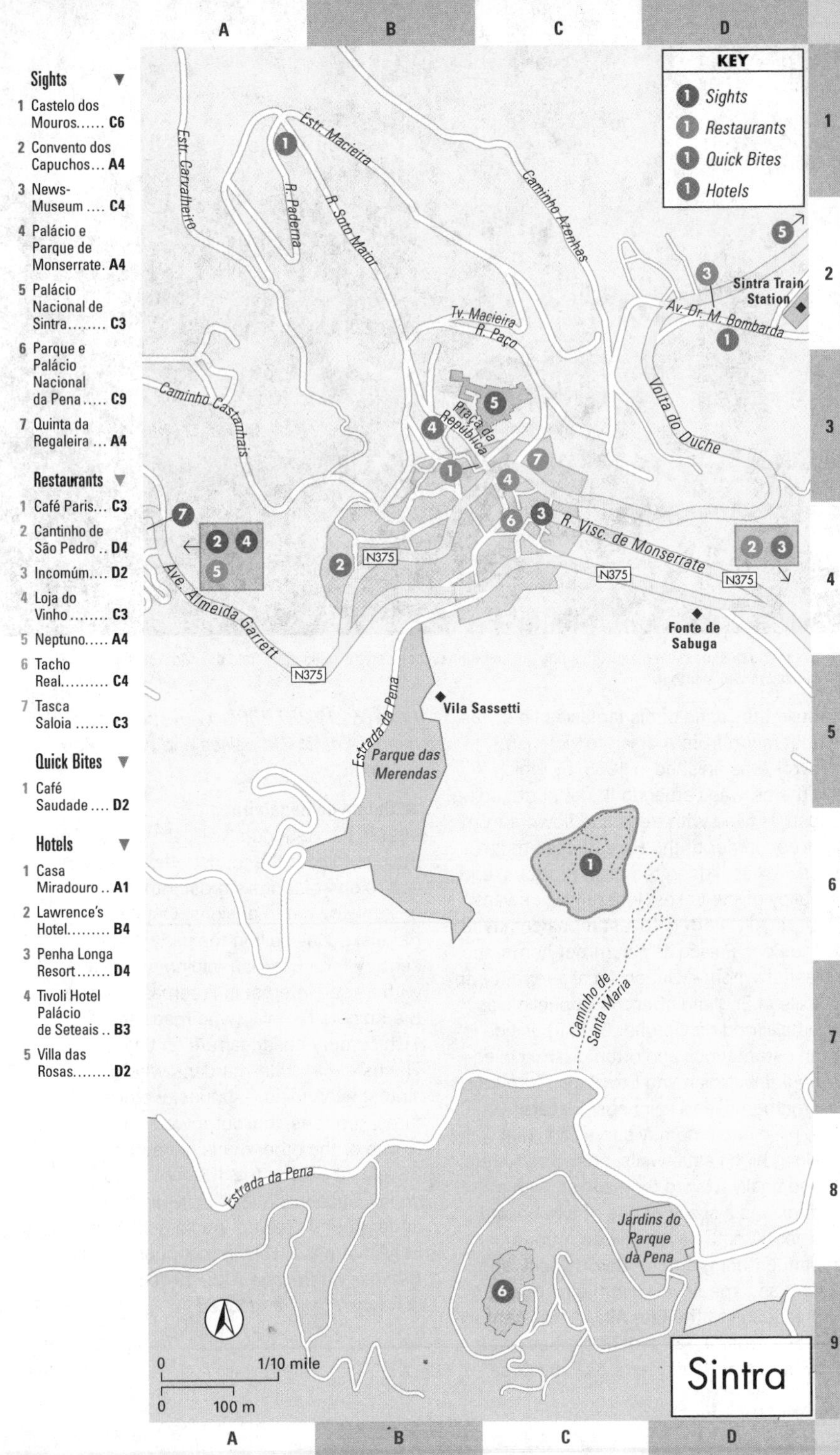
Sights
1 Castelo dos Mouros...... C6
2 Convento dos Capuchos... A4
3 News-Museum C4
4 Palácio e Parque de Monserrate. A4
5 Palácio Nacional de Sintra........ C3
6 Parque e Palácio Nacional da Pena..... C9
7 Quinta da Regaleira ... A4
Restaurants
1 Café Paris... C3
2 Cantinho de São Pedro .. D4
3 Incomúm.... D2
4 Loja do Vinho........ C3
5 Neptuno..... A4
6 Tacho Real.......... C4
7 Tasca Saloia C3
Quick Bites
1 Café Saudade D2
Hotels
1 Casa Miradouro .. A1
2 Lawrence's Hotel......... B4
3 Penha Longa Resort....... D4
4 Tivoli Hotel Palácio de Seteais .. B3
5 Villa das Rosas........ D2
KEY
Sights
Restaurants
Quick Bites
Hotels
Estr. Carralheiro
Estr. Macieira
R. Paderna
R. Soto Maior
Caminho Azenhas
Tv. Macieira
R. Paço
Sintra Train Station
Av. Dr. M. Bombarda
Volta do Duche
Caminho Castanhais
Praça da República
R. Visc. de Monserrate
N375
Ave. Almeida Garrett
Fonte de Sabuga
Vila Sassetti
Estrada da Pena
Parque das Merendas
Caminho de Santa Maria
Jardins do Parque da Pena
0
1/10 mile
100 m
Sintra
A
B
C
D
1
2
3
4
5
6
7
8
9

Coffee and Quick Bites

Cafe Saudade
$ | **CAFÉ** | **FAMILY** | A short stroll downhill from the train station, this cozy spot has marble-topped tables and an elaborately decorated ceiling. It serves delicious scones, cakes, and pastries in a setting that evokes the grandeur of another era. **Known for:** wine is available by the glass or the bottle; strong coffee and hearty breakfasts; stop by for afternoon tea. *Average main: €9* ✉ *Av. Dr. Miguel Bombarda nº6* ☎ *212/428 804* ⏲ *Closed Wed. No dinner.*

Restaurants

Café Paris
$$$ | **INTERNATIONAL** | With an enviable location near the Palácio Nacional de Sintra, this elegant bistro has been attracting a well-heeled crowd since the 1920s. There's a covered area for outdoor dining, while the mirrored walls, ceiling frescoes, and crystal chandeliers of the interior are in keeping with the sense of opulence. **Known for:** the steaks are among the best in the city; ornate touches in dining room; lots of vegetarian options. *Average main: €23* ✉ *Praça da República 32–36* ☎ *219 232 275* 🌐 *www.screstauracao.com/en/venues/Cafe-Paris/29.*

Cantinho de São Pedro
$ | **PORTUGUESE** | A building with white stucco walls and a barrel-tile roof is home to this tavern, said to be one of the oldest in Portugal. Inside are exposed brick walls, expansive windows, and a huge fireplace that keeps the place cozy in cooler weather. **Known for:** anything from the grill is excellent; long and interesting history; plenty for vegetarians. *Average main: €15* ✉ *Praça Dom Fernando II 18* ☎ *219 230 267* 🌐 *www.cantinhosaopedro.com* ⏲ *Closed Wed.*

★ **Incomúm**
$$ | **ECLECTIC** | Not far from the town's main train station, this restaurant's location on one of the major thoroughfares means that it is always busy. The dining room is elegantly lighted with crisp linens on the tables, but the favorite seats are on the street. **Known for:** dishes are a work of art; elegant dining room; perfect location. *Average main: €16* ✉ *Rua Doutor Alfredo Costa 22* ☎ *219 243 719* 🌐 *incomumbyluissantos.pt/en* ⏲ *No lunch Sat.*

Loja do Vinho
$$ | **DELI** | One of the city's first wine shops, Loja do Vinho has a cozy cellar lined with hundreds of bottle from all over the world. Plates of cured meats, boards of local cheeses, and bowls overflowing with olives make good companions to the many varieties of wine on offer here or on the tiny outdoor terrace. **Known for:** tapas-style plates perfect for sharing; huge range of wines from the region; setting is extremely cozy. *Average main: €16* ✉ *Praça da República 3* ☎ *219 244 410* 🌐 *www.screstauracao.com/en/venues/Loja-do-vinho/148.*

Neptuno
$$ | **SEAFOOD** | One of the best ocean-side restaurants in nearby Praia das Maçãs, glass-fronted Neptuno is where sandy-footed diners can feast on freshly grilled fish that was swimming in the surf just hours before. Try *peixe a bulhão pato* (fish with garlic, olive oil, and coriander) and the seafood-rich *arroz de marisco.* **Known for:** huge variety of shellfish dishes; don't pass up the daily catch; lovely beachfront location. *Average main: €18* ✉ *Rua Pedro Álvares Cabral, Praia das Maçãs* ☎ *219 291 222* 🌐 *www.restauranteneptuno.pt* ⏲ *No dinner Mon.*

Tacho Real
$$ | **PORTUGUESE** | Locals make their way up a steep hill to this restaurant for traditional dishes like bacalhau *à brás* (with eggs, onions, and sliced potato) that are cooked with panache and served

Did You Know?

The largest room in the Palácio Nacional de Sintra is the Sala dos Cisnes or Swans Hall, featuring octagonal-shaped ceiling panels with painted swans. The soaring space was traditionally used for receptions and celebrations and is still used today for official banquets.

by a friendly staff. Steaks are a specialty, as are the mouthwatering desserts that include house-made cakes and tarts. **Known for:** elegant dining room bordered with azulejo tiles; delicious grilled fish and freshly caught shrimp; terrace is an escape from the crowds. *Average main: €19 Rua do Ferraria 4 219 235 277 Closed Wed. No dinner Tues. in winter.*

Tasca Saloia

$ | **PORTUGUESE** | **FAMILY** | At this restaurant in the center of town, the handful of tables in the convivial dining room spill out onto the sidewalk in warmer weather. Seafood *petiscos* (the Portuguese version of tapas) and a good wine selection are the main attractions. **Known for:** excellent shrimp and other seafood dishes; relaxed atmosphere; friendly service. *Average main: €14 Largo Doutor Gregório d'Almeida, 2 219 105 863.*

Hotels

★ Casa Miradouro

$ | **B&B/INN** | The Belgian owners of this candy-stripe confection at the edge of the city have a keen eye for style and comfort. **Pros:** fireplaces keep rooms cozy in winter; elegant Victorian architecture; great deals off season. **Cons:** bold decor will not appeal to everybody; extra charge for parking; hotel books up early. *Rooms from: €90 Rua Sotto Mayor 55 914 292 203 www.casa-miradouro.com 8 suites Free Breakfast.*

★ Lawrence's Hotel

$$ | **B&B/INN** | The oldest lodging on the peninsula, this 18th-century grande dame has hosted such illustrious guests as Lord Byron and, more recently, Queen Beatrix of the Netherlands (as well as one former U.S. president who is rumored to be a regular guest). **Pros:** terrace restaurant has spectacular views; light meals served in the cozy bar; good chance of spotting a celebrity. **Cons:** no gym or swimming pool; some rooms are small; decor can feel twee. *Rooms from: €190 Rua Consiglieri Pedroso 38–40 219 105 500 www.lawrenceshotel.com 16 rooms and suites Free Breakfast.*

★ Penha Longa Resort

$$$$ | **RESORT** | **FAMILY** | Hidden among the rolling green hills of the Sintra-Cascais Nature Reserve, this dream resort halfway between Cascais and Sintra has breathtaking views of the surrounding forest or the gorgeous grounds. **Pros:** you're welcomed with a plate of Portuguese pastries; outdoor playground with zipline and trampoline; some of the region's best dining. **Cons:** the huge scale can feel impersonal; you need to drive to town; lots of added costs. *Rooms from: €280 Estrada da Lagoa Azul 219 249 011 www.penhalonga.com 194 rooms Free Breakfast.*

★ Tivoli Hotel Palácio de Seteais

$$$$ | **HOTEL** | Built in the 18th century as a home for the Dutch consul, this suitably grand hotel is surrounded by pristine grounds. **Pros:** ideal location 1 km (½ mile) from the center of Sintra; most memorable entrance in Portugal; excellent facilities for kids. **Cons:** very expensive rates; not near tourist sights; somewhat formal feel. *Rooms from: €270 Rua Barbosa do Bocage 8 219 233 200, www.tivolihotels.com/pt/hoteis/sintra/tivoli-palacio-de-seteais/o-hotel.aspx 30 rooms No meals.*

Villa das Rosas

$ | **B&B/INN** | A 15-minute stroll from the historic center of Sintra, this beautifully restored 19th-century estate sits among carefully maintained gardens with a pool shaded by fruit trees. **Pros:** gorgeous pool area with a relaxing "chill-out zone"; location could not be more peaceful; helpful staff. **Cons:** not quite as luxurious as nearby options; no fitness center or wellness area; a bit isolated. *Rooms from: €95*

✉ *Rua António Cunha 2-4* ☎ *219 100 860* 🌐 *www.villadasrosas.com* *10 rooms* *Free Breakfast.*

Activities

GOLF

★ Penha Longa Golf Courses

GOLF | With magnificent ocean views, the Sintra Hills, and Estoril and Cascais in the foreground, architect Robert Trent Jones Jr. had a wonderful setting in which to create one of Portugal's most memorable courses. The Atlantic Course has great sweeping changes in elevation and often tight fairways that put a premium on driving accuracy. With the elevation often come strong breezes that add another dimension to what is in any case a demanding layout. Lower-handicap players will savor the challenge, but there is plenty of enjoyment here for all abilities. A handicap certificate is required. ✉ *Estrada do Lagoa Azul* ☎ 🌐 *www.penhalonga.com* *€97 weekdays, €130 weekends* *18 holes, 6878 yds, par 72* *Reservations essential.*

Performing Arts

FESTIVALS

Festival de Sintra

FESTIVAL | Approaching its 60th year, Sintra's annual music and dance festival takes place during late summer (usually August or September) at the Centro Cultural Olga Cadaval as well as in the many palaces and gardens around Sintra and Queluz. The Gulbenkian Symphony Orchestra and the Gulbenkian Ballet company as well as other international groups perform. **■ TIP→ Buy tickets at the AskMe Sintra tourist information offices.** ✉ *Praça Dr. Francisco Sá Carneiro* ☎ *707 234 234* 🌐 *festivaldesintra.pt.*

Shopping

Sintra is a noted center for antiques, curios, and ceramics. Keep an eye out for displays of hand-painted ceramics, many of them reproductions of 15th- to 18th-century designs, signed by the artists. As you walk into town from the train station, you'll see people selling all manner of handicrafts, jewelry, and the like. Some of it is mass-produced tat, but some sellers have genuinely interesting wares.

Casa Alegria

CRAFTS | Casa Alegria sells beautiful hand-painted azulejo tiles and can create personalized tiles based on photographs or drawings you supply. ✉ *Escandinhas Felix Nunes 5* ☎ *219 234 726* 🌐 *angeltiles.com/the-shop.*

Maria du Bosque

JEWELRY/ACCESSORIES | Shop for one-off gifts and keepsakes at the intriguing little boutique, whose name means "Maria of the Forest." Delicate handmade jewelry and gauzy clothing capture something of Sintra's "enchanted forest" feel. ✉ *Rua Dr. Alfredo da Costa 4.*

Queluz

15 km (9 miles) east of Sintra, 15 km (9 miles) northwest of Lisbon.

Halfway between Lisbon and Sintra, the otherwise rather unremarkable town of Queluz is dominated by its magnificent palace and gardens, located in the plaza of the town's center. Across from the palace stand the rebuilt royal guard's quarters, which have been turned into a lovely pousada. Unlike its metropolitan surroundings, the rest of the town's buildings still mimic the 18th-century style of the palace, which gives you the unique feeling that you're stepping back in time once you cross the bridge into the area.

GETTING HERE AND AROUND

Queluz is just off N249/IC19, and the drive from Lisbon takes about 20 minutes, making this a good half-day option or a fine stop on the way to or from Sintra. It's also easy to take the train from Lisbon (15 minutes): get off at the Queluz-Belas stop, turn left outside the station, and follow the signs for the 1-km (½-mile) walk to the palace.

Sights

★ **Palácio Nacional de Queluz** (*Queluz National Palace*)

CASTLE/PALACE | This palace was inspired, in part, by the palace at Versailles. The salmon-pink rococo edifice was ordered as a royal summer residence by Dom Pedro III in 1747. Architect Mateus Vicente de Oliveira took five years to make the place habitable; Frenchman Jean-Baptiste Robillon spent 40 more executing a detailed baroque plan that also comprised imported trees and statues, and azulejo-lined canals and fountains. You can tour the apartments and elegant staterooms, including the frescoed Music Salon, the Hall of Ambassadors, and the mirrored Throne Room with its crystal chandeliers and gilt trim. The 90-minute guided tours (€5) begin at 10:30 am throughout the year, and again at 2:30 pm in July and August. ✉ *Largo do Palácio* ☎ *219 237 300* 🌐 *www.parquesdesintra.pt* 🎫 *€10 palace and gardens, €5 gardens only.*

Hotels

Pousada Palácio de Queluz

$$ | **B&B/INN** | The royal guard quarters opposite the palace have undergone a stunning transformation to become this beautiful pousada. **Pros:** Portuguese specialties tempered by a French touch; prime location in the palace grounds; elegant exterior, including a clock tower. **Cons:** rooms can be hot in summer; few activities for children; a bit old-fashioned. 💲 *Rooms from: €145* ✉ *Largo do Palacio Nactional* ☎ *214 356 158* 🌐 *www.pousadas.pt/en/hotel/pousada-queluz* 🛏 *26 rooms* 🍽 *Free Breakfast.*

Activities

GOLF

Belas Clube do Campo

GOLF | Architect Rocky Roquemore built this tough but interesting layout in rolling countryside close to Lisbon and the Palácio de Queluz. Perhaps not the easiest golf course to walk—a golf cart is a must during the heat of summer—it is a serious test and will be better appreciated by lower-handicap players. ✉ *Estrada Nacional, Belas* ☎ *219 626 640* 🌐 *www.belasclubedecampo.pt/golf* 🎫 *Green fees €80 per day high season, €70 low season* ⛳ *18 holes, 6977 yds, par 72* ✍ *Reservations essential.*

Estoril

26 km (16 miles) west of Lisbon, 13 km (8 mi) south of Sintra.

Having long ago established its reputation as an affluent enclave, Estoril is still the place to go for glitz and glamour. In the 19th century, it was favored by the European aristocracy, who wintered here in the comfort and seclusion of mansions and gardens. In the 20th century, it became popular among international stars and was a top playground for Europe's rich and famous. Although the town has elegant hotels, restaurants, and sports facilities, reminders of its genteel history are now few. It presents its best face right in the center, where today's jet set descends on the casino, at the top of the formal gardens of the Parque do Estoril.

Across the busy main road, on the beachfront Tamariz esplanade, are alfresco restaurants and an open-air seawater swimming pool. The best and longest

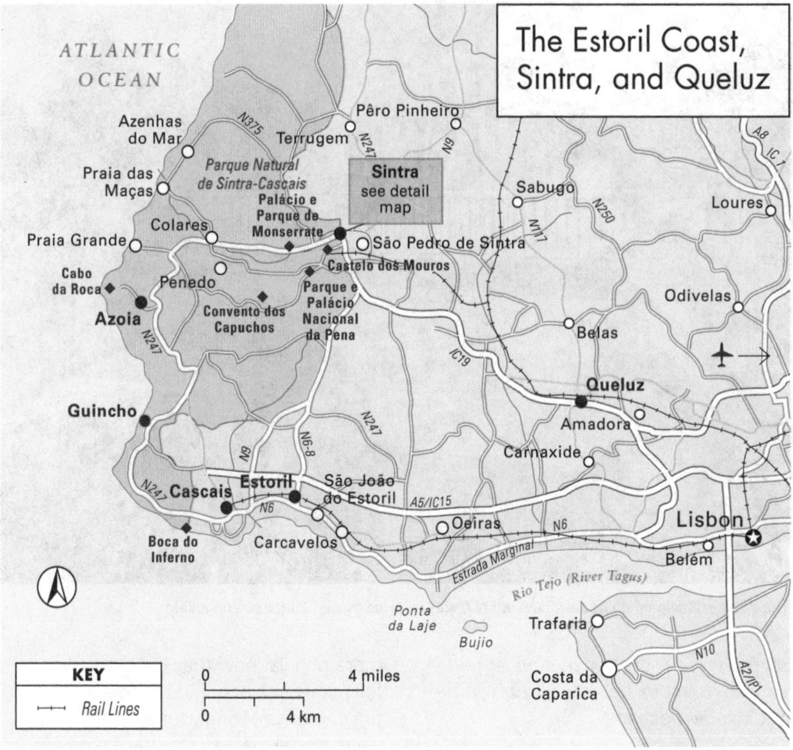

The Estoril Coast, Sintra, and Queluz

local beach is at Monte Estoril, which adjoins Estoril's beach; here you'll find restrooms and beach chairs for rent, as well as plenty of shops and snack bars.

Estoril is also very sports oriented. More than a magnet for golfers, it hosts major sailing, windsurfing, tennis, and equestrian events, as well as motor races at the old Formula 1 track.

GETTING HERE AND AROUND

The best way to arrive is via the CP urban train (Linha de Cascais) departing from Lisbon's Cais do Sodré station in Lisbon. The drive by car will take 25 minutes from Lisbon, either by the A2 highway or the scenic Avenida Marginal running along the coast. Avoid driving during the afternoon on summer weekends, as the traffic is horrendous.

VISITOR INFORMATION Cascais and Estoril Tourism. ✉ *Edifício do Centro de Congressos do Estoril, Av. Clotilde 3°C 2765-211, Estoril* ☎ *214 666 230* 🌐 *www.visitcascais.com.*

Sights

Espaço Memória dos Exílios
MUSEUM | In a striking 1942 Modernist building, this museum focuses on Estoril's community of aristocratic exiles who fled here from Northern Europe during World War II, but its collection of memorabilia relates broadly to Portugal's mid-20th-century history. The exhibit consists mostly of black-and-white photos with captions in Portuguese, and there are also exhibits devoted to the Spanish Civil War, Second World War, and the Holocaust. ✉ *Av. Marginal 7152B*

The Palácio Nacional de Queluz, built in 1747, was inspired by the Palace at Versailles.

☎ 🌐 *www.cm-cascais.pt/equipamento/espaco-memoria-dos-exilios* 🎫 *Free* ⏲ *Closed weekends.*

★ Estoril Casino

CASINO—SIGHT | Thought to have inspired the James Bond novel (and subsequent movie) *Casino Royale,* the glitzy Estoril Casino retains a glamorous allure. It's one of the largest casinos in Europe, with a nightclub, art gallery, bars, and restaurants alongside the gambling salons. You can make an evening of it here, with dinner and a floor show, but it's a pricey night out. To enter the gaming rooms, visitors over 21 must pay a small fee (entrance to the slot rooms is free). ✉ *Av. Dr. Stanley Ho, Estoril* ☎ *214 667 700* 🌐 *www.casino-estoril.pt* 🎫 *Gaming rooms €5, slot rooms free.*

Coffee and Quick Bites

Garrett do Estoril

$ | CAFÉ | FAMILY | This *pastelaria* has been serving delicious cakes, pastries, and other goodies since 1934, and is arguably more popular now than ever. It serves full meals at lunch, but the real pleasure comes in taking your pick from the glass display cases of custard tarts and other confections before sitting down to devour them alongside an espresso, fresh juice, or *ginjinha*. **Known for:** incredibly elaborate fruit tarts and iced macarons; good breakfasts, brunches, and set-lunch plates; handsome design and period furniture. 💲 *Average main: €12* ✉ *Av. de Nice 54* ☎ *214 680 365* ⏲ *Closed Tues. No dinner.*

Restaurants

Água da Cascata Vai Correndo na Ribeira e Acaba no Mar

$$ | ASIAN FUSION | The name—which means "water from the waterfall rushes down the river and ends up in the sea"—is a bit of a mouthful, but sushi fans will want to commit it to memory. In a space that doubles as an art gallery, the food here is prepared using the freshest local ingredients, with an emphasis on vegetarian and vegan-friendly dishes alongside the more traditional shrimp, salmon, and tuna. **Known for:** extensive vegetarian and vegan menu; beautifully presented sushi and sashimi; cozy space with vintage furnishings. *Average main: €17 Rua Nunes dos Santos, Lote C 214 683 736 Closed Mon.*

Cimas

$$$$ | **ECLECTIC** | In a half-timbered building, this family-run estaurant features baronial surroundings of burnished wood, heavy drapes, and oak beams that have played host to royalty, high-ranking politicians, and celebrated authors. The menu spans continents, with everything from French to Indian and Indonesian selections. **Known for:** wine cellar with more than 22,000 bottles; excellent fish and seafood dishes; wonderful wall of windows. *Average main: €28 Av. Marginal 214 681 254 www.cimas.com.pt Closed Sun.*

Miguel Laffan at Atlântico Bar & Restaurante

$$$$ | **PORTUGUESE** | Cascais-born chef Miguel Laffan has won top awards for his creative cuisine, and he seems determined to repeat that success at the InterContinental Cascais Estoril's fine dining restaurant. The Atlântico offers glorious sea views alongside a fish-and-seafood-focused menu that incorporates local produce into elegantly plated contemporary dishes like scallops with wild mushrooms and truffle cream. **Known for:** inventive desserts like goat cheese mousse with honey and lavender; satisfying cocktails and an extensive wine list; gorgeous views from the terrace. *Average main: €30 InterContinental Cascais Estoril, Av. Marginal nº 8023 218 291 100 estorilintercontinental.com/atlantico-bar-restaurant Monte Estoril train station.*

Hotels

Amazonia Hotel

$$ | **HOTEL** | This four-star boutique hotel sits on a hill just far enough off the main drag so that it's hidden from the noise and crowds but still convenient walking distance to all the star attractions, including Estoril Casino and Praia do Tamariz. **Pros:** tucked-away location gives it a tranquil feel; ocean views from top-floor rooms; children's play area. **Cons:** steep walk uphill to the property; restaurant only serves breakfast; some areas in need a refresh. *Rooms from: €160 Rua Engenheiro Álvaro Pedro de Sousa 175, Cascais 214 680 424 www.amazoniahoteis.com/estoril 28 rooms Free Breakfast.*

Estoril Eden

$$ | **HOTEL** | **FAMILY** | Located between Estoril and Cascais, this smart hotel offers comfortable studios and suites. **Pros:** convenient location for beachgoers; plenty of on-site activities; great in-room amenities. **Cons:** it's a drive from the center of town; some rooms look dated; kitchenettes are basic. *Rooms from: €160 Av. Sabóia 214 667 601 www.hotelestorileden.pt 162 units Free Breakfast.*

Hotel Inglaterra

$$ | **HOTEL** | **FAMILY** | The name of this sparkling boutique hotel reflects the long-standing English love affair with the Estoril Coast, but it remains at heart a grand mansion that is unmistakably Portuguese. **Pros:** lovely garden with small playground; offers discounts to a local spa; rooftop pool with sea views. **Cons:** offbeat contemporary decor not to everyone's taste; some rooms are rather small; no on-site parking. *Rooms from: €180 Rua do Porto 1 214 684 461 www.hotelinglaterra.com.pt 70 rooms Free Breakfast.*

★ **Palácio Estoril Golf and Spa Hotel**
$$$ | **HOTEL** | This luxurious 1930s hotel hosted exiled European aristocrats as they waited out World War II; today it draws golfers who play on the nearby course and stressed-out travelers in need of pampering at the spa. **Pros:** impeccable old-world service; excellent dining options; beautiful surroundings. **Cons:** the old-fashioned style will not appeal to everybody; pool area can be very crowded in summer; formal atmosphere can border on stuffy. *Rooms from: €240 ✉ Parque do Estoril, Rua do Parque ☎ 214 680 000 🌐 www.palacioestorilhotel.com 129 rooms, 32 suites Free Breakfast.*

At night, the casino is a big draw; other barhopping typically takes place within the hotels and, during the summer, at a handful of open-late spots along the beachfront.

Tamariz Summer Club
DANCE CLUBS | The biggest and busiest nightspot in the area, at least during high season, the swanky Tamariz Summer Club combines a sushi restaurant, a beachfront lounge, and a dance club. This is a spot where people dress up a bit. *✉ Praia do Tamariz, Rua Olivença.*

GOLF

The superb golf courses near Lisbon attract players from far and wide. Most are the creations of renowned designers, and the climate means that you can play year-round. Many hotels offer golf privileges to guests; some even have their own courses. Package deals abound.

★ **Clube de Golfe do Estoril**
GOLF | Founded in 1929, Estoril Golf Club has an immaculately maintained 18-hole championship course with some very challenging holes. Guests of the Hotel Palácio Estoril receive special rates and privileges. The welcoming clubhouse serves good Portuguese dishes and a good range of drinks, all of which can be enjoyed overlooking the 18th hole and out to sea. *✉ Av. da República ☎ 214 680 176 🌐 www.clubegolfestoril.com 18 holes €82, 9 holes €45 18 holes, 5810 yds, par 69 Reservations essential.*

Feira Internacional de Artesanato do Estoril
CRAFTS | **FAMILY** | From late June to early September, Estoril hosts a huge open-air arts-and-crafts fair near the casino. Vendors sell local art, crafts, and food and drink every evening until midnight. With live music, dancing, and kid-friendly shows, FiARTIL is a major event on Estoril's cultural calendar. *✉ Av. Amaral Estoril ☎ 912 590 249.*

Cascais

3 km (2 miles) west of Estoril.

Once a mere fishing village, the town of Cascais—with three small, sandy bays—is now a heavily developed resort town packed with shops, restaurants, and hotels. Despite the masses of people, though, Cascais has retained some of its small-town character. This is most visible around the harbor, with its fishing boats and yachts, and in the old streets and squares off Largo 5 de Outubro, where you'll find lace shops, cafés, and eateries. Although the water is cold, the beaches are very attractive, from the packed sands in the center of town to wild and windy remote surf beaches and dramatic grottoes like Boca do Inferno.

GETTING HERE AND AROUND

From Lisbon's Cais do Sodré (Linha de Cascais), CP urban trains arrive close to downtown Cascais. To visit the surrounding area, SCOTTurb buses provides connections to Sintra, Estoril, and Oeiras.

The seaside Santa Marta Lighthouse Museum is located in the resort town of Cascais.

Motorists can make the 25-minute drive from Lisbon, either on the A2 highway or the more scenic Avenida Marginal along the coast. Traffic is horrendous on summer weekends.

BUS CONTACTS Cascais Bus Terminal. ✉ *Av. Costa Pinto 74, mall, Cascais* ☎ *214 699 100.*

TAXI CONTACTS Taxis Cascais. ✉ *Av. Júlio Dantas 769, Cascais* ☎ *214 659 500 Landline, 914 659 500 Cellular* 🌐 *site. taxiscascais.com.*

Sights

★ **Boca do Inferno** (*Mouth of Hell*)
NATURE SITE | The most visited attraction in the area around Cascais is the forbiddingly named Mouth of Hell, one of several natural grottoes in the rugged coastline. Located just 2 km (1 mile) west of town, it is best appreciated at high tide or in stormy weather, when the waves crash high onto the surrounding cliffs. You can walk along the fenced paths to the viewing platforms above the grotto and peer into the abyss. A path leads down to secluded spots on the rocks below, where fishermen cast their lines. The bleakly beautiful spot is where English magician Aleister Crowley faked his own suicide in 1930, shocking onlookers when he appeared at a Berlin art gallery three weeks later. A white plaque at the site marks the intriguing occasion, together with the text of the "suicide note" he left behind. ✉ *Av. Rei Humberto II de Itália, Cascais.*

Museu do Mar (*Sea Museum*)
MUSEUM | **FAMILY** | For an understanding of the maritime history of Cascais, head to this modern museum. Here, the town's role as a fishing village is traced through model boats and fishing gear, period clothing, old photographs, and exhibits of curious sea creatures. ✉ *Rua Júlio Pereira de Melho, Cascais* ☎ *214 815 906* 🌐 *www.cm-cascais.pt/museumar* 🎟 *Free* 🕘 *Closed Mon.*

Museu dos Condes Castro Guimarães

(*Museum of the Counts Castro Guimarães*)

MUSEUM | **FAMILY** | Visitors to this grand mansion dating back more than a century can get a peek into how local aristocracy once lived while admiring an impressive display of 18th- and 19th-century paintings, ceramics, and furnishings. ✉ *Av. Rei Humberto II de Itália, Cascais* ☎ *214 815 304* 🌐 *www.cm-cascais.pt/mccg* 🎫 *€4* 🕓 *Closed Mon.*

Parque do Marechal Carmona

CITY PARK | **FAMILY** | Take respite from the crowds at this relaxing park next to the palacial Museu dos Condes. There's tree-shaded spots for picnickers plus a large lawn for sunbathers (expect strolling ducks and peacocks for company). There's also a playground and a pleasant café. ✉ *Praceta Domingos D'Avilez, Av. da Republica, Cascais* 🌐 *www.cm-cascais.pt/equipamento/parque-marechal-carmona.*

Coffee and Quick Bites

★ Santini Cascais

RESTAURANT—SIGHT | **FAMILY** | In the heart of old-town Cascais, Santini Cascais has what many people consider to be the country's best Italian-style gelato. Branches have now opened across Lisbon and in Porto, but Santini Cascais is where it all began when Attilio Santini opened his ice cream parlor on the beach back in 1949. ✉ *Av. Valbom 28F, Cascais* ☎ *214 833 709* 🌐 *www.santini.pt.*

Restaurants

Beira Mar

$$$$ | **SEAFOOD** | One of several well-established restaurants behind the fish market, Beira Mar has won a string of awards for the quality of its fish and seafood. An impressive glass display shows off the best of the day's catch, although hungry diners may pay top dollar as it's sold by weight. **Known for:** lobster and other incredibly fresh seafood; vegetarian options like vegetable risotto; laid-back vibe. 💲 *Average main: €28* ✉ *Rua das Flores 6, Cascais* ☎ *214 827 380* 🌐 *www.restaurantebeiramar.pt* 🕓 *Closed Tues.*

Caffe Itália

$ | **PIZZA** | **FAMILY** | There are plenty of other pizza joints in Cascais, but Caffe Itália is the best of the bunch. In its indoor dining rooms or on its sunny terrace you can choose from a range of authentic thin-crust pizzas and fresh homemade pasta dishes. **Known for:** wide range of salads with fresh produce; outdoor terrace with lovely views; homemade tiramisu for dessert. 💲 *Average main: €14* ✉ *Rua Marques Leal Pancada 16A, Cascais* ☎ *214 830 151* 🕓 *Closed Wed. No lunch Thurs.*

★ O Pescador

$$ | **SEAFOOD** | **FAMILY** | Fresh fish and seafood fills the menu at this relaxed restaurant filled with lobster traps, fishing nets, and other maritime-related artifacts. The *bacalhau assado* (baked salt cod) is one of the specialties of the house, but there are usually also one or two vegetarian options, such as a salad with tofu and asparagus. **Known for:** a local favorite since 1964; well-stocked wine cellar; outdoor patio. 💲 *Average main: €18* ✉ *Rua das Flores 10, Cascais* ☎ *214 832 054* 🌐 *www.restaurantepescador.com* 🕓 *No lunch Wed.*

★ Restaurante Pereira

$ | **PORTUGUESE** | **FAMILY** | Popular though it may be, this longtime favorite remains an unpretentious and inexpensive option for its spectacular food and friendly service. Including much more than the seafood found in most local eateries, the menu features dishes from every region in Portugal. **Known for:** goat, pork, and duck in various dishes; packed with locals all year round; convivial atmosphere. 💲 *Average main: €13* ✉ *Travessa Bela Vista 42, Cascais* ☎ *214 831 215* 🌐 *restaurantepereira.pai.pt* 💳 *No credit cards* 🕓 *Closed Thurs.*

Hotels

★ The Albatroz Hotel

$$$ | **HOTEL** | On a rocky outcrop above the crashing waves, this gorgeous hotel was once the summer residence of the dukes of Loulé. **Pros:** it's worth paying extra for rooms with a sea view; spectacular beach-adjacent location; burnished ambience. **Cons:** one of the most expensive options in the area; nearby beach can get crowded; swimming pool is pretty small. *Rooms from: €260* ✉ *Rua Frederico Arouca 100, Cascais* ☎ *214 847 380* 🌐 *www.thealbatrozcollection.com* *40 rooms* *Free Breakfast.*

Albatroz Villa Cascais

$$$ | **HOTEL** | If Portugal's 18th-century writer Maria Amália de Carvalho could return today to her house on the harbor at Cascais Bay, she wouldn't believe her eyes. **Pros:** excellent breakfast is included in the rates; huge tubs in the bathrooms; friendly staff. **Cons:** less luxurious than the price suggests; street noise seeps into some rooms; some rooms somewhat dark. *Rooms from: €220* ✉ *Rua Fernandes Thomaz 1, Cascais* ☎ *214 863 410* 🌐 *www.thealbatrozcollection.com/villacascais* *11 rooms* *Free Breakfast.*

★ Hotel Cascais Miragem Health & Spa

$$$$ | **HOTEL** | **FAMILY** | Perfectly integrated into the landscape, this luxurious hotel is built in steps up the side of the hill above the sea. **Pros:** great dining options on the premises; indulgent range of spa services; plenty of amenities for kids. **Cons:** some rooms lack individuality; noise from nearby road; parking is pricey. *Rooms from: €270* ✉ *Av. Marginal 8554, Cascais* ☎ *210 060 600* 🌐 *www.cascaismirage.com* *192 rooms and suites* *Free Breakfast.*

★ Pérgola House

$$ | **B&B/INN** | Set amid flower-filled gardens, this intimate town house has been in the hands of the same family for more than 100 years. **Pros:** nice touches like port in the afternoons; extensive breakfast selections; handsome rooms. **Cons:** old-fashioned style not for everyone; books up very quickly; difficult parking. *Rooms from: €150* ✉ *Av. de Valbom 13, Cascais* ☎ *214 840 040* 🌐 *www.pergolahouse.pt* *10 rooms* *Free Breakfast.*

Nightlife

Cascais has plenty of bars on and around the central pedestrian street (Rua Frederico Arouca) and in Largo Luís de Camões. The marina is also a lively place to barhop, with a wide choice of places that stay open until around 2 am.

Bar da Praia

TAPAS BARS | Right on the sand at Praia da Conceição, this is one of the most emblematic beach bars in town. The perfect spot for a sundowner (there are some super-sized cocktails on the menu) while nibbling on *petiscos* and watching beach life go by. Shake off a heavy head in the morning with one of the famous breakfasts followed by a nap on the lounge chairs. ✉ *Rua Frederico Arouca, Cascais* ☎ *214 865 138.*

John Bull

BARS/PUBS | On hot summer nights, patrons of this English-style pub-restaurant spill out into the square. A log fire in the lounge keeps things cozy when the weather turns chilly. ✉ *Largo Luís de Camões 4, Cascais* ☎ *214 833 319* 🌐 *www.johnbullcascais.com.*

Activities

GOLF

★ Oitavos Dunes

GOLF | American architect Arthur Hills built this fine golf course among pine woods and reforested dunes in an area of great natural beauty. The course is consistently rated as one of the top 100 in the world. It lies within the Sintra-Cascais Natural Park, and Hills made the most of three distinct landscape forms: umbrella pine forest, dunes, and the open coastal area. Every hole has a view of the Atlantic Ocean. This was the first course in Europe to be recognized as a Golf Certified Signature Sanctuary, which is awarded by American Audubon International. A handicap certificate is required to play here. ✉ *25 Quinta da Marinha, Cascais* ☎ *214 860 600* 🌐 *www.oitavosdunes.com* 🎫 *€130 weekdays, €155 weekends* ⛳ *18 holes, 5,967mt, par 71.*

SCUBA DIVING

Cascais Dive Center

DIVING/SNORKELING | Scuba courses are available through the PADI-accredited Cascais Dive Center. Other services include specialized dive trips. ✉ *Marina de Cascais, Loja 42a, Cascais* ☎ *919 913 021* 🌐 *www.cascaisdive.com.*

Cascais is arguably the best shopping area on the Estoril Coast, with pedestrian streets lined with small market stalls. For smart fashions and handmade jewelry, browse around Rua Frederico Arouca. Markets with local fruit, vegetables, and cheeses are held north of town at Rua Mercado.

JEWELRY

Torres

JEWELRY/ACCESSORIES | For typical Portuguese handmade jewelry such as delicate filigree, go to Torres, which has its own designers and trademark brand. ✉ *Alameda Combatentes da Grande Guerra 147, Cascais* ☎ *213 243 030* 🌐 *www.torres.pt.*

SHOPPING CENTERS

★ Casa da Guia

SHOPPING CENTERS/MALLS | Housed in a beautiful 19th-century palace, Casa da Guia combines shopping, art, and gastronomy in grand style. It's poised on a cliff edge west of Cascais, beyond Boca do Inferno, and worth the trip out of town for the contemporary art gallery, high-end boutiques, interesting restaurants, and bars with outdoor terraces. ✉ *Av. Nossa Senhora do Cabo 101, Cascais* ☎ *214 843 215* 🌐 *casadaguiacascais.com.*

SPECIALTY STORES

Ceramicarte

SPECIALTY STORES | Fátima and Luís Soares present their carefully executed, modern ceramic designs alongside more traditional jugs and plates at Ceramicarte. There's also a small selection of tapestries and an art gallery. ✉ *Largo da Assunção 3–4, Cascais* ✥ *Near the main Catholic church in the old town* ☎ *214 840 170* 🌐 *www.ceramicarte.pt.*

Vista Alegre

SPECIALTY STORES | Portugal has a long tradition of ceramics, and Vista Alegre, founded in 1824, is one of the country's premium brands. It makes everything from functional pieces such as plates and cups to more decorative collections. ✉ *CascaiShopping, Estrada Nacional 9, Cascais* ☎ *214 692 397* 🌐 *vistaalegre.com.*

Guincho

8 km (5 miles) northwest of Cascais.

The wide beach at Guincho is one of the most famous—and most visited—in the country. Atlantic waves pound the sand even on the calmest of days, providing perfect conditions for windsurfing (the annual world championships are often held here). The undertow is notorious, but the cool summer winds offer a refreshing break from the stuffier beaches on the Cascais line. Whether you go into the water or not, be sure to savor some fresh fish at one of the restaurant terraces overlooking the beach.

GETTING HERE AND AROUND

You can get to Guincho by bus both from Cascais and Sintra (Buses 405 and 415). SCOTTurb buses leave Cascais's train station roughly every hour (25 minutes).

Cascais, with its pedestrian-only streets lined with colorful buildings, is ideal for strolling.

Driving will take 5 to 10 minutes from Cascais, 20 minutes from Sintra, and 35 minutes from Lisbon.

Beaches

★ **Praia do Guincho** (*Guincho Beach*)
BEACH—SIGHT | Cars often line either side of the road behind Guincho Beach on weekends, and surfers can always be seen braving its waves regardless of the season or prevailing weather conditions. The undertow can be dangerous, and even accomplished swimmers have had to summon lifeguards. If you prefer something more sedate, this beach—with the Serra da Sintra serving as a backdrop—is an ideal spot to watch the sunset. **Amenities:** food and drink; parking (no fee); showers; toilets. **Best for:** sunset; surfing; windsurfing. ✉ *N247, Cascais.*

Restaurants

★ **Bar do Guincho**
$ | **PORTUGUESE** | **FAMILY** | Raise a glass to life's simple pleasures as you nibble on freshly caught shellfish at this feet-in-the-sand bar and restaurant. There are grilled slabs of meat and fish on the menu, alongside a lengthy cocktail list and a vast range of small plates that are perfect for sharing. **Known for:** the perfect place for drinks after a day at the beach; open until late on weekends; beautiful spot on the beach. Ⓢ *Average main: €15* ✉ *Estrada do Abono 547, Cascais* ☎ *214 871 683* 🌐 *www.bardoguincho.pt* ⏲ *Closed Mon.*

★ **Monte Mar**
$$$$ | **SEAFOOD** | Superior seafood and steaks come with equally impressive sea views at this highly regarded restaurant in Guincho that attracts everyone from rock stars to heads of state. Situated right at the edge of the ocean, the terrace is the perfect spot for taking in those amazing ocean views. **Known for:** grilled fish and fresh shellfish; amazing

ocean views; reserve ahead. *Average main: €35* *Av. Nossa Senhora do Cabo, Cascais* *214 869 270* *www.montemarrestaurante.com* *Closed Mon.*

Hotels

★ Fortaleza do Guincho
$$$ | **HOTEL** | Standing on the cliffs facing the ocean, this historic fort may look austere from the outside, but walk through the entrance and you'll find all the luxury of an old-world palace. **Pros:** award-winning restaurant serves the best local cuisine; gorgeous location on the ocean; eye-popping architecture. **Cons:** standard rooms are quite small; bathtubs aren't that large; can be pricey. *Rooms from: €230* *Estrada do Guincho, Cascais* *214 870 491* *www.fortalezadoguincho.com* *27 rooms* *Free Breakfast.*

Activities

Guincho Wind Factory
WATER SPORTS | Call ahead for lessons in kitesurfing, windsurfing, and standup paddleboarding from Guincho Wind Factory, where you can also buy or rent boards and all the equipment you need. It also operates a small guesthouse catering to a sporty young crowd. *Rua da Torre 1412, Cascais* *214 868 332* *www.guinchowindfactory.com.*

Azoia

15 km (9 miles) west of Sintra, 9 km (6 miles) north of Guincho.

Azoia is a quaint village in the district of Leira that has maintained a genuine rural charm. Surrounded by flora typical of the Serra de Sintra but perched on the edge of the Atlantic, it is an ideal place for countryside strolls. A stone's throw away is Cabo da Roca—mainland Europe's westernmost point. A lighthouse, originally built in 1772, sits dramatically atop the cape's jutting cliffs.

North of Cabo da Roca, the natural parkland extends through the villages of Praia Grande, Praia das Maçãs, and Azenhas do Mar. The first two have good beaches, and the latter is a postcard come to life, with whitewashed cottages perched on the edge of a cliff. On the way down, the pretty open market with fresh fruit and vegetable stands along the side of a fork in the road makes a nice place to shop with the locals.

GETTING HERE AND AROUND

SCOTTurb Bus 403 will take you to Cabo da Roca from Cascais or Sintra with regular departures from outside either town's train station. The journey takes about 30–40 minutes.

The drive will take 20 minutes from both Sintra and Cascais and 40 minutes from Lisbon.

Sights

Parque Natural de Sintra-Cascais (*Sintra-Cascais Natural Park*)
NATIONAL/STATE PARK | The bleakly beautiful Cabo da Roca and its lighthouse mark the continent's westernmost point and are the main reason that most people make the journey to Sintra-Cascais Natural Park. As with many such places, stalls are laden with gimmicky souvenirs; an information desk and gift shop sells a certificate (€11) that verifies your visit. Even without the certificate, though, the memory of this desolate granite landscape will linger. The cliffs tumble to a frothing sea below, and on the cape a simple cross bears an inscription by Portuguese national poet Luís de Camões. *Estrada do Cabo da Roca s/n, Colares* *219 238 543 Tourist office.*

Restaurants

Moinho Dom Quixote
$ | **CAFÉ** | In the middle of gorgeous gardens, this unusual eatery is built out of an old-fashioned windmill perched on

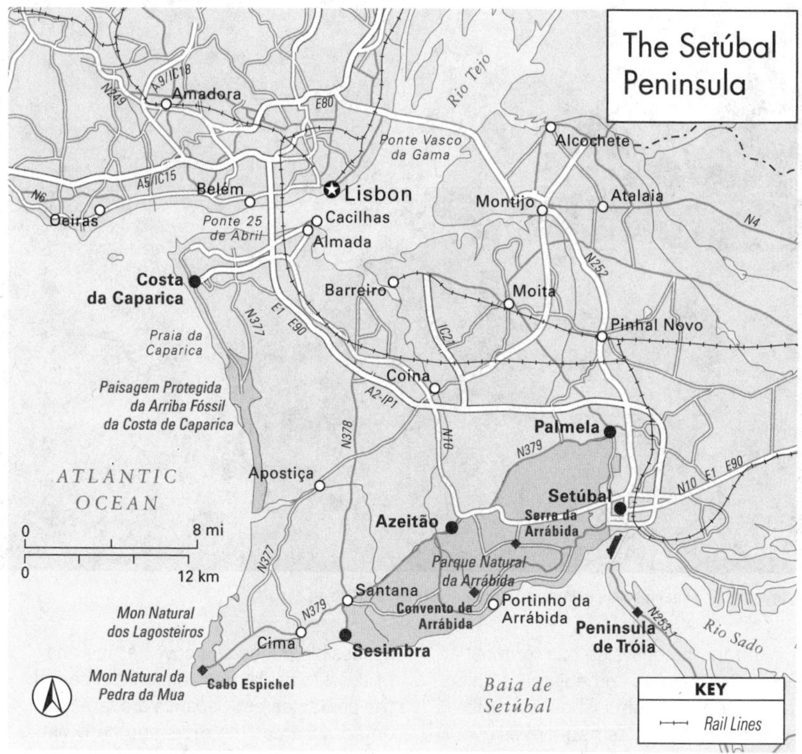

a cliff overlooking the ocean. The outdoor seating area has different seating areas tumbling down the cliff and shaded by pines and flowering cacti. **Known for:** gorgeous setting with stunning views; tasty margaritas and other cocktails; location on the outskirts of Azoia. *$ Average main: €13 ✉ Rua do Campo da Bola-Azoia, Azoia ☎ 219 292 523 ▭ No credit cards.*

Costa da Caparica

14 km (8½ miles) southwest of Lisbon

Costa da Caparica is a 20-km (12-mile) stretch of beach on the northwestern coast of the Setúbal Peninsula. White sand and a laid-back holiday vibe make it Lisbon's answer to the Algarve, and it's often packed with locals on summer weekends. The coastal strip centers on the lively resort of Caparica itself, at the north end of the beach, less than an hour from the capital.

GETTING HERE AND AROUND

Costa da Caparica is served by several TST bus lines that will get you to and from Lisbon; the speediest and most frequent is the 161 from Praça Areeiro. Alternatively, hop on the ferry to Cacilhas and take the express 135 to Caparica town. Several other lines (106, 124, 125, 126, and 127) make stops at at beaches including Fonte da Telha. The drive from Lisbon takes around 25 minutes. Take the minor N377, a slower, more scenic route than the main IC20 route (off the A2/IP1).

Buses to Caparica (45 minutes) depart from the TST terminal at Lisbon's Praça de Espanha, traveling over the 25 de Abril bridge. Regular buses to Caparica also

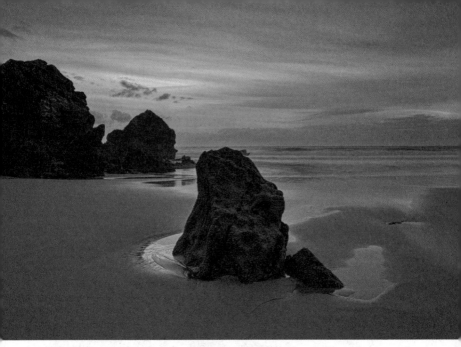

A breathtaking beach scene in Portugal's Parque Natural de Sintra-Cascais.

leave from the quayside bus terminal at Cacilhas, the town immediately across the Tagus River from Lisbon. Departures on both routes are as frequent as every 15 minutes in summer, but can still be very crowded.

From June through September, a small narrow-gauge train departs from Caparica and travels along an 8-km (5-mile) coastal route, making stops along the way; a one-way ticket to the end of the line costs €3.

Beaches

Costa da Caparica Beach

BEACH—SIGHT | FAMILY | When Lisboetas want to go to the beach, more often than not their preferred spot is the Costa da Caparica, which is packed in summer. Formerly a fishing village, the town itself is rather lacking in charm these days, but the beachfront is lively with cafés and bars catering to a relaxed, sandy-footed clientele. You may be able to avoid the crowds by heading south toward the less accessible dunes and coves at the end of the peninsula, Each beach is different: the areas nearest Caparica are family oriented, whereas the more southerly ones tend to attract a younger crowd (there are some nudist beaches, too). **Amenities:** food and drink; lifeguards; parking (fee); showers; toilets; water sports. **Best for:** partiers; sunset; swimming; walking. ✉ *Costa da Caparica.*

★ Praia da Cova do Vapor

BEACH—SIGHT | FAMILY | Still under the radar even among locals, Cova do Vapor is a fishing hamlet perched at the point where the river Tagus meets the Atlantic Ocean. The soft-sand beach is Caparica's closest point to Lisbon, and there are glorious views over the city's domes and towers, but its rustic beach shacks and hand-constructed wooden playground make Cova do Vapor Beach feel like another world. While crowds of surfers pack most of the Costa, there are still vast swaths of space on the sands and gentle dunes here. **Amenities:** food and drink; parking (no fee). **Best for:** solitude;

swimming; walking. ✉ *Praia da Cova do Vapor.*

Restaurants

Borda d'Água
$$ | **ECLECTIC** | This restaurant—a glassed-in wooden cabana built in the sand dunes—has a laid-back beach vibe with colorful pillows, swinging hammocks, and weathered wooden tables. The menu is strong on daily fish specials. **Known for:** caipirinhas and other beachy beverages; sand-in-your-shoes atmosphere; vegetarian and vegan dishes. *Average main: €18* ✉ *Praia da Morena* ☎ *212 975 213* *www.bordadagua.com.pt* *Closed Dec.–mid-Jan.*

Princesa
$$ | **SEAFOOD** | **FAMILY** | Charge your camera: this is one of the most picturesque spots for a meal anywhere in the region. A vast outdoor space is filled with sun loungers and comfy chairs, so you can relax with a sangria and enjoy views across Fonte de Telha Beach as you browse the menu of simple-yet-tasty salads, seafood, and grilled fish. **Known for:** good caipirinhas; spectacular sunset views; family-friendly ambience. *Average main: €17* ✉ *Estrada das Praias* ☎ *No dinner Oct.–May.*

★ **Sentido do Mar**
$$ | **ASIAN FUSION** | This highly regarded sushi spot has sea views, speedy service, and a bright, modern interior with lots of colorful mosaics. Grab a table on the esplanade to dine with the sea breeze in your hair and magical sunsets over the crashing waves just steps away. **Known for:** superfresh fish; excellent sushi and ceviche; tasty cocktails. *Average main: €18* ✉ *Rua Muralha da Praia 7, Praia do Norte* ☎.

Hotels

Aldeia dos Capuchos Golf & Spa
$$ | **HOTEL** | **FAMILY** | This luxury resort stands above Costa da Caparica beach in a verdant spot away from the crowds that throng the sands. **Pros:** beautiful location away from the day-trippers; excellent fitness center and spa; Portuguese and Mediterranean fare. **Cons:** rooms aren't very well soundproofed; furniture too large for smaller rooms; decor feels a little dated. *Rooms from: €145* ✉ *Largo Aldeia dos Capuchos* ☎ *212 909 010* *www.aldeiadoscapuchos.pt* *180 rooms* *Free Breakfast.*

Palmela

38 km (24 miles) southeast of Lisbon.

The small town of Palmela lies in the center of a prosperous wine-growing area, and every September the community holds a good-natured Festa das Vindimas (Grape Harvest Festival) which draws inhabitants from their whitewashed houses onto the cobbled streets. The village is dominated by the remains of a 12th-century castle that was captured from the Moors and enlarged by successive kings. In the 15th century the monastery and church of Sant'Iago were built within the castle walls. The structures were damaged in the 1755 earthquake and lay abandoned for many years. After extensive restoration, a pousada was opened in the monastic buildings. From this height, on a clear day, you can see Lisbon.

GETTING HERE AND AROUND

Public transportation to Palmela includes TST bus routes that take you from Lisbon and Setúbal and Fertagus trains from Lisbon. Driving will take 10 minutes from Setúbal or Azeitão and 30 minutes from Lisbon.

BUS CONTACTS Palmela Bus Station. ✉ *Rua Dona Maria 13* ☎ *707 508 509.*

VISITOR INFORMATION

CONTACTS Palmela Town Hall. ✉ *Largo do Município* ☎ *212 336 600.*

Restaurants

Chateau Cafe

$ | PORTUGUESE | FAMILY | With sweeping views over the nearby hills, this unassuming café has affable owners who serve up simple meals. If you want something more filling than the usual soups and sandwiches, there are also steaks and pasta dishes. **Known for:** views of a whitewashed church; inexpensive set lunches; excellent coffee. *Average main: €7* ✉ *Alameda D.Nuno Alvares Pereira 2* ☎ *212 333 208* *No credit cards.*

Hotels

★ **Pousada Castelo Palmela**

$$ | B&B/INN | Originally a medieval fortress and later a monastery, this pousada makes full use of the colonnaded walkways of the old cloisters, which now make an atmospheric setting for breakfasts with views of the nearby hills. **Pros:** rooms with soaring ceilings and shuttered windows; beautifully restored main building; pretty cobblestone patio. **Cons:** some rooms need updating; no swimming pool or spa; feels like a chain. *Rooms from: €145* ✉ *Castelo de Palmela* ☎ *212 351 226* *www.pousadas.pt* *28 rooms* *Free Breakfast.*

Shopping

Espaço Fortuna

LOCAL SPECIALTIES | Down the road from Palmela is a wonderful little shop selling hand-painted ceramics and azulejos. On the top floor is a café with an outdoor terrace, which is a great place to take a coffee break and savor some local sweets. ✉ *Quinta do Anjo, Estrada Nacional 379* ☎ *212 871 068* *www.espacofortuna.com.*

Setúbal

10 km (6 miles) south of Palmela, 50 km (31 miles) southeast of Lisbon.

A colorful sister city to polished, cosmopolitan Lisbon, Setúbal lacks the tourist hordes of the capital but has plenty to offer the visitor. Along with its famous fresh fish and seafood—notably *choco frito* (fried cuttlefish)—the city has a lively cultural scene and is the starting point for dolphin-spotting trips out into the Sado Estuary.

At the mouth of the Sado River, Setúbal is the country's third-largest port and one of its oldest cities. A significant industrial town in Roman times, it became one again during Portugal's Age of Discovery and took off during the 19th century. The center remains an attractive blend of medieval and modern, and you could spend a day here strolling cobbled pedestrian streets that open onto pretty café-lined squares and lingering in sites like the handsome Igreja de Jesus. Start at the tourist office, which is built atop Roman ruins discovered during a construction project; inside, you'll be standing above and peering down through the glass floor into a 5th-century fish-processing room. Near the port, an agreeable clutter of boats and warehouses is fronted by gardens, where you can stock up for a picnic at a huge indoor fish-and-produce market (Tuesday–Sunday 7–2).

GETTING HERE AND AROUND

Setúbal can be reached by bus from Lisbon and most other cities on the peninsula. It's also the last stop of the Fertagus train, which has an hourly departure from Lisbon. The drive from Lisbon takes 35 minutes, and it's 10 minutes from Palmela or Azeitão.

BUS CONTACTS Setúbal Bus Station. ✉ *Av. 5 de Outubro 44* ☎ *265 525 051.*

VISITOR INFORMATION

CONTACTS Setúbal Centro de Promoção Turística. (*Setúbal Tourist Information Center*) ✉ *Casa da Baía, Av. Luísa Todi 468* ☎ *265 545 010.*

Sights

★ **Convento de Santa Maria da Arrábida** (*Convent of Saint Mary*)
RELIGIOUS SITE | This rather ramshackle 16th-century monastery is built into the hills of the Serra da Arrábida. The glorious views take in the white sandy beaches and turquoise waters of the coast. Tours, which must be booked in advance, take place on Wednesday, Saturday, and Sunday. ✉ *Setúbal* ☎ *212 197 620* 🎟 *€5.*

Igreja de Jesus (*Church of Jesus*)
RELIGIOUS SITE | This 15th-century Church of Jesus, perhaps Portugal's earliest example of Manueline architecture, was built with local marble and later tiled with simple but affecting 17th-century azulejos. The architect was Diogo de Boitaca, whose work here predates his contribution to Lisbon's Mosteiro dos Jerónimos (Jerónimos Monastery). Six extraordinary twisted pillars support the vault; climb the narrow stairs to the balcony for a closer look at the details, which would soon become the very hallmark of Manueline style. Outside, you can still admire the original, although badly worn, main doorway and deplore the addition of a concrete expanse that makes the church square look like a roller-skating rink. The church's original monastic buildings and Gothic cloister—on Rua Balneário Paula Borba—house the **Museu de Setúbal,** a museum with a fascinating collection of 15th- and 16th-century Portuguese paintings, several by the so-called Master of Setúbal. Other attractions include azulejos, local archaeological finds, and a coin collection. ✉ *Praça Miguel Bombarda* ☎ *265 537 890* 🌐 *www.patrimoniocultural.gov.pt/pt/museus-e-monumentos/rede-portuguesa/m/museu-de-setubal-convento-de-jesus* 🎟 *Free (€1 suggested donation)* ⏲ *Closed Mon.*

★ **Parque Natural da Arrábida** (*Arrábida Nature Reserve*)
NATURE PRESERVE | Occupying the entire southern coast of the Setúbal Peninsula is the Parque Natural da Arrábida, dominated by the Serra da Arrábida—a 5,000-foot-high mountain range whose wild crags fall steeply to the sea. There's profuse plant life at these heights, particularly in spring, when the rocks are carpeted with wildflowers. The park is distinguished by a rich geological heritage and numerous species of butterflies, birds, and mammals (you might spot foxes and mongoose, and wild boar have occasionally been spotted). The park is a favorite destination for bikers, hikers, horseback riders, and adventure-sports enthusiasts. There are also some lovely hidden beaches for those prepared to put in the footwork. ✉ *Setúbal.*

★ **Portinho da Arrábida**
TOWN | This small fishing village is a popular destination for Lisboetas, who appreciate the good local beaches, which are famous for their wonderfully clear blue-green waters and white sands that create a dramatic contrast with the green, pine-covered hills. Due to the high number of visitors, cars are banned mid-June to mid-September, but free buses run here from Setúbal to Portinho da Arrábida and other picturesque beaches. Parking can be difficult even outside peak season. ✉ *N10.*

Restaurants

★ **Casa da Baía**
$ | **PORTUGUESE** | **FAMILY** | In an eye-catching blue-and-white building that also houses the tourist information center and a small museum, the Casa da Baía serves cakes and pastries from around the region. You place your order at a small deli (well stocked with Moscatel

and Peninsula de Setúbal wines) and then take a seat in the dining room or head out to a vast terrace complete with comfy deck chairs. **Known for:** affordable set lunches; delicious local products; live music on weekends. *Average main: €11 Av. Luísa Todi 468 265 545 010.*

El Toro

$ | **SPANISH** | This pretty little hacienda is run by Spaniard Alfonso Vasquez and his Portuguese wife, Zélia Marques, who prepares all the food herself in the open kitchen. Outside is an enclosed terrace draped in flowering vines, while inside is a colorful dining room with handsome tiles and original art. **Known for:** excellent paellas and other regional dishes from Spain; generous portions of traditional dishes; tasty homemade liqueurs. *Average main: €13 Rua António José Batista 111–115 restauranteeltoro.wordpress.com Closed Tues. and Wed.*

Rebarca

$ | **SEAFOOD** | **FAMILY** | At the east end of Avenida Luisa Todi, Rebarca is the best of the line of casual restaurants serving inexpensive but delicious fresh seafood—including the titular fried cuttlefish (it's similar to a large, meaty fried squid). Wash everything down with a carafe of the house white wine, which always has a refreshingly light effervescence. **Known for:** the freshest catch of the day is proudly on display; grilled fish like sea bream straight from the market; good variety of regional wines. *Average main: €15 Av. Luisa Todi 70 265 221 309 Closed Tues.*

BOAT TOURS

★ Vertígem Azul

BOAT TOURS | **FAMILY** | The Sado Estuary is famous for its resident bottlenose dolphins, and Vertígem Azul is easily the best of the companies taking you out to see them in their natural habitat. Three-hour dolphin observation trips leave Setúbal at 9:30 and 2:30 every day. The company takes an eco-friendly approach to all its water-based activities, which also include bird-watching trips and sunset cruises accompanied by live music. *Rua Praia da Saúde 11 265 238 000 vertigemazul.com From €38.*

Peninsula de Tróia

20 mins from Setúbal by boat.

Across the estuary from Setúbal is the Peninsula de Tróia—a long spit of land blessed with clean water and fine beaches on both the Sado and the Atlantic side.

GETTING HERE AND AROUND

Car ferries and passenger catamarans to the peninsula run every 30–60 minutes (24 hours a day) from Setúbal's port and cost €7.20 (catamaran) and €5.20 (car ferry) per person. Catamaran passengers pay on the way to Tróia but the return journey is free.

CONTACTS Atlantic Ferries. *Doca do Comércio, Tróia www.atlanticferries.pt.*

★ Praia da Comporta

BEACH—SIGHT | Portugal's Alentejo coast is often overlooked by beachgoers in favor of the Algarve or the Lisbon coast, but this scenic, rural, culinarily rich region is home to some of the finest beaches in Europe. While some are difficult to access, others, such as the beautiful Praia da Comporta, are well equipped to cater for visitors. Here, snow-white sands are dotted with colorful sun loungers and straw-roofed beach huts selling cocktails as well as fresh seafood, and the clear, bright blue invites you to take a cooling dip. Although one of the busier beaches in the Alentejo, this is still quieter than the beaches of the Algarve, and there's plenty of elbow room even during the summer high season. **Amenities:** parking (no fee); toilets; food and drink; water sports. **Best for:** swimming; walking. ✉ *Rua Otelo Saraiva de Carvalho, Tróia.*

Activities

Troia Golf

GOLF | What Robert Trent Jones had in mind when he laid out Troia back in 1981 is sometimes hard to figure out. Built on a peninsula close to the sea, the course has a strategic layout requiring a great deal of thought and first-class shot making, but it might create too much of a test for the average player to find totally enjoyable. Nevertheless, it's ranked highly in several lists of the best courses in Europe. A lot of sand, maritime pines, and flora make for a very beautiful setting. The course is accessible by ferry from Setúbal, which is a much shorter journey than by road around the Sado Estuary. A handicap certificate is required. ✉ *Complexo Turistico de Troia, Carvalhal* ☎ 🌐 *www.troiagolf.com* 🎫 *From €85 weekdays, €102 weekends* 🏌 *18 holes, 6911 yds, par 72* ✍ *Reservations essential.*

Azeitão

14 km (8½ miles) west of Setúbal.

The region around the small town of Azeitão, on the western side of the Serra da Arrábida, retains a disproportionately large number of fine manor houses and palaces. In earlier times, many of the country's noblemen maintained country estates here, deep in the heart of a wealthy wine-making region. Wines made here by the José Maria da Fonseca Company are some of the most popular in the country (and one of Portugal's major exports); the best known is the fortified dessert wine called Moscatel de Setúbal.

GETTING HERE AND AROUND

Azeitão can be reached by the TST buses, from Lisbon, Setúbal, Palmela, and Sesimbra. Driving from Palmela or Setúbal takes 10 to 15 minutes. From Lisbon it will be a 35-minute drive.

Sights

★ **José Maria da Fonseca Company**

WINERY/DISTILLERY | For a close look at the wine business, seek out the manor house and cellars of the José Maria da Fonseca Company. The intriguing tours talk about the long history of the winery and allow you to see all stages of production, including a peek into its dark and mysterious prized Moscatel cellars, where 200-plus-year-old bottles are still aging gracefully. The tour takes 20 to 40 minutes and ends in a shop where select products can be tasted and purchased. ✉ *Rua José Augusto Coelho 11–13* ☎ *212 198 940* 🌐 *www.jmf.pt* 🎫 *€5.*

Praça da República

PLAZA | This pretty square is anchored by the 16th-century Palácio de Tavora (Tavora Palace), which is not open to the public but has an interesting history. In the 18th century, the Marquês de Pombal accused the Duke of Aveiro, who owned the palace, of collaborating in the assassination plot against the king. Subsequently the duke was executed by the marquês, and the Tavora coat of arms was erased from the Sala das Armas in Sintra's National Palace. ✉ *Praça da República.*

Quinta da Bacalhôa

GARDEN | The jewel in the crown of this late-16th-century mansion is its box-hedged garden and striking azulejo-lined paths. Visitors can tours the building, gardens, and wine cellars (advance bookings are advised). Among the highlights are three pyramidal towers, including the so-called Casa do Fresco, which houses the country's oldest azulejo panel. Dating to 1565, it depicts the story of Susannah and the Elders. Scattered elsewhere are Moorish-influenced panels, fragrant groves of fruit trees, and enough restful spots to while away an afternoon. ✉ *N1, 4 km (2½ miles) east of Vila Nogueira de Azeitão* ☎ *212 198 060* 🌐 *www.bacalhoa.pt/enoturismo* 🎫 *€8.*

Coffee and Quick Bites

★ Fábrica De Tortas Azeitonense

$ | PORTUGUESE | FAMILY | When in town, sweet-toothed visitors should be sure to sample the local specialty called *tortas de Azeitão*: little sweet sponge cakes filled with an egg-and-cinnamon custard. Stop by this locally famous café to savor some pastries along with a Portuguese coffee or Moscatel wine, with the option to buy a box to enjoy later. **Known for:** local specialty desserts; wine and cheese; coffee. 💲 *Average main: €8* ✉ *Rua de S. Gonçalo 438* ☎ *212 190 418* 🌐 *www.tortasdeazeitao.com* 💳 *No credit cards.*

Shopping

Azulejos de Azeitão

CRAFTS | Stop here if you're eager to get your hands on some of those distinctive Portuguese tiles. The company uses traditional methods to paint and glaze each of the tiles sold in the shop. Many of the designs for sale originated the 16th to the 19th centuries. You can even try your hand at painting your own tile. ✉ *Rua dos Trabalhadores da Empresa Setubalense 15* ☎ *212 180 013* 🌐 *www.azulejosdeazeitao.com.*

Mercado do Azeitão

MARKET | Vila Nogueira de Azeitão's agricultural traditions are trumpeted on the first Sunday of every month, when a country market is held near the center of town. Apart from the locally produced wine, you can buy several kinds of local cheeses with an *amanteigado* (butterlike) texture. Slice the top rind off and spoon it on hunks of fresh bread from one of the market's bakery stalls. ✉ *R. de Frederico Franco de Paiva 26.*

Sesimbra

40 km (25 miles) south of Lisbon, 30 km (18 miles) southwest of Setúbal.

Sesimbra, a lively fishing village surrounded by mountains and isolated bays and coves, is a popular day trip for Lisboetas. And, despite high-rise apartments that now mar the approaches to the town, its surviving narrow, central streets reflect a traditional past. Moreover, the long beach is lovely, if a little crowded in high summer, and the calm waters are perfect for swimming (the coveted Blue Flag has been raised here since 2016). The waterfront is guarded by a 17th-century fortress and overlooked by outdoor restaurants serving fresh fish. A short walk along the coast to the west takes you to the main port, littered with nets, anchors, and coils of rope and packed with fishing boats—which unload their catches at entertaining auctions. You can also take a 40-minute walk to the hilltop remains of a Moorish castle northwest of town—the grounds have jaw-dropping views over the sea, beaches, and surrounding Serra da Arrábida.

GETTING HERE AND AROUND

Sesimbra can be reached by the TST buses from several locations in the Setúbal Peninsula, including Setúbal, Azeitão, and Cacilhas. Bus 207 will take you to and from Lisbon, or take the more frequent 203 from Cacilhas. The driving time from Lisbon and Setúbal is 40 minutes. Coming from Azeitão will take 20 minutes.

CONTACTS Sesimbra Bus Station. ✉ *Av. da Liberdade 49A* ☎ *707 508 509* 🌐 *www.tsuldotejo.pt.*

VISITOR INFORMATION

CONTACTS Sesimbra Tourist Office. ✉ *Forteleza do Santiago, Rua da Forteleza* ☎ *212 288 540* 🌐 *visitsesimbra.pt.*

Sights

Cabo Espichel

LOCAL INTEREST | This salt-encrusted headland—crowned by a whitewashed convent surrounded by 18th-century pilgrim rest houses—is the southwestern point of the Setúbal Peninsula, marked by a red-and-white lighthouse. It's a ruggedly beautiful spot, where the cliffs rise hundreds of feet out of the stormy Atlantic. To the north, unsullied beaches extend as far as Caparica, with only local roads and footpaths connecting them. It's a good spot for hiking, with marked trails leading down to some clearly visible dinosaur footprints. ✉ *Cabo Espichel* ☎ *800 500 270* 🌐 *www.visitsesimbra.pt/to-visit/62/santu-rio-do-cabo-espichel.*

★ **Castelo de Sesimbra**

CASTLE/PALACE | **FAMILY** | Sitting high above the city is the Castelo de Sesimbra, which was conquered in 1165 by Dom Afonso Henriques but fell back into the hands of the Moors until 1200. The castle lost importance and fell into disrepair during the next several hundred years until Dom João IV ordered that it be adapted for the use of artillery in 1648. Classified as a National Monument, reconstruction was done to restore it to its previous glory after the great earthquake of 1755. From Sesimbra, a steep marked walking trail leads up the side of the pine-covered hill to the castle grounds. Aside from the incredible views of the ocean and the city below, there is a chapel, a small museum, and a café with an outdoor patio where you can enjoy a *bagaço* (a clear Portuguese liquor) as the sun goes down. ✉ *Rua Nossa Senhora do Castelo 11* ☎ *212 680 746* 🌐 *www.museusesimbra.pt.*

Beaches

Praia do Ribeiro do Cavalo

BEACH—SIGHT | Dubbed "the most Thai beach in Portugal," the wild, hard-to-reach Ribeiro do Cavalo has dazzling white sands and crystal-clear water in several shades of turquoise. Curiously formed rocks jutting out of the water are encircled by all manner of colorful fish, so bring your snorkel gear. Until recently a genuine hidden treasure, the beach is now well known among beach lovers. During the summer, regular boat services speed sunseekers to and from the beach and Praia do Ouro in Sesimbra (a 5–10-minute ride), but for the rest of the year it can only be reached by private boat, kayak, or by a half-hour walk/scramble along a very rough track. Look out for the purple markings on the rocks that indicate which way to go. **Amenities:** none. **Best for:** snorkeling; swimming. ✉ *Praia do Ribeiro do Cavalo* ✣ *Follow the main road from Sesimbra, west past Praia do Ouro. Drive or walk and keep a close eye out for the sign for the beach. From here it's a steep clamber downhill. Wear sneakers (not flip-flops) and watch your step.*

Restaurants

★ **Café Filipe**

$$ | **SEAFOOD** | Set back from a lively town square overlooking the ocean, Café Filipe entices seafood lovers with its glass displays of enormous fish and colorful crustaceans. Take a seat in the bright dining room or out on the terrace to make the best of those sea views. **Known for:** freshly caught fish cooked on charcoal grill; seafront location in the very center of town; specialties like swordfish and soft-shell crab. [$] *Average main: €18* ✉ *Av. 25 de Abril* ☎ *212 231 653* 🌐 *www.restaurantefilipe.pt.*

★ **Praiamar**

$$ | **SEAFOOD** | **FAMILY** | Though not right on the ocean, this is an excellent option for for seafood lovers. The extensive menu offers a wide variety of mixed shellfish or grilled fish platters to share, including regional favorites like *sapateira recheada* (whole stuffed stone crab) and *lagosta* (spiny lobster). **Known for:** outdoor seating on a cobblestone street; informal atmosphere; knowledgable servers. $ *Average main: €20* ✉ *Rua Afonso Henriques 16* ☎ *212 234 176* 🌐 *www.praiamar.com.*

★ **Tasca do Isaias**

$ | **SEAFOOD** | The huge queues that form outside this tiny, family-run tavern are a testament to the fact that the fish served here is the best in town. The daily catch is written on a blackboard and cooked to perfection on a charcoal grill out on the flagstones. **Known for:** family-run business; lively local atmosphere; long queues and shared tables if it's busy. $ *Average main: €12* ✉ *Rua Coronel Barreto 2* ☎ ⊙ *Closed Sun.* 💳 *No credit cards.*

Hotels

Quinta do Miguel

$$ | **B&B/INN** | This secluded country estate in the small village of Aldeia do Meco—12 km (7 miles) northwest of Sesimbra—is perfect for a romantic getaway. **Pros:** minutes from one of the area's best beaches; breakfast delivered to your door each morning; private and peaceful setting. **Cons:** a car is a necessity; a bit difficult to find; too quiet for some. $ *Rooms from: €195* ✉ *Rua Do Casalinho, Aldeia do Meco* ☎ *212 684 607* 🌐 *www.quintadomiguel.com* *8 rooms* 🍽 *Free Breakfast.*

Sana Sesimbra Hotel

$$ | **HOTEL** | **FAMILY** | This modern hotel sits directly across from the beach but is still very close to excellent seafood restaurants, lively bars, and the town's major sights. **Pros:** rooftop pool and sundeck; excellent sea views; nice outdoor pool. **Cons:** extra charge for parking; rooms get outside noise; not all views are equal. $ *Rooms from: €160* ✉ *Av. 25 de Abril* ☎ *212 289 000* 🌐 *www.sesimbra.sanahotels.com* *103 rooms* 🍽 *Free Breakfast.*

Sesimbra Hotel & Spa

$$ | **HOTEL** | **FAMILY** | On a cliff overlooking the beach, this luxurious hotel is the only one in the area with a spa. **Pros:** great beachfront location with direct access; beautiful views of the shimmering water; lots of comfortable common areas. **Cons:** massive property can feel impersonal; 10-minute walk to the center of town; feels a little dated. $ *Rooms from: €180* ✉ *Praça da Califórnia* ☎ *212 289 800* 🌐 *www.sesimbrahotelspa.com* *100 rooms* 🍽 *No meals.*

Activities

Sesimbra, a deep-sea-fishing center, is renowned for the huge swordfish that are landed in the area. It's also a top spot for diving, hang gliding, and other adventurous pursuits. The tourist information office at the beachfront fortress can provide details and book lessons and excursions.

FISHING

Clube Naval de Sesimbra

FISHING | **FAMILY** | The Clube Naval de Sesimbra offers fishing trips, sailing lessons, kayaking expeditions, and other excursions on the water ✉ *Porto de Abrigo, Rua Clube Naval de Sesimbra, Edifício Sede* ☎ *212 233 451* 🌐 *www.naval-sesimbra.pt.*

SCUBA DIVING

Nautilus-Sub

DIVING/SNORKELING | **FAMILY** | This PADI-accredited school offers dives and courses at every level, including children's dive classes. ✉ *Porto de Abrigo 1* 🌐 *www.nautilus-sub.com.*

Chapter 5

ESTREMADURA AND THE RIBATEJO

Updated by
Alison Roberts

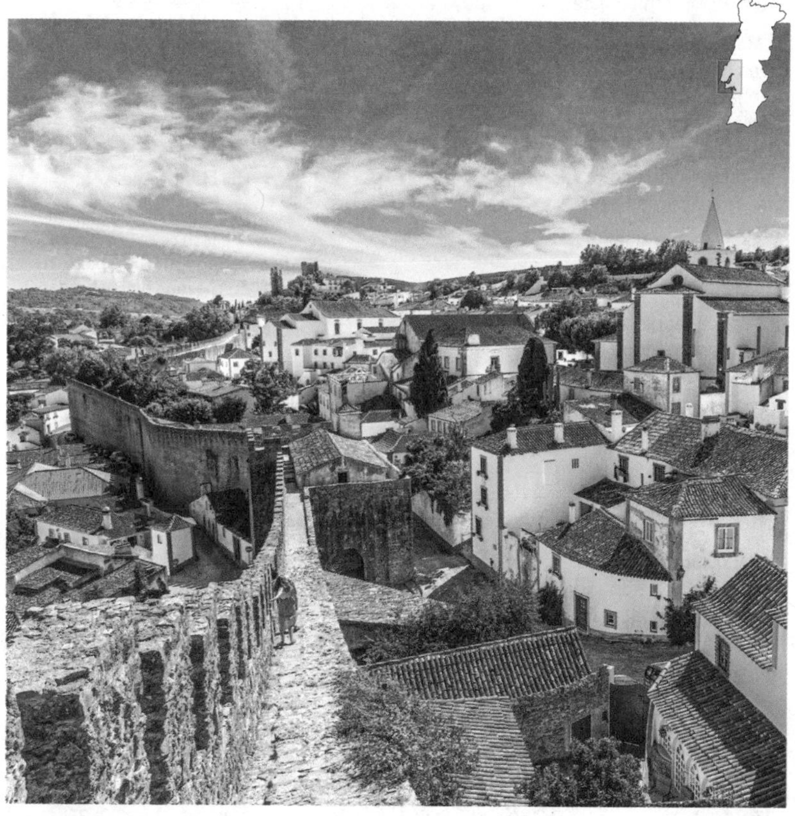

Sights ★★★★☆ | Restaurants ★★★☆☆ | Hotels ★★★☆☆ | Shopping ★★★☆☆ | Nightlife ★☆☆☆☆

WELCOME TO ESTREMADURA AND THE RIBATEJO

TOP REASONS TO GO

★ **Atlantic Coast beaches:** Forty unique beaches dot Estremadura's 100-km (60-mile) coastline, allowing for a variety of choices, including relaxing in the sun or sand, catching some waves, and watching the sunset.

★ **Medieval history:** Cities like Mafra, Tomar, Alcobaça, and Leiria boast medieval monasteries, castles, and royal palaces that provide an incredible view of times past.

★ **Seafood:** The fishing towns of Ericeira, Peniche, and Nazaré are some of the very best places in the country for seafood lovers.

★ **Beautiful countryside:** The landscape along the Tagus and Zêzere rivers is a perfect venue to experience the culture of the Portuguese countryside.

★ **Horseback riding:** The Ribatejo is home to the famous breed of Lusitano horses, used in dressage and bullfighting.

The sea is never far from sight in coast-hugging Estremadura, especially in fishing towns like Nazaré and Peniche. The same holds true for the lively town of Ericeira, where surfing also reigns supreme with its big waves. Coastal valleys witnessed many bloody battles between rival groups, including the Moors, but from them came extraordinary monasteries, such as the ones in Batalha and Alcobaça, built to celebrate Portuguese victories.

The Tagus River flows through the Ribatejo, where vast plains spread out from the riverbanks. The region is dotted with monuments and fortifications that emulate the country's religious history, from the impressive Convento do Cristo of the Knights Templar in Tomar, a UNESCO World Heritage Site, to the most famous pilgrimage site, the sanctuary in Fátima.

1 **Mafra.** One of the oldest towns in Portugal, Mafra has gorgeous architecture from the 18th century.

2 **Ericeira.** The popular seaside resort of Ericeira has wide, sandy beaches that make it popular with both sunbathers and surfers.

3 **Torres Vedras.** This town is best known for its extensive fortifications that were designed to protect the capital from invaders.

4 **Peniche.** Still a fishing village at heart, Peniche is one of the best places around to enjoy delicious fresh fish and seafood.

5 **Óbidos.** Step through the massive city gates and you'll feel like you've been transported to Portugal in the Middle Ages.

6 **Caldas da Rainha.** In the 15th century, Queen Leonor put this spa town on the map by bathing in its "malodorous waters."

7 **Nazaré.** This is the surf capital of the region—even the ancient Forte de São Miguel Arcanjo houses a surf museum.

8 **Alcobaça.** Set in a picturesque valley, Alcobaça is known for its impressive church and monastery.

9 **Batalha.** This quaint village is home to the imposing Mosteiro da Batalha, a UNESCO World Heritage Site.

10 **Leiria.** This otherwise workaday town is overlooked by a wonderfully elegant medieval castle.

11 Benavente. The heart of rural Ribatejo, Benavente is a gateway to the Reserva Natural do Estuário do Tejo.

12 Almeirim. This pretty town is surrounded by gorgeous vineyards and cork-oak forests.

13 Santarém. The "Gothic capital of Portugal," Santarém is blessed with dozens of churches, convents and other landmarks.

14 Constância. At the confluence of the Zêzere and the Tagus rivers, Constância sits near the island Castelo de Almourol.

15 Abrantes. The sweeping views of the entire valley from the top of this town's lofty castle are breathtaking.

16 Tomar. On both sides of the Rio Nabão, Tomar is home to the Convento do Cristo, a UNESCO World Heritage Site.

17 Fátima. This town on the western flanks of the Serra de Aire is an important Roman Catholic pilgrimage site.

Estremadura and the Ribatejo are the two historical provinces north and northeast of Lisbon. Estremadura, with its green rural valleys, is characterized by a mix of maritime activities and where old traditions combine harmoniously with modernity. Meanwhile, on the banks of the Tagus River, Ribatejo is a land of agriculture and livestock, known as a bastion of the famous Lusitano horse.

Water shapes the character of these two provinces. Estremadura stretches itself out along the coast, extending north from Lisbon to include the onetime royal residence of Leiria, 119 km (74 miles) from the capital. Closely tied to the sea, the narrow province is known for its fine beaches, coastal pine forests, and picturesque fishing villages. Some of these have evolved, for better or worse, into popular resorts. Fruits and vegetables grow in fertile coastal valleys, and livestock contentedly graze in rich pastures. But Estremadura hasn't always been so peaceful. During the Wars of Reconquest, which raged from the 8th through the 13th century, it was the scene of a series of bloody encounters between Christians and Moors. The province's name means "farthest from the Douro River," an indication of how far south of the Douro River the Christians had advanced against the Moors. In the aftermath of the wars, Portuguese sovereignty was secured with the defeat of the Spanish at Aljubarrota in 1385 and the turning back of Napoléon's forces in 1810 at Torres Vedras. The bloodshed left behind masterpieces of religious architecture—such as those at Alcobaça and Batalha—which commemorate Portuguese triumphs.

Over the centuries Romans, Visigoths, Moors, and Christians built and rebuilt various castles and fortifications to protect the strategic Tagus River (Rio Tejo). Fine examples of this are along the river at Belver, Abrantes, and Almourol. Spanning the banks of the Rio Nabão (a tributary of the Tagus), Tomar is dominated by the hilltop Convento de Cristo (Convent of Christ), built in the 12th century by the Knights Templar. In the brush-covered hills at the province's western edge lies Fátima, one of Christendom's most important pilgrimage sites. As it flows south approaching Lisbon, the Tagus expands, often overflowing its banks during the winter rains, and the landscape changes to one of rich meadows and pastures and broad, alluvial plains, where grains grow in abundance.

The Ribatejo region developed along both sides of the Tagus, and it is this waterway, born in the mountains of

Spain, that has shaped and sustained the province. In the north, inhabitants tend groves of olive and fig trees in a peaceful landscape that has changed little since Roman times. Ribatejans are said to be more reserved than their fellow Portuguese—that is, until they step into the arena to test their mettle against a ton or so of charging bull. This is bullfighting country, the heartland of one of Portugal's richest and most colorful traditions. On the vast plains along the east bank of the Tagus, you'll encounter men on horseback wearing the traditional waistcoats and stocking caps of their trade. These are *campinos*, the Portuguese "cowboys," who tend the herds of bulls and horses bred and trained for arenas throughout the country.

MAJOR REGIONS

Estremadura. The narrow province surrounding Lisbon and extending north along the coast for approximately 160 km (100 miles) is known as Estremadura, referring to the extreme southern border of the land the Portuguese reconquered from the Moors. This is primarily a rural region, characterized by coastal fishing villages and small farming communities that produce mostly fruit and olives. A tour through the region includes visits to towns with some of Portugal's most outstanding architectural treasures, including Mafra, Alcobaça, Óbidos, Tomar, and Batalha.

The Ribatejo. To the east of Estremadura, straddling both banks of the Tagus River, the Ribatejo is a placid, flat, fertile region known for its vegetables and vineyards. It's also famous for its horses and bulls; you may well see campinos in red waistcoats and green stocking caps moving bulls along with long wooden poles. As a consequence of its strategic location, the Ribatejo is home to a number of imposing castles as well as such diverse sights as the shrine at Fátima.

Planning

When to Go

To avoid the busloads of visitors who inundate major monuments and attractions during July and August, visit the popular ones such as Óbidos and Mafra in the early morning. This also helps to beat the oppressive summer heat, particularly inland. The best time of year for touring is in early spring and from mid-September until late October. The climate during this period is pleasant, and attractions and restaurants aren't crowded. If throngs of people don't bother you, time your visit to Fátima to coincide with May 13, when between 500,000 and 1 million pilgrims overwhelm this otherwise sleepy country town. Less spectacular pilgrimages take place year-round, but particularly on the 13th of the month June through October.

Getting Here and Around

AIR

Estremadura and the Ribatejo are served by Lisbon's Aeroporto Humberto Delgado, 7 km (4½ miles) north of the city.

No trains run directly between the airport and Estremadura and the Ribatejo, but you can catch trains to several towns in the region from Lisbon's Oriente or Santa Apolónia stations, or suburban Agualva-Cacém. Very few regional buses make stops at the airport; most start instead from Campo Grande station, a short taxi ride from the airport. If you are landing in Lisbon and traveling directly to this area, your best bet may be to rent a car.

BUS

There are few places in this region that aren't served by at least one bus daily. Express coaches run by national operator Rede Expressos travel regularly between Lisbon's Sete Rios bus stations and the larger towns such as Santarém, Leiria, and Abrantes, while various regional companies ply those routes and others, many of them from Campo Grande station in Lisbon. Companies serving this region include Barraqueiro Oeste, Boa Viagem, Mafrense, Rede Expressos, Ribatejana, Rodoviária do Oeste, and Rodoviária do Tejo.

BUS CONTACTS Barraqueiro Oeste. ☎ *261 334 150* 🌐 *www.barraqueiro-oeste.pt.* **Boa Viagem.** ☎ *263 730 530 information* 🌐 *www.boa-viagem.pt.* **Mafrense.** ☎ *261 816 152* 🌐 *www.mafrense.pt.* **Rede Expressos.** ☎ *707 223 344, 21 752 4524 for Sete Rios station in Lisbon* 🌐 *www.rede-expressos.pt.* **Ribatejana.** ☎ *263 730 503* 🌐 *www.ribatejana.pt.* **Rodoviária do Oeste.** ☎ *262 767 676* 🌐 *www.rodoviaria-dooeste.pt.* **Rodoviária do Tejo.** ☎ *249 787 878* 🌐 *www.rodotejo.pt.*

CAR

It's easy to reach Estremadura and the Ribatejo from Lisbon because both provinces begin as extensions of the city's northern suburbs. There are two principal access roads from the capital: the A1 (also called E80 and IP1), which is the Lisbon–Porto toll road, provides the best inland access. The A8 (also called IC1) is the fastest route to the coast. From Porto there's easy access via the A1.

The roads are generally good, and traffic is light except for weekend congestion along the coast. Parking can be a problem in some of the towns, but larger hotels don't usually charge for parking.

TRAIN

Travel by train within central Portugal isn't for people in a hurry. Service to many of the more remote destinations is infrequent—and in some cases nonexistent. Even major attractions such as Nazaré and Mafra have no direct rail links. Nevertheless, trains will take you to most of the strategic bases for touring the towns in this chapter. The main line between Lisbon (Santa Apolónia and Oriente stations) and Porto provides reasonably frequent service to Vila Franca de Xira, Santarém, Tomar, and Fátima. Towns in the western part of the region, such as Torres Vedras, Caldas da Rainha, Óbidos, and Leiria, are served on another line to Figueira da Foz from Lisbon's Santa Apolónia station, via Entrecampos and Agualva-Cacém (which is also a stop on the Sintra line that runs from Lisbon's Rossio station).

TRAIN CONTACTS CP. ☎ *707 201 220* 🌐 *www.cp.pt.*

Restaurants

In Estremadura restaurants, the emphasis is on fish, including the ubiquitous *bacalhau* (dried salt cod) and *caldeirada* (a hearty fish stew). The seaside resorts of Ericeira, Nazaré, and Peniche are famous for lobster. In Santarém and other spots along the Tagus River, an *açorda* (bread soup) made with *sável,* a river fish also known as shad, is popular, as are *enguias* (eels) prepared in a variety of ways. Pork is a key component in Ribatejo dishes, and roast lamb and kid are widely enjoyed. Perhaps the result of a sweets-making tradition developed by nuns in the region's once-numerous convents, dessert menus abound with colorful-sounding—although often cloyingly sweet and eggy—dishes such as *queijinhos do céu* (little cheeses from heaven). The straw-color white wines from the Ribatejo district of Bucelas are among the country's finest.

Between mid-June and mid-September, reservations are advised at upscale restaurants. Most moderate or inexpensive establishments, however, don't accept reservations. They also have informal dining rooms, where you may occasionally find yourself sharing a table with other diners. Dress is casual at all but the most luxurious places.

Hotels

Estremadura has plenty of good-quality lodgings, especially along the coast; the Ribatejo is less well endowed. In summer, you definitely need reservations, especially if you're heading to Óbidos and Ourém to stay in one of the beautiful *pousadas* (inns inside historic structures).

Restaurant and hotel reviews have been shortened. For full information, visit Fodors.com. Restaurant prices are per person for a main course at dinner. Hotel prices are for a standard double room, including tax, in high season (off-season rates may be lower).

WHAT IT COSTS In Euros			
$	$$	$$$	$$$$
RESTAURANTS			
under €16	€16–€20	€21–€25	over €25
HOTELS			
under €140	€141–€200	€201–€260	over €260

Tours

ORIENTATION TOURS

Few regularly scheduled sightseeing tours originate within the region, but many of the major attractions are covered by a wide selection of half-day, full-day, or short package tours from Lisbon. Most tour companies can also organzine made-to-measure group tours.

Carristur

BUS TOURS | Carristur offers a full-day Fátima, Óbidos, Batalha, and Nazaré tour from Lisbon, departing Praça do Comércio at 9:30 am Monday, Wednesday, and Friday. ☎ *218 503 225* 🌐 *www.yellowbustours.com* 🎫 *€70.*

Cityrama Gray Line Portugal

BUS TOURS | This well-regarded company offers a half-day trip to Óbidos for €35, as well as a full-day Fátima tour that includes Óbidos, Batalha, Alcobaça, and Nazaré for €72. ✉ *Parque Eduardo VII, Praça Marquês de Pombal, Marquês de Pombal* ☎ *213 522 594* 🌐 *www.cityrama.pt.*

Dianatours

BUS TOURS | For Fátima, Dianatours has a €40 half-day trip departing from Lisbon's Campo Grande, daily at 9 am between March and October. Full-day Óbidos, Nazaré, and Fátima tours are another option. ☎ *217 998 540* 🌐 *www.dianatours.pt.*

Have a Wine Day

SPECIAL-INTEREST | For private half- and full-day tours, with or without a visit to or more one of the region's charming wineries, there's Lisbon-based Have a Wine Day. ☎ *916 470 995* 🌐 *www.en.haveawineday.com.*

Inside Lisbon

BUS TOURS | Inside Lisbon does small group tours to Fátima, Óbidos, and sights in between for €75. ☎ *968 412 612* 🌐 *www.insidelisbon.com.*

Rota Monumental

BUS TOURS | Rota Monumental offers a €70 full-day tour taking in Fátima, Nazaré, Óbidos, and Batalha. ☎ *916 306 682* 🌐 *www.en.rotamonumental.com.*

Visitor Information

CONTACTS Centro Regional Tourist Board. ☎ *232 432 032* 🌐 *www.centerofportugal.com.*

Mafra

40 km (35 miles) northwest of Lisbon, 11 km (7 miles) southeast of Ericeira.

The town of Mafra is one of the oldest in Portugal, with evidence of prehistoric

Great Itineraries

Three days will give you a sense of the region, five days will allow you to include a visit to the shrine at Fátima and the Convent of Christ, and a full week will give you enough time to cover the major attractions as well as explore the countryside. With additional days you can easily extend your itinerary to include Évora and the Alentejo or head north to Coimbra and the Beiras. It's best to explore these regions by car, unless you have a great deal of time and patience: trains don't serve many of the most interesting towns, and bus travel is slow.

If You Have 3 Days

Start with a visit to the imposing monastery and palace at **Mafra**, then head for the coast, with a stop at the resort and fishing village of **Ericeira.** Continue north along the shore to **Peniche**, with its imposing fortress. Head inland to spend the night in the enchanting walled city of **Óbidos.** The next morning continue north, stopping at ceramics shops in **Caldas da Rainha.** En route to **Nazaré**, tour the church and cloister at **Alcobaça.** On your third day head inland to the soaring, multispired monastery church in **Batalha.** Return to Lisbon.

If You Have 5 Days

Follow the three-day itinerary to **Batalha**, and then continue north to **Leiria** and its hilltop castle. Take N113 east to the A1 and drive down to **Fátima**, one of Christendom's most renowned destinations. The next morning, continue east on N113 to **Tomar**, an attractive town dominated by its hilltop convent. Later in the day, follow N110 south and then take N358-2, a scenic road that follows the Rio Zêzere, to its union with the Rio Tejo. Just west of their confluence, on an island in the Tejo, is the **Castelo de Almourol**, one of Portugal's finest castles. From here, follow N118 southwest along the Tejo, stopping in **Alpiarça** to visit the Casa dos Patudos, a large country house containing the art collection of its former owner, and in **Almeirim** to see the winery at the Quinta da Alorna. Spend the night in **Santarém**, an important farming and livestock center with many fine sights. The next day return to Lisbon with a drive along the Tejo on N118 through the region of marshy plains known as the Lezíria.

settlements and remains of Roman and later Moorish occupation. However, it only came to the attention of the wider world with the construction, from 1717 to 1755, of the vast baroque and neoclassical palace and monastery complex that dominates the town to this day.

GETTING HERE AND AROUND

From Lisbon's Campo Grande station, it can take as little as 35 minutes by Mafrense bus to reach Mafra. Most services continue on to Ericeira.

BUS CONTACTS Mafra Bus Station. ✉ *Parque Intermodal, Rua Santa Casa da Misericórdia, Mafra* ☎ *261 105 254* 🌐 *www.mafrense.pt.*

Sights

Palácio Nacional de Mafra (*Mafra National Palace*)
CASTLE/PALACE | Over the centuries the crown, church, and nobility have contested the ownership of the Mafra National Palace and Convent, 8 km (5 miles)

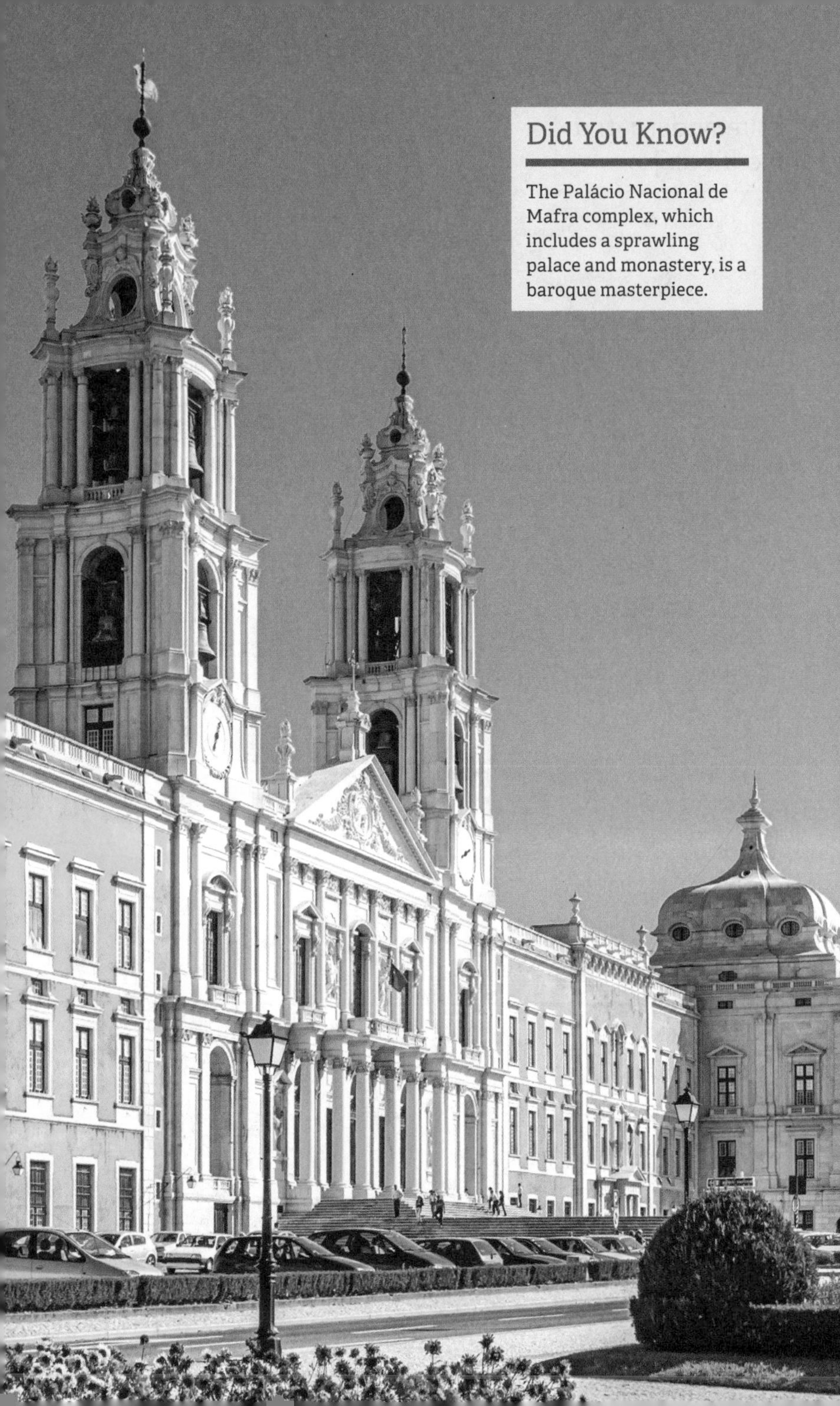

Did You Know?

The Palácio Nacional de Mafra complex, which includes a sprawling palace and monastery, is a baroque masterpiece.

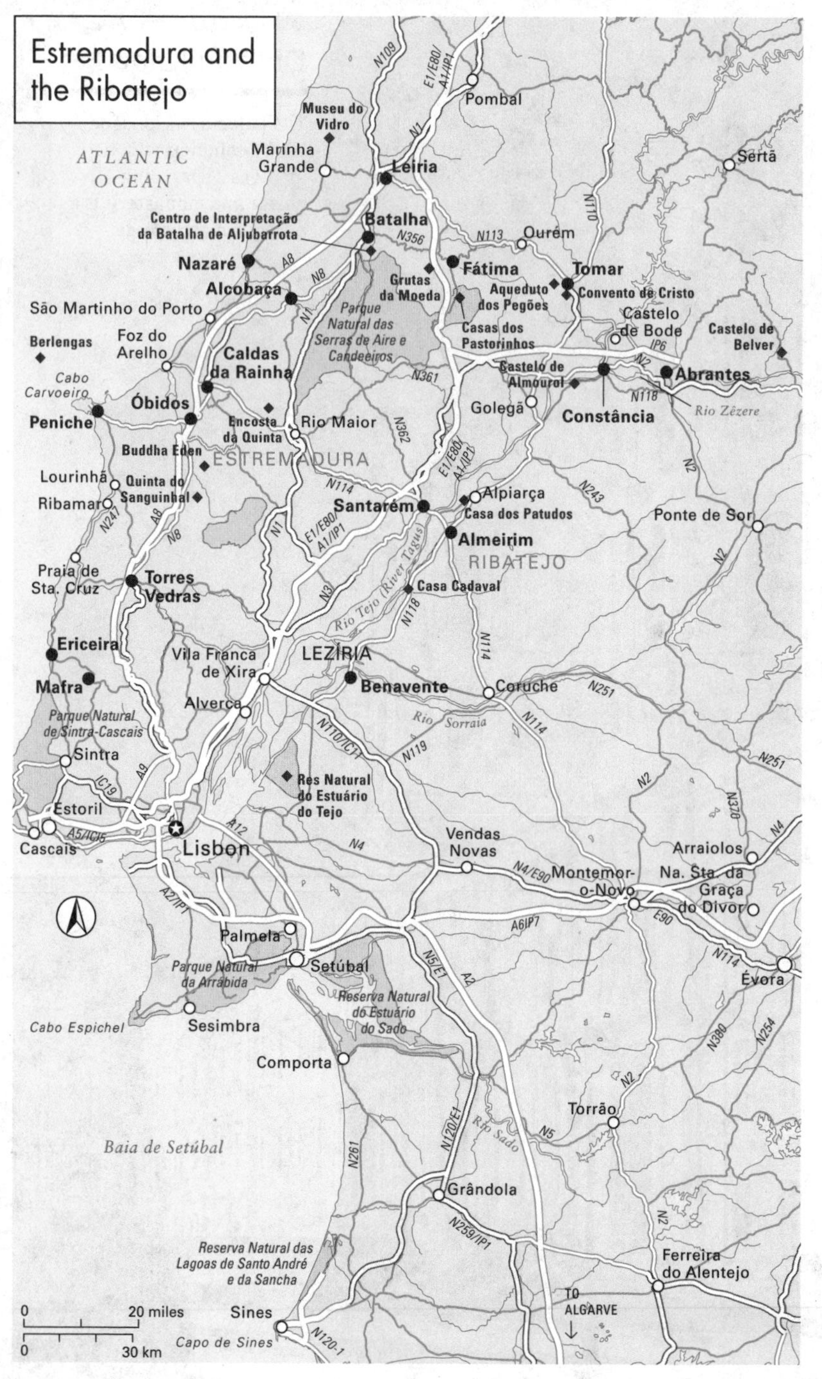
Estremadura and the Ribatejo
ATLANTIC OCEAN
Pombal
Museu do Vidro
Marinha Grande
Leiria
Sertã
Centro de Interpretação da Batalha de Aljubarrota
Batalha
Ourém
Nazaré
Fátima
Tomar
Alcobaça
Grutas da Moeda
Aqueduto dos Pegões
Convento de Cristo
São Martinho do Porto
Parque Natural das Serras de Aire e Candeeiros
Casas dos Pastorinhos
Castelo de Bode
Castelo de Belver
Berlengas
Foz do Arelho
Caldas da Rainha
Castelo de Almourol
Abrantes
Cabo Carvoeiro
Óbidos
Golegã
Constância
Rio Zêzere
Peniche
Encosta da Quinta
Rio Maior
Buddha Eden
ESTREMADURA
Lourinhã
Quinta do Sanguinhal
Ribamar
Alpiarça
Santarém
Casa dos Patudos
Ponte de Sor
Almeirim
RIBATEJO
Praia de Sta. Cruz
Torres Vedras
Casa Cadaval
Rio Tejo (River Tagus)
Ericeira
Vila Franca de Xira
LEZÍRIA
Mafra
Benavente
Coruche
Alverca
Rio Sorraia
Parque Natural de Sintra-Cascais
Sintra
Res Natural do Estuário do Tejo
Estoril
Cascais
Lisbon
Vendas Novas
Arraiolos
Montemor-o-Novo
Na. Sta. da Graça do Divor
Palmela
Setúbal
Évora
Parque Natural da Arrábida
Reserva Natural do Estuário do Sado
Cabo Espichel
Sesimbra
Comporta
Torrão
Rio Sado
Baia de Setúbal
Grândola
Reserva Natural das Lagoas de Santo André e da Sancha
Ferreira do Alentejo
TO ALGARVE
Sines
Capo de Sines
0 20 miles
0 30 km
N109
E1/E80/A1/IP1
N1
N110
N356
N113
A8
N8
IP6
N2
N361
N118
N362
E1/E80/A1/IP1
N114
N243
N247
N3
N251
N110/IC11
N119
A9
IC19
A5/IC15
A12
N4
N370
N4/E90
A2/IP1
A6/IP7
E90
N5/E1
A2
N380
N254
N5
N120/E1
N261
N259/IP1
N120-1

southeast of Ericeira. From the 17th through 19th centuries this was a favorite residence for the Portuguese court. In 1711, after nearly three years of a childless union with his Hapsburg queen, Maria Anna, a despairing King João V vowed that should the queen bear him an heir, he would build a monastery dedicated to St. Anthony. In December of that same year, a girl—later to become queen of Spain—was born; João's eventual heir, José I, was born three years later. True to his word, King João V built an enormous monastery, which still looms above the small farming community of Mafra. The original project—entrusted to the Italian-trained German architect Johann Friedrich Ludwig, invariably known in Portugal as João Frederico Ludovice—was to be a modest facility that could house 13 friars. Construction began in 1717 and continued until 1755, with the final result being a rectangular complex containing a monastery large enough for hundreds of monks as well as an imposing basilica and a grandiose palace that has been compared to El Escorial outside Madrid, Spain. The numbers involved in the construction are mind-boggling: at times 50,000 workers toiled. There are 4,500 doors and windows, 300 cells, 880 halls and rooms, and 154 stairways. Perimeter walls that total some 19 km (12 miles) surround the park.

The highlight of any visit to the monument is the magnificent baroque library: the barrel-vaulted, two-tiered hall holds almost 40,000 volumes of mostly 16th- through 18th-century works and a number of ancient maps. Protection from insects is provided by bats, which slip into the room at night through tiny holes that were bored through stone under the windows for the purpose. The basilica contains 11 chapels and six organs—used simultaneously for splendid concerts at 4 pm on the first Sunday of every month except January and February—and was patterned after St. Peter's in the Vatican. When you're in the gilded throne room, notice the life-size renditions of the seven virtues, as well as the impressive figure of Hercules, by Domingos Sequeira. Guided visits may be booked in advance at an additional cost of €6 per person.

✉ *Terreiro de Dom João V, Mafra* ☎ *261 817 550* 🌐 *www.palaciomafra.pt* 🎫 *€6, organ concerts €3* ⏲ *Closed Tues.*

Ericeira

11 km (7 miles) northwest of Mafra.

Ericeira, an old fishing town tucked into the rocky coast, is a popular seaside resort. Its core fans out from the sheer cliff, beneath which boats are hauled up onto a small, sheltered beach. Along the waterfront are a number of traditional seafood restaurants that are popular with both locals and visitors. Either end of the town has good sand for sunbathing; the south end is preferred by surfers, but about 2 km (1¼ miles) north of Ericeira is Ribeira d'Ilhas, one of Portugal's best surfing beaches. In 2009, Ericeira was declared Europe's first World Surfing Reserve by a global campaign to protect such destinations; there are some fascinating multimedia displays about the reserve upstairs in the tourist office.

Perched atop the cliffs, the town's historic center is a beautiful place to walk around and explore, as it has completely maintained the traditional Portuguese coastal architecture that was popular in the 17th and 18th centuries when the fishing village really thrived. The buildings are all sandblasted white and framed with deep sea blues. The main fishing port in the center is also where the Portuguese royal family departed to exile in 1910 after the Republic was declared, not to return for a couple of generations.

GETTING HERE AND AROUND

There are several daily bus lines between Ericeira, Mafra, and Lisbon run by Mafrense. Driving from Lisbon is close to 45 minutes, and getting to Ericeira from Mafra takes 15 minutes.

BUS CONTACTS Ericeira Bus Station. ✉ *Rua dos Bombeiros Voluntários* ☎ *261 862 717 for Mafrense* 🌐 *www.mafrense.pt.*

ESSENTIALS

VISITOR INFORMATION Ericeira Tourist Office. ✉ *Rua Eduardo Burnay 46* ☎ *261 863 122* 🌐 *www.cm-mafra.pt/en/tourism.*

Beaches

Ribeira d'Ilhas

BEACH—SIGHT | One of Europe's best beaches for surfing—pretty much any time of year—Ribeira d'Ilhas regularly hosts national and world championships. When the surf is up on weekends, expect a crowd. There's a large, modern restaurant where you can grab a bite. The beach is 2 km (1¼ miles) north of Ericeira, set in a picturesque gorge amid tall cane. **Amenities:** food and drink; parking; toilets; water sports. **Best for:** partiers; sunset; surfing. ✉ *Off N247.*

Restaurants

★ Esplanada Furnas

$$$ | **SEAFOOD** | Perched on rocks overlooking the open ocean, on the site of a former shellfish nursery, this fashionable restaurant offers some of the best seafood in the area. As you'd expect, the day's menu depends on the sea's bounty, but it might have *salmonete* (red mullet), *pregado* (turbot), *robalo* (sea bass), or *linguado* (sole). **Known for:** the place has its own own vinho verde; more formal feel during the week; family-friendly atmosphere;. 💲 *Average main: €25* ✉ *Rua das Furnas 2* ☎ *261 864 870* 🌐 *www.restaurantefurnasericeira.com.*

Gabriel

$ | **SEAFOOD** | This family-run restaurant opposite the Vila Galé draws a crowd for its fresh seafood and fish—the latter grilled over charcoal by the owner. The two dozen seats in the original dining room weren't nearly enough space, so the place added a second dining room that's decorated in smart beach-house style. **Known for:** outside of summer, usually open only for lunch; gets crowded, so book ahead; terrace dining. 💲 *Average main: €10* ✉ *Praça dos Navegantes* ☎ *261 863 349* ⏲ *Closed Wed. and Nov. No dinner Tues. No dinner Oct.–May.*

Mar à Vista

$$ | **SEAFOOD** | This Portuguese fisherman's tavern has a genuine feel—fishing nets and baskets hang from walls, and the loud service adds to its character. Seafood is the only option, but it is renowned here—such as spider crab or rock lobster—and many diners come for the *feijoada de marisco*—(shellfish and bean stew). **Known for:** atmosphere feels like the real deal; delicious lemon sorbet for dessert; rich cup of coffee. 💲 *Average main: €19* ✉ *Rua Santo António 16* ☎ *261 862 928* 🌐 *marisqueira-mar-a-vista.negocio.site* ▬ *No credit cards* ⏲ *Closed Wed., 2 wks in May, and 2 wks in Sept.*

Viveiros do Atlântico

$$$ | **SEAFOOD** | Live seafood crawling around in an aquarium shaped like a blue-and-white fisherman's boat gives you an idea of what you'll find on the menu. Pick out the fish or shellfish of your choice to be prepared especially for you, such as a *sapateira recheada* (stuffed crab) brought to the table in its shell. **Known for:** try the cataplanas (mixed seafood served in a copper steamer); fantastic ocean views from all but a few tables; good value. 💲 *Average main: €21* ✉ *N247 Km 46.5, Ribamar* ☎ *261 860 300* 🌐 *www.viveiros-atlantico.com* ⏲ *Closed Mon., and Tues. Oct.–Apr. Closed 2 wks in Nov.*

Hotels

Hotel Pedro O Pescador
$ | **HOTEL** | If you prefer your hotels to have an intimate feel, then you'll love this family-run place a stone's throw from the beach. **Pros:** breakfast is in a large, sunny room; be sure to visit the lively bar; free Wi-Fi and other amenities. **Cons:** parking can be difficult; noisy in the summer; no phone in rooms. *Rooms from: €79* ✉ *Rua Dr. Eduardo Burnay 22* ☎ *261 869 121* 🌐 *www.hotelpedropescador.com* *25 rooms* *Free Breakfast.*

Hotel Vila Galé Ericeira
$$ | **HOTEL** | **FAMILY** | This renowned luxury hotel overlooks the ocean, and a little over half of the rooms have beautiful stone terraces with eye-popping views. **Pros:** prow-shape terrace bar overlooks the sea; playground and other amenities for families; excellent value given the amenities. **Cons:** can get crowded in the summer; some decor is a little dated; not a lot of local charm. *Rooms from: €180* ✉ *Largo dos Navegantes* ☎ *261 869 910* 🌐 *www.vilagale.com* *205 rooms* *Free Breakfast.*

Activities

SURFING

Pure Ocean
WATER SPORTS | This long-established surf school at Ribeira d'Ilhas beach promises to coach everyone from beginners to experts, from €35 per person. ✉ *Praia Ribeira d'Ilhas* ☎ *916 011 111* 🌐 *pocean.pt.*

Torres Vedras

20 km (12 miles) northeast of Ericeira.

A bustling commercial center crowned with the ruins of a medieval castle, Torres Vedras is best known for its extensive fortifications—a system of trenches and fortresses erected by the Duke of Wellington in 1810 as part of a secret plan for the defense of Lisbon. It was here, at the Lines of Torres Vedras, that the surprised French army under Napoléon's Marshal Masséna was routed. You can see reconstructed remnants of the fortifications on a hill above town and throughout the area. The surrounding hills and countryside make for a picturesque drive to one of the several beaches on the coast at and around Santa Cruz, 20 to 30 minutes away.

GETTING HERE AND AROUND

Torres Vedras can be reached from Lisbon by bus (Mafrense, Boa Viagem, Rede Expressos, and local operator Barraqueiro Oeste). Trains from Lisbon run on the regional line from Santa Apolónia or Entrecampos stations via Agualva-Cacém (on the Sintra line) that terminates in Figueira da Foz. Driving from Lisbon takes 30 minutes, from Mafra 20 minutes.

BUS CONTACTS Torres Vedras Bus Station. ✉ *Rua do Parque Regional de Exposições-Expotorres* ☎ *261 334 150* 🌐 *www.barraqueiro-oeste.pt.*

ESSENTIALS

VISITOR INFORMATION Praia de Santa Cruz Tourist Office. ✉ *Rua da Azenha, Silveira, Santa Cruz* ☎ *261 937 524.* **Torres Vedras Tourist Office.** ✉ *Edifício Paços do Concelho, Largo do Município* ☎ *261 310 483.*

Sights

Castelo de Torres Vedras (*Torres Vedras Castle*)
CASTLE/PALACE | Built in the 12th century, this hilltop medieval castle has been reinforced and reconstructed several times throughout the centuries, with the last repairs done in the 1980s. The cement recovered from the cisterns and various coins on display in the municipal museum in town attest to the presence of the Roman occupation here. The castle exhibits both Gothic and Manueline styles in its exterior walls, and a medieval

Bird's-eye city views are visible from the towers of the hilltop Castelo de Torres Vedras.

cemetery once existed where the church of Santa Maria stands. While exploring the towers, don't miss out on the incredible views of the city and surrounding valley and hills. ✉ *Largo Coronel Morais Sarmento* 🎟 *Free* 🕓 *Closed Mon.*

Dino Parque (*Dino Park*)
AMUSEMENT PARK/WATER PARK | FAMILY | Lourinhã, a small town about halfway between Torres Vedras and Peniche, claims the title "Land of the Dinosaurs" because of the rich paleontological finds made in the area's sea cliffs. Since 2018, Lourinhã has been home to the Dino Park, Portugal's largest outdoor museum and a fun attraction for families with kids. Along with 180 life-size models of different species—including several discovered locally and named after the town—there are impressive fossil displays and labs where you can take a closer look at tools and techniques used by paleontologists. ✉ *Rua Vale dos Dinossauros 25 , Abelheira, Lourinhã* ☎ *261 243 160* 🌐 *www.dinoparque.pt* 🎟 *€13.*

Forte de São Vicente (*St. Vincent's Fort*)
MILITARY SITE | On a hill just north of the city, Forte de São Vicente was the first of 152 redoubts built on the Duke of Wellington's orders to form three defensive lines between the Atlantic Ocean and the Tagus, to protect Lisbon from possible invasion by French troops. Since 2017, it has housed a small visitor center for these Lines of Torres Vedras, with fascinating displays such as a model of the system used to communicate between forts. ✉ *Rua Forte São Vicente* ☎ *261 310 483* 🌐 *www.rhlt.pt* 🎟 *€2. Free Sun.* 🕓 *Closed Mon.*

Museu Municipal Leonel Trindade (*Leonel Trindade Municipal Museum*)
MUSEUM | In the 16th-century Convento de Graça, the Municipal Museum has exhibits about the city's historical fortifications, as well as interesting archaeological finds from the castle grounds and all over the region. Audio guides to the city and to the Lines of Torres Vedras are available. ✉ *Convento de Nossa Senhora*

da Graça, Praça 25 de Abril ☎ 261 310 485 🎫 €2. Free Sun. ⊗ Closed Mon.

Beaches

Praia da Areia Branca

BEACH—SIGHT | About 24 km (18 miles) northwest of Torres Vedras, is a broad, light sweep of sand backed by a small settlement with plenty of places to eat and drink. But if you want to get away from it all, there are cliff-top trails that are lovely for hiking. The waves here are suitable both for beginner and advanced surfers. **Amenities:** food and drink; lifeguards; parking (no fee); showers; toilets; water sports. **Best for:** sunset; surfing; swimming; walking. ✉ *Alameda do Golfinho, Lourinhã.*

Praia da Mexilhoeira

BEACH—SIGHT | Hedged in by rocky cliffs topped with the greenest of vegetation, this is one of the region's prettiest beaches. The strand is fairly narrow at high tide, but it rarely gets very crowded because it is served only by a simple café. Access to the beach is via a wooden walkway. The beach is signposted off the N247 north of Santa Cruz, where the beaches are broader but busier. **Amenities:** food and drink; lifeguards; parking (no fee). **Best for:** solitude; sunset; surfing; walking. ✉ *Off N247, Póvoa de Penafirme.*

Restaurants

Foz

$ | **PORTUGUESE** | This bustling restaurant is one of several overlooking the Praia da Areia Branca, the area's prettiest beach, but stands out in terms of its view (due to its elevated position) and the quality of its food, above all the expertly grilled fish. If you want something more elaborate, try the *polvo panado* (battered octopus, served with bean rice), bacalhau *com broa* (with a cornbread gratin), or monkfish rice. **Known for:** servings usually large enough for two; ultrasweet traditional desserts; famous local brandy. $ *Average main: €12* ✉ *Passeio do Mar, Praia da Areia Branco, Lourinhã* ☎ *261 469 348* ⊗ *Closed Mon. Sept.–June. Closed 1st half of Nov.*

Trás d'Orelha

$ | **PORTUGUESE** | Long considered the area's best traditional restaurant, Trás d'Orelha moved to a new location south of the city center without losing its rustic decor or its hearty fare. Among the best dishes are the *burras de porco preto* (slow-cooked cheek from the Iberian black pig), and *cabidela* (chicken cooked in its own blood). **Known for:** delicious desserts include pêra borrachona, or "drunken" pear; meals here are usually big enough for two; in winter try the famous figs in brandy. $ *Average main: €13* ✉ *Rua Cruz de Barro 2, Barro* ✣ *Off N8* ☎ *261 326 018* 🌐 *www.trasdorelha.com* ⊗ *Closed Mon., and 2 wks in Sept. No dinner Sun.*

Hotels

★ **Areias do Seixo**

$$$$ | **RESORT** | Set among the pine trees in front of Mexilhoeira Beach, this small and stylish eco-conscious hotel, 20 minutes from Torres Vedras, was built with a desire to harmoniously integrate it with its surroundings. **Pros:** spa with sauna, steam room, and treatment rooms; heated outdoor pool is a great place to relax; free bicycles for exploring the area. **Cons:** beach is a 10-minute walk and doesn't have a lifeguard; families with kids have limited room options; rates are pricey. $ *Rooms from: €350* ✉ *Praceta Do Atlântico, Mexilhoeira, Póvoa de Penafirme* ☎ *261 936 340* 🌐 *www.areiasdoseixo.com* ⊗ *Closed 2 wks in Nov. and all Dec.* 🛏 *14 rooms, 16 villas* 🍴 *Free Breakfast.*

Ô Hotel Golf Mar

$ | **HOTEL** | **FAMILY** | The idyllic location—on a rise overlooking an absolutely breathtaking view of the ocean, the nearby cliffs, and a lush green valley—is by far the best thing about this hotel near the town of Lourinhã, 16 km (10 miles) northwest of Torres Vedras. **Pros:** staff can arrange for surfing and kitesurfing lessons; beach doesn't get too crowded in the summer; abundant activities for children. **Cons:** interior decor is a bit underwhelming; only superior rooms have a/c; despite its name, the full-size golf course has closed. *Rooms from: €105* *Praia do Porto Novo, Maceira* *261 980 800* *www.hotelgolfmarvimeiro.pt* *234 rooms* *Free Breakfast.*

Stay Hotel Torres Vedras

$ | HOTEL | This bright, cheerfully appointed hotel—part of a small national chain—sits on a pretty downtown plaza. **Pros:** perfect location in city center; laid-back atmosphere; good value. **Cons:** city noise invades some rooms; parking facility is a block away; chain-hotel feel. *Rooms from: €65* *Praça 25 de Abril 17* *261 314 232* *www.stayhotels.pt* *47 rooms* *No meals.*

SPAS

Termas do Vimeiro

FITNESS/HEALTH CLUBS | One of only a few Portuguese thermal centers that welcomes travelers, the Termas do Vimeiro boasts waters with reputed therapeutic properties to tackle respiratory, digestive, circulatory, and skin problems. A wide range of nonmedical wellness treatments are also offered. *Fonte dos Frades, Rua Joaquim Belchior, Maceira* *261 984 484* *www.termasdeportugal.pt.*

Peniche

32 km (20 miles) northwest of Torres Vedras.

In the lee of a rocky peninsula, Peniche is a major fishing-and-canning port that's also a popular summer resort. There are several beaches to choose from in the area as well as the beaches and fishing of the Berlengas archipelago, available to visit in the summer months. Besides Peniche being a major fishing port, locals and tourists know that this is one of the best places around to enjoy delicious fresh fish and seafood, especially sardines. Fans of lace will also want to track down fine examples in local shops of Peniche *renda de bilros*—a traditional craft that is now showcased in a well-appointed museum.

GETTING HERE AND AROUND

Peniche can be reached from Lisbon by express buses run by Rede Expressos and regional operator Rodoviária do Tejo, which along with sister company Rodoviária do Oeste links it with other towns across Estremadura and the Ribatejo. Incoming buses stop first downtown (near the market) before continuing on to the out-of-town terminal; for outgoing Rede Expressos buses you may not board downtown unless you already have a ticket. Driving to Peniche takes 50 minutes from Lisbon, 15 minutes from Óbidos.

BUS CONTACTS Peniche Bus Station. *Rua Dr. Ernesto Moreira* *968 903 861* *rodoviariadooeste.pt.*

ESSENTIALS

VISITOR INFORMATION Peniche Tourist Office. *Rua Alexandre Herculano* *262 789 571* *www.cm-peniche.pt.*

Berlengas

ISLAND | The harbor at Peniche is the jumping-off point for excursions to the Berlenga Archipelago: six islets that are a nesting place for many migratory birds and a favorite spot for anglers and divers. Berlenga Grande, the largest of the group, is the site of a pretty lighthouse and the Forte de São João Baptista, a 17th-century fort built to defend the area from pirates. There are trails around the island, including through caves. You can visit the islands by boat from June to

September, and you can camp overnight or even stay in the fortress if you book ahead. The island has a restaurant and bar, a small guesthouse, and a visitor center. ✉ *Marina de Peniche, Ribeira Velha 2* 🌐 *www.berlengas.eu* 🎫 *From €22.50 round-trip* ⏲ *Closed Oct.–May.*

Fortaleza de Peniche (*Peniche Fort*)
MILITARY SITE | The busy harbor of Peniche is watched over by this sprawling 16th-century fort. During Portugal's dictatorship, which ended in 1974, it was a prison for opponents of the regime, which is why the National Museum of Resistance and Freedom is set to open here in 2020. In the meantime you should be able to tour the former cells and take in temporary exhibits, as well as seeing a memorial inscribed with prisoners' names. There are also some beautiful views of the ocean from its towers. ✉ *Campo da República 609* ☎ *914 145 103* 🌐 *www.museunacionalresistencialiberdade-peniche.gov.pt* 🎫 *Free* ⏲ *Closed Mon. and Tues.*

Igreja de São Leonardo (*Church of Saint Leonard*)
RELIGIOUS SITE | One of the area's most interesting churches is the Church of Saint Leonard in Atouguia da Baleia, a 10-minute drive inland. Dating back to the 12th century, it features Romanesque, Gothic, and Manueline architectural elements, and a ceiling depicting scenes from the Old Testament. ✉ *Largo de São Leonardo, Atouguia da Baleia* ⏲ *Closed weekends.*

Museu das Rendas de Bilros (*Bobbin Lace Museum*)
MUSEUM | One of Peniche's traditional products is *renda de bilros* (bobbin lace)—not a surprise in a port city where making and repairing nets has long been an essential skill. This small but well-organized museum displays every imaginable item relating to the craft—from antique tools to elaborately decorated cushions and draperies—with texts and other explanatory materials in English. The skill is very much alive, with some 100 local craftspeople involved in teaching enthusiasts young and old. Every July, the town hosts an international showcase attended by representatives from 30 countries. ✉ *Rua Nossa Senhora da Conceição 1* ☎ *262 249 538* ⏲ *Closed Mon.*

Peniche Sportagua
WATER SPORTS | **FAMILY** | Open from July to September, this large water-park complex delights with slides and separate pools for adults and children. There's a restaurant and snack bar on-site. ✉ *Av. Monsenhor Manuel Bastos de sousa* ☎ *262 789 125* 🌐 *www.sportagua.com* 🎫 *€12.50.*

Beaches

Praia do Baleal (*Baleal Beach*)
BEACH—SIGHT | This beach on a natural island that's now an artificially created peninsula has long been a surfer hangout thanks to its great waves—it's home to a well-reputed surf school. But Baleal Beach is also popular with families who lounge about under rented umbrellas. Note that there are rocks in the water in some parts of the beach. **Amenities:** food and drink; lifeguards; parking (no fee); showers; toilets; water sports. **Best for:** partiers; sunset; surfing; swimming; windsurfing. ✉ *Av. da Praia, Baleal.*

Restaurants

★ **Tasca do Joel**
$ | **PORTUGUESE** | **FAMILY** | Tucked away on a side street far from the touristy seafront, this tavern attracts diners from far and wide with delicious fresh fish and meat dishes cooked in its wood-burning oven. There are changing daily specials, but regular dishes include bacalhau *à tasca* (fried codfish with onions and potatoes), rice-stuffed cuttlefish, and baked pumpkin risotto. **Known for:** there's also a kids' menu with simpler fare; there are more than 1,000 wines on offer; meet other

diners at the long tables. *Average main: €15* *Rua do Lapadusso 73* *262 782 945* *www.tascadojoel.pt* *Closed Mon. and 2 wks in May–June. No dinner Sun.*

Hotels

MH Atlântico Golfe

$ | **HOTEL** | **FAMILY** | Great for golfers but also anyone who loves waking up to a view, this hotel features balconies (some of them huge) that overlook the links and the long beach at Praia da Consolação. **Pros:** beachfront location perfect for sun lovers; playground and other facilities for kids; bikes for exploring the waterfront. **Cons:** far from bars and restaurants; feels a little impersonal; restaurant is buffet only. *Rooms from: €95* *Complexo Turístico do Botado, Praia da Consolação, Atouguia da Baleia* *262 757 700* *www.mh-hotels.pt* *117 rooms* *Free Breakfast.*

Star Inn Peniche

$ | **HOTEL** | The nicest thing about this modern hotel is that only a street and some sand dunes separate it from the Cova da Alfarroba Beach in the middle of Peniche Bay. Shaped like an L, the hotel has rooms with terraces overlooking the swimming pool or the ocean. **Pros:** not too far from the beach; sea views from upper floors; spacious rooms. **Cons:** far from shops and restaurants; next to a busy thoroughfare; most rooms have twin beds. *Rooms from: €132* *Estrada do Baleal* *262 780 400* *www.hotelstarinn.com/peniche* *102 rooms* *Free Breakfast.*

Activities

BOATING

Viamar

The largest local boat company, Viamar operates round-trips to the Berlengas Archipelago on the 185-seat *Cabo Avelar Pessoa* every day from June through September (from €20). The sea is often rough: hence the rows of buckets under the seats. *Largo da Ribeira Velha 2* *262 785 646* *www.viamar-berlenga.com.*

WATER SPORTS

The clear waters and bizarre rock formations along Estremadura's coast make it a favorite with anglers, snorkelers, and scuba divers. A wet suit is recommended for diving and snorkeling, as the chilly waters don't invite you to linger long, even in summer.

Haliotis

SCUBA DIVING | This outfitter offers diving (from €110) and snorkeling trips (from €60) as well as dolphin watching around the Berlengas Archipelago. *Casal Ponte , Atouguia da Baleia* *262 781 160,* *www.haliotis.pt.*

Óbidos

20 km (12 miles) east of Peniche.

As you enter town through the massive, arched gates of Óbidos, it seems as if you've been transported to Portugal in the Middle Ages, when the fortress was taken by Portugal from the Moors. The narrow Rua Direita, lined with boutiques and white, flower-bedecked houses, runs from the gates to the foot of the castle: you may want to shop for ceramics and clothing on this street. The rest of the medieval-era village is crisscrossed by a labyrinth of stone footpaths, tiny squares, and decaying stairways. Each nook and cranny offers its own reward. Cars aren't permitted inside the walls except to unload luggage at hotels. Parking is provided outside town.

Away from the walled town, two pleasant marked walks enable you to see some rural history and Roman ruins or visit a bird observatory, respectively. It's a 1-km (½-mile) trek from the city gate through farmlands, a grove of poplar trees, and along the Arnoia River to the

Eburobritium Roman ruins (established 1 BC to AD 5), where you can see ancient baths and a forum. Another walk is out to the free Lagoa de Óbidos observatories, from where you can spy aquatic birds and birds of prey. Maps of Óbidos are available at the tourist office in the parking lot at the gate into the city wall.

Once a strategic seaport, Óbidos is now high and dry—and 10 km (6 miles) inland—owing to the silting of its harbor. On the approach to town, you can see bastions and crenellated walls standing like sentinels over the now-peaceful valley of the Ria Arnoia. It's hard to imagine fishing boats and trading vessels docking in places that are today filled by cottages and fields.

GETTING HERE AND AROUND

Óbidos can be reached by bus (Rede Expressos and regional operator Rodoviária do Oeste) from Lisbon. The regional train line from Lisbon's Santa Apolónia and Entrecampos stations (via Agualva-Cacém on the Sintra line) and Figueira da Foz stops in Óbidos as well. Driving from Lisbon takes 40 minutes, and coming from Peniche takes 15 minutes.

ESSENTIALS

VISITOR INFORMATION Óbidos Tourist Office. ✉ *Largo de São Pedro, Rua da Porta da Vila, outside town walls, at entrance to parking lot* ☎ *262 959 231* 🌐 *www.obidos.pt.*

Sights

Buddha Eden

GARDEN | Just about the last thing you'd expect to find in rural Estremadura—about 10 minutes south of Óbidos—this landscaped "Garden of Peace" was inspired by the destruction in 2001 by the Afghanistan Taliban of the giant Buddhas of Bamiyan—one of which is reproduced here. Buddhas of various shapes and sizes dot the lawns and surrounding forest, as well as carved gates, dragons, and hundreds of figures from China's ancient Terracotta Army. There are also sculptures by leading contemporary artists. It all makes for a lovely place to stroll (you can also opt for the hop-on, hop-off miniature train). There's an eatery serving decent Portuguese food and a shop selling wines from the adjoining Quinta dos Loridos estate. ✉ *Quinta dos Loridos, off the A8, Bombarral* ☎ *262 605 240* 🌐 *www.bacalhoa.pt/enoturismo/bacalhoa-buddha-eden* 🎫 *€5.*

★ **Castelo de Óbidos** (*Óbidos Castle*)

CASTLE/PALACE | The outer walls of the fine medieval castle enclose the entire town, and it's great fun to walk their circumference, viewing the town and countryside from above. Extensively restored after suffering severe damage in the 1755 earthquake, the multitower complex has both Arabic and Manueline elements. Most of the keep is now a pousada. ✉ *Óbidos.*

Igreja de Santa Maria (*Church of Saint Mary*)

RELIGIOUS SITE | The 17th-century artist Josefa de Óbidos came to the town as a small child and lived here until her death in 1684. You can see some of her work in the azulejo-lined Church of Saint Mary, which was a Visigoth temple in the 8th century. The church is in a square off Rua Direita. Next door is a small, charming museum dedicated to the work of local artist and theater designer Abílio de Mattos e Silva. ✉ *Praça de Santa Maria.*

Quinta do Sanguinhal

WINERY/DISTILLERY | This family-owned winemaker, founded in the late 19th century, is one of the companies best prepared to receive visitors, with regular tours throughout the week (make sure to book in advance). You'll take in not only the winepresses and cellars but a magnificent antique distillery where *aguardentes* are still made. The tasting features seven wines, and you may also combine it with lunch. The place is south of Óbidos, not far from Buddha Eden.

Óbidos's Fun Festivals

Festival de Chocolate Like a real-life Willy Wonka chocolate factory but even bigger, the outdoor feast that is the annual Festival de Chocolate attracts more than 200,000 people to Óbidos in March and April. There are tons of things to do and see, like an annual chocolate sculpture contest done by locally renowned chefs. Along with the many stands selling all kinds of delicious chocolate goodies, many local restaurants offer chocolate-theme menus. ✉ *Óbidos* 🌐 *www.festivalchocolate.cm-obidos.pt* 🎫 €5.

Festival Internacional Literário de Óbidos Also known as "Fólio," the International Literature Festival was launched as part of a broader initiative to establish Óbidos as a *vila literária* (literary town). The focus was at first on Portuguese-language writers, but organizers have branched out with guests such as Salman Rushdie and Donald Ray Pollock. This annual event is scheduled for late September or October. ✉ *Óbidos* ☎ *262 955 500* 🌐 *www.foliofestival.com* 🎫 *Free.*

Mercado Medieval Every July and August, the Mercado Medieval enlivens the town over two long weekends. There's a parade of people in medieval costumes each day around the city walls. To buy some of the typical products of the region—ceramics, cheeses, hams, and flowers—exchange your euros for replica *torreões* (the first coins struck in Portugal). Battles and court scenes are dramatized daily, and music animates the market until midnight. As for a meal, consider a hunk of the wild boar roasted on a spit. ✉ *Óbidos* 🌐 *www.mercadomedievalobidos.pt* 🎫 €7.

Óbidos Vila Natal All through December, the Óbidos Christmas Village is the perfect miniature winter wonderland for children. There's usually ice-skating, an ice slide, a carousel, puppet shows, and, of course, Santa Claus. There are also several organized games for all ages as well as a market selling traditional sweets and other artisanal crafts. The Bar de Gelo (ice bar) is a popular chill-out spot for adults. ✉ *Óbidos* 🌐 *www.obidosvilanatal.pt* 🎫 €7.

Semana Internacional de Piano de Óbidos This long-running festival offers two weeks in late July to mid-August of top-quality piano music. Most concerts are staged in the compact Casa da Música near the main gate, and given the town's small size you may well end up rubbing shoulders with a star performer during your stay. ✉ *Óbidos* ☎ *914 400 702* 🌐 *www.pianobidos.org* 🎫 €18.

✉ *Rua Principal, off N361, Sanguinhal* ☎ *262 609 199* 🌐 *www.vinhos-sanguinhal.pt.*

Restaurants

★ A Nova Casa de Ramiro

$$$ | PORTUGUESE | This longtime favorite just outside the town walls effortlessly blends modern elegance with rustic decor. For the most part the fare remains reassuringly traditional, with dishes such as *arroz de pato* (rice with duck), fresh grilled fish, and various popular bacalhau options. **Known for:** enjoy a glass of wine on the small terrace; friendly and efficient service; great wine pairings. $ *Average main: €23* ✉ *Rua Porta do Vale* ☎ *262 958 324* ⏲ *Closed Sun., and 1 wk in Sept. No lunch Mon.*

A narrow pedestrian street lined with crafts shops and cafés in the medieval walled village of Óbidos.

Alcaide

$ | **PORTUGUESE** | From the upstairs dining room and terrace of this rustic tavern, enjoy a lovely view of the village's rooftops and the countryside beyond. This isn't a quiet hideaway—Alcaide draws many hungry patrons, especially from May through October. **Known for:** desserts include a heavenly almond cake; unusual use of local ingredients; courteous service. *Average main: €15* ✉ *Rua Direita 60* ☎ *262 959 220* 🌐 *www.restaurantealcaide.com* ⏲ *Closed Wed., and 2nd half Nov.*

★ **Poço dos Sabores**

$ | **PORTUGUESE** | This rustic restaurant in the village of Usseira, 4 km (2½ miles) south of Óbidos, has been serving hearty, mainly regional cuisine in its stone dining room for two decades. The menu changes every few months—some favorites like *arroz selvagem* (wild rice) are always on it—but any lamb or pork dish is a good option. **Known for:** you can't go wrong with polvo (octopus) or bacalhau (cod); local apples, pears, and other fruit in the desserts; live fado music some nights. *Average main: €15* ✉ *Rua Principal 85-B, Usseira* ☎ *262 950 086* ⏲ *Closed Mon and 2 wks in Sept. No dinner Sun. in July and Sept.*

Supatra

$ | **THAI** | This renowned Thai restaurant near Bombarral has an ideal location down the road from the gardens at Buddha Eden. In a spacious former winery, the smiling staff serves the real deal: chicken and pork on skewers, salads brimming with tropical fruit, and specialties like *pla lad prik* (sea bream in a tamarind sauce) and *gaeng kiaw wan kai* (green curry with chicken and coconut). **Known for:** excellent dishes like stir-fried noodles with shrimp and peanuts; chestnut pudding is a tasty dessert; wide range of vegetarian dishes. *Average main: €12* ✉ *Rua Poeta José Ferreira Ventura 73, Carvalhal, Bombarral* ☎ *262 842 920* 🌐 *www.restaurantetailandessupatra.pt* ⏲ *Closed Mon., and Tues.–Thurs. Oct.–June. No dinner Sun.*

Ginja Cherry Liqueur

One cannot visit Óbidos without trying its delicious cherry liqueur, *ginja*. Also known as *ginjinha de Óbidos*, it's made from the ginja sour cherry, whose origin is difficult to establish but is supposedly derived from the banks of the Caspian River and was gradually dispersed among the Mediterranean countries via trade routes. Thanks to the particular microclimate around the area of Óbidos, Portugal actually has the best wild ginja in Europe. As for the drink, it is thought to have originally started in the 17th century by a local friar who took a part of the large quantity of the fruit in the region and refined them into the liqueur that is known today. The liqueur has a deep, dark red color with an intense flavor and aroma perfumed by the fermented cherries. It's produced and sold in two distinct varieties, the liqueur on its own or the liqueur with actual ginja cherries inside, sometimes flavored with vanilla or cinnamon. You can find numerous little shops and cafés in the walled village selling ginja as well as offering tastings. The best thing the locals recommend to have with ginja is chocolate, which they have cutely crafted into little chocolate cups in which to serve the liqueur. Or, you can enjoy it with a big slice of one of the house-made chocolate cakes. The chocolate cups are also sold in packs of 6 and 12 to enjoy the ginja experience at home.

Hotels

Casa das Senhoras Rainhas

$ | **B&B/INN** | As its name suggests, the charming House of Queens just inside the city walls pays tribute to the royalty associated with Óbidos over the centuries. **Pros:** enjoy the welcome drink of the famous local cherry liquor; restaurant serves a delicious cod with potatoes and onions; excellent service. **Cons:** street parking is difficult; limited amenities; hotel entrance can be hard to find. *Rooms from: €135* *Rua Padre Nunes Tavares 6* *262 955 360* *www.senhorasrainhas.com* *10 rooms* *Free Breakfast.*

★ **The Literary Man Óbidos Hotel**

$ | **HOTEL** | This 19th-century convent turned stylish hotel has a bit of a split personality: a quarter of the rooms feature traditional wooden ceilings and floors and wrought-iron beds, while the rest are "eco-chic," employing recycled materials with contemporary flair. **Pros:** well-stocked wine cellar doubles as a treatment room for massages; unusual and engaging literary theme; trendy gin bar. **Cons:** parking in the area can be difficult; can get noisy from outside traffic; books up fast. *Rooms from: €110* *Rua D. João d'Ornelas* *262 959 217* *www.theliteraryman.pt* *30 rooms* *Free Breakfast.*

★ **Pousada Castelo de Óbidos**

$$$ | **HOTEL** | Sleep like royalty in this charming pousada, which occupies parts of the castle that Dom Dinis gave to his young bride, Isabel, in 1282. **Pros:** great location near the town's main attractions; incredible views of the castle; excellent service. **Cons:** no elevator, meaning steps to climb for many rooms; entrance is up a steep hill; pricey rates. *Rooms from: €217* *Paço Real* *262 955 080* *www.pousadas.pt* *17 rooms* *Free Breakfast.*

★ **Praia d'El Rey Marriott Golf & Beach Resort**

$$$ | **RESORT** | **FAMILY** | This top-notch hotel, part of a sprawling luxury resort, is located 16 km (10 miles) west of Óbidos and includes a dazzling array of amenities. **Pros:** lots of water sports to choose from; plenty to keep kids occupied; several excellent eateries. **Cons:** food and drink are very expensive; far from local attractions; gets crowded in summer. *Rooms from: €230 Av. Dona Inês de Castro 1, Vale de Janelas 262 905 100 www.marriott.com/lisdr 177 rooms Free Breakfast.*

★ **Rio do Prado**

$$$ | **HOTEL** | "Eco-chic" is the phrase that best describes this award-winning hotel near the Óbidos Lagoon. **Pros:** unique setting and atmosphere; ecologically sensitive; restaurant serves delicious homemade food. **Cons:** few amenities; far from sights; no shade around pool. *Rooms from: €210 Rua das Poças, Arelho (Lagoa de Óbidos) 262 959 623 www.riodoprado.pt 20 rooms Free Breakfast.*

Activities

GOLF

★ **Praia d'El Rey Golf & Beach Resort**

GOLF | Less than an hour's drive from Lisbon's international airport, Praia d'El Rey is an excellent beachfront complex with one of the most picturesque golf courses in Europe. Undulating greens, natural sand-border areas, and bold, deep bunkers are the hallmarks of this Cabell Robinson design. The architect was at great pains to make the course friendly to women players by creating sensible women's tees that are placed far enough forward. The handicap limit here is 28 for men and women. Reservations must be made by email (*golf.reservations@praia-del-rey.com*) but it is worth phoning ahead to ask about current promotions, or check the website link. *Av. Dom Pedro Primeiro, Vale de Janelas 262 905 005 www.praia-del-rey.com 18 holes, 7110 yds, par 73. Greens fee €110 weekdays, €130 weekends (25% off Nov.–Jan.).*

Shopping

BOOKS

Livraria de Santiago

BOOKS/STATIONERY | Óbidos has ambitions to become Portugal's prime literary town, with a high-profile international festival and bookshops springing up in the most unlikely places. The 18th-century Igreja de Santiago, by the castle keep, has been dramatically transformed, with bookshelves and wooden staircases whose curves echo its baroque interior. It stocks mainly Portuguese literature and glossy coffee-table books, though you will also find some fiction and nonfiction in English. *Igreja de Santiago, Rua da Talhada 262 103 180.*

CERAMICS

Olaria São Pedro

CERAMICS/GLASSWARE | Óbidos is dotted with crafts shops, but this one stands out for its ceramics—many of them very large—by some of the wave of artists who are successfully updating this traditional form in Caldas da Rainha and other towns in the region. Sónia Borga, for example, mixes her own vibrant colors and often fires pieces several times to achieve striking results. The shop also sells jewelry and Andalusia-style azulejo tiles, and will ship any item. *Travessa de São Pedro 2–4 933 867 480 arte-ceramics.com.*

Caldas da Rainha

5 km (3 miles) north of Óbidos.

Caldas da Rainha (Queen's Baths), the hub of a large farming area, is best known for the fantastical, colorful ceramics produced in local factories and—for centuries before that—for its sulfur baths. In 1484 Queen Leonor, en route to Batalha, noticed people bathing in a malodorous pool. Having heard of the healing properties of the sulfurous water, the queen interrupted her journey for a soak and became convinced of the water's beneficial effects. She had a hospital built on the site and was reputedly so enthusiastic that she sold her jewels to help finance the project. There's a bronze statue of Leonor in front of the hospital.

GETTING HERE AND AROUND

Caldas da Rainha can be reached from Lisbon by buses run by Rede Expressos and local operator Rodoviária do Oeste, which serves other towns in the region from a smart downtown hub. The CP regional train line between Lisbon (Santa Apolónia and Entrecampos stations) and Figueira da Foz stops in Caldas da Rainha as well. Driving from Lisbon takes 50 minutes, from Óbidos 10 minutes.

BUS CONTACTS Caldas da Rainha Bus Station. ✉ *Rua Coronel Soeira de Brito 35* ☎ *262 831 067.*

ESSENTIALS

VISITOR INFORMATION Caldas da Rainha Tourist Office. ✉ *Rua Provedor Frei Jorge de São Paulo 1* ☎ *262 240 005.*

Sights

Encosta da Quinta

WINERY/DISTILLERY | One of the region's best small winemakers, Encosta da Quinta is known above all for a prize-winning organic red that goes by the earthy name of Humus. Call ahead to arrange a visit to the estate outside of town (parts of which date back to the 16th century), ending with a tasting with four organic wines—a combination of whites, rosés, or reds, according to visitors' preference—and regional cheeses, all for €20. ✉ *Quinta do Paço, off Rua Principal de Alqueidão, Alvorninha* ☎ *917 276 053* 🌐 *encostadaquinta.com.*

Museu da Cerâmica (*Ceramics Museum*)

MUSEUM | This museum in the Romantic-style former house of the Viscount of Sacavém contains works by the noted 19th-century artisan and artist Rafael Bordalo Pinheiro, as well as ceramics by his Caldas da Rainha contemporaries. Some of his most famous ceramic figurines, done in gaudy colors, are the good-natured peasant Zé Povinho, wet nurse Ama das Caldas, and English aristocrat John Bull. Other amusing figures include a pig's head on a platter and leaping frogs. There are a gift and bookshop and a cafeteria here as well. ✉ *Rua Dr. Ilídio Amado, Apartado 97* ☎ *262 840 280* 🎫 *€3* ⏲ *Closed Mon.*

Museu José Malhoa

MUSEUM | The expansive wooded park surrounding the town's spa contains a museum with works mostly by local José Malhoa (1854–1933), one of Portugal's most prominent Naturalist painters, as well as sculpture, drawings and ceramics from the 19th and 20th centuries. A handheld audio guide with English commentary is available. ✉ *Parque Dom Carlos I* ☎ 🎫 *€3* ⏲ *Closed Mon.*

Beaches

Praia da Foz do Arelho

BEACH—SIGHT | Across the mouth of the Óbidos Lagoon, a large spit of sand juts out into the brackish tidal water. The broad expanse of sand here and the calm waters of the lagoon make it popular with families with young kids, not least because the beaches here have been awarded the coveted Blue Flag (for water quality, safety, and access) several years running. As well as the public facilities, there are several lively esplanades along the promenade. **Amenites:** food and drink; lifeguards; parking (no fee); showers; toilets. **Best for:** partiers; sunset; swimming; windsurfing. ✉ *Foz do Arelho.*

Restaurants

A Lareira

$ | **PORTUGUESE** | With a name that is Portuguese for "fireplace," this elegant, spacious restaurant is nestled in pinewoods between Caldas da Rainha and the Foz do Arelho beach; it's a favorite with locals for special occasions. Try the salmon fillet with caviar sauce, the *tornedó de novilho* tenderloin with one of various sauces, or, for the more daring, the *ensopado de enguia* (eel stew). **Known for:** extensive wine list; affordable weekday set menu; unique eel stew. *Average main: €13* *Rua da Lareira 35, Alto do Nobre, Nadadouro* *www.restaurantealareira.com* *Closed Tues.*

Adega do Albertino

$ | **PORTUGUESE** | **FAMILY** | This bustling tavern in the delightfully named village of Imaginário is no place for fussy eaters: it is renowned for regional dishes such as *polvo na telha* (octopus grilled on a roof tile) and *morcela de arroz* (a type of blood sausage). Leave some space for the eggy desserts, which are all homemade and delicious. **Known for:** unusual seafood dishes like eel stew and whelk salad; generous servings of regional fare; homemade desserts. *Average main: €13* *Rua Júlio Sousa 7, Imaginário* *262 835 152* *adegadoalbertino.pt* *Closed Mon. and 2 wks in Sept. No dinner Sun.*

★ Sabores d'Itália

$$ | **ITALIAN** | Behind a vintage tiled facade is a widely acclaimed restaurant that has long been the country's most popular destination for Italian food. Everything—the pasta, bread, ice cream—is homemade and beautifully presented and served by the owner, Norberto Marcelino, and his wife. **Known for:** roast fig with goat cheese is among mouthwatering starters; Italian wines served by the glass as well as the bottle; weekday set lunch menu is great value. *Average main: €19* *Praça 5 de Outubro 40* *262 845 600* *www.saboresditalia.com* *Closed Mon. in Sept.–July, 3 wks. in Jan.–Feb. No lunch Mon. in Aug.*

Hotels

Casal da Eira Branca

$ | **B&B/INN** | **FAMILY** | This rural retreat is ideal for rest and relaxation, with its sprawling, flower-filled garden and terraces with views. **Pros:** an outdoor pool with a retractable roof for cooler months; run by a friendly couple who live on the premises; has an artsy feel. **Cons:** far from the nearby sights; not many amenities; no restaurant. *Rooms from: €65* *Rua Casal dos Pedreiros 3, 7 km (4 miles) east of Caldas* *934 549 185* *www.casaldaeirabranca.com* *4 rooms, 3 apartments* *Free Breakfast.*

★ Quinta da Foz

$ | **B&B/INN** | A knight serving King Dom Felipe I built this large manor house in the 16th century, and 20-some generations later it is still owned and operated by the original family. **Pros:** a quiet and peaceful base for exploring the area; Foz do Arelho beach is 15-minute walk away; archery or falconry sessions. **Cons:** Wi-Fi is elusive in some rooms; few modern amenities; no restaurant. *Rooms from: €100* *Largo do Arraial, Foz do Arelho* *262 978 506* *quintafozarelho.com* *No credit cards* *4 rooms 2 apartments* *Free Breakfast.*

SANA Silver Coast Hotel

$ | **HOTEL** | A famous Victorian-era showplace that was neglected for years has been transformed into the most highly rated hotel between Lisbon and Leiria. **Pros:** great central location on a pretty park; free Wi-Fi access and Internet terminals; one of the region's most distinctive buildings. **Cons:** rooms at the front get some street noise; extra charge for covered parking; lacks amenities like a pool. $ *Rooms from: €105* ✉ *Av. Dom Manuel Figueira Freire da Câmara* ☎ *262 000 600* 🌐 *www.silvercoast.sanahotels.com* *87 rooms* *Free Breakfast.*

Shopping

CERAMICS

Faianças Artísticas Bordallo Pinheiro

CERAMICS/GLASSWARE | The shop at this factory, once overseen by Rafael Bordalo Pinheiro, has a good range of Caldas-style ceramics, many produced using vintage molds designed by the artist himself. In recent years, leading contemporary artists—most notably Portugal's own Joana Vasconcelos—have worked with the company to produce new works or to use old designs in unexpected ways. There are guided visits to Bordalo Pinheiro's former home, now a museum, on weekdays by appointment only. ✉ *Rua Rafael Bordalo Pinheiro 53* ☎ *262 880 568* 🌐 *www.bordallopinheiro.com.*

Activities

WATER SPORTS

Escola de Vela da Lagoa

WATER SPORTS | This large wooden sailing school on the north bank of the Óbidos Lagoon near Foz do Arelho beach has rentals by the hour: small sailboat from €15, windsurfer €15–€22, canoe €12, and catamaran €25–€33. A kitesurfing course costs €90 for two hours of private lessons. The snack bar here serves hamburgers,sweet and savory crêpes, fresh fruit juices, and cocktails. ✉ *Lagoa de Óbidos, 2½ km (1½ miles) after traffic circle at Foz, Rua do Penedo Furado, Foz do Arelho* ☎ 🌐 *www.escoladeveladalagoa.com.*

Nazaré

24 km (15 miles) northwest of Caldas da Rainha.

Not so long ago you could mingle on the beach with black-stocking-capped fishermen and even help as the oxen hauled boats in from the crashing surf. But Nazaré is no longer a village and has long ceased to be quaint. The boats now motor comfortably into a safe, modern harbor, and the oxen have been put to pasture. The beachfront boulevard is lined with restaurants, bars, and souvenir shops, and in summer the broad, sandy beach is covered with a multicolor quilt of tents and awnings.

You can still catch an interesting piece of culture that has survived: the many *sete saias Nazarenas* or "seven skirts Nazarean women," who can be seen all around the town, dressed in colorful mismatching attire and, of course, wearing seven skirts. These women also sell crafts and souvenirs as well as dried, salted little fish (a local tradition) that they dry on wire racks along the boardwalk. They also have shops selling their particular style of clothing if you're adventurous enough to try them. It's said that the seven skirts represent, in religious terms, the seven virtues, the seven days of the week, the seven colors of the rainbow, the seven waves of the sea, and other biblical and magical attributes.

Nazaré is famed for the giant waves that form in winter thanks to an underground canyon just north of the town, which attracts the most daredevil of surfers. The best place to view the waves—and any surfers up to the challenge—is from the cliff-top fortress of Forte de São Miguel Arcanjo.

GETTING HERE AND AROUND

Nazaré can be reached by Rede Expressos buses from Lisbon; regional routes are served by Rodoviária do Oeste. Driving from Lisbon takes one hour, and the drive from Alcobaça will take you close to 15 minutes. For the most interesting route to Nazaré, head west from Caldas along the lagoon to the beach town of Foz do Arelho, then take the coast road 26 km (16 miles) north.

BUS CONTACTS Nazaré Bus Station. ✉ *Av. do Município* ☎ *967 449 868* 🌐 *rodoviariadooeste.pt.*

ESSENTIALS

VISITOR INFORMATION Nazaré Tourist Office. ✉ *Mercado Municipal, Av. Vieira Guimarães* ☎ *262 561 194* 🌐 *www.cm-nazare.pt.*

Forte de São Miguel Arcanjo

MILITARY SITE | Many travelers make a beeline for this 16th-century fort—which since 1903 has also served as a lighthouse—as the ideal vantage point for watching the waves that attract the world's best surfers. Since 2015, the structure has housed a small surf museum, whose displays include fascinating explanations of how the offshore Nazaré Canyon enables the waves to form. ✉ *Estrada do Farol, Sítio* ☎ *938 013 587* 🎫 *€1.*

Sítio da Nazaré

RELIGIOUS SITE | To catch a glimpse of what was once hailed as "the most picturesque fishing village in Portugal," either climb the precipitous trail or take the Ascensor da Nazaré, a scenic funicular (€1.50 each way), to the top of a 361-foot cliff to visit the settlement called Sítio (literally, "Place"). Clustered at the cliff's edge overlooking the beach is a small community of fishermen who live in tiny cottages and seem unaffected by all that's happening below. On this promontory stands the Igreja de Nossa Senhora da Nazaré, a predominately baroque church with a tiled and gilded interior that houses a figure of the Virgin Mary said to have been carved by Joseph himself in Nazareth—hence the town's name. Its cloisters harbor a free museum with naive paintings of local miracles; in the shrine itself, for €1 you can get a close-up look at the image. ✉ *Sítio.*

A Celeste

$$ | **SEAFOOD** | Owner Dona Celeste likes to personally greet guests—who lately have included record-breaking U.S. surfer Garrett McNamara—at the entrance to her seafood restaurant on the Atlantic seafront. Among popular dishes here are *espadarte à Celeste* (swordfish with cream-and-mushroom sauce) and squid or monkfish on the spit. **Known for:** don't miss the fish baked whole in salt; family-friendly atmosphere; occasional celebrity visitors. 💲 *Average main: €20* ✉ *Av. República 54* ☎ *262 551 695.*

Hotel Mar Bravo

$ | **HOTEL** | This stylish boutique hotel sits across the road from the beach, just steps from both the sea and the center of town. **Pros:** beachfront eatery serves lobsters plucked straight from the tank; location couldn't be more central; free Wi-Fi and other amenities. **Cons:** can get noisy from outside traffic; free parking is off-site; a bit old-fashioned. 💲 *Rooms from: €139* ✉ *Praça Sousa Oliveira 71* ☎ *262 569 160* 🌐 *www.marbravo.com* 🕓 *Closed Christmas wk* 🛏 *16 rooms* 🍴 *Free Breakfast.*

Hotel Maré

$ | **HOTEL** | **FAMILY** | Right in the center of town with access to the beach via the flower-filled gardens, the Maré has rooms that are colorfully decorated and with balconies; family-size rooms are available. **Pros:** generous amenities include free Wi-Fi; offers wide variety of beach activities; off-season packages excellent value. **Cons:** no pool; paid parking 500 meters away; can be noisy. *$ Rooms from: €130 ✉ Rua Mouzinho de Albuquerque 10 ☎ 🌐 www.hotelmare.pt 46 rooms 🍴 Free Breakfast.*

Hotel Oceano

$ | **HOTEL** | Balconies at this pleasantly appointed hotel have unobstructed views of the entire beach. **Pros:** perfect location right on the main drag; restaurant is great for after-beach snacks; excellent value. **Cons:** gets booked up early in summer; not all rooms have the same view; very noisy at times. *$ Rooms from: €120 ✉ Av. da República 51 ☎ 262 561 161 🌐 www.adegaoceano.com 45 rooms 🍴 Free Breakfast.*

Hotel Praia

$$ | **HOTEL** | Along with being only minutes away from the beach, this design hotel has a glass-covered pool and whirlpool tub on the rooftop with views of the ocean and the surrounding city. **Pros:** soundproof rooms guarantee a good night's sleep; guest floors have direct garage access; terrace is a great place to mix and mingle. **Cons:** extra charge for parking; restaurant is pricey; off the beach. *$ Rooms from: €160 ✉ Av. Vieira Guimarães 39 ☎ 262 569 200 🌐 www.hotelpraia.com 76 rooms, 4 duplex apartments 🍴 Free Breakfast.*

Miramar Hotel & Spa

$$ | **HOTEL** | About 1 km (½ mile) *above* Nazaré, in the village of Pederneira, this hotel's views are fantastic. **Pros:** spa with sauna, and steam room, and treatment rooms; one- and two-bedroom apartments are good for families; away from the city crowds. **Cons:** far from the beach; no nightlife nearby; charge for Wi-Fi. *$ Rooms from: €147 ✉ Rua Abel da Silva, Pederneira ☎ 262 550 000 🌐 www.miramarnazarehotels.com 40 rooms 🍴 Free Breakfast.*

Activities

SPAS

Thalasso Nazaré

SPA/BEAUTY | Overlooking the Atlantic, this spa seeks to combine classic thalassotherapy treatments (using seawater) with the latest wellness and beauty therapies. The area's waters have long been valued for their health-giving properties: the existence just offshore of the Nazaré Canyon—a huge submarine gorge—helps bring rich nutrients to the surface. *✉ Av. Manuel Remígio ☎ 262 560 450 🌐 www.thalassoportugal.com.*

Alcobaça

10 km (6 miles) southeast of Nazaré, 20 km (12 miles) northeast of Caldas da Rainha.

Alcobaça is a town that still shows its old-world roots in its downtown architecture—pretty red-tile roofs and French chateau turrets. The town is in a picturesque valley between the towns of Nazaré and Batalha, and is known for its crystal as well as for its impressive church and monastery that date back to the 12th century.

GETTING HERE AND AROUND

Alcobaça can be reached from Lisbon and other cities by buses run by Rede Expressos and local operator Rodoviária do Oeste, which also links it with other towns in the region. Driving from Lisbon takes one hour, while the drive from Nazaré will take you close to 15 minutes.

BUS CONTACTS Alcobaça Bus Station. *✉ Av. Manuel Silva Carolino ☎ 967 449 858 🌐 rodoviariadooeste.pt.*

ESSENTIALS

VISITOR INFORMATION Alcobaça Tourist Office. *✉ Rua 16 de Outubro 7 ☎ 262 582 377 🌐 www.turismodocentro.pt.* **São Martinho do Porto Tourist Office.** *✉ Rua Vasco da Gama, 18, São Martinho do*

Porto ☎ 262 989 110 ⊕ www.turismodo-centro.pt.

Sights

★ **Mosteiro de Alcobaça** (*Alcobaça Monastery*)

RELIGIOUS SITE | Like the monastery at Mafra, the Mosteiro de Alcobaça was built as the result of a kingly vow, this time in gratitude for a battle won. In 1147, faced with stiff Muslim resistance during the battle for Santarém, Portugal's first king, Afonso Henriques, promised to build a monastery dedicated to St. Bernard and the Cistercian Order. The Portuguese were victorious, Santarém was captured from the Moors, and shortly thereafter a site was selected. Construction began in 1153 and was concluded in 1178. The church, the largest in Portugal, is awe-inspiring. The unadorned, 350-foot-long structure of massive granite blocks and cross-ribbed vaulting is a masterpiece of understatement: there's good use of clean, flowing lines, with none of the clutter of the later rococo and Manueline architecture. At opposite ends of the transept, placed foot to foot some 30 paces apart, are the delicately carved tombs of King Pedro I and Inês de Castro.

The graceful twin-tiered cloister at Alcobaça was added in the 14th and 16th centuries. The Kings Hall, just to the left of the main entrance, is lined with a series of 18th-century azulejos illustrating the construction of the monastery. *✉ Praça 25 de Abril ☎ 262 505 120 ⊕ www.mosteiroalcobaca.pt 🎫 €6, €15 combined ticket includes Batalha monastery and Tomar convent.*

Museu do Vinho (*Museum of Wine*)

MUSEUM | Housed in an old winery just outside Alcobaça, the Wine Museum is the country's best showcase of antique implements and presses, dating from the 17th to 21st centuries. Guided tours are offered on the hour from 10 to 5 (except 1 pm), in English and Portuguese, and conclude with a wine tasting. *✉ Rua de Leiria, Olival Fechado ☎ 968 497 832 🎫 €4 ⏲ Closed Mon.*

Beaches

São Martinho do Porto

BEACH—SIGHT | The perfect horseshoe-shape bay here makes this one of Portugal's prettiest beaches and ensures it is lapped by calm waters that are safe for children. The ample strand—patrolled by lifeguards so long as beach cafés are open—has fine, yellow sand (cleaned daily) and areas with sunshades for rent. Much of it is lined with well-preserved dunes; at its northern end, set back from the promenade, are elegant old homes in the typical Caldas style, restaurants, and many hotels. The beach is popular with local families, so don't come in high summer if you dislike crowds. Local companies offer boating and canoeing trips. **Amenities:** food and drink; lifeguards; parking (no fee); toilets; water sports. **Best for:** sunset; swimming; walking. *✉ Av. Marginal, São Martinho do Porto.*

Restaurants

Alcôa

$ | PORTUGUESE | This little café across from the monastery is justly famed for its cakes and pastries, presented in a long glass display case. Since winning a national prize for its *pastéis de nata* (custard tarts) a few years ago, it has opened two offshoots in Lisbon. **Known for:** unique range of regional pastries; beautiful presentation; efficient service. *💲 Average main: €5 ✉ Praça 25 de Abril 44 ⏲ No dinner.*

António Padeiro

$ | PORTUGUESE | This restaurant is best known for showcasing regional cuisine, with dishes such as chicken or partridge *na púcara* (cooked in an clay pot)—many of which evolved in local monasteries. Fans of bacalhau should try the house version: baked with a crust of cornbread and *farinheira* sausage. **Known for:** wide range of traditional eggy desserts as well as fresh fruit; brisk but friendly service; local history. *Average main: €14 Rua Dom Maur Cocheril 27 262 582 295 www.antoniopadeiro.com Closed 2 wks in June.*

Hotels

Casa da Padeira

$ | **B&B/INN** | **FAMILY** | This family-run guesthouse 5 km (3 miles) outside Alcobaça is named after a baker who fought the Spaniards with a wooden shovel—and pushed them into her oven—during the Battle of Aljubarrota in 1385. **Pros:** large swimming pool popular with families; playground for the children; barbecue facilities. **Cons:** far from some of the sights; rooms lack a/c; no elevator. *Rooms from: €85 N8, Aljubarrota 262 505 240 www.casadapadeira.com 8 rooms, 5 apartments Free Breakfast.*

Challet Fonte Nova

$ | **B&B/INN** | This charming B&B, a five-minute walk from the Mosteiro de Alcobaça, has guest rooms in period style, while the more spacious lodgings in the new wing—including two suites with balconies—are more classically decorated. **Pros:** a trellised walkway leads up to leafy garden; small spa where massages are available; toiletries by the luxe Castelbel. **Cons:** free Wi-Fi has elusive signal; no restaurant; no pool. *Rooms from: €120 Rua da Fonte Nova 8 262 598 300 www.challetfontenova.pt Closed 2 wks in Dec. 9 rooms Free Breakfast.*

★ Quinta do Campo

$ | **B&B/INN** | **FAMILY** | This imposing complex in the countryside between Alcobaça and Nazaré housed the country's first agricultural school—founded in the 14th century by Cistercian monks—and is now a comfortable rural retreat. **Pros:** long history that the staff is happy to relate; plenty of outdoor activities; spacious acommodations. **Cons:** restaurant open only in summer; not many facilities; far from sights. *Rooms from: €75 Rua Carlos O'Neill 20, Valado dos Frades, Nazaré 262 577 135 www.aquintadocampo.com 8 rooms, 7 apartments Free Breakfast No credit cards.*

Shopping

CERAMICS AND GLASSWARE

Cristal Atlantis

CERAMICS/GLASSWARE | This outlet shop 8 km (5 miles) north of Alcobaça sells first-rate crystal and secondhand items. There is a free museum and on weekdays you can tour the factory with advance reservations. *Zona Industrial de Casal de Areia, Cós 262 540 269 www.vistaalegreatlantis.com.*

Spal

CERAMICS/GLASSWARE | This factory store on the Nazaré road is a great place to buy porcelain from this leading Portuguese manufacturer. Its outlet section stocks discounted items with minimal defects. The staff will box and ship your purchases. *Ponte da Torre, Valado dos Frades 262 581 339 www.spal.pt.*

Activities

SPAS

Your Hotel & Spa

SPA/BEAUTY | Set between fruit orchards and wooded hills, this hotel spa has an impressive range of treatments, including some with wine and chocolate. There's an indoor pool with jets, Vichy shower, sauna, steam bath, and various relaxation beds. *Rua Manuel Rodrigues Serrazina, Fervença 262 505 376 www.yourhotelspa.com.*

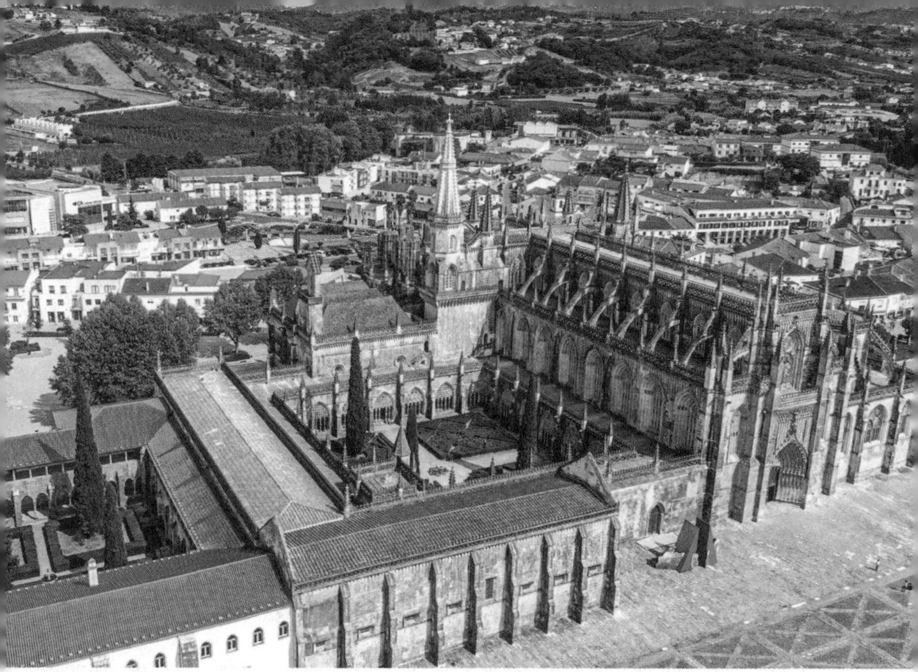

The Mosterio de Batalha is a stunning monastery built to commemorate a battle victory.

Batalha

18 km (11 miles) northeast of Alcobaça.

Batalha, which means "battle" in Portuguese, is the site of another of the country's religious structures that memorialize a battle victory. The monastery, classified as a UNESCO World Heritage Site, is surrounded by the small city center, with several other smaller, historical monuments scattered around the area.

Batalha is right in the Estremaduran countryside, with rolling hills, mountains, old windmills, pastures, and farming villages that create a fairy-tale-like view from higher points of the city. It's a great area to drive around and explore.

GETTING HERE AND AROUND

Batalha is served by the Rede Expressos buses from Lisbon to Leiria as well as other vicinities in between. Driving to Batalha from Lisbon takes 1 hour 10 minutes, 15 minutes if coming from Leiria.

ESSENTIALS

VISITOR INFORMATION Batalha Tourist Office. ✉ *Praça Mouzinho de Albuquerque* ☎ *244 765 180.*

Sights

Centro de Interpretação da Batalha de Aljubarrota (*Battle of Aljubarrota Interpretation Center*)

MILITARY SITE | About 3 km (2 miles) south of Batalha's world-renowned monastery, the Battle of Aljubarrota Interpretation Center is a project of the foundation of the same name, created to preserve and enhance understanding of the history surrounding the São Jorge battlefield. The main focus of the exhibition area (with labels in English) is on the 1385 military engagement that conclusively established Portugal's sovereignty, but it also documents conflicts with Spain from the early Middle Ages through the early 15th century. Audio guides in various languages are always available, and you may also book a guided tour in English in advance. If you plan on visiting the battlefield itself as well, set aside an hour and a half. ✉ *Campo Militar de São Jorge, Av. Nuno Álvares Pereira 120, Calvaria de Cima* ☎ *244 480 062* 🌐 *www.fundacao-aljubarrota.pt* 🎫 *€7* 🕒 *Closed Mon.*

★ **Mosteiro da Batalha** (*Batalha Monastery*)

RELIGIOUS SITE | Dedicated to "Saint Mary of Victory," this UNESCO World Heritage Site was built to commemorate a decisive Portuguese victory over the Spanish on August 14, 1385, in the Battle of Aljubarrota. In this engagement the Portuguese king, João de Avis, who had been crowned only seven days earlier, took on and routed a superior Spanish force. In so doing he maintained independence for Portugal, which was to last until 1580, when the crown finally passed into Spanish hands. The heroic statue of the mounted figure in the forecourt is that of Nuno Álvares Pereira, who, along with João de Avis, led the Portuguese army at Aljubarrota.

The monastery, a masterly combination of Gothic and Manueline styles, was built between 1388 and 1533. Some 15 architects were involved in the project, but the principal architect was Afonso Domingues, whose portrait, carved in stone, graces the wall in the chapter house. In the great hall lie the remains of two unknown Portuguese soldiers who died in World War I: one in France, the other in Africa. Entombed in the center of the Founder's Chapel, beneath the star-shape, vaulted ceiling, is João de Avis, lying hand in hand with his English queen, Philippa of Lancaster. The tombs along the south and west walls are those of the couple's children, including Henry the Navigator. Perhaps the finest parts of the entire project are the Unfinished Chapels, seven chapels radiating off an octagonal rotunda, started by Dom Duarte in 1435 and left roofless owing to lack of funds. Note the intricately filigreed detail of the main doorway. ✉ *Largo Infante Dom Henrique* ☎ *244 765 497* 🌐 *www.mosteirobatalha.pt* 🎫 *€6 (free 1st Sun. of the month); €15 combined ticket, includes Alcobaça monastery and Tomar convent.*

Parque Natural das Serras de Aire e Candeeiros (*Serras de Aire e Candeeiros Natural Park*)

NATIONAL/STATE PARK | This sparsely populated region straddles the border between Estremadura and the Ribatejo and is roughly midway between Lisbon and Coimbra. Within its 75,000 acres of scrublands and moors are small settlements, little changed in hundreds of years, where farmers barely eke out a living. In this rocky landscape, stones are the main building material for houses, windmills, and the miles of walls used to mark boundary lines. In the village of Minde, on weekdays you can visit the Centro de Artes e Ofícios Roque Gameiro (Rua Dr António da Silva Totta 51) to see women weaving the rough patchwork rugs for which this region is known. The park is well suited for leisurely hiking—with many well-marked trails—or cycling. If you're driving, the N362, which runs for approximately 45 km (28 miles) from Batalha in the north to Santarém in the south, is a good route. ✉ *Porto de Mós.*

Restaurants

Dom Duarte

$ | PORTUGUESE | The dishes of the day at this bustling second-floor restaurant are excellent value, and the house wine—from a local producers' cooperative—goes down well, too. Some tables in the main dining room have views of the monastery, but at peak times you may be seated on the covered terrace in back. **Known for:** specializes in a range of tasty bacalhau dishes; everything served in generous portions; friendly service. 💲 *Average main: €12* ✉ *Praça Dom João I, 5C* ☎ *244 766 326* 🌐 *www.restaurantedomduarte.pt.*

★ **Tromba Rija**

$$$ | **PORTUGUESE** | One of Portugal's most famous restaurants, this longtime shrine to traditional cuisine has set up shop in a leafy setting across from the Batalha Monastery. From Friday dinner through Sunday lunch, guests serve themselves from a long table where around 100 regional appetizers are set out in clay pots. **Known for:** specials like lombo de porco recheado com ameixas (pork loin stuffed with prunes); make reservations or be prepared to wait on the large terrace; a special-occasion meal. *Average main: €25 Quinta do Fidalgo Off N1 244 852 277 www.trombarija.com Closed Mon. No dinner Tues.–Thurs., Sun., and holidays.*

Hotels

★ **Cooking and Nature**

$$ | **HOTEL** | "Get connected with nature" is the slogan of this innovative hotel, set amid olive groves in the Parque Natural Serras de Aire de Candeeiros. **Pros:** a wide range of activities, from yoga workshops to horseback riding; great destination for getting away from it all; rooms are decorated with fun themes. **Cons:** far from the historic sights; small swimming pool; no dinner on Sunday. *Rooms from: €179 Rua Asseguia das Lages 181, 20 km (13 miles) south of Batalha, Alvados 244 447 000 www.cookinghotel.com 12 rooms Free Breakfast.*

Hotel Casa do Outeiro

$ | **HOTEL** | This cheerful little hotel in one of the quietest areas of Batalha offers a superb view of the historic monastery and the valley below. **Pros:** it's worth reserving a rooms with a monastery view; breakfast is served beside the pretty swimming pool; small shop sells lovely local handicrafts and jams. **Cons:** some rooms have better decor than others; limited breakfast options; no on-site restaurant. *Rooms from: €64 Largo Carvalho do Outeiro 4 244 765 806 www.hotelcasadooouteiro.com 23 rooms Free Breakfast.*

Hotel Lis Batalha Mestre Afonso Domingues

$ | **HOTEL** | Named for the principal architect of the famous Batalha Monastery, this two-story stucco hotel is full of modern comforts. **Pros:** many rooms look out at the monastery across the street; behind a pretty outdoor shopping area that sells crafts; guests congregate in the lounge or on the outdoor terrace. **Cons:** can get noisy from outside traffic; restaurant is a bit pricey; limited facilities. *Rooms from: €115 Largo Mestre Afonso Domingues 6 244 765 260 www.hotellisbatalha.pt 40 rooms Free Breakfast.*

★ **Hotel Villa Batalha**

$ | **HOTEL** | This smart, modern hotel on the edge of the old city is a great base for exploring Batalha. **Pros:** enjoy a round of golf on the 6-hole pitch-and-putt course; bar serves excellent local and foreign wines and brandies; close to monastery and other sights. **Cons:** sprawling property can feel impersonal; can get crowded from conferences; few amenities. *Rooms from: €85 Rua Dom Duarte I 248 244 240 400 www.hotelvillabatalha.com 93 rooms Free Breakfast.*

Leiria

11 km (7 miles) north of Batalha.

Leiria is a pleasant, modern, industrial town at the confluence of the Rios Liz and Lena, overlooked by a wonderfully elegant medieval castle. The region is known for its handicrafts, particularly the fine handblown glassware from nearby Marinha Grande.

GETTING HERE AND AROUND

The best option to get here is by car. There are two alternative highways between Lisbon and Leiria (A1 and A8), each of which takes about 1 hour 15 minutes; from Batalha it's 15 minutes.

It's also possible to take a Rede Expresso Bus from Lisbon to Leiria. Services within the region are provided by Leiria-based bus operator Rodoviário do Lis and its sister companies Rodoviária do Tejo and Rodoviário do Oeste.

BUS CONTACTS Leiria Bus Station. ✉ *Av. Heróis de Angola* ☎ *244 811 507* 🌐 *www.rodoviariadolis.pt.*

ESSENTIALS

VISITOR INFORMATION Leiria Tourist Office. ✉ *Jardim Luís de Camões* ☎ *244 848 770* 🌐 *turismodocentro.pt.*

Sights

Castelo de Leiria (*Leiria Castle*)
CASTLE/PALACE | Built in 1135 by Prince Afonso Henriques (later Portugal's first king), Leiria Castle was to become an important link in the chain of defenses along the southern border of what was at the time the Kingdom of Portugal. When the Moors were driven from the region, the castle lost its significance and lay dormant until the early 14th century, when it was restored and modified and became the favorite residence of Dom Dinis and his queen, Isabel of Aragon. With these modifications the castle became more of a palace than a fortress and remains one of the loveliest structures of its kind in Portugal. Within the perimeter walls you'll encounter the ruins of a Gothic church, the castle keep, and—built into the section of the fortifications overlooking the town—the royal palace. There's also a small museum in the keep. Lined by eight arches, the balcony of the palace affords lovely views. *Renovations on the castle are expected to continue until 2021, but guided tours will continue with advance bookings.* ✉ *Largo de São Pedro* ☎ *244 839 670* 🎫 *€2.10.*

Museu de Leiria (*Leireia Museum*)
MUSEUM | Housed in a former Augustinian monastery, Leiria's main museum presents the city's development from pre-Roman times through the construction of the castle and the planting of the region's vast pine forests at the behest of medieval kings. Among the most prized items is the "Lapedo child"—a skeleton from the early Upper Paleolithic, excavated locally in 1998, which has fueled debate about the origins of modern humans. Your ticket includes a free audio guide in English and admission to the **Moinho do Papel,** a beautifully restored nearby watermill where you can see cereals being ground and paper made the traditional way. ✉ *Rua Tenente Valadim 4* ☎ *244 839 677* 🎫 *€5.*

Museu do Vidro (*Glass Museum*)
HOUSE | Marinha Grande, just west of Leiria, is known for its fine-quality lead crystal, which has been produced in the region since the 17th century. The palatial 18th-century former home of William Stephens, the Englishman who re-established Portugal's Royal Glass Factory, now houses a museum showcasing glass and crystal from several periods and factories. There is a shop in the reception area. ✉ *Praça Guilherme Stephens, Marinha Grande* ☎ *244 573 377* 🎫 *€1.50* ⏲ *Closed Mon.*

Beaches

★ **Praia de São Pedro do Moel**
BEACH—SIGHT | One of Portugal's most picturesque beaches is framed by steep cliffs and a fast-flowing stream. Strong tides can make the ocean here hazardous, but there are lifeguards on duty in summer. The beach itself bustles with sporting activity, and at night the village bars are lively. Some local houses have an alpine look, thanks to the availability of pine from the forests that blanket the Leiria region—which also makes for lovely fresh air. **Amenities:** food and drink; lifeguards; parking (no fee); showers; toilets; water sports. **Best for:** sunset; surfing; swimming; walking. ✉ *Rua António José Bouça, São Pedro de Moel.*

Restaurants

Casinha Velha

$$ | **PORTUGUESE** | In an old house with rustic Portuguese furniture, this eatery sits in a village that has long been a haven for gourmands. They bake their own bread on the premises—including a delicious *pão chouriço*—and there's a series of tasty starters. **Known for:** pleasant downstairs bar where you can sample an aperitif; extensive wine collection is prominently displayed; everything is beautifully presented. *Average main: €19 Rua Professores Portelas 23, 1 km (½ mile) from the center of town, Marrazes 244 855 355 www.casinhavelha.com Closed Tues., 2 wks in Jan., and 2 wks in July. No dinner Sun.*

★ **O Casarão**

$$ | **PORTUGUESE** | About 5 km (3 miles) south of Leiria, O Casarão occupies a large country house surrounded by gardens where you may take an aperitif before your meal. Try the *ensopado de peixe* (fish stew) or, if there are two of you, split an *espedata de carne com gambas* (skewers of beef and shrimp), which comes with *migas de nabiça* (fried bread crumbs and turnip tops). **Known for:** service and presentation are flawless without being pretentious; several ancient recipes from nearby monasteries; amazing homemade desserts. *Average main: €17 Cruzamento de Azoia, Estrada da Maceira 10, off the N1 244 871 080 ocasarao.pai.pt Closed Mon.*

Hotels

Eurosol Residence

$ | **HOTEL** | **FAMILY** | A five-minute walk from downtown this hotel has studios or one- and two-bedroom apartments that are simply but pleasantly furnished with fully equipped modern kitchenettes. **Pros:** a large fitness center with sauna and steam room; awesome views from rooftop pool; free garage parking. **Cons:** no on-site restaurant; lacking in character; attracts tour groups. *Rooms from: €84 Rua Comissão da Iniciativa 13 244 860 460 www.eurosol.pt 58 apartments Free Breakfast.*

Hotel Casa da Nora

$ | **B&B/INN** | **FAMILY** | This former mill sits next to a small river with a darling little waterfall and waterwheel whose peaceful splashing add to the charm of the house's green, trellised garden. **Pros:** a short drive outside of Leiria; pleasant riverside location; plenty of activities. **Cons:** no telephone in rooms; no elevator; out of town. *Rooms from: €89 Largo José Marques da Cruz 8, Cortes 244 891 189 www.casadanora.com 14 rooms Free Breakfast.*

Benavente

80 km southeast of Óbidos.

Benavente is a small, country town in the heart of rural Ribatejo and of the Lezíria, which is Portuguese for the rich and fertile landscape stretching away from the banks of the Tagus River. The central location of Benavente is a great starting point for exploring the surrounding area, including the beautiful Reserva Natural do Estuário do Tejo. Benavente itself dates back to the 12th century, when Portuguese colonists settled on the southern bank of the Tagus.

GETTING HERE AND AROUND

Benavente is served by Ribetajana Bus 901 from Lisbon (Campo Grande), as well as the 903, which also links the town with Vila Franca de Xira. From Santarém there is the 902. By car it is 35 minutes away from Lisbon and 15 minutes from Vila Franca de Xira.

BUS CONTACTS Benavente Bus Station. *Praça Dr. João Jacinto 263 100 654 www.ribatejana.pt.*

ESSENTIALS

Benavente Tourist Office. ✉ *Edifício dos Antigos CTT, Praça do Município* ☎ *263 519 692.*

Sights

Adega Catapereiro

FARM/RANCH | The 44,500-acre farmstead of Companhia das Lezírias is filled with forests of cork oaks, stone pines, and eucalyptus trees. Rice is also grown and sold under the "Belmonte" and "Bom Sucesso" labels, and the company does organic cattle farming and breeds prize-winning Lusitano stallions. Its winery, Adega Catapereiro, 12 km (7½ miles) south of Samora Correia, offers guided visits with tastings. ✉ *Adega Catapereiro, N118, Km 20, Samora Correia* ☎ *212 349 016* 🌐 *turismo.cl.pt* ☞ *Winery and shop closed Sun.*

Casa Cadaval

WINERY/DISTILLERY | If you're a fan of wine, stop by the prestigious Casa Cadaval between Benavente and Almeirim. This winery, on the Herdade de Muge estate, has belonged to the Alvares Pereira Melo family since 1648. The winery produces red, white, and rosé wines under the Casa Cadaval, Marquesa de Cadaval, and Padre Pedro labels, using both native and international grape varieties, like Pinot Noir. The estate has a wine store with a tasting room, and visits can include a tour of the winery. ✉ *Rua Vasco da Gama, Muge* ☎ *243 588 040* 🌐 *www.casacadaval.pt.*

Reserva Natural do Estuário do Tejo

NATURE PRESERVE | This extensive natural reserve area lies along the banks of the Tagus River and has diverse fauna and flora, great bird-watching, and hiking through the area. The privately run EVOA Visitor Center is one of the best ways to see the park. It can organize tours by foot or electric vehicle from its location beside the park or from Lisbon. ✉ *EVOA Visitor Centre, Lezíria Sul* ☎ 🌐 *evoa.pt/en/home* 🎟 *€12* ⏲ *Visitor center closed Mon., and July.*

Restaurants

A Coudelaria

$ | PORTUGUESE | This restaurant is noted for bacalhau and octopus dishes. On Saturday there is a hearty buffet, and on Sunday, people come from far and near for the *cozido de carnes bravas à Ribatejana* (stew made with meat from local bulls). **Known for:** pretty dining rooms warmed by a stone fireplace; dinner is available only if booked in advance; array of tempting desserts. 💲 *Average main: €13* ✉ *Coudelaria da Companhia das Lezírias, N118, Km 19, Monte de Braço de Prata, Porto Alto* ☎ *263 654 985* 🌐 *www.acoudelaria.com* ⏲ *Closed Mon. and Aug.*

Hotels

Benavente Vila Hotel

$ | HOTEL | This small boutique hotel on Benavente's main square has guest rooms done up in a simple yet modern style with splashes of lime green and other colors. **Pros:** some great package deals for those exploring the region; bistro offers interesting updated Portuguese dishes; staff is happy to help in any way. **Cons:** no designated parking; rooms are a bit small; basic decor. 💲 *Rooms from: €70* ✉ *Praça Da República 39/40* ☎ *263 518 210* 🌐 *www.benaventevilahotel.pt* 🛏 *20 rooms* 🍽 *Free Breakfast.*

Activities

GOLF

RibaGolfe

GOLF | A 20-minute drive from Benavente, RibaGolfe has two 18-hole courses designed by architects Peter Townsend and Michael King. They encompass more than 6,000 yards each and are set in beautiful sloping terrain lined with large cork-oak trees. The golf course also has a training center with a driving range, putting and pitching greens, and a practice bunker. ✉ *Vargem Fresca, N119, Km 23, Infantado, Samora Correia* ☎ *263 930 040* 🌐 *www.orizontegolf.com* 🏌 *Ribagolfe I: 18 holes, 6707 m, par 72. Greens fee €90 (9 holes €64). Ribagolfe II: 18 holes, 6214 m, par 72. Greens fee €90 (9 holes €64)* ✍ *Reservations essential.*

Santo Estêvão

GOLF | This relatively plain but well-designed golf course 12 km (7½ miles) southeast of Benavente makes the most of existing landscape features on these rolling plains with broad fairways and two pleasant lakes. The first few holes are straightforward, but by the 8th things have become rather more challenging on the greens. The 11th hole, a par 4, is generally seen as both the prettiest and the trickiest to play well. ✉ *Vila Nova de Santo Estêvão, CCI 19* ☎ *263 949 492* 🌐 *www.orizontegolf.com* 🏌 *18 holes, 6382 m, par 73. Greens fee: €90 (9 holes €64).*

Almeirim

4 km (2½ miles) east of Santarém.

Almeirim, a pretty country town just across the river from Santarém, is surrounded by vineyards and cork-oak forests. Many people from nearby cities and all over Portugal come to this town dubbed the "capital of stone soup," which is a widely known local recipe that has cute story behind it.

GETTING HERE AND AROUND

Almeirim is served by the Ribatejana Bus 902 from Santarém and Benavente and Rede Expressos from Lisbon. (The stop is at Travessa da Olaria 10A and tickets may be bought at Papelaria Fina at Rua 5 de Outubro 61.) By car, it is about 50 to 60 minutes away from Lisbon,and 10 minutes from Santarém.

ESSENTIALS

VISITOR INFO Almeirim Tourist Office. ✉ *Arena de Almeirim, Largo da Praça de Touros, Loja 9* ✣ *In bullring complex* ☎ *243 594 107.*

Sights

Casa dos Patudos

HOUSE | Alpiarça is a pleasant little town 7 km (4 miles) northeast of Almeirim on the N118. Here you'll have the chance to see how a wealthy country gentleman lived at the beginning of the 20th century. The Casa dos Patudos, now a museum, was the estate of José Relvas, a diplomat and prosperous local farmer. This unusual three-story manor house with its zebra-stripe spire is surrounded by gardens and vineyards and is filled with an impressive assemblage of ceramics, paintings, and furnishings—including Portugal's foremost collection of Arraiolos carpets. ✉ *Rua José Relvas, Alpiarça* ☎ *243 558 321* 🎫 *€2.50* ⏲ *Closed Mon.*

Quinta da Alorna

WINERY/DISTILLERY | This 6,900-acre farm and winery encompasses a vineyard established in 1723 by the Marquês de Alorna, a viceroy of India. It is known particularly for its ripe, floral whites. There's a shop right outside the entrance where you can purchase the wines and other regional products such as honey, jams, olive oil, and sausages. There are no regular tours of the winery, but if you call a day or two ahead, they may be able to arrange a visit and tasting. ✉ *N118, Km 73* ☎ *243 570 700, 243 570 706 for shop* 🌐 *www.alorna.pt.*

Quinta do Casal Branco

WINERY/DISTILLERY | For the gastronome in you, spend a day wining and dining at this 1,630-acre estate; 346 acres are vineyards. The quinta has been owned by the same family for more than 200 years and used to be one of largest royal falconry grounds in the country. The winery produces red, white, rosé, and sparkling

Local Legends

Almeirim is visited mostly because it has a number of restaurants that serve a local delicacy called *sopa da pedra* (stone soup). A local legend says there was once a friar on a pilgrimage traveling through the area who was too proud to beg for food so he knocked on the doors of the houses and asked for only a pot "to make a delicious and filling ... stone soup." Then he took a *pedra* (stone) and dropped it into a boiling pot of water. A little later, he tasted it and approached a housewife, saying, "it just needs a little seasoning." So, she came back with some salt, to which he said "maybe a little bit of sausage or if you also have some potatoes left over from the previous meal then maybe that would make it just a bit better." So she came back with all three and added them to the pot. Eventually, everyone in the village came to contribute to the soup, with carrots, beans, meat, sausage, and other vegetables until it had indeed become a very hearty soup. At the end, the friar fished the stone out of the pot, washed it off, and tucked it into his pocket to save for the next meal. Today Almeirim's sopa da pedra recipe is judged as the best around, and it can easily be eaten as a meal on its own or as a starter to accompany other regional dishes if you have a healthy appetite. Some places still put a small (washed) stone at the bottom. **TIP→ You can find most of the sopa da pedra restaurants across from the bullfighting ring in the Largo da Praça de Touros.** Don't forget to pay a visit to the friar himself. There's a statue of him sitting in front of his soup, located just down the street from the bullfighting plaza on Rua de Coruche.

wines, as well as olive oil under numerous labels which include Capoeira, Terra de Lobos, and their flagship Casal Branco. They use native grape varieties such as Castelão for reds and Fernão Pires for whites, as well as international ones like Syrah, Merlot, Cabernet Sauvignon, and Petit Verdot. Call ahead for a guided tour of the cellar ending with a wine tasting, or for lunch or dinner in the small restaurant. The shop sells its wines and olive oil, as well as homemade jams, cheeses, and traditional sausages. ✉ *N118, Km 69, Benfica do Ribatejo* ☎ *243 592 412* 🌐 *www.casalbranco.com.*

Restaurants

★ O Toucinho

$ | PORTUGUESE | This is Almeirim's most popular traditional restaurant, thanks to its excellent grilled meats—lamb and pork as well as steak—and of course the *sopa da pedra,* which O Toucinho claims to have reinvented back in the 1960s. It is run by a former *forcado* (one of the bullfighters who literally grab the animal by the horns)—as the bull's heads and bullfight posters will remind you. **Known for:** check out the kitchen, where the rustic bread is made all day long; desserts such as arroz doce are cooked in a wood-burning oven; your choice of four handsome dining rooms. [$] *Average main: €12* ✉ *Rua de Timor 2* ☎ *243 592 237* 🌐 *www.toucinho.com* 🕑 *Closed Thurs., 2 wks in June, and 1 wk in Aug.*

Hotels

Quinta da Gafaria

$ | B&B/INN | FAMILY | This homestead midway between Santarém and Almeirim offers modern, tastefully decorated lodgings with plenty of opportunities for contact with the farming and ranching operations. **Pros:** ample opportunity for walks in the surrounding marshland; guests have the use of a large barbecue; gorgeous countryside setting. **Cons:** dining room doesn't serve lunch or dinner; not many facilities; remote location. ⑤ *Rooms from: €90* ✉ *Almeirim* ☎ *919 762 584* 🌐 *www.quintadagafaria.com* *10 rooms, 2 apartments* *Free Breakfast.*

Santarém

7 km (4½ miles) northwest of Almeirim.

Some historians believe that Santarém's beginnings date to as early as 1200 BC and the age of Ulysses. Its strategic location led several kings to choose it as their residence, and the Cortes (Parliament) frequently met here. Thanks to its royal connections, Santarém is more richly endowed with monuments than other towns of its size. The Portuguese refer to it as their "Gothic capital."

Present-day Santarém, high above the Tagus River, is an important farming and livestock center. It holds the largest agricultural fair in the country, just outside town. Even with a tradition of bull breeding and bullfighting, Santarém curiously has what is considered the ugliest bullring on the Iberian Peninsula. Santarém also has bull farms and a working stud farm.

GETTING HERE AND AROUND

Santarém is served by bus (Ribatejana via Vila Franca de Xira and Lisbon and Rede Expressos via Lisbon) and also by the Intercidades, Alfa Pendular, and Regional trains coming from Lisbon, Vila Franca de Xira, and many other stops to and from the north. By car, it's 45 minutes from Lisbon, 25 minutes from Vila Franca de Xira, and five minutes from Almeirim.

BUS CONTACTS Santarém Bus Station. ✉ *Av. Brasil 41* ☎ *243 333 200* 🌐 *www.rodotejo.pt.*

ESSENTIALS

VISITOR INFORMATION Santarém Tourist Office. ✉ *Rua Capelo Ivens 63* ☎ *243 304 258.*

FESTIVALS

Festival Nacional de Gastronomia
FESTIVAL | From late October through to early November, Santarém each year hosts the National Festival of Gastronomy, the longest-running in Portugal. It's held in the Casa do Campino, next to the bullfighting ring, where numerous restaurants from all over the country come to showcase the best gastronomy delights of their area and establishment. The festival includes competitions in various categories of cuisine—often with the opportunity for you to try the winners' wares—and you are guaranteed to eat well here. There is also plenty of handicrafts, folk music, and dancing. ✉ *Casa do Campino, Campo Infante da Câmara* ☎ *243 300 900* 🌐 *www.festivalnacionaldegastronomia.pt* *€2.*

Sights

Igreja da Graça (*Graça Church*)
RELIGIOUS SITE | The 14th-century Gothic church contains the gravestone of Pedro Álvares Cabral, the discoverer of Brazil. (There's also a tomb of the explorer in Belmonte, the town of his birth in northeastern Portugal, but no one is really sure just what—or who—is in which tomb.) Note the delicate rose window whose setting was carved from a single slab of stone. Guided visits to the church may be booked in advance at the city tourist office. ✉ *Largo Pedro Álvares Cabral* ☎.

Igreja de Santa Clara (*Santa Clara Church*)
RELIGIOUS SITE | Santarém is often known as the Gothic capital of Portugal; the Igreja de Santa Clara is an outstanding local example of this medieval architectural style. The 13th-century church was

built by Dom Alfonso III for his daughter Leonor, a nun who took her religious orders there. (Her tomb is one of the highlights of the interior.) Note that this austere stone building has no front door, because the Order of St. Clare did not permit contact with the public. ✉ *Av. Gago Coutinho e Sacadura Cabral* ⏲ *Closed Mon.*

Jardim das Portas do Sol (*Doors of the Sun Garden*)
NATIONAL/STATE PARK | Walk up to this lovely park within the ancient walls. From this vantage point you can look down on a sweeping bend in the river and beyond to the farmlands that stretch into the neighboring Alentejo. ✉ *Santarém.*

Museu Diocesano de Santarém (*Diocese Museum of Santarém*)
MUSEUM | One of the city's treasures, this museum occupies a former seminary. Inside you'll find examples of religious art spanning the centuries, but the best reason to visit is the grandeur of the space itself. ✉ *Praça Sá da Bandeira 1* ☎ *243 304 065* 🌐 *www.museudiocesanodesantarem.pt.*

Restaurants

Adiafa
$ | PORTUGUESE | Near the town's bullring, this typical Ribatejo restaurant is decked out with bullfighting memorabilia. The *ensopado de borrego* (lamb stew) is renowned, as is the *mangusto com bacalhau assado* (a garlickly bread-and-cabbage soup accompanying roasted codfish with fresh herbs). **Known for:** excellent selection of grilled meats; fried shad from the Tagus River; a warming fire in the hearth. 💲 *Average main: €9* ✉ *Campo Emilio Infante da Câmara* ☎ 🌐 *adiafa-restaurante.eatbu.com* ⏲ *Closed Tues., last wk of Aug., and 1st wk of Sept.*

Taberna da Quinzena
$ | PORTUGUESE | Photos of pleased patrons testify to the popularity of this rustic restaurant run by the great-grandson of the original owner, offering hearty traditional fare at low prices. Specialties include *toiro bravo* (wild bull) and *entrecosto com arroz de feijoca* (spareribs with red beans and rice), but the menu is overhauled daily. **Known for:** charmingly old-fashioned interior; lots of bullfighting souvenirs; the place to try local wines. 💲 *Average main: €8* ✉ *Rua Pedro de Santarém 93* ☎ *243 322 804* 🌐 *www.quinzena.com* 💳 *No credit cards* ⏲ *Closed Sun., and 2nd half of Aug.*

Hotels

Quinta M
$$ | B&B/INN | Glamping has been slow to catch on in Portugal, but these gorgeous yurts in a lovely rural setting provide you with creature comforts like a private terraces set in lush gardens. **Pros:** skylights so you can gaze at the stars at night; books ahead for relaxing massages or meditation; pretty pool highlights the grounds. **Cons:** no restaurant, but they can make lunches; rather isolated location; books up fast. 💲 *Rooms from: €180* ✉ *Casal da Avó, Várzea de baixo, Casével* ☎ *243 448 206* 🌐 *www.quinta-m.com* 🛏 *4 yurts* 🍽 *Free Breakfast.*

Santarém Hotel
$ | HOTEL | FAMILY | Three swimming pools, a saunas for men and women, fitness center, and a locally famous tavern are among the draws at this contemporary hotel, where rooms overlook the plains or the town. **Pros:** sparkling after a top-to-bottom renovation; free parking and other perks; excellent restaurant. **Cons:** hotel lacks local character; not in the city center; chain-hotel feel. 💲 *Rooms from: €80* ✉ *Av. Madre Andaluz* ☎ *243 330 800* 🌐 *www.santaremhotel.net* 🛏 *105 rooms* 🍽 *Free Breakfast.*

Constância

18½ km (11 miles) southeast of Tomar, 4 km (2½ miles) east of Castelo de Almourol.

Peaceful little Constância is at the confluence of the Zêzere and the Tagus. It's best known as the town where poet Luís de Camões was exiled in 1548, the unfortunate result of his romantic involvement with Catarina de Ataide, the "Natercia" of his poems and a lady-in-waiting to Queen Catarina. There's a bronze statue of the bard in a reflective pose at the riverbank. The town is surrounded by beautiful Ribatejan countryside and is a 10-minute drive to the famous Castelo de Almourol.

GETTING HERE AND AROUND

Bus services run by Rodoviária do Tejo links Constância with other towns in the region, but from Lisbon you should catch an express bus (Rede Expressos) to Torres Novas and change there. Driving from Lisbon takes about 1 hour 25 minutes, from Tomar about 30 minutes, and from Santarém about 40 minutes on A23 and A1.

ESSENTIALS

VISITOR INFORMATION Constância Tourist Office. ✉ *Av. das Forças Armadas* ☎ *249 730 052.*

National Horse Fair

Feira Nacional do Cavalo About 19 km (12 miles) southwest of Constância is the town of Golegã, one of Portugal's most notable horse-breeding centers. During the first two weeks of November, this is the site of the colorful Feira Nacional do Cavalo, the most important event of its kind in the country, staged for the past 250 years. It has riding displays, horse and trap competitions, and stalls that sell handicrafts. ✉ *Largo Marquês de Pombal 25, Golegã* ☎ *249 976 302* 🌐 *www.feiradagolega.com.*

Sights

★ **Castelo de Almourol** (*Almourol Castle*)
CASTLE/PALACE | For a close look at this storybook castle on a craggy island in the Tagus River, take the 1½-km-long (1-mile-long) dirt road leading down to the water from the N3. The riverbank in this area is practically deserted, making it a wonderful picnic spot. From here, a small motorboat will ferry you across (€4 round-trip); for a more leisurely river cruise, book ahead to board a larger vessel (€6) at the quay just downstream in the village of Tancos. The sight couldn't be more romantic: an ancient castle with crenellated walls and a lofty tower sits on a greenery-covered rock in the middle of a gently flowing river. The stuff of poetry and legends, Almourol was the setting for Francisco de Morais's epic novel *Palmeirim da Inglaterra* (*Palmeirin of England*), about two knights fighting for a princess's favor. ■ **TIP→ Your boat tickets includes admission to the castle and its small museum.** ✉ *Ilhota do Tejo, Almourol* ☎ *249 712 094 for boat reservations* 🌐 *www.cm-vnbarquinha.pt* 🎫 *€4* ⊗ *Castle and Templar Center closed Sun. Oct.–Apr.*

Hotels

★ **Quinta de Santa Barbara**
$ | B&B/INN | Set on some 45 acres of farmland and pine forests overlooking the Tagus River, this property with its several sprawling buildings, a few of which date to the 16th century, is the perfect place to immerse yourself in the Portuguese countryside. **Pros:** peaceful setting a short drive from town; cottages are a good size for families; lovely views from the swimming pool. **Cons:** must

reserve ahead for the popular restaurant; no elevator to the upper floor; few room amenities. $ *Rooms from: €75* ✉ *Estrada da Quinta de Santa Bárbara* ✣ *2 km (1 mile) east of Constância on N3; follow directions on sign at traffic circle to Refeitório Quinhentista* ☎ *249 739 214, 966 039 067* 🌐 *www.quinta-santabarbara.com* *9 rooms* *Free Breakfast.*

Activities

CANOEING

gAventura

TOUR—SPORTS | The experienced English-speaking guides at this canoeing outfitter based at a bar on the east bank of the Zêzere River offer half-day excursions starting at €15 per person ✉ *Glaciar Sports Bar, Av. das Forças Armadas, Parque de Campismo* ☎ *962 503 986* 🌐 *www.gaventura.com.*

Abrantes

16 km (10 miles) east of Constância.

A stroll through the narrow cobblestone streets of Abrantes is a perfect way to spend a lazy afternoon, especially if it winds up at the hilltop castle dating from the 16th century. The views of the valley from the top are nothing short of breathtaking.

Abrantes became one of the country's most populous and prosperous towns during the 16th century, when the Tagus River was navigable all the way to the sea. With the coming of the railroad and the development of better roads, the town's commercial importance waned. It remains a good place to see the country's interesting history and meet friendly locals have also stayed true to traditions.

GETTING HERE AND AROUND

If you're already in the area, Abrantes is an easy 20-minute drive from Constância or 40-minute drive to Tomar. From Lisbon, it's about a 1½-hour drive. There are a few direct trains from Santa Apolónia and Oriente stations, taking at least one hour 30 minutes; you may have to change once or twice. By bus, the Rede Expressos and Rodoviária do Tejo leave daily from Sete Rios and Campo Grande depots, respectively.

BUS CONTACTS Abrantes Bus Station. ✉ *Rua Prof. Dr. Diogo Freitas do Amaral* ☎ *968 692 113.*

ESSENTIALS

VISITOR INFORMATION Abrantes Tourist Office. ✉ *Edifício do Mercado Diário, Esplanada 1° de Maio* ☎ *241 330 100* 🌐 *www.turismo.cm-abrantes.pt.*

Sights

Castelo de Abrantes (*Abrantes Castle*)

CASTLE/PALACE | Walk up through the maze of narrow, flower-lined streets to this 16th-century castle, which is still an impressive structure today. The garden between the twin fortifications, with its panoramic views, is a wonderful place to watch the sun set: the play of light on the river and the lengthening shadows along the olive groves provide a stirring setting for an evening picnic. The Gothic church within the castle walls, the Igreja de Santa Maria do Castelo, houses a museum that showcases sacred art from convents and monasteries around the region, as well as items from a large private collection of Iberian art from prehistoric to contemporary times. ✉ *Praça Dom Francisco de Almeida* ☎ *241 371 724* *Free* *Closed Mon.*

Castelo de Belver (*Belver Castle*)

CASTLE/PALACE | This fairy-tale castle—the fortress of Belver—rests atop a cone-shape hill and commands a superb view of the Tagus River. It was built in the last years of the 12th century by the Knights Hospitallers under the command of King Sancho I. In 1194, this region was threatened by the Moorish forces who controlled the lands south of the river. The expected attack never took place, and the present structure is little changed from its original design. The walls of the keep, which stands in the center of the courtyard, are some 12 feet thick, and on the ground floor is a great cistern of unknown depth. According to local lore, an orange dropped into the well will later appear bobbing down the river. A 30-minute drive from Abrantes, the castle is reached via the N244–3 through the pine-covered hills to Chão de Codes, then the N244 south toward Gavião. There are four trains a day to Belver from Abrantes (a 25-minute ride). *Belver, Gavião, Portalegre 241 639 070 €2 Closed Mon. and Tues.*

Restaurants

Santa Isabel

$ | **PORTUGUESE** | In this warren of stone-flagged rooms, authentic regional dishes are served with flair to well-heeled locals. Specialties include *churrasquinho de porco preto com migas de alheira de caça* (grilled meats from the acorn-fed Iberian black pig, served with a bread-crumb-and-garlic-sausage mixture flavored with game sausage) and *enguias fritas com açorda de ovas* (fried eels with fish-roe bread soup). **Known for:** this old-town spot is mostly off the tourist trail; on winter evening there's a fire in the grate; a good range of Portuguese wines. *Average main: €15 Rua Sta. Isabel 12 241 366 230 Closed Sun., and 1 wk in July.*

Hotels

Luna Hotel Turismo

$ | **HOTEL** | IA 10-minute walk from the castle, this 1950s-era hotel has been transformed into a gorgeous boutique lodging. **Pros:** there's a gym and a spa with a sauna, whirlpool tub, and steam room; pretty pool surrounded by lounge chairs; extensive facilities. **Cons:** mid-century modern exterior not for everyone; location is a bit far from town; lacking in local character. *Rooms from: €80 Largo de Santo António 289 009 400 www.lunahoteis.com 44 rooms Free Breakfast.*

Monte da Várzea

$ | **B&B/INN** | This farmstead 20 km (12½ miles) east of Abrantes is set in fertile land dotted with lagoons near the banks of the Tagus River; its 12 houses—some traditionally decorated, others strikingly modern—take advantage of this peaceful setting. **Pros:** cozy bar is decked out with car-racing memorabilia; staff can arrange canoeing, horse riding, mountain biking; the gem of a pool once stored water for irrigating the fields. **Cons:** remote location; no gym, spa, or indoor pool. *Rooms from: €100 Casa Branca, off N118 241 822 284 www.montedavarzea.com 12 villas Free Breakfast No credit cards.*

Tomar

24 km (15 miles) east of Fátima, 64 km (40 miles) northeast of Santarém.

TOn both sides of the Nabão River, Tomar is linked by a graceful, arched stone bridge. The river flows through a lovely park with weeping willows and an old wooden waterwheel. The town is best known for being the former headquarters of the Order of the Knights Templar and home to their Convento do Cristo, which is a UNESCO World Heritage Site. The town was an important industrial center from medieval times, and its long-abandoned riverside buildings are being transformed into a series of museums called the Complexo Cultural da Levada.

The town hosts the Festa dos Tabuleiros every four years in July. This ancient tradition is also the oldest festival in Portugal and consists of parades of girls carrying large *tabuleiros,* platters piled high with 30 loaves of bread fixed on rods, interspersed with flowers and topped with a crown. They wear these unusual headpieces in honor of the Holy

Spirit, but the festival actually dates back to pagan times.

GETTING HERE AND AROUND

There's a train line between Lisbon (Santa Apolónia and Oriente stations) and Tomar with several daily departures that run through Santarém. Taking the bus (Rede Expressos from Lisbon or other cities, or Rodoviária do Tejo from surrounding towns) is another possibility. Driving to Tomar takes 1 hour 15 minutes from Lisbon and close to 25 minutes from Santarém or Fátima.

BUS CONTACTS Tomar Bus Station. ✉ *Av. Combatentes da Grande Guerra , Varzea Grande* ☎ *924 450 001* 🌐 *www.rodotejo.pt.*

ESSENTIALS

VISITOR INFORMATION Tomar Tourist Office. ✉ *Av. Dr. Cândido Madureira* ☎ *249 329 823* 🌐 *www.cm-tomar.pt.*

Sights

Aqueduto dos Pegões (*Pegões Aqueduct*)
ARCHAEOLOGICAL SITE | Striding across the Ribeira dos Pegões valley, some 5 km (3 miles) northwest of Tomar, is a 5-km-long (3-mile-long) aqueduct, built in the 16th century to bring water to Tomar. It joins the walls of the Convent of Christ. ✉ *Tomar.*

★ **Convento de Cristo** (*Convent of Christ*)
MILITARY SITE | Atop a hill rising from the Old Town is this remarkable UNESCO World Hereitage Site. You can drive to the top of the hill or hike for about 20 minutes along a path through the trees before reaching a formal garden lined with azulejo-covered benches. This was the Portuguese headquarters of the Knights Templar, from 1160 until the order was forced to disband in 1314. Identified by their white tunics emblazoned with a crimson cross, the Templars were at the forefront of the Christian armies in the Crusades and during the struggles against the Moors. King Dinis in 1334 resurrected the order in Portugal under the banner of the Knights of Christ and reestablished Tomar as its headquarters. In the early 15th century, under Prince Henry the Navigator (who for a time resided in the castle), the order flourished. The caravels of the Age of Discovery even sailed under the order's crimson cross.

The oldest parts of the complex date to the 12th century, including the towering castle keep and the fortresslike, 16-sided Charola, which—like many Templar churches—is patterned after the Church of the Holy Sepulchre in Jerusalem and has an octagonal oratory at its core. The paintings and wooden statues in its interior, however, were added in the 16th century. The complex's medieval nucleus acquired its Manueline church and cluster of magnificent cloisters during the next 500 years. To see what the Manueline style is all about, stroll through the church's nave with its many examples of the twisted ropes, seaweed, and nautical themes that typify the style, and be sure to look at the chapter house window, one of the most photographed in Europe. ✉ *Estrada do Convento* ☎ *249 313 481* 🌐 *www.conventocristo.pt* 🎫 *€6; €15 combined ticket includes Alcobaça and Batalha monasteries.*

Igreja de Santa Maria do Olival (*Church of Saint Mary of the Olive Grove*)
RELIGIOUS SITE | The 13th-century Igreja de Santa Maria do Olival—still set in an olive grove, as the name suggests—is where the bones of several Knights Templar are interred, including those of Gualdim Pais, founder of the order in Portugal; his original tomb slab, dated from 1195, can still be seen inside. The church later served the same purpose for the Order of Christ, which succeeded the Templars in the 14th century. Popular belief—supported by some archaeological evidence—has it that the church was once connected with the Convent of Christ by a tunnel. ✉ *Rua Aquiles de Mota Lima* ⏲ *Closed Mon.*

Museu Luso-Hebraico Abraham Zacuto (*Abraham Zacuto Hebrew Museum*)
RELIGIOUS SITE | In the Old Town, a stroll along the flower-lined street of Rua Dr. Joaquim Jacinto takes you to the heart of the Jewish Quarter and this former synagogue, now a modest museum. Built in the mid-15th century for what was then a sizeable community, this is Portugal's oldest extant synagogue, though there are only a handful of Jewish families currently living in Tomar, so it's rarely used as a house of prayer. Inside, exhibits chronicle the Jewish presence in the country, which all but ended in 1496 when Dom Manuel issued an edict ordering Jews to either leave the country or convert to Christianity. Many, who became known as Marranos, converted but secretly practiced Judaism. The building was declared a national monument in 1921 and is open for visits. Call the Tomar Tourist Office in advance to set up a free guided visit in English. *Rua Dr. Joaquim Jacinto 73* *249 329 823* *Free* *Closed Mon.*

Roda do Mouchão (*Mouchão Wheel*)
FACTORY | This enormous working wooden waterwheel—typical of those once used in the region for irrigation—stands in the Parque do Mouchão gardens by the Rio Nabão. The wheel is a replica, but its design is thought to be of either Arabic or Roman origin. *Av. Marquês de Tomar.*

Restaurants

A Bela Vista
$ | PORTUGUESE | The date on the sidewalk out front reads 1922, which was when the Sousa family opened this attractive little restaurant next to the old arched bridge. Carrying on the family tradition, the kitchen turns out great quantities of hearty regional fare. **Known for:** for summer dining there's a small, rustic terrace; views of the river and the nearby convent; traditional local desserts. *Average main: €13* *Rua Marquês Pombal 68 Ponte Velha* *249 312 870* *restaurantebelavista.pai.pt* *Closed Tues. and 2 wks in Oct. No dinner Mon.*

★ **Chico Elias**
$$ | PORTUGUESE | This charmingly rustic restaurant just outside Tomar owes its fame to chef Maria do Céu's creativity. At lunch on weekends there are delicious hearty dishes such as *cabrito assado* (roast kid) and *cachola* (pork rib and loin, served with cabbage); call the day before for dinner, because the dishes take time to prepare in the wood-burning oven. **Known for:** favorite dishes include feijoada de caracoís (bean stew with snails); huge families flock to this longtime favorite; laid-back atmosphere. *Average main: €16* *Rua Principal 70, Algarvios* *249 311 067* *No credit cards* *Closed Tues., last wk in Aug.*

Hotels

★ **Hotel dos Templários**
$ | HOTEL | This sprawling modern hotel in a tranquil park along the Nabão River makes a good base for exploring the whole area. **Pros:** standard rooms so big they look like suites; free Wi-Fi and lots of other amenities; spa offers a range of treatments. **Cons:** large size gives a somewhat impersonal feel; the spa and restaurant are a bit pricey; no covered parking. *Rooms from: €120* *Largo Candido dos Reis 1* *249 310 100* *www.hoteldostemplarios.com* *176 rooms* *Free Breakfast.*

Thomar Boutique Hotel
$ | HOTEL | Across the bridge from the center of the city, this handsome hotel features many decorative motifs that recall the eras of the Romans and the Knights Templars. **Pros:** fabulous view from many parts of the hotel; great location away from crowds; staff is happy to organize tours. **Cons:** breakfast room gets a little crowded; not many amenities; no on-site parking. *Rooms from: €80* *Rua de Santa Iria 14* *249 323 210*

thomarboutiquehotel.pt 24 rooms No meals.

Activities

Barco São Cristóvão

BOAT TOURS | Trips along the Rio Zêzere on the 164-passenger *São Cristóvão* depart in the summer from a dock at the Lago Azul Hotel. Two-hour cruises cost €15 per person, while four-hour cruises including a buffet lunch with wine cost €38. *Lago Azul Hotel, N348, Castanheira, Ferreira do Zêzere 249 310 100 for Hotel dos Templários www.barcosaocristovao.com.*

Fátima

20 km (12 miles) northwest of Torres Vedras, 16 km (10 miles) southeast of Batalha, 20 km (12 miles) southeast of Leiria.

On the western flanks of the Serra de Aire lies Fátima, an important Roman Catholic pilgrimage site that is, ironically, named after the daughter of Mohammed, the prophet of Islam. If you visit this sleepy little Portuguese town in between pilgrimages, it will be difficult to imagine the thousands of faithful who come from all corners of the world to make this religious affirmation, cramming the roads, squares, parks, and virtually every square foot of space. A few pilgrims go the last miles on their knees; many more complete their approach within the sanctuary that way.

GETTING HERE AND AROUND

Rede Expressos and Rodoviária do Tejo buses take you to Fátima from Lisbon or Leiria. Another option is driving, which will take close to one hour from Lisbon and 15 minutes from Leiria.

BUS CONTACTS Fatima Bus Station. *Av. Dom José Alves Correia Silva 249 531 611 www.rodotejo.pt.*

ESSENTIALS

VISITOR INFORMATION Fátima Tourist Office. *Av. Dom José Alves Correia da Silva 213 249 531 139 www.turismo-docentro.pt.* **Santuário de Fátima.** *Rua de Santa Isabel 360 249 539 600 www.fatima.pt.*

Sights

Basílica da Santíssima Trindade (*Basilica of the Holy Trinity*)

RELIGIOUS SITE | One of the largest Catholic churches in the world, seating some 8,500 worshipers, the Holy Trinity was consecrated in 2007 and raised to the state of basilica in 2012. Although it won prizes for engineering rather than architecture, its ample, curved form—designed by Greek architect Alexandros Tombazis—offers a pleasing contrast to its rather run-of-the-mill 1920s predecessor. Much of the iconography, including on the lavish main doors, was inspired by Byzantine and Orthodox motifs, and was produced by artists from Portugal and seven other countries. The Tall Cross crucifix outside the church is by the German artist Robert Schad. *Rua João Paulo II 249 539 600 www.santuario-fatima.pt Free.*

Basílica de Nossa Senhora de Fátima (*Basilica of Our Lady of Fatima*)

RELIGIOUS SITE | At the head of the huge esplanade is the large neoclassical basilica built in the late 1920s, flanked on either side by a semicircular peristyle. Inside you will find the tombs of all three of the "little shepherds" who saw the Virgin Mary. *Cova de Iria 249 539 600 www.santuario-fatima.pt Free.*

Capela das Aparições (*Chapel of Apparitions*)

RELIGIOUS SITE | This tiny chapel—now ringed by benches and covered by a much larger modern canopy—was built in 1920 on the site where the appearances of the Virgin Mary are said to have taken place. A plinth with a statue of the

Luz Charming Houses

| **HOTEL** | Nestled in a nature reserve the outskirts of Fátima, this stylish sort-style lodging has cottages inspired local architecture of the 19th and early th centuries (though their solar panels d open-plan interiors are completely -to-date). **Pros:** a short walk to the me of the little shepherds; activi-s include yoga and pottery classes; lightfully laid-back atmosphere. **Cons:** a le far from the city's main attractions; en-plan rooms not to everyone's taste; oks up quickly. *Rooms from: €140 Rua Principal 78, Moimento 249 532 5 www.luzhouses.pt Closed 1 wk Jan. 15 rooms Free Breakfast.*

The Basílica de Nossa Senhora de Fátima is an important Roman Catholic pilgrimage site.

Virgin marks the exact spot. Encrusted in her bejeweled, golden crown is the bullet extracted from the body of Pope John Paul II after the 1981 assassination attempt on his life. Gifts, mostly wax reproductions of body parts, are burned nearby as offerings to the Virgin in the hope of achieving a miraculous cure. ✉ *Cova da Iria* ☎ *249 539 600* *www.santuario-fatima.pt* *Free.*

Casas dos Pastorinhos (*Little Shepherd Houses*)

HOUSE | These are the cottages, in the nearby hamlet of Aljustrel, where the three shepherd children who saw the Virgin Mary were born. To reach them, from Fátima's Rotunda Sul (south roundabout) take the N360 to Aljustrel for just over 1 km (½ mile) and turn right onto Rua de Aljustrel (signposted "Museu"). At the next major junction, the two houses of the little shepherds are along the street to the left, along with the **Casa-Museu de Aljustrel,** a small museum that aims to give visitors some idea of what life was like in those times. It also displays some the children's own personal items. ✉ *Rua dos Pastorinhos, Aljustrel* ☎ *249 532 828* *€1* *Closed Tues.*

Grutas da Moeda (*Coin Caves*)

NATURE SITE | **FAMILY** | The hills to the south and west of Fátima are honeycombed with limestone caves. Legend has it that many years ago, a wealthy man carrying a bag of coins was traveling through the woods when he was attacked by a gang of thieves. Struggling from the attack, the man fell into one of the grottoes. Through the cave, the lost coins were spread around, thus giving the Grutas da Moeda, 3 km (2 miles) from Fátima, their name. Within about a 25-km (15-mile) radius of the town are four other major caverns—São Mamede, Alvados, Santo António, and Mira de Aire, the country's largest—equipped with lights and elevators. On a guided tour in any of these (ask for an English-speaking guide) you can see the subterranean world of limestone formations, underground rivers and lakes, and multicolor stalagmites and stalactites. ✉ *Largo das*

Catholic Stories

It all began May 13, 1917, when three young shepherds—Lúcia dos Santos and her cousins Francisco and Jacinta—reported seeing the Virgin Mary in a field at Cova de Iria, near the village. The Virgin promised to return on the 13th of each month for the next five months, and amid much controversy and skepticism, each time accompanied by increasingly larger crowds, the three children reported successive apparitions. This was during a period of anticlerical sentiment in Portugal, and after the sixth reputed apparition, in October, the children were arrested and interrogated. But they insisted the Virgin had spoken to them, revealing three secrets. Two of these, revealed by Lúcia in 1941, were interpreted to foretell the coming of World War II and the spread of communism and atheism. In a 1930 Pastoral Letter, the Bishop of Leiria declared the apparitions worthy of belief, thus approving the "Cult of Fátima."

In May 2000, Francisco and Jacinta were beatified in a ceremony held at Fátima by Pope John Paul II, on what was his third and final visit to the shrine. The third secret, which was revealed after the beatification, was interpreted to have foretold an attempt on the life of the pope. In May 2017 the brother and sister were finally canonized by Pope Francis as part of the Fátima centenary celebrations; by then the process to beatify Lúcia, who died in 2005, was well underway, having been fast-tracked in 2008 by Francis's predecessor, Benedict XVI.

On the 13th of each month, and especially in May and October, the faithful flock here to witness the passing of the statue of the Virgin through the throngs, to participate in candlelight processions, and to take part in solemn Masses.

Grutas da Moeda, São Mamede 244 703 838 www.grutasmoeda.com €7.

Museu de Cera (*Wax Museum*)
MUSEUM | FAMILY | In the center of town, the wax museum has 32 tableaux, with a total of 120 figures, depicting the events that took place in Fátima when the child shepherds first saw the apparitions in 1917, and other events. *Rua Jacinto Marto 249 539 300 www.mucefa.pt €7.75.*

Museu Interativo O Milagre de Fátima (*The Miracle of Fatima Interactive Museum*)
MUSEUM | A high-tech rival to the nearby Museu de Cera and its waxworks, the Miracle of Fátima Interactive Museum re-creates the appearance of the Virgin Mary a century ago. Its use of multimedia technologies certainly helps generate a sense of wonder at the apparition of the Virgin and of the Angel of Portugal, and at what became known as the Miracle of the Sun. Visits are guided, with free time towards the end. The museum is under a small shopping mall near the new basilica. *Central Comercial Espaço Fatimae, Av. Dom José Alves Correia da Silva 123 249 406 881 www.omilagredefatima.com €7.50.*

Restaurants

O Crispim
$ | PORTUGUESE | FAMILY | One of Fátima's longest-established restaurants, this place just outside the inner ring road is above all known for the quality of its grilled meat and fish. The vine-shaded esplanade is another big draw, creating a real family ambience. **Known for:** complimentary glasses of Portuguese brandy; main dishes are big enough for two or three; wide range of traditional desserts. *Average main: €14 Rua São João Eudes 23 249 532 781 www.ocrisp-im.com Closed Tues., last week of June, first half of July. No dinner Mon.*

Retiro dos Caçadores
$ | PORTUGUESE | A big brick fireplace, wood paneling, and stone walls set the mood in this cozy hunter's lodge, where the food is simple, but portions are hearty and the flavors are tantalizing. This is the best place in town for fresh game, especially *codorniz* and *coelho* (rabbit), which comes casserole-style with rice or potatoes. **Known for:** dining room has a step-back-in-time feel; huge hearth warms the place in winter; friendly staff. *Average main: €13 Rua São João Deus 44 249 531 323 www.retirodoscacadores.com Closed Wed., Carnival wk, and last 2 wks in July. No dinner Sun.*

Tia Alice
$$ | PORTUGUESE | Considered one of Portugal's best traditional restaurants, Aunt Alice is concealed in an inconspicuous old house with French windows across from the parish church near the sanctuary. A flight of wooden stairs inside leads down to an intimate dining area with stone walls. **Known for:** elegant flower-filled garden provides some outdoor seating; little crafts shop at the top of the stairs; laid-back atmosphere. *Average main: €19 Av. Irmã Lúcia de Jesús 152 249 531 737 www.tiaalice.com Closed Mon., Feb. 1–10, and 3 wks in July. No dinner Sun.*

Hotels

Casa São Nuno
$ | HOTEL | This expansive lodging is run by the Carmelites, but is open to visitors of all faiths. **Pros:** restaurant serves inexpensive meals all day; souven where pilgrims can stock up; inex rates. **Cons:** attracts a mostly religi entele; very few amenities; basic *Rooms from: €56 Av. Beato 271 249 530 230 www.casas no.com Closed mid-Dec.–1st w 130 rooms Free Breakfast.*

★ **Dom Gonçalo Hotel & Spa**
$ | HOTEL | FAMILY | There is a pastc of gardens from most windows c elegant boutique hotel located a ute walk from the sanctuary. **Pros** to the spa's fitness center, heate pool, steam room, sauna; parent ciate the playground and other a for kids; free covered parking. **Co** very close to the sanctuary; chea rooms are small; not much local *Rooms from: €76 Rua Jacin 100 249 539 330 www.hote 71 rooms Free Breakfast.*

Hotel Lux Fátima
$ | HOTEL | A couple of minutes f basilica, this design hotel stands for its contemporary decor highl by pops of bright pink and orang gorgeous outdoor pool surrounc by umbrellas; many rooms have balconies; lots of amenities. **Co** a bit of local character; exterior bland; breakfast is extra. *Roo €70 Av. Dom José Alves Cor Silva, Lote 2, Urbanização das 249 530 690 www.luxhote rooms No meals.*

Hotel Santa Maria
$ | HOTEL | With an eye-catching this contemporary hotel in the of Fátima is a three-minute wal the sanctuary. **Pros:** free underg parking; great value for the loca affordable restaurant. **Cons:** larg makes it feel somewhat imper no fitness room or pool; attract groups. *Rooms from: €64 Santo António 249 530 110 hotelstmaria.com 173 room Breakfast.*

Chapter 6

ÉVORA AND THE ALENTEJO

Updated by
Joana Taborda

Sights ★★★★★ | Restaurants ★★★★☆ | Hotels ★★★★★ | Shopping ★★★☆☆ | Nightlife ★★☆☆☆

WELCOME TO ÉVORA AND THE ALENTEJO

TOP REASONS TO GO

★ **Travel back in time:** Wander amid megaliths erected 2,000 years before Stonehenge, Roman ruins, Moorish forts, and medieval monasteries in the province where Portugal's history is best preserved.

★ **Wide-open spaces:** Stand atop a well-preserved medieval fortress and gaze out at undulating cork and wheat fields.

★ **Traditional rural festivals:** From Portuguese-style flamenco and bullfighting along the border with Spain, to autumn chestnut roasts in northern hill-town squares, and sardine festivals on the coast, every weekend offers another reason to celebrate in rural Alentejo.

★ **Food and wine:** Alentejano cuisine is considered Portugal's best, with centuries-old farming practices that were organic long before it was trendy. The highlight is *porco preto,* free-range black pigs that graze on acorns under Alentejo's ever-present cork trees. Also here are fields of vineyards mostly producing sturdy reds.

1 **Évora.** The capital of Alentejo.

2 **Guadalupe.** This tiny village is named after a 17th-century chapel.

3 **Arraiolos.** See ruins of a walled fortress.

4 **Montemor-o-Novo.** An impressive hilltop castle settlement.

5 **Monsaraz.** Find stone streets and ancient houses.

6 **Vila Viçosa.** Located in the center of Borba Plain.

7 **Estremoz.** This is the seat of the art scene in the Alentejo.

8 **Elvas.** Walls and castles protected this town in the 17th century.

9 **Portalegre.** This town sits at the foot of the Serra de São Mamede.

10 **Marvão.** A village atop a mountain.

11 **Castelo de Vide.** A picturesque hilltop town.

12 **Alvito.** A sleepy town above the Rio Odivelas.

13 **Beja.** Located midway between Spain and the sea.

14 **Serpa.** Medieval town surrounded by vineyards.

15 **Mértola.** An ancient, walled-in town.

16 **Vila Nova de Milfontes.** A resort town lined by beaches.

17 **Alcácer do Sal.** A major producer of salt in the 16th century.

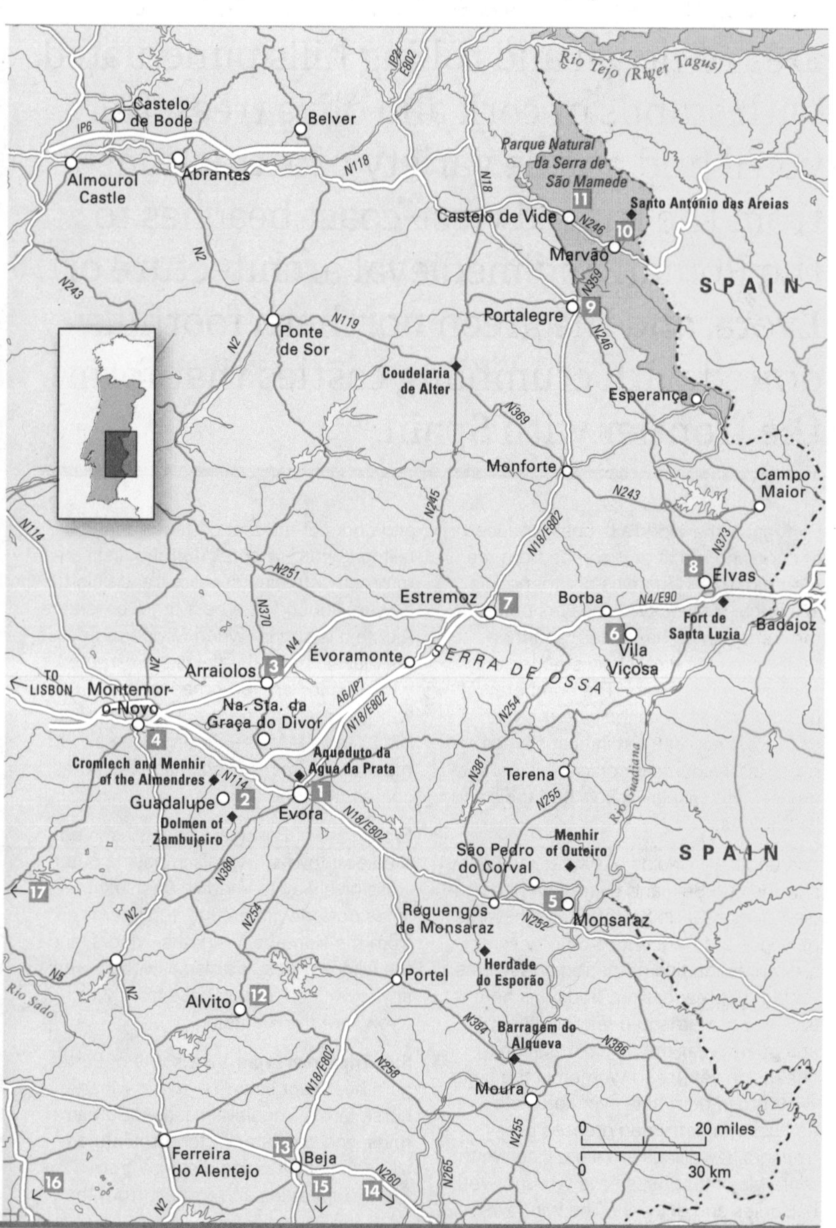
Rio Tejo (River Tagus)
Castelo de Bode
IP6
Belver
IP2/E802
Almourol Castle
Abrantes
N118
N18
Parque Natural da Serra de São Mamede
11
Santo António das Areias
Castelo de Vide
N246
10
Marvão
N2
N243
SPAIN
N359
Portalegre
9
N246
Ponte de Sor
N119
N2
Coudelaria de Alter
Esperança
N369
Monforte
Campo Maior
N243
N245
N114
N18/E802
N373
8
Elvas
N251
N370
Estremoz
7
Borba
N4/E90
Fort de Santa Luzia
Badajoz
6
Vila Viçosa
N4
Évoramonte
SERRA DE OSSA
N2
Arraiolos
3
TO LISBON
Montemor-o-Novo
Na. Sta. da Graça do Divor
A6/IP7
N18/E802
N254
4
Cromlech and Menhir of the Almendres
Aqueduto da Agua da Prata
N114
N381
Terena
Guadalupe
2
1
Évora
N255
Rio Guadiana
Dolmen of Zambujeiro
N18/E802
Menhir of Outeiro
São Pedro do Corval
SPAIN
N380
17
5
Reguengos de Monsaraz
Monsaraz
N254
N252
N2
Herdade do Esporão
N5
Portel
Rio Sado
N2
Alvito
12
N384
Barragem do Alqueva
N386
N18/E802
N258
Moura
N255
0
20 miles
0
30 km
Ferreira do Alentejo
13
Beja
16
15
14
N260
N265
N2

The Alentejo, which means "the land beyond the Rio Tejo" (Tagus River) in Portuguese, is a vast, sparsely populated area of heath and rolling hills punctuated with stands of cork and olive trees. Here you'll find a wide variety of attractions—from the rugged west-coast beaches to the Roman and medieval architecture of Évora, and the green northern foothills dotted with crumbling castles that form the frontier with Spain.

Portugal is the world's largest producer of cork, and much of it comes from the Alentejo. This industry is not for people in a hurry. It takes two decades before the trees can be harvested, and then their bark can be carefully stripped only once every nine years. The numbers painted on the trees indicate the year of the last harvest. Exhibits at several regional museums chronicle this delicate process and display associated tools and handicrafts.

The undulating fields of wheat and barley surrounding Beja and Évora, the rice paddies of Alcácer do Sal, and the vineyards of Borba and Reguengos de Monsaraz are representative of the region's role as Portugal's breadbasket. Traditions here are strong. Herdsmen tending sheep and goats wear the *pelico* (traditional sheepskin vest), and women in the fields wear broad-brim hats over kerchiefs and colorful patterned dresses over trousers. Dwellings are a dazzling white; more elegant houses have wrought-iron balconies and grillwork. The windows and doors of modest cottages and hilltop country *montes* (farmhouses) are trimmed with blue or yellow, and colorful flowers abound. The best time to visit the Alentejo is spring, when temperatures are pleasant and the fields are carpeted with wildflowers. Summer can be brutal, with the mercury frequently topping 37°C (100°F). As the Portuguese say, "In the Alentejo there is no shade but what comes from the sky."

Évora. One of Portugal's best-preserved medieval towns, Évora's imposing outer walls give way to winding cobblestone lanes dotted with architectural gems from the Romans, Visigoths, Moors, and the Middle Ages. It's also a lively university town, and a good base from which to explore the Alentejo.

Side Trips from Évora. Visit some of Portugal's best-kept secrets—rustic wineries, horse farms, medieval castles, Roman ruins, and prehistoric stone sculptures—all within day-tripping distance from Évora. Tapestries and carpets from the unassuming little village of Arraiolos are famous the world over.

Alto Alentejo. Portugal's most stunning walled fortresses and clifftop castles dot the province's northern half, along the frontier with its old archenemy, Spain. With the highest mountains in southern Portugal, this area has a more varied landscape than the flatter south, and is the country's best-kept secret for hiking and mountain biking.

Baixo Alentejo. This is Portugal's breadbasket, with undulating wheat fields, olive groves, and cork forests that stretch to golden dunes and dramatic cliffs over the Atlantic. A network of hiking trails along the coast attracts a new brand of environmentally minded tourists to this previously undiscovered corner of Europe.

Planning

This is the country's largest province, and it's divided roughly into two parts: the more mountainous Alto, or "upper," Alentejo north of Évora, and the flatter Baixo, or "lower," Alentejo that lies to the south. The area stretches from the rugged west-coast beaches all the way east to Spain, and from the Targus in the north to the low mountains on the border of the Algarve, Portugal's southernmost province. Its central hub, Évora, is rich with traditional Portuguese architecture.

When to Go

Spring comes early to this part of Portugal. Early April to mid-June is a wonderful time to tour, when the fields are full of colorful wildflowers. July and August are brutally hot, with temperatures in places such as Beja often reaching 37°C (100°F) or higher. By mid-September things cool off sufficiently to make touring this region a delight.

Getting Here and Around

AIR

You can fly into the Lisbon or Faro airports and then take ground transportation into the region. Évora is roughly 130 km (80 miles) from Lisbon and about 225 km (140 miles) from Faro.

AIRPORT CONTACTS Aeroporto de Faro. (*Faro Airport*) ☎ *289 800 800* 🌐 *www.aeroportofaro.pt.* **Aeroporto Lisboa.** (*Lisbon Portela Airport*) ✉ *Alameda das Comunidades Portuguesas, Lisbon* ☎ *218 413 500* 🌐 *www.aeroportolisboa.pt/en.*

BUS

There are few places in this region that aren't served by at least one bus daily. Express coaches run by several regional lines travel regularly between Lisbon and the larger towns such as Évora, Beja, and Estremoz. Because several companies leave for the Alentejo from different terminals in Lisbon, it's best to have a travel agent do your booking. Standard buses between Lisbon and Évora run at least once every hour between 6 am and 9:30 pm, and cost €12.

BUS CONTACTS Rede Expressos. ✉ *Terminal Rodoviário de Sete Rios, Praça Marechal Humberto Delgado, Estrada das Laranjeiras, Lisbon* ☎ *707 223 344* 🌐 *www.rede-expressos.pt.* **Rodoviária do Alentejo.** ✉ *Terminal Rodoviário, Av. Tulio Espanca, Évora* ☎ *266 738 120* 🌐 *www.rodalentejo.pt.* **Transportes Rodoviários de Évora.** ✉ *Estação Central de Camionagem, Av. S. Sebastião, Évora* ☎ *266 106 923* 🌐 *www.trevo.com.pt.*

CAR

One of the best features of Alentejo is its seemingly untouched beaches and villages—which you'll need a car to reach. Driving will give you access to many out-of-the-way spots. A good network of modern toll roads crisscrossing the country, as well as very little traffic, make driving quick but expensive. A 1½-hour drive on the main A6 toll road from Lisbon to Évora costs about €10 for a standard sedan, and about €16 for an SUV. There are no confusing big cities in which to get lost, although parking can be a problem in some tight town centers, as in Évora.

The toll highway A6, which branches off A2 running south from Lisbon, takes you as far as the Spanish border at Elvas, where it links up with the highway from Madrid. This road provides easy access to Évora and Alto Alentejo. The A2 runs south to the Algarve, as does the non-toll IP1/E01. Farther inland and south of Évora, the IP2/E802 is the best access for Beja and southeastern Alentejo. The N521 runs 105 km (65 miles) from Cáceres, Spain, to the Portuguese border near Portalegre. To the south, the N433 runs from Seville, Spain, to Beja, 225 km (140 miles) away.

TRAIN

Train travel in the vast Alentejo is not for people in a great hurry. Service to the more remote destinations is infrequent—and in some cases nonexistent. A couple of towns, including Évora and Beja, are connected with Lisbon by several trains daily. The Intercidades train leaves from Lisbon's Oriente Station in the Parque da Nações to the Alentejo. You can also catch the Intercidades train at Lisbon's Entrecampos Station.

Restaurants

In the Alentejo, the country's granary, bread is a major part of most meals. It's the basis of a popular dish known as *açorda,* a thick, stick-to-your-ribs porridge to which various ingredients such as fish, meat, and eggs are added. Açorda *de marisco*—bread with eggs, seasonings, and assorted shellfish—is one of the more popular varieties. Another version, açorda *alentejana,* consists of a clear broth, olive oil, garlic, cilantro, slices of bread, and poached eggs. *Cação,* also called baby shark or dogfish, is a white-meat fish with a single bone down the back and is mostly served in a fish soup or as part of a porridge.

Pork from the Alentejo is the best in the country and often is combined with clams, onions, and tomatoes in the classic dish *carne de porco à alentejana.* One of Portugal's most renowned sheep's milk cheeses—tangy, but mellow when properly ripened—is made in the Serpa region. Alentejo wines—especially those from around Borba, Reguengos de Monsaraz, and Vidigueira—are regular prizewinners at national tasting contests.

Elvas, near the Spanish border, is known for its tasty sugar plums. *Ameixas d'Elvas* (Elvas plums) were exported with port wine to England and the Americas and became a popular Christmas sweet among the English. The plums are the green, very sweet Rainha Claúdia variety. The Alto Alentejo region offers the best climate for growing them and pesticides aren't used. As the supply is small and the demand is great, the plums are considered a gourmet treat. They can be eaten fresh, as prunes, dipped in a sugar syrup, candied, or as a jam.

Between mid-June and mid-September, reservations are advised at upscale restaurants. Many moderate or inexpensive establishments, however, don't accept reservations and have informal dining rooms where you share a table with other diners. Dress at all but the most luxurious restaurants is casual. *Prices in the reviews are the average cost of a main course at dinner or, if dinner isn't served, at lunch.*

Hotels

The best accommodations in the Alentejo have long been the *pousadas,* hotels housed in historic properties like medieval convents or castles. Some of the finest pousadas in the country are in the Alentejo, including one in the old

Lóios convent in Évora and another in the castle at Estremoz. But the pousadas' reign has been challenged recently by a new crop of private luxury hotels. There are also a number of private guesthouses in the region. Look for signs that say "turismo rural" or "turismo de habitação." In summer, air-conditioning is absolutely necessary in Évora, where temperatures can soar to more than 44°C (110°F). *Prices in the reviews are the lowest price of a standard double room in high season. For expanded hotel reviews, visit Fodors.com.*

WHAT IT COSTS In Euros			
$	$$	$$$	$$$$
RESTAURANTS			
under €16	€16–€20	€21–€25	over €25
HOTELS			
under €141	€141–€200	€201–€260	over €260

Visitor Information

The Rotas dos Vinhos do Alentejo office is open daily for tastings and can help schedule visits to local wineries.

CONTACTS Alentejo Tourism. ☎ *284 313 540* 🌐 *www.visitalentejo.pt.* **Rotas dos Vinhos do Alentejo.** ✉ *Praça Joaquim Antonio de Aguiar 20-21, Apartado 2146, Évora* ☎ *266 746 498* 🌐 *www.vinhos-doalentejo.pt.*

Évora

130 km (81 miles) southeast of Lisbon.

Dressed in traditional garb, shepherds and farmers with faces wizened by a lifetime in the baking sun stand around the fountain at Praça do Giraldo; a group of college students dressed in jeans and T-shirts chats animatedly at a sidewalk café; a local business executive in coat and tie purposefully hurries by; and clusters of tourists, cameras in hand, capture the historic monuments on film—all this is part of a typical summer's day in Évora. The flourishing capital of the central Alentejo is also a university town with an astonishing variety of inspiring architecture, including pristine Roman ruins. Atop a small hill in the heart of a vast cork-, olive-, and grain-producing region, Évora is a UNESCO World Heritage Site.

GETTING HERE AND AROUND

Évora is, above all, a town for walking. Wherever you glance as you stroll the maze of narrow streets and alleys of the Cidade Velha (Old Town), amid arches and whitewashed houses, you'll come face to face with reminders of the town's rich architectural and cultural heritage. West of Praça do Giraldo, between Rua Serpa Pinto and Rua dos Mercadores you have the old Jewish quarter of narrow streets lined with medieval houses.

For an overview of the city, the hop-on, hop-off tourist bus called Évora City Tour costs €7.50. Cabs charge €1 per kilometer. Note that if you travel to another town from Évora, such as Beja, you'll have to pay for the taxi's return trip. To get a cab, head for one of the many taxi stands around town or call Radio Taxis Évora.

TAXI CONTACT Auto Táxis Modelares Dianenses. ☎ *968 035 386* 🌐 *www.alentejotransfers.com.*

TRAIN CONTACT Évora Train Station. ✉ *Largo da Estação* ☎ *707 210 220* 🌐 *www.cp.pt.*

TOURS

The tourist office in Évora can schedule a variety of guided or unguided tours of megalithic sites, area wineries, and other attractions by bus, van, horse-drawn carriage, or foot. The Association of Tour Guides in Alentejo has well-qualified guides leading daily tours of the city's most popular sights. Led by archaeologists, Ebora Megalithica offers tours of

Great Itineraries

You can make convenient loops starting and finishing in Lisbon, or you can extend your travels by continuing south to the Algarve from Beja or Santiago do Cacém. You should allow 10 days to get a feel for the region, exploring Évora and visiting some outlying attractions such as Monsaraz, Castelo de Vide, and Mértola. This will also allow time for a day or two of sunbathing on a west-coast beach. If you skip the beach, you can cover the most interesting attractions at a comfortable pace in seven days. Three days will give you time to explore Évora and its surroundings along with one or two additional highlights.

If You Have 3 Days

Be sure to include **Évora**, one of Portugal's most beautiful cities, in your first day of exploring. The following morning visit the rug-producing town of **Arraiolos** and then continue on to **Estremoz** and its imposing fortress, which doubles as a pousada. Head east past Borba and its marble quarries to **Vila Viçosa**, site of the Paço Ducal. Then continue south to visit a winery or two in and around **Reguengos de Monsaraz.** In the morning visit the fortified hilltop town of **Monsaraz** before returning to Lisbon.

If You Have 7 Days

After a day and night in **Évora**, head to the **Aqueduto da Agua da Prata** and the prehistoric sites just outside town, which include the **Cromlech and the Menhir of Almendres** and the **Dolmen of Zambujeiro.** On the way to your next overnight stop in **Estremoz**, take a break in **Arraiolos.** From Estremoz head east to the fortified town of **Elvas**, stopping en route at the Paço Ducal in **Vila Viçosa.** The following day continue to **Monsaraz**, with a stop along the way to do some wine tasting in **Reguengos de Monsaraz.** From Monsaraz head south to **Beja**, inspecting the ruins at **Serpa** en route. The next day head west to **Vila Nova de Milfontes** for more Roman ruins and a few hours at the beach. On your seventh day return to Lisbon, stopping along the way to see the castle at **Alcácer do Sal.**

ancient sights in Portuguese, English, and Spanish. Turalentejo is your best choice for carriage tours.

CONTACTS Association of Tour Guides in Alentejo. ✉ *Praça do Giraldo 73* ☎ *963 702 392* 🌐 *www.alentejoguides.com.* **Ebora Megalithica.** ☎ *964 808 337* 🌐 *www.eboramegalithica.com.* **Évora City Tour.** ☎ *266 738 120* 🌐 *www.evoracity-tour.com.* **Turalentejo.** ✉ *Rue Miguel Bombarda 37, Valverde* ☎ 🌐 *www.turalentejo.webnode.pt.*

VISITOR INFORMATION

The Évora tourist office is helpful and can schedule tours or make phone calls to hotels or restaurants.

VISITOR INFORMATION Évora Tourist Office. ✉ *Praça do Giraldo 73* ☎ 🌐 *www.cm-evora.pt/en.*

Sights

Igreja da Nossa Senhora da Graça (*Our Lady of Grace Church*)

RELIGIOUS SITE | A splendid piece of classic Italian-style architecture, this church represents the first breath of the Renaissance in provincial Portuguese architecture. Note the massive figures on columns at either side of the portal. According to local legend, these four figures represent the first victims put to death in the Inquisition in Évora in 1543. The interior is lovely, but not quite as distinctive. ✉ *Travessa da Caraca.*

Igreja de Misericórdia (*Mercy Church*)
RELIGIOUS SITE | Extremely simple on the outside, the interior of this 16th-century church is lined with large azulejo panels in massive gilt frames depicting scenes from the life of Christ. The unsigned 18th-century tiles are thought to be the work of António de Oliveira de Bernardes. ✉ *Rua da Misericórdia.*

Igreja de Santo Antão (*Church of St. Anthony*)
RELIGIOUS SITE | Note the striking white Renaissance facade of this church, which stands near the fountain at the north end of Praça do Giraldo. A medieval hermitage of the Knights Templar was razed in 1553 to make way for this church, which has massive round pillars and soaring vaulted ceilings. The marble altar in bas-relief is a holdover from the primitive hermitage. Packed with locals on Sundays, this is a good place to see a Mass—or a glimpse of a local wedding on a Saturday in spring, if you're lucky. ✉ *Praça do Giraldo.*

★ **Igreja de São Francisco** (*Church of San Francisco*)
RELIGIOUS SITE | After the Sé, this is the most impressive of Évora's churches. Its construction in the early 16th century, on the site of a former Gothic chapel, involved the greatest talents of the day, including Nicolas Chanterene, Oliver of Ghent, and the Arruda brothers, Francisco and Diogo. Magnificent architecture notwithstanding, the bizarre **Capela dos Ossos** (Chapel of Bones) is the main attraction. The translation of the chilling inscription over the entrance reads, "We, the bones that are here, await yours." The bones of some 5,000 skeletons dug up from cemeteries in the area line the ceilings and supporting columns. With a flair worthy of Charles Addams, a 16th-century Franciscan monk placed skulls jaw-to-cranium so they form arches across the ceiling; arm and leg bones are neatly stacked to shape the supporting columns. ✉ *Praça 1 de Maio* ☎ *266 704 521* 🌐 *www.igrejadesaofrancisco.pt* 🎟 *Church free, Chapel of Bones €5.*

★ **Igreja de São João Evangelista** (*St. John the Evangelist Church*)
RELIGIOUS SITE | This small church next to the former Convento dos Lóios, which is now the Pousada dos Lóios, houses one of the most impressive displays of 18th-century *azulejos* (painted and glazed ceramic tiles) anywhere in Portugal. The sanctuary, dedicated to St. John the Evangelist, was founded in the 15th century by the Venetian-based Lóios Order. Its interior walls are covered with azulejos created by Oliveira Bernardes, the foremost master of this unique Portuguese art form. The blue-and-white tiles depict scenes from the life of the church's founder, Rodrigo de Melo, who, along with members of his family, is buried here. The bas-relief marble tombstones at the foot of the high altar are the only ones of their kind in Portugal. Note the two metal hatches on either side of the main aisle: one covers an ancient cistern, which belonged to the Moorish castle that predated the church (an underground spring still supplies the cistern with potable water), and beneath the other hatch lie the neatly stacked bones of hundreds of monks. This bizarre ossuary was uncovered in 1958 during restoration work. ✉ *Palácio Cadaval, Largo do Conde de Vila Flor* ☎ *967 979 763* 🎟 *Church €4; combined ticket €8, includes the adjacent Palácio dos Duques de Cadaval.*

★ **Jardim Diana** (*Diana Garden*)
GARDEN | Opposite the Templo Romano, this restful, tree-lined park looks out over the aqueduct and the plains from the modest heights of what is sometimes

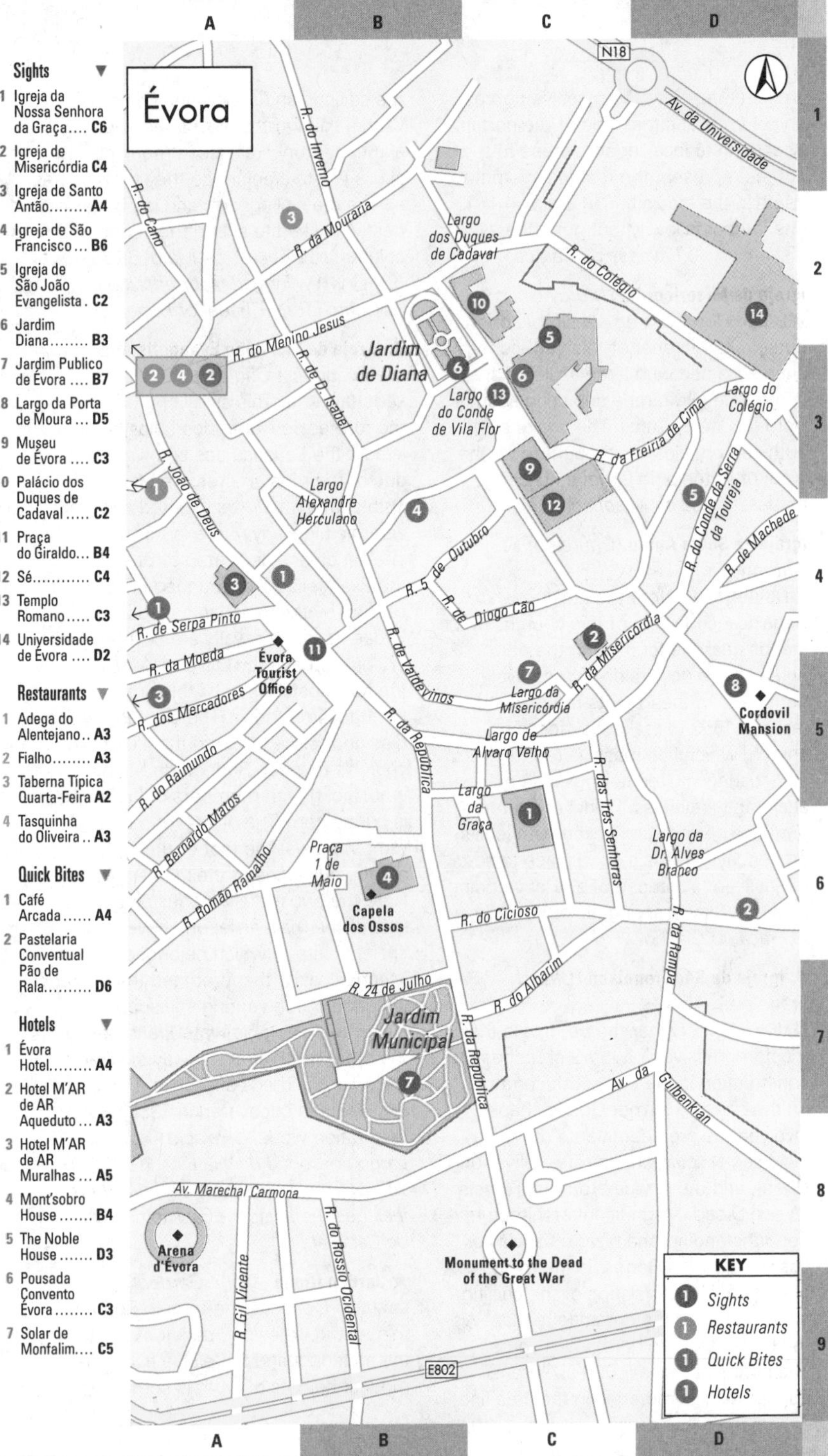
Évora
Sights
1 Igreja da Nossa Senhora da Graça.... C6
2 Igreja de Misericórdia C4
3 Igreja de Santo Antão........ A4
4 Igreja de São Francisco... B6
5 Igreja de São João Evangelista . C2
6 Jardim Diana........ B3
7 Jardim Publico de Évora B7
8 Largo da Porta de Moura ... D5
9 Museu de Évora C3
10 Palácio dos Duques de Cadaval C2
11 Praça do Giraldo... B4
12 Sé........... C4
13 Templo Romano..... C3
14 Universidade de Évora D2
Restaurants
1 Adega do Alentejano.. A3
2 Fialho........ A3
3 Taberna Típica Quarta-Feira A2
4 Tasquinha do Oliveira .. A3
Quick Bites
1 Café Arcada...... A4
2 Pastelaria Conventual Pão de Rala......... D6
Hotels
1 Évora Hotel......... A4
2 Hotel M'AR de AR Aqueduto ... A3
3 Hotel M'AR de AR Muralhas ... A5
4 Mont'sobro House B4
5 The Noble House D3
6 Pousada Convento Évora C3
7 Solar de Monfalim.... C5
A
B
C
D
1
2
3
4
5
6
7
8
9
N18
Av. da Universidade
R. do Inverno
R. do Cano
R. da Mouraria
Largo dos Duques de Cadaval
R. do Colégio
R. do Menino Jesus
R. de D. Isabel
Jardim de Diana
Largo do Conde de Vila Flor
Largo do Colégio
R. da Freiria de Cima
R. João de Deus
Largo Alexandre Herculano
R. do Conde da Serra da Toureja
R. de Machede
R. 5 de Outubro
R. de Diogo Cão
R. de Serpa Pinto
R. da Moeda
Évora Tourist Office
R. de Valdevinos
R. da Misericórdia
Largo da Misericórdia
R. dos Mercadores
Cordovil Mansion
R. da República
Largo de Alvaro Velho
R. do Raimundo
R. das Três Senhoras
Largo da Graça
R. Bernardo Matos
R. Romão Ramalho
Praça 1 de Maio
Largo da Dr. Alves Branco
Capela dos Ossos
R. do Cicioso
R. da Rampa
R. 24 de Julho
R. do Albarum
Jardim Municipal
R. da República
Av. da Gulbenkian
Av. Marechal Carmona
R. do Rossio Ocidental
R. Gil Vicente
Arena d'Évora
Monument to the Dead of the Great War
E802
KEY
Sights
Restaurants
Quick Bites
Hotels

A Bit of History

Although the region was inhabited some 4,000 years ago—as attested to by the dolmens and menhirs in the countryside—it was during the Roman epoch that the town called Liberalitas Julia in the province of Lusitania first achieved importance. A large part of present-day Évora is built on Roman foundations, of which the Temple of Diana, with its graceful Corinthian columns, is the most conspicuous reminder.

The Moors also made a great historical impact on the area. They arrived in 715 and remained more than 450 years. They were driven out in 1166, thanks in part to a clever ruse perpetrated by Geraldo Sem Pavor (Gerald the Fearless). Geraldo tricked Évora's Moorish ruler into leaving a strategic watchtower unguarded. With a small force, Geraldo seized the tower. To regain control of it, most of the Moorish troops left their posts at the city's main entrance, allowing the bulk of Geraldo's forces to march in unopposed.

Toward the end of the 12th century Évora's fortunes increased as the town became the favored location for the courts of the Burgundy and Avis dynasties. It attracted many of the great minds and creative talents of Renaissance Portugal. Some of the more prominent residents at this time were Gil Vicente, the founder of Portuguese theater; the sculptor Nicolas Chanterene; and Gregorio Lopes, the painter known for his renderings of court life. Such a concentration of royal wealth and creativity superimposed upon the existing Moorish town was instrumental in the development of the delicate Manueline-Mudéjar (elaborate, Muslim-influenced) architectural style. You can see fine examples of this in the turreted Ermida de São Brás outside the city walls.

grandiosely referred to as "Évora's Acropolis." You can take in nearly 2,000 years of Portuguese history from here. One sweeping glance encompasses the temple, the spires of the Gothic Sé, the Igreja de São João Evangelista, and the 20th-century pousada housed in the convent. A garden café at the corner of the park is a great spot to reflect on the architectural marvels before you, with a glass of port in hand. ✉ *Largo do Conde de Vila Flor.*

Jardim Publico de Évora (*Évora Public Gardens*)
GARDEN | Off Rua 24 de Julho, the sprawling Jardim Publico is a pleasant place to rest after the rigors of sightseeing. The extensive and verdant gardens are landscaped with plants and trees from all over the world. Here you'll find the lovely Palácio de Dom Manuel, known for its row of gracefully curved Manueline windows. ✉ *Rua 24 de Julho.*

Largo da Porta de Moura (*Square of the Moorish Door*)
PLAZA | One of Évora's most beautiful squares is characterized by paired stone towers that guard one of the principal entrances to the walled old city. The spires of the Sé rise above the towers, and in the center of the square is an unusual Renaissance fountain. The large white-marble sphere, supported by a single column, bears a commemorative inscription in Latin dated 1556. Overlooking the fountain is the Cordovil Mansion, on whose terrace are several particularly attractive arches decorated in the

Manueline-Mudéjar style. ✉ *Largo das Portas de Moura.*

Museu de Évora (*Évora Museum*)
MUSEUM | This handsome museum is in a stately late-17th-century baroque building between the Sé and the Largo do Conde de Vila Flor. Once a palace that accommodated bishops, it contains a rich collection of sculpture and paintings as well as interesting archaeological and architectural artifacts. The first-floor galleries, arranged around a pleasant garden, include several excellent carved pillars and a fine Manueline doorway. ✉ *Largo do Conde de Vila Flor* ☎ *266 730 480* 🌐 *www.visitevora.net/en/evora-museum* 🎫 *€3* ⏲ *Closed Mon.*

Palácio dos Duques de Cadaval (*Palace of the Dukes of Cadaval*)
CASTLE/PALACE | The palace is readily identified by two massive stone towers that have pointed battlements. These towers, once part of a medieval castle that protected the town, were later incorporated into this former residence of kings João I and João IV. A small ground-floor gallery contains historic documents, paintings, and the unusual Flemish-style bronze tomb of Rui de Sousa, a signatory of the Treaty of Tordesillas. In 1494 the treaty divided the world into two spheres of influence: Spanish and Portuguese. ✉ *Largo do Conde de Vila Flor* ☎ *967 979 763* 🎫 *€4, €8 for combined ticket with the adjacent Igreja de São João Evangelista.*

★ **Praça do Giraldo**
PLAZA | The arcade-lined square in the center of the old walled city is named after Évora's liberator, Gerald the Fearless. During Caesar's time, the square, marked by a large arch, was the Roman forum. In 1571 the arch was destroyed to make room for the fountain, a simple half sphere made of white Estremoz marble and designed by the Renaissance architect Afonso Álvares. Nowadays, it's a lovely spot to take in the scenery over coffee or cocktails at one of the many cafés with tables on the square. On the eastern side is a narrow cobblestone pedestrian thoroughfare called Rua 5 de Outubro that leads to the cathedral. ✉ *Praça do Giraldo.*

★ **Sé**
RELIGIOUS SITE | A UNESCO World Heritage Site, this breathtaking cathedral was constructed in 1186 from huge granite blocks. It has been enhanced over the centuries with an octagonal, turreted dome above the transept; a blue-tile spire atop the north tower; a number of fine Manueline windows; and several Gothic rose windows. Two massive asymmetrical towers and battlement-ringed walls give the Sé a fortresslike appearance. At the entrance, Gothic arches are supported by marble columns bearing delicately sculpted statues of the apostles. With the exception of a fine baroque chapel, the granite interior is somber. The cloister, a 14th-century Gothic addition with Mudéjar vestiges, is one of the finest of its type in the country; it might look familiar to those who've visited a similar version at Lisbon's cathedral. Housed in the towers and chapter room is the **Museu de Arte Sacra da Sé** (Sacred Art Museum). Of particular interest is a 13th-century ivory Virgin of Paradise, whose body opens up to show exquisitely carved scenes of her life. ✉ *Largo Marquês de Marialva* ☎ *266 759 330* 🎫 *€2, €4.50 includes museum.*

★ **Templo Romano** (*Roman Temple*)
ARCHAEOLOGICAL SITE | The well-preserved ruins of the Roman Temple dominate Largo do Conde de Vila Flor. The edifice, considered one of the finest of its kind on the Iberian Peninsula, was probably built in the 1st and 2nd centuries AD. The temple, largely destroyed during the invasions of the barbarian tribes in the early 5th century, was later used for various purposes, including that of municipal slaughterhouse in the 14th century. It was restored to its present state in 1871. ✉ *Largo do Conde de Vila Flor.*

The main cathedral of Évora, known as Sé, which dates back to 1186, has been designated a UNESCO World Heritage Site.

Universidade de Évora

COLLEGE | From 1555 until its closure by the Marquis de Pombal in 1759, this university was a Jesuit college; in 1979, after a lapse of more than 200 years, Évora University resumed classes. Although enrollment is small, the college's presence enlivens this ancient city. It's worth a visit to the well-preserved buildings: the large courtyard is flanked on all sides by graceful buildings with double-tier, white-limestone, arched galleries in Italian Renaissance style. From the main entrance you'll see the imposing baroque facade of the gallery known as the Sala dos Actos (Hall of Acts), which is crowned with allegorical figures and coats of arms carved in white marble quarried in the region. Lining the gallery's interior are azulejo works depicting historical, mythological, and biblical themes. ✉ *Largo dos Colegiais 2* ☎ *266 740 800* 🌐 *www.uevora.pt* 🎫 *€3 access to classrooms and chapel when school is not in session* 🕐 *Closed Sun.*

Coffee and Quick Bites

Café Arcada

$ | **PORTUGUESE** | Opposite the fountain on Praça do Giraldo, Café Arcada is a local institution. The large hall, divided into snack bar and restaurant sections, is decorated with photos of the big bands that played here in the 1940s. **Known for:** Portuguese pork sandwiches are a specialty; old-fashioned cup of coffee; outdoor seating. 💲 *Average main: €5* ✉ *Praca do Giraldo 7* ☎ *266 741 777.*

Pastelaria Conventual Pão de Rala

$ | **PORTUGUESE** | A few minutes from Igreja de São Francisco you'll find this pastry shop specializing in regional sweets. Set in a small house between two cobblestone streets, it stands out with its green doors and terra-cotta roof. **Known for:** try the queijinho do céu, an almond-flavored sweet; a little off the beaten path; small but cozy interior. 💲 *Average main: €3* ✉ *Rua de Cicioso 47* ☎ *266 707 778.*

Restaurants

Adega do Alentejano

$ | **PORTUGUESE** | Dine on hearty, simple food with in-the-know locals at this pleasantly rustic Alentejo wine cellar. Walk through the beaded curtain made of wine corks into a simple dining room with red-and-white-checkered tablecloths, blue-and-white-tiled walls, and huge Roman-style clay wine jugs. **Known for:** choose the reasonable local wine from the barrel; delicious pork feet with coriander sauce; agreeably priced menu options. *Average main: €10 Rua Gabriel Victor do Monte Pereira 21-A 266 744 447 No credit cards Closed Sun.*

★ **Fialho**

$$$ | **PORTUGUESE** | The charming elderly owner, Amor Fialho, is the third generation of Fialhos to operate this popular restaurant. He has handed off daily operations to his children, Helena and Rui, but he's still present most evenings in the kitchen, and has been known to give foreign visitors a tour, pointing out photos of the former Spanish king's visit. **Known for:** wide selection of Alentejo wines; homemade sweets for dessert; game dishes like partridge and lamb. *Average main: €25 Travessa das Mascarenhas 14 266 703 079 www.restaurantefialho.pt Closed Mon.*

Taberna Típica Quarta-Feira

$$$$ | **PORTUGUESE** | The street lights will guide you to this family-run tavern in the heart of the city. Exposed brick adds warmth to the intimate dining room, which can accommodate only 28 people. **Known for:** specializes in slow-cooked pork and lamb dishes; end the meal with a glass of Abafado wine; service is friendly and accommodating. *Average main: €30 Rua do Inverno 16 266 707 530 Closed Sun. No lunch Mon. No credit cards.*

★ **Tasquinha do Oliveira**

$$ | **PORTUGUESE** | The charming husband-and-wife duo of Manuel and Carolina Oliveira own and operate this tiny upscale dining room with huge taste. There are only 14 seats in the entire restaurant, creating the atmosphere of a family dining room. **Known for:** delicious codfish fritters and other favorites; excellent selections of Alentejo wines; warm service. *Average main: €18 Rua Cándido dos Reis 45-A Closed Sun. and early Aug.*

Ceramics in Alto Alentejo

The brightly colored, hand-painted plates, bowls, and figurines from the Alto Alentejo are popular throughout Portugal. The best selection of this distinctive type of folk art is in and around Estremoz, where the terra-cotta jugs and bowls are adorned with chips of marble from local quarries. Saturday morning the *rossio* (town square) is full of vendors. Redondo and the village of São Pedro do Corval, near Reguengos de Monsaraz, are also good sources of this type of pottery, as is Évora. Arraiolos is famous for its hand-embroidered wool rugs.

Hotels

Évora Hotel

$ | **RESORT** | **FAMILY** | Just outside town sits this sprawling establishment that is a great option for families—there are huge swimming pools (both indoor and outdoor) and lots of activities for the kids. **Pros:** spa and wellness center attract a weekend-getaway crowd; vegetarian restaurant is a rare find in meat-eating Alentejo; all-inclusive packages make it affordable. **Cons:** far from the city's most popular sights; slow Wi-Fi connection in some rooms; a bit noisy near the pool. *Rooms from: €120 Av. Túlio Espanca*

The ancient Templo Romano archaeological site was restored to its present state in 1871.

Apart. 93 ☎ 266 748 800 🌐 www.evora-hotel.pt ⇆ 170 rooms 🍴 Free Breakfast.

★ Hotel M'AR de AR Aqueduto

$$ | HOTEL | The only five-star hotel within Évora's old city walls, this property's luxury is unmatched, with sleek, modern decor that echoes the city's medieval character. **Pros:** the best rooms have balconies or terraces; supreme luxury at a competitive price; luxurious spa is open to the public. **Cons:** some visitors find the modern style a bit chilly; Wi-Fi signal doesn't reach some rooms; some rooms need freshening up. *$ Rooms from: €200 ✉ Rua Cândido dos Reis 72, Évora Monte ☎ 266 740 700 🌐 www.mardearhotels.com ⇆ 64 rooms 🍴 Free Breakfast.*

Hotel M'AR de AR Muralhas

$$ | RESORT | FAMILY | Often overlooked in favor of its glitzier sister hotel, the Hotel M'AR de AR Muralhas is a gorgeous oasis with balconies and terraces facing a secluded swimming pool and a pretty garden. **Pros:** friendly, multilingual staff is happy to book local tours; swimming pool makes it perfect for families with children; a short walk from the major sights and best restaurants. **Cons:** more of a family atmosphere, rather than for honeymooners or couples; car park is a bit narrow for big cars; not ideal for light sleepers as the rooms aren't soundproofed. *$ Rooms from: €180 ✉ Travessa da Palmeira 4/6 ☎ 266 739 300 🌐 www.mardearhotels.com ⇆ 91 rooms 🍴 Free Breakfast.*

Mont'sobro House

$ | B&B/INN | If you like Portuguese handicrafts, you'll love this impeccable guesthouse run by the owners of one of Évora's most renowned craft shops. **Pros:** authentic antiques and hand-painted beds; all the owner's crafts are on display; near the cathedral and most other sights. **Cons:** some rooms have shared baths; reception closes at 9 pm; no parking. *$ Rooms from: €45 ✉ Rua de Diogo Cão 1 ☎ 266 703 710 🌐 www.montsobro.com ⇆ 6 rooms 🍴 No meals.*

The Noble House

$ | **HOTEL** | The former home of a 17th-century nobleman, this charming hotel offers one of the best values in Évora, with most rooms featuring a view of the city's skyline. **Pros:** central location near the city's main attractions; breakfast includes many regional favorites; rooms with private balconies and spectacular views. **Cons:** some bathrooms are a bit dated; limited parking available; steep staircase to climb. *Rooms from: €70* *Rua da Freiria de Baixo 16, Rua Conde da Serra da Tourega* *266 247 290* *www.thenoblehouse.pt* *24 rooms* *Free Breakfast.*

Pousada Convento Évora

$$ | **HOTEL** | Also known as Pousada de Loios, the former monks' cells in this luxurious convent-turned-pousada have been polished with modern conveniences, retaining their old-world style but leaving no trace of monastic austerity. **Pros:** arguably Portugal's most famous and stately pousada; located in the heart of Évora's historic center; friendly staff caters to your every need. **Cons:** attracts international tour groups; small bathrooms and narrow hallways; poor lighting in some rooms. *Rooms from: €180* *Largo do Conde de Vila Flor* *266 730 070* *www.pousadas.pt* *36 rooms* *Free Breakfast.*

Solar de Monfalim

$ | **B&B/INN** | In a 16th-century nobleman's quarters with a delightful arched gallery overlooking the street, this family-run guesthouse provides quiet, old-fashioned hospitality in the heart of the old city. **Pros:** one of the city's architectural gems; rooms are simple and spacious ; younger kids stay free. **Cons:** winding staircase means a steep climb; no on-site restaurant; no parking. *Rooms from: €80* *Largo da Misericórdia 1* *266 703 529* *www.solarmonfalim.com* *26 rooms* *Free Breakfast.*

Shopping

Just off Praça do Giraldo, the cobblestone Rua 5 de Outubro is lined with shops selling regional handicrafts such as painted furniture, hand-painted ceramics, leather, cork, basketwork, ironwork, rugs, and quilted blankets.

CRAFTS

Mont'sobro

CRAFTS | This shop focuses solely on handmade cork products, and sells everything from frames to handbags to umbrellas—even a cork bikini. And if you really love cork, you can stay in the Mont'Sobro House, owned by the same family, and decorated in cork products. *Rua 5 de Outubro 66* *266 704 609* *www.montsobro.com.*

O Cesto Artesanato

CRAFTS | At the top of the shopping street of Rua 5 de Outubro, O Cesto Artesano specializes in beautiful ceramics and items made with locally produced cork. *Rua 5 de Outubro 57-A* *266 703 344* *www.ocesto.pt.*

O Pierrot

CRAFTS | This store sells Alentejo regional handicrafts, from cork to leather. It's also a good place to pick up some Alentejo wines. *Rua 5 de Outubro 67* *266 703 021.*

Guadalupe

12½ km (8 miles) west of Évora.

The tiny village of Guadalupe takes its name from a 17th-century chapel that is dedicated to Nossa Senhora de Gaudalupe (Our Lady of Guadalupe). Henry the Navigator was known to attend Mass at this chapel. Nowadays this hamlet hosts a boisterous festival during the last 15 days of July, during which the town's population quadruples. The area is better known for its prehistoric relics. There's also a nighttime summer solstice festival each June.

GETTING HERE AND AROUND

Guadalupe can be difficult to find. If you do plan to drive, head northwest from Évora's center on the N114 for about 10 km (6 miles), and then turn left on a tiny road called Estrada do Norte, which takes you into the village of Guadalupe.

Sights

Unless otherwise noted, all sites below are less than a 30-minute drive from Évora, and can be visited as part of a half-day excursion from the city. Évora's tourist office can provide maps and directions.

Anta Grande do Zambujeiro (*Great Dolmen of Zambujeiro*)
ARCHAEOLOGICAL SITE | The 20-foot-high Dolmen of Zambujeiro is the largest of its kind on the Iberian Peninsula. This prehistoric monument is typical of those found throughout Neolithic Europe: several massive stone slabs stand upright, supporting a flat stone that serves as a roof. These structures were designed as burial chambers. ✉ *Off CM1079, Valverde.*

Aqueduto da Água de Prata (*Silver Water Aqueduct*)
ARCHAEOLOGICAL SITE | The graceful arched Silver Water Aqueduct, which once carried water to Évora from the springs at Graça do Divor, is best seen as you drive along the road to Arraiolos (R114-4). Constructed in 1532 under the patronage of Dom João III, the aqueduct was designed by the famous architect Francisco de Arruda and extends 18 km (11 miles) north of Évora. Évora's tourist office has a map of the aqueduct and footpaths alongside it. ✉ *Off the R114-4, Valverde.*

Menhir of Almendres (*Almendres Standing Stone*)
ARCHAEOLOGICAL SITE | In the tiny village of Guadalupe stands the Menhir of Almendres, an 8-foot-tall Neolithic stone obelisk believed to have been used in fertility rites. Several hundred yards away is the cromlech, 95 granite monoliths arranged in an oval in the middle of a large field on a hill. The monoliths face the sunrise and are believed to have been the social, religious, and political center of the agro-pastoral, seminomadic population. The site is also believed to be linked to astral observations and predictions, fertility rites, and the worship of the mother goddess. ✉ *Rua do Cromeleque* ✣ *15 km (9 miles) west of Évora, follow signs from Rua do Cromeleque.*

Arraiolos

22 km (14 miles) northwest of Évora.

Arraiolos, dominated by the ruins of a once-mighty walled fortress, is a typical hilltop village of whitewashed houses and narrow streets. What distinguishes it is its worldwide reputation as a carpet-producing center. In the 16th century, as Portuguese trade with the East grew, an interest developed in the intricate designs of the carpets from India and Persia, and these patterns served as models for the earliest hand-embroidered Arraiolos carpets. The colorful rugs aren't mass-produced in factories but are handmade by locals in their homes and cottages. An authentic Arraiolos rug, made of locally produced wool, has some 4,000 ties per square foot. To discourage imitations, the town council designed a blue seal of authenticity to be affixed to each carpet.

GETTING HERE AND AROUND

Arraiolos is spread over two steep hills, the taller one dominated by the castle and most of the town's center—including carpet shops, restaurants, and guesthouses—just below it, and one housing the impressive pousada. In a valley between the two is a festival parade ground and the bus station.

ESSENTIALS

VISITOR INFORMATION Arraiolos Tourist Office. ✉ *Praca do Municipio 19* ☎ *266 490 254* 🌐 *www.visitevora.net/en/arraiolos.*

Castelo de Arraiolos

CASTLE/PALACE | Nestled on a grassy hill overlooking the village, this medieval castle stands out with its circular walls. The interior has seen better days, especially around the two towers, but the ramparts are still pretty much intact and offer incredible views over Alentejo's countryside. In the middle of the fortress there's a 16th-century church that is occasionally open and has a small souvenir shop. You can drive here or walk from the village, but it's a steep climb. ✉ *Rua do Castelo* 🎫 *Free.*

Centro Interpretativo do Tapete de Arraiolos (*Arraiolos Rug Interpretive Center*)

MUSEUM | For an in-depth history of the intricate weavings produced in and around this community, visit the Centro Interpretativo do Tapete de Arraiolos. Set in an old hospital facing Praça do Município, the small museum displays rugs produced from the 17th to the 21st centuries. Occasionally a local weaver lets you see the process close up. ✉ *Praça do Munícipio 19* ☎ *266 490 254* 🌐 *www.tapetedearraiolos.pt* 🎫 *€1* ⏲ *Closed Mon.*

O Alpendre

$$ | **PORTUGUESE** | Decorated in typical Alentejo style, this quaint eatery serves regional dishes such as *migas* (bread fried in olive oil, garlic, and coriander and served alongside meat or fish) and *sopa de cação* (dogfish soup). Try the *carne de porco preto* (black pork), a specialty of the house. **Known for:** packed on Sunday, when reservations are essential; diverse selection of local dishes; friendly staff. 💲 *Average main: €20* ✉ *Bairro Serpa Pinto 22* ☎ *266 419 024.*

Pousada Convento de Arraiolos

$ | **HOTEL** | If you need to sleep on your decision about which carpet to buy, consider an overnight stay in this picturesque pousada housed in a 16th-century convent that has been beautifully restored and tastefully updated with modern comforts. **Pros:** contemporary restaurant favors traditional regional dishes; all the charm you'd expect at a country inn; free parking and other amenities. **Cons:** modern decor can feel a bit bland; the walk to town is short but steep; pricey restaurant. 💲 *Rooms from: €140* ✉ *Nossa Sra. da Assunção* ☎ *266 419 340* 🌐 *www.pousadas.pt* 🛏 *32 rooms* 🍽 *Free Breakfast.*

The main street of Arraiolos is lined with showrooms and workshops featuring the town's famous hand-embroidered wool rugs.

Casa Quintão

TEXTILES/SEWING | This carpet workshop on the main square of Arraiolos does restoration of traditional carpets, as well as sales of antiques and new ones. ✉ *Praça Municipio 30* ☎ *266 429 250* 🌐 *www.casaquintao.com.*

Casa Tiraz

HOUSEHOLD ITEMS/FURNITURE | One of the town's best rug selections can be found at Casa Tiraz, facing Arraiolos's main town square. ✉ *Praca da Republica 1* ☎ *266 419 057.*

★ **Fábrica de Tapetes Hortense**

HOUSEHOLD ITEMS/FURNITURE | Established in 1985, this shop specializes in traditional rugs from around the region. Over the years, owner Maria Hortense has worked on several high-profile projects, including a rug for Pope Francis. All rugs are handmade by her *bordadeiras* (embroiderers). Clients can select a rug from the shop or order a customized one using their favorite colors and design. ✉ *Rua Alexandre Herculano 22* ☎ *266 043 082.*

Sempre Noiva

HOUSEHOLD ITEMS/FURNITURE | Sempre Noiva–which roughly translates as "Always a Bride"—is not a wedding shop, but a store dedicated to wool carpets. The name comes from a local legend about a maiden living in the hilltop castle whose fiance didn't return from war until she was very old. To hide the signs of age, she covered herself with a rug. This story inspired the original owner, and the shop is now run by her two daughters. ✉ *Rua Alexandre Herculano 33* ☎ *266 490 040.*

Vitorino Paulo

HOUSEHOLD ITEMS/FURNITURE | One of the many tapestry shops along Rua Alexandre Herculano, Vitorino Paulo sells Arraiolos tapestries, along with rugs with Persian and Turkish designs. ✉ *Rua Alexandre Herculano 27* ☎ *266 419 065.*

Montemor-o-Novo

30 km (18 miles) northwest of Évora.

Driving east from the Portuguese capital, the first hilltop castle settlement you'll hit is also one of the most impressive. Montemor-e-Novo, or simply Montemor for short, has been a settlement from the time of the Romans, and its castle has been renovated and expanded by successive generations of Arab rulers, Christian monks, and Portuguese royals since then. Today the town is a prosperous agricultural hub with a surprisingly happening arts scene, and gastronomic festivals throughout the year. Montemor makes a pleasant half-day stop to or from Évora.

GETTING HERE AND AROUND

About 100 km (62 miles) east of Lisbon, Montemor is just past the point where the Portuguese capital's limits disappear into the countryside. It's an easy 90-minute drive from Lisbon, or about 30 minutes west of Alentejo's main city, Évora. Montemor is easily identified from afar by its hilltop castle, on a steep hill towering over clusters of houses hugging its sides.

CONTACTS Montemor-o-Novo Bus Station. ✉ *Carreira de S. Francisco* ☎ *266 892 110.* **Montemor-o-Novo Tourist Office.** ✉ *Largo Calouste Gulbenkian 15* ☎ *266 898 103* 🌐 *www.cm-montemornovo.pt.* **Taxi Montemor.** ☎.

Sights

Biblioteca Municipal (*Municipal Library*)

RELIGIOUS SITE | This former convent houses the municipal library, the town archives, and an art gallery with interesting temporary exhibitions about the city's history. In early March, the building is the hub of a citywide festival celebrating Montemor's patron saint, the 16th-century figure São João de Deus (St. John of God). There's a crypt where the saint is said to have been born and a nave covered with blue-and-white azulejo tiles depicting scenes from his life. ✉ *Terreiro de St. João de Deus 5* ☎ *266 898 103* 🎫 *Free.*

★ **Castelo de Montemor-o-Novo** (*Montemor-o-Novo Castle*)

CASTLE/PALACE | One of the most beautiful in the region, this huge castle towers over the city. It includes an ancient *porta da vila* (city gate) that could be closed during attacks, a *casa da guarda* (guard station), and a dramatic *torre do relogio* (clock tower). You can climb onto the outer fortifications and walk around the complex for a 360-degree view of the town and the sweeping plains beyond. It's also a pleasant walk up to the castle through the winding, steep side streets lined with

17th-century manor houses and ornate doorways. ✉ *Porta de Vila* 🎫 *Free.*

Igreja Matriz de Montemor-o-Novo (*Church of Montemor-o-Novo*)
RELIGIOUS SITE | This church has a splendid Manueline doorway, 17th-century altar pieces, and an 18th-century organ crafted in Italy. Near the front of the church rests a beautiful 15th-century Pietà sculpture carved from local marble. ✉ *Terreiro de St. João de Deus* ☎ *266 898 410* 🌐 *www.scmmn.com* 🎫 *Free.*

Restaurants

Cafe Almansor
$ | CAFÉ | A favorite with locals, this friendly café makes one of the best cups of coffee in town, and its *bifanas* (pork sandwiches seasoned with garlic and spices) are delectable. If you're brave, try the local specialty *caracois* (snails). **Known for:** inexpensive stop for lunch; they take their coffee seriously; quiet atmosphere. [$] *Average main: €3* ✉ *Praca da República 7* ☎ *266 892 209* 💳 *No credit cards* 🕒 *Closed Wed.*

★ **Sociedade Circulo Montemorense**
$ | CAFÉ | There's no better spot to sip a glass of wine than in the front garden of this social club in Montemor's Praça de Republica. In pleasant weather you'll struggle to find a seat at this see-and-be-seen establishment. **Known for:** relaxed outdoor patio; affordable lunch fare; meeting spot for locals. [$] *Average main: €5* ✉ *Rua Alvaro Castelões 6* ☎ *266 896 063* 💳 *No credit cards.*

Monsaraz

50 km (31 miles) southeast of Évora.

The entire fortified hilltop town of Monsaraz is a living museum of narrow stone streets lined with ancient white houses. The medieval town's 150 or so permanent residents (mostly older people) live mainly off tourism, and because they do so graciously and unobtrusively, Monsaraz has managed to retain its essential character.

Old women clad in black sit in the doorways of their cottages and chat with neighbors, their ever-present knitting in hand. At the southern end of the walls stand the well-preserved towers of a formidable 13th-century castle. The view from atop the pentagonal tower sweeps across the plain to the west and to the east over the Guadiana River to Spain.

GETTING HERE AND AROUND

Approaching from any direction, you can't miss the tiny village perched on a hilltop surrounded by steep walls. Drive halfway up to the parking lot, then enter Monsaraz on foot through one of four arched entry gates. This is also where daily buses from Évora will drop you off; check with the tourist office for bus timetables.

VISITOR INFORMATION Monsaraz Tourist Office. ✉ *Rua Direita 24* ☎ *927 997 316* 🌐 *www.cm-reguengos-monsaraz.pt.*

Sights

Barragem do Alqueva (*Alqueva Dam*)
DAM | If the valleys surrounding Monsaraz look flooded, that's because they are. In the late 1990s, Portugal and Spain jointly began work on a huge dam that created the 250-square-km (96-square-mile) Alqueva Reservoir, Europe's largest lake. You can drive or walk across the dam, but one of the best ways to see the lake's expanse is by boat. Visit the nearby town of Amieira, where the **Amieira Marina** offers day trips on the lake, boat rentals, and dining at a waterfront restaurant. ✉ *Amieira Marina, off N255, Amieira* ☎ *266 611 173* 🌐 *www.amieiramarina.com.*

Castelo de Monsaraz
CASTLE/PALACE | The castle and its imposing towers are one of the first things you see when you approach Monsaraz. Dating back to the 14th century, it's among

A gorgeous panorama of the fortified hilltop town of Monsaraz Village in the Alentejo region.

the many fortifications built to protect the border between Portugal and Spain. During the Portuguese Restoration War, the castle was used by the military, but it was abandoned soon after that. It was only around 1830 that locals decided to turn it into a bullfighting ring, a tradition that continues in September during the Festas de Nosso Senhor Jesus dos Passos. For the rest of the year, you can roam around the castle and enjoy the views of the Alqueva Dam. ✉ *Largo do Castelo 1* 🎫 *Free.*

★ Herdade do Esporão

WINE/SPIRITS | This famed wine estate produces Esporão, one of Portugal's top labels. It's on a beautiful, sprawling property overlooking a lake that you won't believe is tucked away in the outskirts of this small town. The winery's driveway cuts across miles of vineyards, up to the main house with an arched portico showcasing the vast property. The winery offers one-hour tours of its facilities several times daily, and they all end with a free glass of wine. You can also sample wines at the bar (you pay according to the number and type of wines tasted). Pair wines with sophisticated Portuguese cuisine in the elegant lunchtime restaurant, where chef Pedro Pena Bastos prepares dishes with wine, olive oil, and vinegar from the estate. ✉ *Herdade do Esporão, Apartado 31, Reguengos de Monsaraz* ☎ *266 509 280* 🌐 *www.esporao.com.*

Menhir of Outeiro (*Outeiro Standing Stone*)

ARCHAEOLOGICAL SITE | The area around Monsaraz is dotted with megalithic monuments. This 18-foot-high menhir (standing stone), is one of the tallest ever discovered. ✉ *Off Rua da Orada* ✥ *3 km (2 miles) north of Monsaraz.*

Museu Do Fresco (*Fresco Museum*)

MUSEUM | This small museum, next to the parish church, displays religious artifacts, well-preserved frescoes, and the original town charter, signed by Dom Manuel in 1512. The former tribunal contains an interesting 15th-century fresco that depicts Christ presiding over

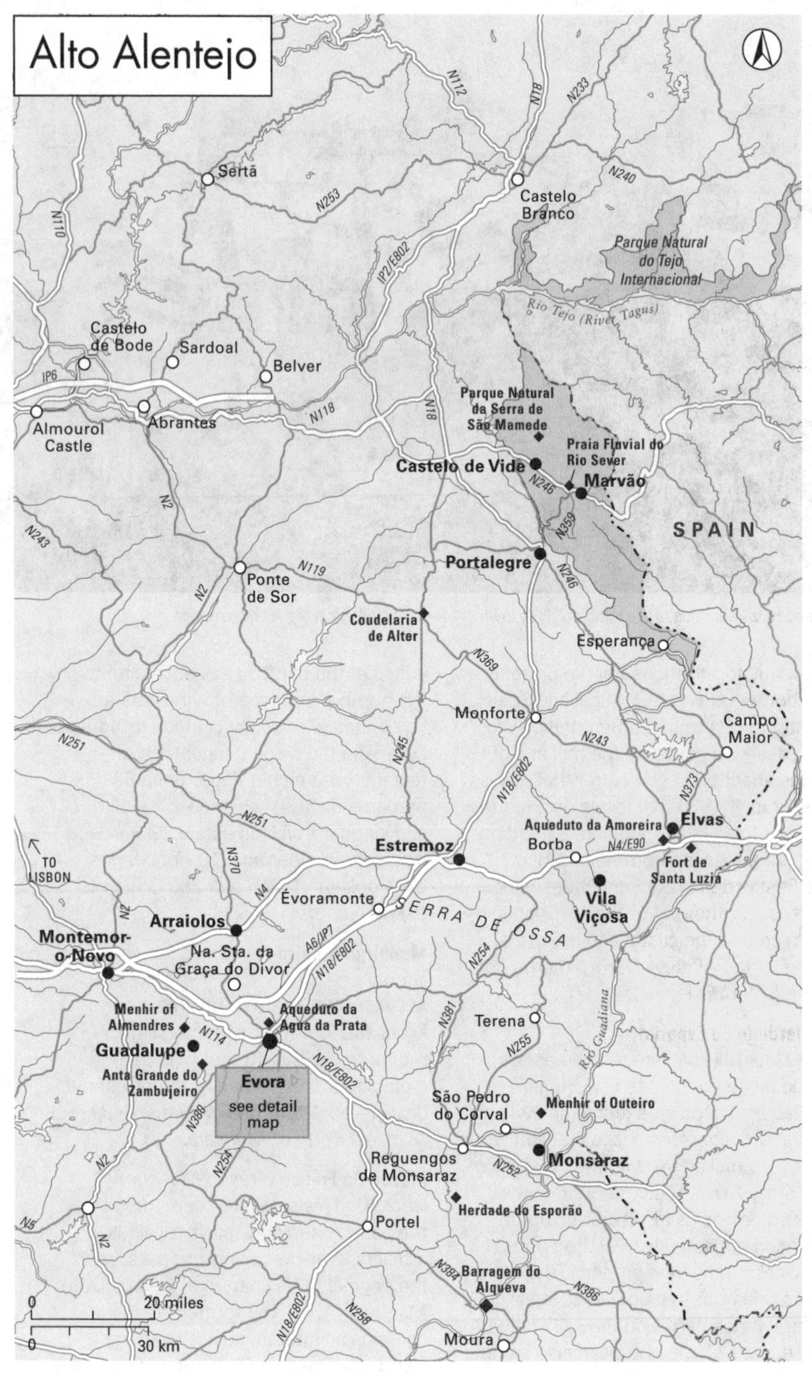
Alto Alentejo
Sertã
Castelo Branco
Parque Natural do Tejo Internacional
Rio Tejo (River Tagus)
Castelo de Bode
Sardoal
Belver
Almourol Castle
Abrantes
Parque Natural da Serra de São Mamede
Praia Fluvial do Rio Sever
Castelo de Vide
Marvão
SPAIN
Portalegre
Ponte de Sor
Coudelaria de Alter
Esperança
Monforte
Campo Maior
Aqueduto da Amoreira
Elvas
Borba
Fort de Santa Luzia
Estremoz
TO LISBON
Vila Viçosa
Évoramonte
SERRA DE OSSA
Arraiolos
Montemor-o-Novo
Na. Sta. da Graça do Divor
Menhir of Almendres
Aqueduto da Agua da Prata
Guadalupe
Terena
Anta Grande do Zambujeiro
Evora
see detail map
Rio Guadiana
São Pedro do Corval
Menhir of Outeiro
Reguengos de Monsaraz
Monsaraz
Herdade do Esporão
Portel
Barragem do Alqueva
Moura
0
20 miles
0
30 km
N112
N18
N233
N240
N253
N110
IP2/E802
IP6
N118
N246
N359
N2
N243
N119
N369
N251
N245
N18/E802
N373
N4/E90
N370
N4
A6/IP7
N254
N114
N381
N255
N380
N252
N5
N384
N386
N258

figures of Truth and Deception. ✉ *Largo Nuno Álvares Pereira 12* ☎ *927 997 316* 🌐 *www.cm-reguengos-monsaraz.pt* 🎫 *€1* ⏲ *Closed Mon.*

Restaurants

Casa do Forno

$ | PORTUGUESE | At the entrance of this popular restaurant is a huge, rounded oven with an iron door, hence the name (*forno* is Portuguese for "oven"). Picture windows line the dining room and afford a spectacular view over the rolling plains. **Known for:** outdoor terrace with great views; ample portions of hearty dishes; lively atmosphere. 💲 *Average main: €15* ✉ *Travessa da Sonabre* ☎ *266 104 008* ⏲ *Closed Tues.*

Lumumba

$ | PORTUGUESE | This little restaurant in one of the old village houses has a devoted clientele that hails from both sides of the Portuguese–Spanish border. The dining room is small, but there is a terrace for outside dining with views over the valley to distant mountains. **Known for:** everything made with lamb is excellent; great views from the terrace; tasty house wine. 💲 *Average main: €12* ✉ *Rua Direita 12* ☎ *266 557 121* ⏲ *Closed Mon.*

O Gato

$ | PORTUGUESE | In the village of Reguengos de Monsaraz, O Gato is a bed and breakfast, pastry shop, and restaurant in a traditional Alentejan white-stucco building with blue awnings. It's a huge favorite with locals, serving traditional fare like lamb stew made with fresh herbs and spices. **Known for:** outdoor terrace with views of the parish church; specializing in meat dishes like lamb stew; generous portions. 💲 *Average main: €11* ✉ *Praça da Liberdade 11–13, Reguengos de Monsaraz* ☎ *266 502 353* 🌐 *www.residencialogato.pt.*

Hotels

★ **Casa Pinto**

$ | B&B/INN | This small and surprisingly sophisticated guesthouse—a true romantic hideaway—occupies a whitewashed row house in the center of the walled town. **Pros:** roof terrace with the best view in town; free Wi-Fi and other amenities; cozy and intimate feel. **Cons:** rooms are on the small side; no space for extra beds; breakfast lacks variety. 💲 *Rooms from: €105* ✉ *Praça Dom Nuno Álvares Pereira 10* ☎ *266 557 076* 🌐 *www.casapinto.pt* 🛏 *5 rooms* 🍽 *Free Breakfast.*

Vila Viçosa

60 (40 miles) northeast of Evora.

A quiet town with a moated castle, Vila Viçosa is in the heart of the fertile Borba Plain. It has been closely linked with Portuguese royalty since the 15th century, and court life in Vila Viçosa flourished in the late 16th and early 17th centuries, when the huge palace constructed by the fourth Duke of Bragança was the scene of great royal feasts, theater performances, and bullfights. Today Vila Viçosa is a pleasant, bustling town that remains affluent because of its ties to the region's wine industry and marble quarries. Most residents still live in the town center, and it's less touristy and untainted by the suburban sprawl that has cropped up on the edges of other provincial towns. The huge Praça da Republica, lined with orange trees and anchored by a castle on one end and a 17th-century church on the other, is one of the finest squares in all of Alentejo.

GETTING HERE AND AROUND

Vila Viçosa lies just past Borba, south of the highway that connects Évora with the Spanish border. Praça da Republica stretches across the town center, with the Paço Ducal and pousada about 300 meters to the northwest. Bus service from Évora is infrequent and slow, and Vila Viçosa is best reached by private car.

BUS CONTACTS Vila Viçosa Bus Terminal. ✉ *R. Dom João IV 2.*

TAXI CONTACT Vila Viçosa Taxis. ✉ *Praça da Republica* ☎ *268 980 115.*

VISITOR INFORMATION Vila Viçosa Tourist Office. ✉ *Praça da Republica 34* ☎ *268 889 317* 🌐 *www.cm-vilavicosa.pt.*

Sights

Castelo de Vila Viçosa

CASTLE/PALACE | In the heart of Vila Viçosa, surrounded by lush gardens, is this medieval-era castle. For a while it was the home of the Bragança family before they settled down in the nearby Paço Ducal. Inside you'll find a 16th-century church and a cemetery where the Portuguese poet Florbela Espanca rests. You can walk around the walls or visit the small museums of archaeology and hunting located inside the castle. ✉ *Av. Duques de Bragança* ☎ *268 980 128* 🌐 *www.fcbraganca.pt* 🎫 *Free entrance to the castle, €3 for museums* ⏲ *Closed Mon. Closed Tues. morning.*

Museu do Mármore Raquel de Castro (*Raquel de Castro Marble Museum*)

MUSEUM | This museum offers an interesting look at Alentejo's local marble industry, which has sustained Vila Viçosa and made it prosperous. It's on the site of a former quarry, near the road out of town toward Borba. There are free guided tours in Portuguese, Spanish, English, and French. ✉ *Av. Duque D. Jaime* ☎ *268 889 310* 🎫 *€1.55* ⏲ *Closed Mon.*

★ **Paço Ducal** (*Doge's Palace*)

CASTLE/PALACE | This opulent palace draws a great many visitors—and for good reason. Built of locally quarried marble, the palace's main wing extends for some 360 feet and overlooks an expansive square and the bronze equestrian statue of Dom João IV. At the north end of the square note the Porta do Nó (Knot Gate) with its massive stone shaped like ropes—an intriguing example of the Manueline style.

The palace's interior was extensively restored in the 1950s and contains all you'd expect to find: intricate rugs, frescoed ceilings, priceless collections of silver and gold objects, Chinese vases, Gobelin tapestries, and a long dining hall adorned with antlers and other hunting trophies. The enormous kitchen's spits are large enough to accommodate several oxen, and there's enough gleaming copper to keep a small army of servants busy polishing. Dom Carlos, the nation's penultimate king, spent his last night here before being assassinated in 1908; his rooms have been maintained as they were. Carlos was quite an accomplished painter, and many of his works (along with private photos of Portugal's last royal family) line the walls of the apartments.

The ground floor of the castle has displays of objects ranging from Paleolithic to 18th century and mainly Roman artifacts discovered during excavations. These include pieces from ancient Mediterranean civilizations—Egypt, Rome, Carthage, and also pre-Columbian. Also on view are coaches from the 17th to the 20th century. Hunting, rather than war, is the dominant theme of the armory that holds more than 2,000 objects. The treasury displays crucifixes from Vila Viçosa and those belonging to Dona Catarina de Bragança as well as more than 200 pieces of jewelry, paintings, crystal, and ceramics. The porcelain collection is made up of blue-and-white china from the 15th to 18th centuries. ✉ *Terreiro do Paço* ☎ *268 980 659* 🌐 *www.fcbraganca.pt* 🎫 *€7.*

Restaurants

Taverna dos Conjurados

$$$ | **PORTUGUESE** | This local favorite serves traditional Alentejo dishes based on old family recipes. Tucked away in a

The Allure of Azulejo

It's difficult to find an old building of any note in Portugal which isn't adorned somewhere or other with the predominantly blue-tone ceramic tiles called azulejos. The centuries-old marriage of glazed ornamental tiles and Portuguese architecture is a match made in heaven.

After the Gothic period, large buildings made entirely of undressed brick or stone became a rarity in Portuguese architecture. Most structures had extensive areas of flat plaster on their facades and interior walls that cried out for decoration. The compulsion to fill these empty architectural spaces produced the art of the fresco in Italy; in Portugal, it produced the art of the azulejo.

The medium is well suited to the deeply rooted Portuguese taste for intricate, ornate decoration. And, aesthetics aside, glazed tiling is ideally suited to the country's more practical needs. Durable, waterproof, and easily cleaned, the tile provides cool interiors during Portugal's hot summers and exterior protection from the dampness of Atlantic winters.

The term *azulejo* comes not from the word *azul* ("blue" in Portuguese), but from the Arabic word for tiles, *az-zulayj*. But despite the long presence of the Moors in Portugal, the Moorish influence on early Portuguese azulejos was actually introduced from Spain in the 15th century.

The very earliest tiles on Portuguese buildings were imported from Andalusia. They're usually geometric in design and were most frequently used to form panels of repeated patterns.

As Portugal's prosperity increased in the 16th century, the growing number of palaces, churches, and sumptuous mansions created a demand for more tile. Local production was small at first, and Holland and Italy were the main suppliers. The superb Dutch-made azulejos in the Paço Ducal in Vila Viçosa are famous examples from this period. The first Portuguese-made tiles had begun to appear in the last quarter of the 15th century, when a number of small factories were established, but three centuries were to pass before Portuguese tile making reached its peak.

The great figure in 18th-century Portuguese tile making is António de Oliveira Bernardes, who died in 1732. The school he established spawned the series of monumental panels depicting hunting scenes, landscapes, battles, and other historical motifs that grace many stately Portuguese homes and churches of the period. Some of the finest examples can be seen in the Alentejo—in buildings such as the university in Évora and the parish church in Alcácer do Sal—as well as at the Castelo de São Felipe in Setúbal. In Lisbon's Museu do Azulejo you can trace the development of tiles in Portugal from their beginnings to the present.

Portuguese tile making declined in quality in the 19th century, but a revival occurred in the 20th century, spearheaded by leading artists such as Almada Negreiros and Maria Keil. Today, some notable examples of tile use by contemporary artists can be seen in many of the capital's metro stations.

former horse stable near the imposing Paço Ducal, it has a rustic decor with granite walls and arched ceilings. **Known for:** the homemade gaspacho is a standout; expansive selection of local wines; friendly host. $ *Average main: €24* ✉ *Largo 25 de Abril 16* ☎ *268 989 530* ⏲ *Closed Mon. No dinner weekends.*

Hotels

★ **Pousada Convento Vila Viçosa**

$$ | **HOTEL** | If you're hooked on Vila Viçosa's history, this 500-year-old convent next door to the Paço Ducal has all the period atmosphere you could want. **Pros:** restaurant serves dishes based on old convent recipes; the friendly, helpful staff can arrange walking tours; spacious rooms filled with antique reproductions. **Cons:** pool area can get a bit noisy in summer; some common areas look a bit run-down; expensive rates. $ *Rooms from: €160* ✉ *Terreiro do Paço* ☎ *268 980 742* 🌐 *www.pousadas.pt* *39 rooms* *Free Breakfast.*

Estremoz

31 km (19 miles) northwest of Vila Viçosa.

Estremoz, which lies on the ancient road that connected Lisbon with Mérida, Spain, has been a site of strategic importance since Roman times, and the castle, which overlooks the town, was a crucial one of the Alentejo's many fortresses.

Today Estremoz is a bustling rural hub that's the seat of eastern Alentejo's growing arts scene, as well as a military garrison town complete with sword-wielding guards outside the cavalry regiment's headquarters across from the main park. Chock-full of history but not resting on its laurels, Estremoz is unfortunately often overlooked in favor of its more touristy sister city Évora, but it shouldn't be. Make Estremoz your base for exploring this half of the Alentejo and you won't be disappointed.

GETTING HERE AND AROUND

Estremoz lies about 45 km (30 miles) northeast of Évora along the nontoll road IP2. Most of the city lies within a low outer protective wall, with the castle, pousada, and some museums atop a central hill with another wall around it. Everything is within walking distance inside town.

TOURS Paladares e Aventuras. ☎ *912 322 911* 🌐 *www.paladareseaventuras.com.* **RSI Viagens.** ✉ *Lg. Combatentes de Grande Guerra 9–10* ☎ *268 333 228* 🌐 *www.rsiviagens.pt.*

VISITOR INFORMATION Estremoz Tourist Office. ✉ *Casa de Estremoz, Rossio Marquês de Pombal* ☎ *268 339 227* 🌐 *www.cm-estremoz.pt.*

Sights

Capela de Rainha Santa Isabel (*Chapel of St. Isabel*)

RELIGIOUS SITE | Across the street from the Castelo de Estremoz, Queen Isabel's personal chapel is a striking, richly decorated enclave lined with azulejo tiles. ✉ *R. da Rainha Santa Isabel 8.*

★ **Castelo de Estremoz** (*Estremoz Castle*)

CASTLE/PALACE | The former royal palace, an impressive hilltop fortress towering over the city, is the highlight of any visit to Estremoz (it now functions as a luxury pousada). The palace was built in the 13th century by Portugal's King Dom Dinis. It's named after his wife, Queen Isabel of Aragon, who died here in 1336. An explosion in 1698 destroyed much of the medieval structure except the **Torre das Tres Coroas** (Tower of the Three Crowns), which you can still climb today for fantastic views of Estremoz and the surrounding countryside. The palace was restored after the ammunition blast and fire. The interior is like a museum, housing an impressive collection of

17th- and 18th-century artifacts and furniture. ✉ *Largo de D. Dinis* ☎ *268 332 075* 🌐 *www.pousadas.pt* 🎫 *Free admission to pousada lobby, tower, and chapel.*

Centro Ciência Viva (*Living Science Center*)

COLLEGE | **FAMILY** | Centuries ago this white stucco building was a convent, but now it's a quirky little science museum—a great stop if you have kids in tow. The exhibits have a special emphasis on local geology, including displays of the interesting dinosaur fossils excavated nearby. Nearly everything is interactive, making it one of the most high-tech museums in the region. ✉ *Convento das Maltezas* ☎ *268 334 285* 🌐 *www.ccvestremoz.uevora.pt* 🎫 *€9* 🕐 *Closed Mon.*

Museu Municipal de Estremoz

MUSEUM | This museum is housed in a lovely 17th-century almshouse across from the castle. Its displays chronicle the development of the region and range from Roman artifacts to contemporary pottery, including a collection of the brightly colored figurines for which Estremoz is famous. ✉ *Largo D. Dinis* ☎ *268 339 219* 🌐 *www.patrimoniocultural.pt/pt/museus-e-monumentos/rede-portuguesa/m/museu-municipal-de-estremoz* 🎫 *€1.55* 🕐 *Closed Mon.*

Rossio

PLAZA | The lower town of Estremoz, a maze of narrow streets and white houses, radiates from the Rossio, a huge, central square. Stands lining it sell the town's famous colorful pottery. In addition to the multicolor, hand-painted plates, pitchers, and dolls, note the earthenware jugs decorated with bits of local white marble. There's a weekly market here on Saturday mornings. ✉ *Rossio Marquês de Pombal.*

Coffee and Quick Bites

Café Alentejano

$ | **PORTUGUESE** | There are several refreshment stands and snack bars along the Rossio, but for more substantial fare try this casual eatery. From this popular 60-year-old art deco–style café and its first-floor restaurant, you can watch the goings-on in the square. **Known for:** generous portions of regional dishes; central location on the main square; lovely outdoor terrace. 💲 *Average main: €5* ✉ *Rossio Marquês de Pombal 13–15* ☎ *268 337 300.*

Restaurants

★ Adega do Isaias

$ | **PORTUGUESE** | Hidden away on a narrow side street a few minutes from the main square, this family-run restaurant is the best place in town for hearty, no-nonsense grilled meats. The front part of the former wine cellar is a rustic brick bar with a pork leg mounted on the counter, and a charcoal grill nestled in the front window alcove. **Known for:** the atmosphere of an old wine cellar; a long list of Alentejo wines; reasonable prices. 💲 *Average main: €15* ✉ *Rua do Almeida 21* ☎ *268 322 318* 🕐 *Closed Sun.*

★ Mercearia Gadanha

$$$$ | **PORTUGUESE** | If you'd like to grab a sandwich, cup of tea, or glass of wine between museum visits, there's no place better than Gadanha. You'll likely end up leaving with more than what you ate, as this deli also sells gift-wrapped gourmet treats like local ham, cheese, and chocolates. **Known for:** friendly and knowledgeable staff; traditional dishes with a modern flair; great regional wine selection. 💲 *Average main: €30* ✉ *Largo Dragoes de Olivença 84-A* ☎ *268 333 262* 🌐 *www.merceariagadanha.pt.*

Venda Azul

$ | **PORTUGUESE** | Even if you're dining solo, Venda Azul will welcome you with open arms. There are daily specials, but for first-timers, the grilled black pork is a must. **Known for:** generous portions made to share; try a shot of local liqueur; warm and friendly service. 💲 *Average main:*

€15 ✉ Rua Victor Cordon 39 ☎ 961 941 394 ⏲ Closed Sun.

Hotels

Monte dos Pensamentos

$ | **B&B/INN** | **FAMILY** | A mile from the historic quarter, this hotel is housed in an 18th-century manor house with sprawling gardens, a heated outdoor swimming pool, and plenty of period charm. **Pros:** babysitting services are available on-site; hearty breakfast buffet is included; beautifully done with local antiques. **Cons:** outside the historic center; cottages are modern and bland; rooms can get cold in the winter. *$ Rooms from: €90 ✉ Estrada Estacao do Ameixial ☎ 917 069 699 🌐 www.montedospensamentos.com 9 rooms 🍴 Free Breakfast.*

Páteo dos Solares

$$ | **HOTEL** | **FAMILY** | In a restored 19th-century manor near the old city walls, this lodging has a huge swimming pool and patio overlooking vineyards and farmland that slope down from the edges of Estremoz. **Pros:** sprawling property retains a historic feel; just steps from the town center; breakfast included in room rate. **Cons:** fills up with corporate conferences; small breakfast selection; poor Wi-Fi in some areas. *$ Rooms from: €150 ✉ Rua Brito Capelo ☎ 268 338 400 🌐 www.pateosolares.com 41 rooms 🍴 Free Breakfast.*

★ **Pousada da Rainha Santa Isabel**

$$ | **HOTEL** | If there's one pousada in all of Portugal that you splurge on, this should be it; dubbed the "museum of all pousadas," this hotel is housed in the medieval Castelo de Estremoz. **Pros:** an architectural gem; a favorite for history buffs; great breakfast selection. **Cons:** few activities for children; room decor is a bit dated; pricey restaurant. *$ Rooms from: €175 ✉ Largo D. Dinis 1 ☎ 268 332 075 🌐 www.pousadas.pt 33 rooms 🍴 Free Breakfast.*

Shopping

Irmas Flores Artesano

MUSEUM | For authentic Estremoz crafts, head to this tiny workshop where you can watch local women molding clay and painting their ceramic creations in the back room. Besides ceramics, the adjacent shop also sells locally handmade blankets, fruit compote, and liqueurs. *✉ Largo da Republica 31-32 ☎ 268 324 239.*

Elvas

40 km (25 miles) east of Estremoz, 15 km (9 miles) west of Spain.

Extensively fortified because of its proximity to the Spanish town of Badajoz, Elvas was from its founding an important bastion in warding off attacks from the east. Portugal's most formidable 17th-century fortifications are characterized by a series of walls, moats, and reinforced towers. The size of the complex can best be appreciated by driving around the periphery of the town. Inside you'll find a bustling, vibrant city with a stately town square, an impressive castle, an array of historic churches and museums, and almost no tourists.

GETTING HERE AND AROUND

Elvas lies on the Spanish frontier, just 15 km (9 miles) west of Badajoz. Praça da República lies at the center, with the castle at the town's northern end. The pedestrian Rua de Alcamim provides a lovely traffic-free entrance by foot from Elvas's southern walls. The bus station lies just outside the city walls, with service several times daily to Évora (check with the tourist office for updated timetable). Inside the city walls, there's a tourist bus that takes you to all the major sites; it costs €5, and runs 10–3 every day but Wednesday and Sunday.

CONTACTS Comboio Turistico. *✉ Praça da República ☎ 268 622 236.*

preserved, and you can
·b horses being trained
he farm. There are also
eresting museums
nts the history of the
llection of horse-drawn
has displays on the
town of Alter do Chão
tlements of a 14th-cen-
king a square, is also
pada do Arneiro, Alter
a dusty track 3 km (2
f Alter do Chão ☎ 245
terreal.pt 🎫 €7.50

Bernardo (*St. Bernard*

in 1518, the Mon-
nard is a beautiful
rty that includes a
ers with a central gar-
nd a mausoleum. The
after the last monk
ince then the building
seminary, a high
museum, and military
sed by the National
s the building to visi-
d hours. ✉ *Av. George*
7 400 🎫 *Free.*

Guy Fino (*Guy Fino*

derful museum holds
lection of the tapes-
talegre world famous.
ned after Guy Fino,
of the city's textile
Figueira 9 ☎ *245 307*
alegre.pt 🎫 *€2.10*

rra de São Mamede
his 80,000-acre nature
km (3 miles) northeast
tends north to the
rvão and the spa
Vide, and south to the
rança on the Spanish
inhabited park region
family plots, and sheepherding is the major occupation. The area is rich in wildlife, including many rare species of birds, as well as wild boars, deer, and wildcats. It's a pristine, quiet place for hiking, riding, or simply communing with nature, and you'll rarely spot another tourist for miles and miles. ✉ *Rua Augusto César de Oliveira Tavares 23, R/C* ☎ *245 309 189* 🌐 *www.icnf.pt.*

Sé de Portalegre (*Portalegre Cathedral*)
RELIGIOUS SITE | About 400 meters north of the castle lies Portalegre's cathedral, a 16th-century church and the town's most prominent landmark. The 18th-century facade is highlighted with marble columns and wrought-iron balconies. Inside are early-17th-century azulejos depicting the Virgin Mary. ✉ *Praça do Município* ☎ *245 309 480* 🎫 *Free.*

Restaurants

★ O Escondidinho
$ | PORTUGUESE | It's worth the time it takes to find this lovely local restaurant, tucked away down a quiet street in Portalegre. Decorated with traditional tiles and brick archways, it's a charming local favorite that serves up amazing Alentejo dishes like migas, porco preto, and grilled fish. **Known for:** great place to sample grilled black pork; kitchen uses old family recipes; rustic atmosphere. 💲 *Average main: €10* ✉ *Travessa das Cruzes 1* ☎ *245 202 728* 💳 *No credit cards* 🕒 *Closed Sun.*

Hotels

★ Quinta da Dourada
$ | HOTEL | This sprawling horse farm and vineyard is 7 km (4 miles) from Portalegre, but it feels like it's way out in the countryside, with 360-degree views of rolling hills, rows of grapevines, and forests from the swimming pool. **Pros:** rural retreat just outside the city; gorgeous pool and gardens; free use of bikes. **Cons:** too far to walk to town; no on-site restaurant; some facilities are a bit run-down. 💲 *Rooms from: €85* ✉ *Parque Natural*

The sprawling Forte de Santa Luzia, outside Elvas's walls, was once an important military fortress.

Sights

Aqueduto da Amoreira
BUILDING | The 8-km (5-mile) Amoreira Aqueduct took more than a century to build and is still in use today. It was started in 1498 under the direction of one of the era's great architects, Francisco de Arruda—who also designed the Aqueduto da Agua da Prata north of Évora. The first drops of water didn't flow into the town fountain until 1622. Some parts of the impressive structure have five stories of arches; the total number of arches is 843. The aqueduct is best viewed from outside the city walls, on the road from Lisbon. ✉ *Av. de Badajoz/N4* ⊕ *1 km (½ mile) west of Elvas, junction between N4 and N246.*

Castelo de Elvas (*Elvas Castle*)
CASTLE/PALACE | At this castle's battlements you'll have a sweeping view of Elvas and its fortifications. There's been a fortress here since Roman times, though this structure's oldest elements were built by the Moors and expanded by a handful of Portuguese monarchs. Touching the border with Spain, it was always on the front line of battles between the two countries. In 1807 it was taken by Napoléon's troops, but the English and the Portuguese quickly fought them off. Despite all the battles it faced, the castle remains in remarkably good condition, thanks to its solid stone walls. There's a small bar inside serving light meals and drinks that's open until late. It gets especially busy in the summer when they set up tables outside. ✉ *Parada do castelo* 🎫 *€2* 🕒 *Closed Mon.*

Forte de Santa Luzia (*Fort of St. Lucia*)
MILITARY SITE | This impressive military fortress on a hill about 1½ km (1 mile) outside Elvas's city walls houses an interesting military museum with an array of artillery and weapons. The fort's rectangular ramparts were first built in the 1640s during Portugal's centuries-long animosity with Spain, and the local governor's residence was at its center. ✉ *Museu Militar de Elvas, Av.*

de São Domingos *268 628 357* *€2* *Closed Mon.*

Igreja da Nossa Senhora da Assunção
RELIGIOUS SITE | The 16th-century Church of Our Lady of the Assumption at the head of the town square, the Praça da República, has an impressive triple-nave interior lined with 17th-century blue-and-yellow azulejos. The church was designed by Francisco de Arruda, architect of the Elvas aqueduct, but underwent subsequent modifications. It was a cathedral until the diocese was moved to Évora in the 18th century. *Praça da República* *Free.*

Museu de Arte Contemporanea de Elvas (*Elvas Contemporary Art Museum*)
MUSEUM | Focusing on 20th-century artists, this musem is definitely worth a visit if you're curious about modern aesthetics in otherwise traditional Alentejo. The well-organized exhibits feature about 300 works that rotate throughout the year. The baroque-style building itself is also exquisite, and used to be a hospital run by a religious order. Upstairs there's a chapel lined with azulejos, and a café with nice views of Elvas. *Rua de Cadeia* *268 637 150* *www.col-antoniocachola.com* *€2* *Closed Mon.*

Museu Municipal da Fotografia João Carpinteiro (*João Carpinteiro Photography Museum*)
MUSEUM | Housed in a 1930s movie theater, the municipal photography museum's permanent collection includes 19th-century cameras, black-and-white images from around Portugal, and an exhibit on the history of global photography. *Largo Luis de Camoes* *268 636 470* *www.museudefotografiaelvas.com.pt* *€2.*

Restaurants

A Bolota Castanha
$$$$ | **PORTUGUESE** | People drive miles to dine at this well-known restaurant 16 km (10 miles) from Elvas in the town of Terrugem. The owner takes pride in the *cozido de grão* (boiled dinner with pork, smoked sausages, cabbage, and chickpeas), but their menu also lists international dishes such as spinach with shrimp au gratin and delicious sorbets for dessert. **Known for:** Sunday buffet draws enthusiastic locals; photo-worthy dishes from the region; the best place for cod. *Average main: €30* *Quinta Janelas Verdes, Rua Madre Teresa, Terrugem* *268 656 118* *Closed Mon. No dinner Sun.*

A Coluna
$ | **PORTUGUESE** | This simple restaurant serves Alentejo classics like grilled pork and veal inside a white stucco dining room decorated with blue-and-white tiles. If you're brave, try the *cabrito* (baby goat), a local delicacy. **Known for:** attentive staff; delicious pork dishes; generous portions. *Average main: €12* *Rua do Cabrito 11* *268 623 728* *No credit cards* *Closed Wed.*

Hotels

★ Hotel São João de Deus
$ | **HOTEL** | Housed in a gleaming white 17th-century convent just inside the city walls, this is Elvas's most luxurious hotel. **Pros:** historic building with a bell tower; flower-filled outdoor terrace; free Wi-Fi and other amenities. **Cons:** some rooms are a bit small; bar closes on the early side; some dated decor. *Rooms from: €110* *Largo S. João Deus 1* *268 639 220* *www.hotelsaojoaodeus.com* *56 rooms* *Free Breakfast.*

Quinta de Santo António
$ | **HOTEL** | **FAMILY** | About 8 km (5 miles) outside Elvas, this palm-shaded estate makes for an restful overnight stop near the Portugal–Spain border. **Pros:** indoor games room and outdoor playground for kids; friendly, multilingual staff; sparkling swimming pool. **Cons:** far from the historic sights; you'll need a car to get here; some facilities are a bit dated. *Rooms from: €85* *Estrada de Barbacena, Apartado 206* *268 636 460* *www.qsahotel.com* *30 rooms* *Free Breakfast.*

Portalegre

60 km (40 miles) north of Elvas.

Portalegre is the gateway to the Alentejo's most mountainous region as well as to the Parque Natural da Serra de São Mamede. The town is at the foot of the Serra de São Mamede, where the parched plains of the south give way to a greener, more inviting landscape. Because it's a larger, more modern town, Portalegre lacks a bit of the charm of the whitewashed hamlets in the south of the province. But the city's vibrant spirit, buoyed by its large university, more than makes up for it. There's a Gothic cathedral, castle, and walled old town to explore.

Portalegre is a great base for outdoors lovers who want easy access to nearby mountains and villages. History buffs will enjoy exploring the remnants of its once-thriving textile industry—Portalegre retains a worldwide reputation for its handmade tapestries, which fetch high prices.

GETTING HERE AND AROUND

Portalegre is Alto Alentejo's largest hub, with good public transportation links. The tourist office can provide an updated bus schedule, with service several times daily from Évora. The city center is divided by the Jardim do Tarro, a public garden, with most historical points of interest to the south within easy walking distance, and residential areas to the north.

The tourist office also offers free guided walking tours at 9:30 on first Saturday of every month. Depending on the size and speed of the group, tours last up to 3½ hours and cover all major tourist sites in Portalegre, except for museums. The

noblest, has be
watch these su
and exercised c
three small but
here: one docur
farm, one has a
carriages, and o
art of falconry. T
itself, with the t
tury castle overl
worth a stroll.
do Chão *Follo*
miles) northwes
610 060 *www*
Closed Mon.

★ Mosteiro de S
Monastery)
MUSEUM | Found
astery of Saint B
Renaissance pro
tiled church, clo
den and fountair
monastery close
died in 1878, an
has been used a
school, a munici
barracks. It's no
Guard, which op
tors during selec
Robinson *245*

Museu de Tapeça
Tapestry Museu
MUSEUM | This w
a contemporary
tries that made P
The museum is r
the founder of o
factories. *Rua*
530 *www.mtp*
Closed Mon.

Parque Natural da
NATURE PRESERVE
park lies roughly
of Portalegre and
fortified town of
town of Castelo c
little hamlet of Es
border. The spars
is made up of sm

Da Serra de S.Mamede ☎ 937 218 654 🌐 www.quintadadourada.pt ▭ No credit cards ⇨ 7 rooms 🍽 Free Breakfast.

Rossio Hotel

$ | HOTEL | You can't overlook this sleek hotel in the historical center: its name extends across the entire facade. **Pros:** gym, spa, and massage services; free Wi-Fi and other amenities; extra beds available for kids. **Cons:** off-street parking costs extra; no on-site restaurant; decor is a bit stark. *$ Rooms from: €85 ✉ Rua 31 de Janeiro 6 ☎ 245 082 218, 🌐 www.rossiohotel.com ⇨ 15 rooms 🍽 Free Breakfast.*

★ **Solar das Avencas**

$ | B&B/INN | This historic manor house is old-world style at its best, exquisitely adorned with local tapestries and chock-full of antiques. **Pros:** historic property with lots of charm; authentic, historic experience; breakfast is included. **Cons:** no central heating; no on-site restaurant; old-fashioned decor. *$ Rooms from: €60 ✉ Parque Miguel Bombarda 11 ☎ 245 201 028 ▭ No credit cards ⇨ 5 rooms 🍽 Free Breakfast.*

Marvão

25 km (15 miles) northeast of Portalegre.

The views of the mountains as you approach the medieval fortress town of Marvão are spectacular, and the town's castle, atop a sheer rock cliff, commands a 360-degree panorama. The village, with some 120 mostly older inhabitants, is perched at 2,800 feet on top of a mountain, and laid out in several long rows of tidy, white-stone dwellings terraced into the hill.

The biggest event of the year here is the boisterous chestnut festival in early November, when marching bands take to the tiny streets and transform Marvão into a homemade wine-swigging, chestnut-roasting party. But be forewarned: parking is impossible, and hotels book up sometimes a year beforehand.

GETTING HERE AND AROUND

Marvão lies north of Portalegre and east of Castelo de Vide, in the Serra Mamede mountains overlooking Spain. For the most scenic approach from Portalegre, take N359 18 km (11 miles) to Marvão. The narrow but well-surfaced serpentine N359 rises to an elevation of 2,800 feet, past stands of birch and chestnut trees and small vegetable gardens bordered by ancient stone walls. At Portagem take note of the well-preserved Roman bridge.

The drive up to Marvão, hugging the side of the mountain, is breathtaking, but can also be hazardous in harsh weather. Although you can drive through the constricted streets, it's best to park in spaces outside the town walls and walk in as Marvão is best appreciated on foot.

VISITOR INFORMATION Marvão Tourist Office. *✉ Rua de Baixo ☎ 🌐 www.cm-marvao.pt.*

Sights

Castelo de Marvão (*Marvão Castle*)

CASTLE/PALACE | You can climb the tower of Marvão's castle and trace the course of the massive Vauban-style stone walls (characterized by concentric lines of trenches and walls, a hallmark of the 17th-century French military engineer Vauban), adorned at intervals with bartizans, to enjoy breathtaking vistas from different angles. Given its strategic position, it's no surprise that Marvão has been a fortified settlement since Roman times or earlier. The present castle was built under Dom Dinis in the late 13th century and modified some four centuries later, during the reign of Dom João IV. *✉ Rua do Castelo 🎫 Free.*

Museu Municipal de Marvão

MUSEUM | At the foot of the path leading to the town's castle is Marvão's municipal museum, in the 13th-century Church of

Saint Mary. The small gallery contains a diverse collection of religious artifacts, traditional costumes, ancient maps, and weapons. ✉ *Igreja de Santa Maria, Largo de Santa Maria* ☎ *245 909 132* 🎫 *€1.90* ⏲ *Closed Mon.*

Praia Fluvial do Rio Sever (*Sever River Beach*)
BEACH—SIGHT | You'll find this riverfront beach in the town of Portagem, 6 km (4 miles) from Marvão. There's a dam holding back the Sever River, creating a natural swimming pool that becomes a popular hangout in the summer. The calm waters make it safe enough for kids, and the temperature is slightly warmer than the Atlantic. Enjoy a meal in one of the cafés nearby overlooking the mountains of São Mamede. Don't miss the Roman bridge over the river, said to be one of Portugal's oldest toll roads. ✉ *Rua da Ponte Romana 3.*

Restaurants

Casa do Povo
$ | **PORTUGUESE** | Nestled in a corner row house, this simple dining room serves up classic Alentejo dishes and local wines. The bar downstairs has a patio with good views for sundowners. **Known for:** outdoor terrace with mountain views; generous portions; delicious baked cod. 💲 *Average main: €10* ✉ *Travessa do Chabouco* ☎ *245 993 160* ⏲ *No dinner Thurs.*

Varanda do Alentejo
$ | **PORTUGUESE** | This boisterous bar and restaurant is a favorite among locals and out-of-town families, especially on Sunday. The cuisine is typical Alentejan, with specialties like migas with potato, grilled pork, and fish. **Known for:** local dishes like lamb casserole; great views of the town; cozy atmosphere. 💲 *Average main: €12* ✉ *Rua das Protas da Vila 12* ☎ *245 909 002* 🌐 *www.varandadoalentejo.com.*

Hotels

Casa Dom Dinis
$ | **B&B/INN** | This 17th-century home has stone arches and thick walls with original murals depicting scenes from the Alentejo. **Pros:** popular with hiking and mountain-biking groups; staff gives you a warm welcome; some of the best views in town. **Cons:** some rooms are cramped and cold; small whirlpool tub; little storage space. 💲 *Rooms from: €100* ✉ *Rua Dr. Matos Magalhães 7* ☎ *245 909 028* 🌐 *www.domdinis.pt* 🛏 *9 rooms* 🍽 *Free Breakfast.*

Hotel Dom Manuel
$ | **HOTEL** | Five of the rooms in this 200-year-old inn inside the castle walls have eye-popping cliff-side views—they're well worth requesting in advance. **Pros:** historic building in quiet location; special rates for families; friendly staff. **Cons:** interior design is a bit dated; some rooms have poor lighting; breakfast selection is sparse. 💲 *Rooms from: €90* ✉ *Largo da Olivença* ☎ *245 909 150* 🌐 *www.turismarvao.pt* 🛏 *15 rooms* 🍽 *Free Breakfast.*

Pousada de Santa Maria
$$ | **HOTEL** | Several old houses within the city walls were joined to create the Pousada de Santa Maria, one of the area's prettiest lodgings. **Pros:** cozy atmosphere, especially in the winter; expansive views of the valley; family-friendly rates. **Cons:** lacks some of the charm of other pousadas; some rooms are small and dated; narrow street makes driving difficult. 💲 *Rooms from: €150* ✉ *Rua 24 de Janeiro 7* ☎ *245 993 201* 🌐 *www.pousadas.pt* 🛏 *31 rooms* 🍽 *Free Breakfast.*

Castelo de Vide

8 km (5 miles) west of Marvão.

A quiet hilltop town, Castelo de Vide is a picturesque place with pots of geraniums and dazzling flower beds throughout

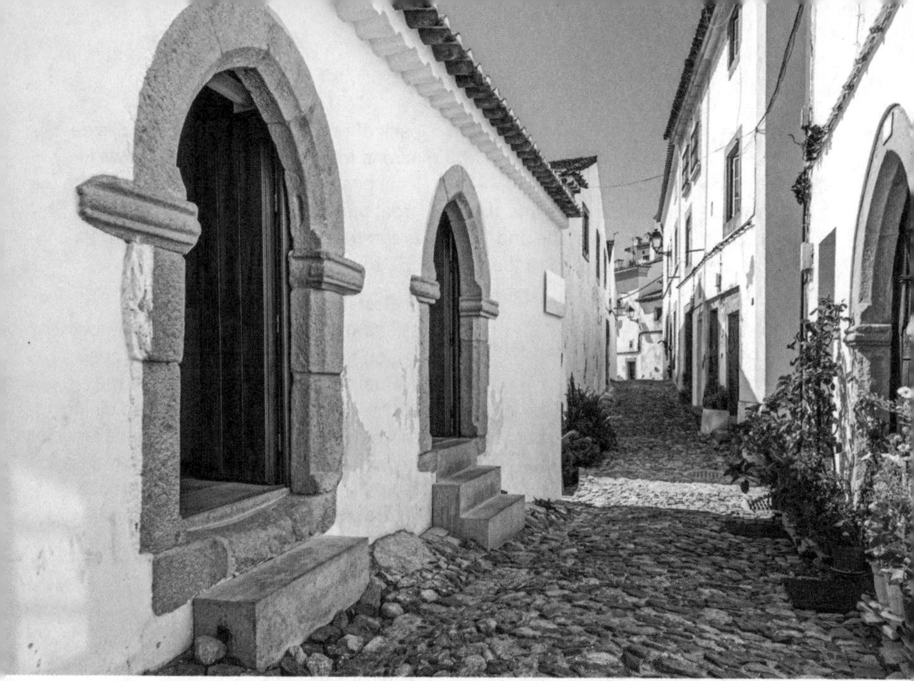

A quaint cobblestone lane in the hilltop town of Castelo de Vide.

town. It's more lively than Marvão, with more options for restaurants, hotels, and sights, but still retains its rustic village feel. When Marvão holds its annual chestnut festival, drawing thousands of tourists from all over Portugal and Spain, Castelo de Vide holds a smaller, more intimate festival in its open-air market, complete with a pig roast and old men in felt hats sharing jugs of their homemade wine. You might be surprised to see a bagpiper strolling through the crowds during Castelo de Vide's festivals; the diverse town still celebrates some traditions from its ancient Gallic and Celtic ancestry.

There are steep cobbled streets that provide beautiful views of the whitewashed town against a backdrop of olive groves and hills. As you walk along, notice the many houses with Gothic doorways in various designs. (The tourist brochures proclaim that Castelo de Vide has the largest number of Gothic doorways of any town in Portugal.) Castelo de Vide's history is as a spa town, renowned for its fresh mountain springs that feed a fountain in the main square today. The town had a sizeable Jewish community in the Middle Ages, and today has one of the oldest synagogues in Portugal.

GETTING HERE AND AROUND

An intriguing backcountry lane connects Marvão with Castelo de Vide. About halfway down the hill from Marvão, turn to the right toward Escusa (watch for the sign) and continue through the chestnut- and acacia-covered hills to Castelo de Vide. If you're traveling from Portalegre, take the N246 directly. At the town's main square is the Praça Dom Pedro V, with the castle to the west and a park to the east.

TAXI CONTACT Castelo de Vide Taxi Service. ✉ *Praça Dom Pedro V* ☎ *245 901 271.*

VISITOR INFO Castelo de Vide Tourist Office. ✉ *Praça Dom Pedro V* ☎ *245 908 227* 🌐 *www.castelodevide.pt.*

Sights

Castelo

CASTLE/PALACE | You can venture into the tower in Castelo de Vide's castle and inside the well-preserved keep to the large Gothic hall, which has a picture window looking down on the town square and the church. ✉ *Rua Direita do Castelo* 🎫 *Free.*

Praça Dom Pedro V

PLAZA | Castelo de Vide's large, baroque central square is bordered by the Igreja de Santa Maria (St. Mary's Church) and the town hall. An alleyway to the right of the church leads to the town symbol: a canopied 16th-century marble fountain. Another cobblestone lane leads from the fountain up to the Juderia (ancient Jewish quarter) On the last Friday of every month the open-air Mercado Franco takes place here. ✉ *Praça Dom Pedro V* 🌐 *www.castelodevide.pt.*

★ **Sinagoga**

RELIGIOUS SITE | A Jewish community is believed to have existed in Castelo de Vide since the 12th century, and reached its peak in the 15th century, bolstered by Jews fleeing the Inquisition in neighboring Spain. This tiny synagogue is believed to be from the late 13th century. There's a small sign outside, but otherwise you might miss it—it looks exactly like all the other row houses. The synagogue was adapted from existing buildings, with two separate prayer rooms for men and women. Although its exact construction year is unknown, this is thought to be one of the oldest in all of Portugal. ✉ *Rua da Judairia* 🎫 *Free.*

Restaurants

Doces & Companhia

$ | BAKERY | FAMILY | This upscale coffee shop with friendly service serves sandwiches and other light lunches, making it the perfect stop between sightseeing trips around town. The outdoor terrace in back offers superb views of the hillside across from Castelo de Vide. **Known for:** local pastries can't be beat; terrace with great views; family-friendly vibe. 💲 *Average main: €7* ✉ *Praça Dom Pedro V 6* ☎ *245 901 408* ⏲ *Closed Sun.*

★ **Restaurante Don Pedro V**

$$ | PORTUGUESE | FAMILY | This is the best option for a traditional Alentejan meal in Castelo de Vide. Walk through the entryway bar into a lovely domed dining room decorated like an old wine cellar. **Known for:** tourist menu is a good value; hearty local dishes; generous portions. 💲 *Average main: €16* ✉ *Praça Dom Pedro V* ☎ *245 901 236* ⏲ *Closed Tues., late Feb.*

Hotels

★ **Casa Amarela**

$ | HOTEL | The beautifully restored 17th-century manor house on Castelo de Vide's main square features a buttery yellow facade and stone stairways to intricately decorated rooms with period antiques. **Pros:** views over Praça Dom Pedro V; great breakfast spread; spacious rooms. **Cons:** some noise in the summer; no on-site restaurant; pool is at another property. 💲 *Rooms from: €100* ✉ *Praça Dom Pedro V 11* ☎ *245 905 878* 🌐 *www.casaamarelath.pt* *11 rooms* 🍽 *Free Breakfast.*

Casa do Parque

$ | HOTEL | This charming, affordable guesthouse is a good option for those who want to absorb local atmosphere close to all the sights. **Pros:** quaint downtown lodging; views of the park; great central location. **Cons:** not very stately; some rooms feel cramped; no elevator access. 💲 *Rooms from: €65* ✉ *Av. da Aramenha 37* ☎ *245 901 250* 🌐 *www.casadoparque.net* *25 rooms* 🍽 *Free Breakfast.*

★ **Vila Maria**

$ | B&B/INN | FAMILY | Named for its friendly owner, Maria Luisa, this historic guesthouse, decorated with antiques and local textiles, offers a great location on the edge of Castelo de Vide. **Pros:** a great spot for sports enthusiasts; free bikes for exploring the area; delicious home cooking. **Cons:** not ideal for large groups; dinner isn't served; some rooms are tight. *Rooms from: €50 Quinta do Patameiro, Bairro da Boavista 960 100 844 www.vilamaria-castelodevide.com 6 rooms Free Breakfast.*

Alvito

40 km south of Evora.

Alvito is a typical, sleepy Alentejo town on a low hill above the Odivelas River. Noted for its fortresslike 13th-century parish church, the town also has a 15th-century castle converted into a pousada and a number of modest houses with graceful Manueline doorways and windows. The castle was built in 1482 by the Baron of Alvito, the first individual permitted to have his own castle. King Manuel I was born and died here.

GETTING HERE AND AROUND

Alvito lies south of Viana do Alentejo on the way to Beja, along the N257 and N258. There is no public transport in this remote, rural part of Portugal, and having your own car is essential for exploring the area. The small village of Alvito stretches just a few blocks out from the castle in all directions.

ESSENTIALS

VISITOR INFORMATION Alvito Tourist Office. *Rua dos Lobos 13* .

Sights

Igreja de Nossa Senhora da Assunção (*Our Lady of the Assumption*)

RELIGIOUS SITE | Set in the middle of a garden facing Largo da Trindade, this 15th-century church combines a variety of architectural styles, featuring elements from the Gothic to the baroque periods. The outdoor facade stands out with its Renaissance entrance and the two stone merlons contrasting against the plastered walls, while inside the church is covered with traditional Portuguese tiles. *Largo da Trindade.*

Restaurants

O Camões

$ | PORTUGUESE | Roughly 7 km (4 miles) northwest of Alvito, the main attraction of this large, popular restaurant is its wood-burning oven in which delicious legs of lamb, pork, and other meats are cooked to perfection. They're first marinated in coriander, oregano, and aromatic herbs that grow in the region. **Known for:** traditional dishes like cabidela de galinha (chicken cooked in its own juices); good selection of Borba wines; room warmed by a fireplace. *Average main: €12 Rua 5 de Outubro 13, Vila Nova da Baronia 964 455 354 No credit cards Closed Mon.*

★ **Taberna do Arrufa**

$ | PORTUGUESE | Enjoy divine traditional Alentejo cooking and local wine under a wood-beamed ceiling and a crystal chandelier, or under a cork tree on a stone terrace alfresco. You'll imbibe alongside 6-foot clay jars, which locals have used to store wine since Roman times. **Known for:** lots of small dishes to share; late-night meals; quirky decor. *Average main: €12 Travessa das Francas 3 967 229 487 Closed Tues.*

Hotels

★ **Pousada do Castelo de Alvito**

$ | HOTEL | FAMILY | The essential architectural elements of a castle—including crenellated battlements and massive round towers—have been retained in this pousada located within the walls of the fortress at the edge of the village. **Pros:** activities include horseback riding and pottery workshops; strolling through the large garden and courtyard; kids love the

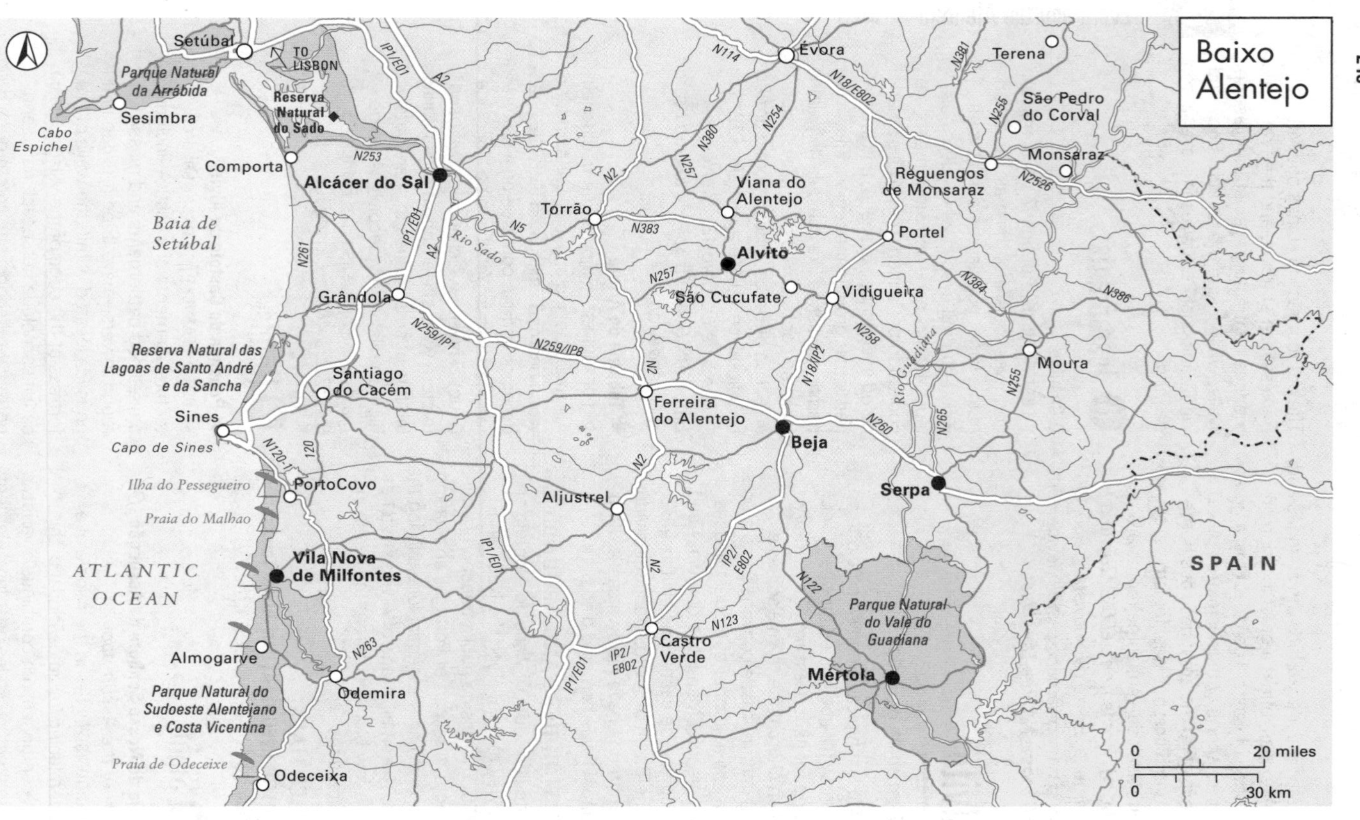

Baixo Alentejo
Setúbal
TO LISBON
Parque Natural da Arrábida
Sesimbra
Cabo Espichel
Reserva Natural do Sado
Comporta
Alcácer do Sal
Baia de Setúbal
Grândola
Reserva Natural das Lagoas de Santo André e da Sancha
Santiago do Cacém
Sines
Capo de Sines
Ilha do Pessegueiro
PortoCovo
Praia do Malhao
ATLANTIC OCEAN
Vila Nova de Milfontes
Almogarve
Odemira
Parque Natural do Sudoeste Alentejano e Costa Vicentina
Praia de Odeceixe
Odeceixa
Évora
Torrão
Viana do Alentejo
Alvito
São Cucufate
Vidigueira
Portel
Reguengos de Monsaraz
Monsaraz
São Pedro do Corval
Terena
Ferreira do Alentejo
Aljustrel
Castro Verde
Beja
Serpa
Moura
Rio Sado
Rio Guadiana
Parque Natural do Vale do Guadiana
Mértola
SPAIN
IP1/E01
A2
N253
N261
N5
N383
N2
N257
N380
N254
N114
N18/E802
N381
N255
N2526
N384
N386
N258
N18/IP2
N260
N265
N259/IP1
N259/IP8
N120-1
120
IP2/E802
N122
N123
N263
0
20 miles
30 km

pool, playground, and board games. **Cons:** not much to do in the evening; pool is on the small side; slow Wi-Fi connection. *Rooms from: €120 Largo do Castelo, Apartado 9 284 480 700 www.pousadas.pt 20 rooms Free Breakfast.*

Beja

36 km southeast of Alvito.

Midway between Spain and the sea is Beja, Baixo Alentejo's principal agricultural center that spreads itself across a small knoll. Much of the oldest part of town retains a significantly Arabic flavor—students of Portuguese even claim that the local dialect has Arabic characteristics—the legacy of more than 400 years of Moorish occupation. Don't miss the stately square called the Praça da República, anchored at one end by the 16th-century Igreja de Misericórdia, whose sprawling stone veranda used to be an open-air market. At one end is an ornate royal pillory from the 16th-century reign of Dom Manuel, restored in the 20th century.

Founded by Julius Caesar and known as Pax Julia, Beja is often overlooked in favor of its more popular and beautiful sister city, Évora, but that just means you'll have the town all to yourself to explore. It's also a classic example of an Alentejo town center that's been emptied of its residents, some of whom have moved to modern apartment complexes on the city's outskirts, and many others who've left altogether, seeking employment in Lisbon or Porto. Walking Beja's streets, it seems like the majority of the population is over 65—a sobering idea when it comes to the future here.

Many of the town's most interesting monuments were destroyed in the 19th century during the population's fury against the church's domination. In spite of that, Beja has an important, valuable heritage, and it can all be explored on foot.

Traditional Music

If you're lucky, you may hear a group of Alentejo men, dressed in typical garb of sheepskin vest and trousers, singing medieval songs (*cante alentejano*), similar to Gregorian chants. These singers are famous all around Portugal.

GETTING HERE AND AROUND

Beja lies in the center of Baixo Alentejo, along the IP2 about halfway between Évora and the Algarve. The city's walkable center is bisected east to west by a public garden and three grand squares: Largo Dom Nuno Alvares Pereira, Largo dos Duques de Beja, and Praça da Republica.

ESSENTIALS

TRAIN TRAVEL Beja Train Station. *Largo da Estação 17 707 210 220 www.cp.pt.*

VISITOR INFORMATION Beja Tourist Office. *Largo Dr. Lima Faleiro 284 311 913 www.cm-beja.pt.*

Sights

Castelo de Beja (*Beja Castle*)
CASTLE/PALACE | Beja's castle is an extensive system of fortifications whose crenellated walls and towers chronicle the history of the town from its Roman occupation through its 19th-century battles with the French. Once inside the central courtyard, climb up the castle's ramparts to the impressive 140-foot **Torre de Menagem,** a stone tower with gorgeous views of the surrounding countryside. The tourist office is also located inside the castle grounds. *Largo Dr. Lima Faleiro Free.*

An Affair to Remember

As the story goes, Mariana Alcoforado (1640–1723), a young Beja nun, fell in love with a French count named Chamilly, who was in the Alentejo fighting the Spaniards. When he went back to France, the nun waited longingly and in vain at the window for him to return. The affair was made public when five passionate love letters to the count, attributed to Mariana, were published in France in 1669 (the popular collection was known as the *Portuguese Letters*). The scandal brought a measure of lasting international literary fame to this provincial Alentejo town. But it's likely that it was actually another Frenchman who penned the infamous letters after hearing of the love story. Nevertheless, French nobles apparently began using the word *portugaise* as a synonym for a passionate love letter.

★ **Convento de Nossa Senhora da Conceição** (*Convent of Our Lady of the Conception*)
MUSEUM | Facing a broad plaza in the oldest part of town, the Convent of Our Lady of the Conception was founded in 1459 by the parents of King Manuel I. Favored by the royal family, this Franciscan convent became one of the richest of the period. It now houses the **Museu Regional de Beja** (Regional Museum of Beja), and if there's one museum you visit in Beja, this should be it. It's tough to decide which is more impressive, the exhibits inside or the building itself. You walk into an ornate, gold-encrusted chapel with saints' relics, and then proceed through the convent's old cloisters covered in azulejos from the 16th and 17th centuries. Some of them comprise panels depicting scenes from the life of St. John the Baptist, and there's also a section of Moorish tiles. At the far end of the second-floor gallery is the famous Mariana Window, named for the 17th-century nun Mariana Alcoforado, whose love affair with a French officer is the stuff of local legend. ✉ *Largo da Conceição* ☎ *284 323 351* 🌐 *www.museuregionaldebeja.pt* 🎫 *€2, includes Museu Visigótico* 🕒 *Closed Mon.*

Museu Visigótico (*The Visigoth Museum*)
MUSEUM | This museum is next to the Castelo de Beja in a 6th-century church—one of Portugal's oldest standing buildings. It houses an impressive collection of tombstones, weapons, and pottery that documents the Visigoth presence in the region. ✉ *Largo de Santo Amaro* ☎ *284 321 465* 🎫 *€2, includes admission to Convento da Conceição.*

Coffee and Quick Bites

Luiz da Rocha
$ | **PORTUGUESE** | This Beja institution, which first opened its doors in 1893, serves great coffee and *conventuais,* sweets made according to recipes from local convents. In a pedestrian-only area just outside the city walls, it's conveniently located next to a few hotels and offers far better breakfasts, including delicious *torradas* (simple white toast with butter). **Known for:** regional pastries like milk tarts and almond cakes; a good spot for a sandwich between museum visits; affordable lunch deals. $ *Average main: €5* ✉ *Rua Capitão João Francisco de Sousa 63* ☎ *284 323 179* 🌐 *www.luizdarocha.com.*

Restaurants

★ Adega Tipica 25 Abril

$$ | **PORTUGUESE** | This rustic restaurant with red-and-white-check tablecloths and cork carvings adorning the walls serves authentic Alentejan dishes. The atmosphere is rustic, with long wooden tables for boisterous families and intimate little two-seaters tucked behind huge clay wine jugs. **Known for:** the grilled black pork is a specialty; the best value eatery in town; laid-back vibe. *Average main: €18 Rua da Moeda 23 284 325 960 No credit cards Closed Mon. No dinner Sun.*

O Arbitro

$ | **PORTUGUESE** | Tucked away behind the castle you'll find this lively local favorite. With a graceful arch, the dining room is decorated in traditional blue-and-white azulejo tiles. **Known for:** generous portions; proximity to the castle; delicious local dishes. *Average main: €12 Rua Conselheiro Meneses 4 284 389 204 Closed Tues.*

Hotels

★ Hotel Bejense

$ | **B&B/INN** | Founded in 1889, this little inn along Beja's pedestrian shopping strip retains retains its old stone doorway covered in vines and vibrant pink flowers. **Pros:** the warmth of a family-run establishment; plenty of period charm; ideal location. **Cons:** rooms have poor soundproofing; no on-site restaurant; no free parking. *Rooms from: €55 Rua Capitão João Francisco de Sousa 57 284 311 570 www.hotelbejense.com 24 rooms Free Breakfast.*

Pousada do Convento de São Francisco

$$ | **HOTEL** | **FAMILY** | Surrounded by spacious gardens is a 13th-century convent that has been tastefully converted into a comfortable pousada. **Pros:** a 10-minute walk from Beja's castle; modern pool surrounded by palm trees; good option for families. **Cons:** more expensive than other options; less historic detail than other pousadas; poor lighting in some rooms. *Rooms from: €160 Largo Dom Nuno Álvares Pereira 284 313 580 www.pousadas.pt 35 rooms Free Breakfast.*

Serpa

27 km (17 miles) southeast of Beja.

One of the most authentic towns on the Alentejan Plain, Serpa's whitewashed medieval center is surrounded by rolling hills and vineyards, well off the tourist path but definitely worth a visit. In cubbyholes along narrow, cobbled streets, carpenters, shoemakers, basket weavers, and other craftsmen work in much the same manner as their forefathers. Townspeople pass the time by gathering together in the compact Praça da República under the shadow of an ancient stone clock tower.

Serpa's sleepy streets explode with life several times a year with festivals that draw visitors from across the Spanish border and around Europe, celebrating Serpa's local delicacies, including one of Portugal's most renowned sheep's milk cheeses.

GETTING HERE AND AROUND

Serpa lies along the IP8 east of Beja, and about equidistant to the Spanish border. It's best to park outside the old city walls near the impressive aqueduct, and navigate the town center by foot.

ESSENTIALS

VISITOR INFORMATION Serpa Tourist Office. *Rua dos Cavalos 19 284 544 727 www.cm-serpa.pt.*

Aqueduto

BUILDING | This impressive structure from the 11th century used to ferry water to

Serpa from wells in the countryside. In the 17th century, a wheel pump was added just outside the city's southern walls, and still stands there today. Follow the aqueduct's walls from the pump out across the city's west side. ✉ *Rua dos Arcos.*

★ **Castelo de Serpa**
CASTLE/PALACE | Serpa's 11th-century aqueduct forms an integral part of the walls of the 13th-century castle, from which there's a stunning view of town. The huge ruined sections of wall tottering precariously above the entrance are the result of explosions ordered by the Duke of Osuna during the 18th-century War of the Spanish Succession. ✉ *Alcáçova do Castelo* ☎ *284 540 100* *Free.*

Museu Arqueológico
MUSEUM | This little gem of a museum located inside the castle walls has light-filled rooms displaying artifacts from Serpa dating from the Paleolithic to the Islamic period. The first floor covers the Prehistoric Period to the Iron Age, and the top floor houses artifacts from the Roman era, Late Antiquity, and the Moorish era. Artifacts include pottery, parts of marble and stone columns, coins, and jewelry. New features include kiosks featuring films by a local filmmaker. ✉ *Alcáçova do Castelo* ☎ *284 544 663* 🌐 *www.cm-serpa.pt* *Free* ⏲ *Closed Mon.*

Museu do Relógio (*The Clock Museum*)
MUSEUM | Housed in a 16th-century convent, this quirky little museum displays a collection of thousands of clocks, with a permanent exhibition titled "400 Years of Clock-Making in Portugal." There's also a workshop where you can watch experts repairing old clocks, or bring in your own to be tinkered with. ✉ *Convento do Mosteirinho, Rua do Assento* ☎ *284 543 194* 🌐 *www.museudorelogio.com* *€2* ⏲ *Closed Mon.*

Restaurants

Cervejaria Lebrinha
$ | PORTUGUESE | At the entrance of town near the Abade Correia da Serra public gardens, this spacious *cervejaria* (beer house) is said to have been pouring the best beer in Portugal since 1957. Old pictures adorning the walls take you back in time to the way Serpa used to be. **Known for:** best draft beer in town; delicious grilled pork; local vibe. *Average main: €8* ✉ *Rua Calvário 6-8* ☎ *284 549 311* ⏲ *Closed Tues., and early Sept.*

★ **Molhó Bico**
$$ | PORTUGUESE | Hands down, this restaurant in a restored wine cellar near Praça da República serves the best food in Serpa, and perhaps even all of Alentejo. Huge wine barrels sit at the entrance to a traditional dining room with domed ceilings, tile floors, and antique farm implements hanging on the walls. **Known for:** rotating exhibits of paintings by local artists; delicious lamb stew and other hearty dishes; great wine selection. *Average main: €20* ✉ *Rua Quente 1* ☎ *284 549 264* ⏲ *Closed Wed.*

Hotels

Bética Hotel Rural
$ | B&B/INN | FAMILY | About a 20-minute drive northwest of Serpa, this big manor house on a cobblestone street offers old Alentejo details and modern amenities. **Pros:** building has charm to spare; great location in a small village; free bikes for exploring the area. **Cons:** no restaurant on the premises; very simple rooms; small pool. *Rooms from: €75* ✉ *Rua Do Outeiro* ☎ *284 858 714* 🌐 *www.beticahotel-rural.com* *14 rooms* *Free Breakfast.*

★ **Cantar do Grilo**
$ | B&B/INN | About a 15-minute drive from Serpa, this modern building just outside the boundaries of the Guadiana Valley Natural Park has traditional Alentejo details like whitewashed exteriors, wood

The Alentejo is known for its pretty landscapes, especially in springtime.

beams, tile floors, and stone fireplaces. **Pros:** lovely owners lend out maps for scenic nature hikes; some of the best views in southern Portugal; grills for outdoor barbecues. **Cons:** you need your own car to get here; two-night minimum stay; no room TVs. *Rooms from: €90 Vale de Milhanos, Correia da Mó, Apt. 668 284 595 415 www.cantardogrilo.com 4 rooms Free Breakfast.*

★ Casa de Serpa

$ | **B&B/INN** | Its labyrinth of passageways, whitewashed walls, vaulted ceilings, and interior open courtyard reflect the Arabic influence in this 200-year-old manor house near the Igreja do Salvador. **Pros:** each room has a character of its own; owner arranges bicycle tours of the town; the area's best breakfast. **Cons:** some noise form other rooms; no on-site restaurant; small bathrooms. *Rooms from: €65 Largo do Salvador 28 963 560 624 www.casadeserpa.com 6 rooms Free Breakfast.*

Shopping

★ Queijaria Bule

FOOD/CANDY | You can buy the famous Serpa cheese in the historic town center at Queijaria Bule, run by the fifth generation of the Bule family. *Rua de Nossa Senhora 4 284 549 612.*

Mértola

56 km (35 miles) south of Serpa.

The ancient walled-in town of Mértola is on a hill overlooking the Guadiana River. At its center is the Praça Luís de Camões, a charming square lined with citrus trees. The town hall sits on the square's western end, with the Torre do Relógio, an impressive clock tower built in the late 16th century, on the opposite side.

Mértola has seen several archaeological excavations in recent years. The artifacts from these digs are all part of the Museu Arqueológico (Archaeology Museum), which has branches—each with displays from different periods—in several locations around town.

GETTING HERE AND AROUND

Mértola lies inside the protected Parque Natural do Vale do Guadiana, about equidistant from Spain and the Algarve. Follow the N122 road into town and park below the hilltop village, which is best explored on foot. The park office can give you helpful maps and advice on how to explore one of Portugal's least touristed—and most spectacular—natural parks.

ESSENTIALS

VISITOR INFORMATION Mértola Tourist Office. ✉ *Rua da Igreja 31* ☎ *286 610 109* 🌐 *www.visitmertola.pt.* **Parque Natural do Vale do Guadiana.** ✉ *Rua D. Sancho II 15* ☎ *286 612 016* 🌐 *www.natural.pt.*

Sights

Castelo de Mértola (*Mértola Castle*)
CASTLE/PALACE | Built in 1292, this castle contains carved stone from the Roman, Moorish, and Christian periods. The courtyard has a very deep cistern in the center. From the castle's **Torre de Menagem,** you can look down on archaeological digs along the sides of the fortress, and out over the river and rolling hills toward Spain. ✉ *Largo da Igreja* 🎫 *Free, €2 for the tower.*

Igreja Matriz (*Central Church*)
RELIGIOUS SITE | Rising from the slopes above the river are the 12 white towers of Mértola's 12th-century house of worship, built on the ruins of a Roman structure. It was once a mosque and retains many of its original Islamic features, including a *mihrab* (a prayer niche that indicates the direction of Mecca). ✉ *Rua da Igreja* ☎ 🎫 *Free* 🕓 *Closed Mon.*

★ **Museu Municipal de Mértola** (*Mértola Municipal Museum*)
MUSEUM | Mértola has a handful of fine museums all within walking distance of one another on the town's hilltop, which together make a wonderful afternoon of sightseeing. The **Núcleo Islâmico** has impressive displays of jewels, metal items, and a collection of ceramics from the 9th to 13th centuries, when Mértola was ruled by the Moors. The **Casa Romana** is a restored, Roman-era house in the basement of the city hall. You can walk through the house's foundations and view a small collection of pottery and kitchen tools excavated nearby. The nearby **Museu de Arte Sacra** has religious statues and carvings from the 16th through 18th centuries, borrowed from Mértola's various churches. The museum group's oldest collection is housed in the **Basílica Paleocristã** and includes funerary stones and other artifacts excavated from the site of the town's paleo-Christian basilica and nearby cemetery. ✉ *Praça Luís de Camões* ☎ *286 610 100* 🌐 *museus.cm-mertola.pt* 🎫 *€2 for Núcleo Islâmico, other museums are free. To access Museu de Arte Sacra on weekends ask the staff at Núcleo Islâmico.*

Restaurants

Restaurante Tamuje
$$ | **PORTUGUESE** | This cozy restaurant serves typical Alentejo delicacies—including *avali à casa* (fried wild boar) and *açorda de perdiz* (partridge bread soup)—made with the finest ingredients. Before you leave, take note of the *açorda* recipe, written on the walls of the restaurant. **Known for:** delicious roasted sheep cheese; dessert is traditional egg pudding; handsome dining room. 💲 *Average main: €20* ✉ *Rua Dr. Serrão Martins 36* ☎ *286 611 115* 🕓 *Closed Sun.*

Hotels

★ **Casa da Tia Amália**
$ | **B&B/INN** | This manor house sits across the river and offers stunning views of the city at sunset. **Pros:** has been in the same family for generations; plenty of options

for families; great views of Mértola. **Cons:** not close to the town's main attractions; thin walls between rooms; breakfast costs extra. *Rooms from: €45 Estrada dos Celeiros 16 www.casadatiaamalia.com 6 rooms No meals.*

Residencial Beira Rio
$ | **B&B/INN** | Some guest rooms in this former mill have balconies overlooking the Guadiana River, while others face the town. **Pros:** wonderful views from many of the rooms; buffet-style breakfast on the terrace; refreshing outdoor pool. **Cons:** some rooms can be a bit cramped; no on-site restaurant; bar is sometimes unattended. *Rooms from: €50 Rua Dr. Afonso Costa 108 913 402 033 www.beirario.pt 24 rooms Free Breakfast.*

Vila Nova de Milfontes

162 km (101 miles) northwest of Mértola.

This small resort town is at the broad mouth of the Mira River, which is lined on both sides by sandy beaches. Overlooking the sea is an ivy-covered, late-16th-century fortress that protected Milfontes from the Algerian pirates who regularly terrorized the Portuguese coast. It was built on ancient Moorish foundations, because it was believed that the spirits there would ward off the pirates. One of the main draws is the coastal Rota Vicentina hiking trail, which passes nearby.

GETTING HERE AND AROUND
Vila Nova de Milfontes lies about halfway between the Setúbal Peninsula and the Algarve, along the N390/N393, and buses make the trip daily from both Lisbon and Faro. The tourist office can provide updated bus timetables. The town center lies north of the Mira River, but its beaches stretch to both sides of the river.

ESSENTIALS
VISITOR INFORMATION Rota Vicentina. *www.rotavicentina.com.* **Vila Nova de Milfontes Tourist Office.** *Rua António Mantas 283 996 599 www.turismo.cm-odemira.pt.*

Beaches

The calm waters of the Franquia beach, extending from the castle all the way to the Farol beach, are good for water sports and families with children. There are several scenic beaches between Porto Covo and Vila Nova de Milfontes. Rock formations stud Ilha do Pessegueiro beach, which is across from a tiny rocky island with a ruined fort, accessible by boat. The Aivados beach attracts anglers, nudists, and surfers. The long Malhão beach is very popular and backed with dunes and fragrant scrubland. There are good access points and plenty of parking.

Praia Das Furnas (*Furnas Beach*)
BEACH—SIGHT | The Praia Das Furnas lies just south of Vila Nova da Milfontes, on the south banks of the Mira River. The southeast current makes it popular with surfers, but the current is calm enough for children to swim here, too. Because it's across the river, the beach is quieter in the busy summer months. You're likely to see hikers, as the Rota Vicentina trail passes through here. You can take a ferry across the Mira River (€4 round-trip; departs hourly) from Vila Nova. If you drive, there's a parking lot and snack bar just behind the dunes. **Amenities:** food and drink; lifeguards; parking. **Best for:** surfing; swimming. *Praia Das Furnas.*

Praia do Farol (*Lighthouse Beach*)
BEACH—SIGHT | Only a five-minute walk from the center of Vila Nova de Milfontes, this is the closest beach to town, named for the lighthouse at the peninsula's tip. It tends to fill up quickly on weekends in summer, and is lined with a seasonal beach bars. The river and ocean currents mixing here can be strong

during winter months, so children should be closely supervised while swimming. **Amenities:** food and drink; lifeguards; parking. **Best for:** sunset. ⊠ *Vila Nova de Milfontes.*

★ **Praia Do Malhão** (*Malhão Beach*)
BEACH—SIGHT | One of the longest beaches in the Vila Nova de Milfontes area, Malhão is popular with surfers, anglers, and a small colony of nudists on the beach's northern end. It's about 5 km (3 miles) north of Vila Nova de Milfontes, inside the coastal national park. The sheer size of these vast sand dunes ensures a sense that you have the place to yourself. **Amenities:** lifeguards. **Best for:** surfing. ⊠ *Estudante da Praia Do Malhão, 5 km (3 miles) north of Vila Nova de Milfontes.*

Restaurants

O Pescador
$$ | **SEAFOOD** | Locals fondly refer to this bustling *marisqueira* (seafood restaurant) as *"o Moura"* (Moura's place, a reference to the owner). He and his wife started off as fish sellers in the nearby market, so you know the seafood quality will be good. **Known for:** freshest seafood in the area; delicious monkfish rice; warm service. $ *Average main: €18* ⊠ *Rua da Praça 18* ☎ *283 996 338* ⏲ *Closed Tues.*

Restaurante Alento
$$ | **PORTUGUESE** | On the way to or from the beach at Praia das Furnas, enjoy a meal at this atmospheric eatery in a former elementary school. Owners Marília Martins and André Silva added a few modern touches to the dining room, but retained the handsome stone walls and wooden ceilings. **Known for:** freshly caught seafood made to order; fish prepared in a wood-burning stove; load up on local souvenirs. $ *Average main: €18* ⊠ *Sítio das Furnas* ✣ *Exit N393 towards Praia das Furnas* ☎ *961 397 462.*

★ **Tasca do Celso**
$$$$ | **SEAFOOD** | This wonderful spot serves up some of the best traditional Portuguese dishes on the entire coastline. The rustic dining room has old-fashioned Alentejan farm tools hanging on the walls, and opens up to the airy kitchen on one side and a small shop on the other that sells gourmet treats and local wines. **Known for:** great wine selection, especially from the Alentejo and the Douro regions; delicious grilled fish from the local market; relaxed setting. $ *Average main: €26* ⊠ *Rua dos Aviadores* ☎ *283 996 753* 🌐 *www.tascadocelso.com* ⏲ *Closed Mon. in winter.*

Hotels

Casa da Eira
$ | **HOTEL** | **FAMILY** | Steps from the beach and the town center, this hotel is a favorite among the surfers, cyclists, kayakers, and hikers making their way along the Rota Vicentina. **Pros:** a shared garden and barbecue area; rooftop terrace with expansive views; great value for families. **Cons:** no on-site restaurant; rooms are a bit small; no breakfast. $ *Rooms from: €70* ⊠ *Rua Eira da Pedra, Lote 7* ☎ *961 339 241,* 🌐 *www.villaeira.pt* *13 rooms* *No meals.*

Duna Parque
$ | **RESORT** | **FAMILY** | A five-minute walk from the beach, this two-story complex features several apartments and villas with fireplaces and other unexpected amenities. **Pros:** plenty of space for families; good option for longer stays; some rooms offer sea views. **Cons:** three-night minimum stay in July and August; some apartments look a bit dated; gym and spa open to the public. $ *Rooms from: €65* ⊠ *Eira da Pedra* ☎ *283 990 072* 🌐 *www.dunaparque.com* *45 units* *Free Breakfast.*

HS Milfontes Beach

$ | **HOTEL** | No matter where you are in this popular hotel you're likely to have a water view, be it the Mira River, the Atlantic Ocean, or the glistening swimming pool. **Pros:** best view in the whole town; gorgeous swimming pool; close to the beach. **Cons:** popular bar is noisy at night; fitness center costs extra; hodgepodge exterior. *Rooms from: €110* ✉ *Av. Marginal* ☎ *283 990 070* 🌐 *www.hsmilfontesbeach.com* *28 rooms* *Free Breakfast.*

Alcácer do Sal

70 km west of Évora.

Salt production here has nearly disappeared, but it was because of this mineral that Alcácer do Sal became one of Portugal's first inhabited sites. Parts of the castle foundations are around 5,000 years old. The Greeks were here, and later the Romans, who established the town of Salatia Urbs Imperatoria—a key intersection in their system of Lusitanian roads. During the Moorish occupation, under the name of Alcácer de Salatia, this became one of the most important Muslim strongholds in all of Iberia. The hilltop castle is the town's most prominent attraction, and from there red-tile-roof buildings descend to the riverbank in horizontal rows.

GETTING HERE AND AROUND

Alcácer do Sal lies upstream from the mouth of the Sado River, a quick drive south from Lisbon on the main north–south highway, the A2. Most of the town lies on the river's northern bank, and there's ample parking in the center. The tourist office can arrange half- or full-day boat trips or guided walks along the Sado River.

ESSENTIALS

TOURS Rotas do Sal. ✉ *Mercado do Livramento, Av. Luísa Todi 163, Loja 14 R/C, Setúbal* ☎ *938 122 190* 🌐 *www.rotasdosal.pt.*

VISITOR INFORMATION Alcácer do Sal Tourist Office. ✉ *Largo Luís de Camões* ☎ *265 009 987* 🌐 *www.cm-alcacerdosal.pt.*

Sights

★ Cripta Arqueológica do Castelo

ARCHAEOLOGICAL SITE | This stunning underground fortress displays archaeological relics from 2,600 years of settlement here. In the mid-1990s, archaeologists discovered traces of an Iron Age settlement from the 6th century BC, underneath the town's castle. Structures are believed to have existed here from Roman times, with later castles being built one on top of another through Moorish and medieval times. The current castle and adjacent church are from the 13th century. ✉ *Castelo de Alcácer do Sal, in basement of Pousada de Dom Afonso II* ☎ *265 612 058* *€3.10* *Closed Mon.*

Reserva Natural do Sado

NATURE PRESERVE | The marshlands and the estuary of the Sado River that extend to the west of Alcácer form this vast nature reserve. The riverbanks are lined with salt pans and rice paddies, and the sprawling park gives shelter to wildlife such as dolphins, otters, storks, and egrets. From the beach town of Comporta, Route N261 runs south along the coast through a mostly deserted stretch of dunes and pine trees with some undeveloped sandy beaches. ✉ *Alcácer do Sal.*

Beaches

Praia da Comporta

BEACH—SIGHT | Portugal's Alentejo coast is often overlooked by beachgoers in favor of the Algarve or the Lisbon coast, but this scenic, rural, culinarily rich region is home to some of the finest beaches in Europe. While some are difficult to access, others, such as the beautiful Praia da Comporta, are well equipped to cater for visitors. Here, snow-white sands are dotted with colorful sun loungers and straw-roofed beach huts selling cocktails as well as fresh seafood, and the clear, bright blue invites you to take a cooling dip. Although one of the busier beaches in the Alentejo, this is still quieter than the beaches of the Algarve, and there's plenty of elbow room even during the summer high season. **Amenities:** parking (no fee), toilets, food and drink, water sports. **Best for:** swimming, walking. ✉ *Rua Otelo Saraiva de Carvalho, Setúbal.*

Restaurants

Porto Santana
$ | **PORTUGUESE** | This restaurant is located just over the old bridge, across the Sado River. You can take your lunch outside with a view of the river. **Known for:** delicious clam soup and razor clam rice; quiet atmosphere; attentive staff. *Average main: €15* ✉ *Rua Senhora Santana* ☎ *265 622 517* *Closed Thurs.*

Hotels

★ **Herdade da Barrosinha**
$ | **HOTEL** | **FAMILY** | This whitewashed country house is on a huge farm estate surrounded by cork and pine trees, about 3 km (2 miles) outside Alcácer do Sal. Red-and-white-striped curtains and bedcovers elegantly match the red-clay-tile floors, while bathrooms are decorated in blue-and-white Alcobaça tiles. **Pros:** organizes horseback riding, hiking, and biking tours; surrounded by a wildlife reserve; quiet atmosphere. **Cons:** reception area closes early; a long walk into the town; pool is off the property. *Rooms from: €110* ✉ *Estrada Nacional 5, Barrosinha* ☎ *265 623 142* *www.herdadedabarrosinha.pt* *37 rooms* *Free Breakfast.*

★ **Pousada de Dom Afonso II**
$$ | **HOTEL** | In the ancient castle overlooking the Sado River, this very attractive pousada has comfortable and tastefully appointed guest rooms with elegant wooden furniture and beauiful handwoven rugs. **Pros:** the well-preserved common areas are worth a visit; some rooms offer river views; beautiful rooms. **Cons:** since it's on a hill, the walk to town can be challenging; not enough lounge chairs by the pool; a bit on the expensive side. *Rooms from: €150* ✉ *Castelo de Alcácer* ☎ *265 613 070* *www.pousadas.pt* *35 rooms* *Free Breakfast.*

Chapter 7

THE ALGARVE

Updated by
Ann Abel

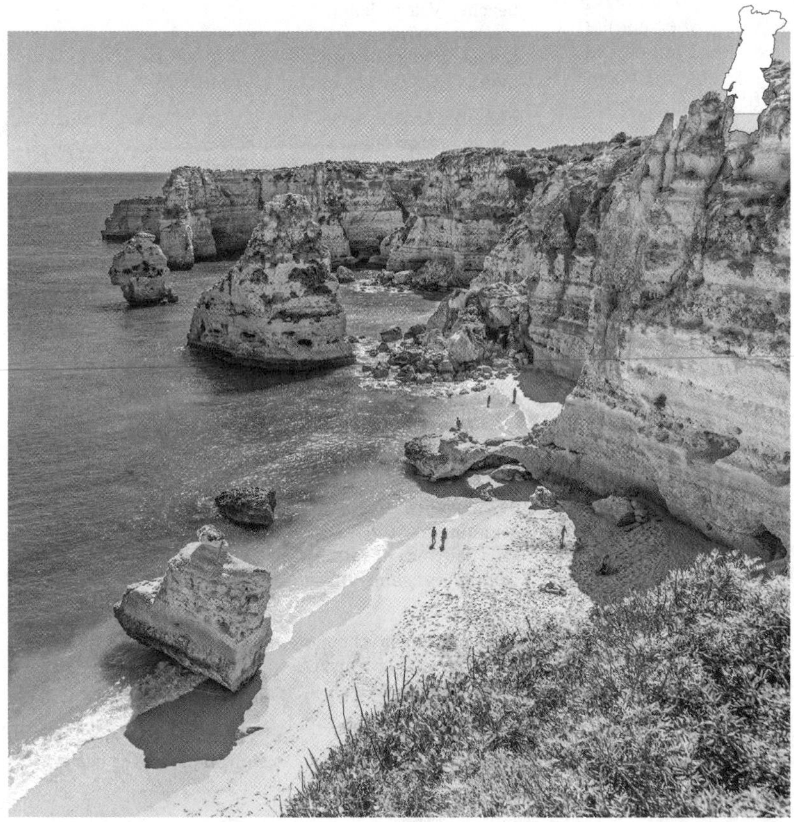

Sights ★★★☆☆ | Restaurants ★★★★☆ | Hotels ★★★★☆ | Shopping ★★★☆☆ | Nightlife ★★★★☆

WELCOME TO THE ALGARVE

TOP REASONS TO GO

★ **Fun in the sun.** One of Europe's sunniest places, the Algarve guarantees great weather pretty much year-round.

★ **Fun in the shade.** Adrenaline junkies are now flocking to the region in winter when comfortable temperatures and bright skies make it an ideal destination for active pursuits like skydiving.

★ **Glitz and glamour.** During peak season, the Algarve rivals Europe's glitziest hot spots. Jetsetters travel from far and wide to attend what are fast becoming world-renowned events.

★ **Green tee.** Golf is a four-season game here. Its 37 acclaimed courses include some of the continent's best.

★ **Festivals galore.** From city-size *festas* to the hundreds of smaller, rural village affairs, there will be something to suit your tastes.

★ **Fantastic food and drink.** The Algarve is home to award-winning restaurants and appealing vineyards.

1 **Faro.** Dotted with historic monuments, this provincial capital is a great base for exploring the Algarve.

2 **Quinta do Lago.** This affluent community has a golden-sand beach and verdent pine forests.

3 **Vale do Lobo.** With one of the region's prettiest beaches, Vale do Lobo attracts the rich and famous from the world over.

4 **Loulé.** An Arabesque indoor market offers a true taste of Algarvian culture.

5 **Vilamoura.** The Algarve's answer to Monaco.

6 **Albufeira.** Albufeira has enough neon lights to rival Las Vegas.

7 **Armação de Pêra.** Seascapes and beautiful beaches make this a popular destination.

8 **Carvoeiro.** With a stunning coastline, Carvoeiro has maintained some of its fishing-village charm.

9 **Lagoa.** Lagoa is home to the region's last surviving wine cooperative.

10 **Silves.** Once the Moorish capital of the Algarve, Silves is unmistakable because of its hilltop fortress.

11 **Portimão.** This town's claim to fame is a stunning stretch of sand backed by a curtain of ocher-red cliffs.

12 **Alvor.** Alvor is the Algarve's best examples of an Arab village.

13 **Monchique.** Many go to Monchique for the healing waters.

14 Lagos. Starting with a dazzling 18th-century church, Lagos has some of the region's most fascinating old buildings.

15 Praia da Luz. See an 18th-century fortress that once guarded against pirates.

16 Sagres. The massive Fortaleza de Sagres is the major landmark in this town.

17 Cabo São Vicente. This spit of land was called "O Fim do Mundo" (The End of the World) by early Portuguese mariners.

18 São Brás de Alportel. Peace and tranquility are the reasons many travelers linger in this town in the Eastern Algarve.

19 Olhão. This town's fishing port is a colorful glimpse of the region's rich history.

20 Tavira. This town's whitewashed 18th-century houses make it one of the prettiest in the region.

21 Vila Real de Santo António. The closest town to the border of Spain.

The Algarve is deservedly popular, with millions of annual vacationers thronging here to enjoy sandy beaches, superb golf, and all the other enticements of seaside resorts. A mere 40 km (25 miles) from top to bottom, Portugal's southernmost province is bordered by the Atlantic to the south and west, the Serra de Monchique (Monchique Mountains) and the Serra de Caldeirão (Caldeirão Mountains) to the north, and the Rio Guadiana (Guadiana River) to the east.

Its coast is cooled by sea breezes in summer, and the province as a whole is much warmer than the rest of the country in winter. The vegetation is far more luxuriant, too; originally irrigated by the Moors, the land supports a profusion of fruits, nuts, and vegetables. Proximity to the ocean, meanwhile, has allowed the fishing industry to flourish. And the region's 300 days of sunshine per year help lure in tourists year-round.

During the past few decades, tourism has flourished, and parts of the once pristine, 240-km (149-mile) coastline are now traffic-clogged and overbuilt. Even where development is heaviest, construction generally takes the form of landscaped villas and apartment complexes, which are often made of local materials and blend well with the scenery. And there are still small, undeveloped fishing villages and secluded beaches, particularly in the west. The west is also home to extraordinary rock formations and idyllic grottoes. In the east, a series of isolated sandbar islands and sweeping beaches balances the crowded excesses of the middle.

To see the Algarve at its best, though, you may have to abandon the shore for a drive inland. Here, rural Portugal still survives in tradition-steeped hill villages, market towns, and agricultural landscapes, which, although only a few miles from the coast, seem a world away in attitude.

MAJOR REGIONS

For touring purposes, the district can conveniently be divided into four sections, starting with Faro—the Algarve's capital—and the nearby beaches and inland towns. The second section encompasses the region east to the border town of Vila Real de Santo António, from which you can cross into Spain. The most built-up part of the coast, and the section with the most to offer vacationers, runs from Faro west to Portimão. The fourth section covers Lagos, the principal town of the western Algarve, and extends to Sagres and Cabo São Vicente.

Faro and Nearby. The capital of the Algarve, Faro is a cosmopolitan city. Home to a pretty marina, the region's only international airport, and several universities, it has a trendy, vibrant feel; the surrounding villages are authentically quaint.

The Eastern Algarve. Better known for its distinctive roof tiles than for roof-raising parties, the eastern Algarve—aka the Sotavento—is quiet and largely less developed, so it's a fine place to visit if you're looking for a slower-paced holiday. Cities are mostly untouched by modernity, and beaches are vast and flat. Shallow waters mean the sea here can be significantly warmer than elsewhere in the Algarve. Enjoying a riverside stroll and bird-watching in the protected Ria Formosa area are the main activities.

The Central Algarve. The central Algarve, between Faro and Portimão, has the heaviest concentration of resorts, but there are also exclusive, secluded hotels and villas. In between built-up areas there are quiet bays and amazing rock formations, including arches, sea stacks, caves, and blowholes. Shell-encrusted ocher-and-red cliffs contrast beautifully with the brilliant blues and greens of the sea. With a car it's easy to travel the few miles inland that make all the difference: minor roads lead into the hills and to towns that have resisted the changes wrought upon the coast.

Lagos and the Western Algarve. From the bustling town of Lagos, the rest of the western Algarve is easily accessible. This is the most unspoiled part of the region, with some genuinely isolated beaches and bays along an often wind-buffeted route that reaches to the southwest and the magnificent Cabo São Vicente. Between Lagos and Sagres a series of quaint villages and hamlets—like Praia da Luz and Burgau—also await.

Planning

When to Go

The Algarvian spring, with its rolling carpets of wildflowers and characteristic almond and orange blossoms, is delightful. Late in the season, you can just about take a dip in the ocean, and there's plenty of space to lay out your beach blanket. Summer (July and August) is high season, when lodging is at a premium, prices are at their highest, and crowds are at their thickest. But summer also brings warmer seas, piercing blue skies, and golden sands at the foot of glowing ocher-red cliffs. Autumn in the Algarve is stunning, with fresh clear days and little rain. The beaches are emptier and the pace of life more relaxed. Accommodation prices start to drop and parking can be found with ease. Winter is mild, so it's the perfect time to visit if you don't mind limiting your swimming to heated hotel pools. On land—or in the air—opportunities for mountain biking and skydiving are also plentiful.

Getting Here and Around

AIR

TAP Air Portugal has several flights each day from Lisbon to Faro (45 minutes); Ryanair has regular service from Porto to Faro (90 minutes). All international and domestic airlines use Faro Airport, which is 6 km (4 miles) west of town. It's easy to find your way into Faro: after around 4 km (2½ miles), signs along the road from the airport direct you right into town.

Public buses run frequently between the airport and Faro city, with tickets costing about €2.30 per person. A taxi from the terminal building to the center of Faro costs around €10, slightly more on weekends. (There's also a small extra charge for baggage.) Ask the staff at the airport tourist office for a list of prices for rides to other destinations in the region. Always make sure that you agree on a price with the taxi driver before setting off.

AIRLINE CONTACT TAP Air Portugal. ☎ *707 205 700* 🌐 *www.flytap.com.* **Ryanair.** ☎ *703 403 363* 🌐 *www.ryanair.com.*

AIRPORT CONTACT Faro Airport. ☎ *289 800 800* 🌐 *www.ana.pt.*

BUS

Various bus companies run daily express buses between Lisbon and Lagos, Portimão, Faro, Tavira, and Vila Real. Allow 3½ to 4½ hours' travel time for all these destinations. Buy tickets online, over the phone, or at ticket offices near the bus terminals. In summer, reserve a seat at least 24 hours in advance.

The main form of public transportation within the Algarve is bus, with the two main companies in the region being Eva and Frota Azul. Every town and village has its own stop, and they are usually close to downtown sights. Individual tickets are relatively inexpensive, but you can save more with a tourist pass (€30.40 for three days, €38 for seven) that covers 16 popular destinations across the Algarve. Some local service doesn't run on Sunday or national holidays.

BUS CONTACTS Eva Buses. ☎ *289 580 611* 🌐 *www.eva-bus.com.* **Frota Azul Algarve.** ☎ *282 400 610* 🌐 *www.frota-azul-algarve.pt.*

CAR

To reach the Algarve from Lisbon—an easy 240-km (150-mile) drive south—cross the Ponte 25 de Abril and take the toll road to Setúbal. The A2 motorway runs directly south, eventually joining the A22, the Algarve's main east–west route. To reach Portimão, Lagos, and the western Algarve, turn right; turn left for Faro and the eastern Algarve. The drive from Lisbon to Faro, Lagos, or Albufeira takes about three hours—longer in summer, on weekends, and on holidays.

In the east, a suspension bridge crosses the Guadiana River between Ayamonte in Spain and Vila Real de Santo António in Portugal. The secondary east–west road, the N125, extends 165 km (102 miles) from the Spanish border all the way west to Sagres. It runs parallel to the coast and the A22, but slightly inland, with clearly marked turnoffs to the beach towns. Be very careful on this route, as it's one of Portugal's most hazardous. In summer expect traffic jams in several places along it.

TAXI

If you intend to take a cab from Faro Airport, there will be plenty of vehicles waiting outside the arrivals area no matter what time you arrive. Fares are set by the government, but double-check with the driver before you depart.

In Faro, you can call for taxis or hail them on the street. A fare of €4 to €5 will get you across town. Uber is now also a convenient option in the larger cities.

TRAIN

The quickest, most comfortable way to travel to and from this region by rail is aboard the Alfa-Pendular—a high-speed train that connects Lisbon, Porto, and other major cities with southern Portugal. The trip from Lisbon to Faro takes around three hours and costs €30.70 for a first-class ticket. Note that the train's gentle rocking makes some passengers feel a bit seasick. Other trains have daily departures from Lisbon, and you can change in Tunes for Silves and points west or at Faro for Vila Real and points east.

Regular trains connects Lagos in the west with Vila Real de Santo António in the east, running close to the N125 motorway. This often-scenic route takes about three to four hours end to end. Most trains have a first-class carriage with individual compartments. Note that express trains don't stop at every station.

The national rail company is Comboios de Portugal (CP). You can buy tickets online, over the phone, at train stations, at travel agencies, and at ATMs (*multibancos*).

TRAIN CONTACT Comboios de Portugal. ☎ *707 210 220* 🌐 *www.cp.pt.*

Restaurants

Algarvian cooking makes good use of local seafood. The most unusual regional appetizer is *espadarte fumado* (smoked swordfish), and you'll find it sliced thin, served with a salad, and usually accompanied by a dry white wine. Other seafood starters include deep-fried sardines, cold octopus salad, and marinated mackerel fillets. Restaurants generally serve their own version of *sopa de peixe* (fish soup), as well as a variety of succulent shellfish, including *perceves* (barnacles), *santola* (crab), and *gambas* (shrimp). Although main courses often depend on what has been landed that day, there's generally a choice of *robalo* (sea bass), *pargo* (bream), and *atum* (tuna).

At simple beach cafés and harbor stalls, the unmistakable smell of *sardinhas assadas* (charcoal-grilled sardines) permeates the air. These make a tempting lunch served with fresh bread and a sparkling *vinho verde* (literally "green wine"), which is indigenous to Portugal. Perhaps the most famous Algarvian dish is *cataplana*, traditionally a stew of clams, pork, onions, tomatoes, and wine, though you can often also find shellfish or mixed fish versions. It takes its name from the lidded utensil used to steam the dish. You have to wait for cataplana to be specially prepared, but once you've tasted it, you won't mind waiting again and again.

Regional desserts are varied and most eateries, right down to the smallest backstreet café, will offer some form of homemade sweet, probably chocolate mousse, caramel flan, *doce da casa*, or a baked cake. Other traditional Algarvian sweets include rich egg, sugar, and almond custards that reflect the Moorish influence, including *doces de amêndoa* (marzipan cakes in the shapes of animals and flowers), *bolos de Dom Rodrigo* (almond sweets with egg-and-sugar filling), *bolo Algarvio* (cake made of sugar, almonds, eggs, and cinnamon), and *morgado de figo do Algarve* (fig-and-almond paste). You will find these on sale in *pastelarias* (cake shops) and in some cafés.

Unless otherwise noted, casual dress is acceptable throughout the Algarve. Reservations are not needed off-season, but they're typically required at the better restaurants in summer. *Prices in the reviews are the average cost of a main course at dinner or, if dinner is not served, at lunch.*

Hotels

Lodgings in the Algarve range from busy beachside hotels to secluded retreats in posh country estates. Villas with luxurious amenities are often built on the most beautiful parts of the coast, and most have bars, restaurants, shops, and other facilities. Budget-friendly lodgings are also available.

In summer, reservations at most places are essential, and rates often rise by as much as 50% above off-peak prices. Since the weather from September through May is still good, you might want to consider a shoulder-season trip to take advantage of the lower rates. *Prices in the reviews are the lowest cost of a standard double room in high season. For expanded hotel reviews, visit www.Fodors.com.*

WHAT IT COSTS In Euros			
$	$$	$$$	$$$$
RESTAURANTS			
under €16	€16–€20	€21–€25	over €25
HOTELS			
under €141	€141–€200	€201–€260	over €260

Tours

Boat tours are very popular, ranging from one-hour tours of local grottoes and rock formations to full-day trips that often involve stops at secluded beaches for lunch. The most popular coastal excursions depart from Albufeira, Vilamoura, Portimão, Tavira, Lagos, Sagres, Vila Real, and Armação de Pêra. Prices and times of the next cruise will be posted at the dock.

Jeep safaris, offered by operators like Rotatur, are a unique way to see fascinating inland villages. Riosul Travel, which arranges cruises up the Guadiana River, also has half-day overland tours by jeep and full-day cruise-jeep tours that take you off the beaten path to the village of Foz de Odeleite.

TOUR CONTACTS Riosul Travel. ☎ *281 510 200* 🌐 *www.riosultravel.com.* **Rotatur.** ☎ *289 810 109* 🌐 *www.rotatur.pt.*

Faro

270 km (168 miles) southeast of Lisbon.

The Algarve's provincial capital combines a smattering of history and ample leisure opportunities in one lively package. It is one of the few places in the region that has a year-round buzz, mainly thanks to the thousands of students who attend universities here. Dotted with historic monuments, Faro is positioned around a small marina where local fishermen and yacht owners keep their vessels. Wander deeper into the city and you will find an attractive shopping street with high-end chains and stores selling local handicrafts, plus a variety of restaurants and bars that remain open in all seasons. Faro is also a great base for exploring the Algarve. It isn't slap-bang in the middle but does offer the best access in terms of public transport and roads to reach both ends of the province.

GETTING HERE AND AROUND

Although Faro is the region's largest city, most of its main attractions (as with all Algarvian cities and towns) can pretty much be covered on foot. Nonetheless, urban buses are frequent and taxis are cheap if you need to get from one end of town to the other quickly. Faro can be reached by train and bus from anywhere in the Algarve.

ESSENTIALS

TAXI CONTACTS Taxis Antral Faro. ✉ *Rua Engenheiro José Campos Coroa 19* ☎ *289 827 203* 🌐 *www.antral.pt.*

TRAIN CONTACTS Faro Train Station. ✉ *Largo da Estação dos Caminhos de Ferro* ☎ *707 210 220* 🌐 *www.cp.pt.*

VISITOR INFORMATION Faro Tourist Office. ✉ *Rua da Misericórdia 8–12* ☎ *289 803 604* 🌐 *www.visitalgarve.pt.*

Sights

Arco da Vila

BUILDING | Beyond this 19th-century gate lies Faro's pretty Cidade Velha (Old Town) with its cobbled streets and white-washed houses. At the top is a niche sheltering a white-marble statue of St. Thomas Aquinas, plus storks that nest here permanently. ✉ *Rua do Municipio.*

Doca de Faro (*Faro Dock*)

PLAZA | The small dock—flanked by Faro's main square, the Praça Dom Francisco Gomes, and the Manuel Bivar Garden—is filled with small pleasure craft rather than working fishing boats. Come at dusk to enjoy a drink as the sun sets dramatically over the lagoon. ✉ *Faro.*

Igreja de São Pedro (*St. Peter's Church*)
RELIGIOUS SITE | This 16th-century sanctuary—perhaps the prettiest of Faro's churches—has an unusual altar set to the left of the main altar. It's entirely carved in gilded chestnut wood and a delicate frieze depicts the Last Supper. ✉ *Largo de S. Pedro* ☎ *289 805 473* 🌐 *www.paroquiasaopedro-faro.org* 🎫 *Free.*

Igreja do Carmo (*Carmo Church*)
RELIGIOUS SITE | Just north of the city center, this baroque church looks very out of place amid the modern buildings surrounding it. Inside, a door to the right of the altar leads to the Capela dos Ossos (Chapel of the Bones) set in an outside garden area. The tiny chapel's walls are covered with more than 1,000 skulls and bones dug up from the adjacent monks' cemetery—an eerie sight, to say the least, but a fairly common custom in Portugal. ✉ *Largo do Carmo* ☎ *289 824 490* 🎫 *€2.*

★ **Sé Catedral de Faro** (*Faro Cathedral*)
RELIGIOUS SITE | This stunning cathedral, flanked by cobblestone streets, whitewashed houses, and fragrant orange trees, is one of Faro's most beautiful monuments. Having survived earthquakes and fires since its construction in 1251, the Sé retains a Gothic tower but is mostly of interest for the 17th- and 18th-century azulejos that fill its interior. On one side of the nave is a red chinoiserie organ, dating to 1751. Best of all, however, is the view from the top of the church tower (up some very steep stairs), looking out over Cidade Velha rooftops and across the lagoon. ✉ *Largo da Sé* ☎ *289 806 632* 🎫 *€3.50 for cathedral, tower, and museum.*

Beaches

Praia de Faro (*Faro Beach*)
BEACH—SIGHT | The closest beach to town is the long, sandy Praia de Faro, which sits on the Ilha de Faro (Faro Island) 5 km (3 miles) southwest of town. The long main road is flanked by the beach on one side and cafés and restaurants on the other. Activities are limited, and in the height of summer, parking can be a struggle. **Amenities:** food and drink; lifeguards; parking (no fee). **Best for:** swimming; walking. ✉ *Av. Nascente Praia de Faro.*

Restaurants

Adega Nova
$ | **PORTUGUESE** | Popular among locals for celebrations, this down-to-earth *adega* (wine cellar) serves typical Portuguese dishes. The seating arrangement on benches around long wooden tables helps keep things lively, and you'll find more good cheer in the tile-covered bar. **Known for:** warm, lively ambience; freshest local seafood; plenty of vegetarian options. 💲 *Average main: €15* ✉ *Rua Francisco Barreto 24* ☎ *289 813 433* 🌐 *www.restauranteadeganova.com* 💳 *No credit cards.*

Dois Irmãos
$ | **PORTUGUESE** | Since 1925, this family-run restaurant has attracted a robust clientele, thanks to its excellent regional dishes and vast national wine selection. The large dining room and plant-filled indoor terrace have a homey vibe, with exposed-brick arches and high-backed chairs. **Known for:** recipes from the region; tasty seafood dishes; homemade desserts. 💲 *Average main: €14* ✉ *Praça Ferreira de Almeida 15* ☎ *289 823 337* 🌐 *www.restaurantedoisirmaos.com.*

★ **Vila Adentro**
$$ | **PORTUGUESE** | In a lovely square near the city's most popular attractions, this charming restaurant in a historic building offers well-prepared traditional dishes with a modern twist. Dine inside surrounded by exposed stone walls, traditional blue-and-white tiles, and exposed wood beams, or outside on the

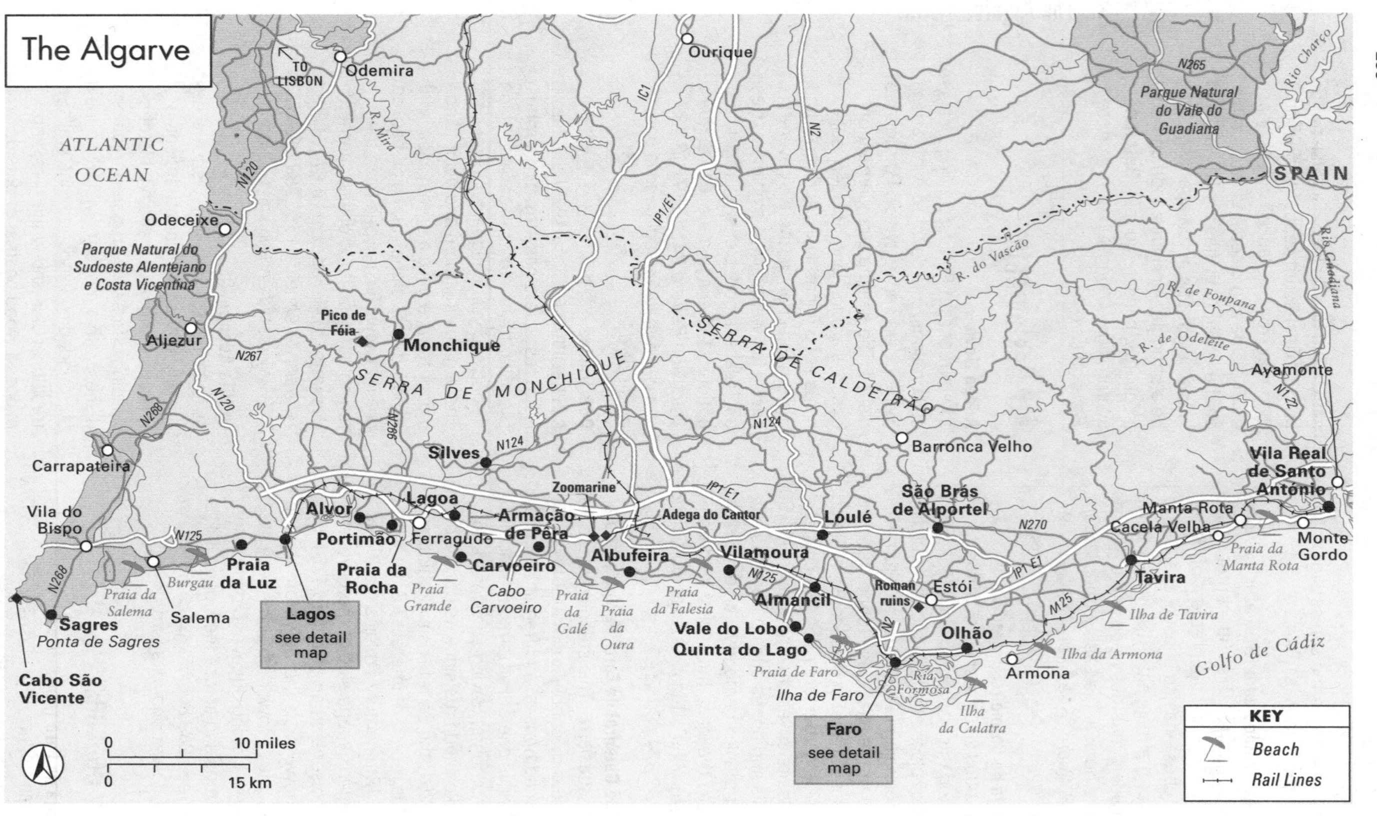
The Algarve
TO LISBON
Odemira
Ourique
N265
Rio Charço
Parque Natural do Vale do Guadiana
SPAIN
ATLANTIC
OCEAN
N120
R. Mira
IC1
N2
IP1/E1
Odeceixe
Parque Natural do Sudoeste Alentejano e Costa Vicentina
R. do Vascão
Rio Guadiana
R. de Foupana
R. de Odeleite
Pico de Fóia
Monchique
Aljezur
N267
SERRA DE MONCHIQUE
SERRA DE CALDEIRÃO
Ayamonte
N122
N268
N266
N124
Barronca Velho
Silves
Carrapateira
Zoomarine
Vila Real de Santo António
São Brás de Alportel
Manta Rota
Vila do Bispo
Alvor
Lagoa
Armação de Pêra
Adega do Cantor
Loulé
N270
Cacela Velha
Monte Gordo
N125
Portimão
Ferragudo
Praia da Manta Rota
Albufeira
Vilamoura
Praia da Luz
Carvoeiro
Tavira
Praia da Rocha
Praia da Salema
Burgau
Praia Grande
Cabo Carvoeiro
Praia da Galé
Praia da Oura
Praia da Falesia
Almancil
Roman ruins
Estói
M25
Ilha de Tavira
Sagres
Ponta de Sagres
Salema
Lagos
see detail map
Vale do Lobo
Quinta do Lago
Olhão
Ilha da Armona
Golfo de Cádiz
Armona
Praia de Faro
Ilha de Faro
Ria Formosa
Ilha da Culatra
Cabo São Vicente
Faro
see detail map
0
10 miles
0
15 km
KEY
Beach
Rail Lines

spacious patio. **Known for:** perfect place for a romantic meal; old recipes adapted to modern tastes; vegetarian, vegan, and gluten-free options. *Average main: €17* *Praca Dom Afonso III 17* *289 052 173* *vilaadentro.pt.*

Hotels

Hotel Eva

$$ | HOTEL | With a cool, contemporary decor, this longtime favorite in the heart of Faro has a sunny rooftop pool and top-floor restaurant with lovely views. **Pros:** within walking distance to all the city's main attractions; short drive to the airport; good fitness center. **Cons:** can be rather noisy because of nearby bus terminal; location not directly on the beach; breakfast buffet often crowded. *Rooms from: €146* *Av. da República 1* *289 001 000* *www.ap-hotelsresorts.com* *134 rooms* *Free Breakfast.*

★ **Hotel Sol Algarve**

$ | HOTEL | Dating from the 1880s, this historic structure is one of Faro's most pleasant budget hotels. **Pros:** private underground garage; two-minute walk to train station; most rooms have a private balcony. **Cons:** rooms are on the small side; hot water can be inconsistent; dated decor. *Rooms from: €99* *Rua Infante Dom Henrique 52* *289 895 700* *www.hotelsolalgarve.com* *38 rooms* *Free Breakfast.*

Nightlife

Rua do Prior is known for its wide selection of late-closing bars. Friday and Saturday nights are the best time for barhopping.

Chessenta Bar

BARS/PUBS | Open very late, this snug bar is very popular and can fill up fast. It offers music for every taste—from rock to traditional Portuguese tunes. The cocktails are refreshing, too. *Rua do Prior 24* *931 194 314.*

Columbus

BARS/PUBS | In a 600-year-old building in the heart of the historic district, this bar draws a trendy crowd. Outside tables are set in a picturesque cobblestone square, while the atmospheric interior—complete with brick-arch ceilings—is impressive and cool. *Praça D. Francisco Gomes 13* *917 776 222* *www.barcolumbus.pt.*

Quinta do Lago

15 km (9 miles) west of Faro.

One of the most affluent communities in the Algarve, the resort of Quinta do Lago is one of the three corners of the Golden Triangle, which also includes Vale do Lobo and Vilamora. It is an area of golden-sand beach, verdent pine forests, an artificial lake, and three award-winning golf courses. It's a very international community, with a variety of restaurants to match. It's a very pleasant place to be, although it can be easy to forget that you're in Portugal here.

GETTING HERE AND AROUND

Given the nature of Quinta do Lago's clientele, there's not much public transportation. You can take a taxi from Faro, since it's fairly close.

Restaurants

Casa Velha

$$$$ | FRENCH | The resort's first restaurant is still one of its best. Casa Velha occupies an old farmhouse and focuses on French-style fine dining. **Known for:** refined setting; romantic terrace; elegant seafood dishes. *Average main: €32* *Quinta do Lago, Rotunda 6, Almancil* *289 394 983* *www.quintodolago.com* *Closed Sun. and Mon. No lunch.*

★ **Gigi's**

$$ | SEAFOOD | This beachfront restaurant—reached via a long wooden bridge that overlooks a tidal lagoon—is the rare Algarve establishment that manages to

Faro

Sights

1 Arco da Vila C4
2 Doca de Faro.......... B4
3 Igreja de São Pedro .. C2
4 Igreja do Carmo ... C2
5 Sé Catedral de Faro...... C5

Restaurants

1 Adega Nova......... B3
2 Dois Irmãos....... C3
3 Vila Adentro C5

Hotels

1 Hotel Eva.... B3
2 Hotel Sol Algarve...... B2

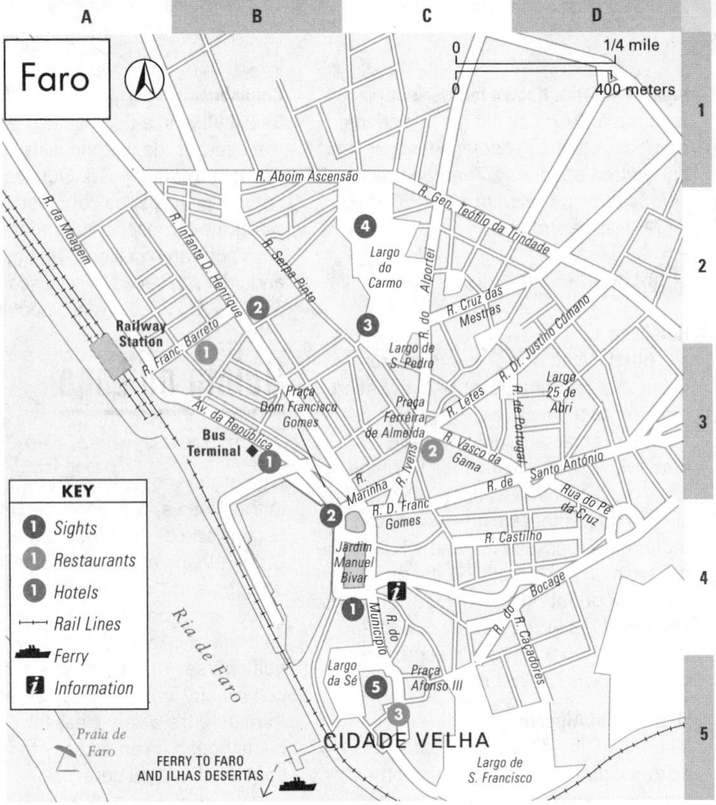

KEY

Sights
Restaurants
Hotels
Rail Lines
Ferry
Information

A B C D
1 2 3 4 5
0 1/4 mile
0 400 meters
R. Aboim Ascensão
R. Gen. Teófilo da Trindade
R. da Moagem
R. Infante D. Henrique
R. Serpa Pinto
Largo do Carmo
R. do Alportel
R. Cruz das Mestras
Railway Station
R. Franc. Barreto
Largo de S. Pedro
R. Dr. Justino Cumano
Largo 25 de Abril
Praça Dom Francisco Gomes
Praça Ferreira de Almeida
R. Letes
R. de Portugal
Av. da República
Bus Terminal
R. Vasco da Gama
R. Marinha
R. Ivens
R. de Santo António
Rua do Pé da Cruz
R. D. Franc Gomes
R. Castilho
Jardim Manuel Bivar
R. do Município
R. do Bocage
R. Caçadores
Ria de Faro
Largo da Sé
Praça Afonso III
Praia de Faro
CIDADE VELHA
FERRY TO FARO AND ILHAS DESERTAS
Largo de S. Francisco

be both authentic and trendy. It serves the quintessential Portuguese beach food, including whole grilled fish, octopus salad, and *amêijoas à bulhão pato* (clams with garlic and coriander). **Known for:** a see-add-be-seen crowd of stylish vacationers; proprietor sometimes breaks into song; lovely ocean views. *$ Average main: €19 Praia da Quinta do Lago, Almancil 964 045 178 www.quintadolago.com No dinner. Closed in winter from end of Nov. No credit cards.*

Pure
$ | **INTERNATIONAL** | The newest restaurant at Quinta do Lago is focused on healthful cuisine so expect nutrient-packed bowls, salads, wraps, and ciabattas. It's all served in a pretty indoor-outdoor dining room. **Known for:** good selection of fresh juices and smoothies; kick-starting breakfast dishes; relaxed atmosphere. *$ Average main: €9 Av. André Jordan, Rotunda 2, Almancil 289 390 708 www.quintadolago.com No dinner.*

Hotels

Magnolia Hotel
$$ | **HOTEL** | An iconic spot in Quinta do Lago, the Magnolia Hotel has a playful vibe that pays homage to the iconic motels of Miami Beach. **Pros:** complimentary access to the resort's golf club; sprawling fitness center; heated saltwater pool. **Cons:** slow service at breakfast; a long walk to the beach; the vibe is not for everyone. *$ Rooms from: €168 € Estrada Quinta do Lago, Almancil 289 005 300 www.themagnoliahotelqdl.com 81 rooms Free Breakfast.*

for exploring the area; good for and their families; staff goes the ile. **Cons:** uninspiring dinners; ated decor; too close to bars. *ns from: €176 ✉ Rua Atlântico 300 780 🌐 www.dompedro.com rooms 🍽 Free Breakfast.*

partamento do Golfe

RT | Positioned around a gener- ized swimming pool, this low-rise x offers affordable studio and droom apartments with their own itchens and dining areas. **Pros:** location in one of the Algarve's esirable postal codes; within a ute drive of a casino, tennis club, rina; free private parking and menities. **Cons:** Wi-Fi and other ies cost extra; design feels a little studios are small. *$ Rooms from: Alto do Golfe ☎ 289 303 140 v.hotelvilamouragolf.com 🛏 59 nents 🍽 Free Breakfast.*

Marina Vilamoura

HOTEL | FAMILY | If you think service include a turned-down bed with ates on the pillow, then this is the for you. **Pros:** direct access to a ful beach; family-friendly atmos- all rooms have balconies. **Cons:** the can make it feel impersonal; pricey amenities; convention hotel vibe. *oms from: €300 ✉ Vilamoura Marina 303 303 🌐 www.tivolihotels.com 3 rooms 🍽 Free Breakfast.*

Nightlife

Vilamoura

OS | Open until the wee hours of norning, Casino Vilamoura is a big f Vilamoura's nightlife scene. Here find two restaurants, a dance club, he usual selection of table games, ell as more than 500 slot machines. s is smart-casual, and you must be enter. *✉ Praça Casino Vilamou- uarteira ☎ 289 310 000 🌐 www. rde.pt.*

Activities

GOLF

Dom Pedro Millennium Course

GOLF | Martin Hawtree extended an existing 9-hole layout to create this visitor-friendly course. It shares the umbrella pine tree backdrop common to the other Vilamoura courses but is a little shorter in length. Reservations are advised. *✉ Caminho da Fonte do Ulme ☎ 289 310 188 🌐 www.dompedrogolf.com 💳 From €82 🏌 18 holes, 6754 yds, par 72.*

Dom Pedro Old Course

GOLF | One of the great golf courses of Europe, this Frank Pennink–designed course is widely regarded as the best of the local layouts because of its subtle routing and challenging holes. Umbrella pines line the fairways, and the crack of ball on timber is almost a signature tune on this famous course. The maximum handicap for men is 28 and for women 36. *✉ Volta do Medronho ☎ 289 310 341 🌐 www.dompedrogolf.com 💳 From €92 🏌 18 holes, 6839 yds, par 73 ✍ Reservations essential.*

SAILING

Algarve Seafaris

SAILING | If you'd like to relax and let someone else do the work, book a sea cave cruise with Algarve Seafaris, which runs three- to six-hour outings along the coast. The company also offers big-game fishing. *✉ Marina de Vilamoura, Escritorio 9/10 ☎ 289 302 318 🌐 www.algarve-seafaris.com.*

Albufeira

12 km (7 miles) west of Vilamoura.

With enough neon lights to rival Las Vegas, the newer sections of Albufeira retain no hint of the old Algarve, but is beloved by fans of English breakfasts, Irish pubs, and karaoke bars. The old town, however, has quaint cobblestone

Activities

The Campus

FITNESS/HEALTH CLUBS | This high-tech sports complex is the winter home for professional sports teams from throughout Europe. The facilities are top-notch, and several of the staffers are champion athletes. A one-day membership is €45. *✉ Av. Ayrton Senna da Silva 20, Almancil ☎ 289 381 220 🌐 www.quintadolago.com.*

Vale do Lobo

3 km (2 miles) west of Quinta do Lago, 18 km (11 miles) from Faro.

Vale do Lobo is one of the Algarve's luxury villa complexes that attracts the super-rich and famous from the world over. The local beach is one of the cleanest in the Algarve and remains relatively quiet during peak months. You can access the beach from below the Dona Filipa Hotel, where most of the restaurants are clustered.

GETTING HERE AND AROUND

There's very little public transportation, but you can take a taxi to Vale do Lobo.

ESSENTIALS

TAXI CONTACT FaroTaxis. *☎ 960 204 709 🌐 www.farotaxi.com.*

Hotels

Dona Filipa Hotel

$$$$ | HOTEL | This luxury property has golf on its mind: guests get reduced green fees and preferential tee times at the prestigious San Lorenzo Golf Club. **Pros:** not quite as expensive as neighboring resorts; a kids' club and other family-oriented perks; good choice for outdoors lovers. **Cons:** cheaper rooms in need of an update; no in-room coffee or tea; no spa or fitness center. *$ Rooms from: €329 ✉ Vale do Lobo ☎ 289 357 200 🌐 www.donafilipahotel.com 🛏 154 rooms 🍽 Free Breakfast.*

Algarve Market Days

All the main towns and villages have regular food markets, usually open daily from 8 until around 2.

Albufeira: first and third Tuesday of the month

Lagos: first Saturday of the month

Loulé: every Saturday

Portimão: first Monday of the month

Sagres: first Friday of the month

Silves: third Monday of the month

Activities

GOLF

Vale do Lobo Ocean Course

GOLF | This challenging course emerged from an earlier design by Sir Henry Cotton and is a combination of the original "orange" and "green" courses of three 9-hole loops. The undulating fairways are fringed by pine, olive, orange, and eucalyptus trees. Accuracy is the key factor, and the correct club selection is always worth a few shots. A handicap certificate is required. There's a driving range, a putting green, golf carts, pull carts, and a pro shop, restaurant, and bar. *✉ Av. do Mar ☎ 289 353 465 🌐 valedolobo.com/en/golf 💳 €91 🏌 18 holes, 6711 yds, par 73.*

Vale do Lobo Royal Course

GOLF | A more demanding course than the Ocean, the Royal is longer and defended by more water and bunkers. Sir Henry Cotton laid out the original course, but significant changes have been introduced by Rocky Roquemore to make it more up-to-date. The pick of the holes is the famous 16th, which requires a carry of 200 yards over three spectacular cliffs to reach the sanctuary green. A handicap limit of 27 for men and 35 for women is enforced here. ✉ *Av. do Mar* ☎ *289 353 535* 🌐 *valedolobo.com/en/golf* *€91* *18 holes, 6626 yds, par 72* *Reservations essential.*

HORSEBACK RIDING

Pinetrees Riding Centre

HORSEBACK RIDING | One of the oldest riding centers in the region, this British-run operation also does noteworthy work with the disabled. Expect lovely treks with experienced guides for riders of all abilities. ✉ *Casa dos Pinheiros, Estrada de Ancão, Almancil* ☎ *289 394 369* 🌐 *pinetrees.pt.*

TENNIS

Vale do Lobo Tennis Academy

TENNIS | The famous Vale do Lobo Tennis Academy has 14 all-weather courts, a bar, a pro shop, a pool, a gym, a steam room, and a restaurant. Court fees start at €32. ✉ *Vale do Lobo* ☎ *289 357 850* 🌐 *www.valedolobo.tennis.*

Loulé

6 km (4 miles) north of Almancil, 17 km (11 miles) northwest of Faro.

Castle walls and three stone towers provide visual evidence of its history, while an Arabesque indoor market—complete with pink turrets—offers a true taste of Algarvian culture. In recent years, Loulé's laid-back vibe has also attracted a growing number of artists and artisans, whose works are displayed in shops and galleries.

GETTING HERE AND AROUND

Trains run straight to Loulé from most major cities and towns in the Algarve, and buses run directly from Portimão, Albufeira, and Faro; tickets cost €3 to €8. A bus from Portimão would take about two hours to Loulé. The good news is that exploring the city does not require a car and can be covered on foot.

Carnival in Loulé

Loulé is famous for being home to one of the oldest and grandest carnival parades in the country. Held every year around the second weekend in February, it attracts thousands of visitors to the city. *www.cm-loule.pt.*

Sights

Castelo de Loulé (*Loulé Castle*)

CASTLE/PALACE | Once a Moorish stronghold, Loulé has preserved the ruins of the medieval castle, which was enlarged in 1268 after the site had been occupied and fortified since Neolithic times. These days, it houses the archaeology museum. ✉ *Rua Dom Paio Peres Correia 17* ☎ *289 400 600* 🌐 *www.cm-loule.pt* *€2* *Closed Sun.*

Igreja de São Clemente (*Church of São Clemente*)

RELIGIOUS SITE | This restored 13th-century church has handsome tiles, wood carvings, and an unusual wrought-iron pulpit. ✉ *Largo da Matriz* 🌐 *www.cm-loule.pt.*

Hotels

Loulé Jardim Hotel

$ | **HOTEL** | Set on a small square, this lovely hotel has a cozy home-away-from-home feel. **Pros:** sunny exterior and comfortable interior; in the center of the old town; free private parking garage. **Cons:** extra charge for in-room coffee and tea; extra charge to use the room safe; the coast is miles away. *Rooms from: €125* ✉ *Largo Manuel D'Arriaga* ☎ *289 413 095* 🌐 *www.loulejardimhotel.com* *52 rooms* *Free Breakfast.*

Shopping

ART GALLERY

Art Catto

ART GALLERIES | Works by internationally renowned artists are displayed—and sold—at the Art Catto gallery. ✉ *Av. José da Costa Mealha 43* ☎ *289 419 447* 🌐 *www.artcatto.com* *Closed Sun.*

MARKETS

★ **Loulé Municipal Market**

OUTDOOR/FLEA/GREEN MARKETS | Believed to be one of the oldest in the Algarve, if not the country, Loulé Municipal Market is a hive of smells, colors, and sounds. The century-old Moorish-style indoor area has added a number of stalls that sell ready-to-eat foods, so you can sample local delicacies as you browse. The best time to come is Saturday morning, when the surrounding outdoor farmers' market bursts into life. ✉ *City Center* ☎ *289 400 600* 🌐 *www.cm-loule.pt.*

Vilamoura

10 km (6 miles) west of Almancil.

Glitzy and glamorous Vilamoura is the Algarve's answer to Monaco. Once a prosperous Roman settlement, today it's an upscale resort community with the Algarve's biggest marina—an enormous complex with hotels, bars, cafés, restaurants, shops, and sports facilities. The town of Vilamoura and the area surrounding it also have several luxury hotels and golf courses as well as a major tennis center and casino.

GETTING HERE AND AROUND

Besides renting a car, you can reach Vilamoura by train, though the nearest stops are Albufeira in the west and Loulé in the east. Once at these stations, catch a bus to Vilamoura.

Sights

Museu de Cêrro (
Museum)
ARCHAEOLOGICAL
the excavations
site known as C
Vilamoura was fi
revealed an elab
as well as severa
The small Museu
you access to the
Vila ☎ *289 312 15*
and Tues.

Restaurai

Purobeach Vilamou
$$$ | **INTERNATIONA**
more than just a g
although it is that,
the terrace and ins
dining room, the st
accomplished men
summer classics, f
to healthy salads. **K**
local seafood; don't
rice; gorgeous sea
main: €24 ✉ *Marina*
303 740 🌐 *purobea*

Hotels

Anantara Vilamoura
$$$$ | **RESORT** | Statel
trees give this mode
of a tropical retreat.
Victoria Golf Course;
restaurants and bars
kids. **Cons:** not within
of the beach; empha
everyone; expensive
Rooms from: €350
brimentos 0 ☎ *289 3*
anantara.com *280*
Breakfast.

Dom Pedro Golf Resort
$$ | **HOTEL** | Golf is clea
the five challenging co
some of the best in th

location
golfers
extra m
rather
Roo
☎ *289*
266

Hotel A
$ | **RES**
ously s
comple
one-be
small k
perfec
most c
10-min
and m
other
ameni
dated;
€110
🌐 *ww*
apartr

Tivoli
$$$$ |
should
choco
place
beaut
phere
scale
beach
Ro
☎ *28*
38

Casin
CASIN
the n
part
you'l
and t
as w
Dres
18 to
ra, C
solv

A street scene in the old town of Albufeira in the Algarve.

streets, traditional restaurants, and its own beach.

Heading east out of Albufeira, you'll come to a slightly quieter, more upmarket part of town (Praia da Falésia–Olhos De Agua), where beautiful beaches are fringed by brand-name hotels.

GETTING HERE AND AROUND

Centrally located Albufeira is an ideal base for exploring the region. Given the sheer number of travelers on any given day, it's no surprise that the biggest bus terminals in the Algarve are found here. Trains are frequent to and from most Algarvian communities.

ESSENTIALS

VISITOR INFORMATION Albufeira Touist Office. ✉ *Rua 5 de Outubro* ☎ *289 585 279* 🌐 *www.visitalgarve.pt.*

Sights

Adega do Cantor

WINERY/DISTILLERY | The "Winery of the Singer," about 10 km (6 miles) west of Albufeira, is now as well known for its wines as it is for its famous owner, British pop legend Cliff Richard. The estate has bottled some seriously strong contenders on the international wine scene, and several of the Adega's Vida Nova wines have gone on to win coveted awards. Reservations are required for tours and tastings. ✉ *Quinta do Miradouro, Guia* ☎ *968 776 971* 🌐 *www.winesvidanova.com* 🎫 *€10* 🕓 *Closed weekends, and mid-Dec.–early Jan.*

Beaches

Praia da Galé

BEACH—SIGHT | Pretty and popular Praia da Galé, 4 km (2½ miles) west of Albufeira, has the classic Algarve rock formations that are characteristic of the region's coastline, plus a smattering of bars and restaurants. Other nice beaches lie on either side of Praia da Galé and can be accessed by foot—the walks from beach to beach are very enjoyable. **Amenities**: food and drink; parking (no fee);

water sports. **Best for:** sunset; walking. ✉ *Estrada da Galé.*

Praia da Oura

BEACH—SIGHT | This pretty beach, 2 km (1 mile) east of Albufeira, is shaped like a bay and surrounded by low-rise hotels and resorts. It's relatively small compared to other beaches, and is extremely crowded most of the year. But it comes equipped with all the summer essentials, like beach beds and water sports. **Amenities:** lifeguards; parking (fee); water sports. **Best for:** partiers. ✉ *Off Rua Oliveira Martins.*

Praia dos Pescadores

BEACH—SIGHT | **FAMILY** | In summer, this beach gets so crowded that it can be hard to enjoy its interesting rock formations, caves, and grottoes, not to mention the sand and sea. Yet it offers the latest in water sports and local children love jumping off the pier. Albufeira's old town encases the beach, which is known as Praia dos Pescadores because fishing boats dock here to supply the local area with their fresh catch. A vast range of eateries and bars are a short stroll away. **Amenities**: lifeguards; water sports. **Best for:** partiers. ✉ *Rua Bairro dos Pescadores.*

A Ruina

$$$$ | **SEAFOOD** | Built in the ruins of an 8th-century castle tower—hence its name—this eatery serves fine renditions of typical Algarvian fare in four dining rooms with balconies overlooking the beach. It's a unique option for a special occasion, but great food in a historic setting comes at a price. **Known for:** wide selection of fresh fish and seafood; boasts an excellent wine list; historic setting comes at a price. *$ Average main: €35* ✉ *Cais Herculano, Praia dos Pescadores* ☎ *289 512 094* 🌐 *www.restaurante-ruina.com* ⊗ *Closed early Jan.–early Feb.*

Cabaz da Praia

$$$ | **PORTUGUESE** | The name of this long-established beachfront restaurant, which means "Beach Basket," seems fitting given the mixed bag of imaginative Portuguese and French creations on the menu. Along with seafood, top choices include the chateaubriand, steak with Roquefort cheese sauce, and salmon in Pernod sauce. **Known for:** terrace overlooking the ocean; perfect for a meal after the beach; friendly service. *$ Average main: €22* ✉ *Praça Miguel Bombarda 7* ☎ *289 512 137* 🌐 *www.cabazdapraia.blogspot.pt.*

Epic Sana Algarve

$$$$ | **RESORT** | **FAMILY** | This resort's low-rise architecture beautifully blends into the landscape, which includes sand dunes and pretty gardens shaded by pines trees. **Pros:** a prime spot overlooking Albufeira's Falésia Beach; decor is cool, contemporary, and comfortable; lot of amenities for famililes with children. **Cons:** fills up with conference attendees; not the place to go for nightlife; far from town. *$ Rooms from: €400* ✉ *Pinhal do Concelho* ☎ *289 104 300* 🌐 *www.algarve.epic.sanahotels.com* *229 rooms* *Free Breakfast.*

Grande Real Santa Eulália

$$$ | **RESORT** | Grand in style, the cliff-top Santa Eulália occupies a privileged position just a stone's throw from shops and bars. **Pros:** direct beach access; four outdoor pools; dedicated kids' club. **Cons:** not within walking distance of town center; lunch and dinner buffets overpriced; the sheer size in daunting. *$ Rooms from: €216* ✉ *Praia de Santa Eulália* ☎ *289 598 000* 🌐 *www.grande-realsantaeulaliahotel.com* *373 rooms* *Free Breakfast.*

Hotel Vila Galé Cerro Alagoa

$$ | **HOTEL** | One of Albufeira's most comfortable lodgings is a 10-minute walk from the main square. **Pros:** central to both old and new towns; on-site spa; family friendly. **Cons:** bar drinks expensive; limited entertainment options; extra charge to use the safe. *Rooms from: €182 ✉ Via Rápida, Rua do Municipio Lt. 26 ☎ 🌐 www.vilagale.pt 310 rooms 🍴 Free Breakfast.*

Pine Cliffs Resort
$$$$ | **RESORT** | Perfect for families, this sprawling resort offers activities ranging from golf to tennis to water sports, along with direct access to a lovely cliff-backed beach. **Pros:** self-contained property with everything that you need; beautiful bar is perched above the red cliffs; boardwalk leads to gorgeous Praia da Falésia. **Cons:** the decor is a bit bland; has an impersonal feel; extra charge for Wi-Fi. *Rooms from: €500 ✉ Pinhal do Concelho ☎ 289 500 300 🌐 www.pinecliffs.com 519 rooms 🍴 Free Breakfast.*

★ **Vila Joya Boutique Resort**
$$$$ | **HOTEL** | Foodies, take note: Austrian chef Dieter Koschina oversees one of Portugal's most highly rated restaurants, and it's right on the grounds of this jewel of a resort; you receive a discount on dinner if you book prior to your stay. **Pros:** service is attentive yet discreet; wonderful list of amenities; memorable meals. **Cons:** not much to do in surrounding area; location is a little difficult to find; pricey rates. *Rooms from: €585 ✉ Estrada da Galé ☎ 289 591 795 🌐 www.vilajoya.com 20 rooms 🍴 Free Breakfast.*

Nightlife

Bizarro
BARS/PUBS | The owner, the music, and the clientele are mellow at this cliff-side club. Rustic on the inside and a traditional blue-and-white Algarvian cottage on the outside, it's the perfect bar from which to watch the sun go down. *✉ Esplanada Doutor Frutuoso da Silva 30 ☎ 289 512 824.*

Casa do Cerro
THEMED ENTERTAINMENT | Think Morocco in the Algarve, complete with swaths of rich fabric, exotic cocktails, and bubbling shisha pipes. This breezy hilltop venue is a world away from the hustle and bustle of the Algarve in summer. *✉ Albufeira Jardim I ☎ 919 596 665.*

Armação de Pêra

14 km (8½ miles) west of Albufeira, 52 km (32 miles) from Faro.

If it weren't for the interesting seascapes, beautiful beaches, and interesting eateries, this massively overdeveloped community wouldn't be worth a visit. Local captains can take you on two-hour cruises to caves and grottoes along the shore past the Praia Nossa Senhora da Rocha (Beach of Our Lady of the Rocks)—a strand named after the Romanesque chapel above it. To arrange tours, head to Praia Armação de Pêra—a wide sandy beach with a promenade—and speak with the fishermen.

GETTING HERE AND AROUND

The town can be reached via Portimão in the west or Albufeira in the east; a bus from either will shuttle you to this seaside resort.

ESSENTIALS

VISITOR INFORMATION Armação de Pêra Tourist Office. *✉ Av. da Beira Mar ☎ 282 312 145 🌐 www.visitalgarve.pt.*

Restaurants

Bollywood Indian Tandoori Restaurante
$ | **INDIAN** | Although it's located directly opposite Praia Nossa Senhora da Rocha, this eatery is a world away. The always-crowded dining room has a romantic feel. **Known for:** one of the Algarve's most popular eateries; lots of vegetarian dishes; reservations are advisable. *Average main: €10 ✉ Rua da Praia, Edifício Vista Mar 1 ☎ 282 313*

755 ⊕ www.bollywoodindianrestaurant.eatbu.com.

★ Ocean Restaurant
$$$$ | PORTUGUESE | Done up in vivid shades of blue and gold, this upscale restaurant at the Vila Vita Parc impresses with its innovative tasting menus, fabulous wine selection, and wonderful ocean views. Choose from two tasting menus of four or six courses featuring interesting riffs on Portuguese classics. **Known for:** one of the top dining experiences in the Algarve; impeccably prepared dishes; creative presentations. *$ Average main: €170 ✉ Vila Vita Parc, Rua Anneliese Pohl, Porches ☎ 282 310 100 ⊕ www.restauranteocean.com ⊙ Closed Mon. and Tues. No lunch.*

Zé Leiteiro
$ | PORTUGUESE | Most *casas de pastos* (loosely translated as "grazing houses") offer big portions of well-cooked regional dishes in no-frills surroundings. Zé Leiteiro is no exception. **Known for:** be prepared to wait awhile for a seat; simple on the outside, basic on the inside; the food and prices do the talking. *$ Average main: €14 ✉ Rua Portas do Mar 17 ☎ 282 314 551 ▭ No credit cards ⊙ Closed Mon., mid-Dec.–mid. Jan., and last wk in May.*

Pestana Viking Resort
$$ | RESORT | About 1 km (½ mile) west of town, the Viking stands on a promontory directly above a lovely beach. **Pros:** direct access to a beautiful beach; ideal location for rest and relaxation; lots of amenities for families. **Cons:** you need a car to get around; restaurant food is pricey; rooms need a refresh. *$ Rooms from: €193 ✉ Praia Nossa Senhora da Rocha, Porches ☎ 282 320 500 ⊕ www.pestanavikingresort.com ⇆ 182 rooms ⑩ Free Breakfast.*

★ Vila Vita Parc
$$$$ | RESORT | Within walking distance of Armação de Pêra, the cliff-top Vila Vita Parc is an award-winning resort. **Pros:** gardens lead down to two sequestered beaches; a true Algarvian experience; 10 on-site eateries. **Cons:** sprawling grounds mean a lot of walking; decor is a bit old-fashioned; room sizes vary. *$ Rooms from: €545 ✉ Rua Anneliese Pohl, Porches ☎ 282 310 161 ⊕ www.vilavitaparc.com ⇆ 170 rooms ⑩ Free Breakfast.*

WATER PARK

Aqualand
WATER SPORTS | FAMILY | Just north of town, this extremely popular water park has a lazy river, wave pools, and a surfing beach. It's home to the Kamikaze, the highest waterslide in Portugal. *✉ Estrada Nacional 125 ☎ 282 320 230 ⊕ www.aqualand.pt ▭ €29 ⊙ Closed mid-Sept.–June.*

Carvoeiro

5 km (3 miles) west of Armação de Pêra, 65 km (40 miles) west of Faro.

This busy resort town has managed to maintain some of its fishing-village charm. Small beaches lie at the foot of steep, rocky cliffs, and waves have sculpted the distinctive yellow rock into intricate archways and stacks encrusted with fossilized shells. Its central location is another of its assets, as it makes a good base for accessing both the east and west coasts.

GETTING HERE AND AROUND

The closest train stations are Silves or Estômbar, with bus services running regularly to this quaint village.

ESSENTIALS

VISITOR INFORMATION Carvoeiro Tourist Office. ✉ *Largo da Praia* ☎ *282 357 728* 🌐 *www.visitalgarve.pt.*

Restaurants

Onze Restaurant

$$ | **GREEK FUSION** | Cool, contemporary Onze offers a tempting array of Mediterranean dishes and one of the best views in the village, right on the cliffs overlooking the beach. Start with the mixed platter of authentic Greek meze, then move onto one of the mouthwatering risottos. **Known for:** prides itself on being family-friendly; impeccable service; excellent wine list. [$] *Average main: €20* ✉ *Rampa da Sra. da Encarnacao 11* ☎ *282 357 427* 🌐 *www.onze-restaurant.com* ⏲ *Closed mid.-Nov.–mid-Dec. and early Jan.–late Feb.*

★ Quinta dos Santos

$$ | **PORTUGUESE** | If you can't decide between a glass of local wine or a craft beer to go with your meal, then this family-run place is for you. What started as a tap room has evolved into a full-fledged restaurant with a gorgeous courtyard ringed by arches and a surprisingly sophisticated dining room serving sharable Portuguese dishes. **Known for:** six taps of house-made craft beer, including three rotating brews; contemporary takes on traditional dishes using seasonal ingredients; a number of Portuguese wines by the glass. [$] *Average main: €18* ✉ *Rua do Pestana Golf 1, Sesmarias* ☎ *282 343 264* 🌐 *www.quintadossantos.com* ⏲ *Closed Mon.*

Hotels

Tivoli Carvoeiro

$$$$ | **HOTEL** | Perched high on a cliff overlooking the dramatic coastline, the Tivoli Carvoeiro has striking modern architecture, stunning ocean views, and well-kept grounds dotted with lots of trees. **Pros:** excellent location overlooking the water; great on-site dive shop; good for families. **Cons:** doesn't have much Portuguese flavor; it's an uphill walk from the town square; a lot of conference attendees. [$] *Rooms from: €300* ✉ *Vale do Covo* ☎ *282 351 100* 🌐 *www.tivolihotels.com* *248 rooms* *Free Breakfast.*

Activities

GOLF

Vale da Pinta Golf Course

GOLF | American designer Ronald Fream carved the Vale da Pinta layout through an ancient grove of 700-year-old olive trees. Fream was the perfect choice for the job, because he is highly regarded for his sensitivity to environmental issues. Five sets of tees on each hole make this an enjoyable course for all skill levels. Booking two weeks in advance is advised for those looking for specific tee times. The greens are large, and there is a feeling of space. Handicap limits are 27 for men and 35 for women. ✉ *Apartado 1011* ☎ *282 340 900* 🌐 *www.pestanagolf.com* *€73–€120* *18 holes, 6409 yds, par 71.*

TENNIS

Carvoeiro Clube de Ténis

TENNIS | The well-regaraded Carvoeiro Clube de Ténis has 10 courts and five mini-courts, as well as padel (a racket sport), a fitness center, a swimming pool, and a restaurant. ✉ *Mato Serrão* ☎ *282 358 236* 🌐 *www.carvoeiroclubedetenis.com.*

Lagoa

15 km (9 miles) northwest of Carvoeiro, 59 km (37 miles) west of Faro.

This market town is primarily known for its wine, called *vinho Lagoa*, with the red being especially good. It is also home to the Algarve's last surviving wine cooperative, a historic structure which now houses an interesting art gallery.

GETTING HERE AND AROUND

Lagoa has a large bus terminal, which connects with Portimão and Albufeira.

ESSENTIALS

BUS CONTACT Lagoa Bus Terminal. ✉ *Rua Jacinto Correia* ☎ *282 341 301.*

Sights

Quinta dos Vales
WINERY/DISTILLERY | Although it's one of the more recent players on the regional wine production scene, Quinta dos Vales has earned an impressive reputation. Free wine tastings are available in the FarmShop, as well as 90-minute guided tastings that must be booked in advance. Visitors who would like to spend more time exploring the beautiful grounds and open-air sculpture garden can book one of the estate's farmhouses. ✉ *Off N125* ☎ *282 431 036* 🌐 *www.quintadosvales.eu* ⏲ *Closed Sun.*

Única-Adega Cooperativa de Lagoa (*Única-Adega Wine Cooperative*)
WINERY/DISTILLERY | The Algarve's last remaining cooperative winery is a piece of living, working history. The Única-Adega Cooperativa do Algarve is a great place for a tour and tasting session. At any time during normal working hours you can pop in to the office to sample the wine and buy a bottle or two. Part of the building has been converted into an art gallery featuring national and international artists. ✉ *Estrada Nacional 125* ☎ *282 342 181* 🌐 *www.vinhosdoalgarve.pt.*

Beaches

★ Praia da Marinha
BEACH—SIGHT | **FAMILY** | At this dreamy beach, crystal clear waters lap against the impressive rock formations. Dramatic coves and caves in orange limestone make for a striking backdrop for snorkeling and sunbathing. Although it's located in prime tourist territory, the relatively challenging descent means it's less visited than other beaches in the region. **Amenities:** food and drink; parking (no fee). **Best for:** snorkeling; sunset. ✉ *Estada da Marinha.*

Shopping

CERAMICS

Olaria Pequena
CERAMICS/GLASSWARE | This pretty little blue-and-white pottery shop embodies the essence of Algarvian ceramics. It is owned and run by a friendly Scot named Ian Fitzpatrick, who has worked in the Algarve for years. He sells handmade pieces at very reasonable prices. ✉ *N125 between Porches and Alcantarilha* ☎ *282 381 213* 🌐 *www.olariapequena.com.*

Silves

7 km (4½ miles) north of Lagoa, 62 km (39 miles) west of Faro.

Silves—once the Moorish capital of the Algarve—is one of the region's most intriguing locales. Small whitewashed villas trickle down from the imposing castle that sits atop town, overlooking the hills beyond. Being inland, Silves is generally warmer than coastal communities, and it has a pretty riverside area where you can enjoy a refreshing stroll or cheap, cheerful meal. In summer, Viking-style canoes run trips down the Arade River to Portimão.

GETTING HERE AND AROUND

The easiest way to get to Silves is by bus via Lagoa, if you're coming from the eastern Algarve. If you're coming from the western end, the easiest route is via Portimão. The train station is 7 km (4½ miles) from the city center; a taxi from the station into Silves should cost no more than €10 at peak times.

ESSENTIALS

BUS CONTACT Silves Bus Station. ✉ *Rua Francisco Pablos, Edifício do Mercado* ☎ *282 442 338* 🌐 *www.eva-bus.com.*

TAXI CONTACT Mega Taxi. ☎ *282 082 587.*

VISITOR INFORMATION Silves Tourist Information. ✉ *Estrada Nacional 124* ☎ *282 098 927* 🌐 *www.visitalgarve.pt.*

Sights

Castelo de Silves (*Silves Castle*)
CASTLE/PALACE | With high red walls that overshadow the little whitewashed houses below, this polygonal sandstone fortress was built between the 8th and 13th centuries and survived untouched until the Christian sieges. You can walk around inside the remaining walls or clamber about the crenellated battlements, taking in bird's-eye views of Silves and the surrounding hills. (Keep an eye open: some places have no guardrails.) Its gardens are watched over by a statue of King Dom Sancho I, and its capacious water cistern is now a gallery space devoted to temporary exhibitions. ✉ *Rua do Castelo* ☎ *282 440 837* 🌐 *www.cm-silves.pt* 🎫 *€3.90.*

Museu Municipal de Arqueológia (*Municipal Archaeological Museum*)
MUSEUM | With most displays in both Portuguese and English, the town's compact archaeology museum provides interesting insights into the area's history. One primary attraction is an Arab water cistern, preserved in its original location, with a 30-foot-deep well. The museum is a few minutes' walk from the cathedral, off Rua da Sé. ✉ *Rua das Portas de Loulé 14* ☎ *282 440 800* 🌐 *www.cm-silves.pt* 🎫 *€2.10; €3.90 combined ticket includes castle.*

Santa Maria da Sé
RELIGIOUS SITE | The 12th- to 13th-century Cathedral of St. Mary, built on the site of a Moorish mosque, saw service as the principal cathedral of the Algarve until the 16th century. The 1755 earthquake and indifferent restoration have left it rather plain inside, but its tower—complete with gargoyles—is still a fine sight. ✉ *Rua da Sé* ☎ *282 442 472* 🎫 *€1.*

Silves Medieval Festival
CULTURAL FESTIVALS | The local council goes all out to make sure the 10-day Silves Medieval Festival feels like a trip back in time. Food merchants and handicraft vendors dressed in traditional garb take over the city in August. Jousting displays and falconry shows are staged, along with fire-eating, traditional dancing, and medieval banquets. Silves's steep, narrow streets are packed during this event. ✉ *Silves* ☎ *282 440 800* 🌐 *www.cm-silves.pt* 🎫 *€2 (extra charge for special events).*

Restaurants

Café Inglês
$ | ECLECTIC | Architectural character, great views, and a broad selection of affordably priced local food combine to make Café Inglês a must-try. In summer make sure you book a table on the rooftop terrace adjacent to the castle. **Known for:** gorgeous dining room; excellent service; fresh salads. $ *Average main: €12* ✉ *Rua do Castelo 11* ☎ *282 442 585* 🌐 *www.cafeingles.com.pt* ⏲ *Closed Mon., and Nov.*

Rui Marisqueira
$$ | SEAFOOD | Although there's no atmosphere to speak of, the fresh fish and shellfish at Rui Marisqueira are a remarkably good value. That's the main reason why the crowds from the coast come inland to dine here alongside in-the-know locals. **Known for:** don't miss the grilled sea bream and bass; specialties include slipper lobster and spider crab; fine selection of Portuguese wines. $ *Average main: €18* ✉ *Rua Comendador Vilarinho 27* ☎ *282 442 682* 🌐 *www.marisqueirarui.pt* ⏲ *Closed Tues., and 1st 2 wks of Nov.*

Portimão, once known for sardine fishing, is now a popular tourist destination due to its beautiful beaches.

Shopping

MARKET

Mercado (*produce market*)

MARKET | Silves's market, by far the liveliest in the morning, sits at the foot of town close to the medieval bridge. If you arrive at lunchtime, have a delicious meal of spicy grilled chicken or typical stews like *cozido á portuguesa* from one of the cheap and cheerful restaurants. After lunch take a long stroll along the city's riverside walk. ✉ *N124.*

Portimão

15 km (9 miles) southwest of Silves, 71 km (44 miles) west of Faro.

Portimão's crown jewel is a 1-km (½-mile) stretch of sand backed by a curtain of ocher-red cliffs, along the top of which stands a series of striking hotels, restaurants, and bars. In summer it buzzes; in winter the locals promenade along the wooden walkway that runs the entire length of the beach, inhaling the invigorating sea air. Year-round Praia da Rocha is popular among youngsters looking for a place to party (though it's nothing like the scale of Albufeira).

Away from the beach, Portimão is an attractive cruise port. There's a lovely riverside area that begs to be strolled. Don't leave without stopping for an alfresco lunch at the Doca da Sardinha ("sardine dock") between the old bridge and the railway bridge. You can sit at one of many inexpensive establishments eating charcoal-grilled sardines (a local specialty) accompanied by chewy fresh bread, simple salads, and local wine.

GETTING HERE AND AROUND

Portimão can be reached by train and bus. The city's impressive Vai e Vem bus service is excellent and enables visitors to zip around at a minimal cost.

ESSENTIALS

BUS CONTACTS Vai e Vem. ✉ *Rua do Comércio 29/31* ☎ *282 470 777* 🌐 *www.vaivem.pt.*

Sights

Fortaleza de Santa Catarina

MILITARY SITE | The eastern end of Praia da Rocha culminates in the 16th-century Fortress of Santa Catarina, which provides wonderful views out to sea and across the Rio Arade to Ferragudo. ✉ *Av. Tomás Cabreira, Praia da Rocha.*

Quinta da Penina

WINERY/DISTILLERY | One of the Algarve's more established wineries, Quinta da Penina is home to the renowned Foral de Portimão wine. Agronomist João Mariano, who mainly uses a blend of Portuguese and French grape varieties, has earned international acclaim since launching the company in 2001. Tours and tastings are possible most days of the week by calling in advance. ✉ *Rua da Angola* ☎ *282 491 070* 🌐 *www.vinhosportimao.com.*

Sardine Festival

FESTIVAL | Portimão stages its renowned Sardine Festival every year at the beginning of August. It's a must for anyone wanting to try the delicious little fish and sample local cuisine while enjoying the sights and sounds of a proper Algarvian party. ✉ *Portimão* ☎ *282 470 700* 🌐 *www.festivaldasardinha.pt.*

Beaches

★ Praia da Rocha

BEACH—SIGHT | Said to be the country's most photographed beach, Praia da Rocha is definitely one of the most popular, and it draws a constant stream of visitors from around the world. Dramatic cliffs provide the backdrop for a wide, golden expanse of sand. Many water sports are available, and there's a long pier to stroll on. Several bars and restaurants can be found along the beach, all jutting off a wooden boardwalk that stretches down the strand. More can be found further east towards the marina. **Amenities:** food and drink; lifeguards; parking (fee and no fee); showers (at the marina); toilets; water sports. **Best for:** partiers; surfing; swimming; walking. ✉ *Av. Tomas Cabreira, 3 km (2 miles) southeast of Portimão, Praia da Rocha.*

Praia Grande

BEACH—SIGHT | The quaint village of Ferragudo, across the river from Portimão, has one of the region's finest beaches: Praia Grande, a long stretch of sand that offers plenty of space for towels even in summer. The 16th-century **Castelo de São João** (St. John's Castle), built to defend Portimão and now privately owned, sits right on the beach. Since many boats dock here, the water can have a slight petrol smell, but it is crystal clear and good for snorkeling. When it's time to dry off, sit and watch the cruise ships glide by as they dock in Portimão. **Amenities:** food and drink; lifeguards; parking (no fee); showers; toilets; water sports. **Best for:** snorkeling; sunset; windsurfing. ✉ *Off M530, 5 km (3 miles) east of Portimão, Ferragudo.*

Restaurants

La Dolce Vita

$ | **PIZZA** | Locals flock to Dolce Vita for its fabulous homemade pizzas, hearty pastas, refreshing sangria, and charmingly old-fashioned decor. Meals are served on bench tables with tiled tops that add extra quirkiness to this popular eatery. **Known for:** be sure to make a reservation in summer; heaping portions of Italian favorites; popular with families. [$] *Average main: €11* ✉ *Av. Tomas Cabreira, Praia da Rocha* ☎ *282 419 444* 🌐 *www.pizzerialadolcevita.pt.*

Nosolo Itália

$ | **PIZZA** | On Portimão's main square, Nosolo Itália is as famous for its massive ice-cream sundaes as it is for its privileged location. The menu is made up almost entirely of ice-cream concoctions and simple Italian fare like pizza, pasta, and salads. **Known for:** elaborate ice-cream sundaes; delicious sweet crepes; interesting flavors. *Average main: €12 ✉ Praça Manuel Teixeira Gomes ☎ 282 427 024 🌐 www.nosoloitalia.com ▭ No credit cards.*

Vista

$$$$ | **INTERNATIONAL** | In an elegant dining room overlooking Praia da Rocha, this Mediterranean-influenced restaurant specializes in meticulously presented dishes that use local ingredients. Chef João Oliveira worked at some of Portugal's most award-winning restaurants, and here he puts his own stamp on refined Algarvian cuisine and serves them in multicourse tasting menus. **Known for:** top-quality seafood from local markets; well-thought-out tasting menus; a full menu for vegetarians. *Average main: €110 ✉ Hotel Bela Vista, Av. Tomás Cabreira ☎ 282 460 280 🌐 vistarestaurante.com ⏲ No lunch. Closed Sun.–Tues. in winter.*

Hotels

Bela Vista Hotel

$$$$ | **HOTEL** | This intimate hotel was designed in 1918 by Graça Viterbo, one of Portugal's leading architects of the time, in grand maximalist style that includes cathedral windows and a soaring tower; the luxe feel continues inside with golden yellow fabrics, vivid blue tiles, and rich wood. **Pros:** one of the region's prettiest buildings; access to the beach; excellent service. **Cons:** over-the-top aesthetic not for everyone; not ideal for families with children; can be pricey. *Rooms from: €570 ✉ Av. Tomás Cabreira ☎ 282 460 280 🌐 www.hotelbelavista.net 38 rooms Free Breakfast.*

Hotel Algarve Casino

$$$$ | **HOTEL** | The sea vistas from this upscale hotel are spectacular, so be sure to book a room with a view. **Pros:** great location on Praia da Rocha's main strip; plenty of spots to lounge around the lovely pool; playground for the kids. **Cons:** somewhat dated decor; overcrowded breakfast buffet; Wi-Fi can be spotty. *Rooms from: €268 ✉ Av. Tomás Cabreira, Praia da Rocha ☎ 282 423 770 🌐 hotelalgarvecasino.solverde.pt 208 rooms Free Breakfast.*

Tivoli Marina Portimão

$$ | **RESORT** | This hotel has a simple but stylish interior cleverly laid out around two large swimming pools complete with wooden decks and palm gardens. **Pros:** stunning views over the river; beach is a 10-minute walk; nice selection at breakfast buffet. **Cons:** bathrooms are a bit cramped; can be noisy from local bars; rooms vary in quality. *Rooms from: €180 ✉ Marina de Portimão ☎ 282 460 200 🌐 www.tivolihotels.com 196 apartments Free Breakfast.*

Nightlife

NoSoloÁgua

BEACHES | At the marina's edge, this Indonesian-inspired club has everything you need to indulge yourself, including a saltwater pool, lovely lounge areas, and delicious food. An adjacent sister retreat on the beach—called NoSoloPraia—holds nightly parties in summer that attract the beautiful people. *✉ Marina de Portimão ☎ 282 498 180 🌐 www.nosoloagua.com.*

Activities

BOATING

Santa Bernarda

SAILING | Take a sailing trip on this twin-masted replica of a pirate ship. Departing from the harbor, the *Santa Bernarda* offers visits to Algarvian caves and barbecues on the beach. *✉ Rua Júdice Fialho 11 ☎ 282 422 791 🌐 www.santa-bernarda.com.*

Alvor

5 km (3 miles) west of Portimão, 75 km (47 miles) west of Faro.

With its maze of alleyways, the handsome old port of Alvor is one of the Algarve's best examples of an Arab village. In summer, many vacationers are attracted to its excellent beaches and appealing nightlife.

GETTING HERE AND AROUND

Alvor is connected by Portimão's Vai e Vem bus service, though taxis are widely used in this popular fishing village.

ESSENTIALS

TAXI CONTACT Taxi Arade. ☎ *282 460 610* 🌐 *www.taxiarade.com.*

VISITOR INFORMATION Alvor Tourist Office. ✉ *Rua Dr. Afonso Costa 51* ☎ *282 457 540.*

Beaches

Praia dos Três Irmãos

BEACH—SIGHT | The covelike Praia dos Três Irmãos has lots of little rocks in the water, which means it can either be great for snorkeling or bad for unwitting toes, depending on the tide. If it gets too crowded, there's always space to spare on one of the beaches to either side. **Amenities:** food and drink; lifeguards; parking (no fee); toilets. **Best for:** snorkeling; walking. ✉ *Off V3, 1½ km (1 mile) from Alvor.*

Restaurants

Atlântida

$$ | SEAFOOD | This charming restaurant has an absolutely lovely location on the eastern edge of a dramatic beach. Specialties here include fresh fish and delicious seafood stews, supported by a selection of fine wines. **Known for:** beautiful wood-paneled dining room; the beach's tastiest sangria; the freshest ingredients. Ⓢ *Average main: €20* ✉ *Praia do Três Irmãos* ☎ *282 459 647* ⏲ *Closed Tues.*

Hotels

Penina Hotel & Golf Resort

$$ | RESORT | With three challenging courses on the property, it's no surprise that the Penina attracts large numbers of golfers (especially because guests get discounted green fees). **Pros:** includes a renowned 18-hole course designed by Henry Cotton; Le Grill restaurant serves excellent Portuguese dishes; lovely pool area and gardens. **Cons:** rooms in need of a refresh; drinks are expensive; sparse evening entertainment. Ⓢ *Rooms from: €184* ✉ *N125, Penina* ☎ *282 420 200* 🌐 *www.penina.com* *188 rooms* *Free Breakfast.*

★ **Pestana Alvor Praia**

$$$$ | HOTEL | Whether you have a room with a sea or a garden view, this cliff-top property looks good from all angles. **Pros:** relaxing heated indoor pool; fresh decor in guest rooms; complimentary sunbeds on the beach. **Cons:** buffet not always quickly restocked; 15-minute walk to town; expensive food by pool. Ⓢ *Rooms from: €350* ✉ *Praia dos Três Irmãos* ☎ *282 400 900* 🌐 *www.pestana.com* *202 rooms* *Free Breakfast.*

Activities

GOLF

★ **Penina**

GOLF | On what was once a flat, uninteresting rice paddy, Sir Henry Cotton created his most famous course. It is considered his masterpiece because of the beautiful setting he created by planting more than 100,000 trees. Cotton held court here for years, welcoming the great and good from the golf world to the lavish resort. The course has had a face-lift and remains a stern test of your skills—the par-3 13th hole has been ranked among the best in the world. Although the course gets busy, golfers on different holes seldom come into contact due to the mature trees and wide fairways. Penina Hotel & Golf Resort guests are entitled to special green fee rates. On the championship course, a handicap of 28 is required for men and 36 for women to play. *Penina Hotel & Golf Resort, N125, Portimão* *282 420 200* *www.penina.com/golf/golf-courses* *€120 high season, €80 low season* *18 holes, 6860 yds, par 73* *Reservations essential.*

Monchique

25 km (15 miles) northeast of Alvor, 85 km (53 miles) northwest of Faro.

The winding road up to Monchique brings the surprise of brightly colored villas surrounded by fruit groves and lush greenery. Steeped in tradition and folklore, Monchique is home to Fóia, the highest peak in the Algarve, as well as the natural springs that are said to have healing properties. In March the town hosts a traditional cured-meats fair to showcase local specialties.

GETTING HERE AND AROUND

Getting to Monchique can be tricky without a car. If you need to use public transportation, travel by bus to Silves or Portimão or by train to Portimão and then take a bus or taxi. The best way to get to Fóia is by taxi from Monchique town center.

ESSENTIALS

TAXI CONTACT Táxis Ginjeira Martins Unipessoal. *282 913 157.*

VISITOR INFORMATION Monchique Tourist Office. *Largo de S. Sebastião* *282 911 189* *www.visitalgarve.pt.*

Sights

Caldas de Monchique

SPA—SIGHT | Monchique's natural springs are renowned for healing waters that bubble out of the ground to create a paradise microclimate where "anything grows." The small chapel of the community of Caldas de Monchique is where many go for a blessing or to pray in thanks for the health of those who drink its waters. The Spa Termal has the healing waters as well as treatments. *Monchique* *282 910 910* *www.monchiquetermalresort.com.*

Feira dos Enchidos

FESTIVAL | Every year on the first weekend in March, Monchique hosts its annual cured-meats fair. The Sausage Fair is a high point on the locals' calendar and people travel from far and wide to sample cured meats, along with jams, dried fruits, liqueurs, and cheeses. It's all rounded off with traditional nightly entertainment. *Monchique* *www.cm-monchique.pt.*

Pico de Fóia

SCENIC DRIVE | A short drive west of Monchique brings you to the highest point in the Serra de Monchique. The towering Pico de Fóia affords panoramic views—weather permitting—over the western Algarve. There's also a café here. *Off N266-3* *www.cm-monchique.pt.*

Restaurants

Teresinha

$ | PORTUGUESE | Just west of Monchique, the simple but elegrant Teresinha has good country cooking and a lofty dining room warmed by a fireplace. An outdoor terrace overlooks a valley as well as the coastline. **Known for:** tasty ham and other locally cured meats; a longtime favorite with locals; good value. *Average main: €10* *N266-3* *282 912 392* *Closed Wed.*

Colorful houses line the way in the town of Monchique, home to natural springs that are said to have healing properties.

Hotels

Inn Albergeria Bica Boa

$ | **B&B/INN** | Inspired by the many springs welling up from the thickly wooded mountain above Monchique, this small roadside hotel has rooms facing the greenery. **Pros:** quiet, relaxing atmosphere; English owner can organize walks for you; range of dishes for vegetarians. **Cons:** you need a car to get around; no Wi-Fi in the rooms; may be too rustic for some. *Rooms from: €60* *Estrada da Lisboa 266* *282 912 271* *www.bica-boa.negocio.site* *4 rooms* *Free Breakfast.*

Monchique Resort & Spa

$$ | **RESORT** | This striking mountain retreat enjoys breathtaking views of the coastline and has become popular with national and international tourists who are looking for privacy and tranquility without being too far from civilization. **Pros:** plenty of activities for those seeking some R&R; a playground and other pluses for families; modern rooms with many amenities. **Cons:** you need a car to explore the area; not much going on in the evenings; kitchens have limited equipment. *Rooms from: €191* *Lugar do Montinho* *282 240 100* *www.monchiqueresort.com* *190 rooms* *Free Breakfast.*

Lagos

47 km (29 miles) southwest of Monchique, 70 km (43 miles) northwest of Faro.

Breezy and cool in every sense of the word, Lagos has an infectious energy and a laid-back feel. This bustling fishing port has many buildings—the Slave Market, Castelo dos Governadores, Forte Ponta da Bandeira, and Igreja de Santo António, to name a few—that evoke the town's long history. The cobblestone streets have a broad assortment of restaurants and bars, and pristine beaches with big waves are nearby.

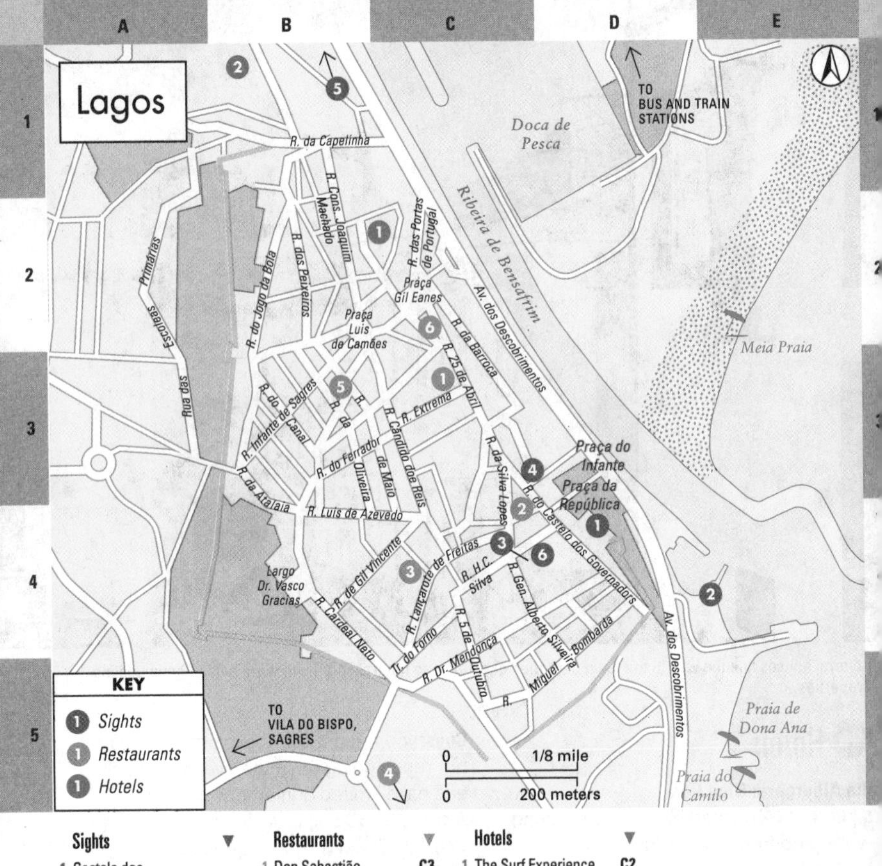

Sights

1. Castelo dos Governadores........... D4
2. Forte da Ponta da Bandeira E4
3. Igreja de Santo António............ C4
4. Mercado de Escravos.................. C3
5. Monte da Casteleja..... B1
6. Museu Municipal Dr José Formosinho............. D4

Restaurants

1. Don Sebastião C3
2. Mar.........................C4
3. No Patio...................C4
4. O Camilo C5
5. O Galeão................. B3
6. Piri-Piri....................C2

Hotels

1. The Surf Experience.....C2
2. Tivoli Lagos Algarve Resort.......... B1

GETTING HERE AND AROUND

Lagos is 80 km (50 miles) from the Faro airport, and you can get here via bus, train, or taxi. The train and bus stations are near each other as well as the marina, from which most of the city can be explored on foot. Alternatively, you can use the local bus system called Onda, which follows 10 routes around town. The tourist train, which departs from the marina, is another great way to see the town.

ESSENTIALS

BUS CONTACTS Onda. ☎ *282 762 944* 🌐 *aonda.pt.*

TAXI CONTACT Lagos Taxi Transfers. ☎ *308 801 277.*

VISITOR INFORMATION Lagos Tourist Office. ✉ *Praça Gil Eanes* ☎ *282 763 031* 🌐 *www.visitalgarve.pt.*

Sights

Castelo dos Governadores (*Governor's Palace*)
HISTORIC SITE | It was from the Manueline window of this palace that the young king Dom Sebastião is said to have addressed his troops before setting off on his crusade of 1578. The palace is long gone, though the section of wall with the famous window remains and can be seen in the northwest corner of the Praça do Infante. The crusade was one of Portugal's greatest-ever disasters, with the king and some 8,000 soldiers killed in Morocco at Alcácer-Quibir. (Dom Sebastião is further remembered by a much-maligned, modernistic statue that stands in Praça Gil Eanes.) ✉ *Praça do Infante.*

Forte da Ponta da Bandeira (*Ponta da Bandeira Fort*)
MILITARY SITE | This 17th-century fort defended the entrance to the harbor in bygone days. From inside you can look out at sweeping ocean views. For an interesting perspective on the rock formations and grottoes of the area's shoreline, take one of the short boat trips offered by the fishermen near the Ponta da Bandeira. ✉ *Av. dos Descobrimentos* ☎ *282 761 410* 🎫 *€3* 🕒 *Closed Mon.*

★ **Igreja de Santo António** (*Church of St. Anthony*)
RELIGIOUS SITE | This early-18th-century baroque building is Lagos's most extraordinary structure. Its interior is a riot of gilt extravagance made possible by the import of gold from Brazil. Dozens of cherubs and angels clamber over the walls, among fancifully carved woodwork and azulejos. ✉ *Entrance via Museu Regional, Rua General Alberto Silveira* ☎ *282 762 301* 🎫 *€3, includes entry to Museu Municipal Dr. José Formosinho* 🕒 *Closed Mon.*

Mercado de Escravos (*Slave Market*)
HISTORIC SITE | Prince Henry the Navigator brought the first African slaves to Portugal for his personal use in 1441. He later established a slave market in West Africa to cope with increasingly large and barbaric slave auctions, and by 1455 around 800 slaves were transported to Portugal each year. The first African slave market in Europe was held under the arches of the old Casa da Alfândega. The building now contains a museum that looks at the history of slavery in the Algarve. ✉ *Praça do Infante Dom Henrique* 🌐 *www.cm-lagos.pt* 🎫 *€4* 🕒 *Closed Mon.*

★ **Monte da Casteleja**
WINERY/DISTILLERY | The motto at this family-run winery—one of the only Algarvian vineyards to produce organic wines—is "think global, drink local." Guided tours and wine-tasting sessions are available by appointment. ✉ *Monte da Casteleja* ☎ *282 798 408* 🌐 *www.montecasteleja.com* 🎫 *€12.50 guided tour* 🕒 *Closed weekends.*

Museu Municipal Dr. José Formosinho (*Dr. José Formosinho Municipal Museum*)
MUSEUM | This small regional museum has an amusing jumble of exhibits,

including mosaics, archaeological and ethnological items, and a town charter from 1504—all arranged haphazardly. ✉ *Rua General Alberto Silveira* ☎ *282 762 301* *€3, includes entry to Igreja de Santo António* ⏲ *Closed Mon.*

Beaches

Meia Praia

BEACH—SIGHT | Curving like a crescent moon the entire distance between Lagos and Alvor, Meia Praia is the largest beach in the area and one of the best centers for water sports. The golden sand extends for 4 km (2½ miles), and the water is calm and clear. You can walk to it from Lagos city center in less than five minutes by crossing the footbridge, but there's also a bus from the riverfront Avenida dos Descobrimentos and a summer-only ferry service a few hundred yards from Forte Ponta da Bandeira. Certain portions are popular with nudists. **Amenities:** food and drink; lifeguards; parking (no fee); showers. **Best for:** nudists; solitude; swimming; walking; windsurfing. ✉ *2 km (1 mile) east of Lagos city center, off M534.*

★ Praia de Dona Ana

BEACH—SIGHT | This beautiful beach has calm, turquoise waters that are perfect for snorkeling and cave-riddled cliffs that can be visited on boat tours. You can reach Praia de Dona Ana by car or on an enjoyable 30-minute walk along a cliff top. This small beach can get packed, especially when the tide comes in and the sand disappears. Parking is difficult and the steep steps down to the sand can be trying, but it's worth the effort to visit what has been voted one of the most beautiful beaches in the world. **Amenities:** food and drink; lifeguards. **Best for:** snorkeling. ✉ *Alameda Dr. Armando Soares Ribeiro, 1 km (½ mile) south of Lagos city center.*

★ Praia do Camilo

BEACH—SIGHT | They say the best things come in small packages, and that's certainly the case here. A short way beyond Praia de Dona Ana, little Praia do Camilo is a hugely popular cove. Just beyond it is the Ponta da Piedade, a much-photographed group of rock arches and grottoes. Praia do Camilo is accessed via a long, wooden walkway through picturesque cliffs. At the top of the cliff restaurant O Camilo offers stunning views over the beach. **Amenities:** none. **Best for:** snorkeling. ✉ *South of Praia Dona Ana.*

Restaurants

Dom Sebastião

$$$ | **PORTUGUESE** | Traditional Portuguese cooking (especially charcoal-grilled fish) is the draw here. You can dine at elegant candlelit tables inside or on a sidewalk out front. **Known for:** fish presented tableside before being prepared; interesting local wine list; unobtrusive service. [$] *Average main: €25* ✉ *Rua 25 de Abril 20-22* ☎ *282 780 480* 🌐 *www.restaurantedonsebastiao.com.*

Mar

$$$ | **PORTUGUESE** | Overlooking the dramatic Praia da Batata, this restaurant has a simple but lovely dining room and a very popular outdoor terrace. A variety of fresh fish is available, including a whole fried fish that locals swear by. **Known for:** perfect place to sample local dishes; great views from the terrace; leisurely vibe. [$] *Average main: €22* ✉ *Av. Descobrimentos* ☎ *282 788 006.*

No Patio

$$ | **ECLECTIC** | Despite the misleading name, this cheerful restaurant actually does have lovely patio (the name translates roughly as "in the courtyard"). The chefs incorporate premium local produce in dishes that have an international flair. **Known for:** alfresco dining at its finest; perfect place for a romantic meal; modern takes on lamb and duck. [$] *Average*

A long wooden walkway leads down to spectacular Camilo Beach in Lagos.

main: €17 ✉ Rua Lançarote de Freitas 46 r/c ☎ 282 763 777 ⏲ Closed Sun. and Mon.

★ O Camilo

$$ | SEAFOOD | If you're looking for fresh fish and a view of the ocean, you can't do much better than this smart restaurant above beautiful Praia do Camilo. Along with fish that's just come from the market, clams, slipper lobsters, and oysters from Ria de Alvor are all local and prepared with skill. **Known for:** reserve a table on the terrace or be prepared to wait; order the seafood cataplanas a day ahead; the day's catch is displayed on ice. *$ Average main: €20 ✉ Praia do Camilo, Estrada da Ponta da Piedade ☎ 282 763 845 🌐 restaurantecamilo.pt ⏲ Closed 2 wks in Nov.*

O Galeão

$ | ITALIAN | Tucked away on a backstreet you'll find this bustling local favorite—it's so popular that you'll wait in line unless you've booked a table well in advance. It has an extensive menu of regional, national, and international dishes from land and sea. **Known for:** reasonably priced wine list; delicious seafood stew; friendly atmosphere. *$ Average main: €15 ✉ Rua da Laranjeira 1 ☎ 282 763 909 ⏲ Closed Tues.*

Piri-Piri

$ | PORTUGUESE | On one of the main streets running through town, this low-key restaurant has an inexpensive but extensive menu. The long list of Portuguese dishes includes a variety of market-fresh fish, but the specialty is the zesty piri-piri chicken that gives the restaurant its name. **Known for:** you've got to try the chicken; moderate prices; speedy service. *$ Average main: €13 ✉ Rua Lima Leitão 15 ☎ 282 763 803.*

Hotels

The Surf Experience

$ | B&B/INN | This spacious, centrally located lodging is open to all who have an interest in surfing, regardless of age. **Pros:** board repair and other must-have amenities for surfers; packages includes meals and airport transfers; great place to meet other travelers. **Cons:** not as much fun for nonsurfers; three-night minimum stay; some rooms have shared baths. *Rooms from: €63 Rua dos Ferreiros 21 919 830 591 Mon., Tues., and Thurs., 916 137 082 Wed., Fri., and Sun. www.surf-experience.com 8 rooms Free Breakfast.*

Tivoli Lagos Algarve Resort
$$ | **HOTEL** | On the eastern edge of the old town, this centrally located hotel has an unusual layout strung across several levels with gardens, lounges, and patios. **Pros:** has its own summer-only beach restaurant and bar; three outdoor pools, including one just for kids; great base for exploring the old town. **Cons:** rooms and public areas are a bit blah; no tea or coffee in the rooms; not enough sunbeds on beach. *Rooms from: €180 Rua António Crisógno dos Santos 282 790 079 www.tivolihotels.com 296 rooms Free Breakfast.*

Nightlife

Bon Vivant
BARS/PUBS | There are a number of boisterous bars at the end of Rua 25 de Abril, most playing music that's brutally loud. Perhaps the most refined of these is Bon Vivant, which has four distinct bar areas and a rooftop terrace way above the din. *Rua 25 de Abril 105 935 718 305.*

★ Mullen's
BARS/PUBS | With wine casks lined up against one wall, this friendly local place has an enthusiastic staff to help keep things swinging until the early morning. *Rua Cândido dos Reis 86 915 045 650 www.mullens-lagos.com.*

Stevie Ray's
MUSIC CLUBS | This lounge is dedicated to blues, jazz, and soul. You can listen while quaffing imported beers and sparkling wine. *Rua Senhora da Graça 9 282 760 673 Closed Sun. and Mon.*

Activities

BOAT TOURS

Algarve Dolphins
WILDLIFE-WATCHING | If you want to spot dolphins in the wild, and do so with a company that supports their well-being, then hop aboard a 90-minute trip with Algarve Dolphins. They guarantee that you'll see dolphins or get another trip for free. Trips depart from Lagos Marina. *Av. Descobrimentos 19 282 764 144 www.algarve-dolphins.com.*

Seafaris
BOATING | Dolphin-watching boat tours depart daily from the Lagos Marina. You can also head to one of the many caves formed by waves crashing into the Algarve's scenic seaside cliffs. Sailing charters, deep-sea fishing excursions, and water-taxi services can be arranged as well. *Marina de Lagos, Loja 5 282 798 727 www.seafaris.net.*

Praia da Luz

6 km (4 miles) west of Lagos, 96 km (60 miles) west of Faro.

Although the fishing boats that were once ubiquitous on these shores are long gone, this is still an agreeable waterfront destination. At the western edge of town is a little church that faces an 18th-century fortress that once guarded against pirates.

GETTING HERE AND AROUND

Praia da Luz is about an hour from the Faro airport by car, and driving is the easiest way to get around town. A regular bus service runs from Faro, stopping right outside the picturesque, seaside church. You can also take the train to Lagos, and then catch a taxi or bus to Praia da Luz.

ESSENTIALS

TAXI CONTACTS Lagos Taxis. *282 583 230.*

Beaches

Praia de Salema

BEACH—SIGHT | The low-key fishing village of Salema, 5 km (3 miles) west of Burgau, is blessed with a 1,970-foot-long beach at the base of green hills. The long, golden strand has cliffs at either end. This area is also popular among hikers for its vast range of trails and breathtaking views. **Amenities:** food and drink; parking (no fee). **Best for:** swimming; walking. ✉ *Travessa do Miramar.*

Praia do Burgau

BEACH—SIGHT | Four kilometers (2½ miles) west of Praia da Luz is Burgau, a fishing village with narrow, steep streets leading to the strand. Although the town has succumbed to the wave of tourism that has swept over the Algarve, its fine beach remains unchanged. High, sloping hills encase the beach, protecting it from the northern winds. **Amenities:** food and drink; parking (fee and no fee). **Best for:** snorkeling. ✉ *Rua 25 de Abril, 4 km (2½ miles) west of Praia da Luz.*

Restaurants

Cabanas Beach Restaurant

$$$ | **INTERNATIONAL** | If you take the rough road west from Burgau, and then an even rougher one down to the Praia Almadena, you'll be rewarded with this delightful hideaway on a deserted cove. The menu features plenty of seafood, including mussels, shrimp, and tuna, along with delicious gourmet burgers. **Known for:** interesting dishes meant to be shared; beach chairs for after-lunch relaxing; play area for children. [$] *Average main: €22* ✉ *Praia Almadena* ☎ *968 871 974* 🌐 *www.cabanasbeachrestaurant.com.*

Hotels

Hotel Belavista da Luz

$$ | **HOTEL** | This family-owned hilltop hotel's horseshoe configuration gives all the spacious guest quarters great sea views. **Pros:** plenty of child-friendly amenities; staff prepared to go the extra mile; walking distance to town. **Cons:** some find the area too quiet; could use a beach shuttle; very hard beds. [$] *Rooms from: €185* ✉ *Praia da Luz* ☎ *282 788 655* 🌐 *www.belavistadaluz.com* *45 rooms* *Free Breakfast.*

Quinta do Mar da Luz

$ | **RESORT** | Set within verdant gardens dotted with sculptures, this holiday village west of Praia da Luz offers a calm, peaceful ambience. **Pros:** spectacular views along the walk to Burgau; three pools, one reserved for children; well-stocked breakfast buffet. **Cons:** no on-site restaurant; you need a car to get around; charge for extra bed. [$] *Rooms from: €130* ✉ *Sítio Cama da Vaca* ☎ *282 697 323* 🌐 *www.quintamarluz.com* *20 rooms, 40 apartments* *Free Breakfast.*

Sagres

30 km (18 miles) southwest of Praia da Luz, 116 km (72 miles) west of Faro.

Sagres has several golden beaches, making this a popular destination despite the fact that the water is always pretty chilly. The massive Fortaleza de Sagres (Sagres Fort) is worth a detour, especially if you have kids who love to explore.

GETTING HERE AND AROUND

Buses are infrequent, so renting a car is recommended for those wishing to travel to the Algarve's westernmost tip. Driving to Sagres takes approximately two hours from Faro.

ESSENTIALS

VISITOR INFORMATION Sagres Tourist Information. ✉ *Rua Comandante Matoso* ☎ *282 624 873* 🌐 *www.visitalgarve.pt.*

★ **Fortaleza de Sagres** (*Sagres Fort*)
MILITARY SITE | FAMILY | The views from the Sagres Fortress, an enormous run of defensive walls high above the crashing waves, are spectacular. Its massive walls and battlements make it popular with kids. The importance of this area dates to as early as the 4th century BC, when Mediterranean seafarers found it to be the last sheltered port before the wild winds of the Atlantic. In the late 8th century, according to local religious tradition, the mortal remains of the 4th-century martyr of Zaragoza, St. Vincent, washed up here. This led to a Vincentine cult that attracted pilgrims until the destruction of the sanctuary in the mid-12th century. The fortress was rebuilt in the 17th century, and although some historians have claimed that it was the site for Prince Henry's famous navigation school, it's more likely that Henry built his school at Cabo São Vicente. But this doesn't detract from the powerful atmosphere. Certainly the **Venta da Rosa** ("Rose of the Winds," a sundial-like stone whose purpose is still unknown) dates to Prince Henry's period. The small chapel of Nossa Senhora da Graça is of the same age. ✉ *Sagres.*

Praia da Baleeira
BEACH—SIGHT | This small, pretty beach is next to the fishing port is dotted with rocks and the sand is not the finest. On top of that, the beach can get quite windy, meaning this is not the most popular spot for sunbathers. Yet it is the perfect spot to sit and watch the fishing boats sailing in and out of the port. **Amenities:** none. **Best for:** solitude; sunset. ✉ *Baleeira Port, ½ km (¼ mile) east of Sagres.*

Praia do Martinhal
BEACH—SIGHT | This long, soft stretch of sand is adjacent to Praia da Baleeira, and hosts several professional surfing events each year. Good wave formations make it very popular among local surf enthusiasts. **Amenities:** lifeguards; parking (no fee). **Best for:** sunrise; sunset; surfing; windsurfing. ✉ *Baleeira Port, 1 km (½ mile) east of Sagres.*

Restaurants

O Retiro do Pescador
$ | PORTUGUESE | With a name that means "fisherman's retreat," this casual eatery serves some of the most flavorful fresh fish in Sagres. The homemade brandy is worth a try, as are the typical regional desserts prepared by the owner's family. **Known for:** opt for anything that comes off the grill; plenty of outdoor seating; homemade desserts. $ *Average main: €14* ✉ *Vale das Silvas* ☎ *282 624 438* ⊙ *Closed Mon., and late Oct.–early Mar.*

Vila Velha
$$ | PORTUGUESE | From the terrace of this laid-back eatery you can watch the sunset over Cabo São Vicente. The traditional Portuguese cuisine here is made from top-quality ingredients, and the recipes have been updated for modern tastes. **Known for:** the bread and just about everything else is homemade; excellent service from the multilingual staff; good range of vegetarian options. $ *Average main: €20* ✉ *Rua Patrão Antonio Faustino* ☎ *282 624 788* 🌐 *www.vilavelha-sagres.com* ⊙ *No lunch. Closed Mon., 2 wks before Christmas, and early Jan.–mid-Feb.*

★ **Martinhal Sagres Beach Family Resort**
$$$$ | RESORT | FAMILY | Direct access to a lovely beach is one of the main perks at this family-friendly resort, which was designed with children in mind with playgrounds and kiddie pools. **Pros:** resort features three laudable restaurants; villas are a great way to take the whole family; individually decorated rooms. **Cons:** not

ideal for those without children; many hills and cobbled walkways; expensive food options. $ *Rooms from: €388* ✉ *Quinta do Martinhal, Apartado 54* ☎ *282 240 200* 🌐 *www.martinhal.com* *238 rooms* *Free Breakfast.*

Pousada Sagres

$$$ | B&B/INN | Occupying a two-story country house across the bay from Fortaleza de Sagres, Pousada Sagres has homey guest rooms, most with balconies and full or partial views of the sea and the craggy cliffs. **Pros:** the well-respected restaurant serves accomplished cuisine; loads of atmosphere and charm; pretty pool area. **Cons:** not as small or intimate as some pousadas; not all rooms have great views; rates can be pricey. $ *Rooms from: €235* ✉ *Ponta da Atalaia, on headland between fishing harbor and Praia da Mareta* ☎ *282 620 240* 🌐 *www.pousadas.pt* *51 rooms* *Free Breakfast.*

Nightlife

Chiringuito Praia da Mareta

BARS/PUBS | This loud, lively beachfront bar is on the list for most merrymakers passing through Sagres. It also claims to be the last place you can get a drink before Madeira. ✉ *Road to Praia da Mareta* ☎ *282 624 113.*

Cabo São Vicente

6 km (4 miles) northwest of Sagres, 123 km (76 miles) west of Faro.

At the southwest tip of Europe, where the land juts starkly into the rough Atlantic, is Cabo São Vicente, called "O Fim do Mundo" ("The End of the World") by early Portuguese mariners. Legends attach themselves easily to this desolate place, which the Romans once considered sacred (they believed it was where the spirits of the light lived because with sunset the light disappeared). It takes its modern name from the martyr St. Vincent, whose relics were brought here in the 8th century; it's said that they were transported to Lisbon 400 years later in a boat guided by ravens. This is not the crowded, overdeveloped Algarve of the south coast. From here you can see the spectacular cliff tops at Murração looking onto seemingly endless deserted beaches. Vast flocks of migratory birds round Cape St. Vincent and the Sagres headlands each year with a navigational precision that would have astounded Columbus. He learned how to navigate at Prince Henry's school after the armed convoy he was traveling with was attacked by pirates off Cape St. Vincent in 1476. Sixteen years later he set sail from here to discover the Americas.

GETTING HERE AND AROUND

Lack of adequate public transportation means renting a car is the only option.

Sights

★ **Farol de São Vicente** (*St. Vincent Lighthouse*)

LIGHTHOUSE | The views from outside this lighthouse are remarkable, and the beacon is said to have the strongest reflectors in Europe—they cast a beam 96 km (60 miles) out to sea. Turquoise water whips across the base of the rust-color cliffs below; the fortress at Sagres is visible to the east; and in the distance lies the immense Atlantic. There's a small museum and café on-site if you want to linger. ✉ *End of N268* 🌐 *www.faros.pt.*

Beaches

Praia do Amado

BEACH—SIGHT | At almost 13 km (8 miles) in length, Portugal's best surfing beach has enough room for the dozens of surfing camps and schools that have sprung up around it. The water is cool and rocky toward the western tip. The area surrounding the beach lacks basic facilities like garbage cans, so sometimes waste

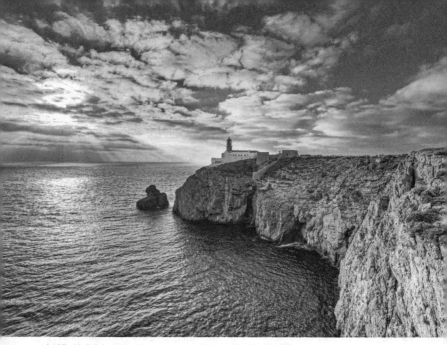

A cliff-side lighthouse creates a photo-worthy scene in Cabo São Vicente.

is scattered around, spoiling an otherwise beautiful beach. **Amenities:** parking (no fee). **Best for:** surfing, windsurfing. ✉ *Parque Natural do Sudoeste Alentejano e Costa Vicentina, 6 km (3 miles) from Vila do Bispo, Vila do Bispo.*

São Brás de Alportel

18 km (11 miles) northwest of Olhão.

Peace and tranquility rule in São Brás, a destination that melds old-fashioned charm with modern amenities. Once the Algarve's largest cork-producing town, it is now more dependent on tourism than trees. A traditional costume museum, a multicultural arts center, and a public picnic area along the sparkling Fonte Férrea springs give visitors a reason to linger.

GETTING HERE AND AROUND

The best way to get to this area is by bus, as the train will only take you as far as Loulé or Faro. A taxi from Faro would cost approximately €30 and would take around 25 minutes, while one from Loulé would be slightly quicker and cheaper.

ESSENTIALS

BUS CONTACT São Brás Bus Terminal. ✉ *Rua João Louro* ☎ *289 842 286.*

TAXI CONTACT Auto Taxis de São Brás. ✉ *Av. Liberdade 43* ☎ *289 842 611.*

VISITOR INFORMATION São Brás de Alportel Tourist Office. ✉ *Largo de S. Sebastião 23* ☎ *289 843 165* 🌐 *www.visitalgarve.pt.*

Sights

Museu do Traje (*Costume Museum*)
MUSEUM | If fashion is your thing, then you'll love this collection of charmingly old-fashioned regional outfits from bygone eras. A short walk from the center of town, it's a great place to learn about the customs of various parts of the country. ✉ *Rua Dr. José Dias Sancho 61* ☎ *289 840 100* 🌐 *www.museu-sbras.com* 🎟 *€2.*

Hotels

Pousada Palácio de Estoi
$$$ | **HOTEL** | About 8 km (5 miles) from São Brás, Pousada Palácio de Estoi provides a comfortable base for exploring the region. **Pros:** rooms have balconies with garden views; lovely pool area; stunning views. **Cons:** quality of restaurant food could be better; need a car to reach the beaches; service can be hit-or-miss. *Rooms from: €245* ✉ *Rua São José, Estói* ☎ *210 407 620* 🌐 *www.pousadas.pt* *63 rooms* *Free Breakfast.*

Olhão

19 km (12 miles) southeast of São Brás de Alportel, 8 km (5 miles) east of Faro.

Visit Olhão's Mercado dos Pescadores (Fish Market) and you'll see why this town is synonymous with fish. Modern construction has marred much of its charm, but the fishing port (the Algarve's largest) is still a colorful glimpse of the past. It's become something of an artists' colony, and sights like the Olhão Art Walls are well worth a look.

GETTING HERE AND AROUND

Olhão can be reached by bus or train from anywhere in the Algarve, though those coming from the western end of the region may have to change buses in Albufeira or Faro.

ESSENTIALS

VISITOR INFORMATION Olhão Tourist Office. ✉ *Largo Sebastião Martins Mestre 6A* ☎ *289 713 936* 🌐 *www.visitalgarve.pt.*

Sights

Associação Cultural Re-Criativa (*Re-Creative Cultural Association*)
MUSEUM | Inside a handsome 19th-century building that was rescued by a group of local artists, this cutural center has lively art openings, interesting concerts, and a sociable small-town bar. ✉ *Av. da República 14* ☎ *289 147 308* 🌐 *www.re-criativarepublica14.pt.*

Festival do Marisco (*Shellfish Festival*)
FESTIVAL | This annual festival is a must for those who are in the Algarve in mid-August. The event, which lasts four to six days, attracts top musicians, and the food on offer features renowned delicacies from the sea. ✉ *Olhão* ☎ *289 090 287* 🌐 *www.festivaldomarisco.com* *€7–€9.*

★ **Olhão Art Walls**
NEIGHBORHOOD | Four local street artists turned the dilapidated walls of the disused Largo da Fábrica Velha into an outdoor art gallery of gorgeous black-and-white murals that depict local fishing traditions. In many cases, the artists worked from period photos, and some locals say they can recognize their parents in the scenes. ✉ *Rua da Fábrica Velha.*

Villa Romana de Milreu (*Milreu Roman Ruins*)
ARCHAEOLOGICAL SITE | The ruins at Milreu, about 10 km (6 miles) northwest of Olhão, were first excavated in 1877. The settlement once known as Roman Ossonoba—including a temple (later converted into a Christian basilica) and mosaic fragments adorning some of the 3rd-century baths—date back to the 2nd through 6th centuries. ✉ *R. de Faro, Estói* ☎ *289 997 823* 🌐 *monumentos-doalgarve.pt* *€2* *Closed Mon.*

Beaches

Adding to the allure of area beaches is the fact that this entire section of coastline—including islands and river inlets—has been designated as a nature reserve, due to the great number of migratory birds that flock in while winging south for the winter. To reach beaches on the nearby islands, take a ferry from the jetty at the east end of the municipal gardens. A small kiosk there posts timetables and sells tickets. If it's closed, buy the tickets on board. From June to September, ferries run about every hour each day; from October through May, there are three or four trips daily. The fare is about €4 round-trip.

Ilha da Armona

BEACH—SIGHT | Tiny white vacation villas dot the pedestrian-only Ilha da Armona, a small island 15 minutes by boat from Olhão. About 9 km (5½ miles) long and just under 1 km (½ mile) wide, the island has some fine, isolated stretches of sand, as well as cafés and bars. It's popular among those who long for a quiet respite from the buzzing throngs of tourists. A wide range of water sports is available, but many people just explore the sandy dunes by foot. **Amenities:** food and drink; showers; toilets; water sports. **Best for:** surfing; walking. *Olhão.*

Ilha da Culatra

BEACH—SIGHT | Sandy Ilha da Culatra is crisscrossed with wooden walkways that guide visitors around the island. It has several ramshackle fishing communities, a number of tasty seafood restaurants, and, at the southern village of Farol, agreeable beaches. Some stretches are supervised by lifeguards, others are not. The car-free island is 15 minutes by ferry from Olhão, and the boat trip itself is a pleasant experience. **Amenities:** food and drink; lifeguards (some). **Best for:** walking. *Olhão.*

Restaurants

7imeio Wine Bar

$ | INTERNATIONAL | With its quirky interior illuminated by dozens of pendant lamps, this lively tapas bar—with inventive cuisine and fine wines—is popular with locals for a big night out. There's a strong focus on Portuguese wines, but the menu ranges further afield, including sushi rolls, shrimp tempura, chicken gyozas. **Known for:** good selection of wines by the glass; bartenders serve creative cocktails; festive vibe. *Average main: €15 Av. 5 de Outubro 38–40 965 258 266 www.7imeiowinebar.com.*

Hotels

Casa Modesta

$$ | B&B/INN | Occupying a building dating from the 1940s, this family-run hotel on the outskirts of Olhão is both rustic and rural, stylish and cosmpolitan. **Pros:** owners have a strong emphasis on sustainable practices; common room warmed by wood-burning oven; freshly baked breads for breakfast. **Cons:** location is outside the city center; not many amenities; small beds. *Rooms from: €200 Quatrum do Sul 289 701 096 www.casamodesta.pt 9 rooms Free Breakfast.*

★ **Vila Monte Farm House**

$$$$ | HOTEL | The Mediterranean-style buildings, lushly planted grounds, and personalized service at Vila Monte Farm House offer a soothing antidote to the sprawling resorts closer to the coast. **Pros:** soak up the relaxed vibe at two pretty swimming pools; two excellent restaurants serving local cuisine; shuttle to nearby beach. **Cons:** need a car to travel around the area; lacks common amenities like a spa; location feels a little remote. *Rooms from: €360 Sitio dos Caliços, Moncarapacho 289 790 790 www.vilamonte.com 55 rooms Free Breakfast.*

Shopping

Mercado dos Pescadores

FOOD/CANDY | One of the Algarve's best food markets, the Mercado dos Pescadores is held in the riverfront buildings in the town gardens. Feast your eyes on the shellfish for which Olhão is renowned; mussels, in particular, are a local specialty. *Av. 5 de Octubre.*

Tavira

28 km (17 miles) east of Olhão, 38 km (24 miles) east of Faro.

With its castle ruins, riverfront gardens, and atmospheric streets, Tavira—at the mouth of the quiet Rio Gilão—is immediately endearing. Many of the town's white 18th-century houses retain their original doorways and coats of arms; others are topped with unusual, four-sided "roof screens," and still others are completely covered in tiles. The town also has more than 30 churches, most dating to the 17th and 18th centuries. One of two river crossings—the low bridge adjacent to the arcaded Praça da República—is of Roman origin, although it was rebuilt in the 17th century and again in recent times after sustaining damage in a flood.

GETTING HERE AND AROUND

Tavira is easily reached by any form of public transport. Once in Tavira there are several types of local transit—including boats and a tourist train—that make touring the city entertaining and enjoyable.

ESSENTIALS

TOUR CONTACTS Delgaturis Tourist Train. ☎ *289 389 067* 🌐 *www.delgaturis.com.* **Séqua Boat Tours.** ☎ *963 106 248* 🌐 *www.sequatours.com.* **Tavira Tours.** ☎ *960 170 789* 🌐 *www.taviratours.com.*

VISITOR INFORMATION Tavira Tourist Office. ✉ *Praça da República 5* ☎ *281 322 511* 🌐 *www.visitalgarve.pt.*

Sights

Castelo de Tavira (*Tavira Castle*)
CASTLE/PALACE | From the battlemented walls of the ruined 13th-century castle you can look down over Tavira's many church spires and across the river delta to the sea. ✉ *Largo Abu-Otmane, off Rua da Liberdade* 🎫 *Free.*

Tavira's Unique Architecture

Take a moment while you're exploring Tavira to look up and admire the peculiar four-sided roofs which rise like pyramids—locals refer to them as roof screens. These unique architectural elements appeared in the late 19th and early 20th centuries. As the town's prosperity grew, so did the popularity of the screens, which are said to project the house's exterior face. The screens are also deemed important elements in the characterization and individualization of the building.

Igreja da Misericórdia (*Mercy Church*)
RELIGIOUS SITE | Widely considered one of the most remarkable examples of the Renaissance movement in the Algarve, this structure has a portal that dates to 1541. ✉ *R. Damião Augusto de Brito Vasconcelos 2, west of Praça da República.*

Santa Maria do Castelo (*St. Mary of the Castle*)
RELIGIOUS SITE | One of the town's two major churches, Santa Maria was built on the site of a Moorish mosque in the 13th century. Although it was almost entirely destroyed by the 1755 earthquake, the church retains its original Gothic doorway. ✉ *Alto de Santa Maria.*

Torre de Tavira (*Tavira Tower*)
VIEWPOINT | This old water tower was converted into a camera obscura of the Leonardo da Vinci fashion in 1931. An oversize photographic camera here takes images of the panoramic views it commands of the town. The visit makes a fascinating exploration into the world of photography and a cool, shady afternoon retreat from the sweltering afternoon sunshine. ✉ *Calçado da Galeria 12* ☎ *281*

322 527 *www.torredetavira.com* €5 *Closed Sat. and Sun.*

 Beaches

★ Ilha de Tavira

BEACH—SIGHT | Directly offshore and extending west for some 11 km (7 miles) is the Ilha de Tavira, a long sandbar with several pleasant beaches. Ferries costing €2 round-trip run to the island every half hour in July and August and every hour May through June and September through mid-October. The island has been awarded a Blue Flag, indicating quality and cleanliness. Several good restaurants and bars are also on the island. **Amenities:** food and drink; lifeguards; showers; toilets; water sports. **Best for:** partiers; nudists; sunrise; sunset. ✉ *Tavira* *www.cm-tavira.pt.*

Praia de Manta Rota

BEACH—SIGHT | About 12 km (7 miles) east of Tavira, Praia da Manta Rota is a small community with a few bars, restaurants, and hotels. But locals swear it has the best beach in the Algarve. Its warm waters and white sands are a magnet for sun worshippers. One particularly nice strand is the offshore sandbar at the village of Cacela Velha. From Manta Rota to Faro the underwater drop-offs are often steep and you can quickly find yourself in deep water. **Amenities:** lifeguards. **Best for:** walking. ✉ *Rua da Praia da Manta Rota.*

 Restaurants

★ Noélia e Jerónimo

$$ | **PORTUGUESE** | Whenever Portugal's most prestigous chefs take their summer holidays in the Algarve, they end up here. From the outside, Noélia's restaurant (which she shares with her partner, Jerónimo) looks like just another unassuming local place, but inside the flavors sing and the senses are delighted, particularly with the tomato rice with seafood or, to be even more indulgent, the rice with champagne and local oysters. **Known for:** beautifully presented dishes; draws foodies from all over; open-air dining room. *Average main: €17* ✉ *Rua da Fortaleza, Edifício Cabanas-Mar, Loja 6* ☎ *281 370 649* *Closed Wed.*

Ponto de Encontro

$ | **PORTUGUESE** | Crossing the Roman bridge, you'll pass by a lot of tempting spots before you reach this typical Portuguese eatery—trust us, it's worth the trip. Here the focus is on fresh fish (the sole in almond sauce is a must-try). **Known for:** prices have remained down-to-earth; close to downtown attractions; efficient service. *Average main: €14* ✉ *Praça Dr. António Padinha 39* ☎ *281 323 730.*

Catch of the Day 

Because Tavira is a tuna-fishing port, you'll find plenty of local color and fresh fish; tuna steaks, often grilled and served with onions, are on restaurant menus all over town at remarkably low prices. In the harbor area, you can sample no-frills dining at its best, alongside the fishermen, at any of the café-restaurants across from the tangle of boats and nets.

 Hotels

★ Fazenda Nova

$$$$ | **HOTEL** | Explore the beaches and vineyards of the Algarve from this country residence and 25-acre farm featuring a swimming pool, fruit orchards, olive groves, and flower gardens. **Pros:** romantic and charming getaway; restaurant showcases local fare; 15 minutes from historic Tavira. **Cons:** two-night minimum stay (five in August); you need a car to explore the area; limited amenities. *Rooms from: €295 Estiramantens, Santo Estevao 281 961 913 www.fazendanova.eu 15 suites Free Breakfast.*

Hotel Vila Galé Albacora

$$ | **RESORT** | Occupying a converted tuna market, the Vila Galé Albacora is a charming hotel that sits at the confluence of two rivers. **Pros:** lovely location right on the water; two restaurants, two bars, and a spa; gorgeous swimming pool. **Cons:** waterfront location attracts insects; extra fees can really add up; shuttle to town doesn't run daily. *Rooms from: €185 Quatro Águas 281 380 800 www.vilagale.com 162 rooms Free Breakfast.*

Marés Residencial e Restaurante

$ | **B&B/INN** | Directly across from the pier (and convenient to the summer ferry to the Ilha de Tavira), this three-story hotel sits above a lively Portuguese restaurant sharing the same name. **Pros:** wonderful waterfront location; free parking a short walk away; sunny rooftop terrace. **Cons:** rooms above restaurant can be noisy; accommodations can feel a bit stark; no elevator to upper floors. *Rooms from: €107 Rua José Pires Padinha 134/140 281 325 815 www.residencialmares.com 24 rooms Free Breakfast.*

Activities

GOLF

★ Quinta de Cima

GOLF | Quite a challenge even for the pros, this course designed by Rocky Roquemore rewards length as well as accuracy in your shots. The difficulty is tempered by some wonderful views in a superb setting. Visitors are required to produce a handicap certificate. *Apartado 161, Vila Nova de Cacela 281 950 580 www.quintadaria.com €107 18 holes, 7202 yards, par 72.*

Vila Real de Santo António

22 km (14 miles) from Tavira, 62 km (39 miles) east of Faro.

This community on the Guadiana River is the last stop before Spain. Like most border towns, it's a lively place, with lots of bars and restaurants and some traffic-free central streets that encourage evening strolls. If you're interested in a short excursion across the border, visit Ayamonte, the town's Spanish counterpart. Just on the other side of the Guadiana River, Ayamonte can be reached during the day and early evening on a charmingly old-fashioned ferry.

GETTING HERE AND AROUND

On the Algarve's eastern end, Vila Real de Santo António is easiest reached by train. From here there's a ferry that carries both vehicles and passengers across the Guardiana River to Ayamonte, Spain. Ferries operate every 30 minutes in summer, less often the rest of the year. Alternatively, you can use a toll-free suspension bridge.

ESSENTIALS

TRAIN CONTACT Vila Real de Santo António Train Station. *Rua da Estação Velha 707 210 220 www.cp.pt.*

VISITOR INFORMATION Vila Real de Santo António Tourist Office. *Rua 5 de Outobro 16 281 510 000 www.visitalgarve.pt.*

TOURS

Riosul Travel

TOUR—SIGHT | This company arranges daylong river cruises to the timeless village of Foz de Odeleite. It also offers jeep safaris, guided walks, and sunset boat trips. *Rua Tristão Vaz Teixeira 15 C, Monte Gordo 281 510 200 www.riosultravel.com.*

Sky Xpedition

AIR EXCURSIONS | This new company offers sightseeing trips in a gyrocopter—a nifty lightweight contraption that is somewhat like a helicopter but smaller, lighter, quieter, and more fuel-efficient. That lets them fly over the Ria Formosa Natural Park, the salt beds of Castro Marim, and the villages along the coast. A 10-minute flight costs €60. ✉ *Pista da Praia Verde, N125, Monte Gordo* ☎ *919 445 868* 🌐 *www.skyxpedition.com.*

 Restaurants

Grand Beach Club

$$$ | INTERNATIONAL | This upscale restaurant and bar, which includes lounge chairs by the infinity pool as well as dining tables inside, is perched on a promontory at the mouth of the Guadiana River. The menu features standards like pizzas and burgers along with more local fare. **Known for:** extremely popular spot for sunset cocktails; cocktails with house-made infused liqueurs; tasty pizzas. $ *Average main: €21* ✉ *Ponta da Areia* ☎ 🌐 *www.grandhousealgarve.com* ⊗ *No dinner.*

Coração da Cidade Hospedaria

$ | HOTEL | This inn in the center of town has a rooftop terrace where you can enjoy the views. **Pros:** basic but spotless rooms; budget-minded rates; good for families. **Cons:** almost no amenities; could use an update; tiny rooms. $ *Rooms from: €65* ✉ *Rua Dr. Sousa Martins 17* ☎ *281 530 470* 🌐 *www.coracaodacidade.com* *21 rooms* 🍴 *Free Breakfast.*

Grand House

$$$$ | HOTEL | After being neglected for decades, the oldest hotel in the eastern Algarve—dating from 1926, when Vila Real de Santo António was the center of the tinned-fish trade—has been transformed into a luxury hotel. **Pros:** beautiful location across from the river; excellent fine-dining restaurant; gorgeous common areas. **Cons:** one of the pricier lodgings in the area; lacks common amenities like a spa; no fitness center. $ *Rooms from: €300* ✉ *Av. da Republica 171* ☎ *281 530 290* 🌐 *www.grandhousealgarve.com* *30 rooms* 🍴 *Free Breakfast.*

Chapter 8

COIMBRA AND THE BEIRAS

8

Updated by
Nora Wallaya

Sights	Restaurants	Hotels	Shopping	Nightlife
★★★☆☆	★★★★☆	★★★☆☆	★★★☆☆	★★★★☆

WELCOME TO COIMBRA AND THE BEIRAS

TOP REASONS TO GO

★ **Fall in love with fado music:** Sway to Coimbra's distinctively romantic style of fado at one of the city's atmospheric fado houses.

★ **Discover the most beautiful forest:** Head for the peaceful beauty of the Buçaco Forest, the country's most revered woods and a monastic retreat during the Middle Ages.

★ **Step back in time in Conímbriga:** Explore the extraordinary mosaics, fountains, and baths at Conímbriga, Portugal's best-preserved Roman site.

★ **Enjoy the sand between your toes:** Take a sunset walk along Portugal's biggest beach at Figueira, or grab a surfboard and ride the waves.

★ **Lace up those hiking boots:** Stride out and discover the vast Parque Natural da Sierra da Estrela, with its extensive, well-marked trails and stunning scenery.

1 **Coimbra.** One of Portugal's most intriguing cities.

2 **Condeixa-a-Velha.** Home to Conímbriga, an important Iberian Peninsula archaeological site.

3 **Montemor-o-Velho.** Impressive castle ruins between Coimbra and Figueira da Foz.

4 **Figueira da Foz.** The area's most famous seaside resort.

5 **Aveiro.** The Venice of Portugal.

6 **Ovar.** A string of beaches and sand dunes in the north.

7 **Curia.** A popular spa town with grand hotels.

8 **Luso.** Home to medicinal water and grand hotels.

9 **Viseu.** The heart of the Dao wine region.

10 **Belmonte.** Highlights include an ancient castle and church.

11 **Sortelha.** The area's best ancient fortified town.

12 **Castelo Branco.** A modern town with gardens, parks, and wide boulevards.

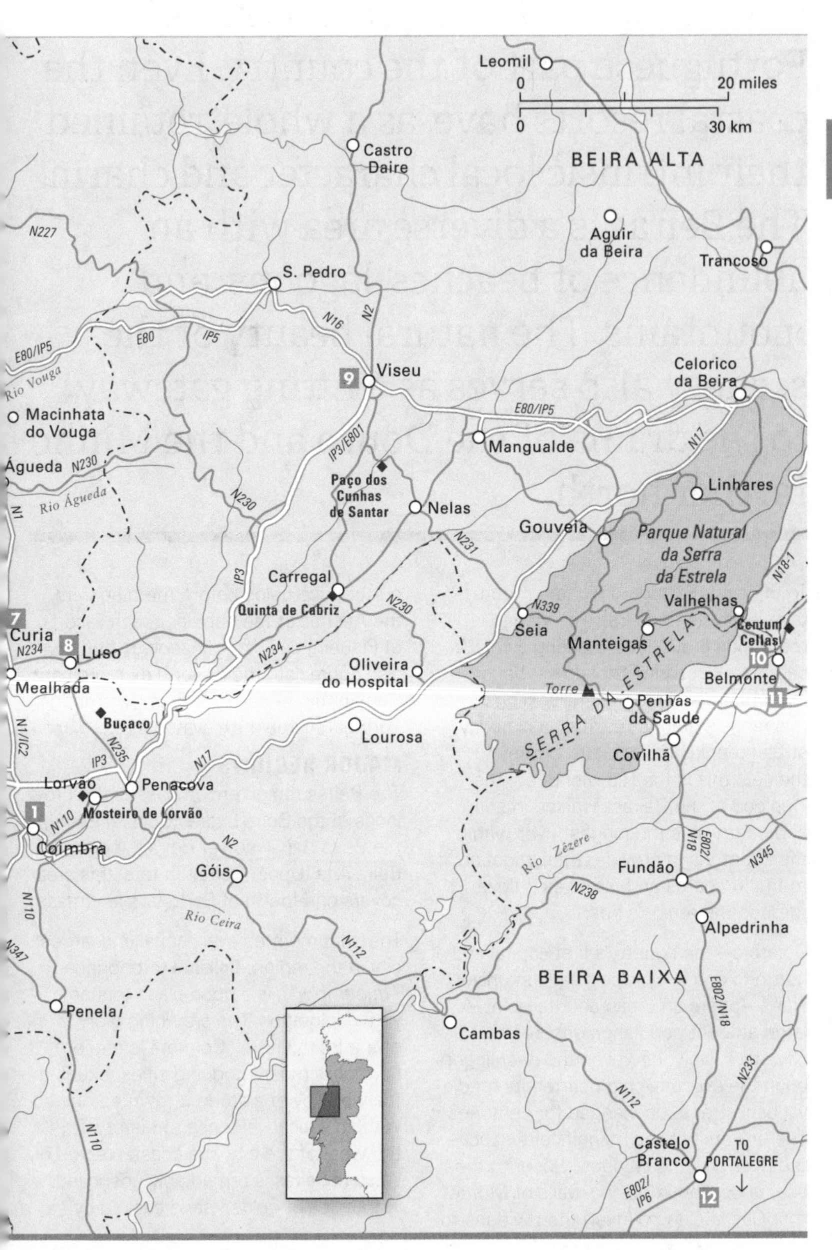
Leomil
0 20 miles
0 30 km
BEIRA ALTA
Castro Daire
Aguir da Beira
Trancoso
S. Pedro
N227
N16
N2
E80
IP5
E80/IP5
Rio Vouga
9 Viseu
Celorico da Beira
E80/IP5
Macinhata do Vouga
Mangualde
IP3/E801
N17
Águeda N230
Paço dos Cunhas de Santar
Linhares
Rio Águeda
N230
Nelas
Gouveia
Parque Natural da Serra da Estrela
N231
IP3
Carregal
N18-1
Quinta de Cabriz
N230
Valhelhas
N339
7 Curia
N234
8 Luso
N234
Seia
Manteigas
Centum Cellas
Oliveira do Hospital
10 Belmonte
Mealhada
Torre
Penhas da Saude
11
Buçaco
Lourosa
SERRA DA ESTRELA
N1/IC2
N235
IP3
N17
Covilhã
Lorvão
Penacova
1
Mosteiro de Lorvão
N110
Coimbra
N2
E802/N18
N345
Rio Zêzere
Fundão
Góis
N238
N110
Rio Ceira
Alpedrinha
N347
N112
BEIRA BAIXA
E802/N18
Penela
Cambas
N233
N112
N110
Castelo Branco
TO PORTALEGRE
E802/IP6
12

While frequently sidestepped by tourists, this region is arguably the most unspoiled and quintessentially Portuguese part of the country. Even the coastal resorts have, as a whole, retained their intrinsic local character and charm. The Beiras is a diverse area with an abundance of beaches, lagoons, and mountains. The natural beauty of the scenery also serves as a fitting gateway to the drama of the Douro and the Minho farther north.

To the east, Portugal's highest mountains—the Serra da Estrela—rise to more than 6,500 feet, creating a colorful patchwork of alpine meadows, haunting forests, and wooded hills. High in this range's granite reaches, a clear icy stream begins its tortuous journey to the sea: this is the Rio Mondego, the lifeblood of the Beiras. Praised in song and poetry, it is the longest river within the country and provides vital irrigation to fruit orchards and farms as it flows through the region's heart.

Coimbra—the country's first capital and home to one of Europe's earliest universities—offers an urban counterpoint. A large student population ensures that the city stays lively; however, the past lingers on in the evocative old quarter, its medieval backstreets unchanged for centuries. The university rises magnificently above the river which continues, closer to the sea, under the imposing walls of Montemor Castle. The *rio* (river) then widens to nurture rice fields before merging with the Atlantic at the popular beach resort of Figueira da Foz. Archaeology buffs will also appreciate the region's extraordinary Roman ruins—particularly at Conímbriga, Portugal's largest excavated site.

MAJOR REGIONS

The Beiras region encompasses the provinces of the Beira Litoral (Coastal Beira), the Beira Baixa (Lower Beira), and the Beira Alta (Upper Beira). In total this area covers one-fourth of Portugal's landmass.

The onetime medieval capital and largest city in the region, **Coimbra** (pronounced "*queembra*"), is a good place to start your exploration. The crowning glory of the Beira Litoral, Coimbra is one of Portugal's most intriguing cities, exuding the vibrancy of a student town combined with an evocative sense of history. To the west of the city, the coastal region of **Western Beiras** is remarkably unspoiled, with miles of golden sand backed by dunes and forests of pine trees and centered around the only sizable resort: **Figueira da Foz.** Between Coimbra and Figueira da Foz, you'll find **Condeixa-a-Velha,** which is home to Conímbriga, one of the Iberian Peninsula's most important archaeological sites, and **Montemor-o-Velho,** another important archaeological site. The canals and lagoons in and around the delightful old port of **Aveiro** are worth exploring. **Ovar** is a good base from which to explore the beaches and the sand dunes in the north. The belle epoque towns of **Luso** and **Curia** are some of the country's most popular spas. Farther inland is the renowned Dão wine region and the must-see city of **Viseu,** with its wonderful parks and historic old quarter.

The more mountainous **Eastern Beiras** region is home to some of the Portugal's most spectacular scenery and is the historic heart of the country. The modern town of **Castelo Branco,** the provincial capital of Beira Baixa, has wide boulevards, parks, and gardens, which is great contrast to the chain of ancient fortified towns like **Sortelha** and **Belmonte** along the Spanish border. The region's eastern area also includes the Serra da Estrela (Portugal's highest mountains).

Planning

When to Go

Although the Beiras's coastal beaches are popular in summer, the crowds are nothing like those in the Algarve. The water along this shore isn't as warm as it is farther south; as a result, the season is considerably shorter. Plan your beach time here between mid-June and mid-September.

With the exception of the eastern regions, the interior is also considerably cooler than that of the Alentejo or the Algarve, so it's well suited for summertime touring. Aside from occasional showers, the weather is comfortable from early April to mid-November. Winters, especially in the eastern mountain towns, are harsh.

Getting Here and Around

AIR

Coimbra is 197 km (123 miles) north of Lisbon and 116 km (72 miles) south of Porto. Both cities are connected to Coimbra via the A1 (E80) highway. Intercontinental flights usually arrive in Lisbon, but Porto has an increasing number of European connections, including ones operated by several budget airlines.

BUS

Buses of various vintages can take you to most destinations within the region, and bus depots—unlike train stations, which are often some distance from the town center—are central. Although this is a great way to travel and get close to the local people, it requires considerable time and patience. Timetables can be found at all the central bus stations, and most of the staff speak good English.

Rede Expressos provides comfortable bus service between Lisbon, Porto, and Coimbra, and to other parts of the Beiras. International as well as regional services are available at the Rodoviário da Beira Litoral bus station in Coimbra and at the Rodoviário da Beira Interior stations in Castelo Branco and Covilhã.

CAR

The Beiras, with their many remote villages, are suited to exploration by car. Distances between major points are short; there are no intimidating cities to negotiate; and except for the coastal strip in July and August, traffic is light. Roads in general are good and destinations well marked; however, parking can be a problem in the larger towns.

Allow plenty of time for journeys the moment you are off the main highways.

A Bit of History

This region has played an important role in Portugal's development. The Romans built roads, established settlements, and in 27 BC incorporated into their vast empire the remote province known as Lusitania, which encompassed most of what is now central Portugal, including the Beiras. They left many traces of their presence: for proof, witness the well-preserved ruins at Conímbriga, near Coimbra. The Moors swept through the territory in the early 8th century and dominated the region for several hundred years. Many of the elaborate castles and extensive fortifications here show a strong Moorish influence. The towns along the Spanish frontier have been the scene of many fierce battles—from those during the Wars of Christian Reconquest to those during the fledgling Portuguese nation's struggle against invaders from neighboring Castile.

The Beiras also played a part in Portugal's golden Age of Discovery. In 1500 Pedro Álvares Cabral, a nobleman from the town of Belmonte on the eastern flank of the Serra da Estrela, led the first expedition to what is now Brazil. Much of the wealth garnered during this period, when tiny Portugal controlled so much of the world's trade, financed the great architectural and artistic achievements of the Portuguese Renaissance. Throughout the region there are fine examples of the Manueline style, a uniquely Portuguese art form that reflects the nation's nautical heritage. The cathedrals at Guarda and Viseu, the Igreja e Mosteiro de Santa Cruz (Church and Monastery of Santa Cruz) in Coimbra, and the Convento de Jesus (Convent of Jesus) in Aveiro are especially noteworthy.

During the 19th-century Peninsular War, between Napoléon's armies and Wellington's British and Portuguese forces, a decisive battle was fought in the tranquil forest of Buçaco. Later in the same century, this area witnessed a much more peaceful invasion, as people from all corners of Europe came to take the waters at such well-known spas as Luso, Curia, and Caramulo. Around the turn of the 20th century, when the now tourist-packed Algarve was merely a remote backwater, Figueira da Foz was coming into its own as an international beach resort.

Many of the mountain roads are switchbacks that need to be treated with extreme caution. In addition, you are almost certain to get lost with appalling signposting (usually hidden around the corner or behind a tree) and nightmarish one-way mazes in every town, from the smallest hamlet to the largest city. If you get to your destination without going around the whole town three times, consider yourself lucky. Even the locals admit to getting lost on a regular basis.

Drive defensively at all times; Portugal has one of Europe's highest traffic fatality rates. Among the worst roads in the country for accidents is the IP5 heading inland from Aveiro to the Serra de Estrela.

TRAIN

Although the major destinations in the Beiras are linked by rail, service to most towns, with the exception of Coimbra, is infrequent. Using Coimbra as a hub, there are three main rail lines in the region. Line 110, the Beira Alta line, goes northeast to Luso, Viseu, Celorico da Beira, and Guarda. Line 100 extends south through the Ribatejo to intersect with Line 130, the Beira Baixa line, which runs from Lisbon northeast through Castelo Branco and Fundão to Covilhã, the gateway to the Serra da Estrela. Going north from Coimbra, Line 100 serves Curia, Aveiro, and Ovar and continues north to Porto and Braga.

Coimbra, Luso, Guarda, Ovar, and Aveiro are on the main Lisbon–Porto line. There are also regular trains linking the principal cities in the Beiras with Madrid, Lisbon, and Porto.

TRAIN CONTACT Comboios de Portugal. ☎ *707 210 220* 🌐 *www.cp.pt.*

Restaurants

With the exception of some luxury hotel dining rooms, restaurants are casual in dress and atmosphere. The emphasis is generally more on the food than on the trappings.

At almost any of the ubiquitous beach bar–restaurants, you can't go wrong by ordering the *peixe do dia* (fish of the day). In most cases it will have been caught only hours before and will be prepared outside on a charcoal grill. You'll usually be served the whole fish along with boiled potatoes and a simple salad. Wash it down with a chilled white Dão wine, and you have a delicious, satisfying, and relatively inexpensive meal. In Figueira da Foz and in the Aveiro region, *enguias* (eels), *lampreia* (lamprey), and *caldeirada* (a fish stew that's a distant cousin of the French bouillabaisse) are popular.

The inland Bairrada region, between Coimbra and Aveiro, is well known for *leitão assado* (roast suckling pig). In Coimbra the dish to try is *chanfana*; this is traditionally made with tender young kid braised in red wine and roasted in an earthenware casserole. In the mountains, fresh *truta* (trout) panfried with bacon and onions is often served, as is *javali* (wild boar). *Bacalhau* (dried, salted cod) in one form or another appears on just about every menu in the region. Bacalhau *à brás* (fried in olive oil with eggs, onions, and potatoes) is one of the many popular versions of this dish.

The Beiras contain two of Portugal's most notable wine districts: Bairrada and Dão. The reds from these districts generally benefit from a fairly long stay in the bottle. The flowery whites from around here should be drunk much younger. Bairrada is also well-known for its superb sparkling wines. *Prices in the reviews are the average cost of a main course at dinner or, if dinner isn't served, at lunch.*

Hotels

There are plenty of high-quality accommodations in the western reaches of the Beiras, but the options thin the farther inland you move; make reservations well in advance if you plan to travel during the busy summer months. That said, the Beiras has a great variety of lodging choices, ranging from venerable old luxury hotels to hip, modern hostels. The *pousadas* (inns that are members of the Turismo de Habitação organization) here make perfect bases for exploring the entire region. In addition, there are Solares de Portugal lodgings, which are family-owned and -run and can range from mansions to cottages. Most establishments offer substantial off-season discounts. (High season varies by hotel but generally runs July 1–September 15.) *Prices in the reviews are the lowest cost of a standard double room in high season. For expanded hotel reviews, visit www.Fodors.com.*

WHAT IT COSTS In Euros			
$	$$	$$$	$$$$
RESTAURANTS			
under €16	€16–€20	€21–€25	over €25
HOTELS			
under €141	€141–€200	€201–€260	over €260

Visitor Information

A few companies lead walking tours and organize activities in the mountains, but otherwise the only regularly scheduled guided tours of the Beiras originate either in Lisbon or in Porto.

Coimbra

197 km (123 miles) northeast of Lisbon.

Coimbra is a fascinating city that combines a tangible sense of history with all of the vibrancy and street life typically associated with a university town. The former is evident in the picturesque medieval quarters, where winding cobblestone streets are flanked by bars, boutiques, and eateries. As for the latter, students are easy to spot as they're traditionally garbed in black capes. Some carry guitars befitting their culture of fado, while others have briefcases adorned with colored ribbons denoting their college. After final exams in May, they burn their ribbons with great exuberance in a ceremony called Queima das Fitas.

The city also has a more cosmopolitan, contemporary side. The riverfront Parque Dr. Manuel Braga is lined with lively clubs and restaurants, while modern shopping malls contrast with idiosyncratic family-owned shops. Providing the soundtrack for it all is Coimbra's romantic, lyrical brand of fado, which you can hear at traditional celebrations, dedicated fado houses, and other venues citywide.

GETTING HERE AND AROUND

To Coimbra, trains run frequently from Lisbon and Porto. Somewhat confusingly, there are two train stations in Coimbra: Coimbra (Estação Nova) is located along the Mondego River, a five-minute walk from the center of town, and Coimbra-B (Estação Velha), located a considerable 5 km (3 miles) west. Some trains to Coimbra will stop at Coimbra-B first, and then depart for Coimbra a few minutes later. Others, including trains from Lisbon and Porto, arrive at Coimbra-B, from where there's a free shuttle to Coimbra. There are also bus links between stations. Schedules for all trains are posted at both stations.

If you're driving, there are parking facilities on and around Avenida Fernão Magalhães. Look for the blue "P" sign. Rede Expressos has buses going to/from Lisbon (2½ hours) and Porto (1½ hours) daily, as well as smaller towns, including Braga (2½ hours). Local buses are operated by several different operators, under the umbrella of the Serviços Municipais de Transportes de Coimbra. Bus tickets also cover the *patufinhas* (electric minibuses running between Baixa and Alta Coimbra) and the Elevador do Mercado (an elevator which connects the Sé Nova area and the Municipal Market area).

ESSENTIALS

BUS CONTACTS Terminal Rodoviário de Coimbra. ✉ *Av. Fernão de Magalhães* ☎ *239 855 270* 🌐 *rede-expressos.pt.* **Transportes Urbanos de Coimbra.** (*SMTUC*) ✉ *Guarda Inglesa* ☎ *239 801 100* 🌐 *www.smtuc.pt.*

TRAIN CONTACTS Coimbra Station (Estação Nova). (*Coimbra A*) ✉ *Av. Emídio Navarro* ☎ *707 210 220* 🌐 *www.cp.pt.* **Coimbra-B Station (Estação Velha).** ✉ *Rua do Padrão-Eiras* ☎ *707 210 220* 🌐 *www.cp.pt.*

VISITOR INFORMATION Coimbra Tourist Office. ✉ *Av. Emídio Navarro* ☎ *239 488 120* 🌐 *turismodocentro.pt.*

A Bit More History (Coimbra)

Since its emergence as the Roman settlement of Aeminium, this city on the banks of the Rio Mondego has played an influential and often crucial role in the country's development. In Roman times, it was an important way station, the midway point on the road connecting Lisbon with Braga to the north, and a rival of the city of Conímbriga, across the river to the south. But by the beginning of the 5th century the Roman administration was falling apart, and Aeminium fell under the dominance of Alans, Swabians, and Visigoths in turn. By the middle of the 7th century, under Visigoth rule, its importance was such that it had become the regional capital and center of the bishopric of Conímbriga. Upstart Aeminium had finally gained ascendancy over its rival Conímbriga.

The Moorish occupation of Coimbra is believed to have occurred around the year AD 714, and it heralded an era of economic development: for the next 300 years or so, Coimbra was a frontier post of Muslim culture. North of the city there are no traces of Moorish architecture, but Coimbra has retained fragments of its Muslim past—remains of old walls as well as a small gate, the Arco de Almedina, once an entrance to a medina—and the surrounding country is full of place-names of Moorish origin.

After a number of bloody attempts, the reconquest of Coimbra by Christian forces was finally achieved in 1064 by Ferdinand, king of León, and Coimbra went on to become the capital of a vast territory extending north to the Rio Douro and encompassing much of what are now the Beiras. The city was the birthplace and burial place of Portugal's first king, Dom Afonso Henriques, and was the point from which he launched the attacks against the Moors that were to end in the conquest of Lisbon and the birth of a nation. Coimbra was the capital of Portugal until the late 13th century, when the court was transferred to Lisbon.

The figure who has remained closest to the heart of the city was the Spanish-born wife of King Dinis, Isabel of Aragon. During her life, while her husband and son were away fighting wars, sometimes against each other, Isabel occupied herself with social works, battling prostitution, and fostering education and welfare schemes for Coimbra's young women. She helped found a convent, and had her own tomb placed in it. She bequeathed her jewels to the poor girls of Coimbra to provide them with wedding dowries. When she died on a peacemaking mission to Estremoz in 1336, her body was brought back to Coimbra, and almost immediately the late queen became the object of a local cult. Isabel was beatified in the 16th century, and then canonized in 1625 by Pope Urban VIII after it was determined that her body had remained undecayed in its tomb.

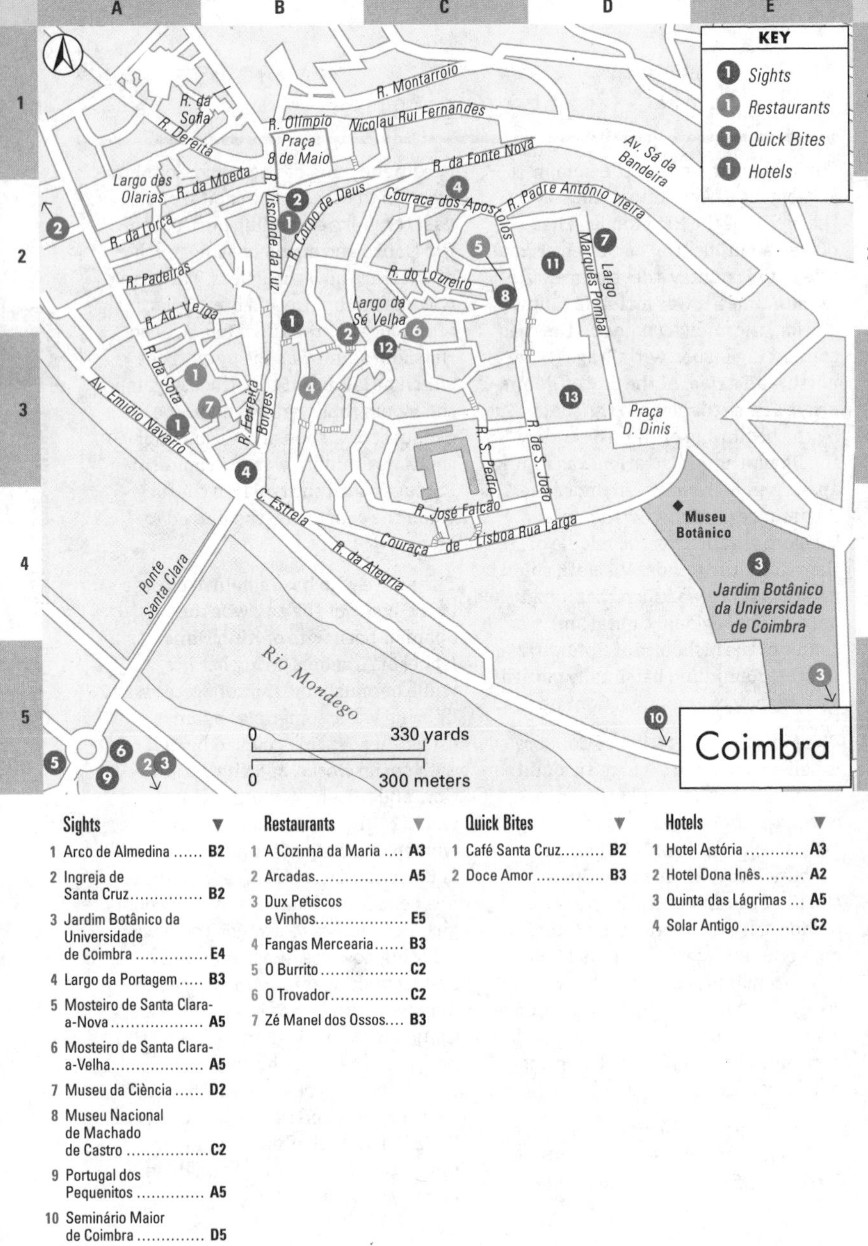

Sights

1 Arco de Almedina **B2**
2 Ingreja de Santa Cruz **B2**
3 Jardim Botânico da Universidade de Coimbra **E4**
4 Largo da Portagem **B3**
5 Mosteiro de Santa Clara-a-Nova **A5**
6 Mosteiro de Santa Clara-a-Velha **A5**
7 Museu da Ciência **D2**
8 Museu Nacional de Machado de Castro **C2**
9 Portugal dos Pequenitos **A5**
10 Seminário Maior de Coimbra **D5**
11 Sé Nova **D2**
12 Sé Velha **C3**
13 Universidade de Coimbra **D3**

Restaurants

1 A Cozinha da Maria **A3**
2 Arcadas **A5**
3 Dux Petiscos e Vinhos **E5**
4 Fangas Mercearia **B3**
5 O Burrito **C2**
6 O Trovador **C2**
7 Zé Manel dos Ossos **B3**

Quick Bites

1 Café Santa Cruz **B2**
2 Doce Amor **B3**

Hotels

1 Hotel Astória **A3**
2 Hotel Dona Inês **A2**
3 Quinta das Lágrimas ... **A5**
4 Solar Antigo **C2**

Sights

Arco de Almedina

BUILDING | On the Baixa district's Rua Ferreira Borges—one of the city's principal shopping streets—the very modest Arco de Almedina opens onto a courtyard. The 12th-century arch is one of the last vestiges of the medieval city walls, and above it are a Renaissance carving of the Virgin and Child and an early Portuguese coat of arms. The *sino de correr* (warning bell) was used from the Middle Ages until 1870 to signal the populace to return to the safety of the city walls. ✉ *Rua Visconde da Luz.*

Igreja de Santa Cruz (*Church of Santa Cruz*)

RELIGIOUS SITE | This is Portugal's National Pantheon, the final resting place of the country's first two kings, Dom Afonso Henriques and his son Dom Sancho I. The lower portions of the interior walls are lined with *azulejos* (tiles) depicting various religious motifs. Look a little closer and you'll notice flaws in the design—that's because the tiles were installed in the 18th century, as a quick fix after flooding damaged the 12th-century frescos that were there originally. The 16th-century baroque organ is a sight to behold. From the sacristy, a door opens to the Casa do Capitulo (Silent Cloister); this double-tier Manueline cloister contains scenes from the Passion of Christ, attributed to Chanterene. ✉ *Praça 8 de Maio* ☎ *239 822 941* 🎫 *Free. €3 cloisters* ⏲ *Closed Sun.*

Jardim Botânico da Universidade de Coimbra (*Coimbra University Botanical Garden*)

GARDEN | From the Old Town, the botanical garden sweeps down the side of the hill to the Mondego River. Designed by British architect William Elsden and two natural history teachers, Domingos Vandelli and Dalla Bella, it was created during the reform of the university in 1772 by the Marquis of Pombal. It's still a place of serious scientific study, with more than 1,200 species of plants covering 50 acres. There is also a foliage-filled greenhouse and a small botanical museum. The walk uphill along the marked trail takes takes around 45 minutes, or half that if you're headed down. ✉ *Alameda Dr. Júlio Henriques* ☎ *239 855 215* 🌐 *www.uc.pt/jardimbotanico* 🎫 *Free.*

Largo da Portagem

PLAZA | This bustling triangular plaza lined with cafés and restaurants sits at the foot of the Ponte Santa Clara over the Mondego River. The statue is of Joaquim António de Aguiar, and the pen in his hand represents the 1833 signing of a decree banning religious orders throughout Portugal. ✉ *Av. Emidio Navarro.*

Mosteiro de Santa Clara-a-Nova (*New St. Clare Convent*)

RELIGIOUS SITE | Repeated flooding of the nearby Mondego River forced the nuns of Mosteiro de Santa Clara-a-Velha to flee to higher ground. Built in the 17th century, the church honors Queen Isabel of Aragon. Her remains are held on the altar in a silver-and-glass sarcophagus that was originally intended to be displayed beneath an ornate arch at the old monastery. The cloisters are by far the most beautiful in Coimbra; arrive early on a weekday and chances are you'll wander the echoing archways and gardens with just the gardeners for company. During the Peninsular War, the French General Massena used the convent as a hospital for hundreds of troops wounded during the battle of Buçaco. The church's carefully hidden treasures escaped the desecration inflicted on so many Portuguese monuments during this period. ✉ *Calçada Santa Isabel* ☎ *239 441 674* 🎫 *€2.*

★ Mosteiro de Santa Clara-a-Velha (*Old St. Clare Convent*)

RELIGIOUS SITE | The evocative ruin of Coimbra's 14th-century monastery has recently undergone extensive restoration to reverse centuries of flood damage. For more than 300 years, the ground floor was completely immersed in water, silt, and mud due to its proximity to the Mondego River. Today, you can safely explore the ruin, observing eerie water stains along the walls. Outside are the excavations of the nuns' private quarters, their refectory, and cloisters, some still with their original tiles visible. There's also a kitchen garden and a contemporary museum displaying relics found during the restoration project. ✉ *Rua das Parreiras* ☎ *239 801 160* 🎫 *€4* ⏲ *Closed Mon.*

Museu da Ciència

MUSEUM | FAMILY | Formerly the Universidade de Coimbra's chemical laboratory, this 18th-century neoclassical building now houses a museum displaying some 250,000 curious and intricate scientific instruments as well as rooms filled with interactive displays and interesting experiments. This is the most important science collection in Portugal, and one of the most important in Europe, covering biology, chemistry, and physics. Across the street is the Colégio de Jesus with an expansive zoological museum housing thousands of flora and fauna specimens—pickled, stuffed, and skeletal. ✉ *Largo Marquês de Pombal* ☎ *239 854 350* 🌐 *visit.uc.pt/turismo* 🎫 *€5, €12.50 (includes all university buildings).*

★ **Museu Nacional de Machado de Castro**

MUSEUM | One of the city's most illustrious museums, the Museu Nacional de Machado de Castro sits on the site of a vast Roman cryptoporticus (a maze of underground storage vaults). The building above, constructed in the 12th century to house the local bishops, was extensively modified over the centuries and finally converted into a museum in 1912. The Bishop's Chapel, adorned with 18th-century tiles and silks, remains a highlight. The museum is notoriously difficult to navigate, although there are plenty of staffers on hand to point you in the right direction. As you exit the museum, note the large 18th-century azulejo panel depicting Jerónimo translating the Bible. ✉ *Largo Dr. José Rodrigues* ☎ *239 853 070* 🌐 *museumachadocastro.gov.pt* 🎫 *€6* ⏲ *Closed Mon.*

Portugal dos Pequenitos (*Portugal of the Little Ones*)

CITY PARK | FAMILY | Coimbra's small, open-air park is made up of scale models of castles and monasteries that children of all ages can play in. The buildings replicate Coimbra's most important and historic buildings, all built to the scale of a five-year-old. It's within walking distance of the Ponte Santa Clara. ✉ *Rossío de Santa Clara* ☎ *239 801 170* 🌐 *portugal-dospequenitos.pt* 🎫 *€10.*

Sé Nova (*New Cathedral*)

RELIGIOUS SITE | This 17th-century cathedral was patterned after the baroque church of Il Gesù in Rome, as were many such churches of the day. It took a century to build and shows two distinct styles as fashion changed from classical cleanliness to the florid baroque. Three enormous and elaborate gilded altarpieces are the highlight of the interior, flanked by 17th-century choir stalls moved here from Sé Velha (Old Cathedral). There's a pair of organs, both from the 18th century. A small and slightly bizarre ecclesiastical museum displays religious figurines in glass boxes. ✉ *Largo Feira dos Estudantes* 🎫 *Free.*

Sé Velha (*Old Cathedral*)

RELIGIOUS SITE | Engaged in an ongoing struggle with the Moors, the Portuguese often incorporated fortifications into their churches—which is why the 12th-century Sé Velha looks more like a fortress than a house of worship. It's made of massive granite blocks and crowned by a ring of battlements, and the harsh exterior is softened somewhat by its graceful 16th-century Renaissance doorway. The somber interior has a gilded wooden altarpiece: a late-15th-century example of the Flamboyant Gothic style, created by the Flemish masters Olivier of Ghent and

The University of Coimbra, Portugal's oldest university, dominates the Coimbra skyline.

Jean d'Ypres. ✉ *Largo da Sé Velha* ☎ *239 825 273* 🎟 *€2.50.*

★ **Seminário Maior de Coimbra** (*Maior de Coimbra Seminary*)

RELIGIOUS SITE | Described as the "jewel of the city," this 250-year-old seminary houses one of Portugal's most impressive collections of 18th-century Italian art, a church, and a library with over 9,000 books. Don't miss the woodcuts of priest and artist Nunes Pereira. In the hills near the botanical gardens, the seminary offers breathtaking views of Coimbra. Guided tours are offered in English. ✉ *Rua Vandelli 2* ☎ *239 792 340* 🌐 *seminariomaiordecoimbra.com* 🎟 *€5* 🕐 *Closed Sun.*

★ **Universidade de Coimbra** (*Coimbra University*)

COLLEGE | Portugal's oldest university—one of the most august academic institutions in Europe—was founded in Lisbon in 1290. It dominates the city both physically (taking up most of the center of the old town) and in terms of numbers (with well over 20,000 students). Built in 1634 as a triumphal arch, the Porta Férrea marks the entrance to the main courtyard and is adorned with statues of Kings Dinis and João III. Walk to the far end of the courtyard for breathtaking panoramic views of the Mondego River. The 18th-century **clock-and-bell tower,** rising above the courtyard, is one of Coimbra's most famous landmarks. The bell, which summons students to class and in centuries past signaled a dusk-to-dawn curfew, is derisively called the *cabra* (she-goat; an insulting term used to express the students' dismay at being confined to quarters).

In the courtyard's southwestern corner is a building with four huge columns framing massive wooden doors. Behind them is one of the world's most beautiful libraries, the baroque **Biblioteca Joanina.** Constructed in the early 18th century, it has three dazzling book-lined halls and stunning trompe-l'oeil decorative features. Knock to gain entrance to the

Fado

The word *fado* means "fate" in Portuguese, and—like the blues—fado songs are full of the fatalism of the poor and deprived, laments of abandoned or rejected lovers, and tales of people oppressed by circumstances they cannot change. The genre, probably an outgrowth of a popular sentimental ballad form called the *modinha*, seems to have emerged in the first half of the 19th century in the poor quarters of Lisbon. Initially, fado was essentially a music of the streets, a bohemian art form born and practiced in the alleys and taverns of Lisbon's Mouraria and Alfama quarters. By the end of the century, though, fado had made its way into the drawing rooms of the upper classes. Portugal's last king, Dom Carlos I, was a fan of the form, and a skilled guitar player to boot.

Strictly an amateur activity in its early years, fado began to turn professional in the 1930s with the advent of radio, recording, and the cinema. The political censorship exercised at the time by Portugal's long-lasting Salazar dictatorship also influenced fado's development. Wary of the social comments *fadistas* might be tempted to make in their lyrics, the authorities leaned on them heavily. Fado became increasingly confined to fado houses, where the singers needed professional licenses and had their repertoires checked by the official censor.

Nowadays, although the tradition of fado sung in taverns and bars by amateurs (called *fado vadio* in Portuguese) is still strong, the place to hear fado is in a professional fado house. Called *casas de fado*, the houses are usually restaurants, too, and some of them mix the pure fado with folk dancing shows. Casas de fado are frequented by the Portuguese, so don't be wary of one being a tourist trap.

There are two basic styles of fado: Coimbra and Lisbon. In both the singer is typically accompanied by three, or sometimes more, guitarists, at least one of whom plays the Portuguese guitar, a pear-shape 12-string descendant of the English guitar introduced into Portugal by the British port-wine community in Porto in the 19th century. It is the Portuguese guitar that gives the musical accompaniment of fado its characteristically plaintive tone, as the musician plays variations on the melody. The other instruments are usually classical Spanish guitars, which the Portuguese call *violas*.

Although the greatest names of Lisbon fado have been women, Coimbra fado is always sung by men, and the style is more lyrical than that of the capital. The themes tend to be more elevated, too—usually serenades to lovers or laments about the trials of love.

nearby **Capela de São Miguel**, where you'll discover the chapel's glorious tiled interior, baroque organ, and rococo side altars in hues of gold and duck-egg blue. ■ **TIP→ There are a set number of daily tickets for the Biblioteca Joanina, so collect your combined ticket early to avoid missing the jewel in the university's crown.** ✉ *Largo da Porta Férrea* ☎ *239 242 744* 🌐 *visit.uc.pt/turismo* 🎫 *€12.50 (includes all university buildings).*

Coffee and Quick Bites

Café Santa Cruz

$ | **PORTUGUESE** | Until its conversion in 1923, Café Santa Cruz was an auxiliary chapel for the monastery. Now its high-vaulted Manueline ceiling and stained-glass windows make it an ideal spot to enjoy your morning cup of coffee. **Known for:** overlooks a bustling city square; grand dining room; good coffee. *Average main: €5 Praça 8 de Maio 239 833 617.*

★ **Doce Amor**

$ | **BRAZILIAN** | This self-proclaimed "brownieria" is owned and run by a friendly Brazilian family that serves a range of squishy, oozing brownies finished with toppings of your own choice and accompanied by filtered coffee. Brazilian *brigadeiros* (traditional fudge balls) are another specialty. **Known for:** dessert here is an event; coffee is top-notch; tasty ice cream. *Average main: €3 Rua do Quebra-Costas 53 918 865 278 Closed Sun. No credit cards.*

Restaurants

A Cozinha da Maria

$ | **PORTUGUESE** | **FAMILY** | A bubbly, friendly atmosphere fills this quintessentially Portuguese restaurant specializing in cod and other dishes from the region. the decor is handsome, looking for all the world like a kitchen from a century ago. The menu is proudly in Portuguese only, so take a phrase book or chat with the friendly staff. **Known for:** big windows let in lots of light; homey dining room; live music. *Average main: €13 Rua das Azeiteiras 65 968 650 253 No lunch No credit cards.*

Arcadas

$$$$ | **PORTUGUESE** | In the former stables of Quinta das Lagrimas, this well-regarded restaurant has two dining rooms, one of which opens onto immaculate gardens. Created by star chefs Vitor Dias and Caroline Zagalo, dishes are immaculately presented and full of powerful and unusual flavors. **Known for:** tranquil views of the well-tended gardens; one of the city's prettiest dining rooms; interesting tasting menus. *Average main: €35 Quinta das Lagrimas, Rua António Augusto Gonçalves 239 802 380 quintadaslagrimas.pt No lunch.*

Dux Petiscos e Vinhos

$ | **PORTUGUESE** | This stylish bar-cum-restaurant specializes in a modern take on Iberian tapas with dishes designed and presented to excite all the senses. The menu changes according to what is fresh in the market that day, but you can expect interesting combinations like chestnut puree topped with grilled shiitake mushrooms. **Known for:** plenty of vegetarian options; good setting for groups; wonderful wines. *Average main: €12 Rua Gen. Humberto Delgado 448 239 402 818 www.duxrestaurante.com.*

★ **Fangas Mercearia**

$ | **PORTUGUESE** | This tucked-away eatery serves up award-winning traditional cod dishes (among the favorites is cod fillet with braised leeks and chickpea puree), plus a range of expertly prepared local delights (including delicious mushrooms stuffed with sausage and almonds). The staff goes out of its way to explain the dishes and provide recommendations. **Known for:** sophisticated setting; staff is full of advice; traditional dishes. *Average main: €8 Rua Fernandes Tomás 934 093 636.*

O Burrito

$ | **MEXICAN FUSION** | As you're heading past Sé Nova, take the first alley on the left to discover this tiny bohemian restaurant tucked behind a church. The Mexican fusion restaurant has a small but delicious range of hot and cold vegan empanadas, quesadillas, and massive burritos. **Known for:** vibrant neighborhood setting; vegan and vegetarian dishes;

The library at the University of Coimbra is famed for its dazzling trompe-l'oeil ceiling.

cash only. *Average main: €5 Largo de São Salvador 239 198 260 Closed Sun. and Mon. No dinner Tues. and Wed. No credit cards.*

O Trovador

$ | **PORTUGUESE** | Seasoned travelers know to avoid restaurants near major sights, but O Trovador—just a step away from the old cathedral—proves everyone wrong. Grab a table with a view of the centuries-old architecture and enjoy generous portions of reliably good regional dishes like pork cheeks with sweet potatoes or cod with cornbread. **Known for:** hard-to-beat location; elegant dining room; excellent service. *Average main: €15 Largo da Sé Velha 15–17 239 825 475 restaurantetrovador.com Closed Sun.*

Zé Manel dos Ossos

$ | **PORTUGUESE** | This hole-in-the-wall has simple wooden tables and chairs squeezed in wherever they will fit, an open kitchen with a jumble of pots and pans, and walls plastered with an intriguing assortment of scribbled poems and cartoons. The food is flavorful and cheap, so don't pass up the chance for a meal here if you can get in (it's a favorite with students). **Known for:** real local character; good house wine; off the beaten path. *Average main: €8 Beco do Forno 12 239 823 790 No credit cards Closed Sun. No dinner Sat.*

Hotels

Hotel Astória

$ | **HOTEL** | The elegantly domed Astória faces the Rio Mondego and has been a striking art nouveau landmark since it first opened its doors in 1917. **Pros:** the definition of a grande dame; handsome facade; Portuguese glazed tiles in the bathroom. **Cons:** restaurant serves breakfast only; no Wi-Fi connections in rooms; not all views are are equal. *Rooms from: €94 Av. Emídio Navarro 21 239 853 020 www.almeidahotels.pt 62 rooms Free Breakfast.*

Hotel Dona Inês

$ | **HOTEL** | **FAMILY** | This modern glass-and-marble hotel complex is just a few minutes from the business district. **Pros:** great if you like to stay active; exellent amenities; efficient staff. **Cons:** not that close to the historic center; large and impersonal feel; far from the sights. *Rooms from: €76* *Rua Abel Dias Urbano 12* *239 855 800* *www.donaines.pt* *122 rooms, 4 suites* *Free Breakfast.*

★ **Quinta das Lágrimas**

$$ | **HOTEL** | The gardens of this elegant castle are part of Portuguese history: it was here where Pedro, son of King Afonso IV, and Inês de Castro, lady in waiting to the royal court, met secretly and fell deeply in love. **Pros:** fairy-tale setting in the truest sense; scrumptuous breakfast buffer; crisp and professional service. **Cons:** not many dining options nearby outside of hotel; rates can be expensive; a bit isolated. *Rooms from: €145* *Rua António Augusto Gonçalves* *239 802 380* *quintadaslagrimas.pt* *57 rooms* *Free Breakfast.*

Solar Antigo

$ | **HOTEL** | Set in the old town, the boutique hotel feels right at home with the city's historic buildings. **Pros:** bursting with character; romantic atmosphere; excellent service. **Cons:** some find the decor a bit over the top; rooms on the small side; on a steep hill. *Rooms from: €70* *Rua Couraça dos Apóstolo* *969 374 875* *solarantigo.com* *40 rooms* *No meals.*

Performing Arts

FADO

àCapella

MUSIC | Once a 14th-century chapel, this atmospheric spot in Coimbra's Jewish Quarter now hosts nightly fado performances. Though the food won't necessarily win prizes, there is an extensive range of Portuguese wines. *Rua Corpo de Deus* *239 833 985* *acapella.com.pt.*

Casa Fado Ao Centro

MUSIC | Here you can enjoy traditional fado in a room that's dark except for the spotlight on the performer. The session begins with a short history lesson on fado, followed by performances of the genre's most famous songs. A small glass of wine is served at the end. *Rua do Quebra Costas* *239 837 060* *fadoaocentro.com* *€10.*

★ **Diligência**

MUSIC | In Coimbra's old town, this dark, musty bar hosts free nightly fado performances in a cavernous underground room. Significantly less formal than its competitors, Coimbra's oldest fado house has an authentic feel. Grab a bar stool and order a beer and some *petiscos*. Performances start at around 10 pm. *Rua Nova 30* *239 827 667* *Free.*

Shopping

One of the Baixa district's busiest and most attractive plazas is Praça do Comércio, once the site of the circus in Roman times. Today it's ringed with fashionable shops in 17th- and 18th-century town houses, and street vendors sell everything from combs to carpets on its corners. The Rua Eduardo Coelho, which fans out from the square, is lined with shoe stores and was once known as the Street of the Shoemakers.

In addition to the ubiquitous lace and cockerels, numerous stores in the city sell delicate blue-and-white Coimbra ceramics, most of them reproductions of 17th- and 18th-century patterns. This style is very distinct from the jolly earthenware associated with Portugal and can be difficult to find in other regions.

★ **Arte e Flor**

CRAFTS | Around the corner from the Museu Nacional de Machado de Castro you'll find this family-run floral art house, selling a delightful collection of handmade products alongside fresh flowers and plants. Black-and-white photography on the walls shows reveals the historic side of the business. ✉ *Rua Borges Carneiro 54* ☎ *239 825 685* ⏲ *Closed Sun. and Mon.*

BOATING

O Basófias

BOATING | **FAMILY** | Leisurely 45-minute boat trips on the river depart from the pier in Parque Dr. Manuel Braga, not far from the Santa Clara Bridge. The cost is €6.50 per person. ✉ *Parque Dr. Manuel Braga* ☎ *969 830 664* 🌐 *odabarca.com.*

O Pioneiro do Mondego

KAYAKING | The student-run O Pioneiro do Mondego conducts kayak trips on the Rio Mondego throughout the year. You're picked up at your hotel and taken to Penacova, a peaceful little river town 25 km (15 miles) north. The trip takes about three hours, but plan on a day for the whole outing. ✉ *Coimbra* ☎ *239 478 385* 🌐 *opioneirodomondego.com.*

HIKING

Trans Serrano

HIKING/WALKING | **FAMILY** | This outfitter provides transportation and English-speaking guides for nature hikes, cultural rambles, and kayaking in the surrounding countryside. There are special programs for seniors. ✉ *Bairro S. Paulo* ☎ *235 778 938* 🌐 *transserrano.com.*

HORSEBACK RIDING

Centro Hípico de Coimbra

HORSEBACK RIDING | **FAMILY** | You can arrange to horseback ride for an hour or two or take longer excursions at the Centro Hípico de Coimbra. It's on the right bank of the Rio Mondego, 2 km (1 mile) or so downstream from the Santa Clara Bridge. ✉ *Mata do Choupal* ☎ 🌐 *facebook.com/centrohipico.coimbra* ⏲ *Closed Aug.*

Condeixa-a-Velha

16 km (10 miles) southwest of Coimbra.

Surrounded by groves of olive trees and rolling hills, Conímbriga is home to one of the Iberian Peninsula's most important archaeological sites. It began as a small settlement in Celtic or possibly pre-Celtic times. In 27 BC, on his second Iberian visit, the emperor Augustus established a Roman province that came to be called Lusitania. It was during this period that, as the Portuguese historian Jorge Alarcão wrote, "Conímbriga was transformed by the Romans from a village where people just existed into a city worth visiting." It still is. There is a café at the on-site museum for refreshments, though you'll find a broader choice of bars and restaurants in the town of Condeixa-a-Velha, where archaeologists believe still more Roman remains await excavation.

GETTING HERE AND AROUND

Transdev runs direct buses from Coimbra to Conímbriga. The journey takes approximately 45 minutes.

ESSENTIALS

BUS CONTACT Transdev. ✉ *Av. Fernão de Magalhães, Coimbra* ☎ *225 100 100* 🌐 *www.transdev.pt.*

★ **Conímbriga**

ARCHAEOLOGICAL SITE | **FAMILY** | At Conímbriga's entrance is a portion of the original Roman road that connected Olissipo (as Lisbon was then known) and the northern town of Braga. If you look closely, you can still make out ridges worn into the stone by cart wheels. The road is just the beginning of the fascinating footprint left behind by the civilization that once dwelled here. A patchwork of mosaics reveals itself as you work your way across the paths. You'll be able to make out the foundations of several villas, including the House of Cantaber, named after a nobleman whose family was captured by invading barbarians in 465. The most extraordinary villa is the 3rd-century House of the Fountains, covered with mosaics depicting Perseus offering the head of Medusa to a monster from the deep. Private baths included a *tepidarium* (hot pool) and *frigidarium* (cold pool). Remnants of the central heating system that was beneath the floor are also visible. An artifact-filled museum in which Conímbriga's Iron Age origins, its heyday as a prosperous Roman town, and its decline after the 5th-century barbarian conquests are chronicled. ✉ *Rua das Ruinas 7, Condeixa-a-Velha* ☎ *239 941 177* 🌐 *conimbriga.gov.pt* 🎫 *€4.50.*

Restaurants

Restaurante do Museu

$ | **PORTUGUESE** | **FAMILY** | You don't need to wander far from the Roman ruins of Conímbriga to enjoy a well-prepared and restorative lunch. The sleek and modern café, located in the museum, offers a basic, though delicious, daily menu of sandwiches and salads. **Known for:** closest eatery to the ruins; relaxed atmosphere; tasty desserts. $ *Average main: €5* ✉ *Rua das Ruinas 7, Condeixa-a-Velha* ☎ *239 948 218.*

Hotels

Conímbriga Hotel do Paco

$ | **HOTEL** | A 16th-century palace houses this elegant pousada in the quiet town of Condeixa-a-Nova. **Pros:** excellent facilities; tranquil location; beautiful pool. **Cons:** popular with tour groups; hard to reach without a car; fills up fast. $ *Rooms from: €132* ✉ *Rua Francisco Lemos, Condeixa-a-Velha* ☎ *239 944 025* 🌐 *www.pousadasofportugal.com/pousadas/condeixa/* *43 rooms* *Free Breakfast.*

Montemor-o-Velho

20 km (12 miles) west of Coimbra, 16 km (10 miles) northwest of Conímbriga.

The small town of Montemor-o-Velho is most notable for its impressive ruined castle which sits high on a hill, overlooking the surrounding huddle of houses backed by agricultural plains. Within the walls lie the ruins of a palace, a restored church, sweeping lawns, and a pleasant café.

GETTING HERE AND AROUND

The most scenic route from Coimbra to the castle, N341, runs along the Rio Mondego's south bank. The route through the village to the castle is complicated; park in the main square and walk up the rest of the way.

It's possible to get here by train, although Montemor-o-Velho is a long, punishing walk from the station.

Sights

Castelo de Montemor-o-Velho (*Castle of Montemor-o-Velho*)

CASTLE/PALACE | **FAMILY** | On a hill between Coimbra and Figueira da Foz lies the well-kept castle of Montemore-o-Velho. Climb to the top and you'll be rewarded with some of the best views of the region.

Montemor-o-Velho figures prominently in the region's history and legends. One popular story tells how the castle's defenders cut the throats of their own families to spare them a cruel death at the hands of the Moorish invaders; many died before the attackers were repulsed. The following day the escaping Moors were pursued and thoroughly defeated.

The castle walls and tower are largely intact. But, thanks to damage done during the Napoleonic invasions in 1811, little remains inside the impressive ramparts to suggest this was a noble family's home that once garrisoned 5,000 troops.

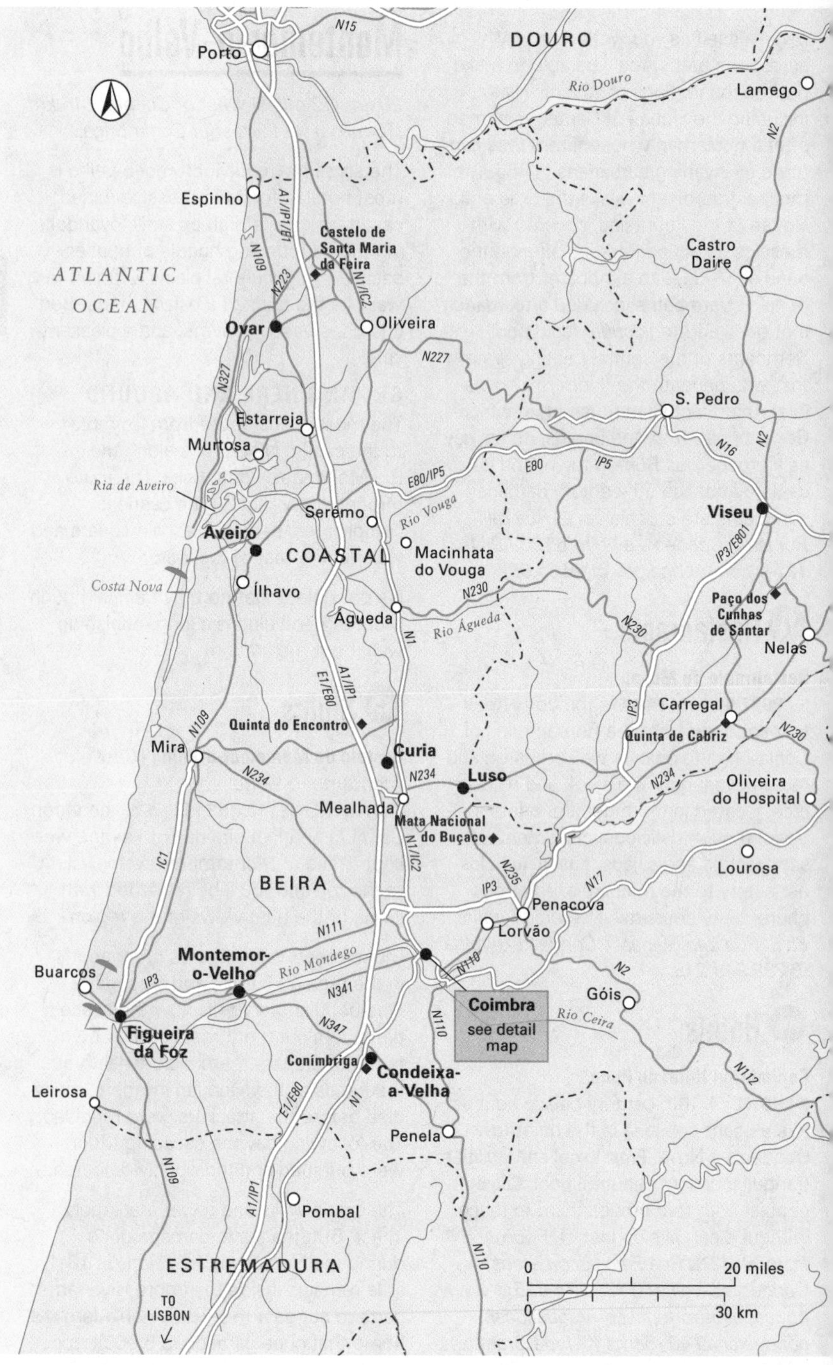
DOURO
Porto
N15
Rio Douro
Lamego
N2
Espinho
A1/IP1/E1
Castelo de Santa Maria da Feira
N109
N223
N1/IC2
Castro Daire
ATLANTIC OCEAN
Ovar
Oliveira
N227
N327
S. Pedro
Estarreja
Murtosa
N16
E80/IP5
E80
IP5
Ria de Aveiro
Serémo
Rio Vouga
Viseu
Aveiro
COASTAL
Macinhata do Vouga
IP3/E801
Costa Nova
Ílhavo
N230
Paço dos Cunhas de Santar
Águeda
Rio Águeda
N1
N230
Nelas
E1/E80
A1/IP1
Carregal
IP3
N109
Quinta do Encontro
Quinta de Cabriz
N230
Mira
Curia
N234
N234
Luso
N234
Oliveira do Hospital
Mealhada
Mata Nacional do Buçaco
N1/IC2
IC1
N235
Lourosa
BEIRA
IP3
N17
Penacova
N111
Lorvão
Montemor-o-Velho
Rio Mondego
N110
Buarcos
IP3
N2
N341
Góis
Figueira da Foz
N347
N110
Coimbra
see detail map
Rio Ceira
Conímbriga
Condeixa-a-Velha
N112
Leirosa
E1/E80
N1
Penela
N109
A1/IP1
Pombal
N110
ESTREMADURA
0
20 miles
0
30 km
TO LISBON

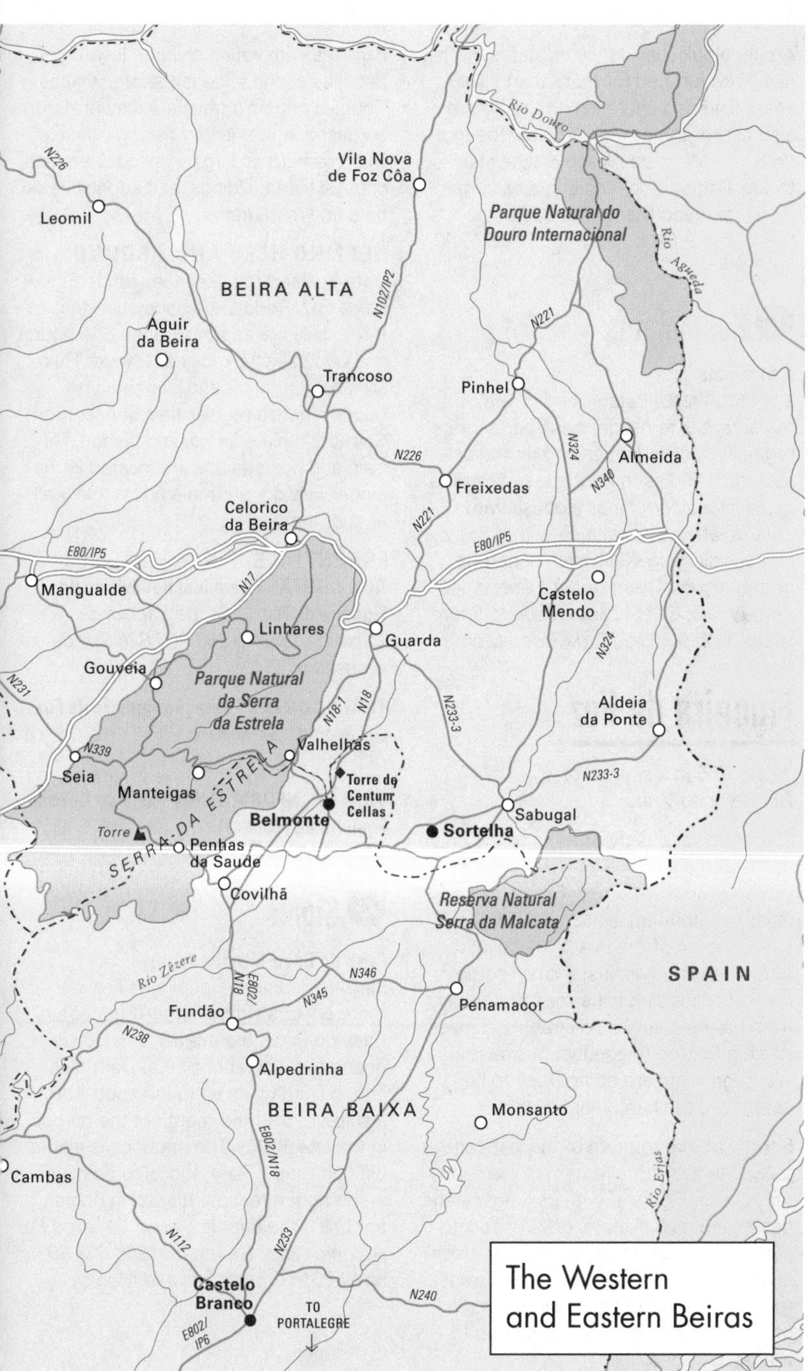

The Western
and Eastern Beiras

Archaeological evidence indicates the hill has been fortified for more than 2,000 years. The two churches on the hill are also part of the castle complex; the Igreja de Santa Maria de Alcaçova dates back to the 11th century and contains some well-preserved Manueline additions. ✉ *R. Infante Dom Pedro* ☎ *239 687 300* 🎫 *Free.*

Restaurants

A Moagem
$ | **PORTUGUESE** | Established in 1987, this restaurant is famed in these parts for its regional cuisine. Depending on the season you'll find such Portuguese favorites as *bacalhau com natas* (codfish with cream), *arroz de pata* (rice with duck), and suckling pig. **Known for:** generous buffet; regional fare; relaxed vibe. $ *Average main: €12* ✉ *Largo Macedo Souto Maior* ☎ *239 680 225* ⏲ *Closed Mon.*

Figueira da Foz

14 km (8½ miles) west of Montemor-o-Velho.

There are various theories as to the origin of the name Figueira da Foz. Locals at this seaside town's busy fishing harbor favor the literal translation: "the fig tree at the mouth of the river." The belief is that when this was just a small settlement, oceangoing fishermen and traders from up the river would arrange to meet at a big fig tree to conduct business. Although there are no fig trees to be seen now, the name has stuck.

Shortly before the turn of the last century, with the improvement of road and rail access, Figueira, with its long, sandy beach and mild climate, developed into a popular resort. Today, a broad four-lane divided boulevard lined with palm trees runs along its length, and large parts of the beach have been designated to tourist activities.

Families with young children love Figueira because of the wide range of activities. Couples and solo travelers may prefer to be based in the nearby fishing village of Buarcos with its largely unspoiled beach, colorful tiled buildings, and sophisticated bars and restaurants.

GETTING HERE AND AROUND

Both bus and train services run to Figueira da Foz. Rede Expressos operates three daily buses from Lisbon (2¾ hours) and two daily from Leiria (1 hour). There are also hourly trips to Coimbra (1¼ hours). There's regular train service from Coimbra, Leiria, Sintra, and Lisbon. The train and bus stations are located in the same building, around a 20-minute walk east of the center.

ESSENTIALS

BUS CONTACT Terminal Rodoviário da Figueira da Foz. ✉ *Av. de Saraiva de Carvalho 1530* ☎ *968 903 826* 🌐 *rede-expressos.pt.*

TRAIN CONTACT Estação Figueira da Foz. ✉ *Largo da Estação* ☎ *707 210 220* 🌐 *cp.pt.*

VISITOR INFORMATION Posto do Turismo Figueira da Foz. ✉ *Av. 25 de Abril* ☎ *233 422 610* 🌐 *cm-figfoz.pt.*

Sights

Casa do Paço (*Palace House*)
BUILDING | One of Figueira da Foz's more curious sights is the 18th-century Casa do Paço, the interior of which is decorated with about 7,000 Delft tiles. These Dutch tiles were salvaged from a shipwreck at the mouth of the harbor in the late 1600s. The entrance is a little difficult to find—ask a local to point you in the right direction. It's worth ringing the bell if the door is closed. ✉ *Largo Pro. Antonio Victor Guerra 4* ☎ *966 913 607* 🎫 *€1.20* ⏲ *Closed Sun and Mon.*

Centro de Artes e Espectáculos (*Performing Arts Center*)
ARTS VENUE | Designed by Luis Marçal Grilo, this impressive modern building sits among the open green spaces of the Parque das Abadias. The interior is flexible enough to host a variety of performance events and also includes exhibition space used for arts, crafts, and photography. There's an on-site restaurant. ✉ *Rua Abade Pedro 2* ☎ *233 407 200* 🌐 *cae.pt* 🎫 *Free.*

Farol do Cabo Mondego (*Cape Mondego Lighthouse*)
LIGHTHOUSE | Drive out to the cape where the Cape Mondego Lighthouse stands for a wonderfully uncluttered view of the coastline. The road traces a loop and returns to Buarcos. ✉ *R. Farol Novo.*

Fortaleza de Santa Catarina (*Santa Catarina Fort*)
MILITARY SITE | The triangular 17th-century Fortaleza de Santa Catarina was occupied by the French during the early days of the Peninsular War. Though it isn't possible to visit the interior, the bar at the top of the fort is a lovely spot to enjoy the breeze. ✉ *Av. de Espanha.*

★ **Museu Municipal Santos Rocha**
MUSEUM | Nestled beside the city park, this modern museum may look a bit stark outside, but it holds one of the province's most diverse and interesting collections. The archaeological section consists mainly of Roman coins sourced from all over the Iberian Peninsula. A second gallery focuses on former Portuguese colonies in Africa, with highlights including some fascinating ritual objects. There is also a gallery dedicated to Portuguese marquetry furniture with exquisite inlaid carvings, plus another devoted to religious items. Exhibits have multilingual explanations. ✉ *Rua Calouste Gulbenkian 70* ☎ *233 402 840* 🌐 *cm-figfoz.pt* 🎫 *€2* ⊙ *Closed Sun. and Mon.*

Beaches

Praia da Claridade
BEACH—SIGHT | **FAMILY** | Figuera´s main draw is the magnificent 2-km-long (1-mile-long) beach that locals claim is the widest in Europe. It has calm waters that offer plenty of shallow areas for paddling tots, making it particularly popular among families. The golden strand is broad (you'll stroll for several minutes just to get your feet wet) and flanked by a promenade that's lined with sprawling terrace cafés. ■ **TIP→ It can get crowded, but walk towards Buarcos to find the quieter stretches. Amenities:** food and drink; lifeguards. **Best for:** sunrise; sunset; swimming. ✉ *Av. 25 de Abril.*

Restaurants

A Plataforma
$ | **SEAFOOD** | Run by a family of fishmongers, this waterfront eatery has seafood that's so fresh it's practically flopping around—expect everything from shrimp and crab to mussels to the fish of the day The old-fashioned service from the jovial staff gives the place an authentic flavor. The nautical paraphernalia around the restaurant is charming. **Known for:** good lunch spot; great beach views; delicious shrimp dishes. $ *Average main: €10* ✉ *Av. Infante Dom Pedro, Buarcos* ☎ *913 065 473* 💳 *No credit cards.*

Caçarola 1
$ | **SEAFOOD** | Dine on superb seafood like juicy prawns, fish stews, and various rice dishes; everything is wonderfully fresh. This restaurant is very popular with locals, particularly on weekends, so you may have to wait for a table. **Known for:** waterfront location; excellent seafood; family friendly. $ *Average main: €15* ✉ *Rua Cándido dos Reis 65* ☎ *233 424 861* 🌐 *cacarola1.com.*

O Peleiro

$ | **PORTUGUESE** | In the peaceful, rather than picturesque, village of Paião, 10 km (6 miles) south of Figueira da Foz, this restaurant decorated with animal skins was once a tannery, and that's what the name means. An institution for over 20 years, the menu is heavy on regional specialties, including *sopa da pedra* (vegetable soup). **Known for:** freshly caught seafood; good wine selection; handsome dining room. *Average main: €15 Largo do Alvideiro 5-7, Paião 233 940 120 Closed Sun.*

★ **Volta & Meia**

$ | **PORTUGUESE** | The brilliant red walls and hand-painted murals might catch your eye, but the savory pies will make you want to stay. That includes a delectable range of "hidden pies" whose ingredients are wrapped like a gift parcel in seasoned pastry crust. **Known for:** ideal for vegetarians and vegans; charmingly disheveled dining room; tasty seafood. *Average main: €12 Rua Dr. Francisco António Diniz 64 233 418 381 voltaemeia.com Closed Mon.*

Hotels

Hotel Atlantida Sol

$ | **HOTEL** | **FAMILY** | With a sloping exterior designed to maximize stunning sea views, this sand castle–shaped hotel also impresses with modern amenities, private balconies, and a beachside location just a mile from the center of town. **Pros:** entrance right on the beach; excellent restaurant and bar; views for days. **Cons:** large and impersonal feel; far from the city's sights; decor is a bit spartan. *Rooms from: €65 Av. D. Joã 11, Buarcos atlantida-sol.com 150 rooms No meals.*

Hotel Aviz

$ | **HOTEL** | With a pretty pink exterior accentuated by traditional wrought-iron balconies, this charming little guesthouse sits a few blocks from the beach. **Pros:** not far from the beach; shiny parquet floors; great breakfast buffet. **Cons:** front rooms can be noisy; decor a little fusty; books up fast. *Rooms from: €60 Rua Dr. A. L. Lopes Guimarães 16 233 422 635 17 rooms Free Breakfast.*

Mercure Figueira da Foz

$ | **HOTEL** | Looking like it it belongs on Miami Beach, this 1950s-era hotel has a sleek mid-century modern exterior and a perfect location on the broad, sandy beach. **Pros:** exhaustive list of facilities; ample ocean views; service is superb. **Cons:** service can seem perfunctory; books up quickly in the summer; no local flavor. *Rooms from: €80 Av. 25 de Abril 22 233 403 900 accorhotels.com 103 rooms Free Breakfast.*

Nightlife

Casino da Figueira

CASINOS | The 1886 gaming room of the Casino da Figueira has frescoed ceilings, chandeliers, and a variety of table games, including blackjack and roulette. Banks of slot machines lie in wait in a separate room. Within the same building there's also a belle epoque show room and a piano bar where you can hear fado music. All visitors are required to show their passports at the door. *Rua Cândido dos Reis 49 casinofigueira.pt Free.*

Activities

You can rent sailboards and other watersports gear from most resorts on the shore of either Figueira or Buarcos. The Quiaios Lakes are also popular for windsurfing. Surfers often find 10- to 12-foot waves at Quiaios Beach (just north of Cape Mondego).

BOATING

Capitão Dureza

KAYAKING | **FAMILY** | Throughout the year, you can enjoy kayaking and rafting on the Mondego River with Capitão Dureza. The company also organizes other activities, including trekking and canyoning. ✉ *Rua Principal 64C, Telhado, Penacova* ☎ *918 315 337* 🌐 *capitaodureza.com.*

SURFING

★ Paintshop Hostel

SURFING | Though it's primarily a hostel, this British-owned establishment also offers top-notch surf lessons and board rentals. A day with a surf teacher and all the equipment you need costs €30 per person. You can also rent bikes for €5. ✉ *Rua Clemência 9* ☎ *916 678 202* 🌐 *paintshophostel.com.*

Aveiro

60 km (40 miles) north of Coimbra.

Aveiro's traditions are closely tied both to the sea and to the Ria de Aveiro—the vast, shallow lagoon that fans out to the north and west of town. Salt is extracted from the sea here, and kelp is harvested for use as fertilizer. Swan-neck *moliceiros* (kelp boats) still glide along canals that run through Aveiro's center, giving rise to its comparison to Venice. In much of the older part of town, sidewalks and squares are paved with *calçada* (traditional Portuguese hand-laid pavement) in intricate nautical patterns. The town's most attractive buildings showcase the art nouveau style that has made Aveiro celebrated by architecture fans around the world. Over the last few years, a massive restoration project has transformed the old fishermen's quarter, just off the main canal, into a delightful little area of small bars and restaurants. A central market square hosts artisan markets and live entertainment during the summer months.

GETTING HERE AND AROUND

Rede Expressos buses run to/from Lisbon (3½ hours), Coimbra (2½ hours), Guarda (1½ hours), and Faro (6 hours). There are train services linking Aveiro to Porto, Coimbra, and Lisbon from the train station northeast of the center.

TRAIN CONTACT Estação de Aveiro. ✉ *Largo da Estação dos Caminhos de Ferro* ☎ *808 208 208* 🌐 *cp.pt.*

ESSENTIALS

VISITOR INFORMATION Turismo Centro de Portugal. ✉ *Rua João Mendonça 8* ☎ *234 420 760* 🌐 *visitportugal.com.*

Sights

★ Convento de Jesus (*Convent of Jesus*)

RELIGIOUS SITE | In 1472, Princess Joana, daughter of King Afonso V, retired against her father's wishes to the Convento de Jesus—established by papal bull in 1461—where she spent the last 18 years of her life. After the last of the holy sisters died, the convent was closed in 1874. It now contains the **Museu de Aveiro,** which encompasses an 18th-century church whose interior is a masterpiece of baroque art. The elaborately gilded wood carvings and ornate ceiling by António Gomes and José Correia from Porto are among Portugal's finest. Blue-and-white azulejo panels have scenes depicting the life of Princess Joana, who was beatified in 1693 and whose tomb is in the lower choir. Her multicolor inlaid-marble sarcophagus is supported at each corner by delicately carved angels. Note also the 16th-century Renaissance cloisters, the splendid refectory lined with camellia-motif tiles, and the chapel of São João Evangelista (St. John the Evangelist). ✉ *Av. de Santa Joana* ☎ *234 423 297* 🎟 *€4* ⏲ *Closed Mon.*

Costa Nova

BEACH—SIGHT | Across the lagoon from Aveiro is a ribbon of small resort towns, the most delightful of which is Costa Nova, which has decked itself out from top to toe in jazzy candy stripes. It's a pleasant place to walk along the ocean and stop for lunch in one of the many seaside restaurants. Hourly buses make the 15-minute trip from Rua Clube dos

Galitos in Aveiro. ✉ *Rua da Quinta do Cravo, Costa Nova.*

Ecomuseu Marinha da Troncalhada (*Marinha da Troncalhada Ecomuseum*)
MUSEUM | Traditional methods of producing salt are on display at this interesting museum. You can try making it yourself using the original equipment and watch workers extracting salt between July and September. ■TIP→ **Bring your bathing suit, because you're allowed to plunge into one of the deeper salt pans. Showers are provided for rinsing off afterward.** ✉ *Cais das Pirâmides* ☎ *234 406 300* *Free* ⏲ *Closed Oct.–June.*

Estação de Caminhos de Ferro (*Old Railway Station*)
MUSEUM | At Aveiro's northeast edge, the old train station displays an adorable collection of azulejo panels depicting regional traditions and customs. ✉ *Av. Dr. Lourenco Peixinho.*

Igreja da Misericórdia (*Mercy Church*)
RELIGIOUS SITE | Facing Praça da República, in a small square a little way from the old town, you'll find the 18th-century Igreja da Misericórdia and its imposing baroque portal. The walls of the otherwise sober interior are resplendent with blue-and-white azulejos. The church isn't officially open to visitors, but if you're lucky you'll find the doors open so you can take a peek inside. ✉ *Praça da República.*

★ **Museu Arte Nova**
MUSEUM | While this museum celebrates the city's rich art nouveau heritage, the main event is the actual building, known as Casa Major Pessoa, a wonderfully flamboyant example of the genre dating to 1909. Notable among the displays are stunning hand-painted tiles decorated with flowers, birds, and animals. The collection itself has a few items of interest, but the biggest plus is that visitors are given a map of various art nouveau landmarks around the city. They're easy to find, marked with silver plaques on the ground. ✉ *Rua Barbosa de Magalhães* ☎ *234 406 485* 🌐 *cm-aveiro.pt* *€2* ⏲ *Closed Mon.*

Aveiro's Canals 

The best place for viewing Aveiro's boats is along the Canal Central and Canal de São Roque, which is crossed by several attractive bridges. On the banks, to the west of these canals, are checkerboard fields of gleaming, white salt pans. The industry dates back to the 10th century, when salt was used for preserving fish. *Bacalhau* (dried and salted cod) is still a staple of the Portuguese menu.

★ **Ria de Aveiro**
BODY OF WATER | This 45-km (28-mile) delta of the Rio Vouga was formed in 1575, when a violent storm caused shifting sand to block the river's flow into the ocean. Over the next two centuries, as more and more sand piled up, the town's prosperity and population tumbled, recovering only when a canal breached the dunes in 1808. Today the lagoon's narrow waterways are dotted with tiny islands. Salt marshes and pine forests border the area, and the ocean side is lined with sandy beaches. In this tranquil setting, colorful moliceiros glide gracefully along, their owners harvesting seaweed. ■TIP→ **The best way to see the lagoon is in one of the boats that depart from the canal across from the tourist office. The cost is €5 for a 45-minute tour.** ✉ *Aveiro.*

Restaurants

Mercado do Peixe
$$ | SEAFOOD | This upscale restaurant is easy to find—just head for the city's fish market. Widely considered to be the best place in town for fresh seafood, its specialties include *caldeirada de enguias* (eel stew) and *arroz de bacalhau e gambas*

Take a ride along one of Aveiro's graceful canals in a traditional moliceiro boat.

(rice with cod and prawns). *Average main: €20* *Largo da Praça do Peixe 1* *968 073 652* *restaurantemercadodopeixeaveiro.pt* *Closed Mon. No dinner Sun.*

★ **Salpoente**

$$$$ | PORTUGUESE | Two former salt warehouses have been lovingly restored to create a sophisticated dining with a lofty ceiling and exposed beams. The specialty at this award-winning space is bacalhau—in fact, it's prepared more than seven different ways. **Known for:** tasting menus are the way to go; options for vegetarians and vegans; gorgeous design. *Average main: €50* *Canal São Roque 82-83* *234 382 674* *salpoente.pt.*

Hotels

Hotel Aveiro Center

$ | HOTEL | This small, modern hotel with a creamy yellow exterior and a barrel-tile roof sits on a quiet backstreet, a few blocks from the main canal. **Pros:** breakfast buffet is more generous than most; staff is extremely courteous; pretty patio area. **Cons:** no on-site parking; no restaurant; a bit basic. *Rooms from: €65* *Rua da Arrochela 6* *234 380 390* *hotelaveirocenter.com* *24 rooms* *Free Breakfast.*

Hotel Aveiro Palace

$ | HOTEL | In an impressive historic building overlooking the main canal, this grand hotel offers slick and comfortable accommodations. **Pros:** unbeatable location; top-notch facilities; efficient staff. **Cons:** rooms are a little bland; small bathrooms; not much charm. *Rooms from: €70* *Rua Viana do Castelo 4* *234 421 885* *hotelaveiropalace.com* *43 rooms, 5 suites* *Free Breakfast.*

★ **Pousada Ria**

$ | HOTEL | About a 30-minute drive north of Aveiro, this lodging sits midway down the narrow, pine-covered peninsula that separates the Ria da Aveiro from the sea. **Pros:** restaurant serves traditional dishes; sparkling swimming pool; tranquil atmosphere. **Cons:** location is a bit isolated; not

Beaches of the Beira Litoral

There's a virtually continuous stretch of good sandy beach along the entire coastal strip known as the Beira Litoral—from Praia de Leirosa in the south to Praia de Espinho in the north. One word of caution: if your only exposure to Portuguese beaches has been the Algarve's southern coast, be careful: west-coast beaches tend to have heavy surf as well as strong undertows and riptides. If you see a red or yellow flag, do *not* go swimming. Note, too, that the water temperature on the west coast is usually a few degrees cooler than it is on the south coast.

You have your choice of beaches here. There are fully equipped resorts, such as Figueira da Foz and Buarcos; if you prefer sand dunes and solitude, you can spread out your towel at any one of the beaches farther north. Just point your car down one of the unmarked roads between Praia de Mira and Costa Nova and head west. The beaches at Figueira da Foz, Tocha, Mira, and Furadouro (Ovar) are well suited to children; they all have lifeguards and have met the European Union standards for safety and hygiene.

all rooms have views; a car is essential. *$ Rooms from: €110 ✉ Bico do Muranzel, Torreira ☎ 234 860 180 ⊕ pousadas.pt 20 rooms Free Breakfast.*

Veneza Hotel

$ | **HOTEL** | You'll find the pleasant, well-run Veneza Hotel near the railway station. **Pros:** rooms are individually decorated; complimentary glass of port; secure parking. **Cons:** 15-minute walk to town center; exterior has more charm; no views. *$ Rooms from: €110 ✉ Rua Luis Gomes de Carvalho 23 ☎ 234 404 400 ⊕ www.venezahotel.pt 49 rooms Free Breakfast.*

Activities

There's no swimming off the lagoon in town, as it's built up with ports, harbors, seafood farms, and salt pans. But within a 20-minute drive you can reach excellent beaches that stretch for miles along the massive sand spit to the north and south of town.

HORSEBACK RIDING

Escola Equestre de Aveiro

HORSEBACK RIDING | FAMILY | In addition to riding classes for all levels, Escola Equestre de Aveiro offers guided horseback treks into the wetlands around Aveiro. Hourly prices are €40 per person. *✉ Rua da Cruz, Vilarinho ☎ 969 428 670 ⊕ escolaequestreaveiro.com.*

Ovar

24 km (15 miles) north of Aveiro.

At Ria de Aveiro's northern end, Ovar is a good jumping-off point for the string of beaches and sand dunes to the north. This small town, with its many tiled houses, is a veritable showcase of azulejos.

GETTING HERE AND AROUND

Head north on N109 from Aveiro to Estarreja, then turn west and follow N109-5 through quiet farmlands, and after crossing the bridge over the Ria, continue north on N327 to Ovar.

ESSENTIALS

VISITOR INFORMATION Poste de Turismo. ✉ *Edifício da Câmara Municipal, Rua Elias Garcia* ☎ *256 572 215* 🌐 *turismocentro.pt.*

Castelo de Santa Maria da Feira (*Castle of Santa Maria da Feira*)
CASTLE/PALACE | The fairy-tale-like Castelo de Santa Maria da Feira sits 8 km (5 miles) northeast of Ovar. Its four square towers are crowned with a series of conical turrets in a display of Gothic architecture more common in Germany or Austria than in Portugal. Although the original walls date to the 11th century, the present structure is the result of modifications made 400 years later. From atop the towers you can make out the sprawling outlines of the Ria de Aveiro. ✉ *Alameda Roberto Vaz de Oliveira* ☎ *256 372 248* 🎟 *€3* ⏲ *Closed Mon.*

Igreja Matriz de Ovar (*Ovar Parish Church*)
RELIGIOUS SITE | The exterior of this late-17th-century church is completely covered with blue-and-white azulejos. ✉ *Av. do Bom Reitor* ☎ *236 588 546.*

Museu de Ovar
MUSEUM | Occupying an old house in the town center, the small Museu de Ovar has displays of traditional tiles and displays scenes from provincial life over the centuries. There's also a collection of mementos relating to popular 19th-century novelist Júlio Dinis, a native of Ovar and its most famous son. ✉ *Rua Heliodoro Salgado 11* ☎ *256 572 822* 🌐 *museudeovar.pt* 🎟 *€2* ⏲ *Closed Sun. and Mon.*

Curia

20 km (12 miles) north of Coimbra.

Just 30 minutes by car from the clamor of the summer beach scene, Curia is a quiet retreat with shaded parks and grand belle epoque hotels. The small but popular spa is in the heart of the Bairrada region, an area noted for its fine sparkling wines and roast suckling pig. The waters, with their high calcium and magnesium-sulfate content, are said to help in the treatment of kidney disorders. For the last 100 years, the spring has been contained within an elaborate treatment center that has provided rejuvenating pampering and medical treatment side by side.

GETTING HERE AND AROUND

Curia-bound trains run throughout the day from Coimbra and Aveiro (less frequently on weekends). The journey takes roughly 25 minutes.

ESSENTIALS

TRAIN CONTACT Comboios de Portugal. ☎ *707 210 220* 🌐 *cp.pt.*

VISITOR INFORMATION Posto de Turismo Curia. ✉ *Largo Dr. Luís Navega* ☎ *231 512 248* 🌐 *turismodocentro.pt.*

Aliança Underground Museum
WINERY/DISTILLERY | This Aladdin's cave of a museum is located in wine cellars that date back some 50 years. Its exhibits—drawn from the private collection of Portuguese billionaire businessman and art collector, José Berardo—include 18th-century Portuguese ceramics, African artwork, and assorted archaeological artifacts. Guided tours are offered in English, but advance reservations are necessary. ✉ *Rua do Comercio 444, Sangalhos* ☎ *234 732 000* 🌐 *bacalhoa.pt* 🎟 *€3.*

Quinta do Encontro
WINERY/DISTILLERY | The eye-popping architecture alone would make this winery, located in a tiny village northwest of Curia, worth visiting. Circular throughout, the building's design is apparently inspired by oak barrels, and the spiral interior walkway is playfully modeled

A Beautiful Geological Phenomemon

Arouca was recognized as a UNESCO Global Geopark in 2009, and it's easy to see why. The spectacular scenery and amazing natural formations make it a higlight of northern Portugal. Although located in Aveiro Province, it's almost equidistant from either Porto or Ovar (and the former has an airport, while the latter does not). Arouca is about an hour from Ovar, and then the Paiva Walkways are another half-hour from the Arouca Geopark entrance station. The park encompasses more than 100 square miles of some of the world's most geologically significant sites. The walkways snake along the Paiva River, offering both a superior (and strenuous) hike and opportunities to see the area in more detail.

Paiva Walkways

Paiva Walkways This zigzag wooden walkway along the Paiva River offering scenic views of the river and the Arouca Geopark has been open less than 10 years, but it's already been recognized as a top site by publications all over the world. From start to finish, the 8-km-long (5-mile-long) trail hike takes about 2½ hours and allows visitors to experience the surrounding landscape—waterfalls, granite cliffs, endangered species, five geosites—without disrupting it. There's river beach access from the walkway, in case you want to take a dip, and there's a suspension bridge that provides amazing views. ■ TIP→ **While there are cafés located at both ends of the trail, make sure you pack enough water and snacks and wear comfortable walking shoes as this is a strenuous hike, requiring you to climb a lot of stairs.** You can access the walkway from either Espiunca or Areinho. ✉ *Arouca Geopark, Arouca* ☎ *256 940 258* 🌐 *www.passadicosdopaiva.pt.*

Arouca Geopark

Arouca Geopark Covering an area of 126 square miles, this UNESCO-recognized park in the north of Portugal is surrounded by the Freita, Montemuro, and Arada Mountains and crisscrossed by several rivers including the Paiva River, which makes it a great place for canyoning, canoeing, kayaking, and mountain climbing. There are 41 significant geosites—including a collection of giant trilobite (ancient marine animals) fossils, some of which are 465 million years old—and 14 mostly easy hiking trails that take visitors to the sites. The park is also home to the world-famous Paiva Walkways. ✉ *Rua Alfredo Vaz Pinto, Arouca* ☎ *256 940 254* 🌐 *arouca-geopark.pt.*

on a corkscrew. Set amid vineyards and gently rolling hills, Quinta do Encontro offers wine tastings and guided tours of its ultramodern wine-making facilities. No advance reservations are necessary, though they're recommended. There is also an excellent restaurant. ✉ *Estr. Principal 16, São Lourenço do Bairro* ☎ *231 527 155* 🌐 *quintadoencontro.pt* 🕓 *Closed Mon.*

Termas da Curia

SPA—SIGHT | Located in the Parque de Curia, this spa has a slightly old-fashioned feel but still offers a range of preventive and regenerative treatments. The calcium salts, sulfur, and magnesium in the waters here are believed to be particularly good for rheumatic and musculoskeletal diseases; programs of varying durations include accommodations at the on-site hotel. Nonguests can enjoy the spa on a drop-in basis, with more general treatments including half-hour massages. ✉ *Parque de Curia* ☎ *231 519 800* 🌐 *termasdacuria.com.*

Restaurants

★ Pedro dos Leitões

$$$ | **PORTUGUESE** | Of the several restaurants specializing in suckling pig, this is the most popular. The size of the parking lot is a dead giveaway that this is no intimate bistro, and the spitted pigs pop out of the huge ovens at an amazing rate (especially in summer). **Known for:** best place to sample leitão à bairrada; massive dining room; speedy service. 💲 *Average main: €21* ✉ *Rua Alvaro Pedro 1, Mealhada* ✣ *3 km (2 miles) south of Curia* ☎ *231 209 950* 🌐 *pedrodosleitoes.com.*

Hotels

★ Curia Palace, Hotel, Spa, and Golf

$ | **HOTEL** | The approach down a tree-lined drive is like the beginning of an old movie. **Pros:** lots of activities geared toward families; well-tended golf course; palatial surroundings. **Cons:** standard rooms on the small side; not a wide range of spa treatments; needs some updates. 💲 *Rooms from: €125* ✉ *Curia* ☎ *231 510 300* 🌐 *almeidahotels.pt* 🌐 *100 rooms* 🍽 *Free Breakfast.*

Quinta de São Lourenço

$ | **B&B/INN** | This delightful 18th-century manor—surrounded by vineyards and pine groves—is in the tiny village of São Lourenço do Bairro. **Pros:** jewel-like swimming pool on the lawn; wonderful gardens and vineyards; lots of kid-friendly amenities. **Cons:** few restaurants and shops nearby; only one room has a four-poster bed; books up fast. 💲 *Rooms from: €75* ✉ *Rua Visconde Seabra 6, São Lourenço do Bairro* ☎ *231 528 168* 🌐 *quinta-de-s-lourenco.pt* *7 rooms* 🍽 *Free Breakfast.*

Luso

8 km (5 miles) southeast of Curia, 18 km (11 miles) northeast of Coimbra.

This charming town, built around the European custom of "taking the waters," is on the main Lisbon–Paris train line, in a little valley at the foot of the Buçaco Forest. Like Curia, it has an attractive park with a lake, elegant hotels, and medicinal waters. Slightly radioactive and with a low-sodium and high-silica content, the water—which emerges from the Fonte de São João, a fountain in the center of town—is said to be effective in the treatment of kidney and rheumatic disorders.

GETTING HERE AND AROUND

Daily buses run from Coimbra bus station to the center of Luso, near the main spa. There are also a limited number of trains from Coimbra (35 minutes); however, the train station in Luso is around a 20-minute hike from the center of town.

ESSENTIALS

BUS INFO Luso Bus Station. ✉ *Rua Emidio Navarro 136.*

VISITOR INFORMATION Posto de Turismo Luso-Buçaco. ✉ *Rua Emidio Navarro 136* ☎ *231 939 122* 🌐 *turismodocentro.pt.*

Sights

Mata Nacional do Buçaco

VIEWPOINT | In the early 17th century, the head of the Order of Barefoot Carmelites, searching for a suitable location for a monastery, came upon an area of dense virgin forest. A site was selected halfway up the slope of the greenest hill, and by 1630 the simple stone structure was occupied. To preserve their world of isolation and silence, the monks built a wall enclosing the forest. Their only link with the outside was through a door facing toward Coimbra, which one of them watched over. The Coimbra Gate, still in use today, is the most decorative of the eight gates constructed since that time. Early in the 20th century, much of the original monastery was torn down to construct an opulent royal hunting lodge under the supervision of Italian architect Luigi Manini. Never used by the royal family, the multiturret extravaganza became a prosperous hotel—now the Palace Hotel do Bussaco—and in the years between the two world wars it was one of Europe's most fashionable vacation addresses. Today many come to Buçaco just to view this unusual structure, to stroll the shaded paths that wind through the forest, and to climb the hill past the Stations of the Cross to the Alta Cruz (High Cross), their efforts rewarded by a view that extends all the way to the sea. ✉ *Estr. Florestal.*

Museu Militar de Buçaco (*Buçaco Military Museum*)
MUSEUM | The small Museu Militar de Buçaco houses uniforms, weapons, and various memorabilia from the Battle of Buçaco. ✉ *N234, Bussaco* ☎ *231 939 310* 🎟 *€2.*

Restaurants

Restaurante O Cesteiro
$ | **SEAFOOD** | At the western edge of town, this popular local restaurant serves simple fare that includes several types of salt cod, roast kid, and fresh fish. **Known for:** Portuguese comfort food; reasonal prices; dated decor. [$] *Average main: €10* ✉ *Rua Monsenhor Raul Mira 78* ☎ *231 939 360* ⏲ *Closed Wed.*

Hotels

★ **Grande Hotel de Luso**
$ | **HOTEL** | Looking a bit like a lighthouse that has lost its way, this hulking complex topped by a towering turret is a mishmash of architectural styles that were popular in 1945. **Pros:** stunningly decorated public areas; restaurant has garden views; free bikes, squash, and snooker. **Cons:** buffet breakfast a little skimpy; attracts a lot of families; unattractive facade. [$] *Rooms from: €75* ✉ *Rua Dr. Cid de Oliveira 86* ☎ *231 937 937* 🌐 *hoteluso.com* 🛏 *132 rooms* 🍽 *Free Breakfast.*

★ **Palace Hotel do Bussaco** (*Palace Hotel Do Buçaco*)
$$ | **HOTEL** | Designed as a royal hunting lodge and set in a 250-acre forest, this bizarrely ornate hotel is an architectural hodgepodge with elements that run the gamut from neo-Gothic to early Walt Disney. **Pros:** a fairy-tale castle down to the smallest of details; dining room aglow from stained-glass windows; beautiful hiking paths. **Cons:** some rooms have over-the-top decor; often booked by groups; some areas look tired. [$] *Rooms from: €145* ✉ *Mata do Bussaco, Bussaco* ☎ *231 937 970* 🌐 *almeidahotels.com* 🛏 *60 rooms* 🍽 *Free Breakfast.*

Residencial Imperial
$ | **HOTEL** | With wrought-iron balconies and a barrel-tile roof, this neat little hotel has plenty of charm. **Pros:** pleasantly furnished rooms; elegant dining room; reasonable rates. **Cons:** lobby decor is a bit dated; rooms are on the small side; books up quickly. [$] *Rooms from: €35* ✉ *Rua Emídio Navarro 25* ☎ *231 937 570* 🌐 *www.residencialimperial.com* 🛏 *14 rooms* 🍽 *Free Breakfast.*

Viseu

82 km (51 miles) southeast of Ovar, 71 km (44 miles) east of Aveiro.

One of Portugal's most impressive squares is Viseu's Largo da Sé. bound by three imposing edifices: the cathedral, the palace housing the Museu de Grão Vasco, and the palacelike Igreja da Misericórdia. Another sight not to miss is the tree-lined Praça da República, framed at one end by a massive azulejo mural depicting scenes of country life. The heroic figure in bronze, standing sword in hand, is Prince Henry the Navigator, the first duke of Viseu.

A thriving provincial capital in the Dão region (one of Portugal's prime wine-growing districts), Viseu has remained the feel of a country town in spite of its obvious prosperity.

GETTING HERE AND AROUND

You can take the scenic but twisting and bone-jarring N227 across the Serra da Gralheira or the smoother, faster, but much less interesting IP1 and IP5. Alternatively there are Rede Expressos buses that run to Viseu from several surrounding towns and cities, including Vila Real (1¼ hours), Coimbra (1¼ hours), and Lisbon (3½ hours). The bus station is located just south of the center.

ESSENTIALS

BUS CONTACT Central de Camionagem de Viseu. ✉ *Av. Dr António Jose de Almeida* ☎ *232 422 822* 🌐 *rede-expressos.pt.*

VISITOR INFORMATION Poste de Turismo Viseu. ✉ *Casa do Adro, Adro da Se* ☎ *232 420 950* 🌐 *turismodocentro.pt.*

Sights

Adega Cooperativa de Mangualde
WINERY/DISTILLERY | This cooperative is a great place to sample locally produced wines. Tours and tastings are available free of charge during the week; on weekends they cost €10 per group. Sessions generally include three to five wines, plus a 45-minute tour of the wine-making facilities. Call ahead if you'd like to add on local cheeses and cold cuts. ✉ *R. Quinta do Melo, Mangualde* ☎ *232 623 845* 🌐 *acmang.com* 🕓 *Closed Sat. pm and Sun.*

Igreja da Misericórdia (*Church of Mercy*)
RELIGIOUS SITE | If the cathedral looks like a fortress, the white, rococo Igreja da Misericórdia across from it looks like a palace. The fussy ornamentation around the windows and unusual entranceway are more impressive than the interior. ✉ *Adro Sé* 🎫 *€1.*

Museu Grão Vasco (*Grão Vasco Museum*)
MUSEUM | Housed in a former seminary beside the cathedral, this palatial museum was originally created to display the works of 16th-century local boy Grão Vasco, who became Portugal's most famous painter. In addition to a wonderful collection of altarpieces by Vasco and his students, the museum has a wide-ranging collection of other art and objects, from Flemish masterpieces to Asian furniture. ✉ *Adro Sé* ☎ *232 422 049* 🌐 *museunacionalgraovasco.gov.pt* 🎫 *€4* 🕓 *Closed Mon.*

Paço dos Cunhas de Santar
WINERY/DISTILLERY | This historic winery in the pretty village of Santar—an easy 16-km (10-mile) drive southwest of Viseu—centers around a magnificent 16th-century Italian Renaissance–style manor. Signature wines include a spicy Casa de Santar Reserva red and several dessert wines. As well as tastings, the winery offers tours of the wine-making facilities. ✉ *Largo do Paço 28* ☎ *914 3520 127* 🌐 *globalwines.pt* 🕓 *Closed Mon.*

★ **Quinta de Cabriz**
WINERY/DISTILLERY | Part of the prestigious Dão Sul company, Quinta de Cabriz is among the best-known wineries in the region. Located 39 km (24 miles) south of Viseu in the community of Carregal do Sal, it produces red, white, rosé, and sparkling wines. The hearty Cabriz Colheita Seleccionada red—which spends six months in French oak and uses primarily local Touriga grape varieties—is one notable award winner. ✉ *Av. Nossa Sra. das Febres, Carregal do Sal* ☎ *232 961 222* 🌐 *cabriz.pt.*

Sé
RELIGIOUS SITE | This massive stone structure with twin square bell towers lends the plaza a solemn air. Construction on this cathedral was started in the 13th century and continued off and on until the 18th century. Inside, massive Gothic pillars support a network of twisted, knotted forms that reach across

the high, vaulted roof; a dazzling, gilded, baroque high altar contrasts with the otherwise somber stone. The lines of the 18th-century upper level are harsh when compared with the graceful Italianate arches of the 16th-century lower level. To the right of the mannerist main portal is a double-tier cloister, which is connected to the cathedral by a well-preserved Gothic-style doorway. The cathedral's Sacred Art Museum has reliquaries from the 12th and 13th centuries. For great views of the cathedral, head a block south to the tiny square of Praça de Dom Duarte. ✉ *Largo da Sé* 🎫 *Free.*

Restaurants

Muralha da Sé

$$ | PORTUGUESE | Within confessional distance of the Igreja da Misericórdia, this elegant eatery is housed in a traditional honey-colored building. The menu has a regional focus, with popular dishes including sausages made in the area. **Known for:** stone-walled dining room; lamb and other local meats; desserts are made daily. 💲 *Average main: €16* ✉ *Adro da Se 24* ☎ *232 437 777* 🌐 *muralhadase.pt* ⏲ *No dinner Sun. Closed Tues.*

O Hilário

$ | PORTUGUESE | FAMILY | Expect a warm welcome and no-frills traditional cuisine at this family-run storefront restaurant with a wood-paneled dining room decorated with photos of the famous 19th-century fado star who once lived on this street. The menu changes according to what is fresh in the market that day, but is, unfailingly, unpretentious home-style cooking with huge portions. **Known for:** desserts are a treat not to be missed; you won't get a warmer welcome than here; Portuguese comfort food. 💲 *Average main: €10* ✉ *Rua Augusto Hilário 35* ☎ *232 436 587* ⏲ *Closed Sun.*

Hotels

Avenida

$ | B&B/INN | Near some of the city's prettiest parks, this elegant town house is a little removed from the hustle and bustle. **Pros:** individually decorated rooms; charming atmosphere; smart decor. **Cons:** front rooms can be noisy; no restaurant or bar; books up quickly. 💲 *Rooms from: €70* ✉ *Av. Alberto Sampaio 1* ☎ *232 423 432* 🌐 *avenidaboutiquehotel.pt* *8 rooms, 1 suite* 🍽 *Free Breakfast.*

Grão Vasco

$ | HOTEL | Once Viseu's leading lodging, the Grão Vasco is still a good choice and a great value. **Pros:** surrounded by lovely gardens; if it's in season, try the wild boar; parking included. **Cons:** Wi-Fi in public areas only; some dated decor; attracts tour groups. 💲 *Rooms from: €75* ✉ *Rua Gaspar Barreiros* ☎ *232 423 511* 🌐 *hotelgraovasco.pt* *106 rooms, 3 suites* 🍽 *Free Breakfast.*

Palácio dos Melos

$ | HOTEL | Built right into the town walls and dating to the 16th century, this stone-walled edifice oozes history. **Pros:** evocative sense of history; elegant public rooms; parking is available. **Cons:** winding downtown streets make it hard to drive here; noise from the street below; not all rooms have charm. 💲 *Rooms from: €90* ✉ *Rua Cháo do Mestre 4* ☎ *232 439 290* 🌐 *montebelohotels.com* *27 rooms* 🍽 *Free Breakfast.*

★ Pousada de Viseu

$$ | HOTEL | One of the latest additions to Portugal's string of historic pousadas, this handsome neoclassical building dates back to 1793 when it served as the town's hospital. **Pros:** one of the best restaurants in the city; nice pool, spa, and fitness area; gorgeous central courtyard. **Cons:** views are unremarkable; a bit removed from the sights; more expensive option. 💲 *Rooms from: €145* ✉ *Rua do Hospital* ☎ *232 457 320* pousadadeviseu.com 84 rooms Free Breakfast.

Quinta da Fata

$ | **B&B/INN** | At this lovely lodging, about 18 km (10 miles) southeast of Viseu, you can reserve either modern apartments or antiques-filled rooms in a 19th-century manor house. **Pros:** immaculately maintained gardens; free bikes for use of guests; hotel has its own vineyards. **Cons:** may be too remote for some; rooms vary in size; you need a car. *Rooms from: €80 Vilar Seco, Nelas 232 942 332 quintadafata.com 9 rooms Free Breakfast.*

Shopping

Narrow Rua Direita, in the old part of town, is lined with shops displaying locally made wood carvings, pottery, and wrought iron. The surrounding rural areas, particularly north toward Castro Daire, are well known for their strong tradition of linen, basketry, and heavy woolen goods.

Belmonte

20 km (12 miles) southwest of Guarda.

Two things catch your eye on the approach to Belmonte: the ancient castle and the church. (There's also an ugly water tower, a reminder that the town is now a major clothing-manufacturing center.) Belmonte's importance can be traced back to Roman times, when it was a key outpost on the road between Mérida, the Lusitanian capital, and Guarda. Elements of this road are still visible.

Ask someone from Portugal—or better yet, from Brazil—what Belmonte is best known for, and the answer will undoubtedly be Pedro Álvares Cabral. In 1500 this native son "discovered" Brazil and, in doing so, helped make Portugal one of the richest, most powerful nations of that era. The monument, in the town center, is an important stop for Brazilian visitors.

GETTING HERE AND AROUND

If you're driving, you'll probably approach Belmonte via the E802 from the north or south. There are daily bus services from Guarda that take about 30 minutes; the stop in Belmonte is around a ½-km (¼-mile) walk from the town center.

ESSENTIALS

VISITOR INFORMATION Posto de Turismo Belmonte. *Largo do Brasil 275 911 488 turismodocentro.pt.*

Sights

Castelo de Belmonte (*Belmonte Castle*)

CASTLE/PALACE | **FAMILY** | Of the mighty complex of fortifications and dwellings that once made up the castle, only the tower and battlements remain. As you enter, note the scale-model replica of the caravel that carried Cabral to Brazil. On one of the side walls is a coat of arms with two goats, the emblem of the Cabral family (in Portuguese, *cabra* means "goat"). Don't miss the graceful but oddly incongruous Manueline window incorporated into the heavy fortifications. The castle ruins are on a rocky hill to the north overlooking town. *Belmonte €2.*

Igreja de São Tiago e Panteão dos Cabrais (*Church of St. James*)

RELIGIOUS SITE | The 12th-century stone church contains fragments of original frescoes and a fine Pietà carved from a single block of granite. The tomb of Pedro Cabral is also in this church. Actually there are two Pedro Cabral tombs in Portugal, the result of a bizarre dispute with Santarém, where Cabral died. Both towns claim ownership of the explorer's mortal remains, and no one seems to know just who or what is in either tomb. **TIP→** If the church is closed, ask at the tourist office. *Largo do Castelo 275 088 698 €1.*

Judaria and Museu Judaico (*Jewish Quarter and Jewish Museum*)
NEIGHBORHOOD | Adjacent to the Castelo de Belmonte, a cluster of old houses makes up the Juderia. Belmonte had (and, in fact, still has) one of Portugal's largest Jewish communities. Many present-day residents are descendants of the Marranos: Jews forced to convert to Christianity during the Inquisition. For centuries, many kept their faith, pretending to be Christians while practicing their true religion behind closed doors. Such was their fear of repression that Belmonte's secret Jews didn't emerge fully until the end of the 1970s. The community here remained without a synagogue until 1995. A small museum situated within a former 18th-century Catholic church includes a permanent exhibition about the Jewish period; it is also an important center for Jewish studies in Portugal. ✉ *Rua da Portela* ☎ *275 088 698* 🌐 *cm-belmonte.pt* 🎫 *€4* 🕒 *Closed Mon.*

Torre de Centum Cellas
ARCHAEOLOGICAL SITE | A strange archaeological sight on a dirt road has kept people guessing for years. The massive framework of granite blocks is thought to be of Roman origin, but experts are unable to explain its original function or provide many clues about its original appearance. Some archaeologists believe it was part of a much larger complex, possibly a Roman villa, and was subsequently used as a watchtower. ✉ *Estrada da Torre* ✢ *Off the N18.*

Hotels

Hotel Belsol
$ | **HOTEL** | **FAMILY** | The views of the Rio Zêzere and the mountains beyond are the selling point of the gleaming white Hotel Belsol. **Pros:** family-friendly atmosphere; sunny swimming pool area; gorgeous balconies. **Cons:** a little distant from the town; could be too quiet for some; decor is a little basic. 💲 *Rooms from: €55* ✉ *N18* ☎ *275 912 206* 🌐 *www.hotelbelsol.com* 🛏 *54 rooms* 🍽 *Free Breakfast.*

★ **Pousada Convento de Belmonte**
$ | **B&B/INN** | On the slopes of the Serra da Esperança, this sumptuous stone-clad pousada occupies a restored Franciscan monastery founded in 1563 by a descendant of Pedro Álvares Cabral, the first European to reach Brazil. **Pros:** has some of the region's best cuisine; gorgeous architectural details; a destination in itself. **Cons:** modern areas not quite as charming; plunge pool is on the small side; can seem too formal. 💲 *Rooms from: €100* ✉ *Serra da Esperança* ☎ *275 910 300* 🌐 *conventodebelmonte.pt* 🛏 *24 rooms* 🍽 *Free Breakfast.*

Sortelha

150 km west of Coimbra, 20 km (12 miles) east of Belmonte.

If you have time to visit only one fortified town, this should be it. From the moment you walk through Sortelha's massive ancient stone walls, you feel as if you're experiencing a time warp. Except for a few TV antennas, there's little to evoke the 21st century. The streets aren't littered with souvenir stands, nor is there a fast-food outlet in sight. Stone houses are built into the rocky terrain and arranged within the walls roughly in the shape of an amphitheater.

GETTING HERE AND AROUND

If you're traveling from Penamacor, follow the N233 north across the high plateau. Regional trains stop at Belmonte-Manteigas station, located around 12 km (7½ miles) away, from where visitors can catch a taxi. There is no regular bus service.

Sights

★ **Castelo de Sortelha** (*Sortelha Castle*)
CASTLE/PALACE | **FAMILY** | Above the village of Sortelha are the ruins of a small yet imposing castle. The present configuration dates back mainly to a late-12th-century reconstruction, done on Moorish foundations; further alterations were made in the 16th century. Note the Manueline coat of arms at the entrance. Wear sturdy shoes so that you can walk along the walls, taking in views of Spain to the east and the Serra da Estrela mountains to the west. The three holes in the balcony projecting over the main entrance were used to pour boiling pitch on intruders. Just to the right of the north gate are two linear indentations in the stone wall. One is exactly a meter (roughly a yard) long, and the shorter of the two is a *côvado* (66 centimeters, or 26 inches). In the Middle Ages, traveling cloth merchants used these markings to ensure an honest measure. ✉ *Rua do Encontro 2.*

Parque Natural da Serra da Malcata
NATIONAL/STATE PARK | The 50,000-acre park along the Spanish border between Penamacor and Sabugal was created to protect the natural habitat of the Iberian lynx, which was threatened with extinction. Although this isn't a place of rugged beauty, it's nevertheless an attractive, quiet region of heavily wooded, low mountains with few traces of human habitation. Although you won't see the lynxes, the park also shelters wildcats, wild boars, wolves, and foxes. The northern boundary begins about 10 km (6 miles) southeast of Sabugal. ✉ *Sabugal.*

Restaurante Dom Sancho
$$ | **PORTUGUESE** | Just inside the gates, this pleasant little restaurant in a restored stone house provides diners with a rustic yet elegant dining experience. It specializes in game dishes like roast wild boar and venison. $ *Average main: €20* ✉ *Largo do Corro* ☎ *271 388 267* ▭ *No credit cards* ⊙ *Closed Mon. No dinner Sun.*

Casa do Campanário e Casa da Villa
$ | **RENTAL** | Just inside the village walls, Casas do Campanário consists of two apartments—one can accommodate two people, the other six. **Pros:** quiet surroundings; central location; on-site bar. **Cons:** advance reservations essential; very basic accommodations; no credit cards. $ *Rooms from: €65* ✉ *Rua da Mesquita* ☎ ▭ *No credit cards* *2 apartments* 🍽 *No meals.*

Castelo Branco

150 km (93 miles) southeast of Coimbra, 68 km (42 miles) south of Belmonte.

The provincial capital of Beira Baixa is a modern town with wide boulevards, parks, and gardens. There are some handsome buildings here, as well as a lovely formal garden and a superb museum. The surroundings are noteworthy for their natural beauty. Lying just off the main north–south IP2 highway, Castelo Branco is easily accessible from all parts of the country.

GETTING HERE AND AROUND

There are regular buses to Castelo Branco from several major travel hubs in Portugal, including Coimbra, Lisbon, Guarda, Portalegre, and Faro. The town is also on the Lisbon–Guardia line with multiple daily trains from Lisbon.

If you're driving from Buçaco, the most scenic route is via the N235, through wooded countryside along the foot of the Serra do Buçaco. If you're coming from Coimbra, take the N110 along the Rio Mondego.

ESSENTIALS

BUS CONTACT Castelo Branco Rodoviária Da Beira Interior. ✉ *Rua Poeta João Roiz* ☎ *272 320 997* 🌐 *rede-expressos.pt.*

VISITOR INFORMATION Posto de Turismo Castelo Branco. ✉ *Av. Nuno Álvares 30* ☎ *272 330 339* 🌐 *turismodocentro.pt.*

Castelo dos Templários (*Templar's Castle*)
ARCHAEOLOGICAL SITE | At the top of the town's hill are the ruins of the 12th-century Castelo Templário. Not much remains of the series of walls and towers that once surrounded the entire community. Adjoining the ruins is the flower-covered Miradouro de São Gens, which provides a fine view of the town and surrounding countryside. ✉ *Rua de Acesso ao Castelo dos Templarios.*

★ **Jardim do Paço Episcopal** (*Garden of the Old Episcopal Palace*)
GARDEN | These 18th-century gardens are planted with rows of hedges cut in all sorts of bizarre shapes and contain an unusual assemblage of sculpture. Bordering one of the park's five small lakes are a path and stairway lined on both sides with granite statues of the apostles, the evangelists, and the kings of Portugal. The long-standing Portuguese disdain for the Spanish is graphically demonstrated here; the kings who ruled when Portugal was under Spanish domination are carved to a noticeably smaller scale than the "true" Portuguese rulers. Unfortunately, many statues were damaged by Napoléon's troops when the city was ransacked in 1807. ✉ *Rua Bartolomeu da Costa 5* ☎ *272 348 320* 🌐 *cm-castelo-branco.pt* 🎫 *€2.*

Museu Francisco Tavares Proença Junior
MUSEUM | This small museum is housed in the old Paço Episcopal (Episcopal Palace). In addition to the usual Roman artifacts and odd pieces of furniture, the collection contains some fine examples of the traditional *bordado* (embroidery) for which Castelo Branco is well-known. Adjacent to the museum is a workshop where embroidered bedspreads in traditional patterns are made and sold. ✉ *Rua Dr. Alfredo Mota* ☎ *272 344 277* 🎫 *€3.*

Retiro do Caçador
$ | PORTUGUESE | This restaurant is a carnivore's delight, something that is abundantly clear from the mounted stag's head on the wall. The the menu is predominantly meat and game, including deer, wild boar, and venison. **Known for:** generous portions; attentive service; simple, filling dishes. 💲 *Average main: €10* ✉ *Rua Ruivo Godinho 9* ☎ *272 343 050.*

Hotel Rainha D. Amélia
$ | HOTEL | One of the only lodging choices in the center of Castelo Branco, Hotel Rainha D. Amélia makes sure you don't pass by its unassuming facade by writing its name in big letters down the sidewalk. **Pros:** perfect downtown location; comfortable rooms; affordable rates. **Cons:** the hotel's size can make it feel impersonal; some rooms don't have much of a view; basic decor. 💲 *Rooms from: €50* ✉ *Rua de Santiago 15* ☎ 🌐 *hotelrainhadamelia.pt* 🛏 *64 rooms* 🍽 *Free Breakfast.*

Chapter 9

PORTO

Updated by
Lucy Bryson

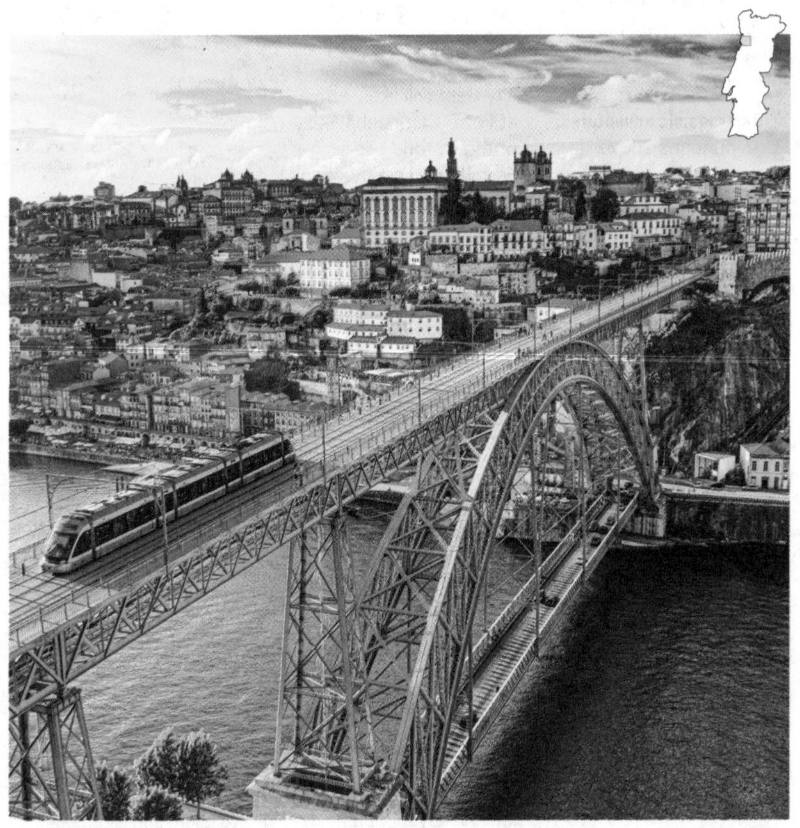

Sights	Restaurants	Hotels	Shopping	Nightlife
★★★★★	★★★★☆	★★★★☆	★★★☆☆	★★★☆☆

WELCOME TO PORTO

TOP REASONS TO GO

★ **Experiencing the old and the new:** Baroque churches and neoclassical palaces sit side by side with some of Europe's best new architecture.

★ **Port wine tastings:** You're never far away from an opportunity to sip port wine in the city that gave the drink its name.

★ **Gastronomic adventures:** Porto punches above its weight in terms of gastronomic achievements. There are several internationally recognized restaurants but also traditional spots offering local specialties like *Francesinhas* and seafood.

★ **Photo-worthy views:** Each steep cobblestone street offers visual rewards in the form of panoramic views, particularly of the glimmering Douro River.

★ **Celebrating at festivals:** On June 23, Porto residents pour into the streets to celebrate the city's patron saint with curbside barbecues, all-night dancing, and curious customs like shaking garlic fronds in the faces of passersby.

Visitors arriving in Porto by plane will find themselves some 11 km (roughly 7 miles) from the city center. The airport's subway station provides a speedy connection to downtown hotels and attractions, and anyone laden down with luggage will find plenty of taxis outside the arrivals lounge. Those arriving by intercity train will likely arrive at Porto-Campanhã, east of the historic center. From here it's a five-minute train ride to the ornately tiled São Bento station, at the heart of the Baixa (downtown). If mobility isn't an issue, the compact city center is best explored on foot. Heading down the slopes takes you to the scenic Ribeira district, and to Vila Nova da Gaia via the Luis I bridge.

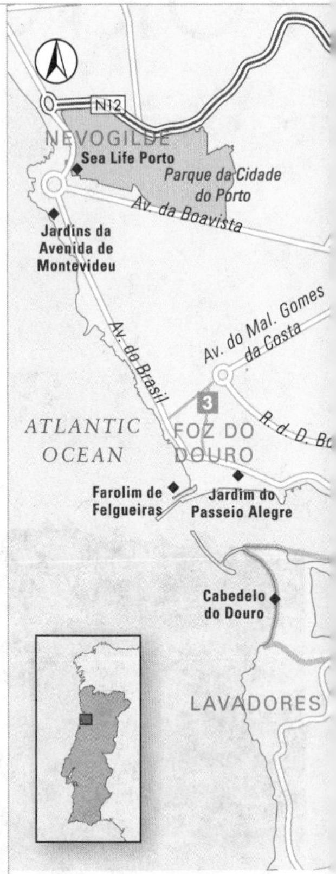

N12
NEVOGILDE
Sea Life Porto
Parque da Cidade do Porto
Av. da Boavista
Jardins da Avenida de Montevideu
Av. do Mal. Gomes da Costa
Av. do Brasil
3
ATLANTIC OCEAN
FOZ DO DOURO
R. d. D. Bo
Farolim de Felgueiras
Jardim do Passeio Alegre
Cabedelo do Douro
LAVADORES

1 Baixa and Ribeira. Home to some of Porto's most famous sights, such as the imposing Torre dos Clérigos, the Sé Cathedral, and the magnificent Livraria Lello (the bookstore that inspired JK Rowling's Harry Potter books), Porto's downtown is also the place for the city's liveliest nightlife and busiest shopping streets. Heading toward the river, the colorful houses spilling down the hillside to the Douro make Ribeira arguably the most picture-perfect part of the city, and the Ponte Luis I spanning the river to Vila Nova de Gaia adds further drama.

2 Vila Nova de Gaia. A town in its own right, Vila Nova de Gaia sits pretty on the river banks facing Porto itself, and is famous for its port wine lodges as well as its dramatically

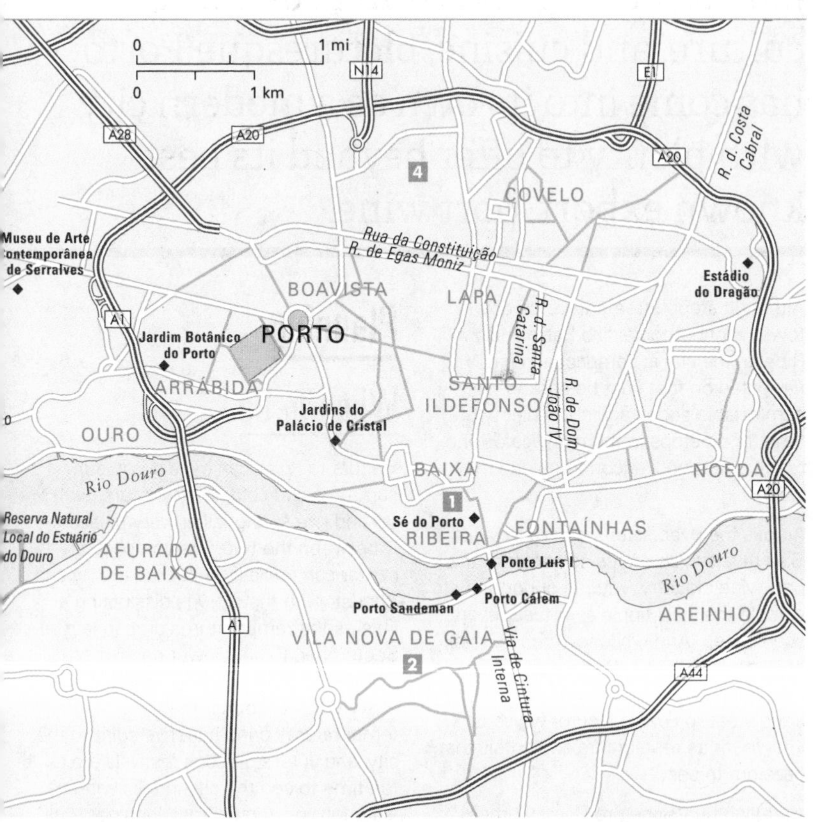

beautiful views. It's a couple of minutes' stroll over the bridge back to Porto's Ribeira, and stopping to snap photos is near-mandatory.

3 Foz do Douro. Few people think of Porto as a beach destination, but the outlying neighborhood of Foz do Douro is a favorite with local sunseekers and a worthy side trip during the summer months. Scenic sandy beaches, upscale shopping, and a lively collection of ocean-facing beach lounges make it the hottest place to be when the sun shines.

4 Greater Porto. Porto's historic center and river-front are the first ports of call for many visitors, but Porto's solid network of subways, trams and buses makes it easy to reach farther-flung points of interest, such as the hip, artsy neighborhood of Cedofeita, the intercity railyway connections at Campanhã, and the upscale shops, pleasant gardens, and impressive cultural scene of Boavista (Porto's longest avenue).

Perched on the steep banks of the River Douro, Porto is many people's favorite part of Portugal. A center for the arts, culture, and cuisine, picturesque Porto has come into its own as a modern city with plenty to offer beyond its best-known export, port wine.

Although steep streets traverse downtown neighborhoods like Baixa and Ribeira, the city is compact and easily navigated on foot (just be sure to wear comfortable shoes and allow plenty of time for pit stops in the many cafés and restaurants you'll encounter along the way).

Across the river, sister city Vila Nova da Gaia revels in its status as center of the port wine industry, with an opportunity to sample the local tipple at virtually every scenic step. And while few people think of Porto as a beach destination, no summer visit to the city is complete without a trip west to Foz do Douro, which is known for its restaurants and hotels that gaze out to sea.

A trading hub since pre-Roman times, vibrant and cosmopolitan Porto has more baroque treasures than Lisbon. Its grandiose granite buildings were financed by the wine trade that made the city wealthy: wine from the upper valley of the Rio Douro (meaning "River of Gold") was transported to Porto, from where it was exported. You can still experience that richness today.

Planning

When To Go

Visitors to Porto can expect hot, sunny summers and cold, rainy winters, with fall and late spring falling very pleasantly between the two. The compact city center can feel a little packed in July and August, with the crowds dissipating a little as the temperatures drop in late September. Expect lower prices from October to April, but be prepared for misty weather to mar the views. Rising temperatures bring a festive spirit to the city, and June's raucous festivals are a fun time to see the city in full swing, although you should book lodgings well in advance if you plan to be here for the the biggest of the parties: the São João festival on June 23.

Planning Your Time

You'll need at least a couple of days to experience central Porto, the wine lodges of Vila Nova de Gaia, and the coast at Foz do Douro. Between *bodega* visits, leave yourself an afternoon or evening free to relax at a riverside bar or restaurant. Art lovers may end up spending hours at the Serralves Contemporary Art Museum, whose extensive gardens also charm visitors. And to really appreciate the Casa da Música, you should take in an evening concert.

Getting Here and Around

The city is congested, so leave your car at the hotel. You can walk around most of central Porto, but be prepared for the steep hills, which can prove tiring in the summer heat. To reach the few outlying attractions, you can use the city's good network of buses, trams, and funicular—all run by Sociedade dos Transportes Colectivos do Porto—or the metro. Its five lines run from 6 am to 1 am, mostly aboveground as a light-rail service outside the center but converging underground at the Trindade stop. The metro offers 24-hour service on weekends and holidays to select stations from June to early October. You can also rent bicycles to pedal out to coastal towns and beaches.

AIR

Porto's Aeroporto Francisco Sá Carneiro, 13 km (8 miles) north of the city, is the gateway to northern Portugal. The airport is served by the metro system (a 30-minute trip downtown, €1.85). Taxis and ride-sharing companies like Uber are also available outside the terminal; the metered fare into town should run €20 to €35 with baggage surcharge. Outside the city limits, tariffs are based on kilometers traveled.

CONTACTS Aeroporto Franciso Sá Carneiro. ☎ *229 432 400* 🌐 *www.aeroportoporto.pt.*

BUS

Buses are a great way to get around this hilly city. One of the most popular tourist routes is Bus 500, which follows the pretty coastal road to the beaches of Foz do Douro and onwards to Matosinhos. Many sightseers opt for hop-on, hop-off buses (€17), with tickets valid for 48 hours after you first validate them. The Red line departs from the Ribeira, while the Blue line leaves from Torre dos Clérigos. For both routes, departures are roughly every half hour.

On buses, you can buy an individual ticket on board (€1.50 one way), but if you're going to use public transport more than once, save money by first buying a €0.60 rechargeable Andante card from a metro station, STCP kiosk, or affiliated convenience stores (look for the Andante decal), then load it up with cash or trips. For both metro and bus journeys with an Andante card, the cost depends on whether trips are within the city limits (€1.20 one way) or beyond (up to €5). On each trip, tickets and Andante cards must be validated.

TAXI

Many Porto locals now use ride-sharing services like Uber rather than calling a cab, but nevertheless you're never far from a taxi stand in downtown Porto. Within the city limits travelers are charged by meter, which starts at €3.25 (rates increase between 9 pm and 6 am, on weekends, and on holidays). Luggage fees are approximately €1.80 per item. Outside the city center (including across the river to Vila Nova de Gaia, where the port wine cellars are located), the rate is €0.50 per km (higher between 9 pm and 6 am, on weekends, and on holidays). Taxis that run outside the city center have a letter "A" on the door. It's considerate, but not obligatory, to tip up to 10%.

TRAIN

Long-distance trains arrive at Porto Campanhã station, east of the center. Note that not all services from Lisbon terminate here; some continue on to Braga. From Campanhã you can take a five-minute connection to the central São Bento station; otherwise, it's a 30-minute scenic walk. From Spain, the Vigo–Porto train crosses at Tui/Valença do Minho and then heads south to Porto, usually stopping at both Campanhã and São Bento.

When leaving Porto, be sure to budget plenty of time from São Bento station to make your connection—or take a taxi straight to Campanhã. For the express service to and from Lisbon, reserve your seat at least a few hours in advance. There are luggage storage facilities at both stations, but are unstaffed and require exact change (you pay on retrieval of your luggage, so don't lose your ticket).

CONTACTS Estação de Campanhã. ✉ *Largo da Estação de Campanhã, Porto* ☎ *707 210 220* 🌐 *www.cp.pt/passageiros/pt/consultar-horarios/estacoes/porto-campanha* Ⓜ *Campanhã.* **Estação de São Bento.** ✉ *Praça Almeida Garrett, Porto* ☎ *707 210 220* 🌐 *www.cp.pt/passageiros/pt/consultar-horarios/estacoes/porto-sao-bento* Ⓜ *São Bento.*

Hotels

Hotels range from boxy but well-equipped business hotels to century-old grande dames in the city center. Gentrification has brought an influx of chic design hotels and small boutique B&Bs, as well as a flurry of homes opening their doors as holiday lets. Visitors who aren't averse to some nighttime noise will find hotels with bags of character and dramatic river views at the colorful (quite literally: the brightly painted buildings are part of its charm) Ribeira neighborhood on the banks of the Douro, while the streets around Aliados are packed with hotels that provide a perfect base for sightseeing. In the summer, Foz do Douro is a good option for those who want to be within easy reach of the beach, while Vila Nova de Gaia, surrounded by wine lodges, is ideal for visitors that are keen to sample Porto's most famous tipple.

Prices in the reviews are the lowest cost of a standard double room in high season. For expanded hotel reviews, visit Fodors.com.

WHAT IT COSTS In Euros

$	$$	$$$	$$$$
RESTAURANTS			
€16 or under	€17–€22	€23–€30	over €30
HOTELS			
€140 or under	€141–€200	€201–€260	over €260

Restaurants

Like Lisbon, Porto is establishing itself as something of a destination for foodies. But while there's plenty of opportunity to enjoy the best of modern cooking techniques, traditional cooking in Porto is rich and heavy. It's typified by the city's favorite dishes, *tripas à moda do Porto* (Porto-style tripe), a concoction involving beans, chicken, sausage, vegetables, and spices, and *Francesinha,* a carb-and-protein bomb involving several types of meat sandwiched between slabs of bread and smothered with a rich sauce, some cheese, and sometimes a fried egg. *Caldo verde* ("green soup") is also ubiquitous; it's made of potato and shredded kale in a broth and is usually served with a slice or two of *chouriço* sausage.

Porto also does a wonderful version of traditional *bolinho de bacalhau* (fried cod and potato patties that are crisp on the outside, soft and fluffy inside) and you're never too far away from a good, strong coffee and a *pastel de nata* (custard tart). Near the riverfront, the focus turns to fish and seafood, with any number of restaurants vying for your attention and most offering a good range of grilled fresh fish which can be washed down with a jug of house wine if you need a break from all that port.

Expect to see breathtakingly beautiful landscapes, complete with terraced vineyards, in the Douro Valley.

Nightlife

Porto nightlife is a lively affair, especially during the summer months when sidewalk cafés and rooftop bars do a brisk trade in jugs of sangria from lunchtime onwards. The real party begins later, however, and it's standing room only at popular bars from midnight until the wee hours of the morning. The waterfront Ribeira district is popular with bohemian barhoppers, and there's been a nightlife renaissance in central Porto in the area just to the north of the Torre dos Clérigos, thanks in part to the vibrant student population. Fashionable bars in this area are open from mid-afternoon until 3 am (4 am on Friday and Saturday). For the liveliest bars and clubs, head to Rua da Galeria de Paris, which might not be quite as chic as the Parisian capital, but does promise a lively night out as revelers wander from bar to bar.

Performing Arts

Noted as a center for modern art, Porto enjoys regular and changing exhibitions at the Museu de Arte Contemporânea, as well as at a variety of galleries, many of which are on Rua Miguel Bombarda. Check local newspapers or with the tourist board for listings of current exhibitions as well as concerts.

Shopping

The best shopping streets are those off the Praça da Liberdade, particularly Rua 31 de Janeiro, Rua dos Clérigos, Rua de Santa Catarina, Rua Sá da Bandeira, Rua Cedofeita, and Rua das Flores. Traditionally, Rua das Flores has been the street for silversmiths, but nowadays they've largely been pushed out by other businesses. Gold-plated filigree is also a regional specialty, found along the same street and along Rua de Santa Catarina. Rua 31 de Janeiro and nearby streets are the center of the shoe trade, and many shops create made-to-measure shoes on request.

You'll see port wine on sale throughout the city, and after sampling a few different types at the caves in Vila Nova de Gaia, you may want to buy a bottle. The more unusual white port, drunk as an aperitif, makes a lovely souvenir as it's not commonly sold in North America or Britain. Try a Portonic, half tonic water and half white port, served in a special glass that you'll see sold in most shops.

Tours

There's no better way to take in the city than from the lovely Douro River. Many short cruises depart several times daily from the Cais da Ribeira, at the foot of Porto's old town. Douro Acima specializes in rides on *rabelos,* centuries-old sailboats traditionally used to transport port wine downriver. The six vessels leave from quays in both Porto's Ribeira district and across the river in Vila Nova de Gaia.

Blue Dragon City Tours
BICYCLE TOURS | The well-regarded Blue Dragon City Tours offers walking tours, as well as trips around the city on bicycles. ✉ *Porto* ☎ *912 562 190* 🌐 *bluedragoncitytours.rezdy.com.*

★ Catavino Tours
SPECIAL-INTEREST | Founder Ryan Opaz is an American wine and food expert based in Portugal, and he's keen to share his deep knowledge of the subject with visitors to the city. ✉ *Porto* ☎ *914 367 836* 🌐 *catavino.net* 🎫 *From €50.*

Douro Acima
BUS TOURS | Sightseeing routes run by Douro Acima (one covering Porto and Vila Nova de Gaia, the other headed to Foz do Douro) depart every half hour. You may hop on and off as often as you wish. ✉ *Porto* ☎ *222 006 418* 🌐 *www.douroacima.pt/en/home* 🎫 *€18.*

Douro Azul
BOAT TOURS | Douro Azul has a wide range of cruises, including trips upriver of up to a week, on air-conditioned hotel boats like the *Invicta* (40 double cabins), the *Douro Queen* (65 double cabins, most with private balconies), and newer *Viking Torgil* (88 cabins). ✉ *Porto* ☎ *223 402 500* 🌐 *www.douroazul.com.*

Helitours Porto
AIR EXCURSIONS | If you want to get above it all, Helitours offers 12-minute flights over Porto. ✉ *Porto* ☎ *225 432 464* 🌐 *portoandlisbon.pt/porto/helitours.*

Living Tours
BUS TOURS | A fun way to see the city, Living Tours has a minitrain you can pick up outside the cathedral. ✉ *Porto* ☎ *228 320 992* 🌐 *www.livingtours.com.*

Porto Free Walking Tours
WALKING TOURS | Those on a budget should look no further than Porto Free Walking Tours, which leave from Praça da Liberdade twice daily Monday through Saturday. ✉ *Porto* ☎ *918 291 519* 🌐 *www.portowalkers.pt/see* 🎫 *Free (gratuity suggested).*

TukTour Porto
PERSONAL GUIDES | This outfitter offers tours on eco-friendly tuk-tuk wagons departing from downtown Porto and across the river in Vila Nova de Gaia. They head out to local beaches, nearby fishing villages, and port wine cellars. ✉ *Cais da Gaia, Vila da Gaia, Porto* ☎ *915 094 443* 🌐 *www.tuktourporto.com/en.*

Visitor Information

The main municipal tourist office is next to the city hall at the top of Avenida dos Aliados, and there are smaller branches at Campanhã Train Station and next to the cathedral. The national tourist office has branches downtown and at the airport. The Vila Nova de Gaia municipality has its own tourist offices with information on the local port wine lodges. The regional tourism board for the whole of the north (including Porto) is based in Viana do Castelo, but there's a small branch at Porto Airport.

CONTACTS Porto Tourism Office. ✉ *Rua Clube dos Fenianos 25, Baixa* ☎ *22 332 6751* 🌐 *visitporto.travel* Ⓜ *Bolhão.*

Baixa and Ribeira

The grandiose baroque architecture of the downtown Baixa gives way to brightly painted buildings along the waterfront in Ribeira, where seafood restaurants serve the catch of the day and visitors goggle at the gorgeous views of the river over a glass of wine. After dark, a lively party scene unfolds in the Baixa, with night owls flocking to the many bars along Rua de Galerias da Paris.

GETTING HERE AND AROUND

The São Bento railway station is not just a handy jumping-off point for exploring the many sights and attractions of downtown Porto, but a major tourist draw in its own right, thanks to the intricate tilework in its vestibule. Most sights in these neighborhoods are within walking distance of each other, but the steep climbs can make it feel like hard work, especially in the heat of summer. The Baixa is well served by subway and by trams, which provide a scenic, if somewhat slow, way to travel between the Ribeira and the Baixa. A funicular railway is a speedier way to make the ascent from the waterfront.

Sights

★ **Cais da Ribeira** (*Ribeira Pier*)
PROMENADE | A string of fish restaurants and *tascas* (taverns) are built into the street-level arcade of timeworn buildings along this pier. In the Praça da Ribeira, people sit and chat at outdoor café tables surrounding a modern, cubelike sculpture; farther on, steps lead to a wide esplanade along the river that's backed by vibrantly hued row houses. The pier also provides the easiest access to the lower level of Porto's most iconic bridge across the Douro, the Ponte Dom Luis I. Those wishing to delve deeper into the Ribeira's 2,000-year past can embark upon informative riverboat tours, leaving from from Cais da Ribeira and across the river in Vila Nova da Gaia, which generally cruise around the city's six bridges and up the river to Peso da Régua and Pinhão. ✉ *Cais da Ribeira, Ribeira.*

★ **Centro Português de Fotografia** (*Portuguese Center of Photography*)
MUSEUM | Housed in a spooky yet stately 18th-century jailhouse, this stellar museum hosts an ever-changing rotation of exhibits of works by modern Portuguese photographers, reflecting their work both at home and abroad. Photography buffs will appreciate the permanent collection of analog cameras housed on the top floor. ✉ *Edifício da Ex-Cadeia e Tribunal da Relação do Porto, Largo Amor de Perdição, Campo dos Mártires da Pátria, Baixa* ☎ *220 046 300* 🌐 *www.cpf.pt* ⏲ *Closed Mon.* Ⓜ *São Bento.*

★ **Estação de São Bento** (*Saint Bento Station*)
TRANSPORTATION SITE (AIRPORT/BUS/FERRY/TRAIN) | This train station was built in the early 20th century (King D. Carlos I laid the first brick himself in 1900) and inaugurated in 1915. It sits precisely where the Convent of S. Bento de Avé-Maria was located, and therefore inherited the convent's name—Saint Bento. The atrium, worth a visit even if you don't have a train to catch, is covered with 20,000 azulejos painted by Jorge Colaço (1916) depicting scenes of Portugal's history—from battles to coronations to royal gatherings—as well as ethnographic images. Designed by Porto-born architect Marques da Silva, it's one of the city's most magnificent artistic undertakings of the early 20th century. ✉ *Praça Almeida Garret, Baixa* ☎ *707 210 220* 🌐 *www.cp.pt* Ⓜ *São Bento.*

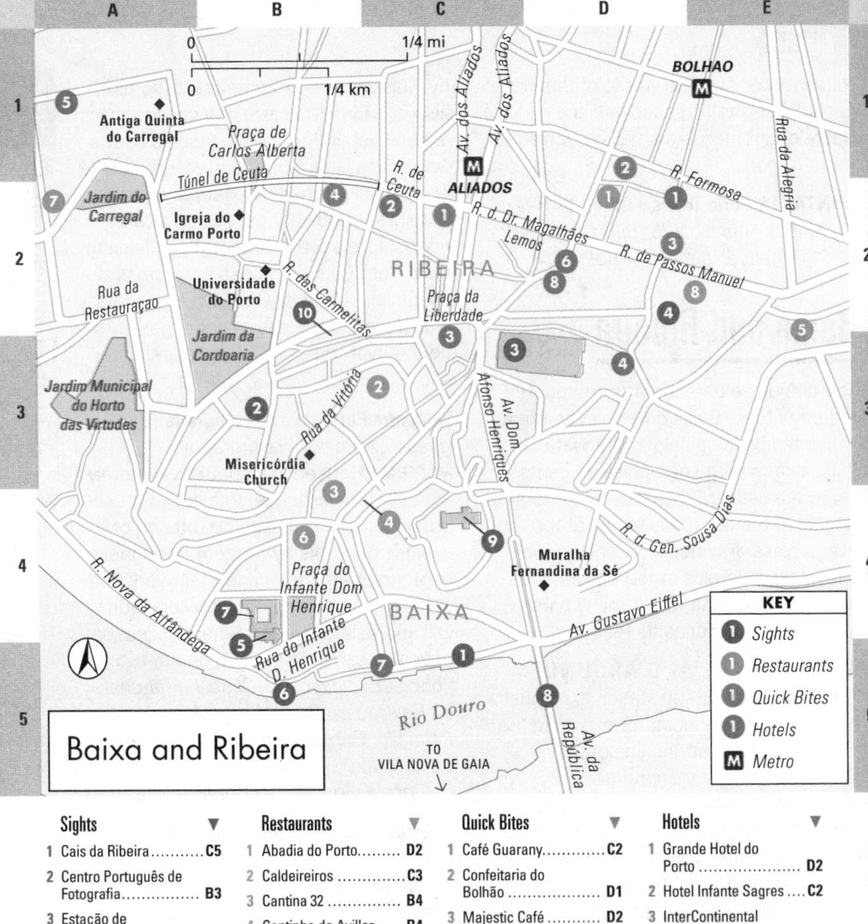

Sights

1 Cais da Ribeira C5
2 Centro Português de Fotografia B3
3 Estação de São Bento C3
4 Igreja de Santo Ildefonso D2
5 Igreja de São Francisco B4
6 Museu do Vinho do Porto B5
7 Palácio da Bolsa B4
8 Ponte Dom Luís I D5
9 Sé do Porto C4
10 Torre dos Clérigos B2

Restaurants

1 Abadia do Porto D2
2 Caldeireiros C3
3 Cantina 32 .... B4
4 Cantinho do Avillez B4
5 Casa Guedes E2
6 DOP B4
7 Época Porto A2
8 O Escondidinho E2

Quick Bites

1 Café Guarany C2
2 Confeitaria do Bolhão D1
3 Majestic Café D2
4 O Diplomata B2

Hotels

1 Grande Hotel do Porto D2
2 Hotel Infante Sagres C2
3 InterContinental Porto-Palacio Das Cardosas C2
4 Mercure Porto Centro Hotel D3
5 Pensão Favorita A1
6 Pestana Porto-A Brasileira D2
7 Pestana Vintage Porto C5
8 PortoBay Hotel Teatro D2

★ **Igreja de Santo Ildefonso** (*Church of St. Ildefonso*)

RELIGIOUS SITE | With the most striking exterior of any church in Porto, Igreja de Santo Ildefonso has a facade covered with some 11,000 blue-and-white azulejo tiles depicting scenes from the Gospels and the life of Saint Ildefonso. The church was completed in the 18th century on the site of a previous chapel from the Middle Ages. While the outside walls are the real attraction, it's worth peeking inside, where you'll find a gilded raised altarpiece by the 18th-century Italian artist Nicolau Nasoni. The church holds a daily mass that's usually packed with locals. ✉ *Praça da Batalha, Baixa* ☎ *222 004 366* 🌐 *www.santoildefonso.org* 🕑 *Closed Mon. until 3 pm.*

★ **Igreja de São Francisco** (*Church of St. Francis*)

RELIGIOUS SITE | During the last days of Porto's siege by the absolutist army (the *miguelistas*) in July 1842, there was gunfire by the nearby Convent of of St. Francis. These shootings caused a fire that destroyed most parts of the convent, sparing only this church. Today the church is the most prominent Gothic monument in Porto. It's a rather undistinguished, late-14th-century Gothic building on the outside, but inside is an astounding interior: gilded carving—added in the mid-18th century—runs up the pillars, over the altar, and across the ceiling. An adjacent museum (Museu de Arte Sacra) houses furnishings from the Franciscan convent. A guided tour (call the day before) includes a visit to the church, museum, and catacombs. ✉ *Rua do Infante Dom Henrique 93, Ribeira* ☎ *222 062 125* 🌐 *www.ordemsaofrancisco.pt* 🎫 *€7.*

Museu do Vinho do Porto (*Port Wine Museum*)

MUSEUM | Not to be confused with the larger, modern port-wine museum upriver in Peso da Régua, this small but worthwhile facility has informative exhibits on the history of the trade that made Porto famous. Displays include implements used in port-wine production—antique glass decanters and textiles, for instance—as well as paintings and engravings depicting the trade. The setting on the Douro River makes for a spectacular walk in the late afternoon, or a scenic ride by Bus 500 or Tram E1. ✉ *Rua de Monchique 98, Ribeira* ☎ *226 057 000* 🌐 *www.cm-porto.pt/cultura/museus-e-arquivos/museu-do-vinho-do-porto* 🎫 *€2* 🕑 *Closed Mon.*

Palácio da Bolsa (*Stock Exchange*)

BANK | Formerly Porto's stock exchange, Palácio da Bolsa is one of the city's most breathtaking historical buildings. Guided tours leaving every half hour are the only way to see the interior of this masterpiece of 19th-century Portuguese architecture, so if you're only in Porto for one day, it's wise to book your tour in the morning for an afternoon time slot. The grand Moorish-style ballroom, with its octagonal dome and ornate arches, is the most memorable chamber. A high-end restaurant called O Commerical serves European dishes in a suitably grand space with high ceilings and elaborate chandeliers. ✉ *Rua Ferreira Borges, Baixa* ☎ *223 399 000* 🌐 *www.palaciodabolsa.com* 🎫 *€10.*

Ponte Dom Luís I (*Luís I Bridge*)

BRIDGE/TUNNEL | Designed by Teófilo Seyrig (who apprenticed for Gustave Eiffel), this two-tiered metal bridge leads directly to the city of Vila Nova de Gaia. On hot summer days some brave souls dive straight into the waters below for a swim, but it's defintiely not for the fainthearted. For most visitors, the real glory is the magnificent view of downtown Porto. The jumble of red-tile roofs on pastel-color buildings is reflected in the majestic Douro River; if the sun is shining just right, everything appears to be washed in gold. By the foot of the bridge is the lower station of the Funicular dos Guindais, the quaintest part of the city's public transportation system, which cranks uphill to the Batalha neighborhood. ✉ *Ponte Dom Luís I, Ribeira.*

Sé do Porto (*Cathedral*)
RELIGIOUS SITE | Originally constructed in the 12th century by the parents of Dom Afonso Henriques (Portugal's first king), Porto's granite cathedral has been rebuilt twice: first in the late 13th century and again in the 18th century, when the architect of the Torre dos Clérigos, Nicolau Nasoni, was among those commissioned to work on its expansion. Despite the renovations, it remains a fortresslike structure—an uncompromising testament to medieval wealth and power. Notice a low relief on the northern tower, depicting a 14th-century vessel and symbolizing the city's nautical vocation. Size is the only exceptional thing about the interior; when you enter the two-story 14th-century cloisters, however, the building comes to life. Decorated with gleaming azulejos, a staircase added by Nasoni leads to the second level and into a richly furnished chapter house, from which there are fine views through narrow windows. Nasono also redesigned the Paço Episcopal (Bishops' Palace) behind the cathedral, adding a famed monumental stairwell. ✉ *Terreiro da Sé, Baixa* ☎ *223 392 330* 🌐 *www.diocese-porto.pt* 🎫 *Free, €5 includes cloisters and palace* ⊙ *Cloisters closed Sun. morning* Ⓜ *São Bento.*

★ **Torre dos Clérigos** (*Clerics Tower*)
VIEWPOINT | Designed by Italian architect Nicolau Nasoni and begun in 1754, the baroque tower of the Igreja dos Clérigos is the tallest in Porto and a landmark on the city's horizon. There are 225 steep stone steps to the belfry, and the considerable effort required to climb them is rewarded by stunning views of the red-roofed Old Town, the river, and the mouth of the Douro River. Binoculars and audio tours are available for an extra charge. The church itself, also built by Nasoni, predates the tower and is an elaborate example of Italianate baroque architecture. Admission includes access to a small museum. ✉ *Rua de São Filipe de Nery, Baixa* ☎ *220 145 489* 🌐 *www.torredosclerigos.pt* 🎫 *€5, €6.50 for guided tour* Ⓜ *São Bento.*

Coffee and Quick Bites

Café Guarany
$$ | CAFÉ | Founded in 1933, this "musicians' café" exudes an old-world charm. The afternoon tea is famous, and if you're lucky you might happen upon a poetry reading or a live concert (often fado music). **Known for:** delicious desserts made with wine; huge selection of teas; bright and colorful decor. 💲 *Average main: €18* ✉ *Av. dos Aliados 89/85, Baixa* ☎ *223 321 272* 🌐 *www.cafeguarany.com* Ⓜ *Aliados.*

Confeitaria do Bolhão
$ | BAKERY | In business for more than a century, the attractively restored Confeitaria do Bolhão is one of the oldest bakeries in town. There's a vast range of breads, pastries, and other local treats, including the featherlight *pão-de-ló* sponge cake. **Known for:** well-regarded in-house bakery; snack bar for light meals; sister restaurant serves larger meals. 💲 *Average main: €14* ✉ *Rua Formosa 339, Baixa* ☎ *223 395 220* 🌐 *www.confeitariadobolhao.com* Ⓜ *Aliados or Bolhão.*

★ **Majestic Café**
$$$ | CAFÉ | Full of art nouveau grandeur—think leaded-glass doorways, elaborately carved woodwork, and ornate chandeliers—the Majestic Café has been the preferred hangout of Portugal's intellectual and social elite since the 1920s. After years of neglect, it was restored to its former glory and is once again an elegant place for coffee, cakes, and evening piano music. **Known for:** belle epoque grandeur; delicious homemade cakes; afternoon tea with scones. 💲 *Average main: €21* ✉ *Rua de Santa Catarina 112,*

Did You Know?

Porto, on the River Douro, is one of Portugal's most popular tourist centers. While known for its charming old town, cultural attractions, and, of course, its port wine production, the city is also emerging as an international culinary powerhouse.

Baixa ☎ *222 003 887* 🌐 *www.cafemajestic.com* ⏲ *Closed Sun.* Ⓜ *Bolhão.*

O Diplomata

$ | **CAFÉ** | Brunch is served until the late afternoon at this relaxed spot, famous for its delicious pancakes and other dishes you can top with a range of sweet and savory treats. All the specials are listed on a massive chalkboard behind the bar. **Known for:** a wide range of coffee beverages; energy boosters like açaí bowls; all-day brunch menu. $ *Average main: €8* ✉ *Rua de José Falcão 32, Baixa* ☎ *960 188 203* ⏲ *Closed Mon. No dinner* Ⓜ *Aliados.*

Restaurants

★ Abadia do Porto

$$ | **PORTUGUESE** | With a cavernous interior, lovely blue and yellow azulejo tiles, and formal staff, this upscale tasca has been a local favorite since 1939. It serves vast portions of typical Portuguese dishes such as *cabrito assado* (roast kid) and *bacalhau à Gomes Sá* (codfish with onions, potato, egg, and olives). **Known for:** good wine list and advice on pairings; excellent fish and seafood dishes; grand building and long history. $ *Average main: €19* ✉ *Rua Ateneu Comercial do Porto 22–24, Baixa* ☎ *222 008 757* 🌐 *www.abadiadoporto.com* ⏲ *Closed Sun. No lunch Mon.* Ⓜ *Aliados.*

Caldeireiros

$ | **PORTUGUESE** | Sharing a half dozen or so *petiscos* (Portuguese-style tapas) is an increasingly popular way to dine in Porto, and there's no better place to sample a wide array of small plates than at Caldeireiros. With long, candlelit tables adding to the communal feel, the restaurant has earned a reputation among a hip young crowd that passes around plates of prawns, sardines, and other local favorites. **Known for:** impressive platters of smoked meats and cured cheeses; sausages and other Portuguese comfort foods; good wine list and sangria by the jug. $ *Average main: €15* ✉ *Rua dos Caldeireiros 139, Baixa* ☎ *223 214074* ⏲ *Closed Sun.* Ⓜ *São Bento.*

★ Cantina 32

$$ | **PORTUGUESE** | Make reservations well in advance, as walk-ins often find themselves out of luck at this industrial-chic spot serving inventive renderings of local classics. Its signature dish is a whole grilled octopus easily big enough for two to share, but there are also favorites like *bacalhau à bras* (a salt-cod-and-shoestring-potato scramble). **Known for:** many dishes served in the pan they were cooked in; perfect location on a pedestrian street; inventive use of Portuguese staples. $ *Average main: €18* ✉ *Rua das Flores 32, Baixa* ☎ *222 039 069* 🌐 *www.cantina32.com* ⏲ *Closed Sun.* Ⓜ *Sao Bento.*

★ Cantinho do Avillez

$$ | **PORTUGUESE** | José Avillez, the head-turning young chef behind the award-winning Belcanto in Lisbon, has made a splash on the Porto culinary scene with Cantinho do Avillez, a homey yet modern dining room located just downhill from São Bento Train Station. Expect moments of molecular gastronomy such as "exploding olives" that burst with flavor on your tongue alongside glammed-up versions of local favorites like steak sandwiches, served here with garlic sauce and fleur de sel. **Known for:** the cuisine is high-end, but the prices are not; trendy but relaxed atmosphere; plenty of vegetarian options. $ *Average main: €22* ✉ *Rua de Mouzinho da Silveira 166, Baixa* ☎ *223 227 879* 🌐 *cantinhodoavillez.pt/en/restaurantes/mouzinho-da-silveira.html* Ⓜ *Sao Bento.*

★ Casa Guedes

$ | **PORTUGUESE** | Without a doubt, one of the most heavenly—and budget-friendly—mouthfuls in Porto is the pulled-pork-and-sheep's-milk-cheese slider from Casa Guedes. Served on a warm country roll and oozing with pungent Serra da Estrela cheese, it's no wonder there are always lines out the door at this unapologetically simple local favorite. **Known for:** grab one of the tables on the sidewalk out front; absolutely delicious roast pork sandwiches; refreshing house wines. *$ Average main: €5 ✉ Praça dos Poveiros 130, Baixa ☎ 222 002874.*

★ DOP

$$$$ | PORTUGUESE | Nationally renowned chef Rui Paula brings his culinary wizardry to traditional dishes like *caldeirada de bacalhau* (Portuguese cod fish stew). The dining room is bright and modern, providing the perfect backdrop for dishes that are always works of art. **Known for:** good use of such traditional ingredients as milk-fed goat; there are always several vegetarian options of the menu; wonderful set-price menus at lunch and dinner. *$ Average main: €35 ✉ Palácio das Artes, Largo de São Domingos 18, Baixa ☎ 222 014 313 🌐 www.doprestaurante.pt ⏲ Closed Sun. No lunch Mon. Ⓜ Sao Bento.*

Época Porto

$ | VEGETARIAN | The city has a smattering of restaurants focusing on plant-based dishes, and the best of the bunch is Época Porto. It's a small, light-filled space serving breakfasts, lunches, and brunches made entirely with organic produce—think barley bowls with mushrooms, goat cheese, and caramelized onion—and there's a range of natural wines to accompany your meal. **Known for:** everything is made from scratch right on the premises; delicious breads served hot from the oven; large selection of coffee and tea drinks. *$ Average main: €8 ✉ Rua do Rosário 22, Baixa ☎ 913 732 038 ⏲ Closed Sun. and Mon.*

O Escondidinho

$$ | PORTUGUESE | FAMILY | In business since 1934, this unpretentious eatery's long history is evident the moment you walk inside and see the dining room's hand-painted tiles from the 17th century. It began winning awards early on, and even though it no longer racks up Michelin stars, its lovingly prepared dishes from northern Portugal still make for hordes of happy diners. **Known for:** delicious regional treats on the dessert trolley; vegetarian options like wild mushrooms au gratin; steaks and seafood served a variety of ways. *$ Average main: €22 ✉ Rua Passos Manuel 142, Baixa ☎ 222 001 079 🌐 www.escondidinho.com.pt Ⓜ São Bento.*

Hotels

Grande Hotel do Porto

$ | HOTEL | If you enjoy shopping, you can't do better than the stately Grande Hotel do Porto, which sits on the city's most popular shopping street. **Pros:** just the right mix of old-fashioned charm and newfangled facilities; on-site restaurant is a sumptuous space; plush lounge for reading or relaxing. **Cons:** style won't appeal to everybody; most rooms are rather small; no swimming pool. *$ Rooms from: €125 ✉ Rua de Santa Catarina 197, Baixa ☎ 222 076 690 🌐 www.grandehotelporto.com 94 rooms Free Breakfast Ⓜ Bolhão.*

★ Hotel Infante Sagres

$$$ | HOTEL | Intricately carved wood, beautiful rugs and tapestries, heavenly stained-glass windows, and a vintage elevator make Porto's first luxury hotel still a standout today. **Pros:** fashion-themed Vogue Cafe has art deco fabulousness; great views from upper floors, sundeck, and pool; individually decorated guest rooms. **Cons:** some rooms get street noise; in a very busy area; small pool. *$ Rooms from: €230 ✉ Praça D. Filipa de Lencastre 62, Baixa ☎ 223 398 500 🌐 www.infantesagres.com 85 rooms Free Breakfast Ⓜ Aliados.*

★ InterContinental Porto–Palacio das Cardosas

$$$ | HOTEL | The InterContinental Porto–Palacio das Cardosas has got it all: location, luxury, and an intriguing history to boot. **Pros:** in a former monastery dating from the 15th century; guest rooms have a regal feel; excellent on-site restaurant. **Cons:** some street noise in front-facing rooms; rates among the city's highest; can feel a bit formal. *Rooms from: €235 Praça da Liberdade 25, Baixa 220 035 600 www.ichotelsgroup.com/intercontinental/en/gb/locations/porto 105 rooms No meals São Bento.*

Mercure Porto Centro Hotel

$ | HOTEL | FAMILY | Overlooking one of Porto's central squares, this upscale chain property is a good choice for its central location, luxurious accommodations, and reasonable price. **Pros:** sleek restaurant serves excellent Portuguese dishes; ideal location for sightseeing; generous breakfast included. **Cons:** rooms overlooking the square can be noisy on weekends; some rooms in need of updating; no pool or fitness center. *Rooms from: €115 Praça da Batalha 116, Baixa 222 043 300 www.accorhotels.com/gb/hotel-1975-mercure-porto-centro-hotel/index.shtml 147 rooms Free Breakfast São Bento.*

Pensão Favorita

$ | B&B/INN | Among the trendy galleries and shops along Rua Miguel Bombarda, this small design hotel has a crisp, contemporary style that highlights works by hot new artists. **Pros:** basement restaurant has an ample terrace; spacious and tastefully decorated rooms; perfect for families. **Cons:** rooms in the front can be noisy; not many amenities; books up quickly in summer. *Rooms from: €80 Rua Miguel Bombarda 267, Baixa 220 134 157 www.pensaofavorita.pt 12 rooms Free Breakfast.*

Pestana Porto-A Brasileira

$$$ | HOTEL | Lots of the original architectural flourishes were retained when this local landmark was transformed into the Pestana Porto, including stained-glass windows, towering columns, and coffered ceilings. **Pros:** painstakingly restored historic building; great location in the heart of downtown; good on-site dining options. **Cons:** fitness center is small; rooms on the small side; can be a little pricey. *Rooms from: €210 Rua de Sá da Bandeira 91, Baixa 218 442 001 www.pestanacollection.com/en/hotel/pestana-porto-brasileira 89 rooms Free Breakfast São Bento.*

Pestana Vintage Porto

$$$ | HOTEL | Located near the waterfront, the Pestana Vintage Porto occupies a restored warehouse that's connected to several neighboring houses; as a result, every room is unique, and many have nice details like restored stone windows or towering French doors. **Pros:** some have stunning river views, while others overlook an alley; good location for sightseeing in Ribeira; tasty on-site restaurant. **Cons:** uphill walk to many nearby sights; no on-site parking; some rooms are small. *Rooms from: €230 Praça da Ribeira 1, Ribeira 223 402 300 www.pestana.com 109 rooms Free Breakfast.*

PortoBay Hotel Teatro

$$ | HOTEL | This glamorous design hotel occupies what was once a 19th-century theater, which means at reception you pick up the ticket to your room, and you can dine in the Palco (stage) restaurant or enjoy a drink at the Plateia (audience) bar. **Pros:** all guests have access to a terrace with gorgeous views; restaurant serves excellent traditional cuisine; great location for sightseeing. **Cons:** only the pricier rooms have private terraces; aesthetic verges on ostentatious; small fitness center. *Rooms from: €155 Rua Sá da Bandeira 84, Baixa 220 409 627 www.portobay.com/en/hotels/porto-hotels/portobay-hotel-teatro 74 rooms Free Breakfast São Bento.*

Nightlife

BARS

Candelabro

BARS/PUBS | At this smoky, bohemian bookstore-turned-bar, drinks run cheaper than most other nightspots in the area. It's supposed to close at 2 am, but hours are elastic on weekends. ✉ *Rua da Conceição 3, Baixa* ☎ *966 984 250* 🌐 *www.cafecandelabro.com* Ⓜ *Aliados.*

Casa do Livro

BARS/PUBS | On the city's liveliest nightlife strips, this speakeasy in a former bookstore is a classic late-night hangout serving creative cocktails against a musical backdrop that ranges from tinkling jazz piano to romantic fado sessions to high-energy DJ sets. ✉ *Rua da Galeria de Paris 85, Baixa* ☎ *919676 969* Ⓜ *Aliados.*

★ Prova

WINE BARS—NIGHTLIFE | At this sophisticated wine bar, sommelier Diogo Amado offers perfect suggestions for the best beverages to pair with plates of carefully chosen petiscos. The gorgeous space with stone walls and bottles displayed like works of art hosts frequent live music. ✉ *Rua Ferreira Borges 86, Ribeira* ☎ *916 499 121* 🌐 *prova.com.pt* Ⓜ *São Bento.*

MUSIC CLUBS

Hard Club

MUSIC CLUBS | For live music from rising stars of the local music scene, head to this club inside a magnificent 18th-century market hall. Weekends feature live music from jazz to indie rock. There's an airy café upstairs that attracts a hip young crowd. ✉ *Mercado Ferreira Borges, Praça do Infante D. Henrique, Baixa* ☎ *220 101 186* 🌐 *www.hardclubporto.com.*

★ Maus Hábitos

MUSIC CLUBS | A meeting place for Porto's leading artists, intellectuals, and alternative types, Maus Hábitos—meaning "Bad Habits"—is a gallery, restaurant, and cultural center—and also the hippest nightlife in town. The mixed bag of nightly events ranges from DJ sets to live theater to dance parties. ✉ *Rua Passos Manuel 178, 4th fl., Baixa* ☎ *222/221 087 268* 🌐 *www.maushabitos.com* Ⓜ *Alidos.*

Performing Arts

Coliseu Porto Ageas

MUSIC | This is one of the biggest showrooms in Portugal, with nearly 3,000 seats. Countless Portuguese and international showbiz legends have appeared here, including Bob Dylan and legendary fado singer Amália Rodrigues. ✉ *Rua de Passos Manuel 137, Baixa* ☎ *223 394 940* 🌐 *www.coliseu.pt.*

Teatro Nacional de São João

MUSIC | Opening its doors for the first time in 1920, this neoclassical theater is one of the city's architectural treasures. It hosts and produces a good range of classical and contemporary concerts and plays all year round. ✉ *Praça da Batalha, Baixa* ☎ *223 401 900* 🌐 *www.tnsj.pt* Ⓜ *São Bento.*

Shopping

With Portugal's large textile and apparel industries concentrated in the north, it's no surprise that Porto is home to a number of the country's leading fashion designers. Several chic shops offer a chance to browse for one-off designs and vintage pieces, keeping the city's fashion-conscious population looking fabulous.

ANTIQUES

Pedro A. Baptista

ANTIQUES/COLLECTIBLES | This elegant shop is a reputable dealer in antique and modern silver pieces. ✉ *Rua das Flores 235, Baixa* ☎ *222 002 880.*

BOOKS

★ Livraria Lello

BOOKS/STATIONERY | Legend has it that one of J. K. Rowling's chief inspirations for the fantasy world of Harry Potter was this century-old bookstore located in the Vitoria district. Although Rowling hasn't confirmed these rumors, an undeniable fairy-tale-like magic permeates this place, whether you're marveling at its 60,000 books, painted-glass ceiling, fanciful facade, or crimson double-helix staircase. In recent years, the bookstore has become so overrun with tourists that there's now a €5 admission fee, which is redeemable against any purchase in the store. ✉ *Rua das Carmelitas 144, Baixa* ☎ *222 002 880* 🌐 *www.livrarialello.pt* Ⓜ *Aliados.*

CLOTHING

Fashion Clinic

CLOTHING | Snappy dressers with cash to spare head here for high-end, fashion-forward clothes, shoes, and accessories. This store specializes in menswear, while a second branch on Avenida da Boavista caters to sharply dressed women. ✉ *Palácio das Cardosas, Praça da Liberdade 39, Baixa* ☎ *227 660 000* 🌐 *www.fashionclinic.com* Ⓜ *São Bento.*

★ The Feeting Room

SHOES/LUGGAGE/LEATHER GOODS | This ultramodern boutique specializes in women's shoes and accessories for both men and women. Of particular interest are the Maria Maleta leather bags, handmade in Porto by two young female entrepreneurs. Wacky flats and platform shoes by Portuguese designer Marita Moreno are also worth seeking out. ✉ *Largo dos Lóios 86, Baixa* ☎ *220 110 463* 🌐 *www.thefeetingroom.com* Ⓜ *São Bento.*

★ La Paz

CLOTHING | Nautical fashions are curated with flair at this inviting menswear store in the heart of the Ribeira. Although founders José Miguel de Abreu and André Bastos Teixeira now sell their Atlantic-inspired pieces as far afield as Korea and Japan, they can often be found here at their flagship store with its beautiful river views. ✉ *Rua da Reboleira 23, Baixa* ☎ *222 025 037* Ⓜ *Tram line 1 to Infante.*

Luis Buchinho

CLOTHING | The comfortable, colorful designs by this Portuguese fashion legend have a strong urban sensibility. The women's wear is particularly stunning. ✉ *Rua de Sá da Bandeira 812, Baixa* ☎ *222 012 776* 🌐 *www.luisbuchinho.pt* Ⓜ *Bolhao.*

CRAFTS

Prometeu Artesanato

CRAFTS | This stylish shop has ceramics, tiles, and other handicrafts from all over the country. Some of the work is done right here in the shop. ✉ *Rua Alexandre Herculano 355, Ribeira* ☎ *222 203 094.*

FOOD AND WINE

Portogalia

FOOD/CANDY | A limited selection of port wines can be had at any supermarket, but to try smaller-production selections that you've never heard of before—plus get expert advice from a French expat—stop by this wine bar and shop in the Ribeira district. The store organizes tastings from a selection of 200 ports, accompanied by cheeses and sweets. ✉ *Rua de São João 28–30, Ribeira* ☎ *222 011 050* 🌐 *www.portologia.pt* Ⓜ *Ribeira.*

GIFTS AND SOUVENIRS

A Vida Portuguesa

CRAFTS | One of Portugal's most talked-about retailers is A Vida Portuguesa, which occupies a magnificent former clothing store. Like its sibling in Lisbon, it carries vintage Portuguese brands of soap and other toiletries, jewelry and accessories, and period toys. ✉ *Rua de Cândido dos Reis 36, Baixa* ☎ *222 022 2105* 🌐 *www.avidaportuguesa.com* Ⓜ *Sao Bento.*

Mercado 48

CLOTHING | A colorful hodgepodge of Portuguese-made apparel and accessories, Mercado 48 is a lovely place to browse. ✉ *Rua da Conceição 48, Baixa* ☎ 🌐 *www.mercado48.pt* Ⓜ *Aliados.*

JEWELRY AND ACCESSORIES

Boutique

JEWELRY/ACCESSORIES | The beautiful window dressing is a clue to the high standard of jewelry, watches, bags, and other accessories at this carefully curated store that brings several acclaimed Portuguese manufacturers and designers together under one roof. ✉ *Rua Mouzinho da Silveira 288, Baixa* ☎ *914 450 094.*

Ourivesaria Eduardo Carneiro

JEWELRY/ACCESSORIES | Rua das Flores is famous for its *ourivesarias* (goldsmiths), and this family-run establishment has been in business here for over 100 years. Beautiful window displays entice you in, and you can choose from finely crafted gold and silver. ✉ *Rua das Flores 225, Baixa* ☎ *222 001 152* Ⓜ *Sao Bento.*

MARKETS AND MALLS

Centro Comercial Bombarda

SHOPPING CENTERS/MALLS | One of the more intriguing venues on Rua Miguel Bombarda, the epicenter of the city's art scene, this shopping center is filled with one-of-a-kind galleries and interesting shops run by local entrepreneurs. Each Saturday there's an organic food market. ✉ *Rua Miguel Bombarda 285, Baixa* ☎ *934 337 703* 🌐 *www.ccbombarda.blogspot.com.*

Galerias Lumière

SHOPPING CENTERS/MALLS | This posh shopping center in a refurbished cinema building boasts some of the most avant-garde boutiques in Porto. Look out for skilled jewelers making artsy one-off pieces. ✉ *Rua José Falcão 157, Baixa* ☎ Ⓜ *Aliados.*

Activities

BIKING

Vieguini Bike Rentals

BICYCLE TOURS | At the bottom of Rua do Infante D. Henrique, Vieguini rents out mountain bikes and scooters. ✉ *Rua Nova da Alfândega 7, Ribeira* ☎ *914 306 838* 🌐 *www.vieguini.pt.*

Vila Nova de Gaia

Across the Rio Douro from central Porto, the city of Vila Nova de Gaia has been the headquarters of the port-wine trade since the late 17th century, when import bans on French wine led British merchants to look for alternative sources. By the 18th century, the British had established companies and a regulatory association in Porto. The wine was transported from vineyards on the upper Douro to port-wine caves at Vila Nova de Gaia, where it was allowed to mature before being exported. Little has changed in the relationship between Porto and the Douro since those days, as wine is still transported to the city downriver (in temperature-controlled trucks nowadays), and matured and bottled in the warehouses. A couple of the traditional rabelo boats are moored at the quayside on the Vila Nova de Gaia side.

It's perfectly possible to spend an entire day visiting and sampling the wares of the many wine cellars here: a couple of the most iconic brands are Sandeman and Cálem, both of which more than merit a visit.

GETTING HERE AND AROUND

Across the river, Vila Nova de Gaia (locals shorten the name to simply Gaia) is easily reached on foot by crossing the Dom Luis I bridge, very much a tourist attraction in its own right. You can also take the Metro Line D across the river to Jardim Do Morro. Many businesses are clustered along the riverbank, called Cais de Gaia, and the views across to Porto make this a lovely place for a stroll. Exploring the hilly streets, with their cobblestone alleyways and abundant wine lodges, is a pleasant way to spend a day, but if hill climbing doesn't appeal, an enjoyable five-minute cable car ride links the riverfront with Jardim do Morro, in the upper echelons of the town.

At Sandeman, a famed port wine-making facility, the cellars have been in use since 1811.

Sights

Casa-Museu Teixeira Lopes (*Teixeira Lopes House and Museum*)
MUSEUM | The former home of the sculptor António Teixeira Lopes (1866–1942) contains some excellent sculpture as well as a varied collection of paintings by Teixeira Lopes's contemporaries. It's worth spending some time perusing the collection of books, coins, and ceramics. ✉ *Rua Teixeira Lopes 32, Vila Nova de Gaia* ☎ *223 751 224* ⏲ *Closed Mon., weekend afternoons* Ⓜ *Camera de Gaia.*

Porto Cálem
LOCAL INTEREST | Cálem is Portugal's biggest port wine producer, and its name is a landmark on the Vila Nova de Gaia skyline. The grand building on the riverbanks is an attraction in itself, and visitors have the option of enjoying fado shows and food-pairing sessions as well as taking tours of the cellars and tasting the wares. ✉ *Av. Diogo Leite, 344, Vila Nova de Gaia* ☎ *916 113 451* 🌐 *tour.calem.pt* 🎫 *€13 tour and tasting* Ⓜ *Jardim do Morro.*

Porto Sandeman
WINERY/DISTILLERY | **FAMILY** | Sandeman's distinctive logo can be seen from across the river, and the image of cable cars soaring over the black, cloaked figure is an unforgettable one. Scotsman George Sandeman founded the brand in London in 1790, and the cellars in Vila Nova de Gaia have been in use since 1811. A museum here re-creates 18th-century London through photographs and other artifacts, and visitors can also explore the cellars and sample the famous tipple. ✉ *Largo Miguel Bombarda 47, Porto* ☎ *223 740 534* 🌐 *www.sandeman.com* 🎫 *Free* Ⓜ *Jardim do Morro.*

Teleférico de Gaia (*Gaia Cable Car*)
VIEWPOINT | **FAMILY** | If your feet are tired, skip climbing up Vila Nova de Gaia's steep hills on foot and hop on the cable car, which offers sweeping views of the Douro River and the Ribeira. ✉ *Calçada da Serra 143, Vila Nova de Gaia* ☎ *223 741 440* 🌐 *www.gaiacablecar.com/* 🎫 *€6 one way* Ⓜ *Jardim do Morro.*

Porto's Wine Trail

Vila Nova de Gaia bodegas include such well-known names as Sandeman, Osborne, Cockburn, Kopke, Ferreira, Calém, Taylor's, Barros, Ramos-Pinto, Real Companhia Velha, Fonseca, Rozès, Burmester, Offley, Noval, and Graham's. All are signposted and within a few minutes' walk of the bridge and each other; their names are also displayed in huge white letters across their roofs. Most bodegas offer free guided tours, which always end with a tasting of one or two wines and an opportunity to buy bottles from the on-site shop. Children are usually welcome and are often fascinated by the huge warehouses and clunky old machinery. From April through September, the major lodges are generally open daily 9:30 to 6, taking a break for lunch. The rest of the year, tours start a little later and end a little earlier. The tourist office at Vila Nova de Gaia offers a small map of the main lodges and can advise you on hours of the smaller operations. Some lodges also have restaurants with quite sophisticated menus; a prime example is Taylor's **Barão Fladgate** (Rua do Choupelo 250 ☏ *223 742 800* 🌐 *www.tresseculos.pt*), whose location uphill means its garden and terrace afford magnificent views of Porto.

Restaurants

The Yeatman Restaurant
$$$$ | PORTUGUESE | You don't need to be a guest at The Yeatman Hotel to dine in its Michelin-starred fine-dining restaurant, but you will need advance reservations and deep pockets (the tasting menus start at €170 per person, and that doesn't include wine pairings). Chef Ricardo Costa's elegant dishes focus on the region's seafood, presenting traditional dishes with imagination and flair. **Known for:** seasonal tasting menus feature the best local produce; elegant dining room with lovely views of the river; one of the most extensive wine lists in Portugal. *$ Average main: €170 ✉ The Yeatman Hotel, Rua do Chopelo, Santa Marinha, Vila Nova de Gaia ☏ 222 133 100 🌐 www.the-yeatman-hotel.com/en/food/restaurant Ⓜ General Torres.*

Hotels

★ The Yeatman
$$$ | HOTEL | If you count wine among your passions, a stay at the British-inspired Yeatman Hotel should be on your itinerary. **Pros:** location is excellent for visiting wine cellars; sweeping views of picturesque Porto; great amenities for families. **Cons:** location on a rather steep hill means a lot of walking; neoclassical decor can seem over the top; prices are not cheap. *$ Rooms from: €250 ✉ Rua do Choupelo, Santa Marinha, Vila Nova de Gaia ☏ 220 133 100 🌐 www.theyeatman.com 82 rooms 🍽 Free Breakfast Ⓜ General Torres.*

Nightlife

Terrace Lounge 360°
BARS/PUBS | With a prime riverfront location at the top of Espaço Porto Cruz, a cultural center dedicated to the country's wines, this is easily among the best of the city's rooftop bars. It serves light meals and snacks by day, then

transforms into a happening nightspot once the sun starts to dip below the horizon. As the name suggests, the views are impressive. ✉ *Largo Miguel Bombarda 23, Vila Nova de Gaia* ☎ *220 925 340* 🌐 *www.myportocruz.com* Ⓜ *Jardim Do Morro.*

Foz do Douro

Literally "Mouth of the Douro," this prosperous suburb is invariably known here simply as "Foz." You haven't gotten under the skin of Porto if you haven't ventured to this beach community: it's a place where city dwellers flock to kick back beside the sea or go for brisk walks on its magnificent promenades.

GETTING HERE AND AROUND

Take Tram 1 from Ribeira, a roughly 20-minute ride that hugs the riverbank and offers some jaw-dropping views. Bus 500 from São Bento is a more practical, if less romantic option.

Sights

Casa de Chá da Boa Nova

BUILDING | Architecture buffs intrigued by Álvaro Siza Vieira's work after visiting the Museu de Arte Contemporânea might consider a trip to this modernist teahouse wedged between boulders just steps from the sea. One of Siza's earliest projects, completed in 1963, it was designed after careful analysis of the surrounding rock formations, tides, and flora. The approach—a series of platforms, steps, and bifold doors—provides a sense of anticipation and views of the structure and the ocean beyond it. In summer, the enormous windows slide down, creating the impression you can step right out into the sea. At the award-winning restaurant you can take in glorious sea views as you tackle huge plates of seafood and grilled fish. ■ **TIP→ To visit the interior of the house you must reserve ahead.** ✉ *Av. da Liberdade, Leça da Palmeira* ☎ *229 940 066* 🌐 *www.casadechadaboanova.pt/en* ⊙ *Closed Sun. and Mon.*

Sea Life Porto

ZOO | FAMILY | The city's top children's attraction, this compact aquarium is at the western end of Avenida da Boavista. Sharks, jellyfish, and seahorses are among the 5,600 or so animals on display, representing more than 100 species. Other highlights include live turtle feeding and an interactive Finding Dory trail. The nearby Parque da Cidade, a large landscaped park dotted with trees and lakes, is a lovely place for a picnic. ✉ *1ª Rua Particular do Castelo do Queijo, Foz do Douro* ☎ *226 190 400* 🌐 *www.visitsealife.com/porto* 🎫 *€13.95.*

Restaurants

Pedro Lemos

$$$$ | **CONTEMPORARY** | A world away from the hustle and bustle of downtown, Pedro Lemos's namesake restaurant occupies a cozy dining room in a stone farmhouse on a scenic riverbank in Foz do Douro. Racking up award after award, his powers are in full force here with decadent, expertly prepared dishes that center around the best the region has to offer: blue lobster, milk-fed lamb, and roasted Iberian pork from Alentejo—available in four-, six-, or eight-course tasting menus. **Known for:** best seats are on the gorgeous rooftop terrace; excellent wine list and advice on pairings; somewhat off-the-beaten track location. $ *Average main: €80* ✉ *Rua do Padre Luís Cabral 974, Foz do Douro* ☎ *220 115 986* 🌐 *www.pedrolemos.net* ⊙ *Closed Sun. and Mon.*

Hotels

Hotel Boa-Vista

$ | **HOTEL** | **FAMILY** | True to its name—which literally means "nice view"—this hotel has eye-popping views from the rooftop pool and sun terrace of the Douro

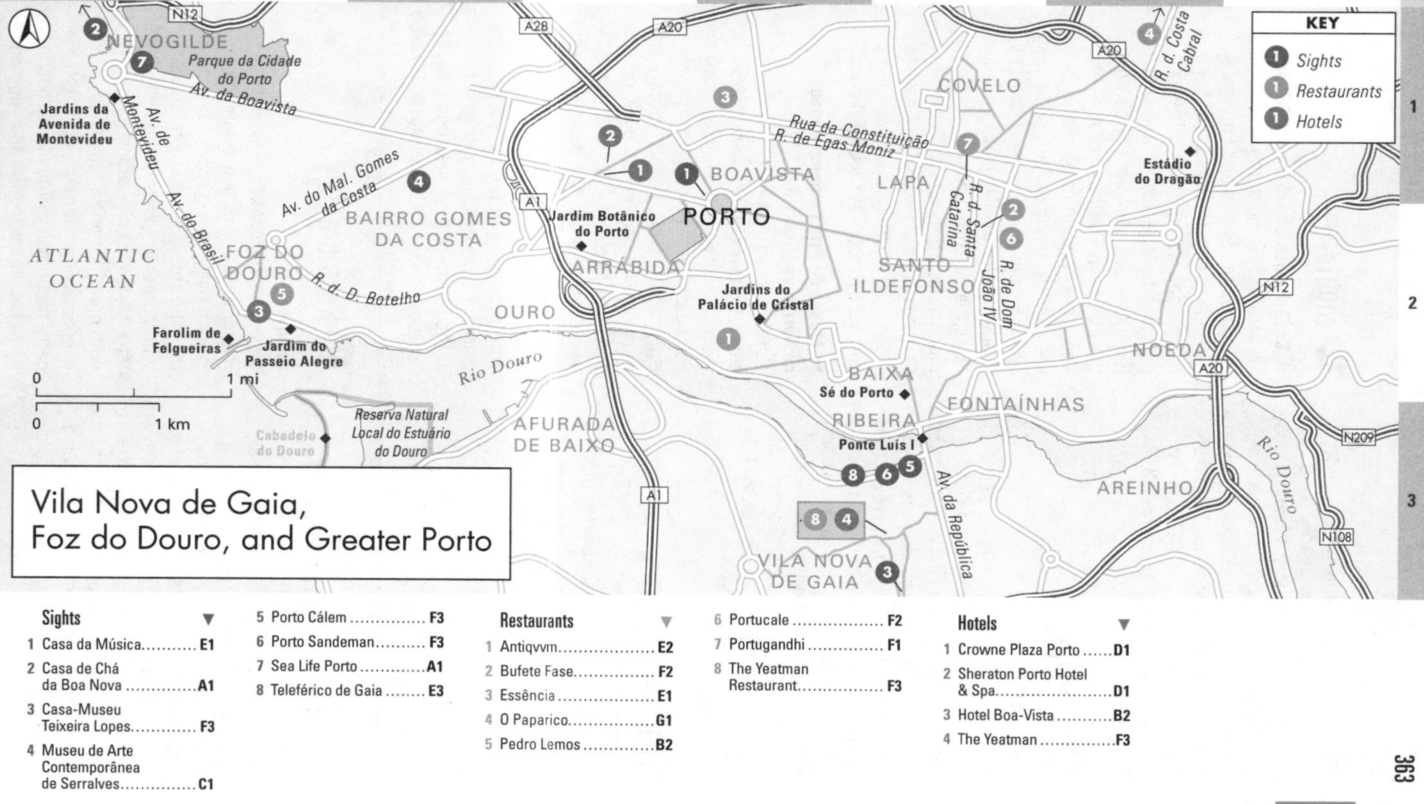

Vila Nova de Gaia, Foz do Douro, and Greater Porto

Sights

1 Casa da Música E1
2 Casa de Chá da Boa Nova A1
3 Casa-Museu Teixeira Lopes............. F3
4 Museu de Arte Contemporânea de Serralves............... C1
5 Porto Cálem F3
6 Porto Sandeman.......... F3
7 Sea Life Porto A1
8 Teleférico de Gaia E3

Restaurants

1 Antiqvvm.................... E2
2 Bufete Fase................. F2
3 Essência E1
4 O Paparico................. G1
5 Pedro Lemos B2
6 Portucale F2
7 Portugandhi F1
8 The Yeatman Restaurant................. F3

Hotels

1 Crowne Plaza Porto D1
2 Sheraton Porto Hotel & Spa........................ D1
3 Hotel Boa-Vista B2
4 The Yeatman F3

Estuary and the Atlantic Ocean. **Pros:** ideal location near the beach; in a quiet location; plenty of history. **Cons:** not close to the downtown sights; rooms are a little small; decor is functional. *Rooms from: €105 ✉ Esplanada do Castelo 58, Foz do Douro ☎ 225 320 020 🌐 www.hotelboavista.com 75 rooms 🍴 Free Breakfast.*

Shopping

FOOD AND WINE

Saboriccia

FOOD/CANDY | For hard-to-get delicacies from the countryside east of Porto, stop at this gourmet food shop whose owners have a farm outside of town where they raise sheep and make many of the products on display. You'll find local cheeses, jams, sausage, and wine, and there are often free tastings. *✉ Rua Senhora da Luz 338–342, Foz do Douro ☎ 220 996 677 🌐 www.saboriccia.pt.*

Greater Porto

While many of Porto's most famous attractions are clustered in and around the historic center of Baixa, exploring the wider reaches of the city pays off for both first-timers and repeat visitors. From fine award-winning dining in the unassuming suburb of Areosa to enjoying music concert and high-end shopping in Boavista, there's a lot to be enjoyed away from downtown.

GETTING HERE AND AROUND

Porto's extensive metro system can whisk you to the city's outer reaches, and the dependable bus service plies routes that the metro doesn't reach. Casa da Musica is the main jumping-off point in Boavista, but Avenida da Boavista stretches for miles, so it can be better to take a bus unless you choose to stroll the avenue to enjoy the excellent shopping.

Sights

★ **Casa da Música** (*House of Music*)

ARTS VENUE | Home to the National Orchestra of Porto and Portugal's Baroque Orchestra, this soaring postmodern temple to music was designed by legendary Dutch architect Rem Koolhaas ahead of Porto's stint as the European Culture Capital in 2001. There are frequent musical events, but the gravity-defying building deserves a visit even when the stage is bare. Book in advance for English-language guided tours that are given twice daily (three times a day from June to September). *✉ Av. da Boavista 604–610, Boavista ☎ 220 120 220 🌐 www.casadamusica.com 🎫 €10 tours Ⓜ Casa da Musica.*

★ **Museu de Arte Contemporânea de Serralves** (*Serralves Museum of Contemporary Art*)

MUSEUM | Designed by Álvaro Siza Vieira, a winner of the Pritzker Prize and Portugal's best-known architect, this is Portugal's leading contemporary art museum. The facility has lovely gardens and interesting exhibitions of works by painters, sculptors, and designers from throughout Portugal and around the world. Visitors can recharge flagging energy levels with tea and cakes at the pleasant Casa de Cha or enjoy a full meal in the tony Serralves restaurant. *✉ Rua D. João de Castro 210, Boavista ☎ 226 156 546 🌐 www.serralves.pt 🎫 €12.*

Restaurants

Antiqvvm

$$$$ | **CONTEMPORARY** | In a handsome manor house, this award-winning restaurant has a dining room set beneath graceful arches and garden terrace with gorgeous views of the river. Chef Vitor Matos uses seasonal ingredients with great flair and imagination on his ever-changing set menus, and the à la carte menu has plenty of interesting dishes to keep meat-eaters and vegetarians

The famed pink villa is a must visit for anyone visiting the Serralves complex, which includes a contemporary museum and park.

happy. **Known for:** artfully presented dishes have a sense of playfulness; gorgeous setting in a formal garden; secluded location. *Average main: €50 Quinta da Macieirinha, Rua de Entre Quintas 220, Porto 226 600 0445 Closed Sun. and Mon.*

Bufete Fase

$ | CAFÉ | Run by a father-and-daughter team, this snack bar near the top of one of the city's main shopping streets has just two things on the menu: the simple *prego* (a steak sandwich) and the belly-busting *francesinha* (a sandwich featuring cheese, cured ham, sausage, and steak, all drenched in a spicy beer-based sauce). Many locals swear they are the best in town. **Known for:** excellent Francesinhas; very friendly service; cozy and unpretentious service. *Average main: €9 Rua Santa Catarina 1147, Baixa 222 052 118 No credit cards Closed Sat. and Sun. Only accepts cash or Portuguese bank cards Marquês.*

Essência

$$ | VEGETARIAN | The cuisine of northern Portugal is notoriously meat-heavy, but local produce is so flavorful that it can easily stand alone. Essência understands this well, and its menu showcases vegetable-driven dishes that run the gamut from curries to salads to risottos, with vegan and gluten-free options available. **Known for:** fresh and wholesome ingredients with focus on local produce; inventive vegetarian cuisine with fish and meat options; pleasant lounge for predinner drinks. *Average main: €17 Rua de Pedro Hispano 1196, Boavista 228 301 813 www.essenciarestaurantevegetariano.com Closed Sun.*

O Paparico

$$$$ | PORTUGUESE | Well worth the taxi ride to its location far from the tourist track, this raved-about restaurant is as delightful to the eye (wood beams across the ceiling, walls of rough-hewn stone, candelabras on the tables) as it is to the taste buds. Alsace-born executive chef Jonathan Seiller infuses the traditional dishes on the menu with more than a little French flair. **Known for:** somewhat hidden entrance adds to the mystique; wine director offers excellent advice on pairings; sharing menus celebrate the country's cuisine. *Average main: €55 Rua de Costa Cabral 2343, Areosa 225 400 548 www.opaparico.com Closed Sun. and Mon. No lunch.*

Portucale

$$$ | PORTUGUESE | Atop a tall building north of the city, the lofty Portucale is known for its sweeping views that take in everything from the Atlantic Ocean to the Marão Mountains. Dining here is like stepping back in time, with mid-century modern furnishings, genteel service, and dishes that harken back to classic French cuisine (foie gras looms large). **Known for:** best tables are beside the wraparound windows; delicious desserts brought around on a trolley; extensive wine list. *Average main: €28 Rua da Alegria 598, Baixa 225 370 717 www.miradouro-portucale.com Marques.*

Portugandhi

$ | INDIAN | At this eatery north of the city center, locals pack the intimate dining room so they can taste dishes from across the Indian subcontinent, all of them with a slight Portuguese twist. There are plenty of vegetarian options on the menu, including a good *saag paneer* (spinach cooked with Indian cheese). **Known for:** the dishes from Goa are especially tasty; wonderfully complex flavors; good value set-lunch menus. *Average main: €12 Rua do Bonjardim 1143, Baixa 223 322 554 www.portugandhi.com Closed Sun. Marquês.*

Hotels

Crowne Plaza Porto

$$ | HOTEL | In a modern tower northwest of the city center, the Crowne Plaza Porto has a handy location near the business district and all the amenities a traveling executive might need. **Pros:** restaurant has won plaudits for its modern Mediterranean cuisine; beautifully landscaped grounds; spacious modern rooms. **Cons:** has a chain-hotel atmosphere; far from most tourist attractions; no swimming pool. *Rooms from: €145 Av. Boavista 1466, Boavista 226 072 500 www.crowneplaza.com/porto 190 rooms, 42 suites No meals Casa da Música or Francos.*

Sheraton Porto Hotel & Spa

$$ | HOTEL | FAMILY | With handy location for the city's business district, the Sheraton Porto Hotel & Spa blends elegant design with plenty of creature comforts. **Pros:** restaurant serves a family-friendly Sunday brunch; wine lovers enjoy the glass-walled cellar; some rooms have private terraces. **Cons:** a little far from the city center; business-hotel vibe; basic decor. *Rooms from: €160 Rua Tenente Valadim 146, Boavista 220 404 000 www.sheratonporto.com 241 rooms, 25 suites No meals Francos.*

Chapter 10

NORTHERN PORTUGAL

Updated by
Gaia Lutz

Sights	Restaurants	Hotels	Shopping	Nightlife
★★★★★	★★★★☆	★★★★☆	★★☆☆☆	★☆☆☆☆

WELCOME TO NORTHERN PORTUGAL

TOP REASONS TO GO

★ **Tasting world-renowned port wines:** Porto and the Douro Valley are the world hub for those sweet red wines that take their name from the region's biggest city.

★ **Shopping for handicrafts:** The Minho is famous even in Portugal for its pottery, embroidery, and other handicrafts, available at local markets and shops in Porto and other major centers.

★ **Seeing the region by boat:** No trip to the north is complete without a boat trip on the Douro River, whose curve after curve of terraced vineyards together form a UNESCO World Heritage Site.

★ **Savoring the best local fare:** From catch-of-the-day fish along the region's western coast to pork and sausage dishes in the countryside, northern Portugal prides itself on its homey and hearty food.

★ **Enjoying the outdoors:** The country's only national park, Peneda-Gerês, has a multitude of marked trails, as well as coastal bird sanctuaries and the remote uplands of Trás-os-Montes.

1 Vila do Conde. This maritime capital's winding streets and centuries-old buildings make it fun to explore.

2 Ofir and Esposende. This pair of beautiful beach towns makes for an extremely popular getaway.

3 Espinho. A series of quiet beaches brings you to Espinho, a resort town with a kid-friendly aquarium.

4 Amarante. On both sides of the Rio Tâmega, Amarante is connected by a narrow 18th-century bridge.

5 Peso da Régua. All the wines from the vineyards of the Upper Douro Valley pass through this town.

6 Lamego. People head here to see the Nossa Senhora dos Remédios, a major religious pilgrimage site.

7 Guimarães. The historic center of Guimarães, dating from the medieval era, is a UNESCO World Heritage Site.

8 Braga. Holy Week festivities, including eerie torchlight processions of hooded participants, are impressive.

9 Viana do Castelo. The region's folk capital specializes in producing traditional embroidered costumes.

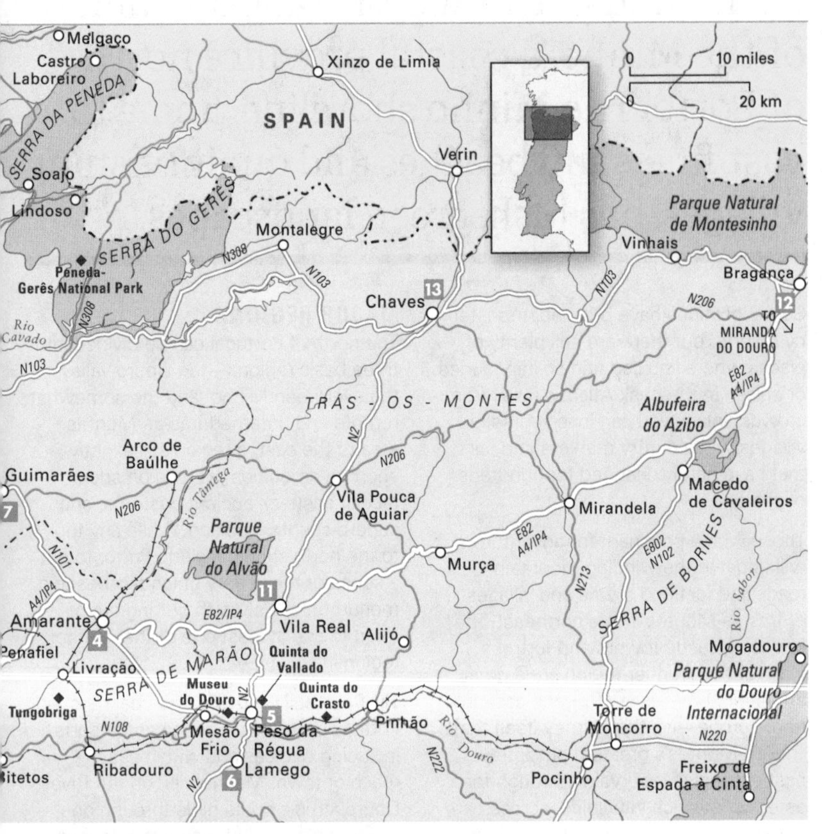

10 **Ponte de Lima.** The graceful bridge that gives this town its name was originally built by the Romans.

11 **Vila Real.** The capital of Trás-os-Montes has somehow managed to retain its small-town feel.

12 **Bragança.** In the northeastern corner of Portugal, this historic town has been inhabited since Celtic times.

13 **Chaves.** This town is renowned for a series of fortifications built during the late Middle Ages.

The remote north is as stark as it is breathtaking, in the arid valley of the Rio Douro and in the deep, rural heartland of the Minho, a coastal province north of Porto. The Minho shoreline, home to vast fine-sand beaches and quaint fishing villages, has lush, green landscapes.

Some locations have been appropriated by resorts, but there are still plenty of places where you can find solitary dunes or splash in the brisk Atlantic away from crowds. Inland you can lose yourself in villages with country markets and fairs that have hardly changed for hundreds of years.

Those with a penchant for adventure will find it in the winding mountain roads and far-flung towns and villages of Trás-os-Montes in the northeast. The imposing castle towers and fortress walls of this frontier region are a great attraction, but—as is often the case in rural Europe—it's the journey itself that's Trás-os-Montes's greatest prize: travel past expansive reservoirs, through forested valleys rich in wildlife, across bare crags and moorlands, and finally down to rustic stone villages where TV aerials sit in anachronistic contrast to the medieval-feeling surroundings.

The uncharted uplands of the northern Trás-os-Montes are called the Terra Fria (Cold Land), where you may spot some unusual forms such as Iron Age sculptures of boars with phallic attributes. It's believed these were worshipped as fertility symbols. There are traces of even more ancient civilizations, in the form of what is believed to be the world's largest open-air museum of Paleolithic rock art.

MAJOR REGIONS

The north of Portugal can be divided into three basic regions—the Douro Valley, the evergreen Minho, and the somewhat remote and untamed Trás-os-Montes area to the east, a region still slightly short on amenities yet long on spectacular scenery, ancient customs, and superb country cooking. While any trip to the north should include Porto, to get a sense of the variety of landscapes and monuments, it's worth getting out of town to see at least one of these other regions.

The Coast and the Douro. The coast around Porto is dotted with dunes and resorts, including two casinos within easy reach of town. Meanwhile, on the River Douro, cruise boats glide through one of Europe's most stunning landscapes, where the grapes used in the world-famous port wine are grown.

The Minho and the Costa Verde. The coastline of Minho Province, north of Porto, is a largely unspoiled stretch of small towns and sandy beaches that runs all the way to the border with Spain. The weather in this region is more inclement than elsewhere, a fact hinted at in the coast's name: the Minho is green because it sees a disproportionate amount of rain. It's a land of emerald valleys, endless pine-scented forests, and secluded beaches that are beautiful, but not for fainthearted swimmers. Summers can be cool, and swimming in the Atlantic is bracing at best. "These are real beaches for real people," is the reply when visitors complain about the water temperature.

Trás-os-Montes. The name means "Beyond the Mountains," and though roads built in the 1980s have made it easier to get here than in the past, exploring this beautiful region in the extreme northeast still requires a sense of adventure. Great distances separate towns, and twisting roads can test your patience. Medieval villages exist in a landscape that alternates between splendor and harshness, and the population, thinned by emigration, retains rural customs that have all but disappeared elsewhere. Some elderly folk still believe in the evil eye, witches, wolf men, golden-haired spirits living down wells, and even the cult of the dead. During winter festivals, masked men in colorful costumes roam village streets, and the region's Celtic roots are evident in the bagpipes traditionally played here.

Planning

From Porto, it's a two-hour drive up the Minho coastline to reach the Spanish border and another three to four hours east to the less visited Trás-os-Montes and the eastern border with Spain. Tack on a few more days to allow excursions to the history-rich towns of Braga and Guimarães or a tour through the lovely Douro Valley. A full week allows you to cover all this territory as well as inland towns and villages along the Lima and Minho Rivers, or you could set off for the remote northeastern Trás-os-Montes and its fascinating towns of Bragança and Chaves.

When to Go

It's best to visit the north in summer, when Porto and the Minho region are generally warm, but be prepared for drizzling rain at any time. Coastal temperatures are a few degrees cooler than in the south. Inland, and especially in the northeastern mountains, it can be very hot in summer and cold in winter.

Getting Here and Around

AIR TRAVEL

Most travelers to this region fly into Porto. Weekday flights from Lisbon to Bragança via Vila Real run twice a day in both directions by Sevenair, in twin-engine turboprop planes for 18 or 36 passengers.

CONTACTS Aeródromo Municipal de Bragança. ☎ *273 304 253* 🌐 *www.cm-braganca.pt.* **Aeródromo Municipal de Vila Real.** ☎ *259 336 620* 🌐 *www.cm-vilareal.pt.* **Sevenair.** ☎ *214 444 545* 🌐 *www.sevenair.com.*

BOAT

Several companies run boat trips up the Douro river, ranging from from two-hour trips to eight-day cruises. Cruzeiros Douro offers the most extensive range of options, while Douro Azul offers luxury trips with the option of renting out a yacht for yourself.

BUS

Rede Expressos operates frequent bus service to and from Lisbon to major towns in the region, with the ride from the capital to Porto, the main regional hub, taking at least 3½ hours and costing €19 one way. Rodonorte links major towns within the northern region, with the trip from Porto to Amarante taking 50 minutes and costing €7.80 and the three-hour ride from Porto to Bragança costing €14.50. Other local operators fill in the gaps. Major terminals are in Porto, Braga, Guimarães, Vila Real, and Chaves;

the staff might not speak English, but timetables are easily decipherable with the aid of a dictionary. Within towns, local buses are generally the way to get around; Porto also has a metro system, a funicular, and a few antique trams aimed mainly at the tourist market.

BUS CONTACTS Autoviação do Minho. ☎ *258 800 340* 🌐 *www.avminho.pt.* **Rede Expressos.** ☎ *707 223 344* 🌐 *www.rede-expressos.pt.* **Rodonorte.** ☎ *259 340 710* 🌐 *www.rodonorte.pt.* **Transdev.** ☎ *225 100 100* 🌐 *www.transdev.pt.*

CAR

The densely populated coast around Porto and the Minho region are well served with roads. A half-hour drive on the A3/IP1 toll highway will take you from Porto to Braga (for Guimarães, peel off just beyond halfway on the A7/IC5) before continuing on to Ponte de Lima and Valença on the Spanish border. The IC1 hugs the coast from Porto almost directly north to Viana do Castelo—a drive of just over an hour.

Inland, the A4/E82 toll road connects Porto to Amarante—again, a drive of about an hour. From here the three-lane IP4/E82 passes through Vila Real, Mirandela, and Bragança en route to the Spanish border at Quintanilha—in all, about four hours from Porto. The IP3 comes up from Viseu in the Beiras through Lamego to Peso da Régua and then Vila Real. You can continue north to Chaves on the N2.

Given the nature of the terrain in this hilly region crisscrossed by river valleys, some journeys will never be anything but slow. Examples are the routes Bragança–Chaves–Braga (N103), Vila Real–Chaves (N2), and Bragança–Mirando do Douro (N218). It's best simply to accept the roads' limitations, slow down, and appreciate the scenery. Off the beaten track, always check with local tourist offices to make sure the routes you wish to follow are navigable. Roadwork and winter landslides can cause detours and delays. In isolated regions, take special care at night, because many roads are unlighted and unpaved.

TRAIN

Trains are run by Comboios de Portugal, the national rail services better known as CP. The picturesque Douro Line is served by trains from Porto's Campanhã station (some with a change at Ermesinde) and pass through Livração, Peso da Régua, and Tua on the four-hour journey to Pocinho, at the far end of the Alto Douro region. On Saturdays from June to October, the Douro Historical Train runs between the Régua and Tua stations, with a stop at Pinhão.

Trains on the main route north along the Costa Verde depart approximately hourly from Porto's Campanhã station and run through Barcelos and Viana do Castelo, as far as Valença do Minho.

Braga and Guimarães are served by Porto suburban services from both São Bento and Campanhã stations. Braga is also served by some long-distance trains through Campanhã.

CONTACTS Comboios de Portugal. ☎ *707 210 220* 🌐 *www.cp.pt.*

Restaurants

As is the case throughout Portugal, pork is the meat most often seen on menus, but nearer the border with Spain, wonderfully tender veal and steak can be found in the form of *posta mirandesa* and *barrosã*. Most dishes will be served with *batatas* (potatoes) or *arroz* (rice), both fine examples of staples being raised to an art form. Potatoes here, whether roasted, boiled, or fried, have an irresistibly nutty and sweet flavor. Rice is lightly sautéed with chopped garlic in olive oil before adding water, resulting in a side dish that could easily be devoured as a main course.

Fresh fish is found all the way up the coast, and every town has a local recipe for *bacalhau* (dried and salted cod); in the Minho it's often *à Gomes de Sá* (cooked with potatoes, onions, and eggs). *Lampreias* (lampreys)—eel-like fish—are found in Minho rivers from February through April and are a specialty of Viana do Castelo and Monção. In the mountains wonderful *truta* (trout) is available in any town or village close to a river.

The wine available throughout the north is of high quality. The Minho region's *vinho verde* is a light, young, slightly sparkling red or white wine. The taste is refreshing, fruity, with good acid—qualities that also make it an excellent starting point for distilling *aguardente* (Portuguese brandy). Both reds and whites are served chilled, and vinho verde goes exceptionally well with fish and shellfish. Port enjoys the most renown of the local wines (ask for *vinho do Porto*), but the Douro region, where the grapes are grown for port, also produces some of Portugal's finest table wines.

Hotels

Lodgings in the Minho and Trás-os-Montes regions are reasonably priced compared with their counterparts elsewhere in the country. The Turismo no Espaço Rural (Rural Tourism) network allows you to spend time at a variety of historic manor houses, country farms, and little village cottages scattered throughout the north. Many of these converted 17th- and 18th-century buildings are found in the lovely rural areas around Ponte de Lima, in the Minho region. *Pousadas* (inns) offer a variety of settings in the north, from a 12th-century monastery in Guimarães to more rustic, hunting-lodge digs in such places as the Marão mountain ridges near Amarante or a hilltop in Bragança.

WHAT IT COSTS In Euros

$	$$	$$$	$$$$
RESTAURANTS			
€16 or under	€17–€22	€23–€30	over €30
HOTELS			
€140 or under	€141–€200	€201–€260	over €260

Visitor Information

CONTACTS Visit Porto and the North. ☎ *300 501 920.*

Vila do Conde

27 km (17 miles) north of Porto.

Vila do Conde has been making wooden boats since the 15th century. The shipyards are probably Europe's oldest, and the traditional boat-making skills used in them have changed surprisingly little over the centuries. It was here that the replica of Bartolomeu Dias's caravel was made in 1987 to commemorate his historic voyage around the Cape of Good Hope 500 years earlier. The city center still has winding streets and centuries-old buildings that make it fun to explore.

Vila do Conde has been known for its lace since the 17th century, and it remains the center of a flourishing lace industry. The tourist office can give you information about the Escola de Rendas (Lace-Making School), where you can see how the famed *rendas de bilros* (bone lace) is made. Local artisans also produce excellent sweaters.

GETTING HERE AND AROUND

Although there is no regular aboveground train, Porto's metro (red line) stops at Vila do Conde on its way to Póvoa, every 20 minutes or so. The trip from the Trindade stop in central Porto normally takes over an hour, but there's an hourly express

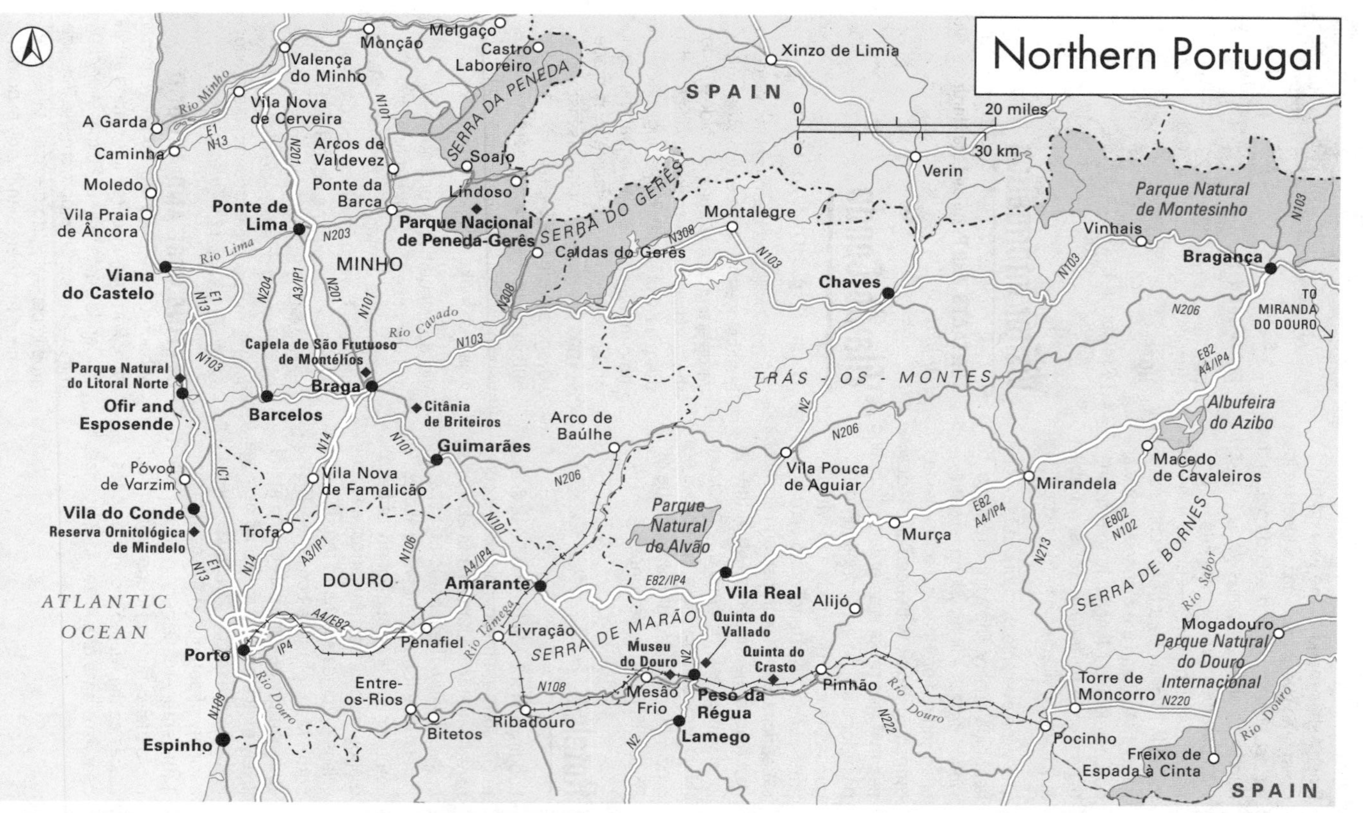
Northern Portugal
0 20 miles
0 30 km
SPAIN
ATLANTIC OCEAN
MINHO
DOURO
TRÁS - OS - MONTES
SERRA DA PENEDA
SERRA DO GERÊS
SERRA DE MARÃO
SERRA DE BORNES
Parque Natural de Montesinho
Parque Natural do Alvão
Parque Natural do Douro Internacional
Albufeira do Azibo
Parque Nacional de Peneda-Gerês
Parque Natural do Litoral Norte
Capela de São Frutuoso de Montélios
Citânia de Briteiros
Reserva Ornitológica de Mindelo
Museu do Douro
Quinta do Vallado
Quinta do Crasto
Melgaço
Monção
Castro Laboreiro
Valença do Minho
Vila Nova de Cerveira
A Garda
Caminha
Moledo
Vila Praia de Âncora
Arcos de Valdevez
Ponte da Barca
Soajo
Lindoso
Ponte de Lima
Viana do Castelo
Barcelos
Braga
Ofir and Esposende
Póvoa de Varzim
Vila do Conde
Trofa
Vila Nova de Famalicão
Guimarães
Arco de Baúlhe
Caldas do Gerês
Montalegre
Xinzo de Limia
Verin
Chaves
Vinhais
Bragança
TO MIRANDA DO DOURO
Macedo de Cavaleiros
Mirandela
Vila Pouca de Aguiar
Murça
Vila Real
Alijó
Amarante
Livração
Penafiel
Porto
Espinho
Entre-os-Rios
Bitetos
Ribadouro
Mesão Frio
Peso da Régua
Lamego
Pinhão
Pocinho
Torre de Moncorro
Mogadouro
Freixo de Espada à Cinta
Rio Minho
Rio Lima
Rio Cavado
Rio Tâmega
Rio Douro
Rio Sabor
E1
N13
N101
N201
N203
N204
A3/IP1
N14
IC1
N103
N308
N206
N2
N106
A4/IP4
A4/E82
IP4
E82/IP4
E82 A4/IP4
N108
N109
N222
N213
E802 N102
N220

train that takes 40 minutes. There are also frequent daily buses from Porto and from Viana do Castelo, run by local companies AVIC and Autoviação Minho. The tourist office can provide schedules.

VISITOR INFORMATION

CONTACTS Vila do Conde. ✉ *Rua 25 de Abril 103* ☎ *252 248 473* 🌐 *www.visitportoandnorth.travel.*

Sights

Convento de Santa Clara (*Santa Clara Convent*)
RELIGIOUS SITE | This impressive structure sprawls along the north bank of the Rio Ave, the river that flows through Vila do Conde. Dom Afonso Sanches and his wife, Dona Teresa Martins, established the convent in the 14th century, and it retains its original cloister and the beautiful tombs of its founders. It reopened as a municipal building in 2017. ✉ *Av. Figueiredo Faria 18.*

Igreja Matriz
RELIGIOUS SITE | With a superb late-Gothic portal, this church in the center of the city has a single solid tower with bells that gleam in the sun. Construction on this church began at the end of the 15th century and was completed in the early 16th. ✉ *Rua 25 de Abril 147* ☎ *252 640 810* 🌐 *www.paroquiadeviladoconde.pt* *Free* *Closed Mon.*

Museu das Rendas de Bilros de Vila do Conde (*Museum of Lace Making*)
MUSEUM | Created in 1919 by António Maria Pereira Júnior, the Escola de Rendas (Lace-Making School) is attached to the Museu das Rendas de Bilros de Vila do Conde. Here you can see beautiful examples of lace from the region and from around the world. ✉ *Casa do Vinhal, Rua de S. Bento 70* ☎ *252 248 470* *€1.10* *Closed Mon.*

International Short Film Festival

Festival Internacional de Curtas Metragens This local film festival, which started in 1993, takes place every July. ✉ *Teatro Municipal, Av. Dr. João Canavarro* ☎ *252 290 050* 🌐 *www.curtas.pt.*

Reserva Ornitológica de Mindelo (*Mindelo Ornithological Reserve*)
NATURE PRESERVE | This part of the coastline is where you'll find the Mindelo Ornithological Reserve, which became Portugal's first protected area in 1957. One of the few remaining swaths of undeveloped land in the region around Porto, it has 1,500 acres of dunes, fields, and wetlands. It's home to more than 150 bird species, especially migratory birds. There's no public transportation, but the reserve is a 20-minute drive from Vila do Conde. ✉ *10 km (6 miles) south of Vila do Conde, Mindelo.*

Beaches

Praia de Mindelo
BEACH—SIGHT | Colorful tents on the clean and coarse sand of the craggy beach Praia de Mindelo create a shield from inconvenient winds. From Vila do Conde, take the EN13 7½ km (4 miles) south to reach the beach's access at the small fishing village of Mindelo. The drive takes about 10 minutes. **Amenities:** food and drink; lifeguards; parking (no fee). **Best for:** walking; windsurfing. ✉ *Praia de Mindelo, R. da Gafa, Mindelo.*

O Cangalho

$$ | PORTUGUESE | Overlooking the river, this longtime favorite has walls that are adorned with old guitars, carvings of saints, ceramic birds, and vintage books—you know the kind of place. In warm weather there's a tiny area with outdoor seating. **Known for:** if they're in season, don't miss out on the fried sardines; the "drunken pears" in port wine are a specialty; friendly and helpful staff. *Average main: €18 Rua do Cais das Lavandeiras 28 912 835 769 Closed Sun. and Mon.*

Santana Hotel

$ | RESORT | FAMILY | Taking full advantage of its location on a hill high above the Rio Ave, this gleaming white lodging's rooms all face the river and have their own balconies. **Pros:** lovely riverside setting; five minutes from the city center; tennis and access to two golf courses. **Cons:** spa can get busy in summer; little nightlife nearby; books up fast. *Rooms from: €75 Monte Santana–Azurara 252 640 460 www.santanahotel.pt 75 fooms Free Breakfast.*

Ofir and Esposende

27 km (17 miles) north of Vila do Conde; 46 km (29 miles) north of Porto.

On the south bank of the Rio Cávado, Ofir has a lovely beach with sweeping white sands, dunes, pinewoods, and water sports—a combination that has made it a popular resort. On the opposite bank of the river, Esposende, which also has a beach, retains elements of the small fishing village it once was. You'll have to drive here to appreciate these twin towns: the train line runs inland at this point, passing through Barcelos.

GETTING HERE AND AROUND

Esposende is on the national express bus network of Rede Expressos, which has a local agent in the market square. Bus services to Esposende from Porto and Viana, meanwhile, are run by Autoviação do Minho. Buses between Esposende and Braga are run by Transdev. The Esposende tourist office can provide more details; it's on the first floor of the main municipal building.

VISITOR INFORMATION

Esposende Tourist Office. *Av. Eng. Eduardo Arantes e Oliveira 62, Esposende 253 961 354.*

Parque Natural do Litoral Norte

NATIONAL/STATE PARK | Extending along 16 km (10 miles) of the coastline north and south of Esposende is the Parque Natural do Litoral Norte, an important haven for birds and plant life. As well as dune habitats through which you can wander on boardwalks, it includes the river beaches of the River Cávado estuary and pine and oak forest. Guided visits of up to 10 people can be arranged. *Off N13, Esposende 253 965 830 www.icnf.pt.*

Beaches

Praia da Apúlia (*Apúlia Beach*)

BEACH—SIGHT | FAMILY | The old windmills that line Apúlia Beach are no longer in use but have been repurposed as charming rental cottages. Sand dunes protect this notoriously windy beach, making it a perfectly sheltered spot for families. The waters here are famous for their medicinal purposes because they contain high levels of iodine. You might see locals collecting seaweed, which is used as fertilizer for nearby farms. There are umbrellas and boat rentals. **Amenities:** food and drink; lifeguards; showers; toilets; water sports. **Best for:** windsurfing. *Rua da Colónia, Apúlia.*

Praia de Ofir (*Ofir Beach*)

BEACH—SIGHT | FAMILY | South of the Cávado River, Ofir's beach is one of the most beautiful stretches of sand along northern Portugal's coast. Huge dunes are bordered by rows of pine trees, which give way to rocks that jut out into the water and are visible at low tide. These rock formations are known locally as "the horses of Fão." Surfers usually hang out on the beach's southern stretch, but there's plenty of room for families farther north. There are also restaurants and beach bars just behind the dunes and huts that rent out umbrellas, windsurfing equipment, and boats. **Amenities:** food and drink; lifeguards; parking (no fee); toilets; water sports. **Best for:** solitude; sunset; windsurfing. ✉ *Parque Natural do Litoral Norte, Rua do Estaleiro, Ofir.*

Espinho

18 km (11 miles) south of Porto.

A string of quiet beaches lead to Espinho, an increasingly fashionable resort. The long, sandy beach is extremely popular in summer, but you can find some space by walking through the pine forest to less developed areas to the south.

GETTING HERE AND AROUND

Espinho is served by frequently stopping trains from Porto Campanhã to points south; some fast trains from Lisbon also stop here. The N109 highway runs nearby, and the town is also served by a four-lane spur off the A1 toll motorway. There is frequent local service from Porto's main bus station.

VISITOR INFORMATION

Espinho Tourist Office. ✉ *Centro Comercial Solverde II, Alameda 8* ☎ *224 901 316* 🌐 *www.cm-espinho.pt.*

Sights

Casino Espinho

CASINO—SIGHT | Right beside the beach, the casino has 500 slot machines, video blackjack, Portuguese dice, and French and American roulette. If these diversions don't do it for you, come for the dining, dancing, and cabaret shows; foreign visitors must present their passports (and be 18 or older), and although there's no formal dress code, smart casual is most appropriate. ✉ *Rua 19 85* ☎ *227 335 500* 🌐 *casinoespinho.solverde.pt.*

Beaches

Praia de Miramar

BEACH—SIGHT | It may lack Lisbon's sunshine, but the Porto coast still has picture-perfect beaches. Just 6 miles south of the city is the pretty seaside town of Miramar, where 17th-century chapel Capela do Senhora Pedra sits proudly amid the waves on a rocky headland that juts out from the sandy beach. Still pleasantly uncrowded, Praia de Miramar is good for swimming in the summer, while the wind whips up surfer-pleasing waves in the chilly winter. **Amenities:** parking (no fee); food and drink; water sports. **Best for:** surfing; swimming; walking. ✉ *Arcozelo, Vila Nova de Gaia.*

Restaurants

★ **Aquário Marisqueira de Espinho**

$$$ | SEAFOOD | Founded in 1954, this oceanfront restaurant is one of the most traditional in Espinho. There's an enormous variety of fresh seafood ready to be grilled, boiled, or roasted in the oven, as well as bacalhau and various fish stews and rice dishes. **Known for:** arroz de tamboril (monkfish) is a specialty; friendly and knowledgeable waiters; ocean views. [$] *Average main: €25* ✉ *Rua 4 540* ☎ *227 321 000.*

Solverde Hotel

Solverde Hotel

$ | RESORT | FAMILY | This plush resort hotel sits atop a hill, so most guest rooms have views of the nearby sandy beach. **Pros:** indoor and outdoor saltwater pools; free shuttle to the casino; 24-hour room service. **Cons:** not convenient to the center of the city; far from train and other transportation; some dated decor. *Rooms from: €120 ✉ Av. da Liberdade 212, Praia da Granja ☎ 227 338 030 ⊕ hotelsolverdespa.solverde.pt 174 rooms Free Breakfast.*

GOLF

Clube de Golfe de Miramar

GOLF | This popular club by the sea has a 9-hole, par-4 course. It's located 5 km (3 miles) north of Espinho. You can make it a full round of 18 holes by doubling the course. The greens fee is €50 for 9 holes and €70 for 18 holes. *✉ Praia de Miramar, Av. Sacadura Cabral, Vila Nova de Gaia ☎ 227 622 067 ⊕ www.cgm.pt 9 holes, 2450 yds, par 36. Greens fee: €50.*

Oporto Golf Club

GOLF | The 18-hole Oporto Golf Club, founded in 1890 by members of the Port Wine Shippers' Association, is 2 km (1 mile) south of Espinho. On weekends, nonmembers can tee off from 11 to 1 only. *✉ Paramos–Espinho ☎ 227 342 008 ⊕ www.oportogolfclub.com 18 holes, 5640 yds, par 71. Greens fee: €80 weekends, €50 weekdays.*

Amarante

78 km (48 miles) northeast of Espinho; 60 km (37 miles) northeast of Porto.

Straddling the Rio Tâmega, the two halves of Amarante are joined by a narrow 18th-century bridge that stretches above the tree-shaded banks. Rowboats and other vessels are available for hire at several points along the riverside paths. The waterfront is also the site of a local market, held every Wednesday and Saturday morning, that clogs the streets of the usually placid town.

GETTING HERE AND AROUND

Regional bus company Rodornorte serves Lamego from Porto and other regional centers such as Guimarães. You can also take the train a good part of the way from Porto Campanhã, getting off at Livração and then catching a local bus to Amarante (about 25 minutes).

VISITOR INFORMATION

Amarante Tourist Office. *✉ Largo Conselheiro António Cândido ☎ 255 420 246 ⊕ www.amarante.pt.*

Convento de São Gonçalo

RELIGIOUS SITE | This imposing convent, built and rebuilt between the 16th and 20th centuries, sits on the north side of the Rio Tâmega. The effigy of its patron saint, in a room to the left of the altar, is reputed to guarantee marriage to anyone who touches it. His features have almost been worn away over the years as desperate suitors try and, perhaps, try again. *✉ Praça da República ☎ 255 437 425 Free.*

★ **Museu Amadeo de Souza-Cardoso**

MUSEUM | The cloisters of a former monastery now house this museum and its excellent collection of modern Portuguese art, including important works by modernist painter Souza-Cardoso, who pursued variations of fauvism, cubism, futurism, and other avant-garde tendencies. He was born in the area and in 1906 shared an apartment with fellow painter Amedeo Modigliani in Paris. He returned to Portugal in 1914 and died four years later at the age of 31. The museum also has some interesting archaeological pieces—the star attractions are the *diabos* (devils), a pair of 19th-century carved

The narrow 18th-century Ponte de São Gonçalo over the Rio Tâmega is the centerpiece of the village of Amarante.

wooden figures connected with ancient fertility rites. They were venerated on St. Bartholomew's Day (August 24), when the devil was thought to run loose. In 1870, the Archbishop of Braga ordered them burned because of their pagan function. The São Gonçalo friars didn't go that far, but they did emasculate the male diabo. ✉ *Alameda Teixeira de Pascoaes* ☎ *255 420 272* 🎟 *€1* ⏲ *Closed Mon.*

Restaurants

★ Adega Regional Quelha

$ | **PORTUGUESE** | The restaurants along or near Rua 31 de Janeiro may have river views, but they don't necessarily serve the best food. This ham-and-garlic-bedecked place—off a square at the end of the main street—has no views, but the regional fare served on its wooden tables make it worth a trip. **Known for:** the roasted rabbit, served on weekends, is a house specialty; try the rabanada, a regional dish similar to French toast; cozy and rustic atmosphere. $ *Average main: €11* ✉ *Rua da Olivença* ☎ *255 425 786* 💳 *No credit cards.*

Amaranto

$$ | **PORTUGUESE** | This spacious, well-appointed restaurant sits on the river near the center of town. The views from here are spectacular, and the menu has excellent regional fare. **Known for:** sophisticated renditions of traditional dishes; snack bar offers less expensive fare; friendly staff. $ *Average main: €20* ✉ *Edifício Amaranto, Rua Acácio Lino 351* ☎ *255 422 006.*

★ Largo do Paço

$$$$ | **PORTUGUESE** | This internationally renowned restaurant in the Casa da Calçada Hotel has won award after award for the innovative Portuguese cuisine by chef Tiago Bonito, including a Michelin star. Carefully constructed tasting menus (including one for vegetarians) are the way to go, but you may also order à la carte. **Known for:** a must-try dish is the suckling pig with potatoes and oranges; dessert includes strawberries with rhubarb and lime; bright colors enliven

the formal dining room. $ *Average main: €80* ✉ *Largo do Paço 6* ☎ *255 410 830* 🌐 *www.largodopaco.com* ⏲ *Closed Sun. and Mon.*

★ **Casa da Calçada**

$$ | B&B/INN | Next to the venerable bridge spanning the river, this carefully restored nobleman's manor is one of Portugal's finest hotels. **Pros:** one of the handsomest buildings in the region; access to one of Portugal's best restaurants; the feel of a luxury resort. **Cons:** the many private events can be noisy; no fitness facilities; a bit pricey. $ *Rooms from: €150* ✉ *Largo do Paço 6* ☎ *255 410 830* 🌐 *www.casadacalcada.com* *30 rooms* *Free Breakfast.*

Pousada de São Gonçalo

$ | B&B/INN | This modern pousada—20 km (12 miles) east of Amarante—is in the dramatic Serra do Marão at an altitude of nearly 3,000 feet. **Pros:** a get-away-from-it-all destination; wide range of activities in the area; pleasant spa area. **Cons:** reachable only by car; less pleasant in winter; next to the highway. $ *Rooms from: €100* ✉ *Curva do Lancete, Serra do Marão, Ansiães* ☎ *255 460 030* 🌐 *www.pousadas.pt* *15 rooms* *Free Breakfast.*

GOLF

Golfe de Amarante

GOLF | This respected course at the property of Quinta da Deveza, 5 km (3 miles) southwest of Amarante, is an 18-hole golf layout with superb mountain views. A handicap certificate is required. ✉ *Quinta da Deveza, Fregim* ☎ *255 446 060* 🌐 *www.golfedeamarante.com* *18 holes, 5500 yds, par 68. Greens fee: €60.*

Peso da Régua

40 km (25 miles) southeast of Amarante; 97 km (60 miles) east of Porto.

This is the true heart of port wine country, and all the bottles from the vineyards of the Upper Douro Valley pass through on their way to Porto. Local wine lodges offer tours of their cellars, which make a nice contrast to the large-scale operations in Vila Nova de Gaia. The Museu do Douro provides a showcase for the wine-making industry. Many boat tours from Porto end in Régua (the town's shortened name); others pause here before continuing upriver to Pinhão, whose train station is lined with beautiful tile panels.

GETTING HERE AND AROUND

Régua is served by Rodonorte, whose routes cover most of the region. There are also local buses from Vila Real. Most visitors using public transport prefer to take the picturesque Douro line, with regular departures from Porto Campanhã (about two hours). The quickest way by car from Porto is to take the A4 motorway toward Vila Real, turning south on the N2 just outside town. A prettier route is the N103 along the north bank of the Douro.

TOURS

Porto-based Douro Azul does day trips to Régua as well as cruises of up to a week. In summer, the Douro Historic Train (with steam or diesel engines) along the Douro from Régua via Pinhão to Tua; the national train company, Comboios de Portugal, or tourist offices can provide details.

Douro Azul. ✉ *Rua de Miragaia 103, Porto* ☎ *223 402 500* 🌐 *www.douroazul.com.*

VISITOR INFORMATION

Peso da Régua Train Station. ✉ *Largo da Estação* ☎ *707 210 220* 🌐 *www.cp.pt/en.*

Sights

★ **Museu do Douro** (*Douro Museum*)
MUSEUM | This stunning museum sits at the center of the Douro Valley, a UNESCO World Heritage Site, underscoring its importance in terms of cultural history and tourism. Housed in the imposing former headquarters of a port-wine company, the institution also has a striking contemporary wing that hosts major exhibitions about the wine-making region, its history, and leading figures connected with it. Those with an appetite can stay for a meal at the riverside restaurant and wine bar overlooking the Douro. The ticket price includes a complimentary glass of port wine. ✉ *Rua Marquês de Pombal* ☎ *254 310 190* 🌐 *www.museudodouro.pt* 🎫 *€6, €20 for guided tour.*

Quinta do Crasto
WINERY/DISTILLERY | Dating back to 1616, this large wine estate on the north bank of Rio Douro, between Régua and Pinhão, was already marked on the first Douro Demarcated Region Map by Baron Forrester. Wines produced here include vintage port, designating wine of exceptional quality made in a single year. It must be bottled between the second and third year after the harvest; it is deep purple in color and full-bodied. It also offers LBV (Late Bottled Vintage) port, wines of a superior quality from a single year which are bottled between the fourth and sixth year after they were made. Reservations must be made to visit this property. ✉ *Gouvinhas–Ferrão, Sabrosa* ☎ *254 920 020* 🌐 *www.quintadocrasto.pt.*

★ **Quinta do Vallado**
WINERY/DISTILLERY | One of the oldest quintas in the region, Quinta do Vallado is on the right bank of Rio Corgo near Rio Douro and has stunning views of terraced hillsides along both river gorges. This wine estate has been in the Ferreira family since 1818 and encompasses 158 acres, some with vines more than 70 years old. Make reservations for a visit, which includes a wine tasting. Like many other quintas throughout the region, it also has rooms for guests, in either a traditional 18th-century manor, or a sleek, modern 21st-century wing. Doubles cost about €190 per night. ✉ *Vilarinho dos Freires* ☎ *254 323 147* 🌐 *www.quintadovallado.com.*

Restaurants

★ **DOC**
$$$$ | **PORTUGUESE** | This riverside restaurant 9 km (6 miles) from Régua, on the south bank of the Douro, draws gourmets from far and wide with chef Rui Paula's take on traditional northern cuisine. Only the best ingredients are used in dishes in which bacalhau, *polvo* (octopus), and seafood often loom large, as well as tender *bísaro* pork and *barrosã* veal. **Known for:** choose between one of the set menus or the à la carte options; award-winning wine list and wine pairings; wooden deck juts out over the river. 💲 *Average main: €55* ✉ *Cais da Folgosa, Estrada Nacional 222, Armamar* ☎ *254 858 123* 🌐 *www.ruipaula.com* 🕒 *Closed Tues. No lunch Wed.*

Gato Preto
$$ | **PORTUGUESE** | With a name that means "black cat," this sleek, family-run restaurant sits on Régua's main street next to the Museu do Douro. The specialty is traditional Douro cuisine, especially *cabrito assado* (roasted kid), which locals line up for once the tourists are gone. **Known for:** the cod is a specialty of the house; friendly staff is eager to help; fair prices for a hearty meal. 💲 *Average main: €20* ✉ *Av. João Franco* ☎ *254 313 367* 🌐 *www.restaurantegatopreto.webnode.pt.*

Hotels

Casa do Visconde de Chanceleiros
$ | **B&B/INN** | **FAMILY** | This 18th-century manor house has lovely gardens bursting with flowers, a swimming pool with views of the valley, and amenities ranging from a sauna to tennis courts. **Pros:** elegant decor balances the old and new; a playground and other facilities for kids; biking, hiking, and boat trips. **Cons:** difficult to reach via public transportation; dining in the hotel can be pricey; a bit formal for some. *Rooms from: €135* ✉ *Largo da Fonte, Pinhão* ☎ *254 730 190* 🌐 *www.chanceleiros.com* *12 rooms* *Free Breakfast.*

Quinta Nova de Nossa Senhora do Carmo
$$ | **B&B/INN** | This hillside estate on the north bank of the Douro is owned by the family that dominates Portugal's cork industry, but its "wine hotel" is on an intimate scale. **Pros:** outdoor pool with views of the terraced vineyards; staff will pick you up at the train station; breathtaking views. **Cons:** few in-room amenities; isolated unless you have a car; pricey restaurant for the region. *Rooms from: €199* ✉ *Quinta Nova de Nossa Senhora do Carmo, Covas do Douro* ☎ *254 730 430* 🌐 *www.quintanova.com* *11 rooms* *Free Breakfast.*

★ **Vintage House**
$$$ | **HOTEL** | About 32 km (18 miles) east of Régua, this lodging in a former port-wine warehouse has a perfect location on the northern bank of the Douro and unrivaled views of the valley. **Pros:** lovely riverside setting in the quaint village of Pinhão; grape picking (and stomping) trips can be arranged; easy to get to from the train station. **Cons:** lacks some common amenities like a gym; some interior decor a bit basic; rates are a bit high. *Rooms from: €245* ✉ *Lugar da Ponte, Pinhão* ☎ *254 730 230* 🌐 *www.vintagehousehotel.com* *50 rooms* *Free Breakfast.*

Lamego

13 km (8 miles) south of Peso da Régua; 110 km (68 miles) southeast of Porto.

A prosperous town set amid a fertile landscape carpeted with vineyards and orchards, Lamego is also rich in baroque churches and mansions. It straddles the River Balsemão, a small tributary of the Douro, and is close to the great river itself. The town is flanked by two hills, one topped by a castle, the other by the Nossa Senhora dos Remédios, a major pilgrimage site. A monumental staircase leads straight up from the town's central avenue to the church steps. The surrounding region has more quintas to visit or stay—plus one of Europe's top spa hotels.

GETTING HERE AND AROUND

Lamego is served by Rodonorte regional buses and fast Rede Expresso buses from Lisbon. Tickets for the latter can be bought at local agent Totolamego. The town is not on the rail network, but it's a short ride on a Transdev bus from Peso da Régua, which is on the picturesque Douro line from Porto.

VISITOR INFORMATION

Lamego Tourism Office. ✉ *Av. Infantaria 9* ☎ *254 099 000* 🌐 *www.cm-lamego.pt.*

Sights

Quinta da Pacheca
WINERY/DISTILLERY | In the heart of the Douro Valley, the wine estate Quinta da Pacheca has existed since 1551. A 17th-century stone marker bears a Feitoria inscription that indicates that the best-quality wine was made here, the only one that could be exported. The estate mansion has a chapel and a beautiful garden with trees that are hundreds of years old. Wine production is still done the old-fashioned way, with grapes crushed by men in a stone tank and aging taking place in oak barrels.

Reservations must be made if you want to tour the cellars. The facility also has an outsanding restaurant and two dozen guest rooms. ✉ *Rua do Relogio de Sol 261* ☎ *254 331 229* 🌐 *www.quintadapacheca.com.*

★ **Santuário de Nossa Senhora dos Remédios** (*Our Lady of Cures Church and Shrine*)

RELIGIOUS SITE | The town's most famous monument is the 18th-century Santuário de Nossa Senhora dos Remédios, which has a marvelous granite staircase of 686 steps decorated with azulejo tiles. Landings along the way have statues and chapels. At the top, you can rest under chestnut trees and enjoy the views. During the Festas de Nossa Senhora dos Remédios, the annual pilgrimage to the shrine, many penitents climb the steps on their knees. The main procession is September 8, but the festivities start at the end of August and include concerts, dancing, parades, a fair, and torchlight processions. Pilgrims use the stairs, but you can always reach the top by car. ✉ *Monte de Santo Estevão* ☎ *254 655 318* *Free.*

Hotels

Six Senses Douro Valley

$$$$ | **RESORT** | This cutting-edge resort 8 km (5 miles) from Lamego has helped the region brush up its image as a fashionable destination. **Pros:** wine tastings and cooking classes can be arranged; stunning setting with views from all over the property; spa included in room rate. **Cons:** not accessible by public transport; is out of reach for many due to its high room rates. $ *Rooms from: €625* ✉ *Quinta do Vale Abrão, Samodães* ☎ *254 660 600* 🌐 *www.sixsenses.com* *60 rooms* *No meals.*

Guimarães

51 km (32 miles) northeast of Porto.

Guimarães is a town proud of its past, and this is evident in a series of delightful medieval landmarks. The old town's narrow, cobbled thoroughfares pass small bars that open onto sidewalks and pastel houses that overhang little squares and have flowers in their windowsills. The historic center of Guimarães is a UNESCO World Heritage Site, and the town has served as the European Capital of Culture and the European Capital of Sport.

Many come for the rich history that the town offers. Afonso Henriques was born in 1110 in Guimarães, and Portuguese schoolchildren are taught that *"aqui nasceu Portugal"* (Portugal was born here) with him. Within 20 years he was regarded as king of Portucale (the united Portuguese lands between the Minho and Douro rivers) and had made Guimarães the seat of his power. From this first "Portuguese" capital, Afonso Henriques drove south, taking Lisbon back from the Moors in 1147.

The volume of tourists in Guimarães is a fraction of what Porto or Lisbon receives, so you'll have many of the city's winding cobblestone streets all to yourself. This truly authentic slice of Portuguese heritage deserves an overnight stay on any trip to the region.

GETTING HERE AND AROUND

Guimarães is served by suburban trains from Porto's São Bento and Campanhã stations, taking about 1 hour 20 minutes and costing €3.10 (or less if you have a €0.50 Andante rechargeable card). Traveling by rail from Braga isn't advisable because you'll have to change, and buses are both quicker and cheaper. Rede Expresso buses serve Guimarães from Porto, Lisbon, and beyond.

The slender Igreja de Nossa Senhora da Consolação e Santos Passos in Guimarães is framed by a lovely garden.

VISITOR INFORMATION

Guimarães Tourism Office. ✉ *Praça de Santiago* ☎ *253 421 221* 🌐 *www.guimaraes-turismo.com.*

Sights

Castelo de Guimarães (*Guimarães Castle*)
CASTLE/PALACE | **FAMILY** | This castle was built (or at least reconstructed from earlier remains) in the 11th century by Henry of Burgundy; his son, Afonso Henriques, was born within its great battlements and flanking towers. Standing high on a solid rock base above the town, the castle has been superbly preserved. A path leads down from its walls to the tiny Romanesque Capela de São Miguel, the chapel traditionally said to be where Afonso Henriques was baptized—in fact it was built well after his death, although the baptismal font may be older. ✉ *Rua D. Teresa de Noronha* ☎ *253 412 273* 🎫 *€2.*

★ **Citânia de Briteiros** (*Celtic Hill Settlement*)
ARCHAEOLOGICAL SITE | About 9 km (5½ miles) northwest of Guimarães you'll find these fascinating remains of a Celtic *citânia* (hill settlement). It dates to around 300 BC and was probably not abandoned until AD 300, making it one of the last Celtic strongholds against the Romans in Portugal, although its residents are now thought to have become gradually romanized. The walls and foundations of 150 huts and a meeting house have been excavated (two of the huts have been reconstructed to show their original size). The site was excavated in the late 19th century by Dr. Martins Sarmento, namesake of a must-see museum in Guimarães where most of the finds from Briteiros were transferred. You can also visit the smaller Museu da Cultura Castreja, housed in Sarmento's 19th-century family home, in the village of São Salvador de Briteiros, down below the Citânia. Several buses travel here daily from downtown Guimaraes, stopping

about 1 km (½ mile) from the Citânia. ✉ *Estrada Nacional 153, Km 55* ☎ *253 478 952* 🌐 *www.csarmento.uminho.pt* 🎫 *€3, includes admission to Museu da Cultura Castreja.*

Igreja de Nossa Senhora da Consolação e Santos Passos (*Church of Our Lady of Consolation and the Holy Steps*)
RELIGIOUS SITE | One of Portugal's prettiest baroque churches, the slim Church of Our Lady of Consolation and the Holy Steps rises up at the end of a long, elegant formal garden. Begun in the 18th century, the building was topped by two pointed towers almost a century later. The steps and balustrade were added at about the same time. The interior is impressively neoclassical. The exterior is especially magical at Christmastime, when every inch of its facade is adorned with decorative lights. ✉ *Largo da República do Brasil* ☎ *253 416 310* 🎫 *Free.*

Igreja de Nossa Senhora da Oliveira (*Church of Our Lady of the Olive Branch*)
RELIGIOUS SITE | This church in the delightful square Largo da Oliveira was founded in the 10th century to commemorate one of Guimarães's most enduring legends. Wamba, elected king of the Visigoths in the 7th century, refused the honor and thrust his olive-branch stick into the earth, declaring that only if his stick were to blossom would he accept the crown—whereupon the stick promptly sprouted foliage. In the square in front of the church, an odd 14th-century Gothic canopy sheltering a cross marks the supposed spot. The square is now surrounded by charming cafés. ✉ *Largo da Oliveira* ☎ *253 423 919* 🎫 *Free.*

Igreja de São Francisco (*Church of St. Francis*)
RELIGIOUS SITE | The Old Town's streets peter out at the southern end of Guimarães in the Almeida da Liberdade, a swath of gardens whose benches and cafés are often full. Here the stunning Igreja de São Francisco has a chancel decorated with 18th-century azulejos depicting the life of the saint. The church also has a fine Renaissance cloister. The complex now houses a home for the elderly, but both chapels are open to visitors. ✉ *Largo de São Francisco* ☎ *253 412 228* 🎫 *Free* ⏲ *Closed Mon.*

Fertile Fields

Little of the green countryside in the Minho is wasted. Vines are trained on poles and in trees high above cultivated fields, forming a natural canopy, for this is *vinho verde* country. This refreshing young "green wine"—light on alcohol but with fine digestive properties—is crisp. There are two types of vinho verde: red and white. Portuguese drink the red more often and export more of the white. Whatever the color, vinho verde is a true taste of the north. The best *aguardente* (Portuguese brandy) is made from distilled vinho verde; when aged, it can rival fine cognacs.

Museu da Sociedade Martins Sarmento (*Martins Sarmento Society Museum*)
MUSEUM | At the top of the Largo do Toural is this excellent archaeological museum contained within the cloister of the the Igreja de São Domingos. The museum has rich finds from the Celtic settlement of Citânia de Briteiros northwest of Guimarães, which makes it a logical stop before or after visiting the Citânia. There are also Lusitanian and Roman stone sarcophagi, a strange miniature bronze chariot, various weapons, and elaborate ornaments. Two finds stand out: the decorative, carved stone slabs known as the *pedras formosas* (beautiful stones)—one of which was found at a funerary monument at Briteiros—and the huge, prehistoric granite Colossus of Pedralva, a figure of brutal power thought

to have been used in ancient fertility rites. ✉ *Rua Paio Galvão 66* ☎ *253 415 969* 🌐 *www.csarmento.uminho.pt* 🎫 *€3* ⏲ *Closed Mon.*

Museu de Alberto Sampaio

MUSEUM | The beautifully preserved convent buildings surrounding the Colegiada de Nossa Senhora da Oliveira house this museum, known for its beautiful displays of religious art, medieval statuary, and coats of arms. The highlight is a 14th-century silver triptych of the Nativity that's full of animation and power. It's said to have been captured from the king of Castile at the Battle of Aljubarrota and presented to the victorious Dom João I, whose tunic, worn at the battle, is preserved in a glass case nearby. ✉ *Rua Alfredo Guimarães* ☎ *253 423 910* 🌐 *culturanorte.gov.pt/pt/patrimonio/museu-de-alberto-sampaio* 🎫 *€3* ⏲ *Closed Mon.*

Paço dos Duques de Bragança (*Palace of the Dukes of Bragança*)

CASTLE/PALACE | This much-maligned 15th-century palace that once belonged to the dukes of Bragança is now the official regional seat of Portugal's president. Critics claim that the restoration during the Salazar regime (1936–59), which turned the building into a state residence, damaged it irrevocably. Certainly the palace's brick chimneys and turrets bear little relation to the original structure, which was an atmospheric ruin for many years. Judge for yourself on an independent or guided tour of the interior, where you'll find much of interest—from tapestries and furniture to porcelain and paintings. You can book guided tours at the main desk. ✉ *Rua Conde D. Henrique* ☎ *253 412 273* 🌐 *www.pduques.culturanorte.pt* 🎫 *€5.*

Teleférico de Guimarães (*Guimarães Cable Car*)

VIEWPOINT | **FAMILY** | For sweeping views of the town, board this cable car that whisks you up to the top of Mount Penha in 10 minutes. The journey ends with a nice view from the gardens that overlook the city. The climb down is steep, so buy a round-trip ticket. ✉ *Estação Inferior do Teleférico, Rua Aristides Sousa Mendes 37* ☎ *253 515 085* 🌐 *www.turipenha.pt* 🎫 *€4 one way, €7.50 round-trip.*

Coffee and Quick Bites

★ Pastelaria Clarinha

$ | **PORTUGUESE** | A local institution, Pastelaria Clarinha is the best place to sample regional cakes and pastries. It has a range of delicious sweets, including traditional *tortas de Guimarães,* which are pastry rolls with an eggy pumpkin filling. **Known for:** a long glass display case filled with just-baked treats; eat at the counter if you want to look like a local; soak up the sun at one of the outside tables. 💲 *Average main: €5* ✉ *Largo do Toural 86/88* ☎ *253 516 513.*

Restaurants

Buxa

$$ | **PORTUGUESE** | **FAMILY** | On one of Guimarães's most scenic squares, this handsome eatery across from the Museu de Alberto Sampaio has tables in a wood-paneled dining room and beneath the arches of a cobbled courtyard. Portuguese specialties include bacalhau baked with corn bread, beef *mirandesa* (stewed with garlic and then grilled—a specialty from the northern city of Miranda do Douro), and grilled *porco preto* (cured ham). **Known for:** weekday lunch menu is an excellent value; excellent renditions of region's classic dishes; extensive wine selection. 💲 *Average main: €20* ✉ *Largo da Oliveira 23* ☎ *252 058 242.*

Café Oriental

$$ | **PORTUGUESE** | On the iconic square of Largo do Toural, this venerable eatery serves tasty regional dishes—the bacalhau baked with cheese and potato slices and the breaded octopus are fantastic—at prices that won't break the bank. If you're not headed to the town of Miranda do Douro, take the chance to sample *posta à mirandesa,* Portugal's tenderest steak, best washed down with a glass of the house wine. **Known for:** housed in a historic stone building; elegantly furnished dining room; excellent lunch buffet. *Average main: €18* *Largo do Toural 11* *253 414 048* *www.restaurantecafeoriental.com* *Closed Sun.*

Nova Nora Zé da Curva

$$ | **PORTUGUESE** | This relaxed restaurant prides itself on cooking bacalhau 1,001 different ways—the only one you need to remember is the house version, which locals call the "best in the world." Behind the traditional exterior you'll find a sleek and modern dining room on the ground floor and a second-floor terrace for alfresco dining. Grilled meats and local wines are the choice of most patrons. **Known for:** terrace has breathtaking sunset views of the city; unbeatable version of duck rice; excellent local wines. *Average main: €17* *Rua da Rainha Doña Maria II 125–129* *253 554 256* *Closed Mon.*

Hotels

★ Casa Dos Pombais

$ | **B&B/INN** | For an unforgettable experience, stay as a guest of the Visconde Viamonte da Silveira in his 18th-century manor house on the edge of the historic quarter. **Pros:** feels like you're sleeping in a well-stocked museum; a window into the country's aristocratic past; unbeatable hospitality. **Cons:** has a decidely old-fashioned feel; may be too formal some some; no restaurant. *Rooms from: €65* *Av. de Londres 100* *258 412 917* *www.solaresdeportugal.pt* *4 rooms* *Free Breakfast.*

★ Hotel da Oliveira

$ | **HOTEL** | Town houses from the 16th and 17th centuries were joined to create this stylish hotel in the heart of town. **Pros:** family-friendly environment; service is courteous and efficient; activities like horseback riding. **Cons:** lacks amenities of bigger hotels; no exercise facilities; basic decor. *Rooms from: €125* *Largo de Oliveira, Rua de Santa Maria* *253 514 157* *www.hoteldaoliveira.com* *20 rooms* *Free Breakfast.*

Hotel de Guimarães

$ | **HOTEL** | Conveniently located steps from the train station, this streamlined hotel about 15 minutes from the center of the city lets you revive yourself with a bracing dip in the indoor pool, a soak in the hot tub, or some time in the separate men's and women's saunas and steam baths. **Pros:** good location near the top attractions; ample free parking; good breakfast menu. **Cons:** uphill walk from the city center; front rooms face a highway; basic decor. *Rooms from: €130* *Rua Eduardo de Almeida* *253 424 800* *www.hotel-guimaraes.com* *116 rooms* *Free Breakfast.*

Hotel Mestre de Avis

$ | **HOTEL** | This family-run hotel has a great mix of historical charm and modern amenities, and its location on a quiet cobblestone street just around the corner from one of the city's main squares is hard to beat. **Pros:** great location on a quiet street; gives you a warm welcome; lots of local flavor. **Cons:** no elevator to third-floor rooms; extremely limited parking; basic decor. *Rooms from: €70* *Rua D. João 40* *253 422 770* *www.hotelmestredeavis.pt* *16 rooms* *No meals.*

★ Pousada Mosteiro Guimarães

$$ | **HOTEL** | **FAMILY** | In a breathtaking 12th-century monastery, this lovely lodging has details like colorful azulejo-tile panels in the public areas and guest rooms that used to be monks' cells. **Pros:** the incredibly elaborate entrance is jaw-dropping; beautiful grounds and sparkling swimming pool; a playground and other activities for kids. **Cons:** location is outside the city center; limited facilities; fussy decor. *Rooms*

from: €160 ✉ Largo Domingos Leite de Castro, Lugar da Costa ☎ 253 511 249 🌐 www.pousadas.pt 51 rooms 🍽 Free Breakfast.

Shopping

Guimarães is a center for the local linen industry. The fabric is hand-spun and handwoven, then embroidered, all to impressive effect; it's available in local shops or at the weekly Friday market.

CRAFTS

A Oficina

CRAFTS | Run by a group of artisans, this embroidery cooperative has a showroom with the best local designs. ✉ *Rua de Rainha Dona Maria II 134* ☎ *253 515 250* Ⓜ *www.aoficina.pt.*

Chafarica

TEXTILES/SEWING | With some of the best local textiles, Chafarica offers handmade pieces for the kitchen, bedroom, and bath. ✉ *Rua Santa Maria 29* ☎ *253 292 912* 🌐 *www.chafarica.pt.*

Braga

25 km (15 miles) northwest of Guimarães; 53 km (33 miles) northeast of Porto.

Braga is one of northern Portugal's nicest surprises. Founded by the Romans as Bracara Augusta, it prospered in earnest in the 6th century—under the Visigoths—when it became an important bishopric. In the 16th century, the city was beautified with churches, palaces, and fountains, many of which were altered in the 18th century.

Today Braga feels like the religious capital it is. Shops that sell religious items line the pedestrian streets around the cathedral. The Semana Santa (Holy Week) festivities here, including eerie torchlight processions of hooded participants, are impressive. There are also several interesting historical sights—most of them religious in nature—a short distance from the city. You can visit all of them by bus from the center of town; inquire at the tourist office for timetables.

GETTING HERE AND AROUND

Some long-distance trains from Lisbon terminate not in Porto but farther north in Braga, so a train is perhaps the least complicated way to make the trip from the capital. From Porto, suburban trains take 50 to 70 minutes from the downtown São Bento Station. As for buses, Transdev serves Braga from Viana do Castelo, while regional bus company Rodornorte plies routes from Porto and other regional towns, and Rede Expressos services come from as far as Lisbon.

VISITOR INFORMATION

Braga Tourism Office. ✉ *Av. da Liberdade 1* ☎ *253 262 550* 🌐 *www.cm-braga.pt.*

Sights

Antigo Paço Arquiepiscopal Bracarense (*Archbishops' Palace*)

BUILDING | Largo do Paço is flanked by the well-proportioned Antigo Paço Arquiepiscopal Bracarense, which overlooks a castellated fountain. Parts of the Gothic building date from the 14th century. Today it's occupied by faculty from the city's university and functions as the public library—one of the country's most impressive, with more than 300,000 volumes. ✉ *Rua da Misericórdia.*

★ **Bom Jesus do Monte** (*Jesus of the Mount*)

RELIGIOUS SITE | Many people come to Braga specifically to see the Bom Jesus do Monte, a pilgrimage shrine atop a 1,312-foot-high, densely wooded hill 5 km (3 miles) east of the city. The stone staircase, a marvel of baroque art that was started in 1723, leads to an 18th-century sanctuary whose terrace commands wonderful views. Fountains placed at various resting places represent the five senses and the virtues,

The Bom Jesus do Monte church in the city of Braga is reached by a magnificent stone staircase (there's also a funicular and bus service).

and small chapels display tableaux with life-size figures illustrating the Stations of the Cross. If you don't want to climb up the staircase, there's a free funicular and buses from the center of town. ✉ *Parque do Bom Jesus* ☎ *253 676 636* 🌐 *www.bomjesus.pt.*

Capela de São Frutuoso de Montélios (*Chapel of Saint Frutuoso of Montélios*)
RELIGIOUS SITE | About 4 km (2½ miles) north of town, this chapel is one of Portugal's oldest buildings. The original structure is believed to have been constructed in the 7th century in the form of a Greek cross. It was partially destroyed by the Moors and rebuilt in the 11th century. ✉ *Av. São Frutuoso.*

Monastery of São Martinho de Tibães (*Monastery of St. Martin of Tibanes*)
RELIGIOUS SITE | Some 6 km (4 miles) northwest of Braga, this impressive Benedictine monastery was built in the 11th century and rebuilt at the end of the 19th century. You can tour four cloisters, which have some fine examples of azulejos. Opt for one of the guided tours, which are the same price as a regular ticket. ✉ *Rua do Mosteiro, Mire de Tibães* ☎ *253 622 670* 🌐 *www.mosteiro-detibaes.org* 🎫 *€2 garden, €4 monastery and garden.*

Museu D. Diogo de Sousa (*D. Diogo de Sousa Museum*)
MUSEUM | One of Braga's newest museums, here you'll find artifacts from the old Roman city known as Bracara Augusta (founded 15 BC), from which Braga derives its name. ✉ *Rua dos Bombeiros Voluntários* ☎ *253 273 706* 🌐 *www.mdds.culturanorte.pt* 🎫 *€3* ⏲ *Closed Mon.*

Palácio dos Biscaínhos (*Palace of the Biscaínhos*)
HOUSE | The elegant rooms in this baroque mansion, which houses a museum of the same name, are furnished in 18th-century style and display silver and porcelain collections. The ground floor of the palace is flagstone, which allowed carriages to run through the interior to the stables beyond. At the back of the

palace is a formal garden with decorative tiles. ✉ *Rua dos Biscaínhos* ☎ *253 204 650* 🎫 *€2.*

Sé de Braga (*Cathedral of Braga*)
MUSEUM | This huge cathedral was originally Romanesque but is now an impressively cohesive blend of styles. The delicate Renaissance stone tracery on the roof is particularly eye-catching. Enter from Rua do Souto through the 18th-century cloister; the cathedral interior is on your left, and there are various interesting chapels. Steps by the entrance to the cathedral lead to the **Museu de Arte Sacra** (Museum of Religious Art), which has a fascinating collection, including a 14th-century crystal cross set in bronze. From the magnificent *coro alto* (upper choir), which you cross as part of the tour, there are views of the great baroque double organ. Across the cloister, you'll see the Capela dos Reis (Kings' Chapel), a 14th-century chapel containing the tombs of Afonso Henriques's parents, Henry of Burgundy and his wife, Teresa. **■ TIP→ Opt for the €5 entrance fee, which includes a personal guide in English.** ✉ *Rua do Souto 38* ☎ *253 263 317* 🌐 *www.se-braga.pt* 🎫 *€2, €5 for guided tour.*

Coffee and Quick Bites

Café Vianna
$ | PORTUGUESE | In business since 1871, this local landmark serves a wide variety of light dishes and has lovely views of the fountain in the square outside. The dining room is refined and elegant, but the tables outside are most in demand. **Known for:** the weekend brunch is popular with locals; a hangout for literary types; lovely spot under the arches. 💲 *Average main: €11* ✉ *Praça da República* ☎ *253 262 336.*

Restaurants

Restaurante Ignácio
$ | PORTUGUESE | Just outside the 18th-century town gate, this well-known restaurant behind a lovely traditional facade serves solid regional fare—bacalhau is a good bet, as is the roast kid. The place also specializes in *lampreia* (lamprey fish) and *sável* (shad or river herring) when in season. **Known for:** service in the dining room is brisk and efficient; reservations are essential on weekends; vegan and gluten-free options. 💲 *Average main: €16* ✉ *Campo das Hortas 4* ☎ *253 613 235* ⏲ *Closed Tues.*

★ **Sameiro O Maia**
$ | PORTUGUESE | A meal in this long-established restaurant is worth a climb (or drive) to the top of the hill that's home to the Santuário Nossa Senhora do Sameiro. Views from the spacious, elegantly decorated dining room are superb, and the menu is unadulterated northern Portuguese cuisine. **Known for:** you can't go wrong with one of the bacalhau dishes; renowned for its efficient service; roaring fire in the stone fireplace all winter. 💲 *Average main: €15* ✉ *Rotunda Monte do Sameiro, Espinho* ☎ *253 675 114* 🌐 *www.restaurantesameiromaia.pai.pt* 💳 *No credit cards* ⏲ *Closed Mon., 2 wks in mid-May, and 1st half of Oct.*

Hotels

Hotel do Elevador
$ | HOTEL | Many seasoned travelers to the country's northern reaches have made this charming hotel their top choice. **Pros:** restaurant scores highly for its food; tennis courts and other amenities; lovely facade. **Cons:** less luxurious than meets the eye; decor could use a refresh; not all rooms have views. 💲 *Rooms from: €85* ✉ *Bom Jesus do Monte* ☎ *253 603 400* 🌐 *www.hoteldoelevadorbraga.com* 🛏 *22 rooms* 🍽 *No meals.*

Hotel Dona Sofia
$ | **HOTEL** | A stone's throw from the cathedral, this pleasant, well-appointed hotel is one of the city's best bargains. **Pros:** breakfast room is bright and airy; bar that's a magnet for guests; inexpensive rates. **Cons:** cathedral bells might wake you up early; limited breakfast buffet; homely exterior. *Rooms from: €70* ✉ *Largo São João do Souto 131* ☎ *253 263 160* 🌐 *www.hoteldonasofia.com* *34 rooms* *Free Breakfast.*

Meliá Braga
$ | **HOTEL** | **FAMILY** | One of the city's most stylish and luxurious lodgings, the Meliá Braga attracts business and leisure travelers with its contemporary style, ample facilities, and professional staff. **Pros:** children's pool and other amenities for families; light meals at the pool bar; spa offers a wide variety of treatments. **Cons:** attracts many tour groups; half-hour walk from the city center; spa can often get pretty crowded. *Rooms from: €110* ✉ *Av. General Carrilho da Silva Pinto 8* ☎ *253 144 000* 🌐 *www.meliabraga.com* *182 rooms* *Free Breakfast.*

Barcelos

24 km (15 miles) west of Braga; 60 km (38 miles) northeast of Porto.

A bustling market town on the banks of the Rio Cávado, Barcelos is the center of a flourishing handicrafts industry, particularly ceramics (above all in the form of the famous Barcelos rooster). The best time to visit is during the famous weekly market—Barcelos is an easy day trip from Braga or Viana do Castelo, and there's not so much to do or see on other days, although the Museu de Olaria (Pottery Museum) is always worth visiting.

GETTING HERE AND AROUND

Barcelos is on the main rail line between Porto to Viana, but there are no direct trains from Braga. Rede Expressos buses serve the town from Lisbon as well as Porto; there is no bus station, but the company has a local agent on Avenida Dr. Sidónio País. Regional operator Transdev also runs buses from Braga, but to get from Viana to Barcelos you have to change in Forjães.

VISITOR INFORMATION

Barcelos Tourist Information. ✉ *Largo Dr. José Novais 27* ☎ *253 811 882* 🌐 *www.cm-barcelos.pt.*

Sights

Feira de Barcelos (*Barcelos Market*)
MARKET | **FAMILY** | Held every Thursday in the central Campo da República, the Barcelos Market is one of the country's largest. Starting at sunup, vendors cry out their wares, which include almost anything you can think of: traditional ceramics (brown pottery with yellow-and-white decorations are a favorite), glazed figurines (including the famous Barcelos rooster), copper lanterns, and wooden toys. There are also mounds of vegetables, fruits, cheese, bread—even live poultry. In fall and winter, the scent of roasting chestnuts wafts across the square. ✉ *Campo da República.*

Museu Arqueologico de Barcelos (*Barcelos Archaeological Museum*)
MUSEUM | The Rio Cávado, crossed by a medieval bridge, is shaded by overhanging trees and bordered by municipal gardens. High above the river stands the ruin of the medieval Paço dos Condes (Palace of the Counts), where you'll find the Museu Arqueologico de Barcelos. Among the empty sarcophagi and stone crosses is the 14th-century crucifix known as the Cruzeiro do Senhor do Galo (Cross of the Lord of the Rooster). According to local legend, after sentencing an innocent man to death, a judge prepared to dine on a roast fowl. When the condemned man said, "I'll be hanged if that rooster doesn't crow," the rooster flew from the table and the man's life was spared. The Barcelos rooster is

on sale in pottery form throughout the town; indeed, it's become something of a national symbol. ✉ *Largo do Município* ☎ *253 809 600* 🎫 *Free.*

Museu de Olaria de Barcelos (*Barcelos Pottery Museum*)
MUSEUM | A five-minute walk from the medieval bridge, this amazing museum contains more than 7,000 pieces of pottery from various epochs. Many are from excavations from all over the world, particularly from Portuguese-speaking countries. It all makes for a fascinating showcase for traditional pottery techniques and styles. ■ **TIP→ If you have trouble finding the place, look for the massive rooster out front.** ✉ *Rua Cónego Joaquim Gaiolas* ☎ *253 824 741* 🌐 *www.museuolaria.pt* 🎫 *Free* ⊙ *Closed Mon.*

Restaurants

Bagoeira
$$ | **PORTUGUESE** | Vendors from the town's weekly market favor this rustic restaurant with its wooden ceiling, wrought-iron chandeliers, and vases of fresh flowers. *Grelhados* (grilled meats and fish) are prepared in full view of hungry customers on a huge range that splutters and hisses. Other regional dishes served here include *rojões* (tender fried pork) and *papas de sarrabulho,* a stew thickened with pig's blood. **Known for:** restaurant seats hundreds of diners; grilled octopus is a specialty; delicious house wine. [$] *Average main: €20* ✉ *Av. Dr. Sidonio Pais 495* ☎ *253 813 088* 🌐 *www.bagoeira.com.*

Hotels

Quinta de Santa Comba
$ | **B&B/INN** | **FAMILY** | About 5 km (3 miles) from Barcelos, this fine 18th-century manor house—known for its beamed ceilings and stone walls—retains its appealing features such as open fireplaces while adding modern touches. **Pros:** two horses that guests may take out for rides; hotel has a real family feel; good value for money. **Cons:** limited in-room amenities; no credit cards; spotty Wi-Fi. [$] *Rooms from: €75* ✉ *São Bento da Várzea* ☎ *253 832 101* 🌐 *www.stacomba.com* 💳 *No credit cards* 🛏 *10 rooms* 🍽 *Free Breakfast.*

Shopping

Centro de Artesanato (*Handicrafts Center*)
STORE/MALL | Ceramic dishes and bowls, often signed by the artist, are a good buy here, as are delicate figurines. ✉ *Torre Medieval, Largo da Porta Nova* ☎ *253 824 261.*

Viana do Castelo

34 km (21 miles) northwest of Barcelos; 71 km (44 miles) north of Porto.

At the mouth of the Rio Lima, Viana do Castelo has been a prosperous trading center since it received its town charter in 1258. Many of its finest buildings date to the 16th and 17th centuries, the period of its greatest prosperity. Viana is regarded as the region's folk capital and specializes in producing traditional embroidered costumes. Although these make colorful souvenirs, you'll also find less elaborate crafts, like ceramics, lace, and jewelry. The large Friday market is a good place to shop.

Like many Portuguese towns, it also has its very own sweet, the *torta de Viana,* a cake roll with a yolk-and-sugar filling—it's served in local cafés. Before or after strolling through town, don't miss the excellent local beach, Praia do Cabedelo (reached by ferry from the riverside at the end of the main street). The city's seaside location makes it a popular spot in August for windsurfers as well as families wishing to combine a little culture and history with a beach holiday.

The Basílica de Santa Luzia takes pride of place in the town of Viana do Castelo.

GETTING HERE AND AROUND

Regional trains from Porto Campanhã are fast and regular; if coming from Braga, you must change at Nine. There are fast Rede Expresso buses from Lisbon, while Autoviação do Minho plies the route from Porto, and Transdev regional buses serve Viana from Braga. Viana is a real hub for transport to smaller Minho towns, with frequent services by local companies such as AVIC and Salvador crisscrossing this densely populated area.

VISITOR INFORMATION

CONTACTS Porto e Norte Tourism Authority. ✉ *Castelo Santiago da Barra* ☎ *258 820 270* 🌐 *www.portoenorte.pt.* **Viana do Castelo Tourist Information.** ✉ *Praça do Eixo Atlântico* ☎ *258 098 415* 🌐 *www.cm-viana-castelo.pt.*

Sights

★ **Basílica de Santa Luzia** (*Basilica of Saint Lucy*)

RELIGIOUS SITE | Sitting high atop a wooded hill, this white granite-domed basilica is one of the most beautiful in Portugal. A funicular railway can carry you up, or you can take the 2-km (1-mile) footpath that winds its way through the trees. The views from the basilica steps are magnificent, and a staircase to the side allows access to the very top of the dome for some extraordinary coastal vistas. ✉ *Estrada de Santa Luzia* ☎ *258 823 173* 🎫 *Funicular €2 one way.*

Castelo de Santiago da Barra (*Santiago da Barra Castle*)

CASTLE/PALACE | The great ramparts of this 16th-century fortification added the words *do castelo* to the town's name and protected it against attack from pirates eager to share in its wealth. It was completed during the reign of King Manuel I, which is why architectural details like the Roqueta Tower are Manueline in style. These days the massive structure serves as a hotel, among other uses. Outside the castle walls, Viana holds a large market every Friday. ✉ *Castelo Santiago da Barra* ☎ *258 820 270.*

Museu de Artes Decorativas (*Museum of Decorative Arts*)
MUSEUM | A 10-minute walk west from the Praça da República takes you to the impressive mansion that houses the beautiful Museu de Artes Decorativas. The early-18th-century interior has been carefully preserved, including some lovely tile panels. The collection of 17th-century ceramics and ornate period furniture shows how wealthy many of Viana's merchants were. ✉ *Largo de São Domingos* ☎ *258 820 678* 🌐 *www.cm-viana-castelo.pt* 🎫 *€2* ⏲ *Closed Mon.*

Praça da República
PLAZA | The town's best face is presented in the old streets that radiate from the Praça da República. The most striking building here is the **Casa da Misericórdia,** an 18th-century almshouse, whose two upper stories are supported, unusually, by tall caryatids (carved, draped female figures). The square's stone fountain, also Renaissance in style, harmonizes perfectly with the surrounding buildings, which include the restored town hall and its lofty arcades. ✉ *Viana do Castelo.*

Coffee and Quick Bites

Zé Natário
$ | **PORTUGUESE** | This small café is the perfect place to soak up the Minho atmosphere. The proprietor makes his own pastries, cakes, and croquettes. **Known for:** this family-run business has become a local institution; the specialty is a sweet pastry called Manjerico de Viana; custard-filled pastries are made fresh throughout the day. 💲 *Average main: €5* ✉ *Av. dos Combatentes da Grande Guerra 20* ☎ *258 826 856* 🌐 *www.zenatario.com.*

Restaurants

Casa d'Armas
$$ | **SEAFOOD** | In a renovated mansion near the waterfront, this eatery is a prime destination for seafood: start with fish soup and continue with main dishes such as *sapateira recheada* (stuffed crab), *polvo com azeite e alho* (octopus with olive oil and garlic), or *arroz de tamboril* (monkfish rice). The house bacalhau is rather unusual: it's fried and stuffed with bacon. **Known for:** a family-run business for three decades; arroz de pato (duck rice) is a specialty; comprehensive list of regional wines. 💲 *Average main: €20* ✉ *Largo 5 de Outubro 30* ☎ *258 824 999* 🌐 *www.casadarmas.com* ⏲ *Closed Wed.*

★ **Os Três Potes**
$$ | **PORTUGUESE** | Taking a seat at one of the tables under the stone arches and massive wood beams, you can choose from a fine range of regional dishes: start with the *aperitivos regionais* (a selection of cod pastries and cheeses), then move on to the exceedingly tender *polvo na brasa* (charcoal-grilled octopus) or the *cabrito à Serra d'Arga* (baby suckling goat with potatoes). On weekends people turn up here for fado music or folk dancing. **Known for:** dining room is in a 16th-century bakery; wine list focusing on local favorites; live music on weekends. 💲 *Average main: €20* ✉ *Beco dos Fornos 7–9, off Praça da República* ☎ *258 829 928* ⏲ *Closed Wed.*

Hotels

Pousada Viana do Castelo
$$ | **HOTEL** | Perched on a wooded hill behind the Basílica de Santa Luzia, this 1920s-era mansion dazzles the eye. **Pros:** fine views of the basilica and the mountains beyond; lovely gardens filled with flowers; plenty of sports facilities. **Cons:** location is a little isolated; funicular stops running early; pricey for the region. 💲 *Rooms from: €165* ✉ *Monte de Santa Luzia* ☎ *258 800 370* 🌐 *www.pousadas.pt* 🛏 *51 rooms* 🍽 *Free Breakfast.*

Rural Tourism

Central Nacional de Turismo no Espaço Rural The Minho region is well known for its *turismo no espaço rural* (rural tourism). There are some 100 properties in the area, with a particular cluster along the Rio Lima's north bank, each no more than several miles from a town. Facilities are usually minimal; houses may have a communal lounge, tennis, a pool or access to local swimming facilities, fishing, and gardens. Rates include a bed and breakfast, and some places will arrange other meals on request. The Central Nacional de Turismo no Espaço Rural is the central booking agency associated with the rural tourism program; its website includes links to the sites of Solares de Portugal (generally grander old houses), Aldeias de Portugal (village lodgings), and Casas no Campo (more remote rural digs), plus suggestions for themed tour routes. ✉ *Praça da República* ☎ 🌐 *www.center.pt.*

Ponte de Lima

35 km (22 miles) east of Viana do Castelo on N203.

Giving the town its name, Ponte de Lima's long, low, graceful bridge is of Roman origin. The main square by the old bridge has a central fountain and benches and is ringed by little cafés—the perfect places to stop for a leisurely drink. The nearby square tower still stands guard over the town, and beyond, in the narrow streets, there are several fine 16th-century mansions and a busy market. Walking around town, you'll return again and again to the river, which is the real highlight of a visit. A wide beach usually displays lines of drying laundry, and a riverside avenue lined with plane trees leads down to the Renaissance-era Igreja de Santo António dos Capuchos. The twice-monthly Monday market, held on the riverbank, is the oldest in Portugal, dating to 1125. On market days and during the mid-September Feiras Novas (New Fairs) you'll see the town at its effervescent best.

GETTING HERE AND AROUND

Local bus companies such as Cura and Autoviação do Minho serve Ponte de Lima from Viana do Castelo, with buses every half hour at peak times. From Braga the firm that provides fairly frequent services is Esteves e Andreia. Regional bus company Transdev also serves Ponte de Lima, as do fast buses from Lisbon run by Rede Expressos; they share a local agent on Rua Vasco da Gama.

VISITOR INFORMATION

Ponte de Lima Tourist Information. ✉ *Torre da Cadeia Velha, Passeio 25 de Abril* ☎ *258 240 208* 🌐 *www.cm-pontedelima.pt.*

Restaurants

A Cozinha Velha

$ | **PORTUGUESE** | It's best to come hungry to this rustic eatery specializing in *orelha de porco* (pig's ear), *favas com fumados* (broad beans with smoked sausage), and *cabrito assado* (kid roasted in a wood oven). The stone-walled dining room is dominated by a massive fireplace that keeps the place warm on chilly evenings. **Known for:** attentive owners and staff;

long list of local wines; convivial atmosphere. $ *Average main: €16 ✉ Caminho da Oliveirinha, Arcozelo ☎ 258 749 664 🌐 www.restaurantecozinhavelha.com.*

Encanada

$ | PORTUGUESE | A covered balcony held aloft by stone pillars makes this one of the most appealing places for outdoor dining in Ponte de Lima. You might start with the *bolinhos de bacalhau,* fried potato cakes with plenty of cod in them, and then try one of the regional dishes, such as *rojões* (fried pork). **Known for:** one of the town's oldest restaurants; good selection of local vinho verde; upper floor has views of the river. $ *Average main: €15 ✉ Mercado Municipal, Passeio 25 de Abril ☎ 258 941 189 ⌚ Closed Mon.*

Parque Nacional de Peneda-Gerês

90 km northeast of Porto.

The northeastern corner of the Minho is quite unlike most of this densely populated, heavily cultivated region. Here several forested *serras* (mountain ranges) rise up, cut through with deep valleys. A significant part of this area is protected, forming Portugal's only national park, the Parque Nacional da Peneda-Gerês. But there are striking landscapes even outside the park's borders, such as the valley of the River Cávado, which harbors Portugal's first five-star rural resort, and the River Homem, with its Vilarinho das Furnas reservoir. The town of Caldas de Gerês has a popular spa and a cluster of lodging options.

GETTING HERE AND AROUND

In terms of access, the national park itself divides into three main sections. The southern, most easily accessible part is a two-hour drive from Braga: turn off the N103 just after Cerdeirinhas, along the N304. There are up to six buses a day from Braga to Cerdeirinhas and Caldas do Gerês, run by local hotel company Empresa Hoteleira do Gerês and by Transdev, both of which have offices in the bus station on Largo de São Francisco in Braga. Buses from Braga also stop in Terras de Bouro, just outside the national park, where there are several restaurants and *pensões,* but gourmets with wheels should cross the River Homem for Brufe, home to a spectacularly sited restaurant.

The park's central region is accessible by car or bus from Ponte da Barca, from which the N203 heads 30 km (18 miles) east to Lindoso, or from Arcos de Valdevez, from which the minor N202 leads to the village of Soajo. Both towns offer basic accommodations and superb hiking. You can reach Lindoso by Salvador bus from Braga, changing in Ponte da Barca or Arcos de Valdevez.

To see the park's northern reaches, which encompass the Serra da Peneda (Peneda Mountains), it's best to approach from Melgaço, a small town on the Rio Minho, 25 km (15 miles) east of Monção. From Melgaço, it's 27 km (17 miles) on the N202 to the village of Castro Laboreiro, at the park's northernmost point. Salvador buses cover this region.

VISITOR INFORMATION

CONTACTS Adere Peneda Gerês. ✉ *Associação de Desenvolvimento das Regiões do Parque Nacional da Peneda-Gerês, Rua D. Manuel I, Ponte da Barca ☎ 258 452 250 🌐 www.adere-pg.pt.* **Empresa Hoteleira do Gerês.** ☎ *253 390 220 🌐 www.hoteisgeres.com.* **Salvador Transportes.** ☎ *258 521 504 🌐 www.salvador-transportes.com.*

Sights

★ **Parque Nacional da Peneda-Gerês**

NATIONAL/STATE PARK | The 172,900-acre park, sitting on the border with with Spain, was created in 1970 to preserve the region's diverse flora and fauna. It remains Portugal's only national park,

A scenic view of the Cávado River in the Peneda-Gerês National Park in northern Portugal.

and even a short trip shows you wild stretches framed by mountains, woods, and lakes. The park's headquarters is in Braga, but you can get a map of the more than 30 marked trails at any local tourism office. ✉ *Sede do Parque Nacional, Av. António Macedo, Braga* ☎ *253 203 480* 🌐 *www.adere-pg.pt.*

Restaurants

★ O Abocanhado

$$$ | PORTUGUESE | Worth a trip for its stunning location and prize-winning design, this restaurant is also renowned for its regional cuisine. Perched in the Serra Amarela, 12 km (7½ miles) from Terras de Bouro, the long building slots into the surrounding slate, its terrace affording panoramic views of the River Homem. **Known for:** incredibly fresh ingredients from local farms; breathtaking views of the surrounding hills; prizewinning architecture. *$ Average main: €30* ✉ *Lugar de Brufe, Brufe* ☎ *253 352 944* 🌐 *www.abocanhado.com* *Closed Mon. and Tues. Sept.–June.*

Hotels

Hotel Carvalho Araújo

$ | B&B/INN | FAMILY | This family-run establishment in the heart of Parque Nacional da Peneda-Gerês is one of the best-value lodging options in the area. **Pros:** family-friendly atmosphere; lots of activities on offer; convenient parking garage. **Cons:** rooms can feel stuffy; not many amenities; breakfast is limited. *$ Rooms from: €60* ✉ *Rua de Arnaçó 6, Parque Nacional da Peneda-Gerês* ☎ *253 391 185,* 🌐 *www.hotelcarvalhoaraujo.com* *23 rooms* *Free Breakfast.*

Vila Real

98 km (61 miles) east of Porto.

The capital of Trás-os-Montes is superbly situated between two mountain ranges, and much of the city retains a small-town air. Although there's no great wealth of sights, it's worth stopping here to stroll down the central avenue, which ends at

The Casa de Mateus mansion in Vila Real is one of the country's finest examples of baroque architecture.

a rocky promontory over the gushing Rio Corgo. A path around the church at the head of the promontory provides views of stepped terraces and green slopes. At the avenue's southern end, a few narrow streets are filled with 17th- and 18th-century houses, their entrances decorated with coats of arms.

GETTING HERE AND AROUND

The Corgo Valley line that runs from the banks of the Douro to Vila Real stopped running in 2009, but the city is served by a plethora of local and regional bus companies including Rodonorte and Auto Viação do Tâmega. Rede Expressos long-distance buses also come here from Lisbon, Porto, and other cities across Portugal. Aero Vip also runs near-daily turbo-prop flights from Lisbon to Vila Real's municipal airport.

ESSENTIALS

BUS CONTACTS Auto Viação do Tâmega. ☎ *276 332 384* 🌐 *www.avtamega.pt.*

VISITOR INFORMATION Vila Real Tourist Information. ✉ *Av. Carvalho Araújo 94* ☎ *259 308 170* 🌐 *www.cm-vilareal.pt.*

Sights

★ **Casa de Mateus** (*Mateus Palace*)
HOUSE | An exceptional baroque mansion believed to have been designed by Nicolau Nasoni (architect of Porto's dashing Clérigos Tower), the Casa de Mateus sits 4 km (2½ miles) east of Vila Real. Its U-shape facade—with high, decorated finials at each corner—is pictured on the Mateus Rosé wine label (though that is the full extent of the association, as the winemaker is not based here). Set behind the main house is the chapel, with an even more extravagant facade. The elegant interior is open to the public, as are the formal gardens, which are enhanced by a "tunnel" of cypress trees that shade the path. ✉ *N322, Mateus* ☎ *259 323 121* 🌐 *www.casadamateus.com* *€13.*

Igreja dos Clérigos (*Church of the Clergy*)
RELIGIOUS SITE | The finest baroque work in Vila Real, this curious fan-shape building is also called the Capela Nova (New Chapel). Its facade is dominated by two heavy columns. Built in the 18th century and dedicated to Saint Peter, it's believed by some to have been designed by Nicolau Nasoni, architect of Porto's emblematic Torre dos Clérigos. ✉ *Rua dos Combatentes da Grande Guerra 74* 🎫 *Free.*

Restaurants

★ **Terra de Montanha**
$$ | **PORTUGUESE** | **FAMILY** | With tables nestled inside oversized wine barrels, Terra de Montanha has an interior design that's as memorable as the food. Try the excellent regional specialties like *bacalhau com presunto e broa no forno* (cod baked with smoked ham and cornbread). **Known for:** upscale dining room resembles a wine cellar; service couldn't be friendlier; vegetarian menu. $ *Average main: €18* ✉ *Rua 31 de Janeiro 16–18* ☎ *259 372 075* 🌐 *www.terrademontanhasite.xpg.uol.com.br* ⏲ *No dinner Sun.*

Hotels

Hotel Miracorgo
$ | **HOTEL** | Once you get past the boxy exterior, this hotel has everything you need: spacious guest rooms with plenty of light shining through the wide windows, handsome common areas where guests actually linger, and a comfortable restaurant and bar. **Pros:** indoor pool is heated with solar power; spacious rooms with private balconies; expansive views from the restaurant. **Cons:** has a chain-hotel feel; rooms lack local charm; some basic decor. $ *Rooms from: €80* ✉ *Av. 1 de Maio 76–78* ☎ *259 325 001* 🌐 *www.hotelmiracorgo.com* *166 rooms* *Free Breakfast.*

Pousada do Barão de Forrester
$ | **HOTEL** | Time fades away as you sit reading by the fire in the lounge, glass of port at your side, at this pousada in Alijó, some 30 km (18 miles) southeast of Vila Real. **Pros:** peaceful setting in the middle of several parks; pleasant location in a smaller village; friendly and efficient service. **Cons:** some areas are beginning to show their age; breakfast buffet could be more varied; not many amenities. $ *Rooms from: €130* ✉ *Rua Comendador José Rufino, Alijó* ☎ *259 959 467* 🌐 *www.pousadas.pt* *21 rooms* *Free Breakfast.*

Bragança

116 km (72 miles) northeast of Vila Real; 212 km (131 miles) northeast of Porto.

This ancient town in the northeastern corner of Portugal has been inhabited since Celtic times (since about 600 BC). The town lent its name to the noble family of Bragança (or Braganza), whose most famous member, Catherine, married Charles II of England—the New York City borough of Queens is named after her. Descendants of the family ruled Portugal until 1910; their tombs are contained within the church of São Vicente de Fora in Lisbon. Unfortunately, since improved roads have encouraged development, the approaches to Bragança have been spoiled by many ugly new buildings.

Just past the town's modern outskirts rises the magnificent 15th-century Castelo (Castle), found within the ring of battlemented walls that surround the Cidadela (Citadel), the country's best-preserved medieval village and one of the most thrilling sights in Trás-os-Montes. Bragança has locally made ceramics, and there's a good crafts shop within the walls of the Citadel. Baskets, copper objects, pottery, woven fabrics, and leather goods are all well made here.

GETTING HERE AND AROUND

Trains to Bragança were discontinued some years ago, much to locals' frustration, but bus company Rodonorte serves the town from major regional centers. There are also Rede Expressos fast services from Lisbon. Aero Vip also runs near-daily turbo-prop flights from Lisbon to Bragança's municipal airport.

ESSENTIALS

VISITOR INFORMATION Bragança Tourist Information. ✉ *Av. Cidade de Zamora* ☎ *273 381 273* 🌐 *www.cm-braganca.pt.*

Sights

★ **Cidadela de Bragança** (*Bragança Citadel*)

MILITARY SITE | FAMILY | Within the walls of the Cidadela, you'll find the Castelo and the **Domus Municipalis** (City Hall), a rare Romanesque civic building dating to the 12th century. It's always open, but you may need to get a key from one of the local cottages for the Igreja de Santa Maria (Church of St. Mary), a building with Romanesque origins that has a superb 18th-century painted ceiling. A prehistoric granite boar, with a tall medieval stone pillory sprouting from its back, stands below the castle keep. The Torre de Menagem now contains the **Museu Militar,** which displays armaments from the 12th century through World War I. The most exciting aspect of the museum is the 108-foot-high Gothic tower with its dungeons, drawbridge, turrets, battlements, and vertiginous outside staircase. ✉ *Rua da Cidadela* ☎ *273 322 378* 🎫 *Free.*

Igreja de São Bento (*Church of St. Benedict*)

RELIGIOUS SITE | Outside the walls of the Citadel is this Renaissance-era church, with fine Mudejar (Moorish-style) vaulted ceiling and a gilded retable. Founded in the 16th century to serve the attached monastery, it also has some 18th-century additions. The church does not have regular opening hours, but is usually open around 5 pm for about two hours. ✉ *Rua de São Francisco* 🎫 *Free.*

Museu do Abade de Baçal (*Abbot of Baçal Museum*)

MUSEUM | Housed in the former bishop's palace, the Museu do Abade de Baçal's collection includes archaeological discoveries such as boarlike fertility symbols, tombstones with pinwheel patterns, and ancient coins. ✉ *Rua Conselheiro Abílio Beça 27* ☎ *273 331 595* 🌐 *www.mabadebacal.com* 🎫 *€3* 🕓 *Closed Mon.*

Museu Ibérico da Máscara e do Traje (*Iberian Museum of Masks and Costumes*)

MUSEUM | If you can't make your visit to the region coincide with one of the festivals in which local lads wearing wooden masks roam the streets, the Museu Ibérico da Máscara e do Traje is definitely worth a visit. A joint Portuguese-Spanish initiative, it has displays on the celebrations in villages across Trás-os-Montes and across the border in Zamora. The many costumes on show are riotously colorful and the masks strikingly carved. Information in English is available. ✉ *Rua D. Fernando O Bravo 24–26* ☎ *273 381 008* 🌐 *museudamascara.cm-braganca.pt* 🎫 *€1* 🕓 *Closed Mon.*

Parque Natural de Montesinho (*Montesinho Natural Park*)

NATIONAL/STATE PARK | These 185,000 acres of rolling hills are one of the most remote, least developed areas of the country. It's home to a growing population of Iberian wolves, which you're not likely to see except on a guided nature tour. In the villages that dot the park, some ancient traditions survive. **Rio de Onor,** right on the Spanish border, has traditional dwellings where livestock inhabit the ground floor and humans live one story up, warmed by the animals' body heat in cold winter months. ✉ *N308* ☎ *938 331 942* 🌐 *www.montesinhovivo.pt.*

Detour: Off the Path

Miranda do Douro, some 80 km (50 miles) southeast of Bragança, is a curiosity: the only city in Portugal to have its own officially recognized language. More closely related to Latin than to Portuguese, Mirandês was always spoken by elders and is now taught in local schools. The old traditions are just as vibrant, with spectacular folk dances taking place during the Festas de Santa Bárbara in mid-August. The town has a hulking ruin of a castle, a museum showcasing local customs, a 16th-century cathedral with lovely decorative elements, and several imposing palaces. The **Turismo** (✉ *Largo do Menino Jesus da Cartolina* ☎ *273 431 132*) has information on daily boat trips on the Douro, where eagles may be spotted nesting on the river cliffs. The valley here forms part of **Parque Natural do Douro Internacional** (🌐 *www.icnf.pt/portal*); its headquarters is farther south in Mogadouro, but it has a branch in Miranda (☎ *273 431 457 or 273 432 833*).

Restaurants

Lá Em Casa

$ | PORTUGUESE | With cool slate walls and a crackling fireplace, this unassuming restaurant sits midway between the castle and the cathedral. As you might expect this far inland, the menu tends to focus on meat, including an unusual recipe for *arroz de pato* (baked duck rice) which features beer. **Known for:** amicable owner is eager to suggest dishes and wine pairings; chestnuts are featured in main dishes as well as desserts; try the alheira—sausage made with wild game. $ *Average main: €12* ✉ *Rua Marquês de Pombal 7* ☎ *273 322 111.*

★ Restaurante Típico Dom Roberto

$ | PORTUGUESE | The wooden sign and the rustic balcony outside may remind Americans of the Old West, but this delightfully rustic restaurant in Gimonde, 8 km (5 miles) east of Bragança, is Portuguese through and through. Hanging on the wall are hams from native *bísaro* pigs, and the menu features local game like hare, wild boar, and pheasants. **Known for:** ingredients are sourced from local farms; old hunting tools adorn the walls; next to a store selling regional goods. $ *Average main: €15* ✉ *Rua Coronel Álvaro Cepeda 1, Gimonde* ☎ *273 302 510* 🌐 *www.amontesinho.pt.*

★ Solar Bragançano

$$$ | PORTUGUESE | In an old manor house overlooking the historic plaza, this family-run establishment starts you out with a complimentary glass of port in the wood-paneled reception area lined with antique bookshelves. The whole place is imbued with old-world elegance, from the ornate silver candlesticks to the fine crystal and lace tablecloths. **Known for:** leafy terrace is perfect for summer evenings; the wild game is always perfectly prepared; excellent selection of regional wines. $ *Average main: €25* ✉ *Praça de Sae 34* ☎ *273 323 875* ⏲ *Closed Mon.*

Hotels

Pousada de São Bartolomeu

$$ | RESORT | FAMILY | On a hilltop to the west of the city center, this modern pousada offers comfortably furnished guest rooms and terrific views. **Pros:** bar is warmed by an open fireplace; a pair of pretty swimming pools; rooms with wide windows. **Cons:** a few miles from the center of town; not a lot of local charm; some basic decor. *Rooms from: €162 Rua Estrada do Turismo 273 331 493 www.pousadas.pt 28 rooms Free Breakfast.*

Chaves

96 km (60 miles) west of Bragança.

Chaves was known to the Romans as Aquae Flaviae (Flavian's Waters). They established a military base here and popularized the town's thermal springs. The impressive 16-arch Roman bridge across the Rio Tâmega, at the southern end of town, dates from the 1st century AD and displays two original Roman milestones. Today Chaves is characterized most by a series of fortifications built during the late Middle Ages, when the city was prone to attack from all sides. The town lies 12 km (7 miles) from the Spanish border. Its name means "keys"—whoever controlled Chaves held the keys to the north of the country.

GETTING HERE AND AROUND

Chaves is served by bus company Rodonorte, which has routes to major towns in the region. Rede Expressos also serves the town from Lisbon and other towns around Portugal.

VISITOR INFORMATION

Chaves Tourist Information
Paço dos Duques de Bragança 276 348 180 www.chaves.pt.

Sights

Igreja da Misericórdia (*Mercy Church*)
RELIGIOUS SITE | This late-17th-century church next door to the Torre de Menagem is lined with huge panels of blue-and-white azulejos depicting scenes from the New Testament. *Praça de Camões 276 321 384.*

Torre de Menagem (*Menagem Tower*)
MUSEUM | The most obvious landmark is this great, blunt, 14th-century fortress overlooking the river. It houses the **Museu da Região Flaviense** (Flaviense Regional Museum), which is made up of the **Museu Militar** (Military Museum); the **Museu Arqueológico,** a hodgepodge of local archaeological finds and relics that tell the town's history; and the **Museu de Arte Sacra** (Sacred Art Museum). Its grounds offer grand views of the town. The tower is surrounded by narrow, winding streets filled with elegant houses, most of which have carved wood balconies on their top floors. *Praça de Camões 276 340 500.*

Hotels

★ **Forte de São Francisco**
$ | HOTEL | FAMILY | The ruins of a 17th-century Franciscan monastery have been transformed into this remarkable hotel with massive walls surrounding extensive gardens and courtyards. **Pros:** perks include an outdoor swimming pool and tennis courts; delicious meals in one of the area's best restaurants; family-friendly environment. **Cons:** some rooms feel a bit dated; spotty Wi-Fi access; tiny gym. *Rooms from: €75 Forte de São Francisco, Rua do Terreiro da Cavalaria 276 333 700 www.fortesaofrancisco.com 58 rooms Free Breakfast.*

Chapter 11

THE AZORES

Updated by
Liz Humphreys

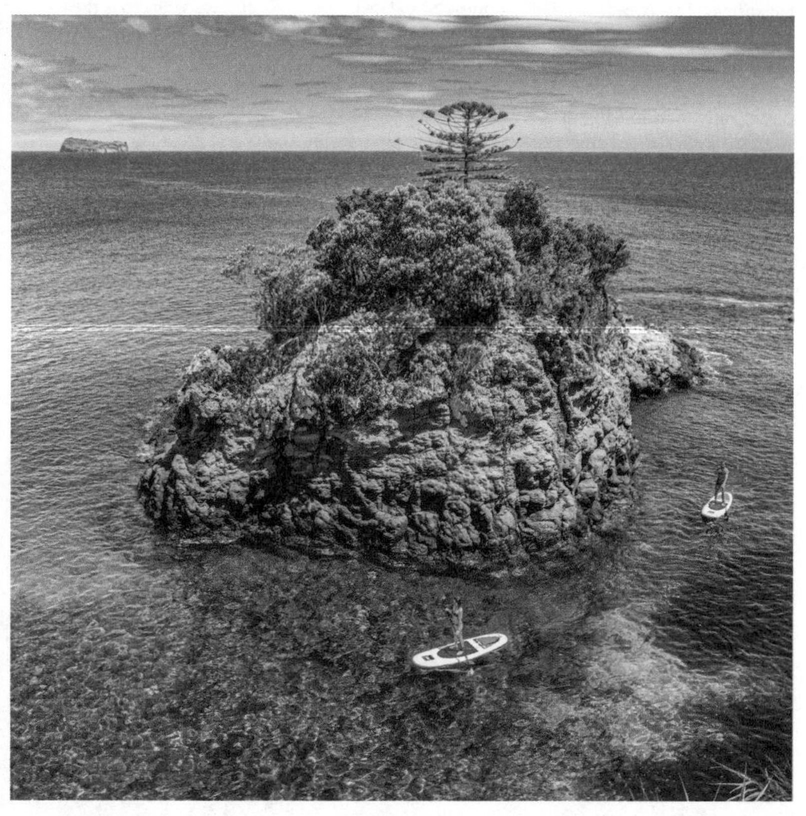

Sights ★★★★★ | Restaurants ★★★★☆ | Hotels ★★★★☆ | Shopping ★★☆☆☆ | Nightlife ★☆☆☆☆

WELCOME TO THE AZORES

TOP REASONS TO GO

★ **Get up-close and personal with volcanoes:** From climbing Mt. Pico's volcanic cone to Terceira's Algar do Carvão cave to the lunar landscape created by Faial's Capelinhos Volcano.

★ **Soak in subtropical hot springs:** The Azores' geothermal activity has resulted in naturally heated waters perfect for a dip, particularly on São Miguel.

★ **Try new-to-you food and wine:** Limpets and barnacles, slipper lobsters and wreckfish. *Bolos lêvedos* (sweet muffins) and *cozido* (stew). Wines made of regional grapes from Pico. And fragrant cheese from every island.

★ **Stop and smell the flowers:** The mild climate supports many types of flowers and plants, which you'll see not only in lovely gardens, but also in the seemingly endless and wondrously colorful hydrangeas from May to October.

★ **Go searching for whales:** At least 24 types of cetaceans have been spotted in the Azores, and can be spotted throughout the year (some from land).

1 **São Miguel.** The Azores' biggest and most diverse island is best known for its relaxing hot springs, beautiful volcanic lakes, leafy tea plantations, and eye-popping flora.

2 **Terceira.** Angra do Heroísmo, Terceira's main city, boasts colorful rows of Renaissance-style buildings, plus an unmissable extinct volcano that offers gentle hikes and lovely views.

3 **Pico.** The Azores' second biggest island is famous for having the tallest mountain in Portugal, volcanic soil vineyards, black stone houses, and some of the best whale-watching around.

4 **Faial.** A seafarers' favorite, this blue hydrangea-laden island hosts boaters who cross the Atlantic and visitors who come to hike its stunning volcanic Caldeira and Capelinhos Volcano.

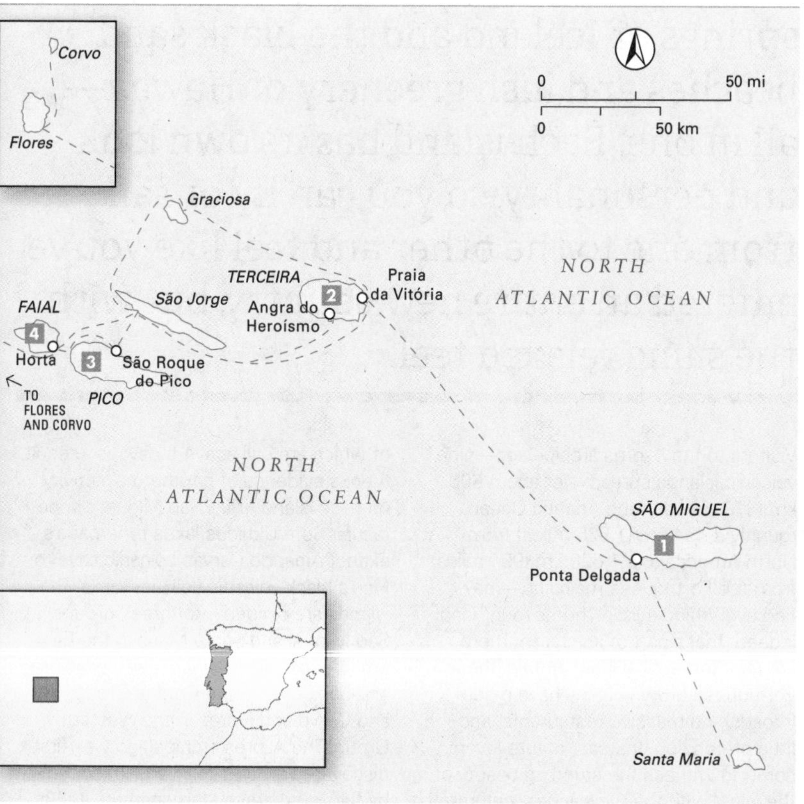
Corvo
Flores
0
50 mi
0
50 km
Graciosa
NORTH
ATLANTIC OCEAN
TERCEIRA
Praia
da Vitória
FAIAL
São Jorge
Angra do
Heroísmo
Horta
São Roque
do Pico
TO
FLORES
AND CORVO
PICO
NORTH
ATLANTIC OCEAN
SÃO MIGUEL
Ponta Delgada
Santa Maria

The Azores offer green, rolling hills straight out of Ireland blended with the dramatic volcanic landscapes and hot springs of Iceland and the black sand beaches and lush greenery of Hawaii—all in one. Each island has its own look and personality, so you can fly or sail from one to the other and feel like you've entered an entire new country, but with the same relaxed feel.

Visitors to the Azores archipelago—nine volcanic islands spread over about 600 km (370 miles) in the Atlantic Ocean, roughly 2,454 km (1,525 miles) from North America and 1,600 km (994 miles) from the Portuguese mainland—may find everything a little "homespun," and indeed, that's part of its charm. There are no international chain hotels (though Portuguese-grown chains have made inroads), no massive restaurants, and little pretension. Instead, nature lovers come to witness the stunning beauty of the isles, with their volcanoes, natural swimming holes, and—in spring—millions of wild, blooming hydrangeas. More adventurous travelers take advantage of the hiking, world-class fishing, and excellent whale-watching available. Still others come for a brief glimpse into a simpler life that is rarely seen today in mainland Europe—small, pretty port towns of cobblestone streets, simple churches, and red-tile-roofed homes that thrive on cottage industries like fishing and cheese making.

The islands were originally formed due to eruptions from 1,766 volcanoes, nine of which are still active today; as a result, there's evidence of geothermal activity on each island, from São Miguel's spectacular Sete Cidades lakes to Terceira's extinct Algar do Carvão volcanic cave to Pico's black volcanic soil vineyards. The islands are divided into three "groups": São Miguel and Santa Maria in the Eastern Group; Terceira, Pico, Faial, Graciosa, and São Jorge in the Central Group; and Corvo and Flores in the Western Group. The Azores archipelago was first discovered around 1427 and inhabited by the Portuguese starting in the 1430s, but due to its far-flung location, development happened at a slower pace than on the mainland, resulting in the unspoiled nature still found there today.

For a first-time visitor, spending time in São Miguel, not only the largest and most diverse island but also the easiest to get to, is a must. For a complete change of pace, a quick flight to Pico and its neighbor Faial showcases the welcoming nature of these smaller islands. If you have time, cap off your trip with a stay in Terceira, a lively island with a more developed feel. Of course, after you visit once, you'll likely want to come back to explore the other islands, too. Just maintain an unhurried pace, and you'll fit right in.

Planning

Getting Here and Around

AIR

São Miguel's João Paulo II Airport, 2 km (1 mile) west of Ponta Delgada, is the major air hub in the Azores. Terceira's Lajes Internacional Airport, 21 km (13 miles northeast) of Angra do Heroísmo, is the second biggest. Direct flights from the United States (from New York, Boston, and Oakland) and Canada (Toronto and Montreal) fly into both Ponta Delgada and Terceira.

Direct flights from European cities (Frankfurt, Brussels, London, Copenhagen, Helsinki) fly into Ponta Delgada, while Amsterdam flights arrive at both Ponta Delgada and Terceira. Flights from Lisbon and Porto fly to Ponta Delgada and Terceira, while those from Lisbon also fly to Pico and Faial. Azores Airlines, also known as SATA Internacional, is the only regional carrier with regular flight links between the islands on well-maintained prop planes. Keep in mind that delays are common due to the changeable North Atlantic weather.

CONTACTS Aerogare Civil das Lajes. (*Lajes Internacional Airport*) ✉ *Praia da Vitoria* ☎ *295 545 454* 🌐 *aerogarelajes.azores.gov.pt.* **Aeroporto da Horta.** ✉ *Castelo Branco, Horta* ☎ *292 943 511* 🌐 *www.ana.pt/en/hor/home.* **Aeroporto de Ponta Delgada.** (*João Paulo II Airport*) ✉ *Ponta Delgada* ☎ *296 205 400* 🌐 *www.aeroportopontadelgada.pt.* **Aeroporto do Pico.** ✉ *Bandeiras, Madalena* ☎ *292 628 380.*

BOAT

Ferries, operated by Atlântico Line, run seasonally between most of the Azores islands. Most convenient is the ferry between Pico and Faial, which takes 30 minutes and sails up to eight times a day year-round. From May to September, there are several sailings a week between São Miguel and Terceira (4½ hours), São Miguel and Faial (14 hours), and Terceira and Faial (8½ hours).

CONTACTS Atlântico Line. ☎ *707 201 572* 🌐 *www.atlanticoline.pt.*

BUS

Though there are buses between all of the major towns on all the islands, they tend to be infrequent and used primarily by locals to get to residential destinations.

CONTACTS Cristiano Limitada. ✉ *Rua 8 de Março 25, Madalena* ☎ *292 622 126* 🌐 *www.cristianolimitada.pt.* **Empresa de Viação Terceirense.** ✉ *Rua Dr. Sousa Meneses 5, Angra do Heroísmo* ☎ *295 217 001* 🌐 *www.evt.pt/index.php.* **Farias.** ✉ *Rua Vasco da Gama 42, Horta* ☎ *292 292 482* 🌐 *www.farias.pt.* **São Miguel Transportes.** ✉ *Rua de Lisboa, Ponta Delgada* ☎ *296 301 800.*

CAR

Renting a car is by far the best way to get around all of the islands. Beyond the flexibility and convenience a car affords, rental prices are also fairly inexpensive compared to the rest of Europe. Local agencies tend to offer the most competitive rates. The roads throughout the four main islands are generally in good shape, though you're bound to get a bit lost when venturing off the main thoroughfares.

CONTACTS Autatlantis Rent-a-Car. ☎ *296 205 340* 🌐 *www.autatlantis.com.* **Ilha Verde Rent-a-Car.** ☎ *296 304 891* 🌐 *www.ilhaverde.com.* **Sixt.** ☎ 🌐 *www.sixt.co.uk/car-hire/portugal.* **Wayzor.** ☎ 🌐 *wayzor.pt.*

TAXI

Taxis are in short supply, other than at airports. The rates are also quite expensive. For instance, in São Miguel, rates are around €1 per minute. Always confirm the fare before you get in, as most taxis don't use meters.

CONTACTS Associação de Profissionais de Automóveis Ligeiros da Ilha Terceira. ✉ *Angra do Heroísmo* ☎ *295 212 004.* **Associação de Taxistas do Faial.** ☎ *292 391 300.* **Associação de Taxistas do Pico.** 🌐 *taxispico.pt.* **Associação de Táxis de São Miguel.** ☎ *296 382 000,.*

Restaurants

Azoreans are rightly proud of the local products found in abundance throughout the islands, particularly their cheeses (though the most famous hails from São Jorge, every island produces several delicious kinds), fish (the Azores boast some of the widest variety around, so you're bound to find types you've never heard of, like wreckfish, guelly jack, and bluemouth rockfish), and seafood, especially octopus, limpets, and barnacles. Pork and beef, often an essential part of a rich stew or casserole, is also popular. Fresh pineapple is served as an unembellished dessert. More decadent desserts often take the form of cakes, like São Miguel's Vila Franca do Campo cheesecakes and Terceira's cinnamon-and-spice Dona Amélias. Other must-try Azores dishes include *cozido*, a meat-rich stew cooked in the ground in São Miguel's volcanic Furnas region, and *alcatra*, pot roast made with red wine, found in Terceira.

Many restaurants in the Azores serve versions of these items, either prepared traditionally or perhaps with modern flourishes, in intimate, simply decorated spaces often run by several generations of the same family. You'll find more variety in the bigger communities of Ponta Delgada and Angra do Heroísmo, while those on the coast or countryside serve up whatever's freshest that day. For higher-end meals (with prices to match), head to one of the upscale hotels.

Reservations are generally a good idea during high season, especially on the larger islands, and as befitting the island pace, service can be on the relaxed side, so make sure to budget in enough time for your meals.

Hotels

The Azores are all about a relaxed, casual approach to living, so don't expect luxurious accommodations (although that's slowly starting to change, particularly on the most touristy island of São Miguel). What you can look forward to are family-run inns and guesthouses where the owner will greet you personally and help sort out your island travel plans, as well as a selection of relaxed hotels (many offering unbeatable views) and atmospheric *pousadas* (lodgings located in old forts and other historic settings). There are limited options outside of São Miguel, so if you're visiting during high season, book as far in advance as you can.

WHAT IT COSTS In Euros

$	$$	$$$	$$$$
RESTAURANTS			
under €16	€16–€20	€21–€25	over €25
HOTELS			
under €141	€141–€200	€200–€260	over €260

Hotel prices in the reviews are the lowest cost of a standard double room in high season. Restaurant prices in the reviews are the average cost of a main course at dinner, or if dinner is not served, at lunch.

Tours

Azores Getaways

EXCURSIONS | This Ponta Delgada–based tour company offers complete packages to the Azores, from daylong tours to individual island specialty excursions like hiking treks, food and wine explorations, and surfing trips to several different islands. ✉ *Av. Natália Correia 51, Ponta Delgada* ☎ *308 804 860* 🌐 *azoresgetaways.com.*

Visitor Information

CONTACTS Associação de Turismo dos Açores. ✉ *Av. Infante D. Henrique 33, Ponta Delgada* ☎ *296 288 082* 🌐 *www.visitazores.com.*

São Miguel

With masses of pink and blue hydrangeas lining the roadways, steaming hot springs tucked away throughout the island, and twin blue-and-green lakes on its western side (the most photographed natural wonders in the Azores), São Miguel is aptly named the "Green Island." Outside the small urban center of Ponta Delgada, São Miguel's very walkable main city, the scenery of the Azores' biggest island varies from the long, sandy beaches of Áqua d'Alto in the south and Santa Bárbara in the north, to the volcanic landscape and gardens of quaint Furnas, to one of Europe's only tea plantations near Ribeira Grande. As you explore, you'll want to save time for one of the island's fantastic hikes and a relaxing hot springs dip or two.

GETTING HERE AND AROUND

Flights arrive into São Miguel's João Paulo II Airport, from where it's about a 10-minute cab ride into Ponta Delgada. To explore the island, a rental car is your best bet, though you can also arrange organized tours to specific sights or prearranged taxi tours around the island if you'd prefer not to drive yourself.

TOURS

Azores Trilhos de Natureza (*Azores Trails of Nature*)

BOAT TOURS | Take a boat around the south coast of São Miguel with an expert skipper to see caves, marine life, and lovely scenery. Tour are four or eight hours. ✉ *Beco da Rua dos Prestes de Cima 1, Ponta Delgada* ☎ *919 02506* 🌐 *www.azorestrailsofnature.com* 🎫 *From €105.*

Greenzone Azores Tours

DRIVING TOURS | Get off the beaten path with these full- and half-day tours to Sete Cidades, Furnas, Lagoa do Fogo, and Nordeste. ✉ *Rua Canada Nova do Pópulo 62, Ponta Delgada* ☎ *918 671 149,* 🌐 *greenzoneazores.com* 🎫 *From €30.*

★ **Hungry Whales**

SPECIAL-INTEREST | Stroll through downtown Ponta Delgada while learning more about its history as you sample some of the island's iconic foods on a three-hour small group walking tour. Hungry Whales also offers a cheese-and wine-experience, a drinks-and-bites jaunt, and customized food tours. ✉ *Rua José Bensaúde 56, Ponta Delgada* ☎ *969 725 337* 🌐 *www.hungrywhales.com* 🎫 *From €37.*

Pure Azores

WALKING TOURS | This 3½-hour walking tour of Ponta Delgada covers the main attractions as well as a botanical garden. It departs from the tourist office on Tuesday, Thursday, and Saturday year-round. ✉ *Rua Agostinho Cymbron 9, Ponta Delgada* ☎ *932 532 200* 🌐 *www.pureazores.com* 🎫 *€30.*

VISITOR INFORMATION

CONTACTS Posto de Turismo de São Miguel. ✉ *Av. Infante D. Henrique, Ponta Delgada* ☎ *296 308 610* 🌐 *www.visitazores.com.*

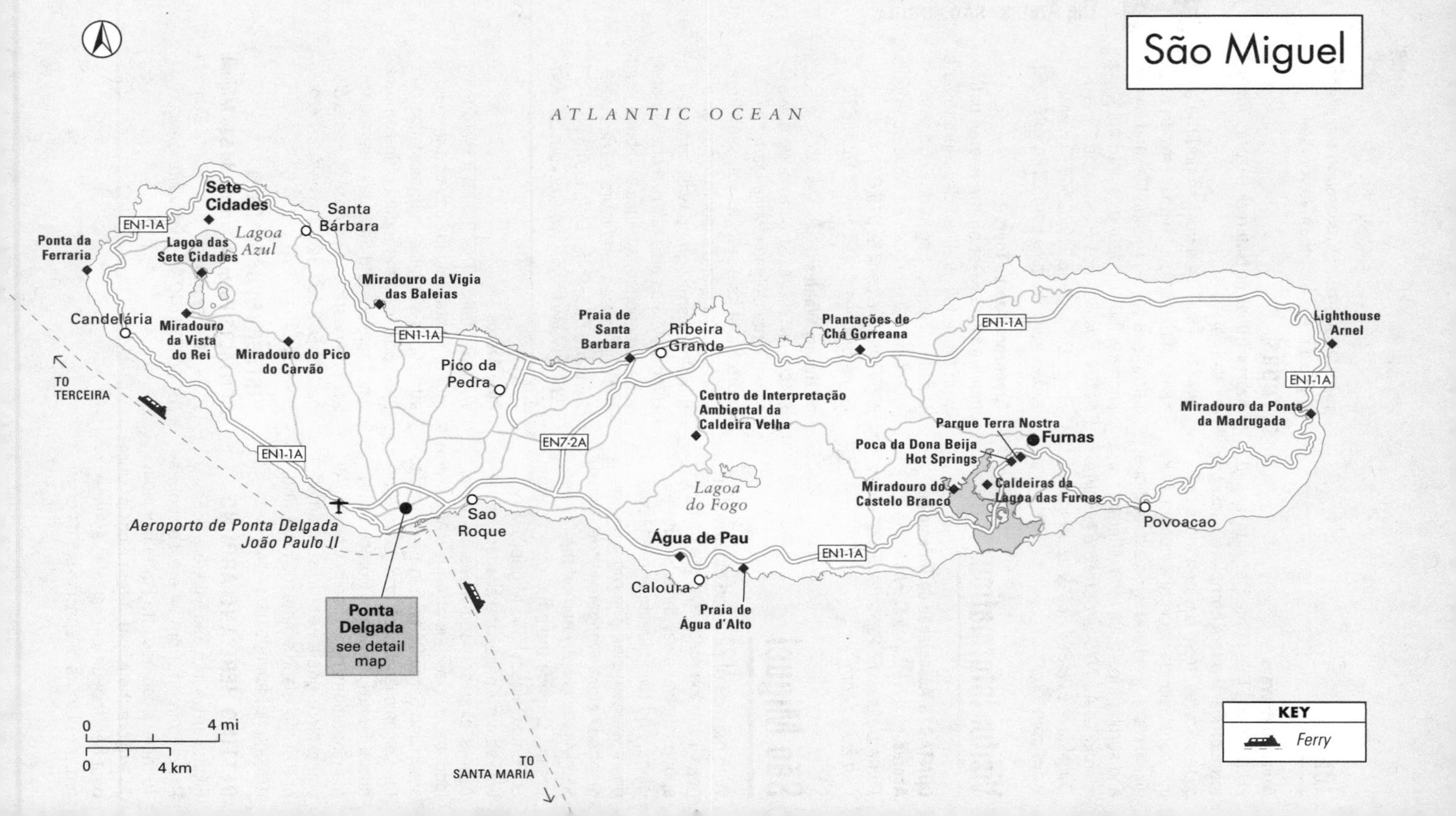

São Miguel

ATLANTIC OCEAN

Sete Cidades
Lagoa Azul
Lagoa das Sete Cidades
Santa Bárbara
Ponta da Ferraria
EN1-1A
Miradouro da Vigia das Baleias
Candelária
Miradouro da Vista do Rei
Miradouro do Pico do Carvão
Praia de Santa Barbara
Ribeira Grande
Pico da Pedra
Plantações de Chá Gorreana
Lighthouse Arnel
Centro de Interpretação Ambiental da Caldeira Velha
EN7-2A
Miradouro da Ponta da Madrugada
Parque Terra Nostra
Furnas
Poca da Dona Beija Hot Springs
Miradouro do Castelo Branco
Caldeiras da Lagoa das Furnas
Lagoa do Fogo
Povoacao
Aeroporto de Ponta Delgada João Paulo II
Sao Roque
Água de Pau
Caloura
Praia de Água d'Alto
TO TERCEIRA
Ponta Delgada see detail map
TO SANTA MARIA

0 4 mi
0 4 km

KEY
Ferry

Ponta Delgada

Sights

Forte de São Brás (*São Brás Fort*)
MILITARY SITE | FAMILY | This 16th-century fort on the far west side of Ponta Delgada's waterfront, used as a military support hub during World War I and II and still partly in use today by the naval forces, houses a compact yet comprehensive museum chronicling the country's military history up to colonial times. Inside the museum, you'll find collections of weaponry, uniforms, photos, and military vehicles, along with temporary exhibits such as the role of the Azores during World War II. Finish your visit with a walk along the ramparts to see the lovely harbor views. ✉ *Av. Infante D. Henrique, Ponta Delgada* ☎ 🌐 *www.cm-pontadelgada.pt* 🎫 *€3.*

Museu Carlos Machado (*Carlos Machado Museum*)
MUSEUM | FAMILY | This eclectic museum's collection is displayed in three buildings within walking distance from each other, with the largest section—the natural history collection—housed within the 16th-century Convento de Santo André, a former convent that retains much of its original charm. The natural history portion focuses on botany, geology, mineralogy, and especially zoology, with many taxidermied specimens that are both fascinating and creepy. The Santa Bárbara location houses more contemporary artworks and temporary displays, while the sacred art museum includes 17th- and 18th-century pieces from Azorean painters, a former chapel with an intricate carved-wood altar, and interesting temporary exhibits. ✉ *Convento de Santo André, Rua João Moreira, Ponta Delgada* ☎ 🌐 *museucarlosmachado.azores.gov.pt* 🎫 *€2, €5 for all three museums* ⏲ *Closed Mon.*

Restaurants

Louvre Michaelense
$ | CAFÉ | This charming all-day café-restaurant-cocktail bar dates from 1904, when it sold products imported from Paris. Today its glass cases are piled high with Azorean creations from tea sets to hats to jewelry, most available for purchase. **Known for:** locally made crafts; delightful historical setting; lively terrace seating. 💲 *Average main: €7* ✉ *Rua Antonio José d'Almeida 8, Ponta Delgada* ☎ *938 346 886.*

Mané Cigano
$ | PORTUGUESE | This authentic yet welcoming locals' favorite—and Ponte Delgada's oldest restaurant—serves up a handful of simple and well-prepared dishes along with rotating daily specials in a bare-bones space. The communal tables at this old-school eatery encourage friendly chats with your neighbors as you dine on fried dishes like sardines, horse mackerel, and moray eel, all washed down with homemade Concord grape wine or moonshine. **Known for:** daily specials like spareribs or stewed octopus; Portuguese diner atmosphere; friendly mix of locals and tourists. 💲 *Average main: €6* ✉ *Rua Engenheiro Jose Cordeiro 1, Ponta Delgada* ☎ *296 285 765* ⏲ *No dinner. Closed Sun.* 💳 *No credit cards.*

★ **Õtaka**
$$$$ | ASIAN FUSION | The sophisticated Nikkei-style tasting menus, which mix South American and Japanese style with Azorean ingredients, combined with knowledgeable servers and a welcoming atmosphere (think minimalist wood tables and an open kitchen) add up to one of the finest dining experiences in Ponta Delgada at this always-packed restaurant. Chef José Pereira, who worked for many years in Geneva before heading home to the Azores, uses as many local ingredients as possible in his artfully presented dishes such as crispy nigiri with tuna tartare and Azorean whitefish

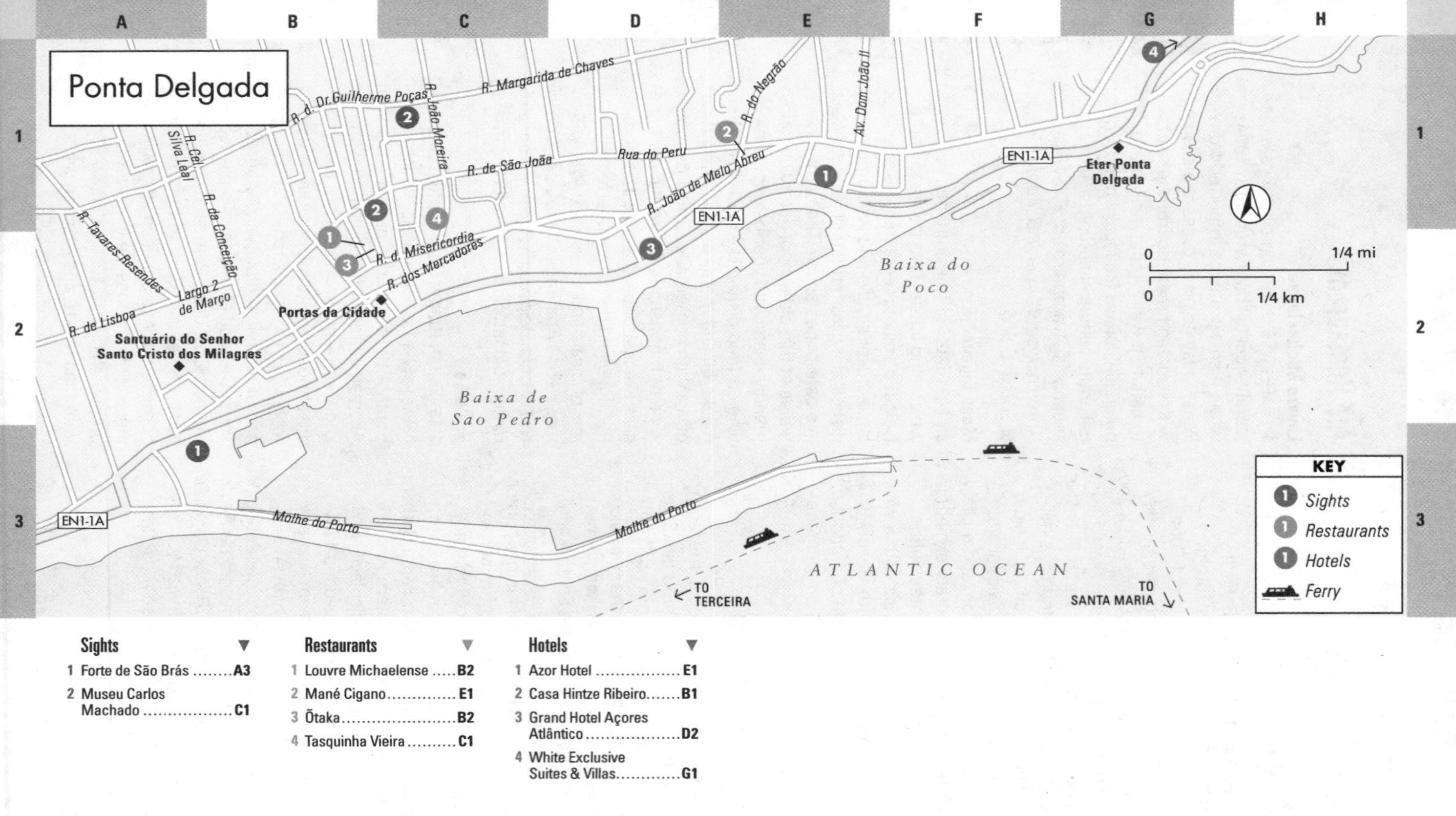
Ponta Delgada
A
B
C
D
E
F
G
H
1
2
3
R. d. Dr.Guilherme Poças
R. Margarida de Chaves
R. João Moreira
R. do Negrão
Av. Dom João II
R. Cel. Silva Leal
R. da Conceição
R. de São Joaõ
Rua do Peru
R. João de Melo Abreu
EN1-1A
Eter Ponta Delgada
R. Tavares Resendes
R. d. Misericordia
R. dos Mercadores
Largo 2 de Março
R. de Lisboa
Portas da Cidade
Santuário do Senhor Santo Cristo dos Milagres
Baixa do Poco
Baixa de Sao Pedro
0
1/4 mi
0
1/4 km
Molhe do Porto
ATLANTIC OCEAN
TO TERCEIRA
TO SANTA MARIA
KEY
Sights
Restaurants
Hotels
Ferry
Sights
1 Forte de São Brás A3
2 Museu Carlos Machado C1
Restaurants
1 Louvre Michaelense B2
2 Mané Cigano.............E1
3 Õtaka.......................B2
4 Tasquinha Vieira..........C1
Hotels
1 Azor Hotel E1
2 Casa Hintze Ribeiro.......B1
3 Grand Hotel Açores Atlântico D2
4 White Exclusive Suites & Villas.............G1

sashimi with miso and yuzu; his wife Anne Teixeira prepares the decadent tropical desserts. **Known for:** unique takes on Japanese cuisine; exquisite food presentations; Azorean wine pairings. *Average main: €35 Rua Hintze Ribeiro 5, Ponta Delgada www.facebook.com/restauranteotaka Closed Sun. and Mon. No lunch.*

★ Tasquinha Vieira

$$ | **PORTUGUESE** | Though the menu is small and the modern space is tiny, the carefully prepared, market-fresh Azorean plates punch way above their weight. Tasquinha Vieira's focus is on a "cuisine of proximity," using top-notch ingredients and innovative techniques while respecting the the islands' culinary culture, and you can't go wrong with any of the constantly changing fish, meat, and vegan options. **Known for:** intimate atmosphere; prime open kitchen views; friendly, attentive service. *Average main: €17 Rua António Joaquim Nunes da Silva 21, Ponta Delgada 296 286 181 www.facebook.com/tasquinhavieira Closed Sun. No lunch.*

Hotels

★ Azor Hotel

$$$ | **HOTEL** | **FAMILY** | This design-focused hotel—the hippest place to stay in Ponta Delgada—offers all sorts of decadent amenities: ocean-facing rooms with balconies, a local cheese and wine selection near the lobby, a nightly sushi bar, and one of the only full-service spas in town. **Pros:** well-equipped fitness center; lovely rooftop pool and bar; bountiful breakfast buffet. **Cons:** an extra charge for the spa area; some guests find the bathrooms dark; a hike to the center of town. *Rooms from: €243 Av. Dr. João Bosco Mota Amaral 4, Ponta Delgada 296 249 900 www.azorhotel.com 123 rooms Free Breakfast.*

Casa Hintze Ribeiro

$$ | **HOTEL** | If you want an easy stroll to the major sights of Porta Delgada, you can't do better than this cozy boutique hotel on one of the town's most charming pedestrian streets; as a bonus, the friendly staff is eager to help with recommendations on what not to miss. **Pros:** central location puts you close to just about everything; some rooms have expansive terraces; inviting outdoor pools. **Cons:** odd layout means little privacy in bathrooms; breakfast buffet on the simple side; rooms facing street can be noisy. *Rooms from: €150 Rua Hintze Ribeiro 62, Ponta Delgada 296 304 340 www.casahintzeribeiro.com 22 rooms Free Breakfast.*

Grand Hotel Açores Atlântico

$$ | **HOTEL** | **FAMILY** | The decor at this aptly named grand hotel overlooking the marina was inspired by the Insulana Navegação shipping company, which sailed between Lisbon, Madeira, the Azores, and the United States in the 19th and 20th centuries; elegant guest rooms and public areas featuring shipping photos and maps further evoke the nautical theme. **Pros:** unique maritime design; extremely helpful staff; lovely marina views. **Cons:** some rooms on the small side; charge for parking at the hotel; breakfast buffet not impressive. *Rooms from: €160 Av. Infante Dom Henrique 113, Ponta Delgada 296 302 200 www.grandhotelacoresatlantico.com 140 rooms Free Breakfast.*

★ White Exclusive Suites & Villas

$$$$ | **HOTEL** | You'll think you've been transported to the Greek island of Santorini when stepping inside the sleek white rooms and chic public spaces in this exclusive 10-room boutique hotel created out of a cluster of 18th-century manor houses perched above the ocean. **Pros:** a 15-minute drive east of Ponta Delgada; unique design for the islands; staff willing to go the extra mile. **Cons:** no gym or spa; extra charge for coffee and

tea in the rooms; dinners in the restaurant are extremely pricey. $ *Rooms from: €350* ✉ *Rua Rocha Quebrada 10, Ponta Delgada* ⊕ *8 km (5 miles) east of Ponta Delgada* ☎ *296 249 153* 🌐 *www.whiteazores.com* *10 rooms* *Free Breakfast.*

Nightlife

Lava Jazz

MUSIC CLUBS | Billing itself as "your living room away from home," this cozy club bar showcases live music five nights a week, including the Lava Jazz Quartet on weekend nights. ✉ *Av. Roberto Ivens, Ponta Delgada* ☎ *917 350 418* 🌐 *www.lavajazz.com.*

★ **Reserva Bar**

MUSIC CLUBS | If you're looking to expand your Portuguese wine knowledge, you can't do better than to stop by this wine bar tucked away down a nondescript alleyway. The owner Bruno or his helpful staff will happily pour you wines by the glass if you let them know your tastes and price points. You can also order Azorean cheeses or meats to accompany your vinho. ✉ *Tv. do Aterro 1, Ponta Delgada* ☎ *910 543 159* 🌐 *www.facebook.com/reserva.bar.*

Tã Gente

CAFES—NIGHTLIFE | This welcoming bar and bistro specializes in classic cocktails and a good selection of gins, plus eclectic tapas-style plates to share. Don't pass up their specialty: broken eggs with asparagus and potatoes. Sit on couches inside, or hang out outside if you manage to snag a spot. ✉ *Rua Manuel Inacio Correia 34/36/38, Ponta Delgada* ☎ *296 707 993* 🌐 *www.facebook.com/tagente.*

Shopping

Com Certeza Gourmet

LOCAL SPECIALTIES | Whether you're looking for jams from the Azores, wines from Madeira, or olive oil from the Douro, this well-stocked shop carries it all, plus chocolate, sausages, and spices. Wines come from across the Azores and throughout Portugal. ✉ *Rua Doutor Francisco Machado de Faria e Maia 22, Ponta Delgada* ☎ *965 810 844* 🌐 *comcerteza.pt.*

★ **O Rei dos Queijos**

FOOD/CANDY | A great place to pick up some items for a picnic, The King of Cheese stocks cheeses from all over the Azores along with other regional products like jams, honeys, cookies, and teas. It's next door to the Mercado da Graça (Graça Market), perfect for browsing the fresh fruit and other produce on offer in the Azores. ✉ *Rua do Mercado da Graça, Ponta Delgada* ☎ *914 298 641* 🌐 *www.oreidosqueijos.com.*

Oficina

ART GALLERIES | For a unique piece of art to take home with you, stop by this petite gallery, studio, and shop in a historical trading house that shows works by local and national artists. The selection ranges from drawings, paintings, and photographs to easy-to-transport postcards and posters. ✉ *Rua António José de Almeida 10, Ponta Delgada* 🌐 *www.facebook.com/oficinagaleria.*

Activities

BIRD-WATCHING

Gerbybirding

SPECIAL-INTEREST | The Azores are known for their great bird-watching opportunities, and Gerbybirding was the first in the islands to specialize in spotting birds. During a walk around São Miguel you'll spot some of the nearly 400 species seen in the archipelago. ✉ *Rua Direita de João Bom 31, São Miguel* ☎ *296 917 444* 🌐 *www.gerbybirding.com* *From €80.*

WHALE-WATCHING

Moby Dick Tours

WHALE-WATCHING | FAMILY | The Azores are one of the best places in the world to spot whales and dolphins, and this family-run company takes passengers out for a minimum of four hours in search of them, while giving you lots of interesting facts about marine life. Boats leave from the Ponta Delgada Marina at 9 am and 2 pm daily. Come prepared if you're prone to seasickness, as the waters can be choppy at times. ✉ *Portas do Mar, Av. Infante Dom Henrique, Ponta Delgada* ☎ *919 94831* 🌐 *www.mobydick-tours.com.*

Água de Pau

16.7 km southeast of Ponta Delgada.

Between Ponta Delgada and Furnas on the southern coast, Água de Pau is a sparsely populated area with some sleepy fishing villages bordering a lush interior. It's worth a stop for one of the most popular beaches on the island and the chance to dine on ultrafresh seafood while gazing out at the ocean.

Beaches

Praia de Água d'Alto

BEACH—SIGHT | This long stretch of beach along the south coast, about 21 km (13 miles) east of Ponta Delgada, is popular with locals and visitors alike for its clear water, beach bar, and proximity to town. **Amenities:** food and drink; lifeguards; parking (no fee); showers; toilets. **Best for:** swimming; walking. ✉ *Estrada Regional 1-1, Áqua d'Alto, Ponta Delgada* 🌐 *www.visitazores.com/en/the-azores/places-to-visit/agua-dalto-beach.*

Restaurants

★ Bar Caloura

$ | SEAFOOD | FAMILY | It's more than worth a trip 20 km (12 miles) east of Ponta Delgada to dine at this popular open-air seafood restaurant with lovely water views; since the place doesn't take reservations, bring your swimsuit for a dip in the adjacent pool while you wait. The friendly staff will grill up your choice of the fresh local fish on display—perhaps tuna, stingray, or barracuda—but you can't go wrong with baked mussels in a buttery garlic sauce or just-caught limpet, plus (a rarity for the islands) a well-stocked salad bar. **Known for:** the freshest fish around; liveliest atmosphere; homemade desserts. 💲 *Average main: €15* ✉ *Rua da Caloura 20, Água de Pau, Ponta Delgada* ☎ *296 913 283* 🌐 *www.barcaloura.com.*

Bar Praia de Água d'Alto

$ | PORTUGUESE | FAMILY | There's nothing fancy about this beach bar where you sit on plastic chairs under umbrellas, but the views over Áqua d'Alto beach more than make up for the basic decor. The extensive menu appeals to all tastes, with choices from local seafood like sardines, cod, and limpets to chicken and pork sandwiches, all of it accompanied by beer or affordable glasses of wine from the islands. **Known for:** lovely location adjacent to the beach; prices couldn't be more reasonable; family-friendly atmosphere. 💲 *Average main: €10* ✉ *Estrada Regional 1, Praia de Água d'Alto, Ponta Delgada* ✣ *21 km (13 miles) east of Ponta Delgada* ☎ *296 581 062* 🌐 *www.facebook.com/barpraiaaguadalto.*

Hotels

Pestana Bahia Praia

$$ | HOTEL | FAMILY | Located about halfway between Ponta Delgada and Furnas, this expansive hotel close to the charming village of Vila Franca do Campo is chock-full of amenities, including tennis courts, a playground, and an outdoor pool area, to name a few. **Pros:** spacious rooms with the right amenities; extensive breakfast buffet; steps to the beach. **Cons:** not many attractions in the nearby area; small and outdated gym and spa; restaurant could be better. 💲 *Rooms from: €141* ✉ *Praia de Água d'Alto, Ponta Delgada* ✣ *21 km (13 miles) east of Ponta Delgada* ☎ *296 539 130* 🌐 *www.pestana.com/en/hotel/pestana-bahia-praia* *102 rooms* *Free Breakfast.*

Furnas

43.4 km east of Ponta Delgada.

The Furnas Valley sits atop a gigantic volcanic crater, much like Yellowstone National Park in the United States. The volcano, which last erupted in 1630, is dormant, but there are geothermal springs all over the area.

GETTING HERE AND AROUND

You can take a bus to Furnas for as little as €3, but the trip might take 90 minutes, and direct buses are infrequent. A taxi may cost €30 to €40 but will take only 45 minutes. You can also drive in the same amount of time, provided you have access to a rental car.

Sights

★ **Caldeiras da Lagoa das Furnas** (*Lake Furnas Hot Springs*)
HOT SPRINGS | FAMILY | Along Lake Furnas you'll see pockets of steam rising from the vents in the volcanic soil, which is used to cook the famous *cozido* (stew, usually made from a variety of meats). If you arrive around noon, you can see the cozido pots being lifted out of the earth after hours of cooking. At other times, the caldeiras are an atmospheric place for a short stroll on the paths constructed around the bubbling mud, or a longer but still relatively easy hike around the lake itself, which takes about 90 minutes. ✉ *Lagoa das Furnas, Furnas.*

★ **Parque Terra Nostra** (*Terra Nostra Park*)
NATIONAL/STATE PARK | FAMILY | These sprawling gardens date back to 1775, when Boston merchant Thomas Hickling built a summer house called Yankee Hall, planted trees brought in from North America, and constructed the thermal water pool, still a highlight of the park today. The gardens were enlarged in the mid-19th century, adding Australian King and Canary Islands palm trees and other imported species still thriving today. The garden is particularly well known for its collections of camellias, cycadales, and ferns, as well as for its thermal pool, which is an orange-brown color due to its high iron content. There are changing rooms and outdoor showers to rinse off after, but be sure to bring a towel and wear a swimsuit that you don't mind getting stained. ✉ *Rua Padre Jose Jacinto Botelho, Furnas* ☎ *296 549 090* 🌐 *www.parqueterranostra.com* 🎫 *€8.*

★ **Poça da Dona Beija Hot Springs**
HOT SPRINGS | FAMILY | These rustic mineral hot springs surrounded by greenery make for a relaxing stop when in Furnas—though they're extremely popular with locals and tourists alike, so it's best to come in the morning to avoid the evening rush and to more easily snag one of the limited parking spots. There are four stone pools with water at 39°C, some with waterfall features, and one cooler pool with 28°C water; all are orange-colored because of the high iron content, so leave light-colored swimsuits and any jewelry back at your hotel to avoid discoloration. Towels are available for an extra fee, as are lockers, for which you'll need to leave a deposit. You'll definitely want to rinse off after bathing in the pools, and while cold showers are free, you'll need to purchase a token to have a hot shower. ✉ *Lomba das Barracas, Furnas* ☎ *296 584 256* 🌐 *www.pocadonabeija.com* 🎫 *€6.*

Restaurants

À Terra Furnas
$$ | FUSION | FAMILY | The chefs at this lively bistro, decorated with jars of preserved fruits and street-style art on the walls, focus on using ingredients from the area, including herbs from the adjacent garden, in their imaginative takes on Azorean cuisine. Choose from a large selection of local fish served with interesting sides like limpet rice, as well as meats grilled in their charcoal oven.

Known for: chefs on full view in the open kitchen; seasonal produce from the areas; upbeat, trendy vibe. *Average main: €18* ✉ *Furnas Boutique Hotel, Av. Doutor Manuel de Arriaga, Furnas* ☎ *296 249 200* 🌐 *www.furnasboutiquehotel.com/a-terra-furnas.*

★ Terra Nostra Garden Restaurant

$$$ | **PORTUGUESE** | **FAMILY** | It seems like everyone at this old-school restaurant tucked into the Terra Nostra Garden Hotel is here to partake of the signature dish: *cozido nas Caldeiras das Furnas*, stew cooked underground in the hot springs, available in both meat and vegetarian versions. Those with less hearty appetites can opt for a fine selection of fresh fish or Azorean beef. **Known for:** lovely art deco decor; pretty garden views; extensive wine list. *Average main: €23* ✉ *Terra Nostra Garden Hotel, Rua Padre Jose Jacinto Botelho 5, Furnas* ☎ *296 549 090* 🌐 *www.terranostra-gardenhotel.com/en/restaurant.php.*

Hotels

★ Furnas Boutique Hotel

$$$ | **HOTEL** | A fine choice for a relaxing vacation in the thermal mecca of Furnas, this modern design-focused hotel offers guest rooms with exceedingly comfy beds and a top-notch restaurant leading to a cool indoor/outdoor lounge perfect for enjoying a cocktail. **Pros:** relaxed vibe; 24-hour thermal pools and gym; extremely helpful service. **Cons:** rooms on the small side; street noise in some rooms; only accessible by car. *Rooms from: €234* ✉ *Av. Doutor Manuel de Arriaga, Furnas, Furnas* ☎ 🌐 *www.furnasboutiquehotel.com* *55 rooms* *Free Breakfast.*

Furnas Lake Forest Living

$$ | **HOTEL** | On the edge of lovely Lake Furnas, this collection of freestanding cedar villas standing on pillars on a reflective pond is set in a former cattle farm, and the mix of peaceful surroundings and contemporary Scandinavian decor attracts those looking for a quiet, nature-filled getaway. **Pros:** unique and charming property; short stroll to Lake Furnas; eager-to-help staff. **Cons:** breakfast an extra €15 charge; bathrooms are basic; Wi-Fi not great inside rooms. *Rooms from: €185* ✉ *Estrada Regional do Sul, Furnas* ☎ 🌐 *www.furnaslake.com* *12 rooms* *No meals.*

★ Terra Nostra Garden Hotel

$$$$ | **HOTEL** | While the art deco décor is extremely pretty and the service as friendly as can be, the main reason to stay at the Azores' first hotel (opened in 1935) is overnight guests' complimentary after-hours access to the namesake botanical garden connected to the hotel, which includes round-the-clock use of the hot springs pool and two thermal Jacuzzis, all without the hectic daytime crowds. **Pros:** unique and lovely garden setting; high-quality, extensive breakfast buffet; fantastic attached restaurant. **Cons:** can feel crowded with tourists during the day; gym needs an update; rates can be expensive. *Rooms from: €434* ✉ *Rua Padre Jose Jacinto Botelho, Furnas* ☎ 🌐 *www.terranostra-gardenhotel.com* *86 rooms* *Free Breakfast.*

Ribeira Grande

19.9 km northeast of Ponta Delgada.

Driving through São Miguel's lush, green interior toward the coast at Ribeira Grande reveals many interesting attractions, including a hot springs surrounded by subtropical forest and a tea plantation. Once you reach the coast, the water's a bit more wild than on the calmer south coast beaches, creating a perfect place for surfers to show their stuff.

The twin lakes of Lagoa das Sete Cidades, which are located in a dormant volcano crater, is a top attraction on the island of São Miguel.

Sights

Centro de Interpretação Ambiental da Caldeira Velha (*Caldeira Velha Environmental Interpretation Center*)

HOT SPRINGS | FAMILY | It's a short walk on a paved path through a subtropical forest to reach the four small pools at Caldheira Velha: three hot pools (about 36°C), and one cooler pool (about 27°C) adjacent to a waterfall. While more compact than the pools at Furnas, the ferns and other greenery give this place an almost prehistoric feel. The interpretation center contains informative displays on the area's volcanic history and biodiversity in the Azores in general. Bring a towel and flip-flops; there are lockers and showers, but with cold water only. ✉ *Estrada Regional da Lagoa do Fogo, Ribeira Grande* ☎ *296 704 649* 🌐 *parquesnaturais.azores.gov.pt/pt/smiguel/o-que-visitar/centros-ambientais* 🎫 *€8 for bathing in pools; €3 for visit without bathing.*

Plantações de Chá Gorreana (*Gorreana Tea Plantation*)

LOCAL INTEREST | FAMILY | Home to one of the only tea plantations in Europe, Gorreana has been cultivating organically grown black and green tea since 1883. A visit here is rather homespun; visitors are welcome to take a self-guided tour (or a free guided tour) of the factory, with machinery dating from the 19th century, before helping themselves to samples of both hot and cold teas. There's also a tearoom that serves light meals (along with tea, of course), and a shop to buy products to take home. ✉ *Plantações de Chá Gorreana, Ribeira Grande* ☎ *296 442 349* 🌐 *gorreana.pt* 🎫 *Free.*

Beaches

★ Praia de Santa Bárbara

BEACH—SIGHT | Stretching for about 1 km (a little over half a mile), this black-sand beach on the Atlantic Ocean is best known as a prime surfing spot—in fact, World Surf League Qualifying Series events are held here every year. You can take a surfing lesson from the school on the beach or rent a paddleboard here, or just grab a drink in the adjacent beach bar. **Amenities:** food and drink; lifeguards; parking (no fee); showers; toilets; water sports. **Best for:** surfing; walking. ✉ *Ribeira Grande.*

Restaurants

Quinta dos Sabores

$$$$ | PORTUGUESE | FAMILY | This charmingly rustic family-run eatery serves an ever-changing menu using produce straight from their gardens, along with other organic ingredients from the surrounding area. The friendly staff serves a fixed menu (cash only) with a tempting selection of homemade dips to start, along with salads, soups, fish, meat, and desserts, plus a reasonably priced selection of wines made by family members on the mainland. **Known for:** farm-fresh ingredients; relaxed atmosphere; excellent tasting menus. *$ Average main: €40* ✉ *Caminho da Selada 10, Ribeira Grande* ☎ *910 331 643* 🌐 *www.facebook.com/QuintadosSabores.Oficial* ⏲ *Closed Sun. and Mon. No lunch* 💳 *No credit cards.*

Hotels

Hotel Verde Mar & Spa

$$$$ | HOTEL | FAMILY | This modern property just a short walk from the center of Ribeira Grande offers comfortable and sharply designed rooms, large indoor and outdoor pools, and views of Monte Verde Beach from some guest rooms, the restaurant, and the bar. **Pros:** some rooms include nice patios; lovely outdoor pool with water views; spacious, comfortable lounge area. **Cons:** hotel feels somewhat impersonal; rooms facing the street can be noisy; no separate showers in most rooms. *$ Rooms from: €270* ✉ *Rua Dr. Jose Nunes Da Ponte, Ribeira Grande* ☎ *296 247 710* 🌐 *verdemarhotel.com* *210 rooms* *Free Breakfast.*

Pico do Refúgio

$ | HOTEL | FAMILY | An interesting blend of a rustic farmhouse setting and contemporary furnishings, this unique boutique hotel created out of several 17th-century buildings hosts artists for five months out of the year, with the wonderful results displayed throughout the property. **Pros:** dive school with entry-level classes; lots of modern art on display; spacious accommodations. **Cons:** no on-site restaurant; two-night minimum stay; far from central attractions. *$ Rooms from: €122* ✉ *Roda do Pico 5, Ribeira Grande* ☎ *296 491 062* 🌐 *www.picodorefugio.com* *8 rooms* *Free Breakfast.*

Santa Barbara Eco-Beach Resort

$$$$ | HOTEL | FAMILY | While this beautifully designed resort sitting between the mountains and the waves of Praia Santa Bárbara is ideal for surfers, nonsurfers will also appreciate the sleek and contemporary guest rooms, the saltwater swimming pool, and the highly regarded sushi restaurant. **Pros:** lovely contemporary design; spacious guest rooms; tasty regional dishes. **Cons:** service seems overwhelmed at times; beds too firm for some guests; flies can be a problem. *$ Rooms from: €300* ✉ *Estrada Regional NO 1-1a 1° Morro de Baixo, Ribeira Grande* ☎ *296 470 360* 🌐 *santabarbaraazores.com* *30 villas* *Free Breakfast.*

Sete Cidades

27 km northwest of Ponta Delgada.

The Caldeira das Sete Cidades, an enormous volcanic crater that collapsed during a prehistoric eruption, is truly an unmissable sight. The major attractions within the crater are the stunning Lagoa Verde and Lagoa Azul, which can be seen from a variety of viewpoints. Drive farther down the west coast to catch glimpses of the gorgeous coastline and stop at a very unique ocean-based thermal springs.

Sights

Lagoa das Sete Cidades (*Sete Cidades Lakes*)

BODY OF WATER | The breathtaking Blue and Green Lakes (Lagoa Azul and Lagoa Verde) of Sete Cidades are one of the most photographed sights on the island of São Miguel—and for good reason. If at all possible, plan your visit for a clear day, when one lake appears to be robin's egg blue and the other jade green. The best way to see the lakes is from one of the vantage points high above, especially Vista do Rei, which has its own parking area. The viewpoint at Boca do Inferno offers what many visitors consider an even better view, overlooking not only the lakes, but also the entire volcano-shaped landscape. You can start a hike from either viewpoint, or at Lagoa Verde itself—though keep in mind that while this hike starts off easy, it becomes more difficult as it climbs up and down through the woods. ✉ *Sete Cidades, Sete Cidades* 🌐 *visitazores.com* 🎫 *Free.*

★ **Ponta da Ferraria**

HOT SPRINGS | This natural hot springs differs from the others on São Miguel because it's actually in the ocean. Surrounded by basalt cliffs, the cold ocean water mixes with the hot thermal water to create a unique bathing experience—just keep an eye on the tides, as at high tide, the waters can feel chilly, while at low tide they can be steamy. But time it right (there's a Ferraria Hot Springs app that can help), and you'll never want to leave. A footpath leads down to the volcanic rock pool and from there, a ladder will take you into the thermal waters. Though it's fairly shallow, wearing waterproof shoes is a good idea, as the rocks can be sharp and slippery underneath. There are ropes to hold on to if needed, and lifeguards on duty. ✉ *Rua Padre Fernando Vieira Gomes 11, Sete Cidades* 🎫 *Free.*

Terceira

Best known for its 16th-century capital city, Angra do Heroísmo, the third-largest island in the Azores in mass (though the second-most populated) has a busier feel than its Azorean neighbors, perhaps because of the American military airbase that's been at Lajes since 1943. Simply exploring Angra, a UNESCO World Heritage Site, along with hiking or driving neighboring Monte Brasil could occupy most of your time, but it's definitely worth venturing inland to clamber down Algar do Carvão, one of the only accessible extinct volcano chimneys in the world.

GETTING HERE AND AROUND

Lajes Airport is located near Praia de Vitória, and is about 21 km (13 miles) northeast of Angra do Heroísmo. If you're concentrating your visit in Angra, you won't need a car; otherwise, it's usually smart to have your own wheels. Buses run regularly from Angra to Praia de Vitória in the east and Biscoitos in the north.

TOURS

Pro Island Tours

DRIVING TOURS | Take a guided half- or full-day tour around the island in a jeep to see volcanoes and waterfalls. Most tours include a barbecue lunch with wine and beer. ✉ *Praia da Vitoria* 🌐 *proislandtour.pt.*

VISITOR INFORMATION

CONTACTS Posto de Turismo da Terceira. ✉ *Rua Direita 70/74, Angra do Heroísmo* ☎ *295 213 393* 🌐 *www.visitazores.com.*

Angra do Heroísmo

Dating from 1534, Angra is a pleasant town of cobblestone streets and colorful Renaissance-style buildings that now house interesting museums, restaurants, and boutiques. Though many buildings were damaged in a 1980 earthquake, they've since been restored, and the town was named a UNESCO Historic World Heritage Site. The extinct volcano of Monte Brasil is worthy of a hike or drive, especially to see the vistas back toward town. The tiny fishing port of São Mateus, just west of Angra, is also worth a stop to try the freshest fish and seafood around with lovely water views.

Sights

★ **Algar do Carvão**

CAVE | FAMILY | Climb deep inside an extinct volcano at this 1,804-foot volcanic cave located toward the middle of Terceira. You'll be guided 148 feet down a set of stairs to the floor of the cavern before descending another 115 feet to a crystal clear lake fed by rainwater (which completely disappears during dry summers). Though the stairs are on the steep side, they have handrails and are not challenging to descend or ascend—just be sure to dress warmly, as the cave becomes colder and wetter the farther down you go. Along the way you'll see unique stalactites and stalagmites. Opening times vary depending on the season, but are generally limited to a few hours in the afternoons, so check before you go. *Estrada Algar Do Carvao, Angra do Heroísmo* *11 km (7 miles) from Angra do Heroísmo* *295 212 992* *www.montanheiros.com/algarCarvao* *€8; €12 with Grutal do Natal* *Closed Mon., Thurs., and Sun. Oct.–Mar.*

Gruta do Natal (*Christmas Caves*)

CAVE | This horizontal lava tube running 2,287 feet is worth a self-guided visit, as long as you wear good footwear and don't feel claustrophobic in tight spaces. Navigating the sometimes dark, narrow, and low-clearance tube requires some ducking and squatting at times (you will be given a helmet for extra protection). Christmas Mass is held here when possible, hence the name. *Altares, Angra do Heroísmo* *10.8 km (6.7 miles) from Angra do Heroísmo* *295 212 992* *www.montanheiros.com/grutaNatal* *€8; €12 with Algar do Carvão* *Closed Mon., Thurs., and Sun. Oct.–Mar.*

Jardim Duque da Terceira (*Duke of Terceira Garden*)

GARDEN | FAMILY | These clearly labeled urban gardens, first created in 1882, showcase plants from around the world and make for a lovely stroll when wandering Angra's historical city center. There are a few terraced levels to explore until you reach the highest point, where you'll find a panoramic view of Angra. You'll find an organic teahouse about halfway up (or down) if you need a reviving cup. There's also a playground. *Rua Direita 130, Angra do Heroísmo* *295 401 700* *www.visitazores.com/en/the-azores/places-to-visit/garden-duque-da-terceira* *Free.*

★ **Monte Brasil** (*Mt. Brasil*)

MOUNTAIN—SIGHT | FAMILY | This extinct volcano on the far west side of Angra, which can be seen from all over town, is now a deer-filled nature reserve with many trails winding throughout the area. Whether you drive or walk from town, you'll first come across the Fortaleza de São João Baptista, a late-16th-century fort that's still in use by the Portuguese army. You can only enter the fort itself by taking a free tour, which runs nearly every hour and is led by a soldier stationed there. Farther up the mountain, the best lookouts to stop at are Pico das Cruzinhas, Pico do Zimbreiro, and Pico do Facho, the highest point on Monte Brasil. There are picnic tables where you can rest, as well as a children's play area. *Angra do Heroísmo* *295 214 001* *www.exploreterceira.com/en/geossitios/reserva-natural-do-monte-brasil* *Free.*

Museu de Angra do Heroísmo

MUSEUM | FAMILY | In the former Convent of São Francisco, this interesting museum tells the history of Terceira and its capital city, from the first settlers to the present day. Exhibits cover military history, transportation, furnishings, and

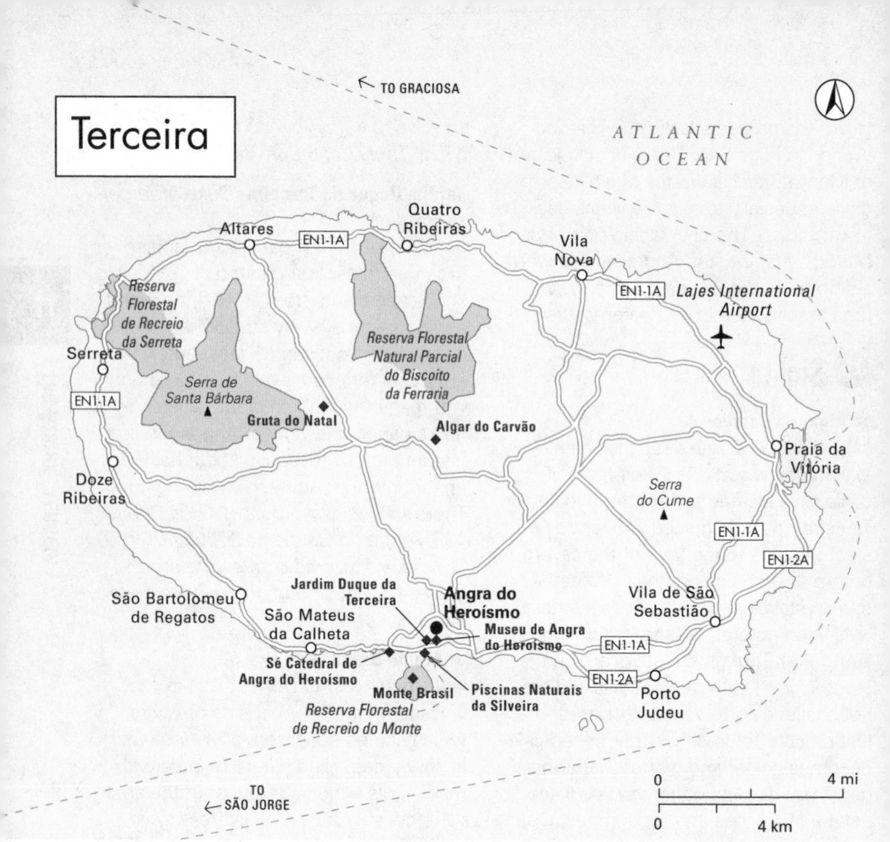

Terceira

TO GRACIOSA
ATLANTIC OCEAN
Quatro Ribeiras
Altares
EN1-1A
Vila Nova
Lajes International Airport
Reserva Florestal de Recreio da Serreta
Reserva Florestal Natural Parcial do Biscoito da Ferraria
Serreta
Serra de Santa Bárbara
Gruta do Natal
Algar do Carvão
Praia da Vitória
Doze Ribeiras
Serra do Cume
EN1-2A
Jardim Duque da Terceira
Angra do Heroísmo
Vila de São Sebastião
São Bartolomeu de Regatos
São Mateus da Calheta
Museu de Angra do Heroísmo
Sé Catedral de Angra do Heroísmo
Monte Brasil
Piscinas Naturais da Silveira
Porto Judeu
Reserva Florestal de Recreio do Monte
TO SÃO JORGE
0 4 mi
0 4 km

artworks, but the wonderful collection of horse-drawn carriages is a definite highlight. Much, though not quite all, of the information is in English as well as Portuguese, and there are always museum staffers available if you have questions. The original chapel contains an 18th-century organ; if you're lucky, your visit will coincide with a free concert. ✉ *Ladeira de São Francisco, Angra do Heroísmo* ☎ *295 240 800* 🌐 *museu-angra.azores.gov.pt* 🎫 *€2; free on Sun.* 🕓 *Closed Mon.*

Sé Catedral de Angra do Heroísmo (*Angra do Heroísmo Cathedral*)
RELIGIOUS SITE | The largest church in the Azores, dating from the late 1500s, is missing much of its baroque interior because it was largely destroyed in Terceira's 1980 earthquake as well as a fire in 1983. Not all was lost, however. The high altar is decorated in 18th-century silverplate, and the Our Lady of the Angels altar also dates from the 18th century. ✉ *Rua da Se, Angra do Heroísmo* ☎ *295 217 850* 🌐 *www.visitportugal.com/en/content/se-catedral-de-angra-do-heroismo* 🎫 *€5 for church, treasury, and towers; €2 for each church, treasury, or towers only.*

Beaches

Piscinas Naturais da Silveira (*Natural Pools of Silveira*)
BEACH—SIGHT | Just west of Angra, you'll find not a beach per se, but rather a former fishing port transformed into a popular swimming area with a large concrete pier jutting out into the ocean. Swimmers can access the water by stairs, by diving in, or by holding a metal handrail as they walk right in. **Amenities:** food and drink; lifeguards; parking (free); showers;

toilets. **Best for:** swimming. ✉ *Silveira, Angra do Heroísmo* ✥ *2 km (1.2 miles) west of Angra do Heroísmo* 🌐 *www.exploreterceira.com/zonas-balneares/zona-balnear-da-silveira.*

Restaurants

★ Beira Mar

$ | **SEAFOOD** | Be sure to make reservations for this always-bustling fish and seafood spot—rightfully thought by many to be the best on the island—with pretty views overlooking the marina in the tiny fishing village of São Mateus. You can't go wrong with any of the freshly caught fish (the restaurant has its own fishing boat), along with limpets, slipper lobsters, and barnacles, which you coax from their shells with tiny forks. **Known for:** save room for the gingerbreadlike "cake of the Indies"; snappy service keeps things moving along; indoor and outdoor seating with water views. [$] *Average main: €13* ✉ *Canada Porto 46, Porto de São Mateus, Angra do Heroísmo* ✥ *5 km (3 miles) west of Angra do Heroísmo* ☎ *295 642 392* 🌐 *www.facebook.com/Beira-Mar-São-Mateus-465356256869367* ⏲ *Closed Mon. and 3 wks in Nov.*

O Chico

$ | **PORTUGUESE** | This is hands down the best place in Angra to try the local dish of *alcatra*—a sort of beef pot roast stewed in a clay pot with wine—along with other regional specialties like steak with egg, grilled swordfish, and octopus. The atmosphere's cozy and traditional, with tiled walls and red-checkered curtains; be sure to make reservations as it's very popular with the locals. **Known for:** traditional dishes; hearty portions; homey vibe. [$] *Average main: €10* ✉ *Rua de Sao Joao 7, Angra do Heroísmo* ☎ *295 333 286* 🌐 *www.facebook.com/restaurante.chico* ⏲ *Closed Sun.*

Quebra Mar

$ | **SEAFOOD** | **FAMILY** | Under the same ownership as the more well-known Beira Mar a short distance away, this simply decorated fish restaurant on the water is more spacious and easy to get into than its sister eatery. Swing by the counter for a look at the fish that's freshest that day, or the grilled squid or octopus are always a good bet. **Known for:** extremely welcoming service; local fish that's never frozen; family-friendly atmosphere. [$] *Average main: €13* ✉ *Canada dos Arrifes 2, São Mateus da Calheta, Angra do Heroísmo* ✥ *6 km (4 miles) west of Angra do Heroísmo* ☎ *295 704 946* 🌐 *www.facebook.com/QuebraMarRestaurante* ⏲ *Closed Tues.*

Hotels

Azoris Angra Garden

$ | **HOTEL** | **FAMILY** | Not only does this comfortable, contemporary hotel have a prime position in the center of Angra's old town and welcome amenities like an indoor pool, fitness center, and roof deck with fabulous views of Monte Brasil, it also backs onto the lovely, peaceful Duque da Terceira Garden. **Pros:** wellness options include a steam room, whirlpool, and massages; location in the center of town; good variety at breakfast. **Cons:** no on-site parking available; street noise in some rooms; gym open limited hours. [$] *Rooms from: €95* ✉ *Praça Velha, Angra do Heroísmo* ☎ *295 206 600* 🌐 *www.azorishotels.com/angragarden* 🛏 *118 rooms* 🍽 *Free Breakfast.*

★ Pousada Forte Angra do Heroísmo

$ | **HOTEL** | **FAMILY** | From the outside, you'd never know that a modern hotel sits inside the walls of a 16th-century fort perched on a hilltop overlooking the sea on the edge of Angra (but only about a 10-minute walk into town); beyond the historical significance, the cool, contemporary guest rooms, outdoor pools and bar, and sea views make the

Pousada a great place to spend the night. **Pros:** highly atmospheric place to stay; spacious rooms and bathrooms; quiet location. **Cons:** very small TVs in rooms; no gym; steep walk up and down the hill to town center. *Rooms from: €120* *Rua do Castelinho, Angra do Heroísmo* *www.pousadas.pt/en/hotel/pousada-angra* *29 rooms* *Free Breakfast.*

Terceira Mar Hotel

$ | HOTEL | FAMILY | The fabulous grounds at this pleasant hotel on Angra's western edge are reason enough to stay here—all rooms have balconies overlooking the sea, Monte Brasil, lots of greenery, and a large-sized saltwater pool—plus the inside amenities are not bad either, including what might be the best hotel gym in the Azores. **Pros:** wonderful setting; amazing fitness center; extensive breakfast choices. **Cons:** could have more outdoor seating in restaurant/bar area; bathrooms don't feel as modern as rest of rooms; lack of umbrellas around outdoor pool area. *Rooms from: €137* *Portões de Sao Pedro 1, Angra do Heroísmo* *www.bestazoreshotels.com/hotel-terceira-mar.php* *139 rooms* *Free Breakfast.*

Activities

OceanEmotion

WHALE-WATCHING | The three-hour whale- and dolphin-spotting cruises that leave from Angra's marina include a marine biologist on board. Whale-watching can be combined with other activities such as snorkeling, swimming with dolphins, and watching the sun set over Monte Brasil. *Marina de Angra do Heroísmo, Angra do Heroísmo* *295 098 119, 967 806 964, 917 072 154* *www.oceanemotion.pt.*

Pico

Dominated by looming Mt. Pico (Portugal's tallest mountain), this is the second-largest of the Azores, 4½ miles from Faial. The island is known for its black volcanic soil. Two industries have dominated Pico's history: wine making and whaling. The whaling industry mostly faded away by 1980 and has now given way to whale-watching. Pico's unique position means you can see cetaceans, especially sperm whales and several species of dolphins and porpoises, virtually year-round. In February and March, baleen whales, blue whales, and humpback whales can be seen, and in early June pilot whales and Atlantic spotted dolphins usually arrive. All this makes for one of the most active whale-watching destinations on earth. The island's wine-making traditions are still active, though grapevines typically run along the ground rather than on rows of trellises (protected by black stone walls), and most of the wines are white (particularly from Verdelho grapes) or fortified. The island's vineyards, some of which have been active since the 16th century, have been designated a UNESCO World Heritage Site.

GETTING HERE AND AROUND

Flights arrive into Pico Airport, about 9 km (5½ miles) east of Madalena. If you're arriving by ferry, there are two terminals, one in Madalena and one in São Roque; the short ferries to Faial generally leave from the Madalena port. A rental car is pretty much a necessity if you want to tour Pico. The roads on the island are in good shape, unless you go off-road to explore some of the volcanic landscapes.

TOURS

Terralta Nature Tours

DRIVING TOURS | Choose one of six routes on a jeep tour through Pico, everything from along the coast to up into the mountains. All tours take a maximum of eight people. *Madalena* *938 972 678*

Topping out at 7,713 feet, Mt. Pico, often shrouded in mist and fog, is the tallest mountain in Portugal.

www.terraltanaturetours.com *From €30.*

Tripix

GUIDED TOURS | This Pico-based company offers guided tours of Pico, including a full-day group tour around the island, a wine tour, and a secret lagoons and volcanoes tour. Every tour includes transport and lunch at a local restaurant. *Cais da Madalena Pico, Madalena* *963 778 109,* *tripixazores.com* *From €75.*

VISITOR INFORMATION

CONTACT Posto de Turismo do Pico. *Gare Marítima da Madalena, Madalena* *292 623 524* *www.visitazores.com.*

Madalena

Nestled on the Atlantic Ocean, Pico's main port town has long been the island's trading center, owing to its proximity to the vineyards. Today it makes a good stop for a lunch or dinner and a place to get a taste (literally) of some of Pico's wine culture at the Pico Wine Cooperative or the Wine Museum, as well as at the Azores Wine Company just outside of town). Otherwise it's a fairly quiet place, with the exception of when the ferries arrive from Faial.

Sights

★ Cooperativa Vitivinícola da Ilha do Pico (*Pico Winemakers Cooperative*)

WINERY/DISTILLERY | This cooperative was formed in 1949 by a group of local winemakers; by 1961, they had started producing wine using the readitional Verdelho, Arinto, and Terrantez grape varieties. Output remained small until the early 1990s, when the production processes were modernized and more varieties were introduced, including in 1997 the first fortified wine with a distilled spirit added (Lajido), and in 2001, the first sweet fortified wine (Angelica). Today, the cooperative is the largest wine producer in the Azores, with about 240 members growing grapes. Book well in advance or try your luck stopping by for a 30-minute tour of the wine production facility. ✉ *Av. Padre Nunes da Rosa 29, Madalena* ☎ *292 622 262* 🌐 *www.picowines.net* 🎫 *€3.50–€10 for wine tasting* ⏲ *Closed Sun.*

★ **Montanha do Pico** (*Mt. Pico*)
MOUNTAIN—SIGHT | Visible from many locations around Pico—unless it's shrouded in fog and clouds, as is often the case—and even more visible from across the water in Faial, 7,713-foot Mt. Pico is the highest mountain in Portugal. Past eruptions have occurred on its flanks rather than from the summit, the most recent back in 1720. If you want to hike up Mt. Pico, you can start at the Casa da Montanha (Mountain House) at 4,035 feet. Though it's not a difficult climb, it can still be quite challenging as the path is steep with uneven rocks; depending on your experience level, consider hiring a guide to accompany you. Come early or book a guide to be guaranteed a hiking spot, as hikers are limited to 120 per day. Bring photo ID to register. ✉ *Casa da Montanha, Caminho Florestal 9, Candelária, Madalena* ☎ *967 303 519* 🌐 *parquesnaturais.azores.gov.pt/en/pico-eng/what-visit/protected-areas/natural-reserve/montanha-do-pico* 🎫 *€20 for hiking permit.*

Museu do Vinho (*Wine Museum*)
LOCAL INTEREST | Set inside and on the grounds of a former convent, this compact but comprehensive museum explains the history of wine on Pico, from its beginnings in the late 15th century to widespread Verdelho wine production—which lasted until the vines were hit by phylloxera in the mid-19th century—to the reintroduction of traditional grape varieties, including Verdelho, in the 1970s. In the adjoining gardens, you'll find magnificent dragon trees—grown throughout the Azores and so named for their red-colored resin—along with examples of vineyards using Pico's traditional "currais" method, where square-shaped areas of volcanic gravel are surrounded by low stone walls that protect them from wind while still allowing sunlight to enter. Other highlights include an interactive display on how to identify the color and aroma of wine, an area devoted to brandy making, and an old winepress. Helpful information sheets in English are available in most of the rooms. ✉ *Canada do Caldeiro 3, Madalena* ☎ *292 622 147* 🌐 *www.museu-pico.azores.gov.pt/museu/museu-do-vinho* 🎫 *€2* ⏲ *Closed Mon.*

Restaurants

★ **Ancoradouro**
$$ | **SEAFOOD** | Come to what's widely regarded as the finest fish and seafood restaurant in town for hearty portions of expertly prepared local delicacies such as *cataplana à ancoradouro* (seafood stew), skewers of grilled fish and shrimp, and seafood rice with crab claws, shrimp, mussels, and clams. Though the decor inside is simple, the large terrace with wonderful water views is the place to be. **Known for:** seafood galore, especially octopus and crab; everything here comes hot off the grill; tempting house-made desserts. $ *Average main: €16* ✉ *Rua Rodrigo Guerra 7, Madalena* ☎ *292 623 490* 🌐 *www.facebook.com/ancoradouropico* ⏲ *Closed Mon.*

Cella Bar
$ | **PORTUGUESE** | This trendy bar and restaurant on the water's edge is worth visiting just to see its unique wood structure, roughly resembling a whale, as well as the prime views of Faial Island. Ask for a seat upstairs on the terrace, especially if you're here before sunset. **Known for:** interesting architecture; lovely oceanfront setting; the freshest seafood. $ *Average main: €12* ✉ *Lugar Da Barca, Madalena* ☎ *292 623 654* 🌐 *www.cellabar.com* ⏲ *Closed last 2 wks of Nov. No lunch weekdays Nov.–Mar.*

Hotels

Alma do Pico Nature Resort
$ | **HOTEL** | **FAMILY** | Though you can't expect luxury, these simple wooden cabins in the woods make a peaceful getaway. **Pros:** popular restaurant serves Italian cuisine using local ingredients; quiet accommodations with plenty of space to spread out; individualized travel suggestions. **Cons:** rooms are extremely basic; odd shower controls; no air-conditioning. *Rooms from: €100* ✉ *Rua dos Biscoitos 34, Madalena* ☎ *914 231 436* ⊕ *www.almadopico.com* ⏲ *Restaurant closed Tues. and Oct.–Apr.* *14 rooms* *Free Breakfast.*

★ **Pocinho Bay**
$$$ | **B&B/INN** | **FAMILY** | Owners Jose and Louisa, former sociologists from Lisbon, have transformed their summer vacation property into a truly unique place to stay, with a collection of six elegant volcanic rock cottages and two sophisticated two-bedroom villas, all decorated with artifacts collected during their extensive travels around the world. **Pros:** beautiful grounds just outside your door; natural rock pool sits nearby; personalized service. **Cons:** somewhat isolated location; no restaurant or bar; no fitness center or spa. *Rooms from: €215* ✉ *Pocinho, Madalena* ✣ *6 km (4 miles) southwest of Madalena* ☎ *292 629 135* ⊕ *www.pocinhobay.com* ⏲ *Closed Dec.–Feb.* *6 rooms, 2 villas* *Free Breakfast.*

Activities

Tripix
CLIMBING/MOUNTAINEERING | If you want to give a climb of Mt. Pico a go but don't want to do it yourself, try a group climb with a guide. The day climb, which takes about seven hours, includes hiking poles, while the night climb, which takes about 10 hours, includes both poles and a headlamp. Both climbs include transfer from Madalena. ✉ *Cais da Madalena Pico, Madalena* ☎ ⊕ *tripixazores.com* ☞ *From €65.*

São Roque do Pico

20.4 km east of Madalena.

As you drive through the district of São Roque do Pico on the island's north coast, you'll see the unique volcanic vineyard configurations, divided into small plots called currais and surrounded by basalt rock walls to protect from wind and rain. This fascinating lava landscape and the nature of volcanoes themselves are explored in two museums in the cute town of Lajido, also worth a wander for its black basalt buildings. Farther east, the former whaling port town of São Roque makes a good stop for lunch as you head down the coast.

Sights

Casa dos Vulcões (*House of Volcanoes*)
MUSEUM | **FAMILY** | The unique volcanic landscape of the nine Azores islands is explored in this jam-packed museum. Visits are by 45-minute guided tour, which must be booked in advance. The topics covered at Casa dos Vulcões range from the broad, like how the universe was formed, to the more specific, like the geological history of tiny Pico, the youngest island in the Azores. The main reasons to visit the museum, however, are to take the journey to the center of the earth, by way of a 360-degree film, and to try the earthquake simulator, which uses VR headsets for a very realistic seismic experience. ✉ *Rua do Lajido, Santa Luzia, São Roque do Pico* ☎ *292 644 328* ⊕ *parquesnaturais.azores.gov.pt/pt/pico/o-que-visitar/centros-de-interpretacao/110-pni-pico/3289-casa-dos-vulcoes* *€7; €8 including Centro de Interpretação da Paisagem da Cultural da Vinha da Ilha do Pico* ⏲ *Closed Mon. Nov.–Mar.*

Pico and Faial

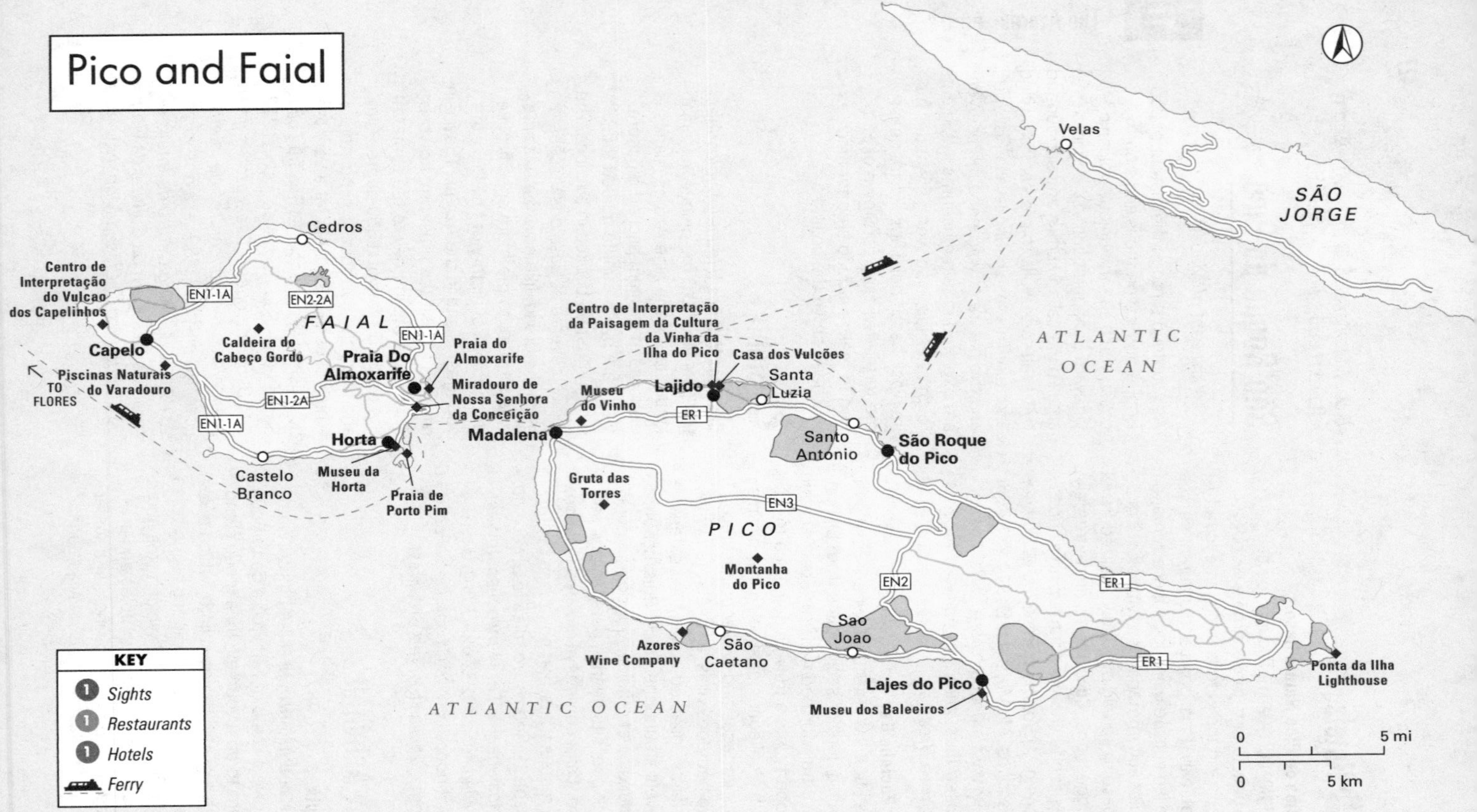

Centro de Interpretação da Paisagem da Cultural da Vinha da Ilha do Pico (*Pico Island Vineyard Culture Landscape Interpretation Center*)
MUSEUM | This small wine museum isn't worth making a detour for, but if you're already visiting the charming town of Lajido it's well worth a short stop. You'll find exhibits in English and Portuguese about wine production in Pico, covering topics including vineyard landscapes, the local climate, and indigenous flora and fauna. The admission price includes a glass of wine at the end, with more available for purchase. The staff offers guided tours of the nearby vineyards and lava fields. ✉ *Rua do Lajido, Santa Luzia, São Roque do Pico* ☎ *965 896 313* 🌐 *parquesnaturais.azores.gov.pt/pt/pico/o-que-visitar/centros-de-interpretacao/centro-de-interpretacao-da-paisagem-da-cultura-da-vinha* 🎫 *€3; €8 including Casa dos Vulcões; €5 for guided tour of Lajida de Santa Luzia UNESCO vineyard area* ⏲ *Closed Mon. Nov.–Mar.*

★ **Lajido**
TOWN | About a 15-minute drive east of Madalena is the postcard-perfect town of Lajido, filled with charming all-black and black-and-white volcanic houses with striking red and green doors and shutters. ✉ *Lajido* ✣ *11 km (7 miles) east of Madalena.*

Restaurants

Casa Âncora
$$ | **PORTUGUESE** | The open kitchen at this minimalist eatery turns out not only traditional Azorean dishes like grilled octopus and fish soup, but also Azorean fusion cuisine using mainly local products with international inspirations—think fish with mint couscous and vegetables. It's a good place to stop for lunch when driving around the island; when the weather's warm, you can sit outside on the water's edge with views of Cais do Pico bay. **Known for:** updated versions of classic dishes; treats like stone crab paté; no reservations. 💲 *Average main: €16* ✉ *Rua do Cais 29B, São Roque do Pico* ☎ *292 644 496* 🌐 *www.facebook.com/casaancorarestaurant* ⏲ *No lunch Mon., Tues., and Thurs.*

Lajes do Pico

22 km southeast of São Roque do Pico.

On the coast in the south of Pico, Lajes is a former whaling town that's now known for its whale-watching excursions. You can explore the history of its former industry in the Whalers' Museum.

Sights

Museu dos Baleeiros (*Whalers' Museum*)
MUSEUM | **FAMILY** | Whaling was a major industry in Pico up until the end of the 20th century. This small museum, set inside a former whaling boat warehouse, screens a movie (available in English) explaining the history of the whaling industry on the island along with historic photos and interesting displays showing some of the tools and equipment used in whale hunting. The exhibits offer an interesting look at this important part of the Azores' history. ✉ *Rua dos Baleeiros 13, Lajes do Pico* ☎ *292 672 276* 🌐 *www.visitazores.com/en/the-azores/places-to-visit/museu-dos-baleeiros* 🎫 *€2; free on Sun.*

Hotels

Aldeia da Fonte Nature Hotel
$ | **HOTEL** | **FAMILY** | Within the lush surroundings of this sprawling complex are six lava stone structures housing the guest rooms, a well-regarded restaurant serving local cuisine, a cliff-top swimming pool, and direct access, down rather steep stairs, to a rocky swimming area by the sea. **Pros:** a small gym and sauna on-site; wonderful swimming pool; popular restaurant. **Cons:** rooms need a refresh; no air-conditioning; steps to climb. 💲 *Rooms from: €93* ✉ *Caminho*

de Baixo, Lajes do Pico ☎ 292 679 500 🌐 *www.aldeiadafonte.com* *40 rooms* *Free Breakfast.*

Activities

★ Espaço Talassa

WHALE-WATCHING | FAMILY | This eco-minded whale-watching outfit offers a variety of whale- and dolphin-spotting packages, including a three-hour boat trip leaving at 10 am and 3 pm daily. Trips start with a multimedia presentation on animal behavior and the island's (not always pleasant) history with whales. It's a great educational experience, especially for kids. ✉ *Rua dos Baleeiros, Lajes do Pico* ☎ *292 672 010* 🌐 *www.espacotalassa.com.*

Faial

Though Faial was originally named for its large number of beech trees, or *faias*, it's also called the "Blue Island" for the beautiful blue hydrangeas that usually bloom in July and August. Faial's main town of Horta is surprisingly cosmopolitan for the Azores, a result of the many yachts that stop here as they cross the Atlantic. The island is also dominated by the huge Caldeira (volcanic crater) at its center, as well as the Capelinhos Volcano, a wonderful chance to see a recently formed volcanic landscape up close before learning more about volcanoes in the underground museum. Add to that some rolling green countryside, pretty beaches (both black and gray sand), basaltic rock pools in which to swim, and phenomenal views of neighboring Pico Mountain, and you'll quickly see the appeal of this compact and easy-to-explore island.

GETTING HERE AND AROUND

Flights from the other islands and the mainland arrive at Horta Airport, about 8½ km (5¼ miles) southwest of Horta. The ferry terminal is on the northeast end of town. Horta itself is very walkable; a rental car is your best option for seeing the rest of the island.

TOURS

★ Endemic Azores

ECOTOURISM | Two engaging marine biologists run this environmentally conscious tour company, They offer a range of excursions, including snorkeling, trekking, bird-watching, and full-island tours, each with a focus on sustainability. ✉ *Rua Conde Dávila 20, Horta* ☎ *918 191 180,* 🌐 *www.endemicazores.com* *From €25.*

★ Naturalist

ECOTOURISM | FAMILY | Combining research data collection with nature and cultural tours, the Naturalist offers guided excursions led by biologists and field researchers. Tours include whale-watching, birdwatching, hiking, and half- and full-day island tours with a focus on geology. ✉ *Largo Manuel de Arriaga Loja 2, Horta* ☎ *968 327 633,* 🌐 *www.naturalist.pt/azores.*

VISITOR INFORMATION

CONTACT Posto de Turismo do Faial. ✉ *Rua Vasco da Gama, Horta* ☎ *292 292 237* 🌐 *turismo.cmhorta.pt/index.php/en/welcome-to-faial.*

Horta

Horta's marina bustles in the late spring and summer when yachts crossing the Atlantic stop here, adding to the vibrancy of this charming maritime town. You'll find a number of worthy restaurants on the cobbled streets near the water, not far from the popular beach Porto Pim—and you can't miss the iconic seafarer's hangout, Peter Café Sport, for some salty talk and local maritime flavor. From here, it's only a short drive north to the spectacular volcanic Caldeira.

The island of Faial is dominated by an enormous volcanic crater, which has a diameter of almost one mile across.

Sights

★ Caldeira

VOLCANO | Located toward the center of the island (and therefore best accessed by car), this stunning ancient volcanic crater with a diameter of 2 km (more than 1 mile) and a depth of 1,312 feet started forming at least 400,000 years ago, with the last volcanic event taking place 1,000 years ago. There's a scenic viewpoint to snap a few pictures, or opt for the fairly easy hike around the 7-km (4-mile) circular trail that winds around the rim's perimeter; there are some narrow sections, so bring your hiking shoes. The perimeter walk takes two to three hours to complete and offers lovely views of the lush laurel forest and, if you're lucky and the day is clear, to Mt. Pico in the distance. ✉ *Horta* ✣ *15 km (9¼ miles) northwest of Horta* 🌐 *www.parquesnaturais.azores.gov.pt/en/faial-eng/what-visit/protected-areas/natural-reserve/caldeira-do-faial* 🎫 *Free.*

Museu da Horta (*Horta Museum*)

MUSEUM | FAMILY | It's worth a stop at this small museum within an 18th-century Jesuit college to learn more about Faial's history, from the first Atlantic seaplane flight that stopped here in the late 19th century to historical submarine telegraph cables used to reduce the communication time between North America and Europe. There's also an interesting collection of elaborate miniatures made out of the pith, or white kernels, from the inside of fig tree branches. ✉ *Palacio do Colégio, Horta* ☎ *292 208 570* 🌐 *www.azores.gov.pt/Portal/en/entidades/pgra-drcultura-mh* 🎫 *€2; free on Sun.*

Beaches

★ Praia de Porto Pim

BEACH—SIGHT | FAMILY | Set in a sheltered bay—with very few waves, making it a great choice for families—Porto Pim Beach is a long, narrow strip of gray sand backed by Monte Queimado and next to Monte da Guia. The first settlers on Faial landed here in the 15th century.

Today it's the most popular beach on the island for swimming and sunbathing, very walkable from the center of Horta and with a number of attractions off its western end, including houses belonging to the once-prominent Dabney family that have been turned into low-key museums. **Amenities:** food and drink; lifeguards; parking (free); showers; toilets. **Best for:** snorkeling; sunset; swimming; walking. ✉ *Praia de Porto Pim, Horta* 🌐 *www.visitportugal.com/en/content/praia-de-porto-pim.*

Restaurants

Canto da Doca

$$ | PORTUGUESE | FAMILY | When visiting a volcanic island, what's better than cooking food on your very own hot lava stone? That's the concept behind this bustling family-owned eatery, in a former fisherman's storage building near the harbor, where you can choose from a wide selection of fish, seafood, and meat (limited vegetarian options are also available) that you grill to your liking at your table. **Known for:** lively atmosphere that make it popular with families; local delicacies like triggerfish and limpets; house-made sauces. $ *Average main: €16* ✉ *Rua Nova, Horta* ☎ *292 292 444.*

★ **Restaurante Genuíno**

$$ | PORTUGUESE | FAMILY | Come to this charming restaurant with views of Porto Pim beach not only for some of the freshest fish in town, but also to chat with owner Genuíno Madruga, a renowned sailor who was the first person from Portugal to sail solo around the world—twice. The helpful servers will point you toward the local fish that's best that day, and you'll dine surrounded by souvenirs collected during Genuíno's travels. **Known for:** eclectic seafaring decorations; largest selection of fish in Faial; homemade fruit ice cream. $ *Average main: €19* ✉ *Areinha Velha 9, Horta* ☎ *292 701 542* 🌐 *www.genuino.pt* ⏲ *Closed Wed.*

Hotels

Azoris Faial Garden

$ | HOTEL | FAMILY | This collection of pale pink buildings, formerly part of the undersea cable company and perched up the hill from Faial's harbor, is a little dated, but the lovely and extensive grounds include lots of amenities: an outdoor infinity pool with harbor views and a poolside bar, an indoor pool with a whirlpool, sauna, and gym, and balconies off of some guest rooms with prime views of Mt. Pico. **Pros:** spacious guest rooms; great mountain views; inviting pool area. **Cons:** restaurant gets mixed reviews; rooms are in need of a refresh; lackluster service. $ *Rooms from: €104* ✉ *Rua Consul Dabney, Horta* ☎ *292 207 400* 🌐 *www.azorishotels.com/faialgarden* *131 rooms* *Free Breakfast.*

Hotel do Canal

$$ | HOTEL | FAMILY | This somewhat old-fashioned hotel makes up for any shortcomings with a prime location across the street from Horta's marina, good-sized rooms with comfortable beds, and a staff ready to help when you need it. **Pros:** sauna, whirlpool tub, and Turkish bath; location in the center of town; free parking. **Cons:** limited breakfast choices; gym has limited options; no swimming pool. $ *Rooms from: €155* ✉ *Largo Doutor Manuel de Arriaga, Horta* ☎ *292 202 120* 🌐 *www.bensaudehotels.com/hotel-docanal* *103 rooms* *Free Breakfast.*

★ **Pousada Forte da Horta**

$$ | HOTEL | This atmospheric hotel inside a 16th-century fort perched directly on the harbor's edge offers rooms with balconies overlooking the military cannons positioned next to the fort's walls. **Pros:** sleep in a nationally recognized treasure; chock-full of historical details; wonderful scenery. **Cons:** no fitness center or spa; staff could be more helpful; parking can be an issue. $ *Rooms from: €180* ✉ *Rua Vasco da Gama, Horta* ☎ *210 407 670* 🌐 *www.pousadas.pt/en/hotel/*

pousada-horta ⏲ Closed Dec.–Feb. 🛏 28 rooms 🍽 Free Breakfast.

Nightlife

★ Peter Café Sport

BARS/PUBS | Locals and tourists alike cap off their evening at this Faial institution, around since 1898, which uses its own brand of passion fruit liqueur–infused gin in the must-try gin and tonics. Grab a seat in the always-packed bar inside, where colorful flags left by sailors stream from the ceiling, or on the covered patio overlooking the harbor. There's also a café serving meals and snacks, and a tiny but fascinating scrimshaw museum—showcasing intricate whale bone and tooth engravings—upstairs. ✉ *Rua José Azevedo 9, Horta* ☎ *292 292 327* 🌐 *www.petercafesport.com.*

Shopping

★ Endemic Store

GIFTS/SOUVENIRS | **FAMILY** | Two marine biologists who run a sustainable tour company on Faial branched out into this charming shop that sells products made by small producers in the Azores, with an emphasis on eco-friendly items and recycled materials. Highlights include their own label of cotton shirts with colorful designs made from recycled African textile scraps and whimsical handmade dog collars. ✉ *Rua Conde Dávila 20, Horta* ☎ *918 191 180* 🌐 *www.endemicazores.com.*

Praia do Almoxarife

6 km north of Horta.

A charming community set alongside a long black sand beach, Praia do Almoxarife makes a lovely setting for lunch and a swim or beach stroll.

Sights

Miradouro de Nossa Senhora da Conceição

VIEWPOINT | Stop at this viewpoint at the Ponta da Espalamaca, a short drive northeast of the town of Horta, for spectacular views on a clear day not only of Horta itself but also of Monte da Guia, Praia do Almoxarife, and Mt. Pico. There's a monument dedicated to Our Lady of Conception along with a 98-foot cross. ✉ *Variante a Estrada Regional NO 1-1a, Horta* 🎫 *Free.*

Beaches

★ Praia do Almoxarife

BEACH—SIGHT | **FAMILY** | Perhaps the most beautiful sandy beach in the Azores, with black volcanic sand, clear water, and views out to Pico Island. Though the Atlantic water can be a bit cold, with the possibility of waves, Praia do Almoxarife makes a delightful stop for lunch at one of the beachside restaurants before or after a stroll, swim, or snorkel. **Amenities:** food and drink; lifeguards; parking (free); showers; toilets. **Best for:** snorkeling; swimming; walking. ✉ *Horta* ✣ *5 km (3 miles) north of Horta* 🌐 *www.visitportugal.com* 🎫 *Free.*

Restaurants

★ Praya Restaurante

$ | **PORTUGUESE** | **FAMILY** | Set alongside pretty black sand beach of Praia do Almoxarife sits this industrial-chic restaurant with floor-to-ceiling windows overlooking the beach and an interesting wood ceiling designed to look like waves. It's not only the architecture that's different from the Azorean norm, but also the food: though still heavy on the cod, prawn, and octopus dishes, many items have an Asian twist, plus there's a good selection of meat and veggie items to round things off. **Known for:** gorgeous setting with views of the crashing waves; try the prawn curry with basmati rice and yogurt; Azorean black tea crème brûlée. $ *Average main: € 15* ✉ *Praia do Almoxarife, Largo Coronel Silva Leal, Horta* ☎ *292 701 037* 🌐 *www.facebook.com/praya.restaurante* ⏲ *Closed Mon. No lunch Tues.–Fri. Oct.–May.*

Capelo

21.2 km west of Praia Do Almoxarife.

The northwestern coast of Faial is dominated by dramatic mountainous volcanic craters—understandable given that the Capelinhos Volcano was the center of the most recent volcanic eruption in the Azores (in 1957 and 1958). Besides exploring the volcano site, the black rock cliffs of Varadouro make a nice spot for a swim if the weather's fine. There are few other amenities on this coast, but the distance is close enough to Horta to be able to return there for a meal.

Sights

Centro de Interpretacao do Vulcao dos Capelinhos (*Capelinhos Volcano Museum Interpretation Center*)
VOLCANO | **FAMILY** | When the Capelinhos Volcano erupted in the 20th century, it completely changed not only the landscape of Faial, but the population as well. The undersea eruption created a lunar-like island that extended the coastal land mass, and resulted in about half of the population leaving Faial, never to return. Today you can visit the innovatively designed Volcano Museum at the site of the volcano—created underground to respect the landscape above—to get a better sense of what happened at that time, as well as to learn more about the geological history of the Azores. If time permits, start with the 10-minute film for an introductory background on volcanoes. Afterward, you can climb to the top of the lighthouse, partially buried during the eruption, for panoramic views. Once back outside, you have the option of taking the steep climb up the volcanic ridge to get an even better sense of the desolate terrain. ✉ *Farol dos Capelinhos, Capelo* ☎ *292 200 470* 🌐 *parquesnaturais.azores.gov.pt/pt/faial/oquevisitar/centros-ambientais/centro-de-interpretacao-do-vulcao-dos-capelinhos* 🎟 *€10; €8 for exhibitions only; €4 for film only; €1 for lighthouse climb only* ⏲ *Closed Mon. Nov.–Mar.*

Beaches

Piscinas Naturais do Varadouro (*Natural Swimming Pools of Varadouro*)
BEACH—SIGHT | **FAMILY** | At these dramatic black basaltic natural rock pools about 20 km (12 miles) northwest of Horta, you'll find two enclosed "pools" created from the ocean water, perfect for a dip without having to worry about waves; one pool is especially for children. It's also possible to access the ocean directly here, though this is recommended only for strong swimmers as the waves can be substantial. There's a concrete area around the pools suitable for lounging between swims. **Amenities:** food and drink; lifeguards; parking (free); showers; toilets. **Best for:** swimming. ✉ *Caminho Varadouro Comprido, Capelo* 🌐 *turismo.cmhorta.pt/index.php/pt/o-que-fazer/praias-e-banhos/piscinas-varadouro* 🎟 *Free.*

Index

A

B

C

N

O

P

Q

Photo Credits

Front Cover: Brady Baker/EyeEm [Description: Illuminated Buildings In Toronto.]. **Back cover, from left to right:** Sean Pavone/Shutterstock, Alena Zharava/Shutterstock, LucVi/Shutterstock. **Spine:** Sean Hsu/Shutterstock. **Interior, from left to right:** SeanPavonePhoto/iStockphoto (1). DaLiu/iStockphoto (2). **Chapter 1: Experience Portugal:** Val Thoermer/Shutterstock (8-9). SeanPavonePhoto/iStockphoto (10). Jacek_Sopotnicki/iStockphoto (11). Tamas Gabor/iStockphoto (11). Manuel Chagas/Shutterstock (12). nikolpetr/Shutterstock (12). iago_Fernandez/iStockphoto (12). Luis Fonseca/iStockphoto (12). Angelina Dobreva/Shutterstock (13). cge2010/Shutterstock (13). 54613/Shutterstock (14). SeanPavonePhoto/iStockphoto (14). hans.slegers/Shutterstock (14). ruivalesousa/iStockphoto (14). trabantos/Shutterstock (15). saiko3p/iStockphoto (16). Romana photographer/Shutterstock (16). Romana photographer/Shutterstock (16). studiof22byricardorocha/iStockphoto (16). pkazmierczak/iStockphoto (17). StockPhotosArt/iStockphoto (17). lhmfoto/Shutterstock (20). nataliaspb/iStockphoto (21). Richie Chan/Shutterstock (22). Sergey Peterman/Dreamstime (22). Município de Elvas (22). StockPhotosArt/Shutterstock (23). Fotoeventis/Shutterstock (23). StockPhotosArt/Shutterstock (24). Carlos Martins (24). tichr/Shutterstock (24). Helena Bilkova/Dreamstime (24). Ricardo Goncalves 2017 (24). agsaz/Shutterstock (25). Alvaro German Vilela/Dreamstime (25). Benny Marty/Shutterstock (25). Joaquin Ossorio Castillo/Dreamstime (25). Martin Lehmann/Dreamstime (25). Fonseca Port – Quinta do Panascal (26). BACALHÔA VINHOS DE PORTUGAL (26). Anabela Rosas Trindade (26). Herdade do Esporão (27). Jorge Castro/Quinta do Vallado (27). Michal Uhlarik/Dreamstime (28). Stevanzz/Dreamstime (29). **Chapter 3: Lisbon:** Zts/Dreamstime (51). Sean Hsu/Shutterstock (56). eskystudio/Shutterstock (66). TTstudio/Shutterstock (69). e X p o s e/Shutterstock (73). Tomas1111/Dreamstime (90). Alexandre Rotenberg/Shutterstock (102). Sean Pavone/Shutterstock (115). **Chapter 4: Sintra, the Estoril Coast, and the Setúbal Peninsula:** Taiga/Shutterstock (123). Andrei Nekrassov/Shutterstock (133). Sean Pavone/Shutterstock (136-137). Yuri Turkov/Shutterstock (142). AWP76/shutterstock.com (145). trabantos/Shutterstock (149). Nuno Maia/Shutterstock (152). **Chapter 5: Estremadura and the Ribatejo:** S-F/Shutterstock (161). Zts/Dreamstime (169). tokar/shutterstock (174). trabantos/Shutterstock (181). Altosvic/Shutterstock (191). StockPhotosArt/Shutterstock (207). **Chapter 6: Évora and the Alentejo:** LucVi/iStockphoto (211). RossHelen/Shutterstock (223). saiko3p/Shutterstock (225). Evgeni Fabisuk/Shutterstock (231). Iakov Filimonov/Shutterstock (239). StockPhotosArt/Shutterstock (245). Carpeira/Shutterstock (253). **Chapter 7: The Algarve:** pkazmierczak/iStockphoto (259). vvoe/Shutterstock (275). Sergio Sergo/Shutterstock (282). Sopotnicki/Shutterstock (287). ruigsantos/Shutterstock (291). Anton Foltin/Shutterstock (296). **Chapter 8: Coimbra and the Beiras:** bennymarty/iStockphoto (303). saiko3p/iStockphoto (315). Benny Marty/Shutterstock (318). DaLiu/Shutterstock (329). **Chapter 9: Porto:** SeanPavonePhoto/iStockphoto (341). Simon Dannhauer/iStockphoto (347). bennymarty/iStockphoto (353). Glen Berlin/Shutterstock (360). TasfotoNL/iStockphoto (365). **Chapter 10: Northern Portugal:** saiko3p/shutterstock (367). Marcelo Ferreira/iStockphoto (379). Sergey Peterman/Shutterstock (384). tane-mahuta/iStockphoto (389). Tsuguliev/Shutterstock (393). Sergey Peterman/iStockphoto (397). Steveheap/Dreamstime (398). **Chapter 11: The Azores:** RavenEyePhoto/Shutterstock (403). peresanz/iStockphoto (418). Robert van der Schoot/Shutterstock (425). Lina Balciunaite/Shutterstock (431). **About Our Writers:** All photos are courtesy of the writers.

*Every effort has been made to trace the copyright holders, and we apologize in advance for any accidental errors. We would be happy to apply the corrections in the following edition of this publication.

Notes

Notes

Notes